GRAMMAR FOR LANGUAGE LEARNING

ELEMENTS of SUCCESS

ANNE M. EDIGER

LINDA LEE

JENNI CURRIE SANTAMARIA

OXFORD

UNIVERSITY PRESS

SHAPING *learning* TOGETHER

We would like to thank the following classes for piloting *Elements of Success*:

University of Delaware English Language Institute
Teacher: Kathleen Vodvarka
Students: Ahmad Alenzi, Bandar Manei Algahmdi, Fadi Mohammed Alhazmi, Abdel Rahman Atallah, Anna Kuzmina, Muhanna Sayer Aljuaid, Coulibaly Sita

ABC Adult School, Cerritos, CA
Teacher: Jenni Santamaria
Students: Gabriela A. Marquez Aguilar, Yijung Chen, Laura Gomez, Terry Hahn, EunKyung Lee, Subin Lee, Sunmin Lee, Jane Leelachat, Lilia Nunezuribe, Gina Olivar, Young Park, Seol Hee Seok, Kwang Mi Song

During the development of *Elements of Success*, we spoke with teachers and professionals who are passionate about teaching grammar. Their feedback led us to create *Elements of Success: Grammar for Language Learning*, a course that solves teaching challenges by presenting grammar clearly, simply, and completely. We would like to acknowledge the advice of teachers from

**USA • BRAZIL • CANADA • COSTA RICA • GUATEMALA • IRAN • JAPAN • MEXICO • OMAN • RUSSIA
SAUDI ARABIA • SOUTH KOREA • TUNISIA • TURKEY • UKRAINE • THE UNITED ARAB EMIRATES**

Mehmet Abi, Mentese Anatolian High School, Turkey; **Anna-Marie Aldaz**, Doña Ana Community College, NM; **Diana Allen**, Oakton Community College, IL; **Marjorie Allen**, Harper College, IL; **Mark Alves**, Montgomery College, Rockville, MD; **Kelly Arce**, College of Lake County, IL; **Irma Arencibia**, Union City Adult Learning Center, NJ; **Arlys Arnold**, University of Minnesota, MN; **Marcia Arthur**, Renton Technical College, WA; **Alexander Astor**, Hostos Community College, NY; **Chris Atkins**, CHICLE Language Institute, NC; **Karin Avila-John**, University of Dayton, OH; **Ümmet Aydan**, Karabuk University, Iran; **Fabiana Azurmendi**; **John Baker**, Wayne State University, MI; **Sepehr Bamdadnia**; **Terry Barakat**, Missouri State University, MO; **Marie Bareille**, Borough of Manhattan Community College, NY; **Eileen Barlow**, SUNY Albany, NY; **Denise Barnes**, Madison English as a Second Language School, WI; **Kitty Barrera**, University of Houston, TX; **Denise Barsotti**, EID Training Solutions, FL; **Maria Bauer**, El Camino College; **Christine Bauer-Ramazani**, Saint Michael's College, VT; **Jamie Beaton**, Boston University, MA; **Gena Bennett**, Cornerstone University, NE; **Linda Berendsen**, Oakton Community College, IL; **Carol Berteotti**; **Grace Bishop**, Houston Community College, TX; **Perrin Blackman**, University of Kansas, KS; **Mara Blake-Ward**, Drexel University English Language Center, PA; **Melissa Bloom**, ELS; **Alexander Bochkov**, ELS, WA; **Marcel Bolintiam**, University of Colorado, CO; **Nancy Boyer**, Golden West College, CA; **T. Bredl**, The New School, NY; **Rosemarie Brefeld**, University of Missouri, MO; **Leticia Brereton**, Kingsborough Community College, NY; **Deborah Brooks**, Laney College, CA; **Kevin Brown**, Irvine Community College, CA; **Rachel Brown**, Center for Literacy, NY; **Tracey Brown**, Parkland College, IL; **Crystal Brunelli**, Tokyo Jogakkan Middle and High School, Japan; **Tom Burger**, Harris County Department of Education, TX; **Thom Burns**, Tokyo English Specialists College, Japan; **Caralyn Bushey**, Maryland English Institute, MD; **Gül Büyü**, Ankara University, Turkey; **Scott Callaway**, Community Family Centers, TX; **Adele Camus**, George Mason University, VA; **Nigel Caplan**, University of Delaware, DE; **Nathan Carr**, California State University, CA; **Christina Cavage**, Savannah College of Art and Design,

GA; **Neslihan Çelik**, Özdemir Sabancı Emirgan Anatolian High School, Turkey; **Shelley Cetin**, Kansas City Kansas Community College, KS; **Hoi Yuen Chan**, University of Wyoming, WY; **Esther Chase**, Berwyn Public Library, IL; **Suzidilara Çınar**, Yıldırım Beyazıt University, Turkey; **Diane Cirino**, SUNY Suffolk, NY; **Cara Codney**, Emporia State University, KS; **Catherine Coleman**, Irvine Valley College, CA; **Jenelle Collins**, Washington High School, AZ; **Greg Conner**, Orange Coast Community College, CA; **Ewelina Cope**, The Language Company, PA; **Jorge Cordon**, Colegio Montessori, Guatemala; **Kathy Cornman**, University of Michigan, MI; **Barry Costa**, Castro Valley Adult and Career Education, CA; **Cathy Costa**, Edmonds Community College, WA; **Julia Cote**, Houston Community College NE, TX; **Eileen Cotter**, Montgomery College, MD; **Winnie Cragg**, Mukogawa Fort Wright Institute, WA; **Douglas Craig**, Diplomatic Language Services, VA; **Elizabeth Craig**, Savannah College of Art and Design, GA; **Ann Telfair Cramer**, Florida State College at Jacksonville, FL; **R. M. Crocker**, Plano Independent School District, TX; **Virginia Cu**, Queens Adult Learning Center, CT; **Marc L. Cummings**, Jefferson Community and Technical College, KY; **Roberta Cummings**, Trinidad Correctional Facility, CO; **David Dahnke**, Lone Star College-North Harris, TX; **Debra Daise**, University of Denver, CO; **L. Dalgish**, Concordia College, NY; **Kristen Danek**, North Carolina State University, NC; **April Darnell**, University of Dayton, OH; **Heather Davis**, OISE Boston, MA; **Megan Davis**, Embassy English, NY; **Jeanne de Simon**, University of West Florida, FL; **Renee Delatizky**, Boston University, MA; **Sonia Delgadillo**, Sierra Community College, NY; **Gözde Burcu Demirkul**, Orkunoglu College, Turkey; **Stella L. Dennis**, Longfellow Middle School, NY; **Mary Diamond**, Auburn University, AL; **Emily Dibala**, Bucks County Community College, PA; **Cynthia Dieckmann**, West Chester East High School, PA; **Michelle DiGiorno**, Richland College, TX; **Luciana Diniz**, Portland Community College, OR; **Özgür Dirik**, Yıldız Technical University, Turkey; **Marta O. Dmytrenko-Arab**, Wayne State University, MI; **Margie Domingo**, Intergenerational Learning Community, CO; **Kellie Draheim**, Hongik University, South Korea; **Ilke Buyuk Duman**, Sehir University, Turkey; **Jennifer Eick-Magan**, Prairie State College, IL;

Juliet Emanuel, Borough of Manhattan Community College, NY; **David Emery**, Kaplan International Center, CA; **Patricia Emery**, Jefferson County Literacy Council, WI; **Eva Engelhard**, Kaplan International Center, WA; **Nancey Epperson**, Harry S. Truman College, IL; **Ken Estep**, Mentor Language Institute, CA; **Cindy Etter**, University of Washington, WA; **Rhoda Fagerland**, St. Cloud State University, MN; **Anrisa Fannin**, Diablo Valley College, CA; **Marie Farnsworth**, Union Public Schools, OK; **Jim Fenton**, Bluegrass Community Technical College, KY; **Lynn Filazzola**, Nassau BOCES Adult Learning Center, NY; **Christine Finck**, Stennis Language Lab; **Mary Fischer**, Texas Intensive English Program, TX; **Mark Fisher**, Lone Star College, TX; **Celeste Flowers**, University of Central Arkansas, AR; **Elizabeth Foss**, Washtenaw Community College, MI; **Jacqueline Fredericks**, West Contra Costa Adult Education, CA; **Patricia Gairaud**, San Jose City College, CA; **Patricia Gallo**, Delaware Technical Community College, DE; **Beverly Gandall**, Coastline Community College, CA; **Alberto Garrido**, The Community College of Baltimore County, MD; **Debbie Garza**, Park University, MO; **Karen Gelender**, Castro Valley Adult and Career Education, CA; **Ronald Gentry**, Suenos Compartidos, Mexico; **Kathie Madden Gerecke**, North Shore Community College, MA; **Jeanne Gibson**, Colorado State University, CO; **A. Elizabeth Gilfillan**, Houston Community College, TX; **Melanie Gobert**, The Higher Colleges of Technology, UAE; **Ellen Goldman**, West Valley College, CA; **Jo Golub**, Houston Community College, TX; **Maria Renata Gonzalez**, Colegio Montessori, Guatemala; **Elisabeth Goodwin**, Pima Community College, AZ; **John Graney**, Santa Fe College, FL; **Karina Greene**, CUNY in the Heights, NY; **Katherine Gregorio**, CASA de Maryland, MD; **Claudia Gronsbell**, La Escuelita, NY; **Yvonne Groseil**, Hunter College, NY; **Alejandra Gutierrez**, Hartnell College, CA; **Eugene Guza**, North Orange County Community College District, CA; **Mary Beth Haan**, El Paso Community College, TX; **Elizabeth Haga**, State College of Florida, FL; **Saeede Haghi**, Ozyegin University, Turkey; **Laura Halvorson**, Lorain County Community College, OH; **Nancy Hamadou**, Pima Community College, AZ; **Kerri Hamberg**, Brookline Community and Adult Education, MA;

ii

Contents

6│Adverb Clauses

7│Nouns and Pronouns

8│Determiners

12 | Noun Clauses and Related Forms

Present, Past, and Future Forms

Twenty years from now you will regret the things that you didn't do more than the things that you did do.

—UNKNOWN

Talk about It Do you agree or disagree with the quotation above? Why?

WARM-UP

A | Read these statements and check (✓) *Fact* or *Opinion*. Then compare answers with your classmates. Do you agree or disagree with the opinions below? Why?

Television: Fact or Opinion?

	FACT	OPINION
1. TV programs **were** much better ten years ago.	☐	☐
2. Most young children **spend** too much time in front of a television.	☐	☐
3. When Neil Armstrong **stepped** onto the surface of the moon in 1969, about 500 million people **were watching** him on TV.	☐	☐
4. Fewer young people **are watching** television, according to a report by media analysts at Ofcom.	☐	☐
5. Television in the future **is going to be** totally different.	☐	☐
6. Sixty-six percent of Americans regularly **watch** television while they **are eating** dinner.	☐	☐
7. The first television sets **were** huge but they **had** very small screens.	☐	☐
8. TV **makes** children less intelligent.	☐	☐
9. In the future, you **won't need** a screen to watch television.	☐	☐

B | Answer these questions about the statements above.

1. The words in **green** above are verbs. Which verb forms do you see? Write the number of the sentence next to each verb form below.

   simple present _____   past progressive _____

   present progressive _____   future with *will* _____

   simple past _____   future with *be going to* _____

2. Which of the statements above give general information that might be true anytime? How do you know?

3. Which statements describe a specific time? How do you know?

C | Look back at the quotation on page 2. Identify any present, past, or future verb forms.

1.1 Useful Things to Remember about Verbs

A

```
                    VERBS
            ┌─────────┴─────────┐
    HELPING VERBS          MAIN VERBS
 be, do, have, can,    learn, change,
    will, etc.         disappear, etc.
```

1 Children **learn** languages easily.

2 Languages **are** always **changing**.

3 Many languages **have disappeared**.

4 How **can** I **improve** my language abilities?

The English language has **main verbs** and **helping verbs**. We describe states, actions, and events with main verbs, as in **1**. Helping verbs primarily give grammatical information. We use helping verbs together with main verbs, as in **2 – 4**.

For a list of irregular verbs, see the Resources, page R-3.

B

COMPARE MAIN VERBS AND HELPING VERBS

5a No one **is** here.
5b No one **is coming** here.

6a Somebody **did** all the work.
6b **Did** you **do** anything yesterday?

7a We **have** plenty of time.
7b I **haven't seen** them all day.

We can use the verbs *be*, *do*, and *have* as either a main verb, as in **5a – 7a**, or a helping verb, as in **5b – 7b**.

GRAMMAR TERM: Helping verbs are also called **auxiliary verbs**. Main verbs are also called **lexical verbs**.

C

8 I **need** a new computer. (1 clause)

9 I **need** a new computer, but I **can't afford** it. (2 clauses)

10 When you **study**, you **should turn** off the TV. (2 clauses)

11 I **don't know** what she **wants**, but I'm **going to find** out.
(3 clauses)

A clause is a group of words with a subject and a main verb. A sentence can have one or more clauses, but each clause needs a main verb, as in **8 – 11**.

D

12 How far **can** you **run**? (run = go quickly on foot)

13 He **runs** a restaurant. (run = manage)

14 This road **runs** south to Dover. (run = extend; reach)

Many main verbs have more than one meaning, as in **12 – 14**.

1 | Identifying Main Verbs and Helping Verbs Is each **bold** word a main verb or a helping verb? Underline the main verbs and circle the helping verbs in this essay. **1.1 A**

The Worst Advice I Have Ever Received

The worst advice I have ever received **was** from a friend. She **told** me not to take an overseas trip I **was planning** because it **would be** too expensive. I **ignored** her advice and **took** the trip anyway. I **had** the most thrilling time of my life. I **am** a classical pianist, and I **was** already **planning** a trip to St. Petersburg, Russia to play in a piano competition there. At the time, I **was living** in Los Angeles, California, so it **was** quite a long journey to Russia. I **thought** to myself, as long as I **would be** 6,000 miles away from home, I **might** as well **stay** longer than just the two-day competition. I **would visit** some other places near St. Petersburg, too.

Because I **am** a classical musician, I **wanted** to visit the homes of some great composers. I **went** to Finland and **saw** the small house where Jean Sibelius **had composed** most of his symphonies. In St. Petersburg, I **took** a tour of the home of Nikolai Rimsky-Korsakov. He **was** a composer and teacher. His most famous student **was** Igor Stravinsky—I actually **played** on Stravinsky's piano. For a pianist like me, it **was** a great thrill.

After three fantastic weeks in Finland and Russia, it **was** time to go home. My friend **was** right—the trip **wasn't** cheap. But I'm **glad** that I **ignored** her advice and **went** on the trip. Now I **have** memories that **will stay** with me for the rest of my life.

2 | *Be, Do,* and *Have*: Main Verb or Helping Verb? Is the **bold** verb in each sentence a main verb or a helping verb? Check (✓) your answer. `1.1 B`

POPULATION FACTS	MAIN VERB	HELPING VERB
1. There **are** about 7 billion people in the world today.	✓	☐
2. The number of people in the world **is** increasing.	☐	☐
3. Populations **have** doubled in many countries over the last 20–30 years.	☐	☐
4. The fastest-growing country **is** Uganda.	☐	☐
5. In some countries, the population **is** decreasing.	☐	☐
6. The U.S. population **has** grown by nearly 18 million since 2000.	☐	☐
7. Many countries **do** a census every 5 or 10 years. That's when the government counts the number of people in the country.	☐	☐
8. Today roughly[1] 301 million people **are** living in the U.S.	☐	☐
9. Some experts believe that in 50 years, the world will **have** 9 billion people.	☐	☐
10. New York City's population **has** passed 8.25 million.	☐	☐
11. "We **have** an enormous population here," said the mayor of New York.	☐	☐
12. Human population **is** a key[2] factor in the health of the planet.	☐	☐
13. Population **has** always been a controversial topic[3].	☐	☐
14. Some countries **don't** have a population problem.	☐	☐
15. During the period from 1877 to 1913, the U.S. population **was** growing at a staggering[4] rate.	☐	☐

3 | Identifying Main Verbs Underline the main verb in each highlighted clause. `1.1 C`

ACADEMIC DEGREES

1. Some students <u>pursue</u> master's degrees, while others <u>study</u> to receive doctorates.
2. For example, business students get an MBA, which means "Master of Business Administration."
3. A doctorate is the highest degree that a student can earn.
4. Most medical doctors train for an MD, which comes from the Latin *medicinae doctor*.
5. Someone with a PhD is a doctor of philosophy.
6. Many students earn a PhD, but not many study the field of philosophy specifically.
7. In 2010, almost 50,000 students received a PhD.
8. Most of the degrees were in science and engineering.
9. Some students complete a master's program before they start a PhD program.
10. A PhD usually requires three years of full-time study, and then students must pass special exams.
11. PhD students also carry out[5] original[6] research.
12. Students present their findings by writing a long research report or dissertation, which can take years to complete.
13. Doctoral students may experience a lot of stress.

Talk about It What other academic degrees do you know about? Tell a partner.

---

[1] **roughly:** about
[2] **key:** important; essential
[3] **controversial topic:** something people disagree about
[4] **staggering:** shocking; amazing
[5] **carry out:** to do
[6] **original:** new

see /si/ *verb* (**saw**, **seen**, **see·ing**)

> *verb (used with an object)*
> 1. to perceive with the eye: *I see something in the distance.*
> 2. find out: *See who is on the phone.*
> 3. to imagine; believe possible: *I see her as a famous writer someday.*
> 4. to attend; view: *We saw a great movie.*
> 5. to visit/meet: *They've been seeing a lot of each other lately.*
> 6. to understand: *I don't see the point.*
>
> *verb (used without an object)*
> 7. to have the power of sight: *I can't see without glasses.*
> 8. to think; consider: *Let's see, what do you want to do next?*

RESEARCH SAYS...

In conversation, the most common main verbs include:

be, buy, come, get, give, go, keep, know, let, like, look, make, mean, need, pay, put, remember, say, see, start, take, talk, tell, think, try, use, want

In academic writing, the most common main verbs include:

be, become, consider, describe, develop, find, follow, give, include, involve, know, make, occur, produce, provide, require, say, see, show, take, use

CORPUS

QUESTIONS

1. What is the simple past form of the verb *see*? _____

2. What is the past participle? _____

3. What is the meaning of the verb *see* in each sentence below? Match the **bold** verbs with the dictionary definitions.

_2_ a. Please **see** if anyone is here yet.

____ b. I'm beginning to **see** the advantages of living in a city.

____ c. I **see** us living in the country in 20 years.

____ d. You can **see** that bus from two miles away.

____ e. You should **see** a doctor right away.

____ f. You must **see** the exhibit before it closes!

____ g. My grandfather doesn't **see** very well.

Write about It Write sentences using three of the definitions above. Then share ideas with a partner.

1.2 The Simple Present

A

1 Most people **need** about eight hours of sleep a night.
2 Adults **have** 206 bones. Babies **have** 270 to 300.
3 An apple a day **keeps** the doctor away.

4 I never **get** to bed before midnight.
5 The class **meets** from 10:00 to 12:00.

6 I **don't want** to go.
7 My arm **hurts**.

We use the **simple present** to describe:

- general statements or timeless truths, as in **1 – 3**
- habits or routines, as in **4 – 5**
- present states, as in **6 – 7**

For a list of spelling rules for the *-s/-es* form of verbs, see the Resources, page R-4.

B

8 **My mother and father like** it here.

9 **The difference between us is** hard to explain.
10 **The programs on television aren't** very good.

11 **Everyone is** here.
12 **Does anything** exciting ever **happen** here?

Sometimes it is difficult to determine correct subject-verb agreement in a sentence. For example:

- when two subjects are connected with *and*, as in **8**
- when there is a prepositional phrase after the subject, as in **9 – 10**
- when the subject is an indefinite pronoun, as in **11 – 12**

C

CORRECT THE COMMON ERRORS (See page R-10.)

13 ✗ Everyone have the duty to vote.

14 ✗ My brother always get what he wants.

15 ✗ I very proud to be a part of this group.

16 ✗ People in a big city has more trouble sleeping at night.

GO ONLINE

5 | Exploring Uses of the Simple Present What kind of information does each sentence give? Write the letter of the correct type from the box. `1.2 A`

> a. general statement or timeless truth   b. habit or routine   c. present state

1. Most people don't get enough sleep. __a__
2. Silence is golden. ____
3. It snows here a lot in the winter. ____
4. I'm a little hungry now. ____
5. I have dark brown hair and brown eyes. ____
6. I don't need anything right now. ____
7. Some scientists say musical training seems to improve communication skills. ____
8. It takes two or three years to get a master's degree. ____
9. I don't always have breakfast. ____
10. You need a license to practice medicine. ____
11. The General Assembly of the United Nations meets for several months every year. ____

> **FYI**
>
> Important! Much of the time, the simple present form does not describe something that is happening right now.

Think about It Do any of the sentences above describe what is happening now?

6 | Spelling Analysis How do you spell the simple present of third-person singular verbs? Study the irregular spellings and answer the questions below. Then compare ideas with a partner. `1.2 A`

Base form	Third-person singular		Base form	Third-person singular
buy	buys		finish	finishes
destroy	destroys		publish	publishes
pay	pays		wish	wishes
carry	carries		catch	catches
copy	copies		touch	touches
cry	cries		watch	watches
fly	flies		discuss	discusses
identify	identifies		pass	passes
reply	replies		quiz	quizzes
try	tries		fix	fixes
worry	worries		tax	taxes

QUESTIONS

1. When the base form of a verb ends in -*y*, we sometimes change the -*y* to -*i* and add -*es*. Other times we just add -*s*. What is the difference between these verbs?

2. For most simple present verbs, we add -*s* to the base form to make the third-person singular. When do we add -*es* instead of -*s*?

3. Write the third-person singular form of each verb below.

a. deny _____denies_____   f. miss _____   k. fax _____

b. match _____   g. fry _____   l. reach _____

c. suggest _____   h. sleep _____   m. push _____

d. relax _____   i. express _____   n. dress _____

e. supply _____   j. modify _____   o. play _____

7 | Subject-Verb Agreement Complete the paragraphs with the simple present form of the verbs.

1.2 B

EXCERPTS FROM RESEARCH REPORTS

1. The caffeine in three cups of coffee _____seems_____ to have a positive
   (seem)
   effect on women but not men. According to one study, female coffee
   drinkers over the age of 60 _____ less likely to experience a
   (be)
   decline in verbal skills.

2. Experts _____ that most people _____ about 8
   (say)   (need)
   hours of sleep a night. Unfortunately, not everyone _____ it.
   (get)
   According to the National Sleep Foundation's annual survey, the average
   adult _____ just 6.9 hours of sleep a night. New research _____
   (get)   (suggest)
   that a decline in sleep time _____ a decline in your health.
   (mean)

3. Tobacco smoke _____ over 4,000 chemicals. Researchers _____
   (contain)   (claim)
   that tobacco smoke _____ as many as 60 substances[7] that may cause cancer.
   (have)

4. Many people today _____ jobs frequently. As a matter of fact[8], some
   (change)
   studies say that the average person _____ at least 7 jobs before he or she
   (hold)
   _____ age 30. What may be more surprising, though, is that many people
   (reach)
   _____ several careers in their lifetime.
   (have)
   People _____ many reasons for making career changes. Some
   (have)
   _____ to the end of their career plan. Others _____ that their
   (come)   (find)
   career plan _____ no longer right for them. Many people _____
   (be)   (want)
   to pursue personal interests or _____ a business of their own.
   (run)

5. Vitamin C in large doses[9] _____ to do little harm. But recent studies also
   (appear)
   _____ that it is largely ineffective.
   (show)

> **RESEARCH SAYS...**
>
> The simple present form is very common in both conversation and academic writing.
>
> CORPUS

Think about It Why did these writers use the simple present form of verbs?

---

[7] **substances:** materials
[8] **as a matter of fact:** in reality; actually

[9] **doses:** portions of a vitamin or medicine

8 | Error Correction Correct any errors in these paragraphs. (Some sentences may not have any errors.)

1. I really admire my father. He is a mechanic, and he know a lot about cars, stoves, and other machines. My father is self-employed, and he travel to people's houses to fix things. Whenever I'm home, I go with him on his jobs so that I can watch him. In my opinion, anybody who know how to fix things is a genius. I guess that make my father a genius.

2. My grandfather take very good care of himself. He is get up early in the morning so he can do tai chi in the park near his house. He try to get his wife, my grandmother, to join him, but she doesn't like to exercise, so he always go by himself.

3. My mother is the most hard-working person I know. She don't have a paying job like my father; she has a job that don't pay. My mother takes care of our house. She take care of everyone and everything in our house. She keep the house clean, and she cook the best food you will ever have. Beyond all this, I think my mother is the only person who understand me.

4. I am from Costa Rica, but my roommate is from the U.S. Needless to say, her English is a lot better than mine. The thing I especially like about her is that she help me with my English. Whenever I say something incorrectly, she just says it correctly for me.

Write about It Write three to four sentences about someone you admire. Explain what you like about this person.

1.3 The Present Progressive

	THE PRESENT PROGRESSIVE	THE SIMPLE PRESENT
A	We use the **present progressive** when we think of an action as temporary or in progress now, as in **1a – 5a**. **1a** I'm **living** with my aunt until I get my own place. **2a** What **are** you **talking** about? **3a** I'm sorry. I'm **not explaining** this very well. **4a** She'll be here soon. She's just **checking** her email. **5a** I see that you **are reading** *The New Yorker*. For a list of spelling rules for the *-ing* form of verbs, see the Resources, page R-4.	In contrast, we use the **simple present** to signal that a state or activity is generally true or habitual, as in **1b – 5b**. **1b** My aunt **lives** near the university. **2b** What **do** you and your friends **talk** about? **3b** Professor Sutton **explains** things very well. **4b** She **checks** her email every hour. **5b** I always **read** *The New Yorker* from cover to cover.
B	**6** It's **becoming** harder and harder to find a job. **7** It's only five, and it's already **getting** dark.	We often use the present progressive with verbs such as *become* and *get* to describe changing states or situations, as in **6 – 7**.
C	**8** He is **forever** taking my things. **9** You **are always** eating! **10** They **are constantly** arguing.	When we use the present progressive to comment on habitual behavior, it can signal our disapproval, as in **8 – 10**. We often use the adverbs *forever*, *always*, or *constantly* in these situations.

9 | Simple Present or Present Progressive? Complete the conversations with the appropriate verb form in parentheses. Then practice with a partner. 1.3 A

1. A: Nice piano. Who _____*plays*_____ it? (plays/is playing)

   B: Nobody anymore.

2. A: That's my favorite piano piece. Who _____ it? (plays/is playing)

   B: That's Uchida.

3. A: David tells us you _____ furniture. (move/are moving)

   B: That's right. It's a family business.

4. A: Why _____ the furniture? (do you move/ are you moving)

   B: Because I need to clean the floor.

5. A: I don't know how to say this.

   B: Say what?

   A: Well, um, I just . . . I just . . .

   B: What _____ to say, James? (do you try/are you trying)

   A: I, um, I lost my job.

6. A: I can't move this thing.

   B: Yes, you can. You just _____ hard enough. (don't try/aren't trying)

7. A: What _____ to? (do you listen/are you listening)

   B: It's a group called the Bald Eagles. Do you like it?

   A: Not especially. Could you turn it down?

8. A: Do you want to choose some music for the trip?

   B: Sure. What kind of music _____ to? (do you listen/are you listening)

   A: Usually jazz, but anything's OK.

9. A: What _____ up so late? (do you do/are you doing)

   B: I have jet lag.[10]

10. A: That's a steep[11] driveway. What _____ when it snows? (do you do/are you doing)

    B: I stay home.

11. A: Why _____ a coat? (do you wear/are you wearing)

    B: Because it's cold in here.

12. A: _____ a school uniform? (do you wear/are you wearing)

    B: Yes, it's brown and white. I'll show it to you someday.

> **RESEARCH SAYS...**
>
> The present progressive is more common in conversation than in writing. Compared to the simple present, however, the present progressive is fairly uncommon.
>
> CORPUS

Think about It Why did each speaker choose the present progressive or the simple present? Choose a reason from the box.

Reasons for using the present progressive	Reasons for using the simple present
The speaker is talking or asking about something: • temporary • in progress now	The speaker is talking or asking about something: • generally true • habitual

[10] **jet lag:** the feeling of being tired or awake due to traveling across time zones   [11] **steep:** almost straight up and down

10 | Habitual or Temporary? Does each situation describe habitual behavior (H) or a temporary event in progress now (T)? Circle your answer and the form of the verb that expresses that meaning. (More than one answer may be possible.) `1.3 A`

H (T)	1. **Amanda sees John at his computer.**

Amanda: Why (do you talk / **are you talking**) to the computer?

John: I (try / am trying) to follow every step correctly to set up this program!

H T	2. **Emma and her husband, Matt, share the housecleaning. This week it is Matt's turn to clean the house.**

Matt: Emma, can you pick up your clothes? You (leave / are leaving) them on the floor all the time!

Emma: But I (pick up / am picking up) my clothes when I clean the house!

H T	3. **Kate sees her husband emptying boxes on the floor of the living room.**

Kate: What (do you do / are you doing)?

Husband: I (look for / am looking for) my cell phone.

Kate: But you (make / are making) a big mess of everything! I just packed those boxes!

H T	4. **Mika and Isabel like to do gardening.**

Mika: When (do roses bloom / are roses blooming) in this part of the country?

Isabel: I think they (bloom / are blooming) in late June.

H T	5. **Sarah has decided to change some things in her life because she wants a healthier lifestyle. Rob notices the change.**

Rob: (Do you exercise / Are you exercising) every day now?

Sarah: Yes, and I (don't eat / am not eating) meat anymore. I (eat / am eating) more vegetables and fruits instead.

H T	6. **Mary is taking her daughter to school in the morning. Mary sees her daughter behind her and calls out to her.**

Mary: Hurry up! Why (do you walk / are you walking) so slowly?

Think about It How do we form statements and questions with present progressive verbs? Work with several classmates to explain the rules.

11 | Present Verb Forms in Essay Responses Complete the paragraph with the simple present or the present progressive form of the verb in parentheses. `1.3 A–B`

Essay Prompt: Is the traditional role of fathers changing? Discuss.

I think that the traditional role of fathers _____*is changing*_____. The most obvious way
　　　　　　　　　　　　　　　　　　　　　　　　　　　(1. change)
it _____ is in work and career. In the past, fathers had a career and
　　　　(2. change)
went to work each day, while mothers stayed at home to take care of the children. But today it

_____ common for mothers to work and have a career just like fathers. Many times
　　(3. be)
when this _____ the case, the children _____ to daycare.
　　　　　　　(4. be)　　　　　　　　　　　　　　　　　　　　(5. go)

But another option _____ available. Some fathers _____
(6. become)   (7. choose)
to stay at home and take care of their children while their wives _____
(8. go)
to work. It _____ not yet a common thing, but more and more fathers
(9. be)
_____ their careers to take care of their children.
(10. leave)

12 | Describing Changes with the Present Progressive Choose six topics from the box. Write one sentence for each topic describing how it is changing. Use the verb *get* or *become* in each sentence. `1.3 B`

TOPICS

air travel	computer power	technology	the news
cars	family life	telephones	the world
children	men	television	women

Air travel is getting less comfortable.   OR   *Air travel is becoming safer.*

Write about It Choose one of your sentences from above and write a paragraph. Give reasons and/or examples to explain your idea.

Air travel is getting less comfortable. Nowadays, the airlines want to save money on fuel, so they are crowding more passengers onto fewer airplanes. To make more money, some airlines are also charging for each suitcase you check. As a result, many passengers are carrying extra luggage onto the airplane. This makes the airplane feel crowded....

13 | Commenting on Habitual Behavior Think of someone you know who fits each general statement below. Write two or more sentences about the person. Include a sentence in the present progressive with *forever*, *always*, or *constantly*. `1.3 C`

GENERAL STATEMENTS

1. Some people can't stop shopping. They feel a need to spend money. _____

_____

Example: My friend Sam is one of those people. He is always buying things he doesn't really need.

2. Some people work all the time. They seem unhappy when they are not working. _____

_____

3. Some people talk on the phone all the time. _____

_____

4. Some people think it's OK to borrow things without asking permission. _____

_____

5. Some people gossip a lot. They love to talk about other people. _____

_____

1.4 Non-Action Verbs

<table>
<tr><td rowspan="2">A</td><td>

ACTION VERBS

1 He's **leaving** now.

2 Most people **don't get** enough exercise.

NON-ACTION VERBS

3 He **appears** to understand the problem.

4 She's **sick**.

5 I **know** him well. (NOT: ~~I am knowing him well.~~)

6 I **own** this car now. (NOT: ~~I am owning this car.~~)

</td><td>

Many verbs describe actions and activities, as in **1 – 2**. We call these verbs **action verbs**. Other verbs describe states or situations, as in **3 – 6**. We call these verbs **non-action verbs**.

With some non-action verbs, we rarely use the progressive form, as in **5 – 6**. Examples of these verbs include:

agree	belong	consist of	know	possess
believe	concern	exist	own	prefer

GRAMMAR TERM: Non-action verbs are also called **stative verbs**. For a list of non-action verbs, see the Resources, page R-2.

</td></tr>
<tr><td>

NON-ACTIVE MEANING

7a He **has** a new computer. (has = owns)

8a She **looks** great. (looks = appears)

9a I **see** something in the distance. (see = view)

ACTIVE MEANING

7b I'm **having** trouble with my computer.
(having = experiencing)

8b Why **are** you **looking** at me? (looking = gazing)

9b My brother **is seeing** a new play tomorrow.
(seeing = viewing)

</td><td>

Some verbs have both an active meaning and a non-active meaning, as in **7a – 9b**. We sometimes use the progressive form with the active meaning of these verbs, as in **7b – 9b**.

Common verbs with both active and non-active meanings include:

appear	doubt	have	love	see	taste
be	feel	look	mind	smell	think

</td></tr>
</table>

<table><tr><td>B</td></tr></table>

14 | Distinguishing Action and Non-Action Verbs Circle the subjects and underline the verbs in these quotations. Then write *A* (action verb) or *N* (non-action verb) over each verb. **1.4 A**

Quotations from Famous People

1. (Everybody) is talking today about the economy. *(Joschka Fischer, politician)*
2. Men and women belong to different species[12], and communication between them is still in its infancy[13]. *(Bill Cosby, comedian)*
3. The Internet is becoming the town square for the global village of tomorrow. *(Bill Gates, businessman)*
4. Whenever people agree with me, I always feel I must be wrong. *(Oscar Wilde, writer)*
5. A man possesses talent; genius possesses the man. *(Isaac Stern, musician)*
6. I buy expensive suits. They just look cheap on me. *(Warren Buffett, businessman)*
7. I know that I am intelligent because I know that I know nothing. *(Socrates, philosopher)*
8. The more I see, the less I know for sure. *(John Lennon, musician)*
9. I don't care what anybody says about me as long as it isn't true. *(Truman Capote, writer)*
10. We hire people who want to make the best things in the world. *(Steve Jobs, businessman)*

Think about It Look at the sentences above. What verb form(s) do we use with active meanings? What verb form(s) do we use with non-active meanings?

[12]**species:** biological categories

[13]**infancy:** the time when one is a baby

15 | Choosing the Correct Meaning Match the **bold** verbs with the correct definitions. (You may not use all the definitions.) 1.4 B

<u>b</u> 1. A: We're **having** some friends over tonight. Can you come?

B: Sure. I'd love to.

_____ 2. A: Do you want to go out to dinner?

B: No, I don't **have** any money.

_____ 3. A: Are you **having** fun?

B: Sure. Why do you ask?

_____ 4. A: So what changes when you **have** a baby?

B: What changes? You mean what *doesn't* change!

HAVE
a. to possess
b. to give; to host
c. to experience
d. to give birth to

_____ 5. A: Are you going anywhere during the break?

B: I **doubt** it.

_____ 6. A: Are you sure you didn't see my ring?

B: Are you **doubting** me?

A: No, of course not.

DOUBT
a. to be uncertain about
b. to disbelieve; to distrust

_____ 7. A: What are you doing tonight?

B: I'm meeting Paul for dinner.

A: When are you **seeing** him?

B: Right after work.

_____ 8. A: Do you **see** anyone out there?

B: No, there's nobody there.

_____ 9. A: There's no reason to do this again.

B: I **see** what you mean.

SEE
a. to view
b. to meet; to go out with
c. to understand
d. to spend time with
e. to imagine

_____ 10. Clive Ellington is **appearing** for the first time at the Everett Theater on Monday, July 13, at 7:30.

_____ 11. A new study, which **appears** in the July issue of the *American Journal of Public Health*, suggests that strong social ties can delay memory problems.

_____ 12. The president and his wife **appear** to be excellent parents.

_____ 13. When I click *Save*, an error box **appears** on the screen.

APPEAR
a. to become visible
b. to seem; to have the appearance of being
c. to perform in public
d. to be published

_____ 14. A: What do you **think** of the new library?

B: It's beautiful.

_____ 15. A: Are you really **thinking** about cutting your hair?

B: Yes, it's much too long.

_____ 16. A: What are you **thinking** about?

B: Nothing special.

THINK
a. to have an opinion
b. to use your mind; to wonder
c. to consider

Think about It Do each of the definitions above have an active or non-active meaning? Share ideas with your classmates.

"For the verb have, *definitions b, c, and d have an active meaning. Definition a has a non-active meaning."*

Write about It Write two sentences or conversations using the verbs above. Read them to your classmates. Ask them which definitions you used.

16 | Usage Note: Present Progressive with _Be_ Read the note. Then do Activity 17.

> We sometimes use the progressive form of the verb _be_ + an adjective to show that a state is temporary or changing.
>
> | Active meaning | Non-active meaning |
> |---|---|
> | You **are being** silly. | You **are** silly. |
> | (= You are acting in a silly manner right now.) | (= In general, you are a silly person.) |
> | | |
> | Why **is** he **being** so rude? | Why **is** he so rude? |
> | (= His rudeness is temporary. He's not usually rude.) | (= In general, he is a rude person.) |

17 | Simple Present or Present Progressive? Complete these conversations with the simple present or present progressive form of the verb in parentheses. (More than one answer may be possible.) Then practice with a partner. ⬛1.4 B⬛

1. A: What are you doing in Los Angeles?

   B: Oh, we _____are seeing_____ some old friends from college. (see)

2. A: Why are you worrying so much about Matt?

   B: Because I _____ how he's going to find a job.

   He's not even trying. (not/see)

3. A: Do you like to travel?

   B: Yes, I _____ to. (love)

4. A: How's your vacation going?

   B: We _____ every minute of it. (love)

5. A: What do you think of your new boss?

   B: She _____ a really nice person. (be)

6. A: Are the children behaving themselves?

   B: No, they _____ unusually naughty today. (be)

7. A: Can I use your phone?

   B: Sorry, but I _____ one. (not/have)

8. A: This is my friend Carlos. He _____ dinner here, too. (have)

   B: Nice to meet you.

9. A: I think we need to talk.

   B: What about?

   A: I _____ that you aren't doing your share of the work. (feel)

   B: Why do you think that?

   A: Well, for one thing, you're never here when I need you.

10. A: I'm really angry about last night.

    B: I'm sorry you _____ that way. (feel)

11. A: Do you know what you are going to do?

    B: Yeah. I _____ of taking some time off to relax. (think)

12. A: What _____ you _____ of the food here? (think)

    B: It's not bad.

18 | Error Correction Correct any errors in these conversations. (Some conversations may not have any errors.)

1. A: Is this your car?
   B: No, I don't own a car.

2. A: The chess club is meeting tonight. Are you going?
   B: No, I'm not belonging to that club.

3. A: Are you preferring to stay home tonight?
   B: I don't care. What do you want to do?

4. A: What's that noise?
   B: I'm not hearing anything.

5. A: Why do you look at me like that?
   B: Like what?
   A: Angry. You look angry.

6. A: What are you thinking of this TV? Do you like it better than the other one?
   B: Well, this one's bigger, but the other one's cheaper.

7. A: What are you looking at?
   B: There's something on the street over there.
   A: What is it?
   B: I'm not sure. It looks like a box.

8. A: Is this wood or plastic? I can't tell.
   B: It's feeling like plastic.

9. A: Are you looking for something?
   B: Yes, I'm needing something to write with.

1.5 The Simple Past

A

1 The modern Olympics **started** in 1896 and **became** an international event in 1924.

2 In 1998, Tara Lipinski **won** an Olympic gold medal. She **was** just 15 years old at the time.

3 We **didn't get** to see the Games.

COMPARE SIMPLE PAST AND SIMPLE PRESENT

4a Did you still **want** to read my novel?
4b Do you still **want** to read my novel?

5a I just **wanted** to say one thing.
5b I just **want** to say one thing.

We use the **simple past** to talk about something that is distant from us in some way. For example, the simple past may signal that:

- an action, event, or state was completed at a definite time in the past (distant in time), as in **1 – 3**. This is the most common use of the simple past.
- the speaker wants to show social or psychological distance, as in **4a** and **5a**. Generally, signaling more distance between people shows more formality or indirectness. Sentences **4a** and **5a** sound more polite and formal than sentences **4b** and **5b**.

For a list of spelling rules for the *-ed* form of verbs, see the Resources, page R-5. For a list of irregular verbs, see the Resources, page R-3.

B

6 In 2002, we **moved** to New York. We **lived** there **for two years**, and **then** we **moved** to India.

7 Mozart **composed** music **throughout his short life**.

8 During the 1800s, many people **moved** across the country.

We often use a time expression in a sentence with the simple past, as in **6 – 8**. These expressions describe a specific time in the recent or distant past.

9 When we moved to India, we **didn't have** much money.

10 When I was younger, I **had** a lot of big plans.

11 He **stopped** playing football **after he hurt his knee during a game**.

When we use a time clause to identify a time in the past, it's important to use the simple past in both parts of the sentence, as in **9 – 11**.

For more information on time clauses, see Unit 6, page 176.

C

CORRECT THE COMMON ERRORS (See page R-10.)

12 ✗ Later I remember that I was not well prepared to take the test.

13 ✗ We didn't want to leave home because we want to take care of our grandparents.

14 ✗ Although she looked nice when she wear that suit, she didn't feel comfortable in it.

15 ✗ When I got there, I sat and think for a while.

19 | Distinguishing Regular and Irregular Verbs Underline the simple past verb forms in this text. Then write each verb under the correct group in the chart below and give the base form. `1.5 A`

Counting Heads

After the American War of Independence, the new government <u>ordered</u> a census—a count of the number of people in each state. Work on the census started in August 1790, about a year after George Washington became president. The law required that census takers visit every family. These workers walked or rode on horseback to gather their data. In all, they counted 3.9 million people.

The first census asked for little more than a person's name and address. Over the years, the government added more questions to the census. By 1820, there were questions about a person's job. Later, questions about crime, education, and wages[14] appeared on the census form.

As the country's population grew and the quantity of data increased, new technology helped census workers. In 1890, clerks began to use a keypunch device to add the numbers. In 1950, the census used its first computer to process data.

Today most people receive a census form in the mail. If they don't fill it out and return it by mail, they still get a visit from a census taker.

REGULAR VERBS		IRREGULAR VERBS	
Base form	Simple past form	Base form	Simple past form
order	*ordered*		

20 | Using the Simple Past Complete this text with the simple past form of the verbs in parentheses. `1.5 A`

WHO WAS LEONARDO DA VINCI?

Leonardo da Vinci (1452–1519) _____*grew up*_____ in a small town near
                               (1. grow up)
Florence, Italy. As the son of a wealthy man, he _____ the best
                                         (2. receive)
education that Florence could offer. Leonardo _____ known
                                     (3. become)
for his ability to create sculptures and paintings that _____
                                        (4. look)
almost lifelike. Much of his success in this area _____ from his
                                       (5. come)

[14] **wages:** salary; money received for work

interest in nature. He also _____ human anatomy and _____ this knowledge
(6. study)   (7. use)
to make his figures realistic.

As a child, Leonardo was fascinated with machines and _____ to draw his own
(8. begin)
inventions. He _____ flying machines, armored tanks[15], and aircraft landing gear. He
(9. draw)
even _____ a diver's suit with tubes and air chambers[16] to allow a swimmer to stay
(10. design)
underwater for long periods of time.

Much of what we know about Leonardo comes from the thousands of pages of notes and

sketches he _____ in his notebooks. He _____ mirror, or reverse, writing,
(11. keep)   (12. use)
starting at the right side of the page and moving across to the left. No one is sure why Leonardo

_____ this way. Some think he _____ to keep people from[17] reading and
(13. write)   (14. want)
stealing his ideas.

Talk about It Write three questions about Leonardo da Vinci. Look for answers to your questions in
books or online and present the answers to your classmates. Pay special attention to your use of simple
past verbs.

21 | Exploring Uses of the Simple Past Write answers to these questions. Then compare ideas with your classmates. `1.5 A`

1. Think of a famous person. What did this person do to become famous?

   _____

   _____

2. What was one important event in the news last year?

   _____

   _____

3. What was the best thing that happened to you last year?

   _____

   _____

4. How could you make these sentences more formal and less direct?

   a. Do you want something? _____

   b. I want to ask you a favor. _____

   c. How do you want to pay for this? _____

   d. What is your name again? _____

   e. Do you need to speak to me? _____

> **FYI**
>
> Most simple past verbs
> end in -ed. Only about
> 200 verbs are irregular.
>
> For a list of irregular
> verbs, see the Resources,
> page R-3.

Think about It How many simple past verbs did you and your classmates use in your answers above?
Which ones are regular verbs? Which are irregular verbs?

[15] **armored tanks:** vehicles for fighting in wars   [17] **keep people from:** to stop people from
[16] **air chambers:** containers filled with air

22 | Using Time Expressions and Clauses Complete each pair of sentences with information about yourself. Make one sentence in each pair false. `1.5 B`

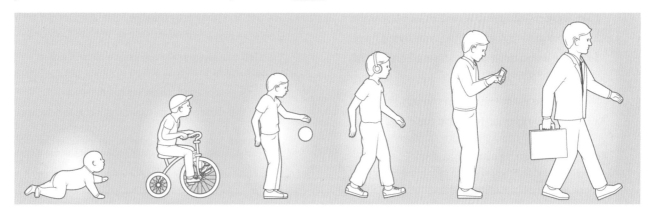

DESCRIBING PAST EXPERIENCES

1. a. I _____ five years ago.

   b. I _____ a year ago.

2. a. I _____ throughout the '90s.

   b. I _____ in 2010.

3. a. During the 2000s, I _____.

   b. Between 2005 and 2010, I _____.

4. a. When I was 5 years old, I _____.

   b. When I was 10 years old, I _____.

5. a. I _____ when I was 15 years old.

   b. I _____ after I graduated from high school.

6. a. _____ before I started school.

   b. _____ when I was a child.

Talk about It Read each pair of sentences you wrote above to a partner. See if your partner can identify the false statement.

23 | Error Correction Correct any errors in these sentences. (Some sentences may not have any errors.)

1. In the past, a woman's place was in the home. Women take care of their families and the house. Men earned the money that supports the family.

2. In high school, we had a lot of clubs. My best friend and I join the chess club even though we weren't really interested in chess.

3. Today I am going to talk about dangerous sports. This topic interested me because I play a dangerous sport.

4. When I was 18, I went hiking in the mountains with my friends. The only thing I take with me was my father's expensive camera because I want to take some pictures from the top of the mountain. I carry that camera very carefully all the way to the top of the mountain, but when I get there, the camera don't work.

5. Jaime is one of my best friends now. I meet him last year when this class began. I think we get along because we like many of the same things.

6. My father's illness affect me a lot because I thought he was a young and healthy person. Everything happen so fast.

1.6 The Past Progressive

A

1 We **were** still **studying** at nine o'clock last night.

2 I **got** my driver's license while I **was living** there.

3 I **was walking** down Water Street when I **heard** footsteps behind me.

COMPARE PAST PROGRESSIVE AND SIMPLE PAST

4a He **was crying** when he **heard** the news.

(= He was crying, and then he heard the news.)

4b He **cried** when he **heard** the news.

(= He heard the news, and then he started to cry.)

We use the **past progressive** to talk about something in progress at a particular time in the past, as in **1**.

We also use the past progressive to talk about something in progress when another action (usually in the simple past) took place, as in **2 – 3**.

Notice the difference in meaning between **4a** and **4b**.

> Remember: For the past progressive, we use a past form of the helping verb *be* (*was / were*) + the *-ing* form of the main verb.

B

COMPARE PRESENT AND PAST PROGRESSIVE

5a **Are** you **looking** for me?
5b **Were** you **looking** for me?

6a **Do** you **need** some help?
6b I **was wondering** if you **needed** some help.

7a **Do** you **want** to go out tonight?
7b I **was wondering** if you **wanted** to go out tonight.

We sometimes use the past progressive to sound less direct and more polite, as in **5b**.

We sometimes use the past progressive of the verb *wonder* + *if* + a past form to make questions, offers, and invitations more polite, as in **6b** and **7b**.

 GO ONLINE

---

24 | Noticing Past Progressive Verbs Underline the past progressive verbs in this text. `1.6 A`

WHAT WERE YOU DOING WHEN . . . ?
by Thomas Thurman

I remember exactly what I <u>was doing</u> when I first heard the news on September 11, 2001. I'd gone to the kitchen at work to get coffee, and I was walking back past co-workers' desks to the other end of the office. As I passed, I caught people's voices: ". . . a plane . . . the North Tower . . . ," and I realized something was up. I got back to my desk, sat down, and looked up BBC News. I got no further work done that day. I was 26.

I remember exactly what I was doing when I heard that Princess Diana had died. I woke up to the news on the radio. I was 22.

I remember exactly what I was doing when I heard that Margaret Thatcher had resigned[18]. I walked, slightly[19] late, into a math class. Ben Anderson, a classmate, looked up and said, "She's resigned." I asked, "Who?" I was almost 16.

I remember what I was doing when my mum told us we were going to have another baby in the family. We were home from school for lunch. I cried with the shock. I was 10.

Think about It The writer uses both the past progressive and the simple past in some of the sentences above. Why?

---

[18] **resign:** to give up a job   [19] **slightly:** a little

25 | Describing Events in the Past Use the pictures to complete each person's answer to the question. (More than one answer may be possible.) **1.6 A**

WHAT WERE YOU DOING AT MIDNIGHT ON DECEMBER 31?

1. "I live in the south of France, so when it was midnight here, it was only 6:00 in New York. Anyway, at that hour a friend and I _____ *were watching TV* _____."

2. "At midnight, as the photo indicates[20], I was out with friends and we _____."

3. "I _____ in a crowded subway car in New York City, somewhere near Times Square."

4. "We _____, and all of a sudden my friend asked, 'What time is it?' I looked at the clock, and it was midnight."

5. "At midnight we _____ the fireworks outside. That went on for about ten minutes!"

6. "To be honest, I _____ at midnight. I had to get up early the next day, so I couldn't stay up until midnight."

7. "I _____ on an airplane. The flight attendant announced that it was midnight, and everyone started cheering."

8. "I had a paper I needed to finish, so _____ in the library until 2:00 a.m. I didn't even notice when it was midnight."

Talk about It What were you doing at midnight on December 31? Tell a partner.

[20] **indicate:** to show

26 | Remembering a Frightening Event Complete these paragraphs with the past progressive or simple past form of the verbs in parentheses. (More than one answer may be possible.) **1.6 A**

The scariest experience I remember was an airplane flight I took many

years ago. I _____ from Istanbul to Prague and I
         (1. travel)

_____ two flights. First, I _____
   (2. have)   (3. fly)

to Zurich, and then I _____ planes to fly to Prague.
                          (4. change)

The first flight was fine, but by the time I _____ in
                                                  (5. land)

Zurich, it _____ heavily.
              (6. snow)

    The snowstorm _____ worse and worse by
                        (7. get)

the minute, but we still _____. As the plane
                              (8. take off)

_____, the turbulence _____.
   (9. climb)   (10. start)

The plane _____ back and forth and up and down.
                (11. shake)

I _____ the armrest as hard as I could. Some of
     (12. squeeze)

the other passengers _____, and one woman
                            (13. cry)

_____ when the plane _____
   (14. scream)   (15. hit)

a big bump.

    When we _____ the final altitude, the
                (16. reach)

turbulence suddenly _____. The passengers
                          (17. stop)

_____ for the pilot and most people
   (18. clap)

_____. But I _____ my seat belt
   (19. relax)   (20. keep)

on for the rest of the flight!

Write about It Think of a frightening event that took place in your life. Write a paragraph about it.

27 | Making Polite Requests Use *I was wondering if* + the simple past to make these requests more indirect. (NOTE: The past form of *can* is *could*.) **1.6 B**

1. Can you help me?

   I was wondering if you could help me.

2. Do you need some help?
3. Can you send me an application form?
4. Can I make an appointment to talk with you?
5. Are you ready to eat?
6. Can you come over and help me for a minute?
7. Do you have a few minutes to talk?
8. Are you doing anything tomorrow night?
9. Can you explain that to me again?

1.7 Talking about the Future with *Be Going To* and *Will*

A

PLANS OR INTENTIONS

1 Don't forget. I'm **going to call** you later.
(= I plan to call you later.)

2 I'm ready to go. I'll **meet** you out front.
(= I plan to meet you out front.)

PREDICTIONS OR EXPECTATIONS

3 Put that down. Someone's **going to get** hurt.
(= I predict that someone is going to get hurt.)

4 Millions of people **will be watching** the program.
(= I expect that millions of people will be watching.)

In English, we use several different verb forms to talk about the future. Two common forms are **be going to** and **will**. We use both *be going to* and *will* to:

• express future plans or intentions, as in **1 – 2**

• make predictions or express expectations about the future, as in **3 – 4**

Remember: We use *will* + the base form of the main verb or *will* + *be* + the *-ing* form to describe future events.

We use a present form of the helping verb *be* (am / is / are) + *going to* + the base form of the main verb to describe future events.

B

PLANS OR INTENTIONS

5 We made a plan for this last week. Let me explain what we're **going to do**.

6 We have a busy schedule for you today. First we're **going to show** you around the office.

7 Oh, I have an idea. Here's what we'll **do**.

8 Wait here. I'll **be** right back.

9 I'll **give** you a ride home from school.

10 **Will** you **excuse** us, please?

11 I'll **call** you as soon as I get home.

We use both *be going to* and *will* to express future intentions or plans, but we use them in different ways.

We often use *be going to* when we:

• talk about a future event that has already been planned or scheduled, as in **5 – 6**

We often use *will* to:

• express a decision made at the moment of speaking, as in **7 – 8**

• offer help or make a request, as in **9 – 10**

• make a promise, as in **11**

Notice: When a decision is made at the moment of speaking, we usually use the contraction *'ll*.

C

PREDICTIONS OR EXPECTATIONS

12 In the future, we're **going to get** most of our food from the ocean.

13 In the future, we **will get** most of our food from the ocean.

14 Look at those dark clouds. It's **going to rain**.
(NOT: Look at those dark clouds. It will rain.)

15 The average child in the U.S. **will eat** approximately 1,500 peanut butter sandwiches by high school.

We can usually use either *be going to* or *will* to make predictions or express expectations, as in **12 – 13**. However, sometimes the choice of *be going to* or *will* depends on the context:

• When we have clear physical evidence that something is going to happen, we usually use *be going to*, as in **14**.

• When we are stating a general belief or an absolute certainty, we often use *will*, as in **15**.

GO ONLINE

28 | Prediction or Future Plan?   Underline the future verb forms in these quotations. Is the person stating a prediction/expectation or expressing a future plan? Check (✓) your answer. **1.7 A**

QUOTATIONS	PREDICTION/ EXPECTATION	FUTURE PLAN
1. I <u>am going to produce</u> a movie of my own. *(Kabir Bedi, actor)*	☐	☑
2. Choose a job you love, and you will never have to work a day in your life. *(Confucius, philosopher)*	☐	☐
3. It's going to be a season with lots of accidents. *(Ayrton Senna, race car driver)*	☐	☐

	PREDICTION/ EXPECTATION	FUTURE PLAN
4. I am not young, but I feel young. The day I feel old, I will go to bed and stay there. *(Coco Chanel, fashion designer)*	☐	☐
5. Look deep into nature, and then you will understand everything better. *(Albert Einstein, scientist)*	☐	☐
6. I'm not going to change the way I look or the way I feel to conform to anything. *(John Lennon, musician)*	☐	☐
7. A quick temper will make a fool of you soon enough. *(Bruce Lee, martial artist)*	☐	☐
8. Give me six hours to chop down a tree, and I will spend the first four sharpening the axe. *(Abraham Lincoln, U.S. president)*	☐	☐
9. I am going to spend my time today just thanking the people that played a role in my career. *(Nolan Ryan, athlete)*	☐	☐
10. America is the most grandiose[21] experiment the world has seen, but, I am afraid, it is not going to be a success. *(Sigmund Freud, psychologist)*	☐	☐
11. In the next 50 to 75 years, people will be living to be 130 or 140. They'll be working until they're 100. *(Willard Scott, entertainer)*	☐	☐
12. At an Olympic Game, you want to enjoy it—especially if you know it's going to be your last one. *(Shannon Miller, Olympic gymnast)*	☐	☐

Think about It In sentence 11 above, it is possible to say either *will be living* or *will live*. Why do you think the speaker chose *will be living*?

Think about It Do an online search for other quotations about future predictions or plans and share them with your classmates.

29 | Expressing Future Plans Complete these conversations with *be going to* or *will* + the verb in parentheses. (Use a contraction where possible.) **1.7 B**

1. A: I'm really tired.

   B: Come on, then. I ___*'ll take*___ you home. (take)

2. A: We need to do something about the car.

   B: Don't worry about it. I _____ it. (take care of)

3. A: Have you heard the news about Lisa and Tim?

   B: No, what news?

   A: They _____ in the fall. (get married)

4. A: Come on. Hurry up. Let's do something.

   B: _____ you _____, please? (relax)

5. A: Did you talk to Bob about the presentation?

   B: No, I forgot. Sorry about that. I _____ him tomorrow. (call)

6. A: Are you ready to order?

   B: Yes, I _____ the fish special and a salad. (have)

> **RESEARCH SAYS...**
>
> In general, *will* is more formal than *be going to*.
>
> Sorry. I'**m going to be** late tonight. (less formal)
>
> I'm very sorry, but I'**ll be** late tonight. (more formal)
>
> CORPUS

[21] **grandiose:** more complicated than necessary; extravagant

7. A: The food looks delicious.

   B: I hope everything is OK. _____ you _____ one of

   the sandwiches and tell me if it tastes good? (try)

8. A: Can you help me next week?

   B: Oh, I didn't tell you?

   A: Tell me what?

   B: We _____ in California all next week. (be)

9. A: Can I get you anything else?

   B: Yes, I think I _____ another cup of coffee. (have)

Think about It Why did you choose *will* or *be going to* in the conversations in Activity 29? Compare ideas with your classmates.

Reason for using *be going to*	Reasons for using *will*
• For a future event that has already been planned or scheduled	• For a decision made at the moment of speaking • For a promise • For a request or offer of help

I chose will *for number one because the person offered to help.*

30 | Analyzing Predictions Underline the uses of *will* in this article. Circle the uses of *be going to*. Why do you think the writer uses each future form? **1.7 C**

Growing Demand for Coal

The demand for coal is growing steadily. Coal accounted for 26 percent of energy consumed in 2004 worldwide, according to the U.S. Energy Information Agency, and will grow to 28 percent by 2030. Total energy consumption, however, will be going up a few percentage points a year, so in the same period of time, coal consumption will rise 74 percent.

India and China will account for 72 percent of the increase, but coal consumption is expected to also rise in Russia, South Africa, and the U.S. In the U.S., the growth could decline, but coal will still be a big part of the energy profile[22].

"Ninety percent of the fossil fuel reserves in the U.S., India, and China are in coal, and China and India are not going to move from this fuel in the future," said Jeremy Carl of Stanford University. "They are not going to turn off the lights."

Think about It Could the writer use either *be going to* or *will* in any of the sentences above? Why?

---

[22] **profile:** a set of data that gives the most important features of something

31 | Making Predictions with *Will* Complete each prediction with *will* and a verb from the box. `1.7 C`

be	be	be able to	become	have	have	make	work

PREDICTIONS FOR LIFE 100 YEARS FROM NOW

1. We _____ control the weather.

2. Most people _____ from their homes.

3. There _____ one kind of money for the whole world.

4. Everyone _____ computers wired to their brains.

5. Space elevators _____ space travel cheap.

6. Deserts _____ tropical forests.

7. We _____ the ability to communicate through thought transmission[23].

8. There _____ only three languages in the world—English, Spanish, and Chinese.

> **F Y I**
>
> We can use *will* with phrasal modals like *be able to*.
>
> You **will be able to** see Mars clearly in October.

Talk about It Choose one of the predictions above. How likely is it to come true in the next 100 years? Choose a number from 10 (very likely) to 0 (not likely at all) and give reasons for your answer.

32 | Using *Be Going To* for Predictions Complete the predictions with *be going to*. Then match the evidence with the predictions. `1.7 C`

EVIDENCE

1. The sun is rising, and there are no clouds in the sky. You think to yourself: _g_

2. It's half an hour after class usually starts, and your teacher still hasn't arrived. One of your classmates says: ____

3. You get to the bus stop in the morning just as the bus is leaving. You say to yourself: ____

4. A friend sees you using a tool incorrectly. He says to you: ____

5. You see a family member eating a second big bowl of ice cream. You say: ____

6. Your friend is cooking fish for dinner, but he bakes it too long, and it burns completely. You say: ____

7. You expected 50 people to come to the lecture, but already there are more than 50 people in the room. You say to your assistant: ____

8. You and your friends are planning to drive to the beach. You try to start the car, but nothing happens. One of your friends says: ____

PREDICTIONS

a. I guess we _____ class today. (not/have)

b. Be careful. You _____ hurt. (get)

c. You _____ yourself sick. (make)

d. I guess we _____ anywhere today. (not/go)

e. We _____ more chairs. (need)

f. Now I _____ late for work. (be)

g. It ____*is going to be*____ a nice day. (be)

h. I guess we _____ fish for dinner. (not/have)

[23] **thought transmission:** the ability to send thoughts from mind to mind

1.8 Using Present Forms to Talk about the Future

A

1 School **starts** on September 3rd **this year**.

2 The plane **leaves** **in an hour**.

3 The library **closes** **at noon today**.

4 When **are** we **meeting** **this week**?

5 Most stores **are closing** early **tonight**.

6 **I'm leaving** for London **tomorrow night**.

In addition to the more common uses of the **simple present** and **present progressive**, we can also use these verb forms to talk about scheduled events and arrangements in the future, as in **1 – 6**.

Notice: We almost always use a time expression (such as *in an hour, this week,* or *tonight*) to show that we are referring to the future, not the present, as in **1 – 6**.

B

SIMPLE PRESENT VS. PRESENT PROGRESSIVE

7 We **meet** at 10 **on Tuesday**. Don't forget to bring your laptop. (= We meet regularly at 10 on Tuesday.)

8 Saturday's game **begins** **at noon**.

9 Don't forget. We**'re meeting** at 9 instead of 10 **on Tuesday**. (= We're meeting at 9 this Tuesday.)

10 Why **is** the game **starting** late **tonight**?

When we talk about a scheduled event that takes place regularly, we usually use the simple present, as in **7 – 8**.

When a scheduled event is temporary or changing, we often use the present progressive, as in **9 – 10**.

C

PRESENT PROGRESSIVE VS. *BE GOING TO*

11 We**'re leaving** next month.

12 We**'re going to leave** next month.

13 It**'s going to rain** tomorrow. (NOT: ~~It's raining tomorrow.~~)

When we talk about personal plans and arrangements, we sometimes use the present progressive instead of *be going to*, as in **11 – 12**.

WARNING! Unlike *be going to*, we do not use the present progressive to make predictions, as in **13**.

D

14 I **am to meet** the president at 10:00. (= I am required to meet the president at 10:00.)

15 The company **is to announce** its quarterly earnings in December. (= The company is obligated to do this.)

In formal contexts, we sometimes use *am / is / are* + **to- infinitive** to refer to the future, as in **14 – 15**. Using this form suggests that the future event is an obligation or requirement.

33 | **Talking about the Future with Present Forms** Listen to these conversations and write the missing words. Then practice with a partner. **1.8 A**

1. A: When _____ *is* _____ your flight tomorrow?

   B: I think it _____ at 6, but I'm not sure.

   A: Nonstop flight?

   B: No, I _____ in London.

   A: _____ you _____ a long layover[24]?

   B: No, only two hours.

   A: Oh, that's not bad.

RESEARCH SAYS...

Common verbs used with the simple present to talk about the future include:

arrive	finish
begin	go
come	leave
depart	start

CORPUS

[24]**layover:** a stop between flights

2. A: _____ you _____

   to the meeting next week?

   B: Yes, I plan to.

   A: What time _____ it _____?

   B: At 7.

3. A: _____ you _____

   anything special this weekend?

   B: Um, I already _____ plans for Saturday,

   but _____ free on Sunday.

   A: Great. _____ a concert in the afternoon. Interested?

   B: Sure.

   A: It _____ at 3, so I'll come by at 2.

   B: OK.

4. A: _____ the last day of school?

   B: June 15.

   A: _____ that a Friday?

   B: No, _____ a Wednesday.

5. A: _____ you _____

   to the concert tonight?

   B: Yeah. What time _____ it _____?

   A: Let me check.

Think about It What time expressions do the speakers use in the conversations in Activity 33? Circle them.

Talk about It Tell your classmates about an event scheduled for later this week.

34 | Present or Future? Listen to ten short conversations. Are the speakers talking about an action in progress now or an event in the future? Check (✓) your answer. `1.8 A`

	Now	In the future			Now	In the future
1.	☐	✓		6.	☐	☐
2.	☐	☐		7.	☐	☐
3.	☐	☐		8.	☐	☐
4.	☐	☐		9.	☐	☐
5.	☐	☐		10.	☐	☐

Think about It Listen to the conversations again. In the future sentences, what time expressions do the speakers use to show that they are talking about the future? Write at least six.

_____ _____

_____ _____

_____ _____

35 | Simple Present or Present Progressive? Complete these conversations with the simple present or present progressive form of the verb in parentheses. (More than one answer may be possible.) `1.8 B`

1. A: When _____ the first train _____ tomorrow morning? (leave)

   B: At seven.

2. A: Where's the train?

   B: You didn't hear the announcement?

   A: No. What did it say?

   B: The seven o'clock train _____ an hour late this morning. (leave)

3. A: Hurry up. We're going to be late.

   B: What time _____ the movie _____? (start)

   A: In 15 minutes.

4. A: Do you want to go for lunch tomorrow?

   B: Um, I _____ tomorrow. I have a doctor's appointment. (not/work)

5. A: Who _____ to the meeting tonight? (come)

   B: I'm not sure.

6. A: I have some good news.

   B: What is it?

   A: They _____ the elevators tomorrow, so the office

   _____ until 11 in the morning. (fix) (not/open)

Think about It In which of the conversations above is a scheduled event temporary or changing?

36 | Present Progressive or *Be Going To*? Complete these quotations. Where possible, use the present progressive to talk about the future. Where you can't, use *be going to*. `1.8 C`

QUOTATIONS FROM FAMOUS PEOPLE

1. I don't know where I _____ from here, but I promise it won't be boring. (go)

   —*David Bowie, musician*

2. If you can't read, it _____ hard to realize dreams. (be)

   —*Booker T. Washington, educator*

3. I _____ to college. I don't care if it ruins my career. I'd rather be smart than a movie

   star. (go) —*Natalie Portman, actor*

4. The desktop market has entered the dark ages, and it _____ in the dark ages for the

   next ten years. (be) —*Steve Jobs, businessman*

5. I know this _____ bad, but I'm going to pretend it _____ good.

   (end/end) —*Johnny Knoxville, actor*

6. It _____ easy to change things. (not/be) —*Daniel Berrigan, activist*

7. Things _____ a lot worse before they get worse. (get) —*Lily Tomlin, actor*

8. Sooner or later I _____, but I'm not going to retire. (die) —*Margaret Mead, scientist*

Think about It In which of the quotations in Activity 36 did you use *be going to* instead of the present progressive? Why?

37 | Talking about Future Requirements Circle the expressions in these sentences that suggest an obligation or requirement. Then rewrite the sentences using *am/is/are* + *to-* infinitive. `1.8 D`

1. Class begins at 9, and you (need to be) here on time.

   Class begins at 9, and you are to be here on time.

2. The school field trip will be on June 15. Your child should bring a lunch and something to drink.

3. The bus is going to leave at 7:15, so everyone should be at the parking lot by 7.

4. Your appointment with the mayor is at noon. You need to arrive at the reception desk by 11:45.

5. I need to go out for a few minutes, but no one should leave the room while I am away. Is that clear?

6. You will have 30 minutes to answer the exam question. When I say stop, you should put down your pencil.

7. Your doctor's appointment is at 10 a.m. Please don't eat or drink anything in the morning.

8. We have important visitors next Monday. Everyone should dress up a bit.

1.9 Using Present Forms in Speaking

A	**USING CONTRACTIONS** **1** Your books're here. **2** The flowers're dying. **3** They're here. **4** What're you doing? **5** Who're they talking to? **6** How're you doing?	In conversation, we usually contract the *am / is / are* after nouns, pronouns, and question words, as in **1 – 6**. By not using contractions, we may sound more formal or insistent than we intend. We sometimes use the full form for special emphasis or in formal speaking situations such as speeches.
B	**NON-ACTION VERBS IN CONVERSATION** **7** I think so. **8** I doubt it. **9** I suppose so. **10** I don't know. **11** It doesn't matter. **12** I don't mind. **13** I don't care. **14** I don't want to.	In conversation, the **simple present** is much more common than the simple past. This is partly because a few verbs are used frequently. Many of these are non-action verbs showing how the speaker feels or thinks about something, as in **7 – 14**.
C	**USING THE PRESENT TO TELL A STORY** **15** So I'm **leaving** the store, and this woman **stops** me and **asks** to use my phone. I **don't know** what to say to her, I mean, I **don't know** her. . . .	We sometimes use the **simple present** and **present progressive** to tell a story that took place in the past, as in **15**. Using present verb forms makes the story seem more vivid.

38 | **Using Contractions** Match the questions with the responses. Listen and check your answers. Then practice with a partner. `1.9 A`

QUESTIONS

1. What are you doing? _e_
2. What is the matter? ____
3. When is she leaving? ____
4. How far is your house from here? ____
5. When is the next exam? ____
6. Where are my shoes? ____
7. How far is Tokyo from here? ____
8. Who are you calling? ____
9. Why are you always yelling at me? ____
10. How long are they going to be there? ____

RESPONSES

a. Not long. I think they are coming back in a week.
b. Because you are always misbehaving.
c. It is on the fifth. That is a Friday.
d. Tomorrow. She is taking the noon train tomorrow.
e. Nothing special. I am just taking a break.
f. My brother. He is in Toronto this week.
g. I think I am going to lose my job.
h. I am not sure, but it is closer than Beijing.
i. They are in the closet.
j. It is just around the corner.

Talk about It Ask a partner four of the questions above again. Give your own answers.

39 | **Common Verbs in the Simple Present** Work with a partner. Take turns saying a sentence from Column A. Your partner responds with a sentence from Column B. (Many responses are possible.) `1.9 B`

COLUMN A

1. Where do you want to go for lunch?
2. Are you coming to class tomorrow?
3. We have a test tomorrow.
4. It's late.
5. It's time to go.
6. You aren't being funny.
7. Does this computer work?
8. Do you know what I mean?
9. What's the matter with you?
10. Why aren't you coming to the concert?
11. Is it cold outside?
12. Somebody's using your computer.
13. I don't have any money.
14. Is it going to rain tomorrow?

COLUMN B

I suppose so.
I doubt it.
I don't care.
I don't mind.
It doesn't matter.
I don't want to.
I know.
I don't know.
I think so.
I don't think so.

Talk about It Work with a partner. Write three more short conversations using verbs in the box below. Then present your conversations to the class.

COMMON VERBS IN THE SIMPLE PRESENT

care	doubt	know	matter	mind	suppose	think	want

40 | Telling a Story Make up a story using these pictures. Use present verb forms to make your story vivid. Tell your story to a partner. Listen to your partner's story. `1.9 C`

Talk about It Tell a partner a story that happened to you. Use present verb forms.

1.10 Using Present and Past Forms in Academic Writing

A	**SUMMARIES AND ABSTRACTS** **1** This paper **examines** the relationship between exercise and mood. Evidence from a number of studies **suggests** that regular exercise **leads** to an improvement in mood. Possible signs of depression **decrease** over the course of a 10-week regular exercise program. The paper also **discusses** other emotional benefits of regular exercise.	We often use the **simple present** in summaries and abstracts of academic papers, as in **1**. Using the simple present signals that the writer views the statement as a fact or general truth.
B	**ADDING DETAILS TO GENERAL STATEMENTS** **2** Lying **is** usually unacceptable behavior, but there **are** rare times when it **is** better to tell a lie than to tell the truth. I **learned** this the hard way. When I **was** 15, . . .	Writers often use the **simple present** to make a general statement, as in **2**. They then explain or support the general statement with specific details and examples using the **simple past**.
C	**WRITING ABOUT RESEARCH** **3** Researchers from University College **studied** brain scans of 105 people—80 of whom were bilingual. The researchers **found** that learning other languages changed the gray matter in the left part of the brain. This research **demonstrates** how learning languages **develops** the brain.	In academic writing, writers often use the **simple past** to describe the steps in a study or experiment, as in **3**. They then evaluate the results of the study using the **simple present**. The simple present signals that the writer believes the information is scientific fact.

41 | Using the Simple Present in Summaries Underline the simple present verbs in these summaries. Then answer the questions on page 34. **1.10 A**

Abstracts of Articles

1. **TITLE:** Real Men Don't Need Work-Life Balance
   AUTHOR: Tanvi Gautam
   SOURCE: *Forbes* magazine
   SUMMARY: This article <u>focuses</u> on the issue of work-life balance for men. Many firms assume that men do not need career flexibility or work-life integration. However, these assumptions are generally not accurate. The author argues that firms need to consider men when they design policies to promote flexibility.

FYI

An abstract is a short summary of a longer piece of writing. Abstracts are used by researchers to understand the main ideas of an article quickly.

2. **TITLE:** Margaret C. Anderson's *Little Review*
   AUTHORS: Sophia Estante; Lorrie Moore
   SOURCE: The Writing Center at the University of Wisconsin–Madison
   SUMMARY: This research looks at the work of Margaret C. Anderson, the editor of the *Little Review*. The research draws upon mostly primary sources including memoirs, published letters, and a complete collection of the *Little Review*. Most prior research on Anderson focuses on her connection to the famous writers and personalities that she published and associated with. This focus undermines[25] her role as the dominant[26] creative force behind one of the most influential little magazines published in the twentieth century. This case example shows how little magazine publishing is arguably a literary art.

---

[25]**undermine:** to injure; to weaken   [26]**dominant:** superior; leading

3. **TITLE:** The Connection between Hypertension[27] and Stress
   AUTHORS: Michael Anderson; Karina Gomez; Peizhu Liu
   SOURCE: *Medical Monthly.* 2014; 58: 556-570.

SUMMARY: It has been established that stressful situations cause temporary spikes[28] in blood pressure, but researchers are unsure of the relationship between stress and long-term hypertension. The purpose of this study is to understand this relationship and to find out if short-term spikes in blood pressure due to stress can add up and cause high blood pressure in the long term. The data for this study comes from a series of tests conducted on forty participants of various backgrounds in the San Francisco Bay Area over a period of twenty years. The researchers also looked at statistical[29] data from the California Board of Health over the past twenty years. Even though the researchers found mixed test results, the study shows that daily exercise and focused stress management lowers the risk of hypertension over time. However, medical researchers must conduct more studies in order to determine the link between the frequency of short term spikes in stress and long-term hypertension.

QUESTIONS

1. Besides the simple present, what other verb forms do the writers use in the summaries above?
2. What kinds of information do these writers include in the summaries?
3. What kinds of information do these writers leave out of the summaries?
4. What is the purpose of an abstract or summary?

42 | Evaluate Read these paragraphs and underline the verbs. Then answer the questions below. `1.10 B`

A	B
A Self-discipline <u>is</u> the most important ingredient for success. When you set a goal for yourself, you have to work to reach it. You need to study, earn money, or do whatever is necessary for your particular[30] goal. You need to make a plan and follow it, even when you feel discouraged[31]. Without self-discipline, it is easy to lose sight of your goal. There is no value in having a goal if you do not have self-discipline.	**B** Self-discipline is the most important ingredient for success. My brother is a good example of the connection between self-discipline and success. When he was only 15, he decided that he wanted to be a doctor. From that point, he stopped playing sports and doing things with his friends so that he would have time to study. Every summer he gave up his vacation so that he could work in a hospital. Because he was self-disciplined, my brother is now a successful family doctor in my hometown.

QUESTIONS

1. What differences in the verbs do you notice between the two paragraphs above? Why?
2. Which paragraph is more interesting to you? Why?
3. Which paragraph provides specific details and examples?

---

[27] **hypertension:** high blood pressure
[28] **spike:** a sudden increase in something
[29] **statistical:** mathematical; numeric

[30] **particular:** specific
[31] **discouraged:** without confidence; hopeless

43 | Using the Simple Past to Give Specific Examples Read these general statements and check (✓) *Agree* or *Disagree*. Then write a short paragraph giving a specific example to explain why you agree or disagree with each statement. `1.10 B`

	AGREE	DISAGREE
1. Athletic competition is not good for very young children.	☐	☐
2. Anger is sometimes beneficial[32].	☐	☐
3. In spite of advances in scientific knowledge, people are still superstitious[33].	☐	☐
4. Learning a second language is not good for young children.	☐	☐

1. Agree: Athletic competition is not good for very young children. When my brother was very young, he played on a children's soccer team. His best friend wanted to play on the team too, but he wasn't a very good player. The other children on the team didn't want my brother's friend to be on the team because they wanted to win. Soccer was a competition for them, not a game, and so at the age of seven, my brother's friend quit playing soccer.

44 | Exploring Verb Forms in Research Reports Complete each research report with the correct form of the verbs in parentheses. `1.10 C`

1. In one report on how intelligence develops in young children, American researchers ____*studied*____ (study) nearly 500 boys and girls born in New Jersey hospitals between 1984 and 1987. When they were born, each child _____ (weigh) less than 2,000 grams, and they were approximately 16 years old when they _____ (participate) in the study. The children _____ (take) intelligence and motor skill tests at home. (Motor skills are skills that require living things to effectively use their muscles.)

   The test results were then compared with test results of other children of the same age. The study _____ (report) that the children with low birth weight often have more problems with motor skills than the other children. This _____ (suggest) that babies with low birth weight may be more likely than other children to have physical and mental problems as they develop.

2. A major study from the University of North Carolina _____ (compare) two groups of children. One group of children _____ (attend) an all-day childcare center from when they _____ (be) a few weeks old until the age of 5. This high-quality program _____ (offer) some social, health, and educational programs, and it _____ (provide) healthy food for the children. The other group of children _____ (not / go) to a childcare center at any time. Both groups _____ (attend) public schools after the age of 5.

   The two groups of children _____ (be) similar when they _____ (be) babies, but different after the age of about 18 months. As babies, both groups _____ (have) similar results in tests for mental and physical skills. However, the children in the childcare program _____ (score) much higher in tests after the age of 18 months. The children _____ (take) tests again at the ages of 12 and 15 years. Again, the children from the childcare center _____ (show) better test scores.

[32] **beneficial:** helpful   [33] **superstitious:** believing in something you can't explain

The study _____ that education during the first months and years of life _____
(suggest)   (be)

important for development later in life. The researchers say that with early education, poorer

children could become more successful and do better in school. They _____ their study
(believe)

_____ a need for the government to spend money on public education at an early age. They
(show)

_____ these kinds of programs _____ better success overall in American schools.
(claim)   (create)

WRAP-UP Demonstrate Your Knowledge

A | WRITE Write three paragraphs with information about yourself ten years ago, now, and ten years from now.

Ten years ago	Now	Ten years from now
I was living in Mexico with my parents. It was a happy time for my family because everyone was healthy....	*I am living here with my wife....*	*I will probably be living here. Hopefully I will have a good job....*

B | SURVEY Choose a topic related to habits. Think of five to ten questions to use in a survey. Ask your classmates the questions and record their answers. What conclusions can you draw? Are there similarities in the answers? Did males and females answer differently?

Topic: Study Habits
How many hours per week do you usually study outside of class?
Did you usually do your homework in high school?

C | PRESENTATION Choose a topic—a person, place, or thing—that interests you. Look for ten interesting facts about this topic and present the facts to your class.

D | WEB SEARCH What happened on the month and day you were born? Do an online search of your date of birth. Choose five interesting things that happened that day and report them to the class.

1.11 Summary of Present, Past, and Future Forms

SIMPLE PRESENT		USES
I You We They	know. do not know. don't know.	We use the simple present to describe: • current habitual behavior • timeless truths • general truths • the state of something now • regular scheduled events in the future
He She It	knows. does not know. doesn't know.	

SIMPLE PAST		USES
I You We They He She It	knew. did not know. didn't know. arrived. did not arrive. didn't arrive.	We use the simple past to: • signal an action, event, or state was completed at a definite time in the past • indicate social or psychological distance

PRESENT PROGRESSIVE		USES
I	am listening. 'm listening. am not listening. 'm not listening.	We use the present progressive to: • signal that a state or activity is temporary or in progress now • talk about planned events in the future
He She It	is listening. 's listening. is not listening. 's not listening. isn't listening.	
You We They	are listening. 're listening. are not listening. 're not listening. aren't listening.	

PAST PROGRESSIVE		USES
I He She It	was listening. was not listening. wasn't listening.	We use the past progressive to: • talk about something in progress at a particular time in the past • describe a developing or changing situation in the past • show social or psychological distance
You We They	were listening. were not listening. weren't listening.	

FUTURE WITH *BE GOING TO*		USES
I	am going to help. 'm going to help. am not going to help. 'm not going to help.	We often use *be going to* to: • talk about planned future events • make predictions
He She It	is going to help. 's going to help. is not going to help. 's not going to help. isn't going to help.	
You We They	are going to help. 're going to help. are not going to help. 're not going to help. aren't going to help.	

FUTURE WITH *WILL*		USES
I He She It You We They	will do it. 'll do it. will not do it. won't do it.	We often use *will* to: • make promises • offer help and make requests • talk about spontaneous plans • make predictions

Perfect Forms

Children have never been very good at listening to their elders[1], but they have never failed to imitate them.

—JAMES BALDWIN, WRITER

(1924–1987)

Talk about It What does the quotation above mean? Do you agree or disagree?

[1] **elders:** people who are older than you

WARM-UP

A | Study the graph on the right. Then read the statements and write *T* (true) or *F* (false). Do you find any of this information surprising? Tell your classmates.

World Population Growth

____ 1. The population of the world **has been increasing** since 1750.

____ 2. Over the past 50 years, the populations of developing and industrial regions **have gone up** at the same rate.

____ 3. In 1800, there were about 1 billion people in the world. By 1900, the population **had** almost **reached** 2 billion.

____ 4. The population of developing regions started to grow more rapidly around 1950. The population of industrial regions **has risen** much less in comparison.

____ 5. By 2050, the population of the world **will have reached** 9 billion people.

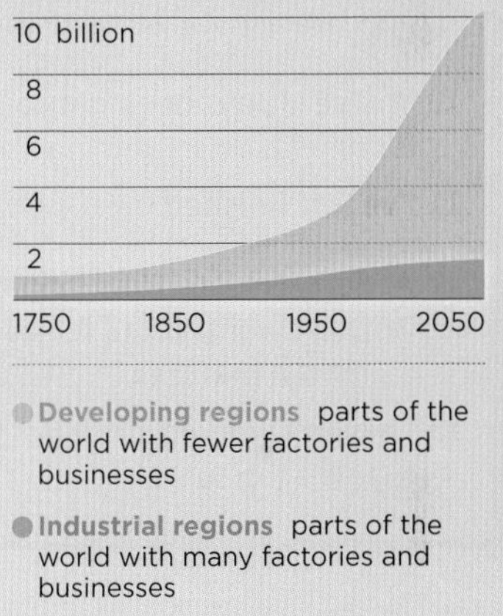

World Population Growth

10 billion
8
6
4
2

1750   1850   1950   2050

● **Developing regions** parts of the world with fewer factories and businesses

● **Industrial regions** parts of the world with many factories and businesses

Sources: United Nations Population Division and Population Reference Bureau, 1993.

B | Answer these questions about the statements above.

1. The words in **green** are perfect forms of verbs. How many different perfect forms do you see in the statements?

2. What time words are used with the perfect verb forms?

3. When do you think we use perfect forms of verbs?

C | Look back at the quotation on page 38. Identify any perfect verb forms.

2.1 Overview of the Present Perfect

A

1 Life expectancy **has increased** since 1900. It's not uncommon for people to live into their eighties now.

2 Technology **has helped** people in many ways, but too much technology isn't healthy.

3 I**'ve watched** that movie too many times. I think I know it by heart.

4 Many roads here **have become** crowded, and this causes frequent traffic jams.

5 A: I need to talk to Barbara for a minute. Is she here?
B: No, she**'s gone** to the library.
(= She went to the library. She isn't here now.)

6 A: Are you hungry?
B: No, I**'ve** already **eaten.**
(= I ate something earlier so now I'm not hungry.)

When we want to show that a past action, event, or state is *connected to now* (the moment of speaking), we use the **present perfect** form of a verb, as in **1 – 6**. The past action, event, or state might be something that:

- started in the past and continues to the present, as in **1 – 2**
- happened repeatedly in the past and has an effect on something in the present, as in **3 – 4**
- started and ended in the past but has an effect on something in the present, as in **5 – 6**

Remember: We form the present perfect with *have / has* (+ *not*) + the past participle (*-ed/-en* form) of the main verb. For a list of past participles of irregular verbs, see the Resources, page R-3.

B

7 A: How's the movie?
B: It**'s been** great **so far.**

8 A: Is Uncle Bill here?
B: No, he **hasn't come** in **yet.**

9 We**'ve spoken** several times **in the past month,** and I think we are now ready to make a decision.

10 You**'ve always been** unhappy with your job. I think it's time to do something about it.

11 I**'ve just finished** my paper.

12 A: Sorry I'm late. How long **have** you **been** here?
B: Don't worry about it. I**'ve** only **been** here **for ten minutes.**

13 I **haven't worked since last December.** I really need to find a job soon.

We often use **adverbs** and **time expressions** with the present perfect, as in **7 – 13**. Some examples include:

already	just	never	yet
always	lately	so far	

in	+	the past few days / the last ten minutes
over	+	the past month / the last two years
for	+	a week / a year / the last two years
since	+	1980 / last year / January / then / my birthday

Notice: We can use some adverbs (such as *already, always, just,* and *never*) between *have / has* and the past participle, as in **10 – 11**.

We use *for* + a period of time, as in **12**. We use *since* + a specific time, as in **13**.

1 | Connecting Past Actions to Now What does each **bold** verb in the conversations below describe? Read the meanings in the box. Then write *a, b,* or *c.* (More than one answer may be possible.) [2.1 A]

The verb describes something that:
- a. started in the past and continues to the present
- b. happened repeatedly in the past and has an effect on something in the present
- c. started and ended in the past but has an effect on something in the present

MEANING

__C__ 1. A: Are you OK?

B: No, I**'ve twisted** my ankle.

A: Does it hurt?

B: Of course it hurts. Can you get me a chair?

_____ 2. A: Ms. James is your academic advisor, isn't she?

B: Yes, but we **haven't had** many meetings.

_____ 3. A: Do you know Isabel Martinez?

B: Yeah, I**'ve known** her for years. Why do you ask?

A: She's my new boss.

_____ 4. A: Do you know Los Angeles very well?

B: Sure. I**'ve been** there several times. What do you want to know?

A: What's the public transportation like?

B: It's not so great. You really need a car.

_____ 5. A: Does your brother still live in Santa Fe?

B: No, he**'s moved** to El Paso, but he still has lots of friends in Santa Fe.

_____ 6. A: Do you want to go to the game tonight?

B: Sorry, I can't. I**'ve made** other plans.

_____ 7. A: **Have** you **seen** my wallet?

B: Yes, it's on the bureau.

_____ 8. A: Ever since the summer, you**'ve been** different.

B: What do you mean?

A: I don't know. You're just more distracted now.

> **F Y I**
>
> When we use the present perfect, the connection to now is not always stated directly.
>
> The exhibit was in California, but now it **has moved on** to New York.
>
> (= now it's in New York)

Think about It What other verb forms do the speakers use in the conversations in Activity 1? What does this say about how we often use the present perfect?

Think about It Think about each situation in Activity 1. For each present perfect verb, what connection(s) to *now* do you think the speaker is making? Write your ideas in this chart. (Many answers are possible.)

Present perfect action, event, or state	Connection(s) to now
1. I've twisted my ankle.	*My ankle hurts.*
2. I haven't had many meetings with Ms. James.	*I don't know Ms. James very well.*
3. I've known Isabel Martinez for years.	
4. I've been to Los Angeles several times.	
5. My brother has moved to El Paso.	
6. I've made other plans for tonight.	
7. I have seen your wallet.	
8. You've been different since the summer.	

2 | Using the Present Perfect Read this essay response and complete it with the present perfect form of the verbs in parentheses. **2.1 A–B**

Essay Prompt: In general, people are living longer now. Discuss the causes of this. Use specific reasons and details to develop your essay.

It's true. People are living longer now. Today it is not uncommon for men and women to live into their eighties or even their nineties. The average life expectancy _____ greatly since 1900. At
(1. increase)
that time, the average life expectancy in this country was 47 years. Today the average life expectancy is 78 years. A few specific things _____ to increase life expectancy. These include vaccinations[2],
(2. help)
a decrease in smoking, and workplace safety rules.

The use of vaccinations _____ greatly to the increase in life expectancy. The law says that
(3. contribute[3])
schoolchildren must be vaccinated against certain deadly diseases. And they must receive these vaccinations before they can start school. This _____ a number of deadly diseases. In addition, the
(4. eliminate[4])
reduction in the number of people smoking cigarettes _____ millions of smoking-related
(5. prevent)
deaths. This change _____ the life expectancy of both former smokers and the people who
(6. raise)
had to breathe secondhand smoke[5].

Another reason for the increase in life expectancy is that workplaces _____ safer. In the
(7. become)
past, it was not uncommon to be injured or even killed on the job. However, in the middle of the twentieth century, the government passed workplace safety laws. As a result, there was a 40 percent decrease in on-the-job deaths in places such as factories and construction sites.

These are three important reasons why people are living longer today. All of these behaviors and others will continue to allow people to live longer and healthier lives.

Think about It Why does the writer use the present perfect in each sentence above? Choose reasons from this box.

The writer uses the present perfect to describe:
1. something started in the past and continues to the present.
2. something happened repeatedly in the past and has an effect on something in the present.
3. something started and ended in the past but has an effect on something in the present.

In #1 the writer uses the present perfect to describe something that started in the past and continues to the present.

Think about It Circle any uses of time expressions with the present perfect above. Are there many uses or only a few? What does this say about how we often use time expressions with the present perfect?

Talk about It Can you think of some other reasons why people are living longer today? Work with a partner to write at least three reasons. Try to use the present perfect in your sentences.

---

[2] **vaccinations:** shots to prevent disease
[3] **contribute:** to help make something happen

[4] **eliminate:** to get rid of; to remove
[5] **secondhand smoke:** smoke from another person's cigarette

3 | Using the Present Perfect Complete these sentences with the present perfect. `2.1 A-B`

1. The United Nations Children's Fund (UNICEF) _____has been_____ very active in vaccinating[6] children around the world. (be)

2. I'm still feeling a pain in my right leg, so I _____ to the gym this week. (not/go)

3. I _____ discouraged before—just like everyone else. (be)

4. I _____ a vacation in years, so I'm really looking forward to this trip. (not/take)

5. My sister _____ more in five years than most people do in a lifetime. (do)

6. It is my hard work that _____ me a success. (make)

7. Thank you for the interest you _____ in my work. (show)

8. My boss is very serious about the project. She _____ about it a lot. (talk)

9. I walk everywhere and I play basketball. I do that three times a week, and I _____ 30 pounds so far. I feel so much better. (lose)

10. It _____ much for the past few years, and a number of ski resorts are closing. (not/snow)

11. Improvements in technology _____ us to determine that Pluto is not a planet. (allow)

12. Scientists are just now discovering some of the strange living things that _____ to life in the deep ocean. (adapt)

13. The basic design of a bicycle _____ pretty much the same since the 1800s. Most bikes still use a foot-powered system that powers the back wheel. (remain)

14. Modern technology _____ it easier for businesspeople to succeed. However, they still have problems getting money to start businesses. (make)

15. China _____ the world's dominant producer of solar panels[7] in the last two years. It was responsible for half the world's production last year. (become)

Think about It Underline the time expressions in the sentences above. (Some of the sentences don't have a time expression.) Then write each time expression under the correct group in this chart.

Time expressions with the simple present	Time expressions with the present progressive	Time expressions with the present perfect	Time expressions with the simple past
	still		

Think about It Which of the time expressions above can be used with more than one verb form?

---

[6] **vaccinating:** giving a shot to prevent disease   [7] **solar panels:** devices used to gather energy from the sun

4 | Using Time Expressions with the Present Perfect Complete the sentences below with a time expression from the box. (More than one answer may be possible.) 2.1 B

| already | for | since | so far | yet |

SCIENCE AND RESEARCH

1. Thousands of people visited the King Tutankhamun exhibit when it was in Chicago. _____*Since*_____ then, the exhibit has moved to Philadelphia, and it is going to move to London in November.

2. Children learn new words at a very fast rate. Scientists have wondered _____ a long time how this is possible.

3. According to the *World Book Encyclopedia*, scientists have named more than 1½ million animals _____. Over half of these are types of insects.

4. Someone with a PhD is a doctor of philosophy. Many people earn PhDs, but they aren't all philosophers. The name has survived _____ the Middle Ages when many areas of study were called philosophy.

5. _____ scientists have not found a way to determine the exact age of the Earth.

6. Antarctica may help us solve some of the most difficult problems of the past and future of our planet. For example, scientists have _____ found that Antarctica is the largest storehouse of fresh water on the planet.

7. _____ ancient times, people have used parts of the willow tree to reduce pain.

8. Researchers have _____ found cures for many deadly diseases, but they haven't found a cure for skin cancer _____.

9. Researchers haven't _____ discovered how to cure the illness, but there are ways to treat the symptoms.

10. Scientists have discovered other stars with orbiting planets, but _____ they have only discovered one place that supports complex life forms: Earth.

mask of
King Tutankhamun

FYI

Time expressions with the present perfect help to show "time up to now."

I **haven't worked** since last December. (= last December up to now)

I **haven't finished** it yet, but I will soon. (= not finished in the past up to now)

5 | Error Correction Correct any errors in these sentences. (Some sentences may not have any errors.)

1. My parents been here for only three years, but they like it very much.

   My parents have been here for only three years, but they like it very much.

2. I has only been here for a month, so I still get lost a lot.
3. My sister doesn't live with me anymore. She gone to live in another state.
4. My mother is very smart even though she was never been to college.
5. I've try to make a lot of new friends here, but it isn't easy.
6. My father has always give me help when I needed it.
7. I admire my professor because she have taught me to express my ideas better.

8. My parents have always give me good advice. I know I can go to them when I have a problem.

9. I want to go someplace I never been to before.

10. I miss my brother a lot. I haven't seen him for more than a year because he is been in Asia.

11. My brother doesn't know I have a new job because I not told him.

12. Computers are changed our lives in many different ways. For example, in the past, it took days or weeks to communicate with someone on the other side of the world.

2.2 The Simple Past vs. the Present Perfect

A

SIMPLE PAST

The **simple past** is a past form. We usually use it to describe an action, event, or state that was completed in the past. It is *separate from now* (the moment of speaking), as in **1 – 2**.

1 A 2009 study **showed** that a diet high in fruit and vegetables **decreased** the risk of heart failure by 37 percent.

2 In 1652, the first samples of tea **reached** England. By then, tea drinking **was** already popular in France.

PRESENT PERFECT

The **present perfect** is a present form. We usually use it to describe an action, event, or state that happened or started in the past and is *connected to now*. We are thinking of how the past affects the **present**, as in **3 – 4**.

3 Research in the last several years **has shown** that people with some diseases often **have** low levels of vitamin D. More doctors **are now having** their patients tested for their vitamin D levels.

4 He's **been** a teacher here for ten years, and the students **love** him. He definitely **deserves** a raise.

B

SIMPLE PAST

We usually use the simple past with **time expressions** that indicate a finished time period, as in **5**.

SIMPLE PAST OR PRESENT PERFECT

Some **time expressions** can be used with either the simple past or the present perfect, as in **6**.

PRESENT PERFECT

We use the present perfect with **time expressions** that indicate a time period "up until now," as in **7**.

5
- **in** 1990 / 2010 • **yesterday**
- **last** night / week / month / year
- a week / several days / a year **ago**
- **from** 1850 **to** 1860 / 7:00 **to** 10:00
- **when** I was a child / he was ten

6
- **already** • **before** • **recently**
- **always** • **ever** • **never**
- **today** • **this** week / month
- **for** two years / a long time

7
- **lately** • **so far** • **yet**
- **before now** • **until now**
- **in the past** month / few years
- **over the past** few days / year
- **(ever) since** I was a child / he was ten

With the time expressions in **6**, the choice of verb form depends on how we interpret the event and when it happened, as in **8 – 9**.

SIMPLE PAST

8a I **didn't see** him **today**.
(I didn't see him at any time today.)

9a I **didn't see** him **for ten years**.
(I didn't see him from 1990 to 2000.)

PRESENT PERFECT

8b I **haven't seen** him **today**.
(I haven't seen him at any time from this morning until now.)

9b I **haven't seen** him **for ten years**.
(I haven't seen him from ten years ago until now.)

C

CORRECT THE COMMON ERRORS (See page R-11.)

10 ✗ I have seen many things when I was a child.

11 ✗ I have been here since three weeks.

12 ✗ I lived in Toronto for three years. I really love it here.

13 ✗ He is the most optimistic person I ever know.

GO ONLINE

◀)) 6 | Pronunciation Note: Simple Past or Present Perfect? Listen to the note. Then do Activity 7.

In conversation, it is sometimes difficult to distinguish **simple past** and **present perfect** verbs. Compare:

1 I **lost** my keys.   I've **lost** my keys.   **3** She **left.**   She's **left.**

2 He **hurt** his leg.   He's **hurt** his leg.   **4** They **called.**   They've **called.**

The other words in a conversation can help you understand a speaker's meaning.

PAST CONTEXT

5 A: Why didn't you drive home?
   B: Because I **lost** my keys.

PRESENT CONTEXT

6 A: Where are your keys?
   B: I don't know. I think I've **lost** them.

◀)) 7 | Simple Past or Present Perfect? Listen and write the missing verbs. Use contractions. `2.2 A`

1. He _'s lost_____ a lot of weight.

2. They _____ to go.

3. We _____ about it.

4. I _____ that house.

5. The game _____.

6. I _____ several movies.

7. We _____ not to go.

8. He _____ a lot of new friends there.

9. She _____ her phone number.

10. We _____ an hour for them.

11. I _____ to go there.

12. She _____ him.

13. He _____ a lot of money.

14. They _____ their house.

Talk about It Work with a partner. Choose one of the sentences above and use it to create a short conversation. Present your conversation to the class.

8 | Finished Time or Time Up Until Now? Check (✓) the time period that the **bold** expressions describe. Then complete the sentences with the correct verb form. `2.2 B`

TEN FACTS ABOUT U.S. HISTORY	FINISHED TIME PERIOD	TIME PERIOD UP UNTIL NOW
1. Washington, D.C., __has been__ the U.S. capital **since 1800.** (was / has been)	☐	☑
2. **From 1790 to 1800,** Philadelphia, Pennsylvania _____ (was / has been) the capital.	☐	☐
3. The U.S. Constitution was written in 1789, but it _____ (changed / has changed) **over the years.**	☐	☐
4. **From 1800 to 1900,** the U.S. _____ tremendous (experienced / has experienced) growth.	☐	☐
5. The U.S. _____ one civil war **since it became a nation.** (had / has had)	☐	☐
6. The U.S. Civil War _____ **in the mid-1800s.** (took place / has taken place)	☐	☐

7. **Ever since the Civil War began in 1861**, people _____
(argued / have argued)   ☐   ☐

over what caused the war.

8. **In the past 200 years**, Supreme Court decisions and laws   ☐   ☐

_____ the duties of the U.S. president.
(increased / have increased)

9. **In the past few years**, the government _____ the   ☐   ☐
(used / has used)

Supreme Court for new purposes, such as determining the

outcome of an election.

10. **In 2005**, the president _____ a new chief justice   ☐   ☐
(appointed / has appointed)

of the Supreme Court, John Roberts.

---

9 | Simple Past or Present Perfect? Complete these sentences with the simple past or present perfect form of the verb. Use contractions where possible. Then check (✓) if each sentence is *True* or *False* for you. `2.2 A–B`

PERSONAL FACTS	TRUE	FALSE
1. I _'ve lived_ here for the past five years. (live)	☐	☐
2. I _____ to Egypt yet, but I hope to go someday. (not/go)	☐	☐
3. I _____ in junior high school from 2009 to 2012. (be)	☐	☐
4. When I was a child, I sometimes _____ trouble. (get into)	☐	☐
5. I _____ a lot of new words since I started school here. (learn)	☐	☐
6. I _____ to study English when I was 15 years old. (begin)	☐	☐
7. So far I _____ to eight different countries. (be)	☐	☐
8. Last year _____ a great year for me. (be)	☐	☐
9. I _____ anything since I had dinner last night. (not/eat)	☐	☐
10. I _____ my phone at all yesterday. (not/use)	☐	☐
11. I _____ very much over the past three years. (not/travel)	☐	☐
12. I _____ any homework since we took the test a week ago. (not/do)	☐	☐

Write about It Change the information in the false statements above to make them true for you.

I haven't lived here for the past five years. OR *I have lived here for the past two years.*

Write about It Write three true statements and one false statement using the time expressions in the box. Read your sentences to the class, and ask your classmates to identify the false statement.

a year ago	in 2010	over the past few years	since I was a child

10 | Simple Past and Present Perfect in Context Read this essay response. Circle the simple past verbs. Underline the present perfect verbs. Then answer the questions below. `2.2 A–B`

Essay Prompt: The twentieth century saw great change. In your opinion, what was one of the biggest changes that took place in the twentieth century? Use specific reasons and details to explain your choice.

The development of new and more advanced technology (increased) rapidly in the twentieth century. In the beginning of the 1900s, people relied on horses to get around. Letters took days or weeks to arrive, and traveling to other countries wasn't easy. However, by the end of the century, people had cars, subways, and buses to get where they wanted to go. They communicated instantly by email. Travel from one country to another took hours, not months. Because of these things, I think that the growth in technology was one of the most important changes in the twentieth century.

Advances in technology have done more than make travel and communication quicker and more convenient; they have saved lives. People live much longer now than they did just 100 years ago. Some diseases that were once deadly have now been cured or can at least be treated with medications. Doctors have learned to keep individuals alive longer using new technologies.

Although technology has been very positive for the health of people, in some ways it has had a negative effect on the planet. The technological advances of the nineteenth and twentieth centuries have caused great damage to the earth's atmosphere[8]. There is also a shortage of natural resources caused by the rapid growth of the human population. Today scientists are working on ways to solve these problems. Hopefully, the twenty-first century will see the development of new technologies that can solve the problems created by the old.

QUESTIONS

1. Why does the writer use a lot of simple past verbs in the first paragraph?
2. Why does the writer use a lot of present perfect verbs in the second and third paragraphs?
3. What time expressions do you see in the sentences with the simple past or the present perfect? Write them under the correct group in this chart.

Time expressions with the simple past	Time expressions with the present perfect
in the twentieth century	

4. Is a time expression always necessary with the present perfect? Why do you think this?
5. According to the writer, how have advances in technology changed the way we live?

11 | Simple Past or Present Perfect? Complete these paragraphs with the words in parentheses. Use the simple past or present perfect form of the verb. `2.2 A–B`

1. Hayao Miyazaki _____*began*_____ his career as an animator in 1963.
   (begin)
   He _____ his first feature anime[9] film 16 years later. Then
   (direct)
   he _____ a movie company of his own in 1985. In 2001,
   (start)
   his movie *Spirited Away* _____ Best Film at the Japanese
   (win)
   Academy Awards.

a scene from *Spirited Away*

[8] **atmosphere:** the mixture of gases that surrounds a planet

[9] **anime:** Japanese style of cartoons or animation

2. I _____ collecting comic books when I was young. My grandfather often took me to
   (start)

   comic book stores, and I _____ a fan ever since. I know it's not the deepest reading in the
   (be)

   world, but that's why comic books are a great stress reliever.

3. History tells us a lot about ourselves. We can see how people _____ things a hundred
   (do)

   years ago and figure out what we want to keep and what we want to change. Look at how different

   everything is today from what it was a hundred years ago. We _____ some things like
   (keep)

   schools and family but changed many other things.

4. My grandparents were born in Poland and later immigrated to the U.S. They _____ their
   (leave)

   families behind to start a new family here. I have many cousins in Poland but I _____
   (never / meet)

   them. I think it would be fun to meet them and see how they live. I would also like to see where my

   grandparents _____ in Poland and learn about what life was like for them when they
   (live)

   were growing up.

5. Bicycles _____ a great form of transportation. They're safe, fun, and economical.
   (always / be)

   Today they're also more convenient than ever. Bicycle designers _____ a way to
   (come up with)

   fold them so that now you can ride your bike to work, fold it up, and take it in with you.

6. Water shortages are a serious problem. Many areas _____ droughts[10] because of
   (experience)

   climate change. Other places have access to water, but the water is polluted.

12 | Asking Questions Read this information. What *else* do you want to know about the person? Write six
questions to ask for more information. Use the present perfect and the simple past. `2.2 A–B`

FACT FILE

Name: Edwidge Danticat
Date of Birth: 1/19/1969
Birthplace: Port-au-Prince, Haiti

Academic degrees: Received a bachelor of arts degree in French
literature from Barnard College and a master of fine arts degree from
Brown University.

Awards: Finalist for a National Book Award for novel *Krik? Krak!* and
memoir *Brother, I'm Dying*; 1995 Pushcart Short Story Prize; 1998 Oprah's
Book Club selection for novel *Breath, Eyes, Memory*.

Other: Moved to the U.S. ten years after her parents moved to the U.S.
Employment: Taught at New York University and the University of Miami.

Examples: When did you get your bachelor of arts?   *How long have you lived in the U.S.?*

Talk about It Look online for answers to the questions you wrote above. Tell your classmates what
you learned.

---

[10] **droughts:** periods of extremely dry weather

13 | Using Different Verb Forms Complete these common job interview questions. Use the simple present, simple past, or present perfect form of the verb. Then answer the questions below. **2.2 A–B**

FREQUENTLY ASKED JOB INTERVIEW QUESTIONS

1. What goals _____have_____ you _____set_____ for your career? (set)

2. What _____ you _____ best about your previous job? (like)

3. What _____ your major strengths? Your major weaknesses? (be)

4. How _____ you _____ your last job? (get)

5. What _____ you _____ with your free time? (do)

6. What _____ your biggest professional achievement[11]? (be)

7. Describe the best boss you _____ in your professional career. (have)

8. _____ you ever _____ for a difficult person? (work)

9. How will the academic program and course work you _____ benefit your career? (take)

10. Where _____ you _____ to be professionally in five years? (hope)

QUESTIONS

a. Which verb form is a person most likely to use to answer each of the questions above? Is the verb form used in the answer the same as or different from the form in the question?

b. In a job interview, the interviewer often asks questions with present perfect verbs. Why is this?

Talk about It Using some of the questions above, role-play a job interview with a classmate.

14 | Error Correction Correct any errors in these sentences. (Some sentences may not have any errors.)

1. I arrived in the U.S. in 2002. Since I came here, I had trouble communicating with people because I don't speak English very well.

2. One of my favorite movies is the film *Australia*. I can't tell you how many times I saw the movie, but every time I see it, I like it better.

3. While computers have made life easier, they also made it more stressful.

4. My mother has always encouraged me to do big things. I wanted to get a job when I finished high school, but my mother told me to continue my education. She said I could do more with my life with a university education. She also encourage me to get a scholarship to pay for my education.

5. Since I came here, I have made a lot of friends, but one person in particular has helped me a lot. I have met Jennifer at the Learning Center at the beginning of the semester. She was looking for a Spanish tutor, and I needed help with my English. Since then, we got together several times a week just to talk.

6. One person who has had a great effect on my life is my father. He owns a clothing store, and I have worked with him at his store every time I have a holiday. From this experience I learn a lot about the business world.

[11] **achievement:** something that someone has done after trying hard

7. My parents have always encourage me to do what I want to do. When I have needed help, they support me. When I have decided to become an engineer, they helped pay for my education.

8. The Internet made communication faster and cheaper. Today you can use programs such as email or Skype to get an immediate response from someone, and they are much cheaper than a telephone call.

2.3 The Present Perfect Progressive vs. the Present Perfect

A

We form the **present perfect progressive** with **have / has** (+ **not**) + **been** + the **-ing form of the main verb**, as in **1 – 2**.

		have (+ not)	been	verb + -ing	
1	I	**have** **'ve**	**been**	**working**	all week.
	You				
	We / Bill and I	**have not** **haven't**			
	They / My friends*				

		has (+ not)	been	verb + -ing	
2	He / My brother	**has** **'s**	**been**	**working**	all week.
	She / His wife				
	It / The car	**has not** **hasn't**			

*In writing, we don't contract nouns like *My friends* with *have*.

B

COMPARE

3a I've been writing for this magazine for 14 years, and I still don't have my own office.

3b I've written for this magazine for 14 years. I can't imagine working anywhere else.

With most verbs, we can use either the **present perfect** or the **present perfect progressive** to talk about an activity that started in the past and continues to the present, as in **3a – 3b**. However, the progressive form emphasizes that the action is ongoing.

4 I've known him for several years, but we don't get together very often. (NOT: I've been knowing him . . .)

5 I've finished three books so far, but I have four more to read. (NOT: I've been finishing . . .)

We don't normally use the present perfect progressive:
- with verbs that have a non-active meaning, as in **4**
- with verbs that describe a single point in time (such as *leave, start, stop, finish*, etc.), as in **5**

For a list of non-action verbs, see the Resources, page R-2.

C

COMPARE

6a I've tried to call Jack all day.

6b I've been trying to call Jack all day.

6c I've tried to call Jack **several times** today. (NOT: I've been trying to call Jack several times . . .)

We can often use either form to describe an activity that happened repeatedly in the past and has an effect on the present, as in **6a – 6b**. However, with frequency words such as *once, twice,* or *several times*, we use the present perfect, as in **6c**.

7a Someone **has used** my name to apply for a credit card. I don't know what to do. (= started and ended in the past)

7b Someone **has been using** that credit card I lost. I don't know what to do. (= continues up to now)

We can use the present perfect to show that something started and ended in the past (but affects the present), as in **7a**. Using the present perfect progressive shows that the activity was repeated or ongoing up to now, as in **7b**.

15 | Forming the Present Perfect Progressive Complete these conversations with the present perfect progressive. Use contractions where possible. Then practice with a partner. `2.3 A`

1. A: When do you want dinner?

   B: Not for a while. I _'ve been eating_ all day. (eat)

2. A: What _____ you _____ all day? (do)

   B: Not much. What about you?

3. A: Somebody _____ my computer. (use)

   B: How do you know?

   A: It was off when I left this morning but now it's on.

4. A: Want something to drink?

   B: I'd love a cup of coffee.

   A: I thought you didn't drink coffee.

   B: Oh, come on. I _____ coffee for years. (drink)

5. A: Have you ever heard of the movie director Sam Giorgio?

   B: Sure. He _____ films for years. (make)

6. A: I'm worried about David.

   B: Why?

   A: Well, I _____ to reach him for three days, and he hasn't called me back. (try)

   B: Hmm. That's strange.

7. A: How long _____ the children _____ television? (watch)

   B: Only for half an hour.

8. A: Have you found a new apartment yet?

   B: No, but we _____ only _____ for a few days. (look)

9. A: How's your back?

   B: It _____ better but it's still bothering me. (get)

10. A: Do your parents know where they are going on vacation?

    B: They _____ about going to visit my brother, but they haven't decided yet. (talk)

Think about It Did the speakers use any time expressions in the conversations above? Underline them.

16 | Using the Present Perfect or Present Perfect Progressive Complete these conversations with the present perfect or present perfect progressive. Use contractions where possible. (In some sentences, either form may be possible.) Then practice with a partner. `2.3 B`

1. A: Where _____ _have_ _____ you _____ _been_ _____? (be)

   B: What do you mean?

   A: I _____ all over the place for you. (look)

   B: Sorry. I just went out for a minute.

2. A: Where have you been?

   B: At the gym. Why?

   A: I _____ to reach you for the last 20 minutes. (try)

   B: Sorry, I turned my phone off.

Where have you been?

3. A: Who's Amanda talking to?

   B: Her friend in Japan.

   A: Japan! That's going to be expensive.

   B: Yeah, I know. And she _____ to him for an hour. (talk)

4. A: Is the soup ready to eat?

   B: Almost. It _____ for about 30 minutes. (cook)

5. A: Do you know Sam Bradford?

   B: Of course. I _____ him for years. How do you know him? (know)

   A: I met him last week at a conference.

6. A: _____ you _____ the remote? I can't find it anywhere. (see)

   B: I think it's on the floor next to the couch.

7. A: Are you having a good time?

   B: Absolutely. I _____ so much fun in years. (not/have)

8. A: Are you going out with us this weekend?

   B: Of course. I _____ it all week. (look forward to)

9. A: What do you think of this music?

   B: I don't know. It's OK, I guess. I _____ just never _____ jazz. (like)

10. A: Aren't you finished yet?

    B: Be patient. I _____ on it for an hour. (only/work)

11. A: Did you know that your doorbell isn't working?

    B: Oh, right. I _____ to fix it. (mean)

12. A: How long have you been studying here?

    B: Not long. My class just started a week ago. What about you?

    A: My class _____ yet. (not/start)

13. A: I hear you won your last three races.

    B: Yeah, I _____ on a lucky streak lately. (be)

14. A: Have you decided what you are going to do next year?

    B: Yeah. My parents _____ finally _____ to let me study overseas. (agree)

Think about It For which verbs in Activity 16 did you **not** use the progressive form? Why not?

Think about It Is the speaker annoyed or complaining in any of the conversations in Activity 16? Which ones?

F Y I

As with other progressive forms, the present perfect progressive can indicate that the speaker is annoyed or complaining.

Hurry up. I**'ve been waiting** for you all afternoon, and now we're going to be late.

17 | Present Perfect or Present Perfect Progressive? Complete one sentence in each pair with the present perfect form of the verb in the box. Complete the other sentence with the present perfect progressive. Use contractions where possible. **2.3 C**

1. a. I _'ve drunk_____ four cups of coffee since I got up this morning, so I
       shouldn't drink any more.

   b. I _____ coffee since I got up this morning. Maybe that's why I can't
      sit still.

   | drink |

2. a. I _____ *The Call of the Wild* for a few days. I just can't put it down.

   b. I _____ *The Call of the Wild* twice. I highly recommend it.

   | read |

3. a. We _____ to the gym several times this week, so we're going to take
       tomorrow off.

   b. We _____ to the gym since January, and we already feel a lot better.

   | go |

4. a. She _____ already _____ at them twice today for making too
       much noise. I hope they behave now.

   b. She _____ at them all day. It's really irritating.

   | yell |

5. a. I _____ to Toshi several times this week, but he still doesn't want
       to come.

   b. I _____ to friends about taking a trip to Istanbul this summer.

   | talk |

6. a. I hope Hassan's OK. He _____ sick several times this winter.

   b. I can tell winter is coming. The nights _____ colder and colder.

   | get |

7. a. My brother thinks that I _____ his phone all week, but it's not true.

   b. If you need help with your new phone, I think Carlos _____ one a
      few times.

   | use |

8. a. I _____ you to clean your room three times this week. I'm not going
       to ask you again.

   b. I _____ you to clean your room all week. Could you please just
      do it?

   | ask |

9. a. You don't need to cook anything. I _____ dinner already.

   b. I _____ phone calls all day, so now I have a bad headache.

   | make |

10. a. I _____ several time to fix this computer, but it still won't work.

    b. Why didn't you answer your phone. I _____ to call you all morning.

    | try |

2.4 The Past Perfect and the Past Perfect Progressive

We use the **past perfect** to make the order of two past events clear. The past perfect signals the earlier event. The later event is often in the **simple past**, as in **1 – 2**. We can also use the past perfect in a sentence with a time phrase, as in **3**.

A

	earlier event	later event
1	Somebody **had left** a newspaper on a chair,	so I **took** it and **sat** down.

	later event	earlier event
2	By the time Thomas **arrived** in Phoenix,	his parents **had** already **left**.

	later time	earlier event
3	By the 1960s,	the population of the world **had reached** 3 billion.

4 By the time we got there, they **had eaten** all the sandwiches and **drunk** all the juice.

Remember: We form the past perfect with *had (+ not)* + the past participle (*-ed /-en* form) of the main verb.

When we use two past perfect verbs together, it's not necessary to repeat the helping verb *had*, as in **4**.

B

5 She **was** angry **because** he **had forgotten** to call.

6 He **looked as though** he'd hardly **slept** at all.

7 **When** I met him, he **hadn't graduated** from college yet.

8 I met him **before** he **graduated** from college.

9 I met him **after** he **graduated** from college.

COMPARE

10a We **left** when he **got** there. (He got there and then we left.)

10b We'd **left** when he **got** there. (We left and then he got there.)

We often use the past perfect in sentences with *because, as though,* or *when*. The past perfect signals which past event happened first, as in **5 – 7**.

The words *before* and *after* make the order of events clear. We can use the simple past after these words, as in **8 – 9**. The past perfect is not necessary.

Notice the difference in meaning when we use the simple past compared to the past perfect, as in **10a – 10b**.

C

COMPARE

11a He was sure that someone **had used** his computer.

(Someone had used his computer at least one time.)

11b He was sure that someone **had been using** his computer.

(Someone had been using his computer repeatedly or for an ongoing period of time.)

We can use the **past perfect progressive** instead of the past perfect to emphasize that an earlier activity was ongoing or repeated, as in **11b**.

We form the past perfect progressive with *had (+ not)* + *been* + the *-ing* form of the main verb.

18 | Using the Past Perfect Underline the verbs in these quotations. Then write the number *1* above the event in each sentence that took place first. **2.4 A**

QUOTATIONS ABOUT FAMILIES AND GROWING UP

1. We <u>were</u> a family who <u>had come</u> from nothing, and now we <u>had</u> respect
                           ¹
   from French people of all sorts¹². *(Zinedine Zidane, soccer player)*

2. My grandmother had wanted to be a music teacher herself, and so she
   steered¹³ my mother into that profession. *(Renée Fleming, singer)*

3. My mother had meant to be an opera star or even a movie star . . . but the
   [birth] of a baby put an end to that. *(Renée Fleming, singer)*

4. By the time I was 15, my mother had turned me into a real
   clotheshorse¹⁴. *(Gloria Swanson, movie star)*

Zinedine Zidane

---

¹²**sorts:** different kinds
¹³**steer:** to guide

¹⁴**clotheshorse:** someone who loves clothes

5. My mother had been a country and western singer, but when she moved out to Hollywood she found it very difficult to get work, so when I was born they put me into dance classes and singing classes as soon as I could walk, actually. *(Morgan Brittany, actor)*

6. My mother had always taught me to write about my feelings instead of sharing really personal things with others, so I spent many evenings writing in my diary, eating everything in the kitchen and waiting for Mr. Wrong to call. *(Cathy Guisewite, cartoonist)*

7. I had traveled 10 states and played over 50 cities by the time I was 4. *(Sammy Davis, Jr., entertainer)*

8. Interestingly enough, I met and had classes from several professors that my father had had many years before. *(Daniel J. Evans, politician)*

9. My mother was a very literate person who had educated herself. *(Lynn Johnston, cartoonist)*

10. Music was around in my family in two ways. My mother would occasionally sing to me, but I was mostly stimulated[15] by the classical music my father had left behind. *(Tom Glazer, musician)*

Think about It What is similar about the form of the verbs you labeled "1" in Activity 18?

Write about It Think of a way to complete these sentences with information about yourself. Then share your sentences with your classmates.

By the time I was 15, _____ .

I _____ by the time I was 4.

19 | Using the Past Perfect with *Because* and *As Though* Match the beginnings of these sentences with their endings. `2.4 B`

REASONS AND CONTRASTS

1. His clothes were wet because he __*h*__
2. She quit her job because her boss ____
3. He didn't call me because he ____
4. I felt sick last night because I ____
5. He was ashamed because he ____
6. He was angry because she ____
7. His back hurt so much he felt as though a car ____
8. The house looked as though it ____
9. She was breathless as though she ____
10. The child cried out as though she ____

a. had run there.
b. had run over him.
c. had been empty for years.
d. had criticized her.
e. had insulted him.
f. had eaten too much at dinner.
g. had been rude to his parents.
h. had fallen in the river.
i. had hurt herself.
j. had lost my phone number.

Talk about It Work with a partner. Think of another way to complete each sentence above.

"His clothes were wet because he had forgotten to bring an umbrella."

---

[15] **stimulate:** to energize

20 | Sentences with *When* Write the number *1* above the event that happened first in each sentence. Then rewrite the sentence using *when* and the past perfect. 2.4 B

1. She called me after I left the house.

   When she called me, I had already left the house.

2. After 20 minutes went by, we finally got a table at the restaurant.

3. The sun came up before we did all our work.

4. I still have the watch my father gave me before I left home.

5. After the smoke cleared, we saw the house in the distance.

6. After my cousin got her PhD, she got a job in the high-tech industry.

7. Everyone got out of the bus before it burst into flames.

8. After the last person left, we went inside and had lunch.

9. After the plane landed, the person next to me suddenly started laughing.

> **F Y I**
>
> When we give a series of past events in chronological order, we can usually just use the simple past because the order of events is clear.
>
> Tamae Watanabe **was** 63 years old when she **climbed** Mount Everest for the first time. Then, when she **was** 73 years old, she **climbed** it again.

21 | Simple Past or Past Perfect? Complete this article. Use the simple past or the past perfect form of the verb. 2.4 A–B

PATSY CLINE: 1932–1963

FANS[16] LOVED THIS YOUNG COUNTRY MUSIC STAR

Patsy Cline, born Virginia Patterson Hensley, _____*recorded*_____ her first
(1. record)

big hit[17] in 1957. It was called "Walkin' After Midnight" and it became No. 2

on the list of country music hit recordings and No. 16 on the list of most

popular music.

Patsy _____ for many years to make that first successful record.
(2. work)

She _____ singing when she was a young girl in her hometown of
(3. begin)

Winchester, Virginia. Patsy sang anywhere she could. If there was a stage, she

tried to sing there. She sang at weddings, dances, restaurants, and other public

places. She earned $8 a night. Her friends and family said she worked hard to

improve her singing and make a successful record.

In 1947, she _____ if she could perform on a local radio show.
(4. ask)

People loved her performance, and the radio station soon _____ her
(5. invite)

back to perform again. Patsy continued to perform and in 1954 she _____
(6. win)

a country music competition near her home. She _____ 22 years old. She
(7. be)

was then invited to sing on a country music TV show in Washington, D.C. She also

performed on radio shows in Virginia and recorded some records.

---

[16] **fans:** people who like someone or something very much   [17] **hit:** very successful

Patsy Cline _____ on a national television show in New York City. It was on
(8. appear)
this show in 1957 that millions of people first _____ her sing. She sang a song she
(9. hear)
_____ called "Walkin' After Midnight." This performance helped make her career
(10. recently / record)
a major success. Patsy continued to record more songs, and soon made another major hit called "I Fall to

Pieces." By this time, her voice _____ something special. Patsy _____ to
(11. already / become)   (12. learn)
control not only the sound of her voice, but also the feelings expressed in her songs. People especially loved

her slow, sad love songs like "I Fall to Pieces." "I Fall to Pieces" became Patsy's first No. 1 hit, and she was

now a major star. She also _____ performing at the Grand Ole Opry, a famous country music
(13. begin)
theater in Nashville, Tennessee.

The people who knew her after she _____ a star say Patsy Cline was a great friend. Many
(14. become)
young musicians _____ important stars with her help. At the age of 30, Patsy Cline was killed
(15. become)
in a plane crash on March 5, 1963. Earlier, she _____ in a special show in Kansas City
(16. take part)
to raise money for the family of a country music performer who recently _____, and she was
(17. die)
flying home to Nashville. Thousands of people _____ to her funeral near her hometown. Ten
(18. come)
years after her death, she became the first female musician elected to the Country Music Hall of Fame.

Think about It Answer these questions about the article in Activity 21.

1. Which event in each pair of sentences took place first? Check (✓) the sentence.
   a. ☐ She recorded her first big hit.
      ☐ She worked hard for many years to make a successful record.
   b. ☐ She appeared on a national television show.
      ☐ She recorded the song "Walkin' After Midnight."
   c. ☐ She recorded the song "I Fall to Pieces."
      ☐ She learned to control the sound and feelings in her songs.
2. What had Cline accomplished by the time she was 30 years old?

Write about It Use these time expressions to write four sentences about Patsy Cline. Make three sentences true and one false. Read your sentences to a partner, and let your partner identify the false statement.

1. (by 1957) _____

   _____

2. (in 1957) _____

   _____

3. (by 1963) _____

   _____

4. (in 1963) _____

   _____

22 | Using the Past Perfect Progressive Underline the past perfect progressive verbs in these sentences. Then decide if the action was ongoing or repeated. Check (✓) your answers. **2.4 C**

	ONGOING	REPEATED
1. After I <u>had been working</u> at the bank for a few years, I decided I wanted a more interesting job.	✓	☐
2. Before I moved to Australia, I had been teaching myself English.	☐	☐
3. I had been drawing pictures the whole time I was in Italy, so when I returned home, my parents were very pleased.	☐	☐
4. I had been feeling a little ill, but I didn't think it was anything serious.	☐	☐
5. I had been thinking for a while how much I missed my family.	☐	☐
6. When she joined the band, the other members had been playing together for years.	☐	☐
7. When I got home in the morning, I discovered that my parents had been waiting up all night.	☐	☐
8. The car that hit the tree had been going too fast.	☐	☐
9. We had been going there every Saturday for the past six months.	☐	☐
10. According to the police, the driver had been texting just before he went off the road.	☐	☐

Think about It Look at the past perfect progressive verbs you underlined above. Which part of each verb shows the "perfect" meaning? Which part shows the "progressive" meaning?

23 | Error Correction Correct any errors in these sentences. (Some sentences may not have any errors.)

1. My father grown up in the U.S., but his mother always speaks to him in Spanish when he was a baby.

   My father grew up in the U.S., but his mother had always spoken to him in Spanish when he was a baby.

2. In the story, the main character lose a lot of money.
3. My parents have never gone abroad, but they wanted their children to see the world.
4. By the 1900s, traveling became easier because there were better roads.
5. I have been studying English for many years before I came here.
6. I liked to sing when we got together.
7. By the time I was born, my parents got married for three years.
8. I didn't pass my first exams even though I been studying every night for weeks.
9. My cousin was living in this country for five years when his father died.
10. I was very lonely when I arrived here because I left all my friends.

2.5 The Future Perfect and the Future Perfect Progressive

A

FUTURE PERFECT

	will (+ not)	*have*	past participle	
1 I You He She It We They	**will** **'ll** **will not** **won't**	**have**	**finished**	by the end of the day.

We form the **future perfect** with *will* (+ *not*) + *have* + the **past participle of the main verb**, as in **1**.

2 By next October, we **will have lived** here for ten years. It's hard to believe.

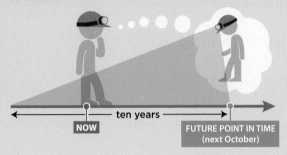

←—— ten years ——→
NOW **FUTURE POINT IN TIME** (next October)

We use the future perfect when we imagine ourselves at a future point in time. From this future viewpoint, we describe an event that will be completed by or before that time, as in **2 – 4**.

Notice that we often describe the future point in time using *by*. We may use:
- a time clause with *by*, as in **3**
- *by* + a time word or phrase, as in **4**

3 By the time they finish building the new school, the town **will have spent** $10 million.

4 I'm sure I **will have talked to her by the end of the week**.

WARNING! We use a present form in the time clause even though we are talking about a future time, as in **3**.

FUTURE PERFECT PROGRESSIVE

5 By 5 o'clock, I **will have been driving** for three hours. I think I'll be ready for a stop.

6 By 6, we **will have been waiting** for an hour.

The **future perfect progressive** is very rare. It emphasizes that an activity will be ongoing up to a future point in time (and may continue after that time), as in **5 – 6**.

We form the future perfect progressive with *will* (+ *not*) + *have* + *been* + the *-ing* form of the main verb.

GO ONLINE

---

24 | Noticing Future Perfect Forms Underline the future perfect forms in these predictions. Then decide how likely each prediction is. Check (✓) *Very Likely*, *Somewhat Likely*, or *Not Likely*. **2.5 A**

FUTURE PREDICTIONS	VERY LIKELY	SOMEWHAT LIKELY	NOT LIKELY
By the year 2050,			
1. the population of the world <u>will have reached</u> 10 billion.	☐	☐	☐
2. the world will have become paperless[18].	☐	☐	☐
3. we will have found a cure for all cancers.	☐	☐	☐
4. we will have stopped using coal, oil, and gas for energy.	☐	☐	☐
5. we will have had another world war.	☐	☐	☐
6. the number of fish in the oceans will have decreased by a large amount.	☐	☐	☐
7. people will have lived on Mars for many years.	☐	☐	☐
8. the world will have become a better place.	☐	☐	☐

[18]**paperless:** using computers instead of paper

Talk about It What else will have happened by the year 2050? Share ideas like the ones in Activity 24 with your classmates.

Think about It Look back at the diagram of the future perfect in Chart 2.5 on page 60. Can you draw similar diagrams to show the meaning of sentences 1, 3 and 4? How would they be different from the diagram for sentence 2?

25 | Using Future Perfect Forms Complete these sentences with the future perfect form of the verb in parentheses. **2.5 A**

The Average Person

1. By 18 months of age, most children _____ *will have learned* _____ 5 to 20 words—mostly nouns. By 24 months, the vocabulary of most children _____ to between 150 and 300 words. (learn/expand)

2. In a 65-year lifespan, the average person _____ 9 years watching television. (spend)

3. By the age of 20, most people _____ video games for 10,000 hours. (play)

4. The average person _____ to 10,500 hours of music by the end of his or her teen years. (listen)

5. The average person _____ for 91,250 hours by the end of his or her life. (work)

6. By the time you stop working, you _____ ten different jobs. (have)

7. By the time you retire, you _____ careers three to five times. (change)

8. By the age of 65, the average person _____ 2 million television commercials. (see)

9. By age 70, the average person _____ a distance equal to four times around the world. (walk)

10. By the end of his or her life, the average person _____ 7,163 baths. (take)

Talk about It What kind of "average person" are the statements above about? Do you think all of these statements describe your life?

Write about It What are some other things that the average person will have done by the time he or she is 65? What are some things he or she won't have done? Write four to six sentences.

The average person will probably have eaten a lot of junk food by age 65.
The average person probably won't have traveled into space.

Talk about It What will you have accomplished in 10 years? In 20 years? Tell your classmates.

"In 10 years, I will have finished college and found a job."

2.6 Using Perfect Forms in Speaking

A	**STARTING A CONVERSATION** **1** What **have** you **been** up to? **2** **Haven't** we **met** before? **3** **Haven't** I **seen** you somewhere before? **ENDING A CONVERSATION** **4** It's **been** good to talk to you. **5** I've **enjoyed** talking with you. **6** It's **been** great seeing you again.	We often use the **present perfect** when we ask general questions or make general statements. General questions and statements are common when we are trying to start a conversation, as in **1 – 3**, or end a conversation, as in **4 – 6**.
B	**OMITTING HELPING VERBS AND SUBJECTS** **7** You **seen** my purse? (= Have you seen my purse?) **8** He always **been** this selfish? (= Has he always been this selfish?) **9** How you **been**? (= How have you been?) **10** **Been** married long? (= Have you been married long?)	In casual conversation, speakers sometimes omit the helping verbs *have* and *has* from the present perfect, as in **7 – 9**. This is especially common with the main verb *be*. Speakers may also omit the subject, as in **10**.

C	**COMPARE**
	
	11a Computers **have gotten** a lot better.
	   (= Computers have become a lot better.)
	11b **Have** you **gotten** your paycheck yet?
	   (= Have you received your paycheck yet?)
	11c I've **got to** leave. (= I must leave. It is necessary.)
	11d I've **got** some money. (= I have some money.)
		Be careful not to confuse these forms:
		
		• *have / has gotten* (the present perfect of *get*), as in **11a – 11b**
		
		• the phrasal modal *have / has got to* (similar in meaning to *must* or *have to*), as in **11c**
		
		• *have / has got* for possession, as in **11d**

26 | Starting a Conversation Complete these conversation starters with the words in parentheses. Use the present perfect form of the verb. ▮2.6 A▮

CONVERSATION STARTERS

1. ___*Have you been*___ keeping busy? (you/be)

2. _____ any good movies recently? (you/see)

3. How long _____ here? (you/live)

4. _____ any good books lately? (you/read)

5. _____ any good music recently? (you/hear)

6. _____ at any good restaurants lately? (you/eat)

7. _____ any trips this year? (you/take)

Talk about It Use one of the questions above to start a conversation with a partner. Ask more questions to continue your conversation. Then use one of the sentences in the box to end your conversation.

A: Hi, James.
B: Hey, Hassan. How are you? Have you been keeping busy?
A: Well, actually, it hasn't been so bad lately. . . .

> It's been good to talk to you.
> I've enjoyed talking with you.
> It's been great seeing you again.

27 | Omitting _Have_ and _Has_ in Conversation Listen and write the missing words in each casual conversation. After you finish listening, write the complete form of each sentence. **2.6 B**

CASUAL CONVERSATION	COMPLETE FORM
1. A: _You always lived_ _____ here?	1. A: _Have you always lived here?_
B: No, I lived in California before this.	B: No, I lived in California before this.
2. A: How long _____ here?	2. A: _____
B: Not long. Just a few minutes.	B: Not long. Just a few minutes.
3. A: _____ OK?	3. A: _____
B: Yeah, not bad.	B: Yeah, not bad.
4. A: How are you?	4. A: How are you?
B: _____ better.	B: _____
5. A: _____ here before?	5. A: _____
B: No. Have you?	B: No. Have you?
6. A: Where _____?	6. A: _____
B: At the library.	B: At the library.
7. A: _____ outside yet?	7. A: _____
B: No, why?	B: No, why?
A: It snowed last night.	A: It snowed last night.
8. A: _____ any good movies lately?	8. A: _____
B: No, I haven't. What about you?	B: No, I haven't. What about you?
A: No, I haven't either.	A: No, I haven't either.
9. A: _____ about Amanda?	9. A: _____
B: No, what?	B: No, what?
A: She's going to marry some guy named Joe.	A: She's going to marry some guy named Joe.
B: _____ him long?	B: _____
A: Oh, I don't know. A year or so.	A: Oh, I don't know. A year or so.
10. A: _____ to James recently?	10. A: _____
B: No, why?	B: No, why?
A: I think he has a surprise for all of you.	A: I think he has a surprise for all of you.

Talk about It Practice the conversations above with a partner.

28 | Dictation Listen and write the sentences you hear. Then check (✓) the correct meaning. **2.6 C**

	PRESENT PERFECT OF GET	NECESSITY	POSSESSION
1. _____	☐	☐	☐
2. _____	☐	☐	☐
3. _____	☐	☐	☐
4. _____	☐	☐	☐

5. _____ ☐ ☐ ☐
6. _____ ☐ ☐ ☐
7. _____ ☐ ☐ ☐
8. _____ ☐ ☐ ☐

Talk about It Work with a partner. Choose one of the sentences in Activity 28 and use it to create a short conversation. Present your conversation to the class.

2.7 Using Perfect Forms in Academic Writing

A

WRITING INTRODUCTORY STATEMENTS

1 I **have had** a lot of problems since I came here. During my first month here, I **had** to find a job and a place to live. I **didn't have** anyone to help me, and I **wasn't** familiar with apartment hunting here.

2 You probably **have seen** garlic in the kitchen. It is about the size of a small onion, and it **has** a strong flavor. But people **prize** garlic for more than its taste. Doctors in ancient Rome **recommended** garlic for 61 different problems.

Writers often use the **present perfect** to make a general introductory statement or to ask a general question at the beginning of a piece of writing. They then use the **simple present** or the **simple past** to give examples and details, as in **1 – 2**.

B

ESSAY WRITING

3 Essay Prompt: Discuss the influence that advertising has **had** on your life.

4 Answer: Advertising tries to get us to buy things we don't really need and do things we don't really want to do. Thanks to my parents, I **have learned** to stand up to the power of advertising. . . .

Essay test questions and prompts often use the present perfect to ask how something in your past has affected you or how something has changed, as in **3**.

When you answer, it is often a good idea to use the same form in the first paragraph of your essay, as in **4**.

C

SCIENCE AND RESEARCH WRITING

5 Scientists **have** already **established** that good-looking people find it easier to get a job and are generally viewed as smarter and more likable. Now a new study **has found** that even parents favor more attractive children.

6 Researchers **observed** interactions between parents and children and **found** that prettier children **received** more attention and care.

Writers use the present perfect to describe important findings and accomplishments in science or research. Using this form emphasizes that the results of an experiment are still true and important now, as in **5**.

When writers describe the specific steps in an experiment, however, they often use the simple past, as in **6**. This is because they are describing actions that took place at a finished time in the past.

D

GIVING BACKGROUND INFORMATION

7 Tori McClure took on the adventure of a lifetime when she attempted to be the first woman to row across the Atlantic Ocean. McClure was no stranger to adventure. She **had** already **skied** across Antarctica and **done** a lot of mountain climbing.

Writers sometimes use the **past perfect** to give background information to support an idea or explanation, as in **7**.

Remember: When we use two past perfect verbs together, it's not necessary to repeat the helping verb *had*.

29 | Supporting General Statements Complete these essay outlines. Give two examples to support each general statement. Provide two or three details to explain each example. Pay special attention to the form of the verbs you use. 2.7 A

1. GENERAL STATEMENT: Computers have made life easier.

   Example 1: _You can go shopping without ever leaving your home._

   Detail 1: _I now buy most of my books online instead of at a bookstore._

   Detail 2: _Last year I bought most of my holiday gifts online._

   Detail 3: _Some people buy their groceries online. I haven't tried this yet, but it would save me a lot of time._

   Example 2: _____

   Detail 1: _____

   Detail 2: _____

   Detail 3: _____

2. GENERAL STATEMENT: The automobile has created serious problems.

   Example 1: _____

   Detail 1: _____

   Detail 2: _____

   Detail 3: _____

   Example 2: _____

   Detail 1: _____

   Detail 2: _____

   Detail 3: _____

3. GENERAL STATEMENT: Telephones and email have made communication between people less personal.

   Example 1: _____

   Detail 1: _____

   Detail 2: _____

   Detail 3: _____

   Example 2: _____

   Detail 1: _____

   Detail 2: _____

   Detail 3: _____

Write about It Choose one of the general statements above and develop your ideas into a cohesive paragraph or essay.

30 | Answering Essay Questions Think of two ways to begin a response to each essay question using the same verb form that is in the question. Then answer the questions below. `2.7 B`

ESSAY QUESTIONS

1. Have your attitudes changed much in the last few years? Explain.

   My attitudes have changed significantly in the last few years.
   OR
   Over the past five years, I have lived in three different countries. This experience has changed the way I think about my own country.

2. Has the automobile been harmful to our society? Discuss.
3. Television has made the U.S. a nation of watchers, not doers. Do you agree or disagree with this statement?
4. In your opinion, what invention has caused the most important changes in our society? Explain.
5. Have computers made our lives easier or more complicated? Explain.
6. Discuss the influence that advertising has had on your life or the lives of your friends.
7. In what ways has information technology changed work and working practices in the past ten years?

QUESTIONS

a. Why is it a good idea to begin your response to an essay question using the same verb form?
b. Do you always need to do this? Why or why not?

31 | Analyzing Verb Choices Circle the present perfect verbs in these excerpts from newspaper articles. Underline the simple past verbs. Then explain why you think the writer used each form of the verb. `2.7 C`

Does Vitamin C Help Fight the Common Cold?

A large review of medical trials[19] has concluded that Vitamin C is largely ineffective in the prevention and treatment of the common cold.

In 30 trials with 11,350 participants who took at least 200 milligrams of vitamin C a day, researchers found that vitamin C did not reduce the occurrence[20] of the common cold. Vitamin C did slightly reduce the duration and severity[21] of cold symptoms, but the effect was very small.

Lecture or Interactive Teaching? New Study of an Old Issue

Professors have lectured for centuries. But how effective is lecturing to students compared to working with them?

A new study compared two classes of a beginning physics course at the University of British Columbia in Canada. There were more than 260 students in each section. Both were taught by popular and experienced professors.

[19] **trials:** experiments
[20] **occurrence:** something that happens
[21] **severity:** the strength of something

Humans Have Been Making Art for a Lot Longer Than We Thought

A new study has revealed that Spain's El Castillo Cave contains the oldest known cave paintings in Europe, with a handprint dating back 37,300 years.

Instead of testing the paint's age, a team of British and Spanish researchers measured the age of the stone that had formed around the drawings.

Scientists Able to Study Atmosphere of Planet Outside Our Solar System

Scientists have detailed the atmosphere of a planet outside our solar system. The team, based in Chile, was able to measure the amount of carbon monoxide on *Tau Bootis b*—one of the first "exoplanets" discovered back in 1996. They were able to measure the atmosphere without relying on a "transit" of the planet—where it passes in front of its star. That is important as, up to now, astronomers and scientists have had to rely on transits to measure the atmosphere.

32 | Providing Background Information Read these sentences from student essays. Then write another sentence giving background information to support the first one. Use a past perfect form in your new sentence. `2.7 D`

SENTENCES FROM STUDENT ESSAYS

1. Her grandfather was a great businessman.
   He had started his own business at age 24, and he had helped his brothers start their own businesses.

2. The athletes were in great shape when they got to the competition.
   _____

3. He was nervous when he moved here by himself.
   _____

4. When he was a young man, he witnessed something that changed his life.
   _____

5. She was tired, but her first days in this new country were very exciting.
   _____

6. It was a real accomplishment when her mother finally graduated from college.
   _____

7. When she was a child, her father didn't know how to act around her.
   _____

8. When he came to this country, he couldn't get a job.
   _____

A | DISCUSSION Look in a magazine or newspaper for a paragraph that uses a variety of verb forms. Read the paragraph to your classmates. Together, identify the verb forms and suggest why the writer used each form.

Eating Well: Less Science, More Common Sense

Food **is** life. Food **gives** us energy to **do** everyday activities, but not all food ← simple present

is created equal. Studies **have shown**, for example, that children who eat a nutritious

breakfast do better in school than those with a poor diet. Research **has** also **shown** . . . present perfect

B | WRITING Write three opinions about someone you know. Then give three reasons or examples to support each opinion. Think carefully about whether you need to use the simple present, simple past, present perfect, past perfect, or some other verb form.

Opinions	Examples
My sister Elena is very smart.	1. She has several academic degrees. 2. She has been a teacher for ten years. 3. She graduated from college at the top of her class.

C | WRITING Choose one of the essay topics in Activity 30, and write an essay in response. Think carefully about whether you need to use the simple present, simple past, present perfect, past perfect, or some other verb form in your writing.

D | INTERVIEW Choose an interesting or unusual job. What kinds of skills, knowledge, or experience would a person need in order to do this job? Write your ideas. Then make a list of interview questions for this job, and practice interviewing a partner.

Job: a cook on a sailboat
Skills/Experience: has experience on sailboats, likes to cook, has cooked for large groups of people . . .
Interview Questions: Have you ever been on a sailboat? Do you like to cook? Have you ever cooked in a very small kitchen? Have you ever cooked for a large group of people?

2.8 Summary of Perfect Forms

SIMPLE

PRESENT PERFECT

I You We They	have gone. 've gone.
	have not gone. haven't gone.
He She It	has gone. 's gone.
	has not gone. hasn't gone.

PAST PERFECT

| I You He She It We They | had left 'd left | by 6. |
| | had not left hadn't left | |

USES
We use the present perfect to describe something that:
- started in the past and continues to the present
- happened in the past but has an effect on the present

USES
We use the past perfect to show that one event in the past took place before another past time or event.

PROGRESSIVE

PRESENT PERFECT PROGRESSIVE

I You We They	have been waiting. 've been waiting.
	have not been waiting. haven't been waiting.
He She It	has been waiting. 's been waiting.
	has not been waiting. hasn't been waiting.

PAST PERFECT PROGRESSIVE

| I You He She It We They | had been waiting. 'd been waiting. |
| | had not been waiting. 'd not been waiting. hadn't been waiting. |

USES
We use the present perfect progressive to emphasize that something happened:
- repeatedly in the past and has an effect on the present
- continuously from a time in the past up until now

USES
We use the past perfect progressive to show that an earlier activity in the past was ongoing or repeated.

FUTURE

FUTURE PERFECT

| I You He She It We They | will have finished. 'll have finished. |
| | will not have finished. won't have finished. |

FUTURE PERFECT PROGRESSIVE

| I You He She It We They | will have been sleeping. 'll have been sleeping. |
| | will not have been sleeping. won't have been sleeping. |

USES
We use the future perfect to describe something that will be completed by or before a time in the future.

USES
We use the future perfect progressive to emphasize that something will be ongoing until a time in the future.

3

Modals

If we are not ashamed to think it, we should not be ashamed to say it.

—MARCUS TULLIUS CICERO,
ROMAN STATESMAN
(106–43 BCE)

Talk about It What does the quotation above mean? Do you agree or disagree?

WARM-UP

A | Match the beginnings and endings of the quotations. Which quotation is the most memorable to you? Why?

Famous Quotations

1. A man **should** look for what is, _f_
2. You **must** be the change ____
3. If you want to understand today, ____
4. An inch of time is an inch of gold, ____
5. No one **would** have crossed the ocean ____
6. While we **may not be able to** control all that happens to us, ____
7. The less one **has to** do, ____

a. you wish to see in the world.
(*Mahatma Gandhi, Indian statesman*)

b. if he **could** have gotten off the ship in a storm.
(*Charles Kettering, U.S. inventor*)

c. the less time one finds to do it in.
(*Lord Chesterfield, British statesman*)

d. we **can** control what happens inside us.
(*Benjamin Franklin, writer, scientist, and statesman*)

e. but you **cannot** buy that inch of time with an inch of gold. (*Chinese proverb*)

f. and not for what he thinks **should** be.
(*Albert Einstein, physicist*)

g. you **have to** search yesterday. (*Pearl S. Buck, U.S. novelist*)

B | The words in green in the quotations above are simple modals. The words in blue are phrasal modals. Based on the examples, check (✓) *True* or *False* for these sentences.

	TRUE	FALSE
1. Simple modals are followed by the base form of the verb.	☐	☐
2. A simple modal changes form after different subjects.	☐	☐
3. A phrasal modal changes form after different subjects.	☐	☐
4. We can place a simple modal next to a phrasal modal in a sentence.	☐	☐
5. Some simple modals and phrasal modals have similar meanings.	☐	☐

C | Look back at the quotation on page 70. Identify any modal forms.

3.1 Overview of Simple Modals and Phrasal Modals

We can use **simple modals** and **phrasal modals** (+ the base form of a main verb) to express different beliefs and attitudes about what we say.

A

1 He **can speak** English very well already.
2 He **has to take** an English class. It's a requirement.
3 He really **should take** an English class.
4 You **might want to take** an English class, too.
5 **Could** you please **help** me with my English homework?
6 They're **allowed to take** English if they want to.

7 He's **going to take** English 101 next fall.
8 He **may take** an English class in the fall—I'm not sure.
9 She **should be** here by 7:00. She left an hour ago.

We use simple modals and phrasal modals to express different social purposes, such as:
- ability, as in **1**
- obligations, as in **2**
- advice, as in **3**
- softening advice, as in **4**
- requests, as in **5**
- permission, as in **6**

We also use these forms to express how sure or likely an event is, as in **7 – 9**.

B

10 Students **should get** a good night's sleep before exam day.
11 She **may be** at work right now. I'm not sure.
12 He **must be taking** a shower. I can hear the water.
13 They **might arrive** at 7:00 instead of 6:00. Their flight is late.
14 I'll **take** those to the office for you.
15 She **has to get** up at 5:00 tomorrow. Work starts at 6:00.
16 We **won't be able to meet** on Monday. Anne is sick.

Most **simple modals** can refer to things that are:
- generally true, as in **10**
- true or in progress at the moment, as in **11 – 12**
- future actions, as in **13 – 14**

When we use modals to refer to past time, we use verb forms in a special way. See Charts 3.3, 3.5, 3.6, and 3.9.

Unlike simple modals, **phrasal modals** include a helping verb, *have* or *be*. We show time by using the correct past, present, or future form of the helping verb, as in **15 – 16**.

1 | Identifying Simple Modals in a Passage Underline each simple modal and its main verb in this passage. `3.1 A`

Choosing a Major . . . and a Career

At many universities, students <u>can choose</u> from dozens of majors and minors. Nowadays, when they are making that important decision, students often focus on the subjects that can provide the best careers because they want to be sure they have jobs after they graduate. But some experts say that students should think about doing something they love instead. Research has shown that students may not do well at studies they don't care about. Before you choose a major, ask yourself: Would you really enjoy doing this as a career? If you don't have a strong interest in the topic, you might want to consider a different choice. For the moment, it may not be clear where your interest will lead you, but passion[1] inspires hard work, which often leads to success.

[1] **passion:** a strong feeling of excitement for something

2 | Identifying Speakers' Attitudes Match each statement on the left with a description on the right. `3.1 A`

1. "They'll bring the potato salad." __e__

2. "He might not remember how to get here." ____

3. "I have to call my sister tonight." ____

4. "You can stay out until 11 p.m." ____

5. "You might want to try a different approach." ____

6. "You shouldn't eat so much sugar." ____

7. "She can do advanced mathematics." ____

8. "Could you please send me a copy of that?" ____

The speaker is:

a. giving advice

b. not sure about something

c. making a request

d. saying that something is necessary

e. sure about something

f. softening advice

g. talking about ability

h. giving permission

3 | Identifying Time References Circle the simple modal and phrasal modal forms in these conversations. Then check (✓) the time that the modal(s) refer to. `3.1 B`

	PRESENT/ GENERAL TIME	FUTURE
1. A: Are you calling the store? B: Yes, but they're not answering. They (must be closed).	✓	☐
2. A: Where are you going on vacation? B: We might go to Hawaii.	☐	☐
3. A: Seems as if Alex always eats pizza for lunch. B: He must really like it.	☐	☐
4. A: I can't decide which one to buy. B: You should get the blue one.	☐	☐
5. A: We won't be able to get reservations this late. B: Let's go tomorrow, then.	☐	☐
6. A: People shouldn't be so quick to judge each other. B: That's true.	☐	☐
7. A: Is he here? I don't hear any noise from his room. B: He might be sleeping.	☐	☐
8. A: The company may have to change its hiring policies. B: I hope so. We'll see what happens.	☐	☐
9. A: What does the handbook say? B: It says, "Employees must report any problems to the proper authorities."	☐	☐
10. A: You can come over after lunch if you want to. B: Great! I'll see you then.	☐	☐
11. A: Did you hear that Sheila quit yesterday? B: Wow, I can't believe that. I thought she liked it here.	☐	☐
12. A: How does your brother feel? Any better? B: Yeah, actually, I think he may be feeling pretty good. He went to work today.	☐	☐

4 | Usage Note: Simple Modal vs. Phrasal Modal Sentence Patterns Study the note. Then do Activities 5–6.

We use the base form of a main verb after simple modals.

Phrasal modals include *to* before the base form of a main verb.

STATEMENTS

	subject	modal / phrasal modal	base form of main verb	
1	I	can(not)	understand	the problem.
2	The manager	is (not) supposed to	tell	us about the problem.

YES/NO AND WH- QUESTIONS

	wh- word	modal / first helping verb	subject	other parts of phrasal verb	base form of main verb	
3		Should	we	—	meet	at 7?
4		Are	you	allowed to	leave	early?
5	When	can	we	—	go	home?
6	How	is	she	able to	communicate	with him?

5 | Error Correction Correct any errors in these sentences. (Some sentences may not have any errors.) `3.1 A`

1. You must to think about that a little more carefully.

   You must think about that a little more carefully.

2. Sal should calls the office in the morning.
3. When do I should place the order?
4. They can to see both sides of the argument.
5. I think the corporations should trying a little harder to solve this problem.
6. Passengers don't must stand near the doors when they are opening and closing.
7. Do students supposed to eat and drink in the library?
8. That color might not is the best choice for you.
9. When we can take another break?
10. If they practice, they might to do a little better next time.

6 | Forming Negatives and Questions Read these sentences. Write a new sentence with a similar meaning. Use the **bold** modal form. (More than one answer may be possible.) `3.1 A`

1. I don't believe I **can** come over tonight.

   I can't come over tonight.

2. Did someone say we **could** wait here?
3. Do you think I **will** be able to finish later?
4. I don't believe the plan **will** work.
5. I don't think I **may** be ready for the test.
6. Is it true that you **can** eat more and lose weight?
7. I don't think we **should** go out tonight.
8. Is it possible that we **could** talk now?

3.2 Willingness and Intent

A

STATEMENTS OF INTENT WITH *WILL*

1 A: I can't understand this problem.
B: **I'll help** you.

2 A: You were late again today.
B: **I'll be** on time tomorrow, I promise.

3 A: Do you want to stay and finish?
B: No, **I'll come** back tomorrow.

4 In Academic Writing: I **will describe** the experiment in more detail later.

In informal conversation, we use **will** to make offers, promises, or general statements of intent, as in **1 – 3**. We usually contract *will* to **'ll**.

Speakers and writers also use *will* in academic contexts to describe something they intend or plan to do later, as in **4**.

For more information on the use of *will*, see Unit 1, page 23.

B

PRESENT AND FUTURE COUNTERFACTUAL STATEMENTS WITH *WOULD*

5 **I'd help** you, but I just don't have any time.
(= I want to help you but I can't.)

6 Following this plan **would reduce** greenhouse gases in the atmosphere.
(= This plan hasn't been followed.)

A counterfactual statement can describe something that will not happen. We use **would (not)** to describe:

- something that someone wants to do, but can't, as in **5**
- the results of something that has not been done, as in **6**

We often contract *would* to **'d**.

C

PAST COUNTERFACTUAL STATEMENTS WITH *WOULD*

7 We **would have gone** to the show, but we didn't have enough money.
(= We didn't go to the show.)

8 I **would have stayed** later, but I got too tired.
(= I didn't stay later.)

We can also use counterfactual statements to describe something we were willing to do in the past, but did not actually do, as in **7 – 8**. We use **would (not)** + **have** + the **past participle of a main verb**.

In past counterfactual statements, it is possible to contract *I would* to *I'd*, but it is not common.

7 | Making Statements with *Will* Work with a partner. Complete each conversation with a statement of intent, promise, or offer, using *I'll*. Then practice with your partner. **3.2 A**

1. A: Can you bring something for the potluck dinner?

   B: Sure. _I'll make a salad._

2. A: Amal is late. I wonder where he is.

   B: I don't know. _____

3. A: How will I know what time to show up?

   B: Don't worry. _____

4. A: Bye! It was nice seeing you again.

   B: You too! _____

5. A: Please don't tell anyone I said this.

   B: I promise. _____

6. A: How are you going to find a job?

   B: Well, _____.

7. A: I don't think Sara can do this alone.

   B: That's OK. _____

a potluck dinner

8. A: I don't have time to make all those copies.

   B: I have time. _____

9. A: Are you sure you can go? You look tired.

   B: I _____. I promise.

Think about It Is each statement you wrote in Activity 7 an offer, promise, or general statement? Write *O* (offer), *P* (promise), or *G* (general statement) next to each one.

8 | Using *Will* to State Intentions Write eight meaningful sentences telling what an essay will be about. Use *will*, a verb from Column 1, and phrases from Columns 2 and 3. (Many different answers are possible.) `3.2 A`

SENTENCES FROM ACADEMIC ESSAYS

1	2	3
address describe discuss explore focus on outline refer to	how the virus spreads the effects of an unhealthy diet the government's policies the important points of the novel the process of cell division the relationship between the two countries the research on carbohydrates two of Shakespeare's sonnets[2]	below in depth[3] in the following section in this paper throughout this essay

I will focus on two of Shakespeare's sonnets in depth.

Talk about It Share the sentences you wrote above with a partner. Which of these subjects is each one about?

biology	English literature	nutrition	political science

A: I will focus on two of Shakespeare's sonnets in depth.
B: That's about English literature.

9 | Distinguishing *Will* from *Would* Complete these conversations with *'ll* (will) or *'d* (would). Then practice with a partner. `3.2 A–B`

1. A: Your essay was due today.

   B: I know. I ____ do it tomorrow, when I have time.

2. A: You need to work on your essay.

   B: I know. I ____ do it today, but I don't have time.

3. A: Tomas couldn't make it?

   B: No, I'm sorry. He ____ be here if he could.

4. A: I can't decide what to order.

   B: I ____ have the chicken. That looks delicious.

5. A: Where is Alexander?

   B: He ____ be here any minute.

6. A: I have no interest in that movie.

   B: Really? I ____ love to see it.

7. A: Where are the extra blankets?

   B: Hmm. Ask Rafa. He ____ know.

8. A: I'm sorry we're out of time.

   B: Me too. I ____ stay longer if I could.

Think about It What helped you choose between *would* and *will* in the sentences above? Share ideas with your classmates.

[2] **sonnets:** 14-line poems   [3] **in depth:** deeply

76

10 | Using *Would* to Describe Possible Results The left column of this chart contains proposals for new laws. Use *would* to write possible positive and negative results of each law. `3.2 B`

Proposals for new laws	In favor	Against
1. Make cigarettes illegal.	*Stores would not sell cigarettes, so people would smoke less.*	*Some people would smoke anyway.*
2. Require all citizens to vote.		
3. Don't allow cars in downtown areas.		
4. Allow advertising on school websites.		
5. Increase taxes on gasoline.		
6. Stop the sale of candy at children's schools.		
7. Spend public money on a high-speed railway.		
8. Raise the minimum wage.		

Talk about It Share your ideas above with a partner. Do you agree about the possible results?

11 | Using Counterfactual *Would Have* Complete these conversations with *would have* and the past participle of the verb in parentheses. Then practice with a partner. `3.2 C`

MAKING EXCUSES

1. A: You know, I was in Toronto last weekend.

   B: I didn't know you were in town! I _____would have invited_____ you over for dinner. (invite)

2. A: We missed you at the concert last night.

   B: I _____, but I had a lot of homework. (go)

3. A: I didn't see you in class yesterday.

   B: I know. I _____, but I didn't hear my alarm go off. (come)

4. A: Selena was here yesterday.

   B: Oh, I didn't know that. I _____ her. (call)

5. A: How'd you do on the test?

   B: Not too well. I _____ more, but I left my book in the library. (study)

6. A: I walked all the way over here.

    B: Why didn't you call me? I _____ you up! (pick)

7. A: We're out of apples.

    B: Oh, I didn't know. I _____ some when I was at the store. (buy)

8. A: Whew! That was hard!

    B: Why didn't you tell me? I _____ you. (help)

12 | Using *Will*, *Would*, or *Would Have* Complete the conversations below with *will*, *would*, or *would have* and the correct form of a verb from the box. Use contractions where you can. (More than one answer is possible.) Then practice with a partner. **3.2 A–C**

be	call	come back	eat	have	like	pay	stay

CAFÉ CONVERSATIONS

1. A: Sorry I'm late. I _____*would have called*_____ you, but my

    phone is dead⁴.

    B: That's OK.

2. A: So what are you getting?

    B: I think I _____ the garden salad.

3. A: This place is kind of expensive.

    B: Don't worry. I _____ for this.

4. A: Are you leaving already?

    B: I _____, but I have a class in 15 minutes.

5. A: This place is fantastic.

    B: Yeah, I know I didn't know about it or I _____

    here before.

6. A: Could you excuse me for a moment? I _____ right back.

    B: Of course.

7. A: So what did you think of this place?

    B: It was great. I _____ absolutely _____ again.

8. A: I think I'll get dessert.

    B: I _____ some pie, but I don't have time.

Think about It What helped you choose between *will*, *would*, and *would have* in the conversations above? Share ideas with your classmates.

---

⁴**dead:** not working or not charged

3.3 Possibility with *Can* and *Could*

<table>
<tr>
<td rowspan="2" valign="top">A</td>
<td valign="top">

POSSIBILITY WITH *CAN* AND *COULD*

1 Spinal cord injuries **can** severely **damage** the central nervous system.

(= Severe damage is possible, but it doesn't always happen.)

2 This treatment **could** really **help** you.

3 The manager **can do** an inspection whenever he wants to. He **could do** an inspection today.

</td>
<td valign="top">

We use *can(not)* and *could* to suggest that something is possible or impossible, as in **1** – **3**. We often use:

- *can* to talk about general possibilities
- *could* to talk about the possibility of a particular thing happening in the present or future

WARNING! Don't confuse this meaning of *could* with the meaning of past general ability: *In the old days, people couldn't stay in touch so easily.*

</td>
</tr>
</table>

<table>
<tr>
<td rowspan="2" valign="top">B</td>
<td valign="top">

PAST POSSIBILITY (COUNTERFACTUAL)

4 A: That driver wasn't even looking. She **could have hit** us!
   B: Thank goodness she didn't.

5 A: Sorry I forgot to tell you about the movie!
   B: That's OK. I **couldn't have gone** anyway. I was working.

</td>
<td valign="top">

Sometimes we use **could (not) have** + the **past participle of a main verb** to say that something was possible in the past but didn't happen, as in **4**.

We also use it to say that something was not possible in the past, as in **5**.

WARNING! We also use *could (not) have* to express a past possibility that is NOT counterfactual. This use of *couldn't have* is discussed in Chart 3.5.

</td>
</tr>
</table>

 ONLINE

13 | Using *Can* for Possibility The verbs underlined in the first paragraph of this passage are too definite. Rewrite them using *can*. In the second paragraph, use your own ideas to decide which verbs should use *can*. **3.3 A**

WHAT CAN WE EAT?

We all want to be healthy and to look good, and we all know that exercise and a healthy diet are essential. But specific advice about food and

       can be

nutrition <u>is</u> overwhelming[5] at times. Research shows that high-fat foods like red meat <u>raise</u> cholesterol[6], which leads to heart disease. And refined carbohydrates[7], like white flour and white rice, <u>raise</u> blood sugar levels. Many foods, like milk, nuts, eggs, and fish, <u>cause</u> serious allergies.

    In addition to these more serious problems, some people think that foods like onions, garlic, and cabbage give you bad breath. Others believe that eating meat and refined carbohydrates leads to bad body odor. Tomatoes, citrus fruits, and chocolate make your stomach hurt. Coffee keeps you awake, but dairy products and bananas make you sleepy. If you drink soda and eat candy, you damage your teeth.

FYI

We often use *can* in academic writing to say that something is possible, but not definite.

Specific advice about food and nutrition **is** overwhelming. (definite)

Specific advice about food and nutrition **can be** overwhelming. (possible)

---

[5] **overwhelming:** so much that you don't know how to react to it
[6] **cholesterol:** a substance found in blood, fat, and most body tissues

[7] **carbohydrates:** sugars or starches found in foods such as bread, rice, and potatoes

Talk about It What can people eat to stay healthy? Share your ideas with your classmates.

Write about It What do you know about the effects of these behaviors? Write two or three sentences about each topic with *can*. If necessary, research your topic online.

drinking plenty of water	eating a lot of vegetables	exercising every day

Exercising every day can increase your energy level.

14 | Using Counterfactual *Could Have* Complete these sentences with *could(n't) have* and the past participle of the verb in parentheses. `3.3 B`

1. We _____ could have seen _____ the movie last night, but we weren't in the mood. (see)

2. It was a beautiful day, so we _____ a walk on the beach. (take)

3. I don't know where my parents are, but they _____ very far. (go)

4. I _____ you last weekend. I wasn't in town. (help)

5. I _____ to the office, but I decided to stay home. I just wasn't feeling well. (go)

6. We _____ soccer today. We just didn't have time. (play)

7. I didn't know the restaurant was going to be crowded. We _____ at home instead. (eat)

8. The concert was fantastic. I _____ to them for another hour. (listen)

9. I _____ Jon, but I didn't think he'd want to come with us. (call)

10. Thank you for all your help. I _____ this without you. (do)

Write about It Write two sentences about plans you had that didn't happen. Use *could(n't) have*.

15 | Present Possibility vs. Past Possibility Which sentences refer to the present or future, and which refer to the past? Circle the modal forms and check (✓) the correct column. `3.3 A-B`

	PRESENT/FUTURE POSSIBILITY	PAST COUNTERFACTUAL
1. A fall from that height could result in a broken arm.	☐	☐
2. He could have hurt himself.	☐	☐
3. We could get a raise this year.	☐	☐
4. The new policies could have a good effect on our neighborhood.	☐	☐
5. They say it could rain.	☐	☐
6. He could have been a very important man.	☐	☐
7. You really could have told me about this before.	☐	☐
8. She could take the day off to relax.	☐	☐

Think about It For each counterfactual sentence above, what *didn't* happen?

Write about It Rewrite the present and future sentences above using a past form. How does the meaning change?

16 | Error Correction Correct any errors in these sentences. (Some sentences may not have any errors.)

1. I'm so tired that I can fall asleep right now.
2. It's too bad he didn't try a little harder yesterday. He could win that race.
3. My brother could got a job anywhere after he graduated.
4. I would buy tickets, but I just couldn't afford them.
5. There is a lot left to do. This job can take seven or eight more days.
6. The team could have went to the finals this year, but Rodriguez broke his leg.
7. The neighbors could move out later this year.
8. In many areas around the world, earthquakes can causing major damage.

3.4 Degrees of Certainty about the Present and Future

We can use **simple modals** and **phrasal modals** to show how certain we are that something is true or is likely to happen, as in **1 – 15**. We often provide evidence or a reason for what we are saying. Notice that some modals show different degrees of certainty in positive and negative sentences.

		POSITIVE	NEGATIVE
STRONGER CERTAINTY	*will/won't*	1 She'**ll be** home at 6:00. Her schedule never changes.	3 She **won't get** home early. She has too much work to do.
	be going to/ be (not) going to	2 She'**s going to be** home at 6:00. She told me so.	4 She'**s not going to come** home early.
	*must/ must not**	5 She's not here, so she **must be** at work.	6 She **must not be** at her desk— I called and she didn't answer.
	can't	—	7 She **can't be** home already. I saw her at work five minutes ago.
	couldn't		8 She **couldn't be** home already. I just saw her.
EXPECTATION	*should/ shouldn't*	9 She **should be** at work by now. It usually takes her 30 minutes.	10 She **shouldn't be** home yet. She usually works until 7:00.
WEAKER CERTAINTY	*may/ may not**	11 She **may be** there already— she left before we did.	14 She didn't get paid. She **may not have** enough money to go out.
	*might/ might not**	12 They **might visit** tomorrow. I have to call to find out.	15 They **might not visit** tomorrow after all.
	could	13 I don't know him. He **could be** a new student, I guess.	—

*We don't usually contract *must not*, *may not*, and *might not*.

GO ONLINE

17 | Identifying Degrees of Certainty Circle the Speaker B response that indicates a higher degree of certainty. 3.4 A

1. A: Why haven't they gotten here yet?
   B: They may not know about the time change.
   B: They must not know about the time change.

2. A: I wonder if he's coming to the lecture.
   B: He'll come.
   B: He might come.

3. A: Do you think we'll get a raise next year?
   B: We could.
   B: Oh, we're going to get a raise.

4. A: Does he have enough money?
   B: He may.
   B: He should.

5. A: I don't think I know her.

   B: You must know her! You took a class together.

   B: You might. You took a class together.

6. A: I think we should get Diana the chocolate cake.

   B: She won't like chocolate. Let's get vanilla.

   B: She might not like chocolate. Let's get vanilla.

7. A: That's Koji's car.

   B: It couldn't be Koji's. His car is in the shop.

   B: It could be Koji's. It looks just like it.

8. A: Why is he so tired?

   B: He shouldn't be. He slept for ten hours.

   B: He might not sleep well.

Talk about It Practice the conversations in Activity 17 with a partner. Choose either answer. Try to also show certainty or uncertainty with your voice, facial expression, and body language.

Think about It Which of the statements in Activity 17 are about the future? Which are about the present?

18 | Expressing Degrees of Certainty Write responses to these statements. Use a variety of modals to show different degrees of certainty. Try to provide a reason as well. **3.4 A**

GIVING REASONS

1. A: Why is the classroom empty?

   B: _It's almost 4. The class must be over already._

2. A: Why is everyone outside?

   B: _____

3. A: Why is the store closed?

   B: _____

4. A: Why does Tara look so confused?

   B: _____

5. A: Why does the soup taste funny?

   B: _____

6. A: Why isn't there anything good on TV?

   B: _____

7. A: Why is Arif reading so much?

   B: _____

8. A: Why is Sarah so pale[8]?

   B: _____

Think about It Take turns reading the responses you wrote above to a partner. Do your partner's reasons match the modal he or she used? Could you use a different modal with the same reason?

Write about It Which of the responses you wrote above could you rewrite using *maybe*?

> **WARNING!**
>
> *Maybe* is an adverb similar in meaning to *may*. We usually use *maybe* at the beginning of a sentence.
>
> He **may have** a new address.
> **Maybe he has** a new address.

---

[8] **pale:** having skin that is lighter than usual

19 | Writing about Degrees of Certainty Choose five topics from this box and write sentences about events in your life. Use modals to show how certain you are about the events. Try to add an explanation or reason for your statements. Then share some of your statements with the class. `3.4 A`

a celebrity	events in the news	technology	the weather	your country
a sporting event	politics	the environment	your city	your school

My school might raise tuition rates next year. They are building a new library, so they must need money.

3.5 Past Certainty

We can use **modal** + *have* + the **past participle of a main verb** to express probability in the past, as in **1 – 8**. As with present and future modals, we often give evidence or a reason for our degree of certainty.

A

		POSITIVE	NEGATIVE
STRONGER CERTAINTY	*must have/ must not have**	**1** They **must have seen** us. We were only a few feet away from them.	**2** She's not up yet. She **must not have** set her alarm clock.
	couldn't have	—	**3** It was the first time you met her. You **couldn't have known** about her problems.
WEAKER CERTAINTY	*may have/ may not have** *might have/ might not have** *could have*	**4** I'm not sure why he went home early. He **may have been** tired. **5** You **might have seen** him. Did you notice a guy in a blue jacket? **6** The temperature differences **could have affected** the data, but we're not sure if they did.	**7** She **may not have noticed** the stop sign. It was very dark. **8** They didn't do the project correctly. They **might not have understood** the directions. —

*We don't usually contract *must not*, *may not*, and *might not*.

GO ONLINE

---

20 | Identifying Time Frames Circle the modal forms. Then check (✓) the time frame. `3.5 A`

GLOBAL WARMING	PAST	PRESENT	FUTURE
1. We (might see) more extreme weather in the coming years.	☐	☐	✓
2. The earth's temperature may have risen too much to stop the effects of climate change.	☐	☐	☐
3. Past human activity must have helped change the climate.	☐	☐	☐
4. Natural weather cycles could also have contributed.	☐	☐	☐
5. The Arctic ice should continue to melt at the same speed.	☐	☐	☐
6. New energy policies could affect the speed of global warming.	☐	☐	☐
7. Although the earth is warmer, the weather can be colder in particular areas.	☐	☐	☐
8. Climate may be difficult to predict, so scientists have developed complicated models to help them with predictions.	☐	☐	☐

Think about It What kinds of information in each sentence above helped you identify the time frame?

21 | Degrees of Certainty with Modals Match the statements with the responses. Then practice with a partner. `3.5 A`

PHONE PROBLEMS

1. I can't find my phone. ____
2. My phone keeps freezing[9]. ____
3. Whose phone is this? ____
4. She never answered my text message. ____
5. He's not answering. ____
6. I forgot to call you! ____
7. My battery is almost dead. ____
8. I must have left her five messages! ____

a. He might have turned off his ringer.
b. It must be Tina's.
c. You must have forgotten to charge it.
d. It's OK. You couldn't have anyway. I left my phone at home.
e. She may not have gotten it.
f. You might need to update the software.
g. She may not check her voicemail.
h. It should be in your bag. I saw you put it there.

Think about It Which responses above refer to past time? Which refer to present or future time?

Talk about It With a partner, write a short conversation (five to six sentences) about a problem with a phone. You can use one of the statements in the left column above to start the conversation. Read your conversation to another pair.

A: *I must have left her five messages!*
B: *She might be busy.*
A: *It shouldn't take that long to check her voicemail.*
B: *Well, maybe she doesn't want to talk to you.*
A: *Gee, thanks.*

> **FYI**
>
> We can also use *should*(*n't*) or *can't* + *have* + **past participle** to talk about past certainty, but it is less common.
>
> She **should have called** by now. I wonder where she is.
>
> He **can't have called** them already! It's too early.

22 | Usage Note: Different Uses of *Could* and *Could Have* Read the note. Then do Activity 23.

> We can use **could** (*not*) and **could** (*not*) **have** to express many different present, past, or future meanings.
>
> **PRESENT OR FUTURE TIME**
>
> **A** Possibility: This class **could** really **help** you with your writing.
> **B** Weaker certainty: He **could be** at work now, but it's pretty early. He's probably still at home.
> **C** Strong negative certainty: She **couldn't be** the manager. She's too young!
>
> **PAST TIME**
>
> **D** General ability: When I was a kid, I **could understand** Spanish.
> **E** Possibility (counterfactual): We **could have visited** my parents but we didn't have time.
> **F** Weak certainty: I don't know how many people were at the lecture. There **could have been** 20 or 30 maybe.
> **G** Strong negative certainty: They **couldn't have fit** more people in the lecture hall. It was really crowded.

[9]**freezing:** stopping movement; becoming still

23 | Identifying Meanings of Could Label each sentence A, B, C, D, E, F, or G according to the meanings in Activity 22. `3.5 A`

1. I guess I didn't study enough. I could have passed that test easily. _E_
2. They say it could snow tomorrow. ____
3. I don't see the dictionary. Malai could have taken it to school. ____
4. He could lift a hundred pounds easily when he was younger. ____
5. I'm not sure who ate the cookies. It could have been my brother. ____
6. Don't eat that. It could be spoiled. ____
7. I could start working tomorrow. ____
8. She could have a lot of money in the bank, but I doubt it. ____
9. In those days, you could travel many miles without seeing a city. ____
10. She's exhausted. She couldn't have worked any harder last night. ____
11. She couldn't have written that. That's not even her handwriting. ____
12. That looks like my sister, but it couldn't be her. She doesn't even live in this town. ____
13. We really got lucky. That accident could have a caused a lot of problems. ____
14. He couldn't have any money left now. He spent a fortune last night! ____

I didn't study enough.

24 | Using Could/Could Have Work with a partner. Write B's responses. Use *could* or *could have* and your own ideas. Then practice with your partner. `3.5 A`

1. A: I wonder why Marcos is so happy today.
   B: _____

2. A: What should we do tomorrow?
   B: _____

3. A: Who is that man?
   B: _____

4. A: Did you go home last weekend?
   B: _____

5. A: What were you good at when you were a kid?
   B: _____

6. A: Is that woman a doctor?
   B: _____

7. A: What happened to the computer?
   B: _____

8. A: What was that noise?
   B: _____

Talk about It Look at the responses you wrote above. Could you have written a response in a different time frame or with a different meaning of *could/could have*? Discuss the possibilities with a partner.

25 | Error Correction Correct the errors with modals in these sentences. Some sentences have errors in form, and some have errors in meaning.

1. They might go to the celebration last night, but I didn't see them there.
2. He could have gone to work tomorrow. He's not very sick at all.
3. I don't know where your keys are. They must be in the kitchen.
4. It's a good thing she raised so much money. Otherwise, she could lost the election.
5. It's 9 a.m. The store can be open, but I'm not sure.
6. This book is torn. The baby could do it. He was looking at it this morning.
7. We saw someone who looked like you on Friday, but we knew it can't be you.
8. They may not had enough time to finish yesterday.

3.6 Advisability with *Should, Ought To,* and *Had Better*

<table>
<tr><td rowspan="2">A</td><td>

ADVISABILITY IN THE PRESENT/FUTURE

1 A: You **should get** a haircut.
B: Yeah, I probably **should**.

2 Future research **should investigate** the effects of air pollutants.

3 A: I think that we **ought to have** a choice about this.
B: I agree. We **should**.

4 You **had better get** ready for this storm. It's going to be bad.

5 I**'d better hurry** or I'm not going to get there on time.

</td><td>

We use the modal **should** (**not**) to give and request advice. We use *should* in informal speech, as in **1**, and in academic writing, as in **2**.

Ought to has a similar meaning to *should*, but we use it much less frequently. We usually use *ought to* in positive statements, as in **3** (but not usually in negative or question forms).

Had better (**not**) is a very strong form of advice. We often use it to say that something should happen soon, as in **4**. We also often use it to talk about things we should do ourselves, as in **5**.

We usually contract *had better* to *'d better* in speaking.

</td></tr>
</table>

<table>
<tr><td rowspan="2">B</td><td>

ADVISABILITY IN THE PAST (COUNTERFACTUAL)

6 The other team members **should have asked** her for her opinions. Instead, they ignored her.

7 I'm sorry about waking you up. I **shouldn't have called** so early.

8 **Should** I **have contacted** Greg? I didn't call him because I thought someone else was going to.

</td><td>

Should + have + the **past participle of a main verb** means that something was advisable, but didn't happen, as in **6**.

We often use *should / shouldn't have* to express regret, as in **7**. We can also ask questions with *should / should have*, as in **8**.

It is possible to use *ought to have* but it is not very common: *They ought to have helped him, but they didn't.*

</td></tr>
</table>

 ONLINE

26 | Giving and Requesting Advice Complete the questions and advice with *should* (*not*) + a verb from the box. Include a subject if necessary. Then practice with a partner. `3.6 A`

ACADEMIC ADVISOR

1. Advisor: You need to take Writing for Business and Economics 101.

   Student: Which one _____*should I take*_____ first?

2. Student: When _____ for an internship[10]?

   Advisor: You really should do that in your junior year.

STORE CLERK

3. Clerk: You _____ our accessories[11] table. Everything is on sale.

   Customer: That's OK. I'll just take this.

4. Customer: Where _____ to return an item?

   Clerk: You can do that at the register.

CUSTOMER SERVICE AGENT

5. Customer: Where _____ this item?

   CSA: I can help you with that.

6. Customer: What number _____ for technical service?

   CSA: I'll transfer you.

> apply
> bring
> call
> change
> contact
> go
> look at
> put
> return
> take

> **F Y I**
>
> In speaking, we often use **really** together with **should** when we give advice.
>
> A: He really **should see** a doctor.
>
> B: I know. I'm worried about him.

---

[10] **internship:** a job that a student has for a short time in order to get experience

[11] **accessories:** small clothing items, like jewelry or belts

7. Customer: What documents _____?

   Teller: You just need your ID and your account number.

8. Teller: We'll stop the check, but you _____ the merchant.

   Customer: OK. I'll do that.

REPAIRPERSON

9. Customer: How often _____ the oil?

   Repairperson: Every three months.

10. Repairperson: You _____ too much laundry in the dryer.

    Customer: I'll keep that in mind.

Write about It Write one more question you could ask each person in Activity 26. Role-play asking and answering your questions with a partner.

27 | Expressing Opinions with *Should* or *Ought To* Write a positive and a negative opinion statement in response to each question. Use *should* (*not*) or *ought to*. `3.6 A`

ADVICE FOR SUCCESS

1. How should colleges prepare students for the future?

   Colleges ought to provide students with a general education and teach them a variety of skills. They shouldn't just focus on career preparation.

2. How should parents prepare their children for the future?
3. What should a new restaurant do to attract customers?
4. What should teachers do to keep students interested in class?
5. What should people do to meet new friends?
6. What should people do to maintain contact with old friends?
7. What should cities do to attract tourism?
8. What should airlines do to improve the customer experience?
9. What should people do to be happy?
10. How should a person spend his/her early twenties?

Talk about It Share the statements you wrote above with a partner. Do you agree?

28 | Using *Had Better* Write a response to each statement with *had* ('*d*) *better* or *had* ('*d*) *better not*. `3.6 A`

1. A: It looks like it's going to rain.

   B: _We'd better get inside._

2. A: What did your father say?

   B: _____

3. A: Tom's boss is pretty mad at him right now.

   B: _____

4. A: Marta got sick at that restaurant.

   B: _____

5. A: It looks like the store is going to close soon.

   B: _____

6. A: That might be my boss calling.

   B: _____

7. A: The president of my bank was just caught in a big scandal[12].

   B: _____

8. A: Uh-oh. I forgot about my sister's birthday tomorrow.

   B: _____

FYI

Often we use **had better** to report what other people have said.

He called me and told me **I'd better get** moving.

We may use *had better* when someone else is putting pressure on us.

29 | Expressing Regret with *Should(n't) Have* Write one or two regrets for each situation. **3.6 B**

REGRETS

1. Tony stayed up late watching TV and overslept this morning.

   He shouldn't have stayed up so late. He should have turned off the TV earlier.

2. Kara didn't read the directions carefully and failed the test.
3. Sarah turned her application in late, so she didn't get an interview.
4. Kate lost touch with her best friend. Now she misses her.
5. John didn't accept the job offer. Now the company is doing really well.
6. Mika didn't write down the address. Now she doesn't know where to go.
7. Angela bought a new TV last week. This week the price dropped by 20 percent.
8. Khalid left his laptop on a table in the library. Somebody took it.

Talk about It Tell a partner your own regrets. Talk about two things you should or shouldn't have done when you were younger and two things you should or shouldn't have done recently.

30 | Using Past and Present Advisability with *Should* Complete these conversations with *should/shouldn't* or *should have/shouldn't have* and the verb in parentheses. Then practice with a partner. **3.6 A–B**

1. A: You forgot to buy bananas.

   B: Darn! I _____*should have made*_____ a list before I went to the store. (make)

2. A: Are you going shopping?

   B: Yeah, in a few minutes. I _____ a list first, though. (make)

3. A: I'm so glad we finally talked.

   B: Me too. We _____ this earlier. (do)

4. A: Ken didn't look very happy this morning.

   B: I know. Maybe I _____ him about the layoffs. (tell)

5. A: You don't look very well.

   B: I'm not. I _____ that fish. (eat)

6. A: My interview is tomorrow. I'm so nervous!

   B: You _____ so much. You'll do fine. (worry)

[12] **scandal:** something that is shocking, upsetting, or unacceptable

7. A: Sounds as if you guys had a lot of fun.

   B: We did. You really _____ with us. (come)

8. A: We're not going to get there on time.

   B: I know, I know. We _____ earlier. (leave)

Think about It What helped you choose between *should* and *should have* in the conversations in Activity 30? Share ideas with your classmates.

---

31 | Usage Note: Different Uses of *Should* and *Should Have* Read the note. Then do Activity 32.

> We can use *should* and *should have* to express many different present, past, or future meanings.
>
> **PRESENT OR FUTURE TIME**
>
> **A** Advisability: She's sick. She **should go** home and rest.
> **B** Expectation (not met): He left work an hour ago. He **should be** here by now. Where is he?
> **C** Expectation (strong certainty): Ask Benny that question. He **should know** the answer.
>
> **PAST TIME**
>
> **D** Past advisability (counterfactual): We **should have brought** more cash. They don't take credit here.

---

32 | Identifying Uses of *Should* and *Should Have* Label each sentence *A*, *B*, *C*, or *D* according to the meanings in Activity 31. `3.6 A–B`

1. You're under a lot of stress. You should relax and take some time for yourself. ____

2. I'm sorry we missed the beginning of the show. We should have come earlier. ____

3. What have you been doing all day? You should be finished with your work by now! ____

4. Try SuperMart. They should have the brand you're looking for. They have a huge selection. ____

5. I've been saving all year. I should have more money than this! ____

6. You should have seen the moon last night. It was beautiful. ____

7. She should call her father. I think he's lonely. ____

8. Just wait here, please. He should be available in a couple of minutes. ____

---

33 | Pronunciation Note: Modal + *Have* Listen to the note. Then do Activity 34.

> When we use *have* after a modal, we usually pronounce it as /əv/ or /ə/.
>
> | **1** She **couldn't have** known. | *sounds like* | "She couldn'tuv known." | or | "She couldn'tuh known." |
> | **2** They **should have** called earlier. | *sounds like* | "They shoulduv called earlier." | or | "They shoulduh called earlier." |
> | **3** I **would have** told him. | *sounds like* | "I woulduv told him." | or | "I woulduh told him." |
>
> You don't have to use the reduced form, but you need to understand it in conversation.

---

34 | Using *Could Have*, *Would Have*, and *Should Have* Listen and write the complete verb for each sentence. Then listen again and repeat. `3.6 B`

1. Marcia _should have come_ to dinner with us.

2. She _____ enough money.

3. I _____ with you.

4. You _____ out for the team.

5. They _____ ready.

6. He _____ that.

7. She _____ that.

8. You _____ surprised.

9. He _____ me.

10. She _____ that.

11. You _____ me.

12. Carlos _____ it.

Write about It Work with a partner. Write a short conversation for each sentence in Activity 34. Make clear what happened or did not happen in each situation. Read your conversations to another pair.

1. A: *Marcia should have come to dinner with us.*
   B: *She couldn't. She had to work.*

3.7 Obligation and Prohibition

We can use **must** (**not**), (**don't / doesn't**) **have to**, and **has / have got to** for strong obligation (requirement) or prohibition, as in **1 – 10**.

	EXAMPLES OF OBLIGATION / PROHIBITION	USE
must (not)	**1** Employees **must sign in** when they arrive. (= necessary) **2** Visitors **must not enter** the employee area. (= not allowed)	• Rare in speaking, but common in writing. • Usually refers to present or general time. • The question form is not common.
has to / have to *had to*	**3** They just **have to accept** his decision, whether they like it or not. (= necessary) **4** You **don't have to bring** your laptop. Computers will be provided. (= not required) **5 Does** she **have to talk** so loudly? **6** I **had to accept** the decision. **7** He **didn't have to go**. **8** We'll **have to leave** early today.	• Common in speaking, but rare in writing. • Can refer to past, present, or future time. • Used in positive, negative, and question forms.
has got to / have got to	**9** You've just **got to** be tough. (= necessary) **10** She's **got to finish** soon. Time is almost up! (= necessary)	Usually only used: • in speaking. • in simple present positive statements. • in the contracted form (*'s / 've got to*).

Column A label: **A**

COMPARING OBLIGATION / PROHIBITION TO CERTAINTY

We use **must** (**not**), **have to**, and **have got to** for obligation / prohibition, but we can also use them to express strong certainty, as in **11 – 15**.

	EXAMPLES OF CERTAINTY	USE
must (not)	**11** You **must be** new here. (present time) **12** The new land **must not have looked** very promising to the settlers. (past time)	• Commonly used in speaking to express strong certainty. • Also commonly expresses strong certainty in academic writing. • Can refer to past, present, or future time.
has to / have to *had to*	**13** He's not here so he **has to be** at work. (present time) **14** She **has to have written** it. I recognize her handwriting. (past time)	• Common in speaking, but rare in writing. • Can refer to past or present time. • Usually only used in positive statements.
has got to / have got to	**15** He's **got to be** there already—I saw him leave hours ago. (present time)	Usually only used: • in speaking. • in simple present positive statements. • in the contracted form.

Column B label: **B**

See Charts 3.4 and 3.5 for more information on the use of modals for certainty.

35 | Using *Must* for Obligation in Writing Work with a partner. Complete these sentences with *must* (*not*) + a verb from the box. Then match each sentence with a source below. `3.7 A`

SENTENCES FROM WRITTEN SOURCES

be	reach
boil	reconsider
cut	resign
have	retake
pay	use

_e_ 1. For this reaction to occur, temperatures _____*must reach*_____ 80 degrees.

____ 2. The potatoes _____ dry before you put them in the oil.

____ 3. The government _____ the sales tax on luxury items. We need the revenue[13], and the tax only affects people who can afford it.

____ 4. Hundreds of students _____ the test this year.

____ 5. Students _____ university computers in unlawful[14] ways.

____ 6. The human body _____ a good supply of oxygen.

____ 7. The administration _____ the campus parking rules.

____ 8. The mayor is terrible and _____ immediately.

____ 9. The cream sauce _____ or it will be ruined.

____ 10. Undergraduates _____ their full tuition by October 15.

◄ 80° Celsius

a chemical reaction

a. cookbook	b. political blog	c. school newspaper	d. school policy handbook	e. science text

Write about It Choose two or three sources from the box above. Search online for sentences from that source that use modals for obligation.

36 | Using *Have To* Complete the conversations with a form of (*not*) *have to* and an appropriate verb. `3.7 A`

1. A: _____ late last night?

   B: Yeah, I did. Jason never showed up for his shift.

2. A: Where's Sun-Hee?

   B: She left about an hour ago. She _____ to class.

3. A: What is Carlos so happy about?

   B: He _____ the final exam tomorrow because he has an A in the class.

4. A: _____ the manager _____ tonight?

   B: Yeah, he does. And he's not happy about it!

5. A: Thank you. That's so nice! You _____ me a present.

   B: I know, but I wanted to.

6. A: I _____ the window. It's so hot in here.

   B: I wish you wouldn't. It's really cold outside.

7. A: I'm so glad I _____ that medicine anymore.

   B: Oh, that's good. It was making you sick, wasn't it?

8. A: Emma has been going to the gym a lot lately.

   B: She _____ in shape for the big game.

Think about It Which two sentences above could be restated with *have got to*?

[13] **revenue:** money that a government or company receives   [14] **unlawful:** not legal

37 | Usage Note: Other Ways to Express Obligation and Prohibition Read the note. Then do Activities 38–40.

We can express obligation or prohibition with other **phrasal modals**.

OTHER WAYS TO EXPRESS OBLIGATION AND PROHIBITION

be required to + base form of main verb (similar to *have to*)

1 Jillian **is required to attend** all practices and home games during the season.

2 Participants **were required to rate** their agreement with each statement on a 6-point scale.

be not allowed to + base form of main verb (similar to *must not*)

3 You're **not allowed to bring** food on the plane.

4 We **were not allowed to enter** the building.

be supposed to + base form of main verb (similar to *should*)

5 Students **are supposed to take** three years of a foreign language.

6 I **was supposed to take** a test yesterday, but I stayed home because I was sick.

> We use these forms to describe external obligations or prohibitions—things that come from an outside authority. These phrasal modals do not describe internal obligations such as *I must try to be more positive* or *She has to think about the effects of her actions.*

38 | Using *Be Required To* and *Be Not Allowed To* These activities are required or permitted at many workplaces. For each activity, write a "work rule" for employees using *be required to* or *be not allowed to.* Choose a job from the box or use your own ideas. `3.7 A`

WORK RULES

1. accept gifts from students

   Teachers are not allowed to accept gifts from students.

2. call a substitute for absences
3. eat or drink in the work area
4. shred[15] many documents
5. talk about work to people outside the company
6. wash their hands before returning to work
7. wear jewelry or loose clothing
8. wear protective clothing

JOBS
chemists
engineers
factory workers
government employees
machine operators
public service workers
restaurant servers
teachers

Write about It Compare the sentences you wrote above with a partner. Then write two more rules for another job using your own ideas.

39 | Using *Be Supposed To* Complete these sentences with information that is true for you. Include the correct form of *be supposed to* if one isn't provided. `3.7 A`

1. When I was younger, I _____, but sometimes I didn't.

2. Recently, I _____, but I didn't because _____.

3. I _____ every day, but sometimes I don't.

4. Tomorrow I _____.

5. My _____ was supposed to _____, but _____.

6. My _____ is supposed to _____, but _____.

7. _____ were supposed to _____, but _____.

8. The _____ was supposed to _____, but _____.

[15] **shred:** to cut or tear into small pieces (usually with a machine called a shredder)

40 | Expressing Prohibition and Obligation Write a sentence for each rule. Use *must, have to, be required to, be not allowed to,* or *be supposed to.* Then compare with a partner. `3.7 A`

RULES FOR STUDENTS

1. try your best to succeed

    You must try your best to succeed.

2. bring all materials to every class
3. don't get discouraged if you fall behind
4. don't copy writing from the Internet
5. be considerate and polite to classmates
6. make wise decisions about how to spend your time
7. believe in yourself
8. attend class regularly

41 | Identifying Meanings of *Must (Not)*, *Have To*, and *Have Got To* Circle the modal forms. Then check (✓) *Strong Certainty* or *Obligation* for each sentence. `3.7 B`

AT THE AMUSEMENT PARK	STRONG CERTAINTY	OBLIGATION
1. "Do you hear those people screaming? That ride must be scary!"	☐	☐
2. "You must be over four feet tall to go on this ride."	☐	☐
3. "You've got to try this roller coaster. It's really fun."	☐	☐
4. "They must employ thousands of people here. This place is huge."	☐	☐
5. "You look exhausted. You must have been here all day."	☐	☐
6. "I'm not surprised they charge so much. It has to cost a lot to maintain this place."	☐	☐
7. "We'll have to stand in that long line if we want to go on the new ride."	☐	☐
8. "This has got to be the most exciting place in the world for little kids."	☐	☐

3.8 Combining Modals

A

SIMPLE MODAL + PHRASAL MODAL

1 I **would be willing to pay** for better service.

2 We **may be able to develop** strategies to overcome this problem.

3 Students **should be allowed to form** their own groups.

4 Have you called your cousin? He **might be able to fix** that computer for you.

5 Physicians **must be permitted to practice** medicine the way they choose.

6 City workers **will have to wait** until next year for a salary increase.

We generally do not use two simple modals together. However, we can use most **simple modals** together with a **phrasal modal**, as in **1 – 6**.

SIMPLE MODALS		PHRASAL MODALS
can	could	be able to
may	might	be allowed to
will	would	be permitted to
—	should	be required to
must	—	be willing to
		have to

WARNING! We do not usually combine *can/could* with *be able to* or *can* with *have to.*

42 | Using Combinations of Modals Work with a partner. Complete these sentences with a positive or negative phrasal modal. (More than one answer may be possible.) `3.8 A`

Facing a Water Shortage

1. In the near future, citizens may _____ pay fines if they use too much water.

2. Homeowners will _____ water their lawns or wash their cars.

3. Each member of the household will _____ take one shower every day.

4. Every one of us should _____ make these changes for the good of the community.

5. City officials must _____ enforce these rules.

6. In some instances, individuals might _____ apply for an exemption[16] from the water limitations.

7. People who are growing fruits and vegetables could _____ use more water.

8. If you have an exemption, you should _____ pay over-use fines.

Think about It What other modal combinations could be used in each sentence? Share ideas with your classmates.

Write about It Choose one of these events. Write four sentences about the effects of this event on the community. Use combinations of modals.

- The Olympics are coming to town.
- A very important person is going to visit your school.
- City officials are putting in a large park near the city center.
- There will be a lot of road construction in the area this summer.

43 | Using Combinations of Modals Complete these sentences with your own ideas. `3.8 A`

OPINIONS

1. Our teacher may not be able to _take a vacation soon_____.

2. Students should be able to _____.

3. I would be willing to _____.

4. I would never be willing to _____.

5. Teenagers should sometimes be permitted to _____.

6. University students must be allowed to _____.

7. Any good friend would be willing to _____.

8. Pretty soon, people in this country will have to _____.

9. All companies should have to _____.

[16]**exemption:** official permission not to do something or pay for something

10. Children shouldn't be permitted to _____.

11. The government might have to _____.

12. Someday, people won't be able to _____.

Talk about It Rewrite each statement you wrote in Activity 43 as a question. Ask a partner the questions. Do you and your partner agree?

A: *Do you think our teacher will take a vacation soon?*
B: *Maybe, but she might not be able to until the summer.*

FYI

We do not usually ask questions with *might* or *may* (for degrees of certainty). You can ask those questions with *will*.

3.9 Modals with Progressive Verb Forms

A

MODALS OF CERTAINTY OR PROBABILITY

1 The medical treatment **must be working.** She's getting better.

2 This is an old address. He **may not be living** there anymore.

3 It **might be confusing** at first, but you'll get it eventually.

4 The company is going bankrupt. Thousands of employees **could be losing** their jobs soon.

5 She didn't hear the phone ring. She **might have been sleeping.**

6 The government shut that company down. It **must have been operating** illegally.

7 He **must know** that already. (NOT: He must be knowing . . .)

We can use **progressive verb forms with modals** to express degrees of certainty, as in **1 – 6**. This form is more common in speaking than in writing. For present forms, we use:

| modal | + | (not) | + | be | + | the *-ing* form of the main verb |

For past forms, we use:

| modal | + | (not) | + | have been | + | the *-ing* form of the main verb |

We don't usually use non-action verbs such as *believe, own,* and *know* in the progressive, as in **7**.

B

MODALS OF ADVISABILITY

8 You **should be spending** more time on your work.

9 I don't know why they're upset. They **ought to be celebrating.**

10 You **should have been listening** while the teacher was talking!

We can also use the progressive verb forms with *should* and *ought to* when we are:

• giving advice or making recommendations in the present, as in **8 – 9**

• making past counterfactual statements, as in **10**

GO ONLINE

44 | Using Modals for Certainty in the Present Read the Speaker A statement. Then circle the appropriate response. **3.9 A**

1. A: He's been on the computer for quite a while.

    B: He might be writing an essay.

    B: He might write an essay.

2. A: The meeting is going long[17].

    B: They must be arguing about the budget.

    B: They must argue about the budget.

3. A: That guy seems to really know what he's doing.

    B: He must be coming here a lot.

    B: He must come here a lot.

[17]**go long:** to last longer than expected

4. A: Mark looks really frustrated.

   B: He must be having trouble with his assignment.

   B: He must have trouble with his assignment.

5. A: Someone said they're going to close the store.

   B: They might have been talking about the one on Hill Street.

   B: They might have talked about the one on Hill Street.

6. A: Mina never wants to go to the games.

   B: She may think sports are boring.

   B: She may be thinking sports are boring.

7. A: What was she doing at the park?

   B: I'm not sure. She might have been playing soccer.

   B: I'm not sure. She might have played soccer.

8. A: How did she finish the game so quickly?

   B: She must be playing a lot.

   B: She must play a lot.

Write about It Work with a partner. Write a new response for each Speaker A statement in Activity 44. If possible, use a progressive form with a modal.

---

45 | Using Modals for Certainty in the Past Choose verbs from the box to complete these conversations. Use a modal of certainty with *have* + a past participle verb form or *have* + *been* + an *-ing* verb form. Then practice with a partner. `3.9 A`

1. A: I lost my keys.

   B: You _____*must have left*_____ them in the car.

2. A: Sara's eyes are all puffy and red.

   B: Yeah, I noticed. She _____ before class.

3. A: All the lights are off.

   B: They _____ early.

4. A: I saw Tony at the lake on Saturday.

   B: He _____.

5. A: Do you think this chicken is still good?

   B: I wouldn't eat it. It _____ there for hours.

6. A: Why did she buy that ugly sweater?

   B: I don't know. She _____ it as a gift.

7. A: Why didn't they hear me knocking?

   B: They _____ to music.

8. A: Why isn't there any cereal in the cabinet?

   B: David _____ it.

close
cry
eat
fish
get
leave
listen
sit

46 | Expressing Opinions with _Should_ Choose a verb from the box to complete each statement below. Use _should_ and a progressive verb form. (More than one answer may be possible.) Then check (✓) whether you agree or disagree with each statement. `3.9 B`

ask	cut	eliminate	hire	lower	offer	provide	spend

HOW TO IMPROVE THE ECONOMY   YES   NO

1. Our government officials _____*should be hiring*_____ people to build roads and bridges.   ☐   ☐

2. They _____ taxes so people have more money to spend.   ☐   ☐

3. They _____ money on education so that young people can find better jobs.   ☐   ☐

4. They _____ unemployment benefits so people are motivated to work.   ☐   ☐

5. They _____ tax incentives to companies to encourage growth.   ☐   ☐

6. They _____ low-interest loans to people with good business ideas.   ☐   ☐

7. They _____ many government programs to save money.   ☐   ☐

8. They _____ people to spend instead of save.   ☐   ☐

Talk about It Compare your answers above with a partner and discuss. Suggest some other ideas for improving the economy.

Write about It With a partner, brainstorm a list of problems that your school, community, or country is currently facing. Write eight sentences about what leaders should be doing right now to deal with the problems.

47 | Using _Should_ to Express Opinions about the Past Work with a partner. Complete each response. Use _should_ with _have_ + a past participle verb form or _have_ + _been_ + an _-ing_ verb form. Then practice with your partner. `3.9 B`

CRITICIZING OTHERS

1. A: Mark lost some money yesterday. It fell out of his pocket.

   B: Well, he _____*should have put*_____ it in his wallet.

2. A: Sue spent all morning ordering stuff online instead of working. Ed caught her and now he's furious.

   B: What does she expect? She _____.

3. A: Poor Julia worked nine hours last night and now she's even sicker.

   B: I'm not surprised. She _____.

4. A: Paul caught Misha reading his email last night.

   B: That's terrible! He _____ someone else's email.

5. A: Ana started looking for a summer job last week. She hasn't found anything yet.

   B: Why did she start so late? She _____ for the last month.

6. A: Yuri got rear-ended yesterday. He was texting and didn't notice the light had changed.

   B: Well, he _____ in the car.

   A: True, but the other driver _____ attention.

7. A: Hassan called at the last minute to cancel.

   B: I know. He _____ us yesterday.

8. A: Mary threw the book to me and knocked over my cup of coffee.

   B: She _____ the book.

3.10 Other Ways to Express Modality

A

ORDER OF ADVERBS OF CERTAINTY

POSITIVE STATEMENTS

	subject	*be* or first helping verb	adverb	main verb	
1	She	was	probably	—	frustrated.
2	This	will	most likely	change	later.
3	The people	can	certainly	decide	themselves.
4	He	—	definitely	knows	the answer.

NEGATIVE STATEMENTS

	subject	—	adverb	helping and main verbs	
5	Listeners	—	obviously	can't understand	her.
6	The phone	—	clearly	isn't working.	

We sometimes use **adverbs** to express degrees of certainty. We can place these adverbs:

- after a positive *be* verb, as in **1**, or the first helping verb, as in **2 – 3**
- before positive main verbs (besides *be*), as in **4**
- in negative sentences before any verb, including *be*, as in **5** and **6**

ADVERBS OF CERTAINTY

STRONG CERTAINTY	certainly clearly definitely	evidently obviously
MODERATE CERTAINTY	most likely probably	
WEAK CERTAINTY	possibly	

B

PREPOSITIONAL PHRASES

7 **In a way**, I understand their decision. But I don't agree with it.

8 He has grown up a lot, but he has the same personality and character. **In a sense**, he hasn't changed at all.

9 Their jobs are different, but they both achieved success quickly. **In some respects**, their careers have followed the same path.

With some **prepositional phrases**, we can suggest that a statement is only partly true, as in **7 – 9**.

We often use these prepositional phrases at the beginning of a sentence.

48 | Using Adverbs of Certainty Rewrite these sentences using the adverb in parentheses instead of the modal. **3.10 A**

Restaurant Reviews

1. This might be the best fish stew I've ever had. (possibly)

   This is possibly the best fish stew I've ever had.

2. The chef must have trained in France. (obviously)

3. These strawberries must have just been picked. (clearly)

4. This has to be one of the best restaurants in town. (definitely)
5. They must be offering some new dishes this week. (evidently)
6. Soon they might start serving lunch as well as dinner. (possibly)
7. This place must get excellent reviews from everyone. (probably)
8. I should come back very soon. (most likely)

49 | Placing Adverbs of Certainty in a Sentence Write a complete sentence in response to each question. Include an adverb of certainty. **3.10 A**

MODERN LIFE

1. Do most people spend too much time online?

   Some people clearly spend too much time online, but most people don't.

2. Do social media do more good than harm?
3. Is television better today than it was in the past?
4. Can you learn any useful skills from video games?
5. Is it important for everyone to have a smartphone?
6. Should a 13-year-old have a smartphone?
7. Should people have to pay for online newspaper subscriptions?
8. Is it a good idea to buy brand-new technology?

Talk about It Share the sentences you wrote above with a partner. Explain the reasons for your opinions.

"There are obviously people who spend too much time online. They just look at a screen all day and it's not healthy. But most people I know do other things, too."

50 | Using Adverbs and Prepositional Phrases of Certainty Complete these sentences with your own ideas. Share your sentences with a partner. **3.10 A–B**

1. In a way, the past year _____.
2. The people in my classes are clearly _____.
3. _____ will obviously _____ very soon.
4. _____ should definitely _____.
5. In some respects, _____ and _____ are very similar.
6. In a sense, my friends are _____.
7. Tomorrow, I probably _____.
8. Next week, I'm most likely to _____.
9. In a way, I really like _____.
10. In some respects, _____ was the best _____.

3.11 Using Modals in Speaking: Modals for Social Purposes

A

POLITE SUGGESTIONS

1 A: I'm having trouble with my math class.
B: You **could always get** a tutor.

2 A: I can't get to sleep at night.
B: You **may want to stop** drinking coffee.

3 A: I keep running out of money.
B: **Maybe** you **should ask** your boss for more hours.

4 A: I don't know anyone here.
B: You **may as well introduce** yourself to a few people. Maybe you'll make a new friend.

We sometimes use **modals with other words** to soften suggestions, as in **1 – 4**. Some phrases that make suggestions a little less direct and more polite include:

> You could always . . .
> You may want to . . .
> You might want to . . .
> Maybe you should . . .
> You might as well . . .
> You may as well . . .

B

SOFTENING SUGGESTIONS WITH NEGATIVE QUESTIONS

5 A: I'm afraid she's not going to see this email in time.
B: **Can't you text** her instead?

6 A: **Shouldn't you call** your brother today?
B: You're right. I should.

Asking questions with **can't**, **couldn't**, and **shouldn't** is another way to soften suggestions, as in **5 – 6**.

C

OTHER SOCIAL USES OF MODALS

7 Could I have another fork, please?

8 Would you mind turning the music down?

9 Can I help you with that?

10 May I speak to you for a moment?

We often use the modals **can**, **could**, **would**, and **may** in speaking for:

- requests, as in **7 – 8**
- offers, as in **9**
- permission, as in **10**

 GO ONLINE

---

51 | Using Softening Strategies to Make Suggestions Write a suggestion for each problem. Use a polite form with a modal. `3.11 A`

PROBLEMS WITH SOLUTIONS

1. "I don't have time to exercise."

   Maybe you could start walking to school.

2. "I can't stop eating chocolate."

3. "I always oversleep in the morning."

4. "I'm really shy."

5. "I have trouble getting organized."

6. "I'm always late to class."

7. "I can't decide what to major in."

8. "I can't find a job."

9. "I have a friend who is constantly calling and texting me."

10. "I want to ask for a raise, but I'm nervous."

11. "This class is really hard for me."

12. "I can barely afford to pay my rent these days."

Talk about It Compare the advice you wrote above with a partner. For each problem, which piece of advice is the most helpful?

---

52 | Using Negative Questions to Make Suggestions Work with a partner and take turns. One of you reads a statement in Activity 51 aloud. The other uses negative questions to give advice for the situation. `3.11 B`

A: *I don't have time to exercise.*
B: *Couldn't you walk to school in the morning?*

53 | Using Modals for Requests, Offers, and Permission Write a short conversation for each situation. Use *can, could, would,* or *may.* `3.11 C`

AROUND TOWN

At a restaurant

1. Customer: Ask for permission to exchange a menu item.

   A: Could I get fresh fruit instead of potatoes?
   B: Yes, of course.

2. Customer: Request a new table.
3. Server: Offer to clean up a spill on the table.

At work

4. Employee: Ask for permission to take a day off.
5. Co-worker: Offer to help a co-worker with a big job.
6. Employer: Request that the employee do some additional work.

At a clothing store

7. Customer: Ask to see a different item.
8. Customer: Ask for permission to try something on.
9. Clerk: Ask if the customer wants to pay with a credit card.
10. Clerk: Offer to show other styles.

At an acquaintance's house

11. Visitor: Ask for permission to look at the garden.
12. Visitor: Offer to help with dinner preparations.
13. Host: Request that a guest put his or her jacket/purse in the bedroom.

3.12 Using Modals in Academic Writing

To **hedge** a statement means to make it less definite. Hedging is a very common way we use **modals** in academic writing, where it's necessary to be precise.

A

COULD / MIGHT

1 You **could say** that they have run out of ideas.
2 One **might conclude** that no peaceful options remain. But that is not the case.

We sometimes use *could* or *might* to make a less definite conclusion, as in **1**. Sometimes we use them to introduce an idea that we are going to argue against, as in **2**.

MAY

3 After the procedure, patients **may notice** an increase in energy levels.

We can use *may* in writing to show that something is possible, as in **3**. *May* shows a higher degree of certainty than *might* or *could*.

WOULD

4 We **would argue** that the point is valid.
5 I **would suggest** that we need to review this topic.
6 One **would assume** that the answers are obvious.

We can use *would* with verbs like *say, suggest, assume,* and *argue* when we are making a point that others might disagree with, as in **4 – 6**.

SHOULD

7 Our experiment **should show** the effects of carbon monoxide.
8 These studies **should demonstrate** the usefulness of our procedure.

We can use *should* to describe our expectations, as in **7 – 8**. It shows more certainty than *might* or *may*, but less than *will* or statements without modals.

54 | Identifying Hedges with *Could* and *Might* Underline the hedging expressions. Then match the statements with the conclusions. `3.12 A`

DRAWING CONCLUSIONS

1. The two birds look extremely similar. ____
2. This is the author's most well-known novel. ____
3. She rarely left the house and avoided all contact with strangers. ____
4. The mice began to solve the maze more quickly. ____
5. Six months after the shopping center was built, stores along Main Street began to close. ____
6. The company's closure affected the lives of hundreds of people. ____
7. Every year, more students are passing the entrance examination. ____
8. The two documents have a similar writing style and use much of the same vocabulary. ____

a. One <u>could say</u> that it's also his most important work.
b. One might assume that she was deeply depressed during this period.
c. We might assume that the new diet was increasing their intelligence.
d. One could say it is the worst disaster this city has ever faced.
e. This might suggest that they were written by the same person.
f. We might conclude that secondary schools are doing a better job of preparing them.
g. This might suggest that customers feel little loyalty to local business owners.
h. We could conclude that they are closely related.

Write about It Choose three sentences from this box to write a conclusion about. Hedge your conclusions with *could* or *might*, using three of the phrases you underlined above.

> 1. Gas prices have risen in the last two years.
> 2. High-end televisions have gotten cheaper.
> 3. Computing power has increased rapidly over the last five years.
> 4. More and more businesses have moved into this area recently.
> 5. The traffic problems downtown continue to get worse.
> 6. The number of students applying to the university goes up every year.

55 | Hedging with *May* Write two to three sentences about possible results for each situation. Use *may*. Share your sentences with a partner. `3.12 A`

LIFESTYLE

What happens when people . . .

1. take long naps in the afternoon

   They may have difficulty sleeping at night.

2. sit at the computer for hours every day
3. begin a dance class
4. move to a new city
5. lose a job
6. get plenty of exercise
7. become very famous
8. start college

56 | Hedging with *Would* Write an opinion statement about each issue. Use *would argue that, would suggest that, would assume that,* or *would say that.* `3.12 A`

> ### SOLVING CAMPUS PROBLEMS
>
> 1. There is an increase in the number of students cheating on exams.
>
>   *I would suggest that we need to put cameras in the classrooms.*
>
> 2. Student residences are overcrowded.
> 3. Students are not happy with the food choices in the cafeteria.
> 4. There are long lines in the bookstore at the beginning of every semester.
> 5. The registration process is confusing.
> 6. There is not enough for students to do on weekends.
> 7. Some of the classrooms are old and lack modern technology.
> 8. Classes often fill up very quickly.

Write about It Think of a real problem on your campus. Suggest an idea for a solution. Use *would.*

57 | Hedging with *Should* Rewrite these statements with *should* to make them less certain. `3.12 A`

1. The patient's quick recovery will demonstrate the usefulness of the procedure.

   The patient's quick recovery should demonstrate the usefulness of the procedure.

2. Our research will show the negative effect of the oil spill on wildlife.
3. This treatment will make the patient much more comfortable.
4. The new software will solve most of the problems we have been experiencing.
5. The presentation is going to help students understand the material.
6. The team will finish the first research by early next year.
7. The new fertilizer[18] will add nutrients to the soil.
8. Our profits will increase over the next year.

Write about It Complete these sentences with your own ideas. Write about your expectations.

1. _____ should show _____.
2. _____ should make _____.
3. _____ should finish _____.

WRAP-UP Demonstrate Your Knowledge

A | ROLE-PLAY Work with two partners. Role-play these situations. Use *can, could, might want to, have to, will, should,* or *be going to.* Take turns being Student A.

1. Student A: You are going on a two-week vacation. You will be staying in three different hotels and taking public transportation. It's summer. Ask your friends for advice.

   Students B and C: Give advice.

2. Student A: You want to look for a new job but aren't sure when to tell your boss. Ask for advice.

   Students B and C: Give advice about when to tell the boss and about how to find a new job.

[18]**fertilizer:** something added to soil to make plants grow more successfully

3. Student A: You want to buy a birthday gift for a friend, but it can't be too expensive. Ask for advice.

   Students B and C: Give advice about what to buy and how to celebrate the birthday.

4. Student A: You have visitors coming to town, and you want to show them the perfect weekend in your city. Ask for advice.

   Students B and C: Give advice about where to go, what to do, and what to eat.

B | SENTENCES Write a paragraph for each picture to answer these questions. Use various verb forms with modals.

1. What probably happened?
2. What should have happened?
3. What should happen now?
4. What might happen next?

Her child must have left the toy on the floor....

C | SURVEY Work with a partner. Write an opinion statement about each group of people in this chart. Use modals and *be required to, be permitted to, (not) be allowed to,* or *be supposed to*. Then read your statements to your classmates. Find out how many people agree or disagree with you.

	Do you agree with these statements?	Yes	No
professional athletes	*Professional athletes should not be allowed to participate in the Olympics.*		
drivers			
flight attendants			
landlords			
parents			
politicians			

SIMPLE MODALS

She **can speak** English well. →

She **could speak** Chinese when she was a child. →

They say it **will rain** tomorrow. →

They said it **would rain**, but it didn't. →

Employees **must arrive** on time. →

Employees **may take** two 15-minute breaks. →

We **might finish** by 4:00, but I'm not sure. →

He **should help** his mother. →

PHRASAL MODALS

Many immigrants **are able to speak** English very well.

She **was able to speak** Chinese when she was a child.

They say it's **going to rain** tomorrow.

They said it **was going to rain**, but it didn't.

Employees **have to arrive** on time.

Employees **are permitted to take** two 15-minute breaks.

—

He **is supposed to help** his mother.

SOCIAL PURPOSE MEANINGS

CAN(NOT)

Ability **I can swim.**

Permission We **can stay** for a few more hours.

Prohibition You **can't stay** any longer.

Offer **Can I help** you?

WILL

Offer **I'll help** you with that.

MUST (NOT)

Obligation Employees **must sign** in when they arrive.

SHOULD (NOT)

Advice You **should take** Walker Boulevard.

MAY (NOT)

Permission **May I continue?**

Prohibition You **may not talk** during the test.

Offer **May I help** you?

MIGHT (NOT)

Suggestion You **might want to try** calling him again.

COULD

Permission **Could I sit** here?

Suggestion We **could try** that new restaurant downtown.

Request **Could you say** that again?

DEGREE OF CERTAINTY / LOGICAL PROBABILITY MEANINGS

CAN(NOT)

General possibility Honey **can make** your throat feel better.

very certain / very likely
strong probability

WILL / WON'T

They **will come** home soon.

They **won't be** out much longer.

MUST / CAN'T / COULDN'T

She has so many flowers. She **must love** to garden.

That **can't be** our train. It's too early.

SHOULD (NOT)

I **should be** home by 5:00. I **shouldn't be** late.

MAY (NOT)

I **may take** accounting next year. I haven't decided.

MIGHT (NOT) / COULD

They **might drop** by tomorrow, but I'm not sure.

The meeting **could last** for an hour.

WOULD (NOT)

Counterfactual I **would help** you, but you haven't asked.

not certain / not likely
weak probability

OTHER WAYS OF SHOWING PERMISSION / PROHIBITION / OBLIGATION

Permission On Fridays, we **were allowed to wear** casual clothing at work.

You **are permitted to turn** right on a red light here.

Prohibition Employees **are not allowed to eat** at their desks.

Obligation He **is required to take** a final exam for this class.

Children **are supposed to obey** their parents.

OTHER WAYS OF SHOWING CERTAINTY / UNCERTAINTY

ADVERBS

Strong certainty They are **certainly / definitely / clearly** going to enjoy this wonderful meal.

Moderate certainty He is **probably / most likely** going to come home tomorrow.

Weak certainty They are **possibly** going to get new uniforms.

PREPOSITIONAL PHRASES

In way, this is the most difficult class I've ever taken.

In a sense, he is representing the class.

In some respects, nothing has changed.

4 The Passive

Nothing great was ever achieved without enthusiasm.

—RALPH WALDO EMERSON,
ESSAYIST, POET,
AND PHILOSOPHER
(1803–1882)

Talk about It What does the quotation above mean? Do you agree or disagree?

WARM-UP

A | Match each time on the timeline with an event. Then compare answers with your classmates. How many do you agree on?

TIMELINE OF GREAT ACHIEVEMENT

1839   1895 1903   1928   1952 1954 1960   the future

1. The first open-heart surgery was attempted in ___1952___.

2. The first airplane was flown by the Wright brothers in _____.

3. The camera was invented in _____.

4. Penicillin, the first antibiotic, was discovered by accident in _____.

5. The first nuclear power plant was built in _____.

6. The first motion pictures were shown to a paying audience in _____.

7. Lasers had been developed by about _____.

8. A cure for cancer will probably be found in _____.

RESEARCHERS FIND CURE FOR CANCER
_____
_____
_____

B | The verb in blue in each sentence above is a passive verb form. Based on these examples, what can you say about passive verb forms? Check (✓) *True* or *False*.

	TRUE	FALSE
1. A passive verb form has a form of the verb *be*.	☐	☐
2. In a sentence with a passive verb form, the subject causes the action.	☐	☐
3. A sentence with a passive verb form always has *by* + a noun phrase.	☐	☐

C | Look back at the quotation on page 106. Identify any passive forms.

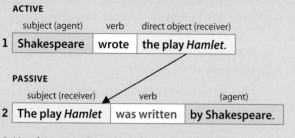

A

ACTIVE

| subject (agent) | verb | direct object (receiver) |
| Shakespeare | wrote | the play *Hamlet*. |

1

PASSIVE

| subject (receiver) | verb | (agent) |
| The play *Hamlet* | was written | by Shakespeare. |

2

3 *Hamlet* **was written** between 1599 and 1601.

In most sentences, the subject is the performer of the action, or agent, as in **1**. When the subject performs the action, we call the sentence an **active sentence**. The direct object is the receiver of the action.

A **passive sentence** lets us change the focus to what happened or who received the action, as in **2**.

• The receiver of the action becomes the subject of the sentence.

• When the agent is included, it follows the word *by*.

In passive sentences, however, the agent is usually omitted, as in **3**.

B

We form the passive with *be* + the **past participle of the main verb**. The form of *be* signals the time frame we are talking about.

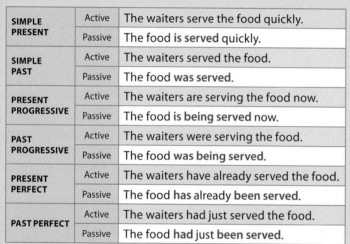

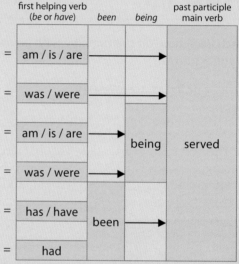

			first helping verb (*be* or *have*)	been	being	past participle main verb
SIMPLE PRESENT	Active	The waiters serve the food quickly.				
	Passive	The food **is served** quickly.	= am / is / are →			
SIMPLE PAST	Active	The waiters served the food.				
	Passive	The food **was served**.	= was / were →			
PRESENT PROGRESSIVE	Active	The waiters are serving the food now.				
	Passive	The food **is being served** now.	= am / is / are →		being	served
PAST PROGRESSIVE	Active	The waiters were serving the food.				
	Passive	The food **was being served**.	= was / were →			
PRESENT PERFECT	Active	The waiters have already served the food.				
	Passive	The food **has already been served**.	= has / have	been →		
PAST PERFECT	Active	The waiters had just served the food.				
	Passive	The food **had just been served**.	= had			

For a list of past participles of irregular verbs, see the Resources, page R-3.

 ONLINE

1 | Performer or Receiver of the Action? Decide if each **bold** subject is the performer of the action or the receiver of the action. Write *P* (performer) or *R* (receiver) above the subject. **4.1 A**

FACTS ABOUT WILLIAM SHAKESPEARE

1.   *P*
   Many people think that William Shakespeare was the greatest writer in the English language.

2. **Nobody** knows Shakespeare's actual birthday, but scholars think he was born on April 23, 1564.

3. As far as we know, **Shakespeare** never went beyond grammar school.

4. **Shakespeare and his wife** had three children: Susanna and twins Judith and Hamnet.

5. Although **Shakespeare's son Hamnet** died at age 11, **his name** lives on.

6. **The name Hamnet** was sometimes written as *Hamlet*, the title of one of Shakespeare's greatest plays.

7. **"Shakespeare"** was spelled 80 different ways, including "Shaxpere" and "Shaxberd."

8. **Shakespeare's work** has been translated into many languages.

9. **His plays** are read in at least 80 languages.

10. **Shakespeare** is thought to be the author of 39 plays. **About half of them** were printed before his death.

11. **Some of Shakespeare's most famous works** were not published until after his death.

Think about It Which of the sentences in Activity 1 are passive? How do you know?

2 | Noticing Passive Forms Read this email message and underline the passive forms. Then write each verb under the correct group in the chart below. **4.1 B**

From: Williams, Judy

To: All

Subject: State of the office

These emails are annoying, I know, but it's your own fault that I have to send them. Here is your semiannual list of bad office behavior.

1. Paper <u>is</u> still <u>being wasted</u>. Print jobs are piled at the printer for days and weeks. If you don't need it, don't print it!
2. The conference rooms are often left in a mess. Please put used paper in the recycling bin.
3. Last week some confidential materials were found in the copier room. Please keep all confidential materials with you.
4. Paper towels are being thrown on the floor in restrooms. Please throw them in the garbage.
5. Lengthy conversations are being held in office cubicles, to the dismay of nearby people. Move to a conference room.
6. Some strange things have been found in the recycling bins. Please remember that the remains of your lunch are not recyclable.
7. The same dirty dishes have been left in the kitchen sink for the past four days. Will the owner please wash them?
8. Lights aren't being turned off in empty offices. Please turn off all lights when you leave a room.

Simple present passive	Simple past passive	Present progressive passive	Present perfect passive
am / is / are + past participle of verb	*was / were +* past participle of verb	*am / is / are + being +* past participle of verb	*have / has + been +* past participle of verb
		is being wasted	

Talk about It What other examples of bad office behavior can you think of? Share ideas with your classmates.

Think about It Why do you think the writer used the passive forms in the sentences in Activity 2?

3 | Forming Simple Present Passive Sentences Complete these sentences with the simple present passive form of the verbs in parentheses. **4.1 B**

IT'S A FACT!

1. Every year, about 70 million tons of fish and other sea animals
   _____*are caught*_____ in the oceans. (catch)

2. Nuclear energy _____ when atoms of a nuclear fuel,
   such as uranium, _____ apart. (produce/split)

3. There is enough food in the world for everybody. The problem is
   getting it where it _____. (need)

4. More than half of the world's languages _____ by
   less than 1 percent of the population. (speak)

5. When land _____ by water on three sides,
   it _____ a peninsula. (surround/call)

6. Modern bridges _____ with materials that can expand
   and contract¹ as the temperature changes. (build)

7. When air _____, it expands and takes up more space. (heat)

8. One large body of water covers about 71 percent of the earth. It _____ by scientists into
   four oceans: the Pacific, the Atlantic, the Indian, and the Arctic. (divide)

9. A tide is the movement of water toward and away from land. Ocean tides _____ mostly
   by the pull of the moon's gravity on the earth's water. (cause)

10. Reykjavik, Iceland, is located in a cold northern climate. Buildings in this city _____ by
    the hot-water springs in the ground below. (heat)

11. Ice covers about 10 percent of the earth's land surface. Nearly all of it _____ in Greenland
    and Antarctica. (find)

12. About 80 percent of microwaves from mobile phones _____ by your head. (absorb²)

13. Trees _____ just for wood. They do many other important things such as releasing
    oxygen for us to breathe. (not need)

14. A battery uses special chemicals to make electricity. When the chemicals _____,
    the battery stops working. (use up)

15. Three of Switzerland's official languages are German, French, and Italian. All national laws
    _____ in these three languages. (publish)

Talk about It Which facts above were new to you? Which was the most interesting to you? Why?

---

¹ **contract:** to become smaller   ² **absorb:** to take something in like liquid or heat and hold it

4 | Using Simple Past Passive Verb Forms Complete these sentences with the simple past passive form of the verbs in parentheses. `4.1 B`

FAMOUS FIRSTS

1. The first pulley ___*was*___ probably ___*invented*___ in ancient Greece. Pulleys _____ first _____ to help construct buildings. (invent/employ)

2. Toothbrushes _____ probably first _____ in Egypt and Babylonia about 3500 BCE. (use)

3. The first books _____ in China and Korea about 700 CE. (print)

4. The first English newspaper _____ in 1621, but it wasn't until 1643 that the first newspaper with pictures _____. (publish/print)

5. The first photograph of land from above _____ from a balloon over a village in France in 1858. (take)

6. The first record player _____ a phonograph, and it played cylinders[3] instead of discs[4]. (call)

7. The first gasoline _____ about 1864, but it wasn't until the automobile _____ in 1885 that gasoline became really useful. (produce/invent)

8. Wristwatches _____ about 1890, but for many years they _____ only _____ by women. (introduce/wear)

9. The first contact lenses[5] _____ by a Swiss doctor. They were thick and not very comfortable. (develop)

10. The first plastic _____ "Parkesine" because it _____ by a scientist named Alexander Parkes. (call/invent)

11. The first World Cup _____ in 1930, and Uruguay _____ to host it. (hold/choose)

12. In 1797, André-Jacques Garnerin made the first parachute jump ever. He _____ from a balloon at about 3,200 feet above Paris. (drop)

13. The world's first skyscraper _____ in Chicago in 1885. This ten-story building _____ inside and outside by a metal frame. (complete/support)

14. The first photograph _____ in 1826 by a French scientist. It's a picture of the view from an upstairs window of his house. (take)

<aside>
FYI

When we use an adverb to describe a passive verb form, we often place it after the first helping verb.

The building was **almost** destroyed.

The city was **completely** rebuilt.
</aside>

pulley

phonograph

Talk about It What other famous inventions or discoveries do you know about? When were they invented or discovered?

---

[3] **cylinders:** long, round shapes like tubes or cans
[4] **discs:** flat, round objects

[5] **contact lenses:** small, round pieces of plastic that you wear in your eyes so you can see better

5 | Using Different Forms of the Passive Which monument does each sentence describe? Check (✓) your answers. Then rewrite each sentence to make it passive. Leave out the agent (the performer of the action) in your passive sentence. **4.1 B**

TWO FAMOUS MONUMENTS

	PYRAMID OF GIZA	EIFFEL TOWER
1. Today, people recognize it as a symbol of France.	☐	✓
Today, it is recognized as a symbol of France.		
2. The builders used more than 2.3 million stone blocks to build it.	☐	☐
More than 2.3 million stone blocks _____.		
3. The builders completed it more than 4,500 years ago.	☐	☐
4. People built it for a world's fair.	☐	☐
5. It opened in 1889.	☐	☐
6. People designed it as a tomb[6] to protect a king's body.	☐	☐
7. In 1909, the government almost tore it down.	☐	☐
8. They covered it with limestone.	☐	☐
9. The government repaints it every seven years.	☐	☐
10. The United Nations has identified it as a World Heritage Site.	☐	☐
11. In ancient times, people considered it one of the Seven Wonders of the World.	☐	☐
12. Architects are completely redesigning the first floor.	☐	☐

Think about It What verb form did you use in each sentence above? Why?

---

[6] **tomb:** a place where a body is buried after the person dies, often with a large decorated stone

6 | Pronunciation Note: Sentence Rhythm Listen to the note. Then do Activity 7.

English speakers usually stress the content words (nouns, verbs, adjectives, adverbs, etc.) in a sentence. They don't usually stress function words (articles, helping verbs, prepositions, etc.). The length of time it takes to say a sentence depends on the number of STRESSED syllables—not the length of the sentence. Notice:

──────── TAKE THE SAME AMOUNT OF TIME TO SAY ────────

1 The WAITers SERVED DINner at SIX.

Number of syllables in the sentence: 8
Number of stressed syllables: 4

2 The WAITers are going to SERVE DINner at SIX.

Number of syllables in the sentence: 11
Number of stressed syllables: 4

Notice that a passive sentence may have more syllables than an active sentence, but the two sentences take about the same amount of time to say.

3 Active: AMANda MADE the deCIsion.

Number of syllables in the sentence: 8
Number of stressed syllables: 3

4 Passive: The deCIsion was MADE by AMANda.

Number of syllables in the sentence: 10
Number of stressed syllables: 3

7 | Pronouncing Passive Sentences Count the number of syllables in each sentence, and write the number. Then underline the stressed syllables in each sentence, and write the number on the next line. Finally, listen and check your answers. 4.1 B

	NUMBER OF SYLLABLES IN THE SENTENCE	NUMBER OF STRESSED SYLLABLES
1. a. <u>John</u> <u>fin</u>ished it.	4	2
b. It was finished by John.	___	___
2. a. A switch turns on the light.	___	___
b. The lights are turned on by a switch.	___	___
3. a. Toni Morrison wrote the novel *Sula*.	___	___
b. The novel *Sula* was written by Toni Morrison.	___	___
4. a. The workers are cleaning the streets today.	___	___
b. The streets are being cleaned by the workers today.	___	___
5. a. The storm destroyed the house.	___	___
b. The house was destroyed by the storm.	___	___
6. a. A friend introduced them.	___	___
b. They were introduced by a friend.	___	___
7. a. Their employer is organizing a conference.	___	___
b. A conference is being organized by their employer.	___	___
8. a. The committee has recently honored Dr. Bell.	___	___
b. Dr. Bell has recently been honored by the committee.	___	___
9. a. One of his students made the furniture.	___	___
b. The furniture was made by one of his students.	___	___
10. a. Scientists have discovered other stars with planets.	___	___
b. Other stars with planets have been discovered by scientists.	___	___

Think about It There are more syllables in each passive sentence, yet it takes about the same amount of time to say the active sentence. What do speakers do differently when they say the passive sentences?

8 | Error Correction Correct any errors in these sentences. (Some sentences may not have any errors.)

1. This picture is painted about 100 years ago, but it still looks very modern.

2. My father was left the country after the war ended, and he didn't go back until he was in his sixties.

3. All of the work was finish before noon, but we were told to stay anyway.

4. This photo taken by my parents in 1990. You can see my sister next to the car and my brother with a soccer ball.

5. My grandfather was very important to me when I was a child. He was the only person who were helped me.

6. When my father was a young man, he was ask to set up a school in my city. This school has become one of the best schools in the area.

7. My sister admires by many of her friends because she has appeared on national TV several times.

8. After the storm, our house was surround by water. We weren't able to get into town for over a week, and even then we had to walk.

9. My parents were always willing to give me advice, but they are encouraged me to make my own decisions.

4.2 Using the Passive

Passive sentences are much less common than active sentences, but they are very useful when we want to focus on what happened and to what or whom. The first sentence in **1** below focuses on the agent or performer of the action (*My brother*) and uses an **active verb form**. The second sentence in **1** focuses on what happened (*was designed*) and to what/whom (the *house*) and uses **passive verb forms**.

1 My brother just **bought** an unusual house. It **was designed** and **built** in the 1950s.

A

2 Their car **was stolen.** (by someone unknown)

3 Dr. Henry, one of our most prominent scientists, **was honored** with an award last night.
(We aren't interested in who gave the award.)

4 What **is** this **called** in English? (by everyone)

5 Sam Edwards, 32, **was arrested** at his home last night.
(by the police)

We often use the passive because the agent:
- is unknown, as in **2**
- is unimportant in a particular context, as in **3**
- refers to people in general, as in **4**
- is obvious from the context, as in **5**

B

COMPARE

6a David didn't notify anyone about the meeting.
6b No one **was notified** about the meeting.

7a We have made many mistakes in this war.
7b Many mistakes **have been made** in this war.

We sometimes use the passive:
- to avoid blaming someone for something, as in **6b**
- to avoid taking responsibility for something, as in **7b**

C

8 Ega is an endangered language. It **is spoken** in Ivory Coast **by only 300 people.**

9 The engine **is started** by an electric device.

Because the focus of a passive sentence is on what happens and to what / whom, we rarely mention the agent. The few times that we do, it is because the agent is worth noticing. This might be because the agent is:
- new, unique, or unexpected, as in **8**
- nonhuman, as in **9** (We expect agents to be human.)

114

9 | Using the Passive Complete the sentences below with the passive form of the verbs in parentheses. Then explain why the writer wanted to focus the sentence on what happened or to whom. Write one or more reasons from the box. `4.2 A`

> **REASONS TO USE THE PASSIVE**
> a. because the agent is unknown
> b. because the agent is unimportant
> c. because the agent refers to people in general
> d. because the agent is obvious from the context

HOT CHOCOLATE   REASON(S)

1. The Aztec emperor Montezuma drank hot chocolate every day. The hot chocolate   _a, b_
   _____was made_____ with chili peppers and dyed red. (make)

2. Hot chocolate was valued very highly by the Aztecs; in fact, cocoa beans   _____
   _____ in place of money. (use)

3. In some Central American villages back then, no one under the age of 60   _____
   _____ to drink hot chocolate. (allow)

TEA

4. Over the years, tea _____ as part of different ceremonies. (serve)   _____

5. When tea _____ in the American colonies, many people served the   _____
   tea leaves with sugar and threw away the water. (introduce)

6. Tea was so expensive in seventeenth-century Europe that it _____   _____
   in locked boxes. (keep)

COFFEE

7. The beans of one entire coffee tree _____ for a single pound of   _____
   ground coffee. (require)

8. The amount of coffee you can safely drink _____ yet.   _____
   (not/determine)

9. Today, coffee _____ commercially in more than 50 countries. (grow)   _____

Think about It Which passive verb forms did you use in the sentences above? Write them under the correct group in this chart. Then explain why you chose each verb form.

Simple present passive	Simple past passive	Present perfect passive
	was made	

10 | Using the Passive Rewrite each sentence to avoid blaming someone or taking responsibility. **4.2 B**

1. I think Anna broke the window on purpose.
   I think the window was broken on purpose.

2. My best friend broke my arm during a soccer game.
   _____

3. I can't believe the parents left their children at home alone.
   _____

4. Emma hasn't returned the keys.
   _____

5. The car seat is all wet because James left the window open.
   _____

6. Rob left the door open and the dog got out.
   _____

7. I didn't lock the front door this morning.
   _____

8. Matt accidentally deleted all the files.
   _____

9. Kate didn't pay the bill on time.
   _____

10. We didn't clean up the room after the meeting.
    _____

Think about It For each sentence you wrote above, decide if the speaker uses a passive form to avoid blaming someone or to avoid taking responsibility for something.

11 | Identifying the Agent Match the beginning of each passive sentence on the left with the agent that best completes the sentence. Then listen to the news reports and check your guesses. **4.2 C**

1. Much of the city was destroyed __c__   a. by a park.
2. A swimmer was hurt ____   b. by a crowd of cheering fans.
3. In the 1800s, the city was surrounded ____   c. by a fire.
4. The movie has been ignored ____   d. by a shark.
5. The house is heated ____   e. by the critics.
6. The winning team was met ____   f. by a dog.
7. The music was written ____   g. by a ten-year-old girl.
8. A man in the park was attacked ____   h. by the sun.

Think about It Why do you think the speaker included the agent in each sentence above? Is the agent new, unique, or unexpected, or is the agent nonhuman?

Talk about It Think of three different ways to complete each sentence above.

1. *"Much of the city was destroyed by a flood. Much of the city was destroyed by the enemy. Much of the city was destroyed by an earthquake."*

4.3 Transitive and Intransitive Verbs

Many verbs need a direct object in order to be complete, as in **1 – 2**. We call these verbs **transitive verbs**. Most (but not all) transitive verbs can be used with a **passive form**, as in **3 – 4**. Some verbs make sense without an object, as in **5 – 6**. These verbs, called **intransitive verbs**, cannot be used with a passive form.

A

TRANSITIVE VERBS

ACTIVE FORM

subject	verb	direct object
1 Scientists	have discovered	a new planet.

subject	verb	direct object
2 Someone	took	my book.

PASSIVE FORM

subject	verb
3 A new planet	has been discovered.

subject	verb
4 My book	was taken.

For a list of common transitive verbs, see the Resources, page R-5.

INTRANSITIVE VERBS

ACTIVE FORM

subject	verb	adverbial
5 Everyone	arrived	early.

subject	verb
6 Something	happened.

NO PASSIVE FORM

For a list of common intransitive verbs, see the Resources, page R-6.

B

COMPARE

subject	verb	direct object
7a We	're going to smoke	the fish. (transitive use)

subject	verb
7b That pile of leaves	is smoking. (intransitive use)

8a I can't run. I'm too tired. (intransitive use)
8b The same family **has run** the company for 50 years. (transitive use)
8c The company **has been run** by the same family for 50 years. (passive form / transitive use)

We can use many verbs both transitively and intransitively, as in **7a – 7b**.

The transitive and intransitive uses of the same verb may have different meanings, as in **8**. Only when you are using the transitive meaning of the verb can you use a passive form, as in **8c**.

C

VERBS WITH TWO OBJECTS

subject	verb	indirect object	direct object
9 Someone	gave	the library	a lot of books.

subject	verb	direct object	indirect object
10 Someone	gave	a lot of books	to the library.

subject	verb	indirect object
11 A lot of books	were given	to the library.

subject	verb	direct object
12 The library	was given	a lot of books.

Some transitive verbs can have two objects: an indirect object and a direct object, as in **9**. With many of these verbs, the indirect object can come before or after the direct object, as in **9 – 10**. For example:

ask	give	offer	pay	read	serve	teach
bring	lend	owe	promise	send	show	tell

With the verbs above, either the direct object or the indirect object can become the subject of a passive sentence, as in **11 – 12**. However, it is more common for the direct object to become the subject.

GRAMMAR TERM: Verbs with two objects are also called **ditransitive verbs**. The indirect object is the person/thing to or for whom the action was performed.

D

CORRECT THE COMMON ERRORS (See page R-11.)

13 ✗ They thought she was died.
14 ✗ These things were happened on Friday evening.
15 ✗ The paintings appeared several people.
16 ✗ Three people injured in the accident.

12 | Transitive or Intransitive Verb? Circle the verbs in these paragraphs. Then write each verb under the correct group in the chart below. `4.3 A`

BIOGRAPHIES

1. Naomi Shihab Nye (grew up) in St. Louis, Missouri, and Jerusalem and now lives in San Antonio, Texas. A graduate of Trinity University, Nye has published nearly two dozen books including *Come with Me: Poems for a Journey*, *Fuel*, and *Habibi*. Daughter of a Palestinian father and an American mother, she has edited six prize-winning collections of poetry for young readers. She has worked as a visiting writer in schools for 37 years.

2. Julia Alvarez was born in New York City but spent part of her childhood in the Dominican Republic before returning to the United States, and her Spanish-speaking heritage[7] has influenced her literary work in English. She has published novels, poetry, and books for young readers. Alvarez received a BA degree from Middlebury College in Vermont and master's degrees from Syracuse University and the University of Illinois. She has held teaching positions at the University of Vermont and George Washington University. She currently has a position as writer-in-residence at Middlebury College.

Transitive verb (needs/has an object)	Intransitive verb (doesn't need/have an object)
	grew up

Write about It Choose another person, and write a similar paragraph with biographical information. Read your paragraph to the class, and ask your classmates to identify the transitive and intransitive verbs.

[7] **heritage:** important traditions, history, and culture of a country

13 | Usage Note: Understanding Linking Verbs Read the note. Then do Activity 14.

Linking verbs such as **be**, **become**, **remain**, and **seem** are neither transitive nor intransitive. Linking verbs are followed by a complement—a noun phrase, adjective, or adverb that refers back to the subject—not by a direct object. For this reason, we don't use linking verbs with a passive form.

subject	verb	complement
She	**was**	a great president.

She = a great president

subject	verb	complement
He	**became**	my best friend.

He = my best friend

subject	verb	complement
They	**remained**	behind.

They = behind

For a list of linking verbs, see the Resources, page R-2.

14 | Identifying Transitive Verbs Underline the verbs in these sentences. Then decide if each verb is a transitive verb, an intransitive verb, or a linking verb. Write *T*, *I*, or *L* above the verb. `4.3 A`

Albert Einstein

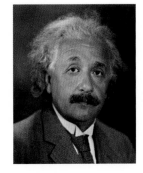

1. When Einstein <u>was</u> 5 years old, his father showed him a simple compass[8]. This sparked his interest in science.

2. A physics journal published his articles when he was just 26 years old.

3. He became a citizen of Switzerland in 1901 and a citizen of the U.S. in 1940.

4. Einstein often had a pipe[9] in his mouth. Wherever he went, a trail of smoke followed him.

5. Albert Einstein won the Nobel Prize in 1921.

6. Einstein spent the last 22 years of his life at Princeton University in the U.S.

7. He died in 1955.

Pablo Picasso

8. The artist Pablo Picasso grew up in Spain.

9. He completed his first painting at the age of 9.

10. His father sent him to the Royal Academy of San Fernando in Madrid to study art.

11. He was very smart but he wasn't a very good student.

12. Picasso's paintings were unconventional.

13. His unconventional painting style annoyed his father.

14. Picasso's paintings influenced the direction of modern art.

Write about It Where possible, rewrite the sentences above to make them passive.

---

[8] **compass:** a tool for finding direction, with a needle that always points north

[9] **pipe:** a tube with a small bowl at one end that is used for smoking tobacco

15 | Distinguishing Transitive and Intransitive Verbs Write each verb from this box under the correct group in the chart below. Then use each word in a sentence. `4.3 A`

allow	come	die	find	happen	involve	occur	say	stare
bring	describe	exist	go	include	mean	pull	smile	wait

Transitive verb	Sample sentence	Intransitive verb	Sample sentence
allow	*My parents allowed me to drive their car.*		

Think about It Where possible, rewrite the active sentences you wrote above as passive sentences.

16 | Transitive or Intransitive Meaning? Decide if the verb in each sentence has a transitive or an intransitive meaning. Write *a*, *b*, or *c*. `4.3 B`

1. The children opened the door.   *a*
2. The door opened in front of us.   ___

open	—*tr*	**a.** to cause (something) to no longer be covered
	—*intr*	**b.** to move and no longer cover something

3. She spoke at our annual meeting. ___
4. He speaks English and Spanish. ___
5. She always speaks clearly. ___

speak	—*tr*	**a.** to use or be able to use
	—*intr*	**b.** to give a speech
	—*intr*	**c.** to communicate by voice

6. The movie starts at 9:00. ___
7. I started that book a month ago. ___

start	—*tr*	**a.** to begin work on
	—*intr*	**b.** to begin

8. I usually walk to work. ___
9. I need someone to walk my dog tomorrow. ___

walk	—*tr*	**a.** to cause to travel on foot; to lead
	—*intr*	**b.** to travel on foot

10. We leave for Brazil next week.   ——

11. I think I left the door open.   ——

| leave | —tr | **a.** to cause or allow someone or something to stay in a particular place or condition |
| | —intr | **b.** to depart |

12. Did I hurt you?   ——

13. My neck hurts.   ——

| hurt | —tr | **a.** to cause pain |
| | —intr | **b.** to feel pain |

14. Bananas are selling for a dollar a pound.   ——

15. The neighbors finally sold their car.   ——

| sell | —tr | **a.** to exchange money for goods and services |
| | —intr | **b.** to have a specific price |

Think about It Where logical, rewrite the active sentences in Activity 16 as passive sentences.

17 | Using Verbs with Two Objects Rewrite each complaint in two ways. Use passive forms. `4.3 C`

COMPLAINTS ABOUT A COMPANY

1. The company doesn't pay the employees a fair salary.

   The employees aren't paid a fair salary. A fair salary isn't paid to the employees.

2. My company doesn't offer employees health insurance.

   _____

   _____

3. This company doesn't give people proper training.

   _____

   _____

4. The company hasn't always told the workers the truth.

   _____

   _____

5. The company has never paid overtime[10] to its employees.

   _____

   _____

6. The company didn't give employees a bonus last year.

   _____

   _____

7. The company gave a huge raise to the president.

   _____

   _____

8. The company promises a lot of things to the employees.

   _____

   _____

> **RESEARCH SAYS...**
>
> The choice of indirect object or direct object as the subject of a passive sentence often depends on which is mentioned in the previous sentence.
>
> The company doesn't treat its **employees** well. For example, **they** aren't paid a fair salary.
> (vs. A fair salary isn't paid to them.)
>
> CORPUS

---

[10] **overtime:** extra time you spend at work

18 | Error Correction Correct any errors in these sentences. (Some sentences may not have any errors.)

1. My father is the person who grew me.
2. In this photograph appears all of my relatives at home.
3. It was a very bad accident and two people were died.
4. A strange thing happened me yesterday.
5. How did you injure?
6. What was appeared on the screen when you turned on your computer?
7. When was the accident occurred? Does anyone know?
8. The money was meant to be payment for my work.
9. After the war started, my brothers were run away to the countryside.
10. All my photographs, school assignments, and telephone numbers saved on my computer.

4.4 The Passive with Modals

We often use the passive with modal and phrasal modal forms, as in **1b – 13b**.

MODAL + *BE* + PAST PARTICIPLE

WILL	Active	**1a** The organizers **will hold** the meeting tomorrow at 10:00.
	Passive	**1b** The meeting **will be held** tomorrow at 10:00.
SHOULD	Active	**2a** Somebody **should deliver** the package in two weeks.
	Passive	**2b** The package **should be delivered** in two weeks.
MUST	Active	**3a** Somebody **must tell** him soon.
	Passive	**3b** He **must be told** soon.
CAN	Active	**4a** We **can prevent** heart disease.
	Passive	**4b** Heart disease **can be prevented**.
MAY	Active	**5a** No one **may copy** any part of this publication.
	Passive	**5b** No part of this publication **may be copied**.
MIGHT	Active	**6a** They **might make** this offer again.
	Passive	**6b** This offer **might be made** again.
COULD	Active	**7a** The writer **could improve** this essay.
	Passive	**7b** This essay **could be improved**.
WOULD	Active	**8a** They said they **would hold** the election as promised.
	Passive	**8b** They said the election **would be held** as promised.

PHRASAL MODAL + *BE* + PAST PARTICIPLE

BE GOING TO	Active	**9a** They **are going to give** us another chance to play.
	Passive	**9b** We're **going to be given** another chance to play.
BE SUPPOSED TO	Active	**10a** We **are supposed to keep** this outside.
	Passive	**10b** This is **supposed to be kept** outside.
HAVE TO	Active	**11a** Somebody **has to do** something.
	Passive	**11b** Something **has to be done**.
BE ABLE TO	Active	**12a** Teachers **are** easily **able to use** this method in all schools.
	Passive	**12b** This method **is able to be used** easily in all schools.
BE ALLOWED TO	Active	**13a** No one **is allowed to take** photographs.
	Passive	**13b** No photographs **are allowed to be taken**.

A

19 | Active or Passive? Decide if the underlined verb is a passive or active form. Write *P* above the passive verb forms. Write *A* above the active forms. Then choose the correct sport. `4.4 A`

Describing Sports

1. This sport <u>can be played</u> [P] indoors or outdoors, but it <u>has to be played</u> on a hard surface. Each team <u>is made up</u> of five players.
   - a. baseball
   - b. basketball
   - c. soccer

2. Players of this sport <u>wear</u> a protective jacket, or *hogu*. This jacket <u>is able to be fitted</u> with sensors that <u>signal</u> hits to the body.
   - a. boxing
   - b. diving
   - c. tae kwon do

3. Jumps and turns <u>have to be performed</u> perfectly to win at this sport. You definitely <u>aren't supposed to fall down</u>—you <u>lose</u> points for that.
   - a. archery
   - b. cycling
   - c. figure skating

4. In this sport, athletes <u>are supposed to be judged</u> on their takeoff, flight, and entry. The score <u>is</u> then <u>multiplied</u> by a degree of difficulty factor.
   - a. diving
   - b. judo
   - c. weight-lifting

5. Women <u>were allowed to participate</u> in the Olympics for the first time in 1900, but they <u>could only play</u> these two sports.
   - a. golf and lawn tennis
   - b. canoeing and sailing
   - c. figure skating and badminton

6. In this sport, gloves <u>must be worn</u>, and a punch[11] <u>must be landed</u> with the white part of the glove.
   - a. boxing
   - b. fencing
   - c. judo

7. In this sport, a serve <u>must be made</u> from below the waist, with the racket head below the hand and with both feet on the ground.
   - a. badminton
   - b. table tennis
   - c. tennis

8. This sport <u>has been played</u> at every Olympic Games though the rules <u>have changed</u> over the years. Today, penalties[12] <u>can be awarded</u> for deflecting hits with the hand or refusing to salute one's opponent.
   - a. archery
   - b. fencing
   - c. volleyball

9. This sport <u>can be played</u> on a soft or hard surface. Players <u>are supposed to hit</u> the ball back and forth over a net without letting it touch the ground. Any part of the body above the waist <u>may be used</u> to hit the ball, but the ball <u>isn't allowed to be held</u>.
   - a. basketball
   - b. football
   - c. volleyball

10. In this sport, 85 percent of the bat or racket <u>is supposed to be made</u> of wood. The other 15 percent <u>can be made</u> of other materials.
    - a. football
    - b. table tennis
    - c. water polo

---

[11] **punch:** a hit with a closed hand

[12] **penalties:** punishments for one team and advantages for another team when a player breaks a rule

Talk about It Work with one or more classmates. In three minutes, think of as many sports as you can for each category. Then compare ideas with your classmates.

It's played with a ball but players aren't allowed to kick it.	It can be played indoors or outdoors.	Special shoes have to be worn.
tennis		

It is supposed to be played by teams of 11 people.	It isn't going to be played at the next Olympic Games.	It must be played on ice.

Write about It Write several sentences about a sport, but don't identify the sport. Try to use the passive with modal or phrasal modal forms. Then read your sentences to your classmates and let them identify the sport.

20 | Using the Passive with Modals Complete these descriptions with the passive form of the words in parentheses. `4.4 A`

Course Descriptions

1. **ENGL 242 English Grammar and Conversation I**

   This course _____*is intended*_____ to help foreign students in acquiring fluency in spoken English.
   (intend)

   All four language skills (listening, speaking, reading, and writing) _____.
   (will / practice)

2. **ENGL 243 English Grammar and Conversation II**

   This course is a continuation of ENGL 242. It _____ prior to ENGL 256.
   (should / take)

   Some students whose assessment scores qualify them for ENGL 256 _____
   (may / advise)

   to take this course as a companion course.

3. **ENGL 245 Advanced Conversation**

   Students discuss current events in English. Pronunciation, vocabulary development, and group

   discussion skills _____. This course _____ concurrently[13]
   (stress)   (may / take)

   with other English courses.

4. **ENGL 256 Grammar and Composition**

   This intermediate course in English grammar and composition _____ to help
   (design)

   students acquire a greater facility in written English. This course is for the student who is pursuing

   a college career. It _____ with ENGL 243 or 245.
   (can / take)

Think about It Passive forms are common in course descriptions. Why might this be?

---

[13] **concurrently:** at the same time

21 | Using the Passive with *Can, Can't, Could,* and *Couldn't* Write the passive form of each sentence using *can, can't, could,* or *couldn't* + the past participle of the verb in parentheses. 4.4 A

1. These questions were unanswerable. (answer)

   These questions couldn't be answered.

2. This place was indescribable. (describe)

3. Her absence is inexcusable. (excuse)

4. The problem was solvable. (solve)

5. The results were measurable. (measure)

6. War is preventable. (prevent)

7. Sometimes delays are unavoidable. (avoid)

8. The consequences were unpredictable. (predict)

9. His goal is achievable. (achieve)

10. These walls are movable. (move)

FYI

The most common modals used with the passive are *can* and *could* (for possibility).

Write about It Choose three verbs used in the passive sentences above, and write your own sentences.

4.5 Special Passive Structures

A

ACTIVE VERB + *THAT* CLAUSE

1 At one time, people **believed** that the earth was flat.

2 In the 1600s, Europeans **thought** that tomatoes were poisonous.

PASSIVE FORM + *TO-* INFINITIVE

3 At one time, the earth **was believed** to be flat.

4 In the 1600s, tomatoes **were thought** to be poisonous.

We use certain verbs (e.g., *believe, consider, say, think, understand*) to identify a common belief. In an **active** sentence, we often use a ***that* clause** after these verbs, as in **1 – 2**. In these sentences, the *that* clause functions as a kind of direct object.

In a **passive** sentence, we sometimes use a **to- infinitive** after these verbs, as in **3 – 4**.

For more information on *that* clauses, see Unit 12.

B

IT + PASSIVE FORM + *THAT* CLAUSE

5 It **has been reported** that this year will be warmer than usual.

6 It is commonly **believed** that children are better language learners than adults.

7 In Shefley (1999), **it is argued** that children are better language learners than adults.

We sometimes use **it + passive form + *that* clause**, as in **5 – 7**. Verbs used with this pattern include:

argue	estimate	report	suppose
believe	expect	say	think
consider	know	show	

In academic writing, this pattern is sometimes used to introduce an argument, as in **7**.

22 | Using the Passive to Identify Common Beliefs Match the sentence beginnings with the sentence endings. (More than one answer may be possible but only one is correct.) `4.5 A`

COMMON BELIEFS

1. Tobacco was once considered __*a*__
2. Carrots were once thought ____
3. The planet Venus was once believed ____
4. Television was once thought ____
5. Earth was once believed ____
6. Bathing was once considered ____
7. Thinking was once understood ____
8. Centuries ago, a child was said ____
9. Your personality was once thought ____

a. to be a cure[14] for a toothache.
b. to be related to your blood type.
c. to be the death of the movie industry.
d. to be covered with oil.
e. to be a small adult.
f. to be the center of the solar system.
g. to take place in the heart.
h. to be bad for your health.
i. to improve your vision.

Think about It Why does it make sense to use passive rather than active forms in the sentences above?

Write about It Identify three more things that were thought to be true in the past and write sentences about them. Read your sentences to the class.

23 | Using *It* + Passive Form + *That* Clause Rewrite each sentence using *it* + a passive verb form. Pay special attention to the form of the verb. `4.5 B`

MEDICAL BELIEFS

1. Experts say that more than 20,000 different plants are used for health purposes.

   It is said that more than 20,000 different plants are used for health purposes.

2. For a long time, people believed that the evil "influence" of the stars caused influenza, or the flu.

   _____

3. In sixteenth-century England, people thought the color red helped sick people get well.

   _____

4. Doctors have reported that some dogs are able to smell skin cancer.

   _____

5. Researchers believe that doctors prescribe antibiotics[15] too frequently.

   _____

6. Researchers estimate that one in two Americans will get cancer.

   _____

7. Many people think cancer is the most frightening disease.

   _____

8. Many people expect that researchers will find a cure for AIDS.

   _____

Think about It Why might a writer choose to use the passive rather than the active form in the sentences above?

---

[14]**cure:** something that makes an illness go away

[15]**antibiotics:** medicines that fight illness in a person's body

4.6 Passive Form or *Be* + Adjective?

A

PASSIVE FORM

1 The door **is locked** every evening at 9:00.
(= Someone locks the door every evening.)

2 The atoms **were excited** by the X-rays.
(= The X-rays excited the atoms.)

BE + ADJECTIVE

3 I was **exhausted** after the hike.

4 I can't sleep. I'm too **excited**.

5 The front door **is** always **locked** in the evening.
(= appears locked or is locked by someone)

A **passive verb form** is made with *be* + past participle, as in **1 – 2**. In these sentences, the past participles *locked* and *excited* describe actions.

A past participle can also function as an **adjective**, as in **3 – 4**. In these sentences, the past participles *exhausted* and *excited* follow *be* and describe a state—how something is. In these sentences, you can often use *very* before the past participle.

Sometimes it is difficult to tell whether a past participle is an adjective (describes a state) or a true passive form (describes an action), as in **5**.

B

PASSIVE WITH *BY* + AGENT

                              agent
6 She **was frightened by** the loud noise.

                              agent
7 Everyone **was confused by** the instructions.

BE + ADJECTIVE + PREPOSITION

8 He's **interested in** science.

9 The table **was covered with** a dark cloth.

10 The committee **is composed of** instructors from each faculty.

Remember: In a passive sentence, we sometimes use the preposition *by* to introduce the agent, as in **6 – 7**.

However, when a past participle functions as an adjective, we use other prepositions, as in **8 – 10**. Common *be* + participle + preposition combinations include:

be annoyed with	be dressed in	be known for
be bored with	be excited about	be made of
be composed of	be filled with	be opposed to
be concerned about	be finished with	be pleased with
be covered with	be interested in	be satisfied with
be dedicated to	be involved in	be worried about
be disappointed with/in		

GO ONLINE

24 | Passive Verb Form or *Be* + Adjective? Decide if the underlined words in these sentences are passive verb forms or *be* + adjective. Check (✓) your answers. **4.6 A**

Rudolph Nureyev

	PASSIVE	BE + ADJECTIVE
1. Rudolf Nureyev, the famous dancer, <u>was born</u> in a train in 1938.	✓	☐
2. From an early age, Nureyev <u>was interested</u> in music and ballet.	☐	☐
3. When he was 17, he <u>was accepted</u> at a famous ballet school in Leningrad.	☐	☐
4. His instructor, Alexander Pushkin, <u>was renowned</u> in the world of ballet.	☐	☐

		PASSIVE	BE + ADJECTIVE

5. Pushkin's students <u>were not scolded</u>[16] when they made mistakes. ☐ ☐

6. In 1958, at the age of 20, Nureyev <u>was asked</u> to join the Kirov Ballet. ☐ ☐

7. For the most part, his colleagues at the Kirov Ballet <u>were unimpressed</u> with his dancing. ☐ ☐

8. Nureyev's early style <u>was unrefined</u>. ☐ ☐

9. In early films of Nureyev, his shoulders <u>are hunched</u>[17] and his landings[18] are heavy. ☐ ☐

10. Nureyev <u>was dedicated</u> to ballet and he worked hard to become one of the best dancers in the world. ☐ ☐

RESEARCH SAYS...

Some verbs are almost always used in the passive form. Examples include:

be approved
be associated with
be based on
be born
be classified as
be composed of

CORPUS

Think about It Which of the underlined verb forms in Activity 24 were easy to classify as a passive form or *be* + adjective? Why? Which were difficult?

25 | Listening for Past Participles Read these conversations and guess the missing past participle. (Many different answers are possible.) Listen and check your guesses. Then practice with a partner. **4.6 A**

1. A: What's the matter? You look _____*bored*_____.

   B: I am. There's nothing to do.

2. A: What happened to this chair? It's all wet.

   B: Yeah, it was _____ outside in the rain last night.

3. A: Look. You've made your sister cry. You should be _____!

   B: Sorry, Mom.

4. A: I hear your brother didn't get that job.

   B: Yeah. They gave it to someone with more experience.

   A: He must have been very _____.

   B: Yeah, he was.

5. A: Why are you so _____ about money?

   B: Because I don't have any.

   A: That's a good answer.

6. A: Do you want to go with us to the lecture?

   B: Thanks, but no thanks. I'm really not _____.

7. A: It's getting late. Are you _____?

   B: I'm just putting on my shoes.

   A: OK. I'll wait for you downstairs.

---

[16] **scold:** to tell a person in an angry way that he or she has done something wrong

[17] **hunched:** bent over
[18] **landings:** acts of coming down onto the ground

8. A: How did your speech go?

   B: It was all right. At least the audience seemed _____.

9. A: Did you hear? Carlos and Sarah are getting married.

   B: I'm not _____. They've been talking about it for months.

10. A: Are you going to the conference next spring?

    B: I hadn't thought about it. Where is it being _____?

    A: In London.

11. A: I heard there was an accident last night.

    B: Yeah, a car went through a red light and hit another car.

    A: Was anyone _____?

    B: Luckily, no.

Think about It In which conversations in Activity 25 does a speaker use a passive form?

26 | Choosing the Correct Preposition Complete each sentence with the correct preposition. Then check (✓) *True* or *False* for you. `4.6 B`

ALL ABOUT ME	TRUE	FALSE
1. I am very interested ___*in*___ politics.	☐	☐
2. I am concerned _____ the state of the world.	☐	☐
3. I am engaged _____ a wonderful person.	☐	☐
4. I have never been involved _____ a car accident.	☐	☐
5. I am known _____ my generosity.	☐	☐
6. I am opposed _____ gun control.	☐	☐
7. I am pleased _____ my progress at school this year.	☐	☐
8. I am worried _____ the environment.	☐	☐
9. I am dressed _____ casual clothes today.	☐	☐
10. I am satisfied _____ the amount of money I have.	☐	☐
11. I have never been annoyed _____ anyone.	☐	☐
12. My parents were never disappointed _____ my schoolwork.	☐	☐
13. My bedroom is filled _____ books.	☐	☐
14. My shoes are made _____ leather.	☐	☐
15. I am bored _____ the news about climate change.	☐	☐
16. I am excited _____ my plans for this coming weekend.	☐	☐

Write about It Write three statements about yourself using *be* + participle + preposition. Make two of your statements true and one false. Read your statements to the class, and ask your classmates to identify the false statement.

Today, I'm dressed in my best clothes.
I'm interested in chess.
I'm satisfied with my life so far.

4.7 Using the Passive in Speaking

A

1 A: Who **got offered** the job?
B: I haven't heard.

2 A: What happened to Jeremy?
B: He **got caught** skipping class.

3 A: How did you **get hurt**?
B: I **got hit** by a golf ball.

4 A: Are you going to Yan's dinner?
B: No, I **didn't get invited**.

5 Did she **get fired**? (= Was she fired?)

6 They **didn't get paid** for their work.
(= They weren't paid for their work.)

In conversation, we sometimes use **get** + **past participle** instead of *be* + past participle for the passive, as in **1 – 2**. We usually use *get* + a past participle to express a change of situation or condition. For example:

get asked	get fired	get left
get blamed	get hit	get offered
get caught	get hurt	get paid
get done	get invited	get promoted
get elected	get killed	

The passive with *get* is often (but not always) used when there is a negative result, as in **3 – 4**.

Notice that we use the helping verb *do* in questions and negative statements with *get*, as in **5 – 6**.

27 | Listening for *Get* Passives Read these conversations and guess the missing past participle. (Many different answers are possible.) Listen and check your guesses. **4.7 A**

1. A: Did you hear about the accident?

   B: Yeah, it was on the news.

   A: Did anyone get _____*hurt*_____?

   B: I don't think so.

2. A: Why don't you stay home today?

   B: Are you kidding? I could get _____.

3. A: Why are you driving so slowly?

   B: Because I've already gotten _____

   by the police once today.

4. A: Why are you celebrating?

   B: Because Toshi just got _____.

   A: Really? That's great!

5. A: What's that smell?

   B: I think it's the trash. It didn't get _____ out yesterday.

6. A: What are you looking for?

   B: My dark-blue shirt.

   A: Look in the closet. It just got _____.

7. A: Do you know if the lights got _____ off?

   B: Yeah, I'm pretty sure they did.

8. A: How did you break the window?

   B: I didn't do it. Why do I get _____ for everything?

9. A: I wonder why we haven't received those books yet. It's been three weeks.

   B: Maybe they got _____ to the wrong address.

> **WARNING!**
>
> We use *get* in a number of expressions that don't have a passive meaning. In these contexts, *get* means *become*. The word used with *get* is an adjective.
>
> | get dressed | get lost |
> | get engaged | get married |
> | get involved | get tired |

10. A: Can I borrow some money?

    B: Again? I thought you just got _____.

    A: I did but I had some bills to pay.

11. A: Are you going to vote tomorrow?

    B: Yes, but I'm not sure why. No one I vote for gets _____.

12. A: Don't forget to wash the car today.

    B: I'm not sure I can do it today. Is tomorrow OK?

    A: As long as it gets _____ this week, I'm happy.

Talk about It Practice the conversations in Activity 27 with a partner.

28 | Using *Get* Passives Rewrite these questions with the *get* passive. `4.7 A`

1. Were you ever punished as a child?

   Did you ever get punished as a child?
   _____

2. Were you ever yelled at by an adult?

   _____

3. Were you ever caught cheating on a test?

   _____

4. Were you ever treated unfairly by someone?

   _____

5. Were you ever hit by someone?

   _____

6. Were you ever elected to something?

   _____

7. Were you ever sent home from school?

   _____

8. Were you ever blamed for something you didn't do?

   _____

> **WARNING!**
>
> We don't normally use *get* in the passive with non-action verbs (*hate, know, like, own, see, want,* etc.).
>
> You were seen at the beach. (NOT: ~~You got seen at the beach.~~)

Talk about It Ask a partner the questions you wrote above. If your partner answers yes, ask a follow-up question.

A: *Did you ever get punished as a child?*
B: *Sometimes.*
A: *When?*
B: *...*

4.8 Using the Passive in Academic Writing

A

MAKING WRITING COHESIVE

1 Dr. Bell is one of our most prominent scientists. His research focuses on the role of the environment in the development of cancer. Because of the importance of his work, Dr. Bell **was honored** with a research award last night.

2 The researchers selected 209 compositions for the study. All of the compositions **were written** in 50-minute class sessions.

In a cohesive paragraph, each sentence connects smoothly to the sentences before and after it. The passive is one of several techniques that writers can use to make a connection between sentences, as in **1 – 2**.

- In **1**, the writer connects the sentences by keeping the focus on the same topic: *Dr. Bell / His research / Dr. Bell*. To do this, the writer uses a passive form in the third sentence.

- In **2**, the writer connects the sentences by using the new information in the first sentence (*209 compositions*) as the subject of the next sentence (*All of the compositions*). To do this, the writer uses a passive form in the second sentence.

For more information on cohesion, see Units 5, 6, and 7.

B

USING THE PASSIVE IN ACADEMIC WRITING

3 For this study, 107 young adults **were divided** into three groups. For three weeks, they all they drank the same type of coffee. Then the participants **were randomly assigned** to different groups. Each of these groups **was given** a different type of coffee.

The passive is often used in academic writing, especially in the sciences where the focus is more on what happened than on who did something, as in **3**.

Using the passive gives the impression that the person doing the research is unimportant. It suggests that the results of the research will be the same for anyone.

C

USING PARALLEL STRUCTURE

4 For each composition, the errors **were counted**, **classified**, and later **analyzed**. (NOT: For each composition, the errors were counted, classified, and ~~later they analyzed them.~~)

In a sentence with a series of verbs, it's important to be consistent or parallel, as in **4**. Use all passive or all active verbs.

29 | Using the Passive to Connect Sentences Check (✓) the sentence in each pair that best follows the first sentence. `4.8 A`

1. Several people complained about the new schedule.
   - ☑ a. The first complaint was made by a member of the school committee.
   - ☐ b. A member of the school committee made the first complaint.

2. This year's graduation celebration cost $6,549.
   - ☐ a. The parents of the graduates raised this money.
   - ☐ b. This money was raised entirely by the parents of the graduates.

3. Frederick Tyler designed the new furniture for the town library.
   - ☐ a. One of his students made it.
   - ☐ b. It was made by one of his students.

4. Football has a long history in Europe.
   - ☐ a. In fourteenth-century England, authorities banned the sport for being too violent.
   - ☐ b. In fourteenth-century England, it was banned for being too violent.

5. A typical grocery store in 1928 stocked about 870 items.
   - ☐ a. Today's supermarkets carry up to 30,000 items.
   - ☐ b. Today, up to 30,000 items are carried.

6. For many years, bicycle racers wore leather helmets. Then, in the mid-1980s, they started wearing helmets made of strong, dense materials.

   ☐ a. Engineers designed them to protect the racers' heads if they fell.

   ☐ b. They were designed to protect the racers' heads if they fell.

7. Pollution causes poor air quality.

   ☐ a. It can be bad for your health.

   ☐ b. Your health can be affected by it.

8. Antibiotics are important tools in the fight against illness, but some bacteria change.

   ☐ a. Therefore, we need new medicines to kill them.

   ☐ b. Therefore, new medicines are needed to kill them.

9. There are two types of fats: saturated and unsaturated. Saturated fats, such as butter and coconut oil, are solid at room temperature. Unsaturated fats, such as olive oil and corn oil, are liquid at room temperature.

   ☐ a. Doctors consider unsaturated fats better for you.

   ☐ b. Unsaturated fats are considered better for you.

10. The first U.S. flag had 13 white stars.

    ☐ a. A new star has been added for every new state.

    ☐ b. The government has added a new star for every new state.

11. The president is the head of the executive branch of the government.

    ☐ a. He or she is elected by the entire country.

    ☐ b. The entire country elects the president.

12. There are nine justices, or judges, on the U.S. Supreme Court.

    ☐ a. The president nominates them and the Senate approves them.

    ☐ b. They are nominated by the president and approved by the Senate.

13. In this study, French researchers looked at more than 7,000 men and women.

    ☐ a. They recorded information on their education, income, and tobacco use, among other factors.

    ☐ b. Information on their education, income, and tobacco use, among other factors, was recorded.

14. Michelle Kwan became famous when she was quite young.

    ☐ a. She was asked to represent the U.S. as a skater when she was just 13 years old.

    ☐ b. The U.S. Olympic team asked her to represent the U.S. as a skater when she was just 13 years old.

15. In this study, researchers tested students both outdoors in natural settings and inside buildings.

    ☐ a. The students were found to have more energy after spending time in nature.

    ☐ b. Spending time in nature increased the students' energy level.

16. Although he worked as an engineer in the U.S. for 20 years, Gilberto Cetina never forgot the food of his native country.

    ☐ a. Eleven years ago, a restaurant was opened by Gilberto and his son.

    ☐ b. Eleven years ago, he and his son opened a restaurant.

Write about It What do you think the third sentence in each item above might be?

Several people complained about the new schedule. The first complaint was made by a member of the school committee. This person felt that the new schedule didn't give students enough time for lunch.

30 | Identifying Reasons for Using the Passive An obituary is a news report on someone's death. Underline the passive verb forms in this obituary. Then tell why the writer used the passive in each case. Choose one or more reasons from the list on the right. 4.8 A

Marmaduke Hussey, Former Chairman of the BBC, Dies Aged 83

By Mark Herlihy and Chris Peterson

Dec. 27 (Bloomberg)—Marmaduke Hussey, the former chairman of the BBC and managing director of Times Newspapers, has died at the age of 83.

Hussey, who lost a leg in in World War II, <u>was educated</u> at Trinity College, Oxford. He was trained as a journalist and worked as chief executive and managing director of Times Newspapers, owner of the Times of London, from 1971 to 1980.

"He will be remembered for his great vision, his integrity and his forthrightness, but also for his great personal kindness," BBC Director General Mark Thompson said in an e-mailed statement today. His contribution to public life was immense, Thompson said.

Hussey was appointed chairman of the BBC in 1986 thanks in part to his connections to the then ruling Conservative Party under the leadership of Margaret Thatcher. During his time as BBC chairman, he sacked Alasdair Milne as director general in 1987 after a series of rows with the government over the BBC's independence.

Hussey was made a life peer in 1996, following his retirement from the BBC. He was married to Lady Susan Waldegrave, a lady in waiting to Queen Elizabeth II and godmother to Prince William, who is next in line to the throne after Prince Charles.

REASONS
1. because the agent is unknown
2. because the agent is unimportant
3. because the agent refers to people in general
4. because the agent is obvious from the context
5. to keep the focus on the same topic
6. to use new information in the previous sentence as the subject of the following sentence

Think about It Compare your answers above with your classmates. Was it difficult to choose between reasons for any of the passive uses? Why?

31 | Analyzing Passive Forms in Academic Writing Read this text from a psychology textbook. Underline any passive forms. Then answer the questions on page 135. 4.8 A–B

A STUDY OF STEREOTYPES

It <u>has recently been shown</u> that stereotypes can have negative, long-lasting effects on the people who experience them. A new study has found that people who experience negative stereotypes and insults in one situation may continue to experience the effects of those insults in a later, unrelated situation. "Past studies have shown that people perform poorly in situations where they feel they are being stereotyped," said lead researcher Michael Inzlicht of the University of Toronto in Canada. "What we wanted to do was look at what happens afterwards." Inzlicht's study asked if there are any lasting effects of prejudice and if being stereotyped has an impact after the moment when the stereotyping occurs.

The researchers divided female participants into two groups. The women were asked to take a test that would determine their math abilities. One group of women was exposed to negative stereotypes about women and their math abilities. After the test began, the researchers made negative statements about women in order to make them feel more stress. In contrast, another group of women was given the same test, but they were offered strategies to deal with the stress of taking the exam. The researchers were very supportive with this group. After the math test ended, both groups of women were given ice cream samples and were asked to describe the flavors. Next, they were asked to play a video game that allowed them to shoot other players with a loud noise for as long as they wanted.

The women who were discriminated against performed more poorly on the math test. They also ate more ice cream than the women in the supported group, and they showed more hostility and aggression when they played the video game than the other group. These effects were particularly noticeable for the women who experienced negative stereotypes during the math test.

In the end, the study results show that stereotypes have negative effects, even for individuals who leave the environments where they experienced the stereotyping. These effects can be long-lasting. When people are affected by negative stereotyping, they are more likely to be aggressive and show a lack of self-control. After they've faced prejudice, they have trouble making good decisions, and they are more likely to make unhealthy food choices and overeat. Researchers hope the study will make people more aware of these effects of stereotyping. They hope this will help people to better manage their emotions and thoughts when they are faced with stereotypes so that they can show more self-control in later situations.

QUESTIONS

1. How many passive verb forms did you find in this text? Compare answers with your classmates.
2. How many of these passive forms appear with *by* + agent?
3. Did the writer use a passive form to help connect two sentences? Give an example.
4. Did the writer use any intransitive verbs? Which ones?

Write about It Write a one-paragraph summary of the article in Activity 31.

32 | Using a Series of Verbs Complete these sentences with the appropriate form of the verb in parentheses. **4.8 C**

1. The letter was written and _____*sent*_____ before the due date. (send)

2. Stone can be carved, chipped, and _____. (smooth)

3. Penicillin was created and _____ to fight infection. (use)

4. Ice reduces the swelling around an insect bite and _____ the itching. (ease)

5. Their children were raised and _____ in London. (educate)

6. The house was designed and _____ in the 1860s. (build)

7. Scientists have already established that good-looking people are paid better

    and _____ as smarter and more likeable. (view)

8. The book was written in 1968 and _____ in 1982. (revise)

A | ANALYZE Look for an interesting news story—a story that focuses on what happened and to whom. Bring the story to class and identify the passive verb forms.

National Zoo Names Panda Cub

WASHINGTON—The giant female panda cub at the Smithsonian National Zoo <u>has been given</u> a name—Bao Bao. The name <u>was selected</u> after it received more than 123,000 votes online from the public.

Panda mother Mei Xiang (may-SHONG) has been caring for her cub since Bao Bao <u>was born</u> on August 23. Bao Bao <u>will be shown</u> for short periods of time beginning early next year.

The public <u>was asked</u> to vote for one of five names for the new cub. The others were Ling Hua (ling-HWA), Long Yun (long-YOON), Mulan (moo-LAHN), and Zhen Bao (jen-BAO). The names <u>were submitted</u> by the Chinese ambassador.

B | WEB SEARCH Complete this question and then look online for the answer. Tell your classmates what you learned.

When and where was the first _____ used?

C | RESEARCH AND REPORT Choose three countries and look for the information to complete this chart. Present your findings to the class.

	Country *Cambodia*	Country _____	Country _____	Country _____
What language is spoken?	*Khmer*			
What percentage of the land is used for agriculture?	*30.9%*			
What is grown or produced there?	*rice, rubber, clothing*			
What natural resources are found there?	*oil, gas, timber, fish*			

D | COMPARE Study the "before" and "after" pictures below. How many changes can you find? Describe them.

The birdhouses were taken out of the room.

4.9 Summary of the Passive

USES

We sometimes use the passive:

- to focus a sentence on what happened and to what or whom
- because we can't or choose not to identify the performer of the action, or agent
- to avoid blaming someone for something
- to avoid taking responsibility for something
- to connect sentences in a paragraph

SIMPLE PRESENT PASSIVE:
BE (AM, IS, ARE) + PAST PARTICIPLE

I	am	paid	twice a month.
He / She / It	is		
We / You / They	are		

SIMPLE PAST PASSIVE:
BE (WAS, WERE) + PAST PARTICIPLE

I / He / She / It	was	paid	last week.
We / You / They	were		

PRESENT PROGRESSIVE PASSIVE:
BE (AM, IS, ARE) + *BEING* + PAST PARTICIPLE

I	am	being helped.
He / She / It	is	
We / You / They	are	

PAST PROGRESSIVE PASSIVE:
BE (WAS, WERE) + *BEING* + PAST PARTICIPLE

I / He / She / It	was	being helped.
We / You / They	were	

PRESENT PERFECT PASSIVE:
HAVE / HAS + *BEEN* + PAST PARTICIPLE

I / We / You / They	have	been helped.
He / She / It	has	

PAST PERFECT PASSIVE:
HAD + *BEEN* + PAST PARTICIPLE

I / He / She / It	had been helped.
We / You / They	

MODALS:
MODAL + *BE* + PAST PARTICIPLE

The package	will should can must may might could would	be delivered	soon.

PHRASAL MODALS:
PHRASAL MODAL + *BE* + PAST PARTICIPLE

The package	is going to is supposed to has to is able to is allowed to	be sent	by air.

Adverbs and Adverbials

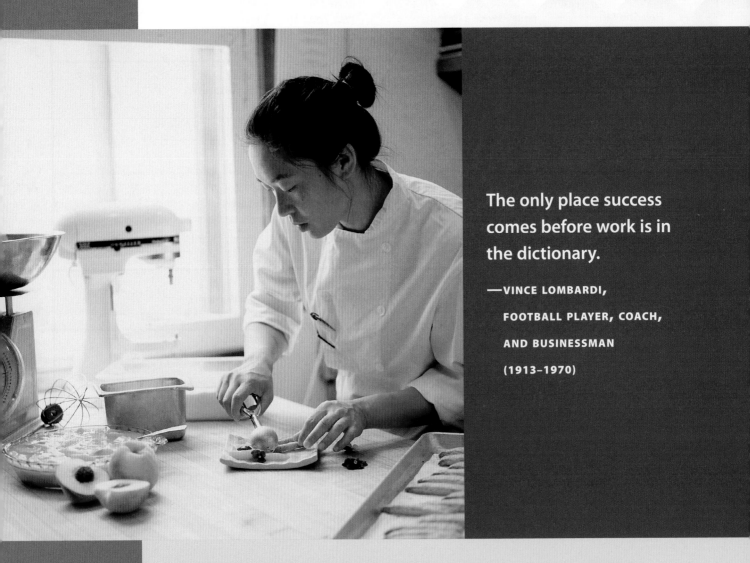

The only place success comes before work is in the dictionary.

—VINCE LOMBARDI,
FOOTBALL PLAYER, COACH,
AND BUSINESSMAN
(1913–1970)

Talk about It What does the quotation above mean? Do you agree or disagree?

WARM-UP

A | Match each description with a topic on the right. (You will not use all of the topics.)

What are they describing?

1. It's a medium-sized place **near my apartment**. **For very little money**, you can get a sandwich and a bowl of soup. ____

2. There was nothing I could do **to calm my fear**. I squeezed the armrest of my seat **until my knuckles were white**. I drank some bottled water **to settle my stomach**. I tried to read a book and listen to music. No luck. **Finally**, I started talking to an elderly woman **across from me**. ____

3. He had problems with his GPS, and then he had to stop **to change a flat tire**. He traveled **very slowly**—only 10 miles in five hours—and **along the way** his camera got destroyed. ____

4. It has **fairly** new tires and **only** 2,400 miles **on the odometer**[1]. ____

a. a motorcycle
b. a city
c. a classroom problem
d. a plane ride
e. a difficult trip
f. a restaurant

B | The words in green in the descriptions above are adverbials. Based on these examples, what can you say about adverbials? Check (✓) *True* or *False*.

	TRUE	FALSE
1. Adverbials are always single words.	☐	☐
2. A prepositional phrase can be an adverbial.	☐	☐
3. Some adverbials begin with a *to-* infinitive.	☐	☐
4. Adverbials add different kinds of information to a sentence.	☐	☐
5. Adverbials are common in writing.	☐	☐

C | Look back at the quotation on page 138. Identify any adverbials.

[1] **odometer:** an instrument that shows the distance that a car has traveled

5.1 Overview of Adverbs and Adverbials

A

We use some **adverbs** to add information to verbs, adjectives, and other adverbs, as in **1 – 3**.

verb	adverb
1 | Go | ahead. |

adverb	adjective
2 | You look | **really** | familiar. |

adverb	adverb
3 | She isn't here | right | now. |

We use other adverbs to show our feelings or attitude about the information in a clause or whole sentence, as in **4 – 5**.

adverb	sentence
4 | Unfortunately, | I couldn't call you. |

sentence	adverb
5 | I'm OK, | honestly. |

And we use other adverbs to connect clauses or sentences, as in **6**. (We call these linking adverbs.)

sentence	adverb	sentence
6 | Food is not allowed on the trains. | However, | mobile phones can be used. |

WARNING! Sometimes the same adverb can be used in different ways.

7 He told me a **really** funny story. (*really = very*; it strengthens the meaning of the adjective *funny*)

8 I **don't want to go**, **really**. (*really = honestly*; it shows our feelings or attitude about the whole sentence)

B

DIFFERENT KINDS OF ADVERBIALS

9 I'll come **later**.

10 The car is running **much better**.

11 She can't be here **on Tuesday**.

12 Can you come **this weekend**?

13 They're coming **to see you**.

14 **Since everyone is here**, let's get started.

Any word, phrase, or clause that can function like an adverb is called an **adverbial**. Forms of adverbials include:

- one-word adverbs, as in **9** (and **1 – 8** above)
- adverb phrases, as in **10**
- prepositional phrases that function as adverbs, as in **11**
- noun phrases that function as adverbs, as in **12**
- to- infinitive phrases that function as adverbs, as in **13**
- adverb clauses, as in **14**

For information on to- infinitives, see Unit 11.
For information on adverb clauses, see Unit 6.

C

15 I think he writes **well**. (adverbial)

16 She doesn't feel **well**. (adjectival)

17 He appeared **on TV**. (adverbial)

18 The man **on TV** was funny. (adjectival)

Sometimes a word or phrase can be **adverbial** in one context but **adjectival** (function like an adjective) in another, as in **15 – 18**.

For more information on the kinds of words and phrases we use to add information to nouns, see Unit 9.

 ONLINE

1 | Noticing How Adverbs Add Information Draw an arrow from the **bold** adverbs to the words they describe or connect. Some adverbs may describe a whole sentence or connect two sentences. 5.1 A

Hurricanes

1. Hurricanes are storms with **extremely** strong winds.

2. In the Indian Ocean, these storms **generally** are called cyclones.

3. A storm **officially** becomes a hurricane when winds reach above 75 miles an hour.

4. Hurricanes **usually** start in the North Atlantic and move **westward**.

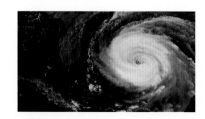

5. They move at about 10 miles an hour in the beginning and **gradually** gain speed.

6. A **fully** mature hurricane is **almost** circular.

7. In the center, or eye, the sky **often** looks blue.

8. **Remarkably**, the air is **very** calm in the eye of the hurricane.

9. The Atlantic hurricane season starts on June 1 and ends on November 30.
   However, most hurricanes form between August 15 and October 15.

Think about It What is the purpose of each **bold** adverb in Activity 1? Write each adverb under the correct group in this chart.

Describes a verb	Describes an adjective	Describes the writer's attitude about the information in the sentence	Connects two sentences
	extremely		

2 | Categorizing Adverbials Read the text below. Match each **bold** adverbial with a form from the box. Write the number of the form over the adverbial. 5.1 B

1. one-word adverb	3. prepositional phrase	5. *to-* infinitive phrase
2. adverb phrase	4. noun phrase	6. adverb clause

My Scariest Experience

The scariest experience I can remember was an airplane flight I took
3
many years ago. I was **at my university** and decided to spend the
holidays **with my father**. I was studying **in Los Angeles**, and he lived
in a small city near Phoenix, Arizona. My trip was divided into two
flights. **First**, I flew **from Los Angeles to Phoenix**. **Then** I had to change
planes **to fly to the smaller city**. The first flight was on a large jet and
was **very** smooth. **By the time I landed in Phoenix, however,** it was
snowing. I walked **to my connecting flight**, and imagine my surprise
to discover that the plane was small—it **probably** sat ten people.

We took off **in the middle of a snowstorm. From the first moment,** the plane shook **back and forth,
up and down**. There was nothing I could do **to calm my fear**. I squeezed the armrest of my seat **until my
knuckles were white**. I drank some bottled water **to settle my stomach**. I tried to read a book and listen

to music. No luck. **Finally**, I started talking to an elderly woman **across from me**. She didn't seem bothered by the turbulence **at all**. She revealed that, **many years ago**, she had **also** attended my university. **In fact**, she had been its first female graduate! I was so absorbed with her story that I calmed down. **Thankfully**, the flight was short! **When we landed**, I was relieved to be on the ground and I thanked my new friend.

Think about It Which of the **bold** adverbials in Activity 2 show the writer's feelings about the information in the sentence? Which connect two sentences?

3 | Adverbial or Adjectival? Decide if the **bold** words and phrases in these sentences are used in an adverbial or adjectival way. Check (✓) your answers. [5.1 C]

	ADVERBIAL	ADJECTIVAL
1. a. The temperature **in there** was unbearable.	☐	☐
b. Don't go **in there** until it cools off.	☐	☐
2. a. Don't you feel **well**?	☐	☐
b. I don't think I did **well** on the test.	☐	☐
3. a Lots of people use their cell phones **at the grocery store**.	☐	☐
b. People **at the grocery store** are always talking on their cell phones.	☐	☐
4. a. I hope this test isn't going to be **hard**.	☐	☐
b. I was breathing **hard** after running for so long.	☐	☐
5. a. On Sundays we usually eat **early**.	☐	☐
b. We usually have an **early** dinner on Sundays.	☐	☐
6. a. There isn't anything **on the table**.	☐	☐
b. The things **on the table** are yours.	☐	☐
7. a. Travelers **without a guide** can't visit this area.	☐	☐
b. You can't travel there **without a guide**.	☐	☐
8. a. There are many opportunities for work and education **in a large city**.	☐	☐
b. Apartments **in a large city** are usually quite expensive.	☐	☐
9. a. **On the radio**, you can hear many different kinds of programs.	☐	☐
b. I can't hear the music **on the radio**.	☐	☐

Write about It Write questions using each of these words or phrases in both an adverbial and an adjectival way. Then ask a partner your questions.

hard	on your desk	well

5.2 Using Adverbials to Explain *When*, *Where*, *How*, and *Why*

A

TIME ADVERBIALS

1 **Now** it's my turn. (when)

2 Reports in the natural sciences **often** begin with the results. (how often)

3 She arrived **this morning**. (when)

4 They're going to stay **for a while**. (how long)

We use some **adverbials** as time expressions. Time adverbials answer the question *when*, *how often*, or *how long*, as in **1 – 4**. The adverbial may be:

- an adverb or adverb phrase, as in **1 – 2**
- a noun phrase, as in **3**
- a prepositional phrase, as in **4**

B

PLACE ADVERBIALS

5 Everyone's **here**. (where)

6 Could I see you **in my office**? (where)

7 He's gone **to England**. (where)

8 They live **ten miles away**. (how far)

Some adverbials indicate location or distance. These place adverbials answer the question *where* or *how far*, as in **5 – 8**. The adverbial may be:

- an adverb or adverb phrase, as in **5**
- a prepositional phrase, as in **6 – 7**
- a noun phrase, as in **8**

C

MANNER ADVERBIALS

9 You need to do something **quickly**. (how)

10 Please handle this **with care**. (how)

11 She talks **like a businessperson**. (in what way / manner)

12 Did you come **by car**? (by what means)

Some adverbials answer the question *how*, *in what way / manner*, or *by what means*, as in **9 – 12**. We call them manner adverbials. The adverbial may be:

- an adverb or adverb phrase, as in **9**
- a prepositional phrase, as in **10 – 12**

D

REASON/PURPOSE ADVERBIALS

13 Classes were canceled **because of the weather**. (why)

14 **As a result of changing trends**, automobile sales have decreased. (why)

15 There were 50,000 deaths last year **due to car crashes**. (why)

16 **On account of the snow**, he hadn't even gone outside. (why)

17 We called **to invite them to dinner**. (for what purpose / reason)

18 I'm waiting **to finally have some free time**. (why)

We can also use adverbials to answer the question *why* or *for what purpose / reason*, as in **13 – 18**.

- In **13 – 16**, the adverbials are multi-word prepositional phrases.
- In **17 – 18**, the adverbials are to- infinitive phrases.

For information on *to-* infinitives, see Unit 11.

GO ONLINE

4 | Explaining *When*, *How Often*, *Where*, and *How Far* Decide if each underlined adverbial answers the question *when*, *how often*, *where*, or *how far*. Write your answers in the boxes. `5.2 A–B`

From: Professor Collins

To: All students

Subject: Biology field trip

Hi class,

This is a reminder about the biology field trip <u>next week</u>. We'll be collecting
₁

samples <u>on Thursday</u>, so be sure to write the date <u>on your calendar</u>. We only
₂ ₃

do this <u>once a semester</u>, so you don't want to miss this trip. We'll be meeting
₄

1. *when*

2.

3.

4.

at the <u>entrance</u> to <u>Poplar Pond</u> <u>at 7:30</u>. (See picture below.) Be sure to arrive
⁵   ⁶

<u>early</u>. <u>Every year</u> a few students show up <u>late</u> and hold up everyone else.
 ⁷   ⁸   ⁹

Don't forget to wear comfortable shoes as we will be walking <u>several miles</u>.
                                           ¹⁰

If you have any questions or problems, send me an email <u>before Friday</u>.
                                            ¹¹

I'll be checking my email <u>frequently</u> and will answer you <u>as soon as possible</u>.
                         ¹²   ¹³

You can also come to see me <u>during my office hours</u>.
                               ¹⁴

EBC

5.
6.
7.
8.
9.
10.
11.
12.
13.
14.

Think about It Is each underlined adverbial in Activity 4 an adverb, an adverb phrase, a noun phrase, or a prepositional phrase?

Write about It Write a formal email message like the one in Activity 4 in which you remind a class of students about an upcoming event. Remember to explain when and where the event takes place.

5 | Explaining *When*, *How Often*, and *How Long* Match the questions with the answers. 5.2 A

WHAT DO YOU KNOW?

Questions

1. How many times a day does the human eye blink[2]? <u> b </u>
2. How long do the Olympic Games last? ____
3. How often does a presidential election take place in the United States? ____
4. How long does it take to drive across the U.S.? ____
5. How long does it take to become a medical doctor? ____
6. When did the first modern Olympic Games take place? ____
7. How often do strong earthquakes happen worldwide? ____
8. How often do small earthquakes occur? ____
9. How long does it take the earth to go around the sun? ____
10. How often does the earth stop moving? ____

Answers (time adverbials)

a. Four to five days.
b. On average, 17,000 times.
c. In 1896.
d. 365 days.
e. At least 11 years.
f. Never.
g. Every 4 years.
h. Generally for 12 to 17 days.
i. About once a month.
j. Several hundred times a day.

[2] **blink:** to close and open your eyes very quickly

Think about It Identify the form of each adverbial in the answers in Activity 5. Write *A* (adverb), *NP* (noun phrase), or *PP* (prepositional phrase) next to it.

Write about It Try to use a different adverbial to answer each question in Activity 5. Are there any questions that are difficult to answer differently?

> 1. *How many times a day does the human eye blink?*
>   *About 17,000 times a day.*

Write about It Write five questions that begin with *when*, *how often*, or *how long*. Ask a partner your questions.

> A: *How often do you eat out?*   A: *How long does it take to get from your home to school?*
> B: *Once a week.*   B: *About 20 minutes.*

6 | Explaining *How* Complete each sentence with an adverbial from the box. Then compare answers with your classmates. Which facts were the most surprising? 5.2 C

FACT FILE

1. The only planet that rolls on its side _____*like a ball*_____ is Uranus.

2. It can take the body over 50 hours to digest[3] food _____.

3. A rabbit can see on both sides of itself _____ _____.

4. The left side of your body is controlled _____ _____.

5. Eating _____ can improve your ability to remember things.

6. The average cough comes out of the mouth _____.

7. It's almost impossible to sneeze _____.

8. When you don't get enough sleep, your brain can't function _____.

9. A moderately severe[4] sunburn damages the blood vessels[5] _____.

10. A candle flame typically burns _____.

11. In nearly every language, the word for *mother* begins _____.

12. Women can identify smells _____ than men.

ADVERBIALS

> at 60 miles (96.5 km) per hour
> by the right side of your brain
> completely
> like a ball
> well
> without moving its head

> at about 1000° C
> at full capacity
> extensively
> more easily
> with an *m* sound
> with your eyes open

Write about It Try to think of a different adverbial to complete each sentence above.

> 1. *The only planet that rolls on its side like a wheel is Uranus.*

---

[3] **digest:** to change food in your stomach so your body can use it
[4] **severe:** very bad or strong

[5] **blood vessels:** tubes in the body that blood moves through

7 | Explaining *When*, *Where*, and *How* Decide if each **bold** adverbial answers the question *when*, *where*, or *how*. Write your answers in the boxes. `5.2 A–C`

Letter of Complaint

August 25, 2014

Sound Systems Electronics
Consumer Complaint Division
500 Derby Drive
Cullman, AL 35056

Dear Sir or Madam:

I would like to call your attention to a problem I am having. **Last month**,
1
I ordered a radio from your company. I paid for the radio **by credit card**
2
when I ordered it. It was my understanding that I would receive the
radio **within five days**. It is now **four weeks later** and I still don't have it.
3 **4**
However, my records show that you charged my credit card account
on August 1. Enclosed is a copy of my credit card statement as proof.
5
   If the radio has not been sent, please deliver it **by September 10**. If
6
there is a problem, please contact me **by email** at **dsmith@arkmail.net**.
7 **8**
Thank you for your attention to this matter.

Sincerely,

David Smith

1.	*when*
2.	
3.	
4.	
5.	
6.	
7.	
8.	

Write about It Write your own letter of complaint using the example above as a model.

8 | Explaining *Why* Choose an adverbial from the box to complete each sentence below. `5.2 D`

as a result of global warming	due to the demands of the workplace	because of quickly changing job markets
as a result of the growth of cities	due to the lack of snow	because of the distractions they cause
as a result of the weak economy	because of a possible problem with the brakes	on account of age
due in part to the animal's diet	because of advances in medicine	on account of darkness

1. The earth's polar regions[6] have begun to change drastically
   as a result of global warming   .

2. Many schools have banned cell phones from classrooms

   _____ .

3. The government began an investigation of the car after two people died

   in accidents _____ .

[6] **polar regions:** areas around the top and bottom of the earth

4. Human life expectancy[7] has increased steadily, mainly

   _____ .

5. Taking a nap after the midday meal used to be a common practice in
   many countries. Unfortunately, this practice is now less common

   _____ .

6. Giraffes vary in color from light brown to almost black.
   The difference is _____ .

7. _____ ,

   housing has become more expensive.

8. In the future, many ski resorts may be unable to operate

   _____ .

9. In the U.S., it's against the law to discriminate[8] against someone

   _____ .

10. The tennis match was stopped at 7 p.m. _____

    _____ .

11. _____ ,

    businesses are hiring fewer people.

12. _____ ,

    education is an ongoing, lifelong process.

Think about It What other adverbials can you find in the sentences in Activity 8? Circle them.

Write about It Write three sentences using *as a result of*, *due to*, *because of*, or *on account of*. Then read your sentences to your classmates.

9 | Identifying *To-* Infinitives of Purpose Match the first part of each sentence with a *to-* infinitive on the right. (More than one answer may be possible.) `5.2 D`

HELPFUL HINTS FOR GIVING A SPEECH

1. Practice your speech several times _d_
2. Just before your speech, do some breathing
   exercises ____
3. Use pictures and diagrams ____
4. Keep your eyes on your audience ____
5. Use facial expressions and gestures[9] ____
6. Use your voice like a musical instrument ____
7. Increase and decrease the volume of your voice ____
8. Ask questions ____
9. Start your speech with something interesting ____
10. Include some personal stories ____

a. to communicate difficult information.
b. to help communicate your message.
c. to keep the sounds interesting.
d. to hear how it will sound to the audience.
e. to watch for signs of confusion or boredom.
f. to help yourself relax.
g. to emphasize your main points.
h. to get the audience's attention.
i. to add fun to your speech.
j. to involve your audience.

[7] **life expectancy:** how long one is believed to be able to live
[8] **discriminate:** to treat one person or group in a worse way than others

[9] **gestures:** movements of your head or hands to show how you feel or what you want

Think about It Think of different *to-* infinitives to complete the sentences in Activity 9.

Practice your speech several times to find out how much time it will take.

Write about It Choose a different topic and write a list of helpful hints. Try to use *to-* infinitives in your list.

10 | Usage Note: *Because of* vs. *Because* Read the note. Then do Activity 11.

COMPARE

We use the multi-word prepositions *as a result of*, *because of*, *due to*, and *on account of* + a **noun phrase**.

			noun phrase
1a	We didn't go	because of	the heat.

			noun phrase
2a	She plays well	due to	years of practice.

However, we use *because* when we introduce an **adverb clause**.

		adverb clause	
1b	We didn't go	because it was very hot.	(NOT: ~~because of it was hot~~)

		adverb clause	
2b	She plays well	because she has practiced for years.	(NOT: ~~due to she has practiced for years~~)

11 | Using Adverbials to Explain *Why* Rewrite each sentence using *as a result of*, *because of*, *due to*, or *on account of*. (Many different answers are possible.) `5.2 D`

1. Classes were canceled because the weather was terrible.

   Classes were canceled because of the terrible weather.

2. Fewer people can travel nowadays because the price of gasoline is very high.

3. A cell phone can last for many hours because it has a rechargeable battery.

4. A lot of people take naps here in the summer because it gets so hot.

5. I wasn't successful in learning Chinese because I lacked self-discipline.

6. Because farms have become more efficient, people here have plenty of food.

7. California is the top producer of food in the U.S. because it has such a great climate.

8. Some scientists say we are having more storms because the weather has gotten warmer.

9. I would like to visit Poland someday because my ancestors lived there.

10. Because they share a lot of experiences, brothers and sisters get to know each other well.

11. Because these scissors are very small, you can carry them in your pocket.

5.3 Degree and Focusing Adverbials

A

DEGREE ADVERBIALS

1 You're **absolutely right**.

2 The bridge is **extremely unsafe**.

3 We are all working **pretty hard**.

4 You look **really familiar**.

5 It's **rather late** to go out, don't you think?

We use **degree adverbials** to explain *to what degree*, as in **1 – 9**. Notice that we usually use degree adverbials before an adjective or adverb.

Some degree adverbials make a statement stronger, as in **1 – 5**.

absolutely	extremely	perfectly	really	terribly
completely	highly	pretty	reasonably	totally
considerably	incredibly	quite	significantly	truly
entirely	much	rather	so	very

6 You **almost hit** that car.

7 I think it's **about 50 years old**.

A few degree adverbials show an approximation, as in **6 – 7**.

about	almost	approximately	nearly

8 I'm **fairly certain** about this.

9 Be careful. The floor is **slightly wet**.

Some other degree adverbials can make a statement weaker, as in **8 – 9**.

a (little) bit	less	somewhat
fairly	slightly	to an extent

B

FOCUSING ADVERBIALS

10 A: Can I help you?
   B: No, I'm **just** looking.

11 Smoking increases the risk of many diseases, **especially** heart disease and cancer.

12 Football is known as soccer **only** in North America.

Sometimes we want to focus attention on one word or phrase in a sentence, as in **10 – 12**. When we use adverbials to do this, we call them **focusing adverbials**. Adverbials used in this way include:

especially	even	just	only	particularly

COMPARE

13a Some people can communicate complicated ideas in **only** a few words.

13b Some people can **only** communicate complicated ideas in a few words.

13c **Only** some people can communicate complicated ideas in a few words.

Focusing adverbials usually come immediately before the words they describe. Changing the position of these adverbials can change the meaning of the sentence, as in **13a – 13c**.

GO ONLINE

---

12 | Choosing Degree Adverbials Complete each sentence with the correct adverbial in parentheses. (You may want to look up information online.) Then compare answers with your classmates and together agree on the correct answer. **5.3 A**

GEOGRAPHY

1. From the moon, the earth looks _____*very*_____ smooth, like a ball. (very / a bit)

2. China covers an area _____ larger than that of the U.S. (significantly / slightly)

3. The Nile River is _____ longer than the Amazon River. (considerably / a little bit)

4. Mount Everest is _____ higher than Mount Fuji. (considerably / somewhat)

5. Brazil is _____ bigger than Venezuela. (much/a little bit)

6. Annual rainfall varies _____ around the world. (greatly/slightly)

7. An island is _____ surrounded by water. (a little bit/completely)

8. It's _____ cold in Antarctica. In some places the average temperature is -58 degrees Celsius. (extremely/fairly)

9. The population of Mexico City is _____ larger than the population of Paris. (significantly/somewhat)

10. Although the sun doesn't rise on parts of Greenland for three whole months, it is never _____ dark there. (slightly/totally)

Think about It Which adverbials in Activity 12 describe an adjective or adverb? Which describe a verb? Do the adverbials come before or after the words they describe?

13 | Usage Note: Collocations with Degree Adverbials Read the note. Then do Activity 14.

Degree adverbials collocate strongly with specific adjectives, adverbs, and verbs. Notice some of the adverbs that are used with these five adjectives.

adverb + adjective		adverb + adjective		adverb + adjective		adverb + adjective		adverb + adjective	
fairly highly so completely extremely reasonably generally quite pretty totally really relatively entirely truly somewhat very	reliable	fairly extremely totally almost quite really relatively completely perfectly pretty so very	clean	absolutely incredibly quite really so very	beautiful	bitterly extremely pretty quite particularly rather really so terribly very	cold	pretty rather extremely fairly quite very	lively

14 | Using Degree Adverbials Underline the degree adverbials in these sentences. Then rewrite each sentence using a different adverbial. (Don't change the meaning of the sentence.) `5.3 A`

Describing Cities

1. The public transportation system here is <u>fairly</u> reliable.

   The public transportation system here is somewhat reliable.

2. The subway stations are extremely clean.

3. The streets are pretty clean.

CORPU

4. It gets quite cold here in the winter.
5. The buses here are never on time, but the subways are extremely reliable.
6. I stayed in a very lively part of town.
7. It's quite beautiful here in the summertime.
8. The mountains in the distance are incredibly beautiful.
9. Although the city is rather quiet during the week, the streets get pretty crowded on the weekend.
10. Because of the bitterly cold weather in winter, people spend a lot of time indoors.

Write about It Write three sentences describing a city you know. Use a degree adverbial in each sentence.

15 | Noticing Focusing Adverbials Which of the **bold** adverbials in these conversations are focusing adverbials? Circle them. `5.3 B`

1. A: Do you **ever** get homesick?

   B: Sure—(especially) on holidays.

2. A: Where's Amanda?

   B: She's **already** gone.

   A: You're kidding! She didn't **even** say goodbye.

   B: I think she was in a hurry.

3. A: Did you tell James about the meeting?

   B: Yeah, but he didn't seem **particularly** interested.

4. A: Do you want something for breakfast?

   B: No, thanks. I **only** eat breakfast **on weekends**.

5. A: Want to go **to a movie tonight**?

   B: Can't we **just** stay **home**?

   A: Sure. That's fine with me.

6. A: Have you heard anything about our new boss?

   B: Not a word. I don't **even** know her name.

7. A: Wow! That was a big bird.

   B: **Really**? I didn't **even** see it.

8. A: Don't you need a rest?

   B: No, why?

   A: **Because you're always doing something**.

   I get tired **just** watching you.

9. A: What did you think of the movie?

    B: It was **pretty** good. I **particularly** liked the ending.

10. A: Want to try some of my macaroni and cheese?

    B: Thanks, but no thanks. I'm not **especially** fond of cheese.

Talk about It Practice the conversations in Activity 15 with a partner.

16 | Usage Note: Adverbials with Multiple Meanings Read the note. Then do Activity 17.

Many adverbials have more than one meaning; the adverbial can function in different ways in a sentence based on the meaning of the word. Notice in this dictionary entry how the word *just* can function as:

- a degree adverbial (definition 1)
- a time adverbial (definition 2)
- a focusing adverbial (definitions 3 and 4)

Sometimes the meanings overlap, and it can be difficult to know how the adverbial is functioning.

just /dʒʌst/ *adverb*

1. exactly: *This jacket is just my size.* • *You're just in time.* • *He looks just like his father.*
2. a very short time before: *I just heard the news.* • *Jim isn't here. He just went out.*
3. only: *It's just a small gift.*
4. a word that makes what you say stronger (positive or negative): *Just look at that funny little dog!*

17 | Choosing the Correct Meaning Read the sentences below and choose the correct meaning of *just* from the box. `5.3 B`

1. exactly	3. only
2. a very short time before	4. a word that makes what you say stronger

1. Excuse me for interrupting. I **just** wanted to ask a quick question. __3__

2. This room is **just** a mess. ____

3. No one came to the meeting. It was **just** me and 20 empty chairs. ____

4. It was really cold there **just** as you said it would be. ____

5. John is fine. I **just** talked to him. ____

6. I brought something **just** for you. ____

7. After she was kicked out of school, she **just** disappeared. ____

8. I'm **just** not interested in poetry. ____

9. He cut his leg **just** above the ankle. ____

10. Chicago is **just** north of here. ____

11. We did it **just** for fun. ____

12. I'm not really hungry—I **just** had lunch. ____

Write about It Write four more sentences using each meaning of *just* in the box above.

5.4 Stance Adverbials

We use **stance adverbials** to express our attitude about the information in a clause or sentence.

A

GIVING AN OPINION OR EVALUATION

1 Unfortunately, I couldn't contact her.
(= It was unfortunate that I couldn't contact her.)

2 The president believes, **quite rightly,** that we have a serious problem. (= I think the president is right to believe that we have a serious problem.)

We use some stance adverbials to give an opinion or evaluation of what we are saying, as in **1 – 2**. For example:

(un)fortunately	luckily	thankfully
hopefully	surprisingly	

We often use commas before and after stance adverbials.

B

SHOWING CERTAINTY OR DOUBT

3 They wanted me to be there, but **of course** I had to work.

4 It was **definitely** too late to do anything.

5 Without a doubt, Yosemite is one of the most beautiful places in the world.

COMPARE

6a I thought he was here, but **maybe** he went out.
6b I thought he was here, but he **may have gone out**.

We use some stance adverbials to show certainty or doubt about what we are saying, as in **3 – 5**. For example:

	to show certainty		to show doubt
certainly	no doubt	undoubtedly	maybe
clearly	obviously	very likely	perhaps
definitely	of course	without a doubt	possibly
			probably

Notice that stance adverbials are similar to modal verbs in the ways we use them to show certainty or doubt, as in **6a – 6b**.

C

OTHER STANCE ADVERBIALS

7 I **honestly** didn't see anything.

8 Seriously, I want you to leave now.

9 Eating too much **actually** reduces your ability to hear.

10 A: Is there an easy way to get downtown?
B: Yes, there is. **In fact**, there's a very easy way.

COMPARE

11a Don't take life too **seriously.** (adverb of manner)
11b Seriously, I want you to be home by 10:00.
   (stance adverbial)

12a I think something is **really** wrong. (degree adverb)
12b I **really** need to talk to you. (stance adverbial)

Other adverbials that speakers and writers use to comment on the information in a whole clause or sentence include:

actually	really	technically speaking
honestly	seriously	to tell you the truth
in fact		

Remember: An adverbial can function in more than one way, as in **11a – 12b**.

GO ONLINE

18 | Using Stance Adverbials to Give an Opinion or Evaluation Choose a stance adverbial from the box to complete each quotation below. (More than one answer may be possible, but only one is correct.) **5.4 A**

QUOTATIONS FROM FAMOUS PEOPLE

fortunately	luckily	sadly	thankfully	to my surprise	unfortunately

1. _Luckily_____, in my case, I have managed, by writing, to do the one thing that I always wanted to do. (*Jonathan Coe, novelist*)

2. _____, it's much easier to create a desert than a forest. (*James Lovelock, environmentalist*)

| fortunately | luckily | sadly | thankfully | to my surprise | unfortunately |

3. _____, it doesn't seem to have made a lot of difference to my audience that I'm as bald as a billiard ball! (*James Taylor, musician*)

4. _____, my 70s are nicer than my 60s and my 60s than my 50s, and I wouldn't wish my teens and 20s on my enemies. (*Lionel Blue, clergyman*)

5. Dad taught me everything I know. _____, he didn't teach me everything he knows. (*Al Unser, athlete*)

6. _____, I have my mom and a small group of close friends who are there for me 24/7[10] and whom I can trust and depend on. (*Christina Aguilera, musician*)

James Taylor

| happily | hopefully | luckily | oddly | sadly | unfortunately |

7. I would've loved to have been in a band, but _____ I just wasn't good enough. (*Tony Blair, British prime minister*)

8. I've broken my nose, I've broken ribs. You name it. In fact, we just got back from South America, and I fell over a monitor speaker[11] on the stage and almost ended up in the front row of the audience. I managed to sprain[12] my wrist on that one but _____ nothing was broken. (*Keith Emerson, musician*)

Tony Blair

9. Winning is a habit. _____, so is losing. (*Vince Lombardi, football coach*)

10. I think maybe ten years from now, I'm _____ going to be, in like, Tahiti or something. Kicking back[13] like in my huge mansion, if everything goes right, it's all up to me. (*Corey Haim, actor*)

11. I love having a big family. I think it's easier, _____, in some ways, having three children as opposed to one. (*Patrick Dempsey, actor*)

12. A sense of freedom is something that, _____, comes with age and life experience. (*Diane Keaton, actor*)

Think about It Compare answers with your classmates. In which sentences in Activity 18 could you use more than one adverbial?

19 | Using Stance Adverbials to Show Certainty or Doubt Underline the stance adverbials in these conversations and sentences. Then practice conversations 1–6 with a partner. 5.4 B

IN CONVERSATION

1. A: How was your plane trip?
   B: Scary. Next time I'll <u>definitely</u> go by train.

2. A: Have you eaten at the new restaurant?
   B: Yeah, and I'd definitely go again.

---

[10] **24/7:** 24 hours per day, seven days per week
[11] **monitor speaker:** the part of the audio system where sound comes out; it is used onstage during a performance
[12] **sprain:** to hurt part of your body by turning it suddenly
[13] **kick back:** to relax

3. A: Are you going to the meeting tomorrow?

   B: Probably. What about you?

   A: I don't know yet.

4. A: Do you still want to look at my photos?

   B: Oh, yeah. Sure. Of course.

5. A: I'm going to Matt's house tonight. Maybe you'll come?

   B: No, not tonight.

6. A: How well do you know Rob?

   B: Pretty well.

   A: What's he like?

   B: Well, he's usually good-natured and funny. Of course, he can be a little moody at times.

IN WRITING

7. Clearly, it's both advantageous and enjoyable to have a brother or sister, especially if you are close in age.

8. Some people prefer vigorous exercise, such as running. Others prefer less strenuous[14] activities, such as walking. Of course, more strenuous activities burn more calories.

9. I am especially concerned about the spread of consumer culture[15] in the twenty-first century. There are certainly many other important problems in the world today, but consumerism is one of the least noticed.

10. Students should be encouraged to learn a second and possibly even a third foreign language.

11. Slang and other informal spoken language obviously has no place in school reports.

12. Without a doubt, recreation is essential to a healthy life.

13. The smartphone has changed the way people communicate, and it will surely see many innovations in the future.

Think about It Based on sentences 7–13 in Activity 19, when do writers use a comma after a stance adverbial?

Write about It Rewrite sentences 7–13 in Activity 19 using a different stance adverbial.

20 | Identifying Other Stance Adverbials Underline the stance adverbials in these conversations and sentences. Then practice conversations 1–6 with a partner. `5.4 C`

IN CONVERSATION

1. A: I can't believe you wrote this.

   B: But I did, <u>really</u>.

2. A: Will you still be here in an hour?

   B: Actually, I won't. I'm leaving in a few minutes and I won't be back until this evening.

3. A: Is that your money over there?

   B: I don't honestly know. It might be.

4. A: Did you like my speech?

   B: Yeah, it was great. Seriously, I'm kind of jealous. I wish I could speak in public like that.

5. A: Hey, Sam. Do you have a few minutes? I have some questions.

   B: Yeah, I need to talk to you, too. In fact, I've been trying to get in touch with you all week.

6. A: That was a good movie, don't you think?

   B: To tell you the truth, I thought it was really strange.

---

[14] **strenuous:** requiring physical effort and strength

[15] **consumer culture:** the belief that it is good for people to spend a lot of money on goods and services

7. Technically speaking, your brain has the capacity to store everything you experience.

8. Your brain processes pain signals but it doesn't actually feel pain.

9. It may seem impossible to come up with a single definition of psychology, but actually we can: psychology is the scientific study of mental processes and behavior.

10. Many people change careers at some point. In fact, many people have several careers in their lifetime.

11. Humans are social animals. We aren't supposed to live alone. Relationships stimulate our brains—in fact, socializing with others is a great form of brain exercise.

12. The Romans invented indoor plumbing using lead pipes. In fact, the word *plumbing* comes from the Roman word for lead, *plumbum*.

Write about It Write your own sentences using the stance adverbials in Activity 20.

21 | Using Stance Adverbials Rewrite these sentences. Replace the **bold** words with a stance adverbial. (More than one answer may be possible.) `5.4 A–C`

1. **It's not surprising that** your skin is thickest on the bottom of your feet.

   Not surprisingly, your skin is thickest on the bottom of your feet.

2. **It is obvious that** mothers who work outside the home have less time to spend with their children.

3. **I'm going to tell you exactly what I think**. I think you are making a big mistake.

4. **I'm being honest when I say that** I didn't break it.

5. **I'm being truthful when I say** I don't know how long I will be here.

6. **She is lucky that** she didn't break her leg.

7. **I don't doubt that** you will do well on the exam.

8. **Everyone can see that** you aren't happy here.

9. I don't want you to go. **I'm serious about that**.

10. **I'm very thankful that** I didn't have to go.

11. **It's possible that** they will get here in time.

5.5 Sentence Patterns with Linking Adverbials

Linking adverbials have a special function. We use them to link or connect ideas within and across sentences, most often in academic writing. We can connect ideas in a number of different ways. For example:

A

PATTERN 1

independent clause / period (.) + linking adverbial / comma (,) + independent clause

1 | We haven't received the information. | **Therefore,** | we won't be able to comment on it. | (two sentences)

PATTERN 2

independent clause / semicolon (;) + linking adverbial / comma (,) + independent clause

2 | We haven't received the information; | **therefore,** | we won't be able to comment on it. | (one sentence)

PATTERN 3

independent clause / semicolon (;) + part of independent clause / comma (,) + linking adverbial / comma (,) + rest of clause

3 | We haven't received the information; | we won't, | **therefore,** | be able to comment on it. | (one sentence)

WARNING! Not all linking adverbials can be used with each pattern.

GRAMMAR TERMS: Linking adverbials are also called **transition words**, **connecting words**, or **conjunctive adverbials**.

22 | Connecting Sentences in Different Ways Read each sentence. Write the number of the pattern from Chart 5.5 that the writer uses. Then rewrite each sentence using the pattern in parentheses. 5.5 A

1. The island of Greenland belongs to Denmark. **However**, if it were a separate country, it would be the thirteenth largest country in the world. _1_
   (Use pattern 2.) _____
   _____

2. China covers an area only slightly larger than that of the U.S.; the population of China, **however**, is nearly five times greater. ____
   (Use pattern 1.) _____
   _____

3. The gravity[16] of the moon is one-sixth that of Earth; on the moon, **therefore**, you would weigh one-sixth of what you weigh on Earth. ____
   (Use pattern 2.) _____
   _____
   _____

4. We use linking adverbials to connect ideas in writing. **However**, it's important not to overuse them. ____
   (Use pattern 3.) _____
   _____

5. An environmentalist is defined as someone who is interested in preserving[17] the environment; to me, **however**, simply being interested is not enough. ____
   (Use pattern 1.) _____
   _____
   _____

6. The tropical deserts are the hottest places on earth; **however**, nights can be very cold there. ____
   (Use pattern 3.) _____
   _____

7. There isn't much food for animals in Antarctica. **Therefore**, most animals live in or near the sea. ____
   (Use pattern 3.) _____
   _____

8. The acting in this movie was terrible and the plot was entirely predictable; I wouldn't, **therefore**, recommend this movie to most people. ____
   (Use pattern 1.) _____
   _____
   _____

---

[16] **gravity:** the force that pulls everything toward the earth   [17] **preserving:** keeping safe or in good condition

5.6 Linking Adverbials That Signal a Result or Contrast

A

SIGNALING A RESULT OR CONSEQUENCE

1 There is twice as much hydrogen as oxygen in water. **Therefore**, its chemical formula is written as H_2O.

2 The author points out that we value some abilities over others; **as a result**, we often fail to develop our children's potential.

3 My father was born in Italy, but he grew up in California. **Consequently**, he feels more American than Italian.

We use **linking adverbials** to show a connection between two sentences or clauses. Different linking adverbials signal different kinds of connections. Some linking adverbials signal that a result or consequence of something in the first clause or sentence is coming in the second clause or sentence, as in **1 – 3**.

as a result	consequently	therefore	thus

B

SIGNALING A CONTRAST

4 A few years ago it seemed likely that computers would replace books. Now, **however**, most experts think that books are here to stay.

5 A professional cyclist can cover 30 miles in one hour. **In contrast**, the average cyclist covers only 16.

6 Cities are generally noisy, dirty, and expensive. **In spite of that**, the number of people moving to cities is increasing.

7 Many cities are dirty, noisy, and dangerous. **Nonetheless**, many people prefer cities because of the job opportunities and the excitement.

Some linking adverbials signal a contrast between two clauses, as in **4 – 5**.

however	in contrast	on the contrary
in comparison	instead	on the other hand

Certain other linking adverbials signal a contrast that is surprising or unexpected, as in **6 – 7**.

after all	besides	nevertheless
anyhow	in any case	nonetheless
at any rate	in spite of that	still

C

OTHER WAYS TO EXPRESS A RESULT OR CONTRAST

independent clause / comma (,) + *so* + independent clause
8 I'm going to graduate soon, **so** I'll probably relocate.

independent clause / comma (,) + (*and*) *yet* + independent clause
9 Everything was going wrong, **and yet** I was still happy.

independent clause / comma (,) + *but* + independent clause
10 Televisions were expensive at first, **but** they eventually became much cheaper.

GO ONLINE

23 | Using Linking Adverbials to Signal a Result Choose the answer in parentheses that best completes each sentence. 5.6 A

1. Foldable scissors are very small; consequently, they _____*fit*_____ easily in a purse or pocket. (don't fit/fit)

2. I practiced the piano several hours a day. Therefore, I made progress _____. (slowly/quickly)

3. For me, a good job is one where I can help others become smarter. Thus, I can think of nothing better than being a _____. (singer/teacher)

4. Centuries ago, children were considered to be small adults. As a result, _____ done to help address the special emotional needs of young children. (lots of things were/very little was)

5. Much of the surface of Mars is covered by reddish rocks and sand. As a result, people often call Mars the _____ planet. (old/red)

6. Living in another country gave me the opportunity to meet new people and to learn about another culture. As a result, I now _____ to travel to foreign countries. (hate/love)

7. The number of overweight children is increasing. As a result, schools are serving _____ junk food. (less/more)

8. In psychology, the term *behavior* refers to almost any activity. Thus, the blink of an eye _____ an example of a behavior. (is/isn't)

24 | Result or Contrast? Choose the linking adverbial in parentheses that best completes each sentence.
`5.6 A–B`

1. The tallest tree in the world today is a redwood tree. In the nineteenth century, _____*however*_____, much taller eucalyptus trees existed. (however/thus)

2. Japan is a popular tourist spot for many Koreans. _____, bookstores in Korea carry a lot of travel books for Japan. (as a result/in contrast)

3. Both humans and giraffes have seven neck vertebrae[18]. For giraffes, _____, each one can be more than 10 inches (25.4 centimeters) long. (however/therefore)

4. I've never thought of him as being sad. _____, he seems happy and full of life. (on the contrary/thus)

5. Something always went wrong on our family vacations. One year, everyone got sick. Another year, it rained the whole time. _____, now we look back on these incidents and laugh. (as a result/nevertheless)

6. My sister got into all the schools she applied to. I, _____, didn't get into any of them. (on the other hand/thus)

7. Spanish and Italian male colleagues may embrace when they greet each other. _____, the Japanese usually bow. (consequently/in contrast)

8. The western calendar is based on the length of the seasonal year. The lunar calendar, _____, is based on the cycle of the moon. (as a result/in contrast)

9. When I first moved to Canada, I was very homesick. _____, once I started school, I made a lot of friends, and I began to feel more comfortable. (as a result/however)

10. Divorce has become common in some countries. _____, the traditional role of the father as wage-earner[19] and the mother as homemaker continues to be viewed as the norm. (consequently/still)

redwood trees

embrace

---

[18] **vertebrae:** the small bones that are connected together to form the line down the middle of your back

[19] **wage-earner:** a person who gets money from working

11. The universe is so large that we can't measure it in miles or kilometers.
_____, we measure it in light years. (nevertheless/instead)

12. I am a good judge of character. I can tell if someone is trustworthy.
_____, I am not very organized. (consequently/however)

Think about It In which sentence(s) in Activity 24 is there a surprising contrast?

25 | Other Ways to Express a Result or Contrast Rewrite these sentences using a linking adverbial to connect the clauses or sentences. 5.6 C

Sentences from Student Essays

1. Running your own business can be difficult, but it can prove to be extremely rewarding.

   Running your own business can be difficult; however, it can prove to be extremely rewarding.

2. His mother worked for a university, so they didn't have to pay tuition.
3. Modern technology has freed us from many chores[20], so we have more time to enjoy ourselves.
4. Several years ago I was thinking of taking a trip to Russia. At the time, I was living in California, so it was going to be quite a journey just getting there.
5. She was very young and small, yet she was able to skate beautifully with the eyes of the whole world on her.
6. He worked 20 hours every day to make his business successful, but after several years, he finally gave up.
7. Most people have more than one skill or talent, and yet they stay in the same profession for their whole life.
8. I most often get sick when I am run down, so I try to make sure I eat well, exercise daily, and get plenty of sleep.
9. It's often a difficult decision to leave children in the care of others—and yet millions of women do it.

Write about It Rewrite the second clause in each sentence you wrote above. (You can also use a different linking adverbial.)

   1. Running your own business can be difficult; as a result, many businesses fail during their first year.

[20] **chores:** small jobs or routine tasks

5.7 | Linking Adverbials That Signal Additional Information

A	**SIGNALING AN EXAMPLE** **1** Not all plants are gentle on the environment. Cotton plants, **for instance**, are often covered with chemicals. **2** Skilled public speakers use hand gestures for emphasis. **For example**, a speaker may point a finger or use a chopping motion.	We use some **linking adverbials** to signal that an example is coming next, as in **1 – 2**. for example for instance
B	**SIGNALING NEW RELATED INFORMATION** **3** Biking is a good way to get around Berlin because many parts of the city are hard to get to via public transportation. **Moreover**, the city is almost entirely flat, so it is easy to use a bike. **4** The study found that healthy employees are more productive during work hours. **In addition**, they take fewer sick days. **5** Diabetes rates are rising quickly and an increase in heart disease cannot be far behind. **Furthermore**, new evidence suggests that sitting all day is bad for your health.	Some linking adverbials signal that we are adding new information that is related to what we said before, as in **3 – 5**. furthermore likewise in addition moreover
C	**OTHER WAYS TO SIGNAL ADDITIONAL INFORMATION** *such as* + noun phrase **6** In some countries, activities **such as bullfighting** are part of the culture. *besides* + noun phrase **7** **Besides being the largest city in Canada**, Toronto has a multicultural population. *in addition to* + noun phrase **8** **In addition to self-discipline**, a self-employed person needs to have a lot of motivation.	

26 | Adding Examples Match the linking adverbials with the examples they introduce. `5.7 A`

1. Our ears can't hear every sound. For instance, _c_

2. Efforts to use recycled products haven't always been successful. In the 1990s, for example, ____

3. When you visit another country, it's interesting to learn about cultural differences. For example, ____

4. I think that feeling a little stress can be a good thing. For example, ____

5. Rubber is a common material used in sports equipment. For example, ____

6. Because of the Internet, we can find out how people in other countries are dealing with events. For instance, ____

7. Some places have very old laws that don't make any sense. For instance, ____

8. At times it's natural to feel angry. For example, ____

a. worrying about a test might actually make me study harder.

b. we can hear stories from people who have been affected by earthquakes or typhoons[21].

c. ultrasonic sounds are too high-pitched[22] for humans to hear.

d. in one state in the U.S., it is against the law to carry an ice-cream cone in your pocket.

e. recycled wool came and went, mostly because the clothes were very itchy[23].

f. it is the main ingredient in bicycle tires and basketballs.

g. the food may be very different from what you are used to.

h. being treated unfairly upsets most people.

---

[21] **typhoons:** violent storms with strong winds in hot countries
[22] **high-pitched:** at a very high sound frequency

[23] **itchy:** producing the feeling in your skin that makes you want to scratch it

Think about It Think of another example to complete each statement in Activity 26. Share your ideas with a partner.

27 | Signaling New Related Information Circle the answer that best completes each sentence. 5.7 B

Hong Kong

1. When you are visiting Hong Kong, Kowloon Peninsula may be a better place to stay because it is less crowded. Moreover, ____

   a. Hong Kong has some great hotels.

   b. it doesn't have as many good restaurants.

   c. it has great museums and good views of the Hong Kong skyline.

Hotel Review

2. The bedrooms are comfortable but very dark. The closets are tiny, so good luck if you want to hang up any clothes. And housekeeping could be better. During our entire stay, the floors were never cleaned. In addition, ____

   a. the staff was very friendly.

   b. the furniture in our room was covered with a thick layer of dust.

   c. the floors were very dirty.

Student Essay

3. Coping with stress is very important, and I have a few main methods of helping myself stay relaxed. The first things I always try to do are to slow down my breathing, quiet my thoughts, and relax my muscles. I also try to speak more calmly and slowly. Furthermore, ____. For me, the best thing to do is to take a quiet walk alone or to exercise.

   a. this isn't always easy to do

   b. I often try to take myself out of the stressful environment

   c. I feel more relaxed when I do this

Think about It What other adverbials can you find in the sentences above? Circle them. Then tell a partner what kind of information they add to the paragraph.

28 | Signaling Additional Information Choose the word or phrase in parentheses that best completes each sentence. Add the correct punctuation if necessary. `5.7 A–C`

1. There are many interesting things to do in Washington, D.C. A visitor can tour the White House, the home of the president, visit the many historical museums, or walk around government buildings such as the Supreme Court and the Capitol. _____*Besides*_____ touring the educational sites in the city, visitors can do fun activities such as visiting the zoo. (besides/in addition)

2. In the past, people spent many hours taking care of basic chores _____ cooking and cleaning. (for instance/such as)

3. I would need a very good reason to fire an employee. _____ I would fire an employee who was stealing from the company. (for example/such as)

4. Many forms of exercise, _____ running, playing sports, and swimming, are good for the body. (for example/besides)

5. Cape Town in South Africa is a great place to visit. _____ the spectacular mountains, you will find some beautiful beaches there. (in addition/in addition to)

6. Whatever your profession is, you can find work in a large city. _____ there are many different kinds of schools. (in addition/in addition to)

7. People in different cultures value different things. _____ in some countries people value punctuality—they expect you to be on time. (for instance/such as)

8. You should encourage her to avoid bad habits _____ smoking and drinking. (for instance/such as)

Write about It Rewrite each sentence above using the other word or phrase in parentheses. (You may write one or two sentences.)

1. In addition, visitors can do fun activities such as visiting the zoo.

5.8 Linking Adverbials That Signal a List or Summary

A	**SIGNALING A LIST** **1** The popularity of Arabic coffee is due to several of its characteristics. **First**, it is easy to grow. More importantly, however, Arabic coffee has the best flavor. **2** It was not a typical lunch. **For one thing**, I was in a small boat. **For another**, my boat was tied to 16 other boats.	Some **linking adverbials** signal that a list or sequence of ideas is coming next, as in **1 – 2**. <table><tr><td>first</td><td>first of all</td><td>to begin with</td></tr><tr><td>second</td><td>second of all</td><td>next</td></tr><tr><td>firstly</td><td>for one (thing)</td><td>lastly</td></tr><tr><td>secondly</td><td>for another (thing)</td><td>finally</td></tr></table>
B	**SIGNALING A SUMMARY OF PREVIOUS INFORMATION** **3** . . . **In conclusion**, something must be done to ensure that children's toys are safe. **4** . . . **All in all**, it has been a good year.	We can also use certain linking adverbials to signal that a summary of previous information is coming, as in **3 – 4**. <table><tr><td>in sum</td><td>in conclusion</td><td>all in all</td></tr><tr><td>in summary</td><td>to conclude</td><td>overall</td></tr><tr><td>ultimately</td><td>to summarize</td><td></td></tr></table>

29 | Noticing Linking Adverbials Read these paragraphs and underline the linking adverbials. (The number in parentheses indicates the number of linking adverbials in the paragraph.) Then answer the questions below. `5.8 A`

What would you do if you knew that you would die in a few months?

1. If I knew that I would die in a few months, I would stop worrying about long-term goals. I think that knowing I would die soon could help me to focus on the here and now[24]. The first thing that I would do is to stop worrying about jobs and careers; if I am going to die soon, I will have little need for money. Secondly, I would want to spend a lot more time in quiet, either alone or with close friends. I hope that this would make me a wiser and calmer person. Lastly, I would try to share what wisdom I have gained in life with the people I trust most. If I did these things, I think it could help others live happier lives after I'm gone. (2)

What do you want to accomplish in the next ten years?

2. There is a lot that I would like to accomplish in the next ten years. I think that this will be a very busy time for me. The first thing that I will do is complete my education. I will go to college and study to become a teacher. I have always wanted to be a teacher; I think this is because I've always liked school and my teachers have been important figures in my life. Getting my degree will be hard work, but it is very important to me. Once I've received my teaching degree, I will try to find a job in a public school. I think it will be fun to have my own students, and I will work hard to be the best possible teacher. Finally, once I am settled into a teaching career, I will think about starting my own family. I would like to get married and have children someday. Hopefully my future spouse will be easy to find. We will get married, find a home, and settle down. (1)

MAKING LITERATE[25] SOCIETIES

3. There are two primary purposes of this chapter. First, it reviews the development of widespread literacy in various countries, examining the influences that have accelerated this process and, more briefly, those that have hindered[26] it. Second, it examines the broader social context of literacy: how it is learned and practiced in particular social settings, how it serves different individual and group purposes, and how it is influenced by public policies and family circumstances. In particular, the chapter focuses on language issues, literacy practices, and literate environments. (2)

QUESTIONS

1. Writers use different forms to signal a list or sequence, not just adverbials. They do this to give variety to their writing. In the first and second paragraphs above, what other forms does the writer use to signal a sequence or list? Circle them.
2. What other linking adverbials could you use in the paragraphs above? Compare ideas with your classmates.

[24] **here and now:** the present time
[25] **literate:** able to read and write
[26] **hinder:** to make it more difficult to do something

30 | Adding a Summary Statement Read each paragraph and choose the best summary statement.

5.8 B

Paragraphs from Student Essays

1. **Essay Prompt: Do you have the skills to run your own business? Explain.**

   To run your own business, you must be very organized and hard-working. If you are involved in the hiring process, you must also be a good judge of character. I do have some of these skills. I am one of the most hard-working people I know. Even if it isn't necessary, I always try to do a job to perfection. I am also a good judge of character. I can tell when someone is trustworthy or when a person is not. Unfortunately, I am not very organized. I would have a difficult time keeping track of everything related to the business, like legal documents and receipts. In addition, I have a hard time making a budget and keeping to it. This skill is essential for a business owner. In conclusion, ____

   a. I think that I could run my own business, but I would need an assistant and a financial advisor.

   b. I am not a good decision maker and this is a liability in business.

   c. most people do not have the skills to run their own business.

2. **Essay Prompt: Explain why you would or would not want to live in a large city.**

   For me, the choice of whether or not to live in a big city is easy to make: Why would I want to live where there is such a high concentration of people? Why would I want to spend so much money to live in a tiny apartment? And why would I want to be exposed to noise and air pollution? Obviously, you get less for your money in the city. Overall, ____

   a. it's more expensive to live in a large city.

   b. it's not very pleasant to live in a big city.

   c. there are a lot of good reasons to live in a big city.

Think about It Compare your answers above with your classmates. Explain your choice of the best summary statements.

Write about It Write your own answer to one of the essay prompts above.

5.9 Using Adverbials in Speaking and Academic Writing

A

HEDGING

1 A: What do you think of this shirt?
B: I **kind of** like it.

2 A: Do you **by any chance** have a piece of paper?
B: Sure. Just one?

COMPARE 3A–3B

3a Some people claim they never dream, but that is not true.

3b Some people claim they never dream, but that is **generally** not true.

4 Most scientists think that a sudden event—**perhaps** caused by a crashing meteor or planet—led to the extinction of dinosaurs.

5 The average person spends about nine hours a day using some kind of media. This is **arguably** more than was expected ten years ago.

In conversation, we sometimes use an **adverbial** to hedge, or soften, our words, as in **1 – 2**. We often do this to sound more polite.

In academic texts, writers need to make sure their claims are not too strong. A claim that is too strong becomes unbelievable, as in **3a**. Adverbials are one of many tools that writers can use to qualify, limit, or hedge a claim, as in **3b – 5**.

B

CONNECTING IDEAS

6 The coal question remains perhaps the most difficult issue in the energy world. Supporters of solar, wind, and even nuclear power say these are cleaner and safer sources of energy. **On the other hand**, the use of coal continues to climb.

7 A number of experiments suggest that the brain is very malleable. **However**, all were carried out on animals.

In academic writing, linking adverbials are just one of many tools that writers use to connect ideas in a text, as in **6 – 7**.

WARNING! Don't use too many linking adverbials in your writing. This makes the writing choppy. Instead, use linking words, phrases, and clauses together with other cohesive tools like pronouns, repetition of key words, etc.

31 | Hedging a Statement in Speaking Choose a word or phrase from the box to soften each question or response. (Many different answers are possible.) Then compare with your classmates. **5.9 A**

1. You should come back later.

   Maybe you should come back later.

2. You called the wrong number.
3. Are you driving to the meeting tomorrow?
4. She didn't like my essay. In fact, she said it was boring.
5. Aren't you young to own your own business?
6. He has a loud, unpleasant voice.
7. You're mistaken.
8. Is Dr. Martin at home?
9. You upset her.
10. Can I borrow ten dollars?

> by any chance
> kind of
> maybe
> perhaps
> probably
> sort of

Think about It For each sentence above, which expressions do not work well? Why not?

32 | Hedging a Statement in Writing What words do these writers use to hedge, or limit, their claims? Underline them. `5.9 A`

SENTENCES FROM ACADEMIC SOURCES

1. Deserts are dry regions, <u>generally</u> receiving less than ten inches of precipitation a year.
2. Mothers who work outside the home obviously have less time to spend with their children. According to a recent study, however, this does not necessarily have a negative effect on their children.
3. This is arguably the best museum in the whole country.
4. In general, smoking is no longer fashionable in Canada. In many other parts of the world, however, smoking is still growing in popularity.
5. Researchers have found these substances almost everywhere they have looked for them.
6. The risk to humans is uncertain in part because few tests have been done.
7. In most cases, the assumption that wealthy countries have better education systems than poorer countries is correct.
8. Researchers have long suggested that in "noun-friendly" languages including English, infants' attention is focused mainly on objects, typically marked by nouns.
9. The number of farm workers has decreased steadily over the years. This is primarily because the use of sophisticated machines has reduced the need for labor.

Write about It Rewrite the sentences above using a different adverbial to hedge.

33 | Using Linking Adverbials in Writing Choose the linking adverbial in parentheses that best completes each sentence. `5.9 B`

Facts about Japan

1. Many people think Japan is one large island; _____*however*_____, it is actually thousands of islands. (however/thus)

2. Much of Japan is mountainous; _____, there is little farmland. (as a result/in addition)

3. Japan has only a small supply of minerals. It is _____ one of the world's richest nations. (for example/nonetheless)

4. Volcanic eruptions take place frequently. _____, earthquakes are common occurrences. (in contrast/in addition)

5. Japanese trees are often cultivated[27] as miniatures; _____, gardens are often designed as smaller versions of the surrounding landscape. (on the other hand/likewise)

[27]**cultivate:** to grow

6. The largest of the main islands, Honshu, is less than 200 miles wide at its greatest width; _____, no part of Japan is more than 100 miles from the sea. (consequently/nevertheless)

7. Few inlets are found on the east coast north of Tokyo; _____, south of Tokyo are many of the best harbors. (however/therefore)

8. Every valley in Japan has a stream; _____, there aren't any long, navigable[28] rivers in Japan. (as a result/however)

9. In the Japanese mountains, there are about 200 volcanoes; _____, only about 60 are still active. (however/moreover)

34 | Choosing Linking Adverbials Choose linking adverbials from the box to complete each textbook excerpt below. (There is one extra adverbial for each text. More than one answer may be possible.) Then answer the questions on page 169. **5.9 B**

as a result	consequently	however	in addition

Parenting Styles

There are three basic styles of parenting: permissive, dictatorial, and authoritative. Generally, each style has fairly predictable effects on children.

Permissive parents have very few demands of their children. They don't make many rules, and when they do, they often fail to enforce[29] them. These parents generally act more like friends rather than parents. _____, their children don't learn much about good behavior and the consequences for bad behavior. Children raised in this way can be impulsive[30] and irresponsible.

Dictatorial parents are inflexible. They make strict rules and demand obedience[31]. When their children disobey, they are usually punished very harshly. Dictatorial parents don't trust their children to make decisions for themselves, and they often don't explain why they make such strict rules. _____, their children are often not very good at making decisions.

FYI

Many linking adverbials are used almost exclusively in writing. They are more formal and sound strange in informal conversation. Examples include *consequently*, *furthermore*, *moreover*, *nevertheless*, and *thus*.

[28] **navigable:** deep and wide enough to provide passage for boats and/or ships
[29] **enforce:** to make sure that people follow the law or rules

[30] **impulsive:** doing things suddenly and without thinking carefully
[31] **obedience:** the state of doing what someone tells you to do

Authoritative parents are in the role of authority figures, but they are not dictators. They expect their children to obey their rules. _____, they are caring, flexible, and often willing to listen to their children's opinions.

| for example | furthermore | in conclusion | instead |

Emotions

According to psychologists, all humans show distinctive facial expressions for six basic emotions: disgust, sadness, happiness, fear, anger, and surprise. _____, these expressions appear to be universal. This means that people from different cultures across the world use and recognize the same expressions for the same emotions. Of course, not every person will have the same emotional responses to the same things, but we do seem to have the same way of showing these six emotions without using language.

In general, when we experience an intense feeling, we don't just feel "normal" after that feeling passes. _____, we often go beyond that middle ground[32] and experience the opposite emotion. _____, if you have just given a presentation to your classmates, one that you have dreaded[33] for weeks, you might feel wonderful when it's over instead of feeling just OK. Similarly, it is not unusual to feel a little sad or depressed after experiencing a lot of joy or excitement for a period of time. If your parents live far away and they visit you only once a year for a short time, you might feel very happy during their visit. However, once they leave, you may experience some sadness or depression in their absence.

FYI
Some linking adverbials require several sentences or even a paragraph to build up to them. Examples include *furthermore, in conclusion, on the contrary*, and *therefore*.

QUESTIONS

1. Do you think each writer above uses too many linking adverbials or just enough? Why?
2. How many other adverbials can you find in the paragraphs above? Circle them.
3. What adverbials does each writer use to hedge some of the claims in these textbook excerpts?

[32] **middle ground:** halfway point; intermediate position

[33] **dread:** to be afraid of something that is going to happen

A | TIC-TAC-TOE Follow these instructions.

1. Work with a partner. Student A is X. Student B is O.

2. Student A: Choose a square. On another piece of paper, write a sentence with an example that supports the statement in the square. Use *for example* or *for instance* in your sentence.

3. Students A and B: Check the sentence together. If the sentence has no errors, write an *X* in the square. If the sentence is not correct, do not write an *X* in the square.

4. Student B: Take your turn. Write an *O* for each correct answer.

5. The first person to get three *X*s or three *O*s in a line is the winner.

Professional athletes are paid a lot of money.	Not all languages use the Roman alphabet.	There are a number of things you can do to improve your memory.
Some cities have great public transportation.	Not all animals need to drink water every day.	You need a lot of different skills to run your own business.
People use a variety of facial expressions to show their emotions.	Some actors are also good singers.	You can learn a lot from living in a different country.

You need a lot of different skills to run your own business.
For example, you need to be good at making a budget.

B | WRITING Consider this essay test prompt and take notes on your ideas. Then write a paragraph in which you present your ideas to your classmates. Use adverbials where appropriate. (Look again at the sample essay responses in Activity 29.)

Essay Prompt: If your doctor told you that you had only a few months to live, how would you change your way of life? Discuss.

C | WEB SEARCH Choose a free online academic course and download a transcript of the first lecture. Look for examples of adverbials that the speaker frequently uses. Share what you learned with your classmates.

TYPES OF ADVERBIALS	PURPOSE	COMMON EXAMPLES			
TIME ADVERBIALS	Explain *when, how often,* or *how long*	then always already usually	now still ever this morning	never today sometimes	again yesterday often
PLACE ADVERBIALS	Explain *where* or *how far*	here	there	outside	upstairs
ADVERBIALS OF MANNER	Explain *how, in what way, in what manner,* or *by what means*	fast	significantly	together	well
ADVERBIALS OF PURPOSE	Explain *why, for what purpose,* or *for what reason*	as a result of because of	due to on account of	to let everyone know *to* + base form of verb (*to-* infinitive)	
DEGREE ADVERBIALS	Explain *to what degree*	absolutely quite rather truly significantly about fairly somewhat	completely incredibly pretty perfectly much almost slightly	entirely extremely really reasonably approximately less	considerably highly so very nearly a (little) bit
FOCUSING ADVERBIALS	Focus attention on a word or a phrase	especially particularly	even	just	only
STANCE ADVERBIALS	Express an attitude about or comment on the information in a clause or sentence	hopefully fortunately of course undoubtedly perhaps actually	luckily certainly obviously clearly maybe really	surprisingly definitely very likely probably honestly in fact	thankfully no doubt without a doubt possibly seriously technically speaking to tell you the truth
LINKING ADVERBIALS	Connect ideas within and across sentences	**Result/Consequence** as a result **Contrast** however instead anyhow still **Additional information** for example in addition **List** first first of all to begin with **Summary** in sum in summary ultimately	consequently in contrast though nevertheless nonetheless for instance likewise second secondly second of all in conclusion to conclude to summarize	therefore in comparison on the contrary at any rate in any case furthermore firstly lastly finally all in all overall	thus on the other hand besides in spite of that moreover for one thing for another thing next

Adverb Clauses

Never look back unless you are planning to go that way.

—HENRY DAVID THOREAU, WRITER AND PHILOSOPHER (1817–1862)

Talk about It What does the quotation above mean? Do you agree or disagree?

WARM-UP

A | Match the beginnings and endings of the proverbs. Then choose one proverb and tell a partner what it means to you.

PROVERBS FROM AROUND THE WORLD

1. Knowledge is the most valuable treasure __d__

2. Don't count your chickens ____

3. When spider webs unite, ____

4. A snake will emit[1] poison ____

5. The eyes are of little use ____

6. Make hay ____

7. Even though the old man is strong, ____

a. they can tie up a lion. *(Ethiopian)*

b. even though you feed it on milk. *(Indian)*

c. while the sun shines. *(English)*

d. because it can't be stolen or consumed. *(Sanskrit)*

e. he will not live forever. *(Ghanaian)*

f. if the mind is blind. *(Arabic)*

g. before they hatch[2]. *(Greek)*

B | The words in blue in the proverbs above are adverb clauses. Based on these examples, what can you say about adverb clauses? Check (✓) *True* or *False*.

	TRUE	FALSE
1. An adverb clause has a subject and verb.	☐	☐
2. Adverb clauses always come at the end of a sentence.	☐	☐
3. An adverb clause is connected to another clause.	☐	☐
4. Adverb clauses always begin with *when* or *while*.	☐	☐

C | Look back at the quotation on page 172. Identify any adverb clauses.

[1] **emit:** to send out something such as gas, heat, light, or a sound   [2] **hatch:** to come out of an egg

6.1 Overview of Adverb Clauses

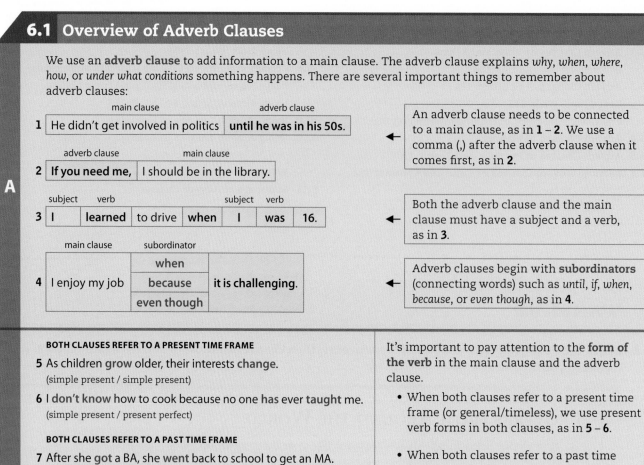

A

We use an **adverb clause** to add information to a main clause. The adverb clause explains *why*, *when*, *where*, *how*, or *under what conditions* something happens. There are several important things to remember about adverb clauses:

	main clause	adverb clause
1	He didn't get involved in politics	until he was in his 50s.

An adverb clause needs to be connected to a main clause, as in **1 – 2**. We use a comma (,) after the adverb clause when it comes first, as in **2**.

	adverb clause	main clause
2	If you need me,	I should be in the library.

	subject	verb		subject	verb	
3	I	learned	to drive	when	I	was 16.

Both the adverb clause and the main clause must have a subject and a verb, as in **3**.

	main clause	subordinator	
4	I enjoy my job	when / because / even though	it is challenging.

Adverb clauses begin with **subordinators** (connecting words) such as *until*, *if*, *when*, *because*, or *even though*, as in **4**.

B

BOTH CLAUSES REFER TO A PRESENT TIME FRAME

5 As children **grow** older, their interests **change**.
(simple present / simple present)

6 I **don't know** how to cook because no one **has** ever **taught** me.
(simple present / present perfect)

BOTH CLAUSES REFER TO A PAST TIME FRAME

7 After she **got** a BA, she **went** back to school to get an MA.
(simple past / simple past)

8 The store **wasn't doing** very well when my father **bought** it.
(past progressive / simple past)

THE TWO CLAUSES REFER TO DIFFERENT TIME FRAMES

9 This book **is** special to me because it **was** a gift from my uncle.
(simple present / simple past)

10 This book **has** always **been** special to me because it **was** a gift from my uncle. (present perfect / simple past)

It's important to pay attention to the **form of the verb** in the main clause and the adverb clause.

- When both clauses refer to a present time frame (or general/timeless), we use present verb forms in both clauses, as in **5 – 6**.

- When both clauses refer to a past time frame, we use past verb forms in both clauses, as in **7 – 8**.

- When the two clauses refer to different time frames, we can use different verb forms, as in **9 – 10**.

For information about future time frames, see Chart 6.2.

1 | Noticing Adverb Clauses Read this information and take notes in the timeline on page 175. Then answer the questions on page 175. **6.1 A**

VANESSA-MAE

Like many famous musicians, Vanessa-Mae started playing music at a very young age. She was only 3 years old **when she had her first piano lesson**, and she started playing the violin **when she was just 5**. Then, at the age of 8, she had to make a difficult decision. She had to choose between the violin and the piano. **Although she had just won a prize at an important piano competition**, Vanessa-Mae decided to focus on the violin. **Once she made her decision**, she worked hard to improve her playing, and **by the time she was 12**, she had made three recordings of classical music. **Although she loved classical music**, she wanted to play other kinds of music, too. To many people's surprise, she got an electric violin and started playing rock music. Today Vanessa-Mae is known as both a great classical violin musician and a great rock musician. That's quite a combination.

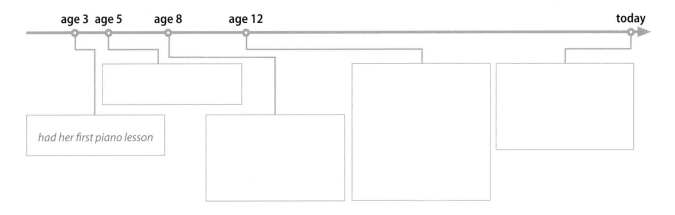

age 3 age 5   age 8   age 12   today

had her first piano lesson

QUESTIONS

1. What are the subject and verb in each **bold** adverb clause in the Activity 1 text on page 174? Circle them.

2. What subordinator (connecting word or phrase) begins each adverb clause? Underline it.

3. Which adverb clauses come before the main clauses? What punctuation marks does the writer use in these sentences?

4. Vanessa-Mae was a child prodigy—a person who develops a special skill at a young age. Can you think of other child prodigies? What did they accomplish at a young age? Try to use adverb clauses in your answers.

2 | Identifying Verb Forms Underline the verb in each main clause and each adverb clause in the sentences below. Then identify the form of each verb. **6.1 B**

PRESENT VERB FORMS	simple present	present progressive	present perfect
PAST VERB FORMS	simple past	past progressive	past perfect

1. When I <u>have spent</u> a lot of time exercising, I <u>sleep</u> better at night. _____ *present perfect / simple present* _____

2. When I was younger, I thought a lot about my future. _____

3. My parents are important to me because they have always been my best friends. _____

4. Once I start something, I don't stop until I'm done. _____

5. I try to stay completely focused while I'm studying. _____

6. My hometown has always been special to me because it's so beautiful. _____

7. Once I've made a decision, I never change my mind. _____

8. I didn't have any friends while I was growing up. _____

9. A year after I had finished high school, I started college. _____

10. Shortly after I moved here, I got a job. _____

11. Although I worked hard yesterday, I don't feel like working this morning. _____

12. I am applying to this college because my father attended the same school. _____

Talk about It Are any of the sentences above true for you? Tell a partner.

Think about It Which sentences above have actions that take place in different time frames? What verb forms are used in each clause?

6.2 Adverb Clauses of Time and Reason

A

ADVERB CLAUSES OF TIME

1 One study shows that babies can learn **before they are born**.

2 **Once the process began**, it was irreversible.

3 The lights automatically turn off **when people leave the room**.

4 **As plastic bags break down**, they release poisonous material into the water.

An **adverb clause of time** tells when one event happens in relation to another event in the main clause, as in **1 – 4**.

- We use some subordinators to show that one event happens before or after another event:

after	before	once	until
as soon as	by the time	since	when

- We use some subordinators to show that two events happen at the same time:

as	when	whenever	while

B

FUTURE ADVERB CLAUSES OF TIME

5 Nobody **will care** when you get there tomorrow.
(NOT: ~~Nobody will care when you will get there tomorrow.~~)

6 What **are** you **going to do** while we're away?
(NOT: ~~What are you going to do while we will be away?~~)

7 **After you read this**, you**'ll** probably **have** some questions.

8 We **aren't going to leave** until you get back.

When we make a prediction or talk about a future plan, we usually use a future verb form in the main clause but a present (not future) verb form in the adverb clause, as in **5 – 8**.

C

ADVERB CLAUSES OF REASON

9 My watch is important to me **because it was a gift from my father**.

10 **Since we have some new people here today**, let's start with introductions.

11 The meeting was canceled as **no one could get there**.

12 **Now that prices have gone up**, we can't afford to travel.

We can also use an adverb clause to give a reason for something in the main clause. **Adverb clauses of reason** usually begin with the subordinator *because*, *since*, *as*, or *now that*, as in **9 – 12**.

D

OTHER WAYS TO GIVE REASONS

because of + noun phrase
13 **Because of the increase in prices**, we can't afford to travel now. (*because of* = phrasal preposition)

independent clause + *so* + independent clause
14 **Prices have increased, so** we can't afford to travel now. (*so* = conjunction)

two separate sentences
15 We can't afford to travel now. **Prices have increased too much**.

---

3 | Noticing Adverb Clauses of Time Read these sentences and underline the adverb clauses of time. Then check (✓) *Good Advice* or *Bad Advice*. **6.2 A**

ADVICE FOR UNIVERSITY STUDENTS	GOOD ADVICE	BAD ADVICE
1. <u>Before you turn in an assignment</u>, check it over carefully.	☐	☐
2. It's important to review your notes from class as soon as you get home.	☐	☐
3. Don't study for a test until your instructor tells you to.	☐	☐
4. Take notes while you are reading assigned texts.	☐	☐
5. Study with a large group of classmates whenever you can.	☐	☐

	GOOD ADVICE	BAD ADVICE
6. Ask to meet with your instructor whenever you are confused about the course material.	☐	☐
7. As you read your class assignment, you should listen to loud music to help you think.	☐	☐
8. Ask questions in class when you don't understand something.	☐	☐
9. Always stay up late while you are studying.	☐	☐
10. Once you have read a text, don't look at it again until you need to study for a test.	☐	☐

Talk about It Which advice in Activity 3 was good or bad? Compare with a partner and say why.

Write about It Write new sentences using the time clauses in the sentences in Activity 3. Use your own words to write a different main clause.

Before you turn in an assignment, be sure to put your name on it.

4 | Understanding Subordinators Choose the subordinator on the right that best completes each sentence. Then answer the questions on page 178. 6.2 A–B

QUOTATIONS FROM FAMOUS PEOPLE

1. __As_____ you grow older you will discover that you have two hands: one for helping yourself, the other for helping others. *(Sam Levenson, writer and humorist)*

> as
> before
> whenever

2. _____ I crave³ junk food, I want salty things like peanuts or potato chips. *(Tyra Banks, model)*

> after
> until
> whenever

3. There's only one way to have a happy marriage and _____ I learn what it is, I'll get married again. *(Clint Eastwood, actor)*

> as soon as
> by the time
> while

4. _____ you are over 30, 35 years old, I think everyone should get down to the gym and start moving again. *(Warren Cuccurullo, musician)*

> once
> until
> whenever

5. Life is what happens _____ you are busy making other plans. *(John Lennon, musician)*

> before
> until
> while

6. I've now been in this country . . . _____ I was 17. So this is my second home. *(Hakeem Olajuwon, athlete)*

> by the time
> since
> when

³**crave:** to need something strongly or urgently

7. I still love making hamburgers on the grill⁴. I guess _____ I eat them, childhood memories come up for me. *(Bobby Flay, chef)*

before
until
whenever

8. Champions keep playing _____ they get it right. *(Billie Jean King, athlete)*

before
until
whenever

9. _____ you do the common things in life in an uncommon way, you will command the attention of the world. *(George Washington Carver, scientist)*

after
since
when

10. _____ I hear music, something in me starts to vibrate⁵.
    (Suzanne Farrell, dancer)

as soon as
by the time
until

11. I could develop a picture _____ I was 12. *(David Bailey, photographer)*

by the time
since
whenever

12. A lie gets halfway around the world _____ the truth has a chance to get its pants on. *(Winston Churchill, statesman)*

before
until
when

QUESTIONS

1. In which sentences in Activity 4 do the two events happen at the same time?
2. What verb form does each speaker use in the main clause and the adverb clause of time?
3. In which sentences in Activity 4 is the speaker making a prediction or a plan? How do you know?

Talk about It Which quotation in Activity 4 is the most interesting to you? Tell your classmates why.

5 | Using Adverb Clauses of Time to Talk about the Future Complete these sentences with the correct form of the verbs in parentheses. Then check (✓) *Prediction* or *Plan*. 6.2 B

UNDERGRADUATES DISCUSS THE FUTURE

	PREDICTION	PLAN
1. When the economy _____improves_____ (improve), more people _____ (have) jobs.	☐	☐
2. It _____ (be) years before the economy _____ (become) steady again.	☐	☐
3. I _____ (not / get) a job unless I _____ (be) very lucky.	☐	☐
4. Most students _____ (start) at low salaries when they _____ (leave) college.	☐	☐
5. When I _____ (graduate), I _____ (get) a job right away.	☐	☐
6. As soon as I _____ (finish) school, I _____ (apply) for as many jobs as possible.	☐	☐

⁴**grill:** a metal frame that you put food on to cook over a fire   ⁵**vibrate:** to move very quickly from side to side or up and down

7. I _____ for employment until I _____
      (not / look)   (graduate)
   from college.   ☐   ☐

8. We _____ good jobs unless we _____ new skills. ☐   ☐
      (not / get)   (learn)

9. I _____ to get some work experience while I   ☐   ☐
      (try)
   _____ in school.
      (be)

10. I _____ after I _____ my final exams.   ☐   ☐
       (travel)   (pass)

Talk about It Work with a partner. For each prediction in Activity 5, agree or disagree. For each plan, say true or false for you.

Write about It Rewrite each sentence in Activity 5 using a different main clause.

When the economy improves, people will start taking vacations overseas again.

6 | Noticing Adverb Clauses of Reason Underline the adverb clauses of reason. Then circle the subordinator in each clause. 6.2 C

Tips for Staying Healthy in Hot Weather

1. Avoid very cold drinks (as) they can cause stomach pain.
2. Don't assume the heat won't make you sick just because you never had a problem before.
3. Avoid high-protein foods since they increase body heat.
4. Don't exercise in very hot, humid weather. Your body will sweat because it is hot, but the sweat won't evaporate[6] because of the high humidity.

Tips for Staying Healthy in Cold Weather

5. Since you lose most of your body heat through your head, it's important to wear a hat in cold weather.
6. Wearing layers[7] of clothing helps keep you warm because your body heat gets trapped[8] between the layers.
7. Don't wear tight shoes or boots as they increase your chances of getting frostbite[9].
8. Be especially careful on cold, windy days because the wind can carry heat away from the body.

[6] **evaporate:** to change from a liquid into steam or gas and disappear
[7] **layers:** things that lie on other things or between other things

[8] **trapped:** caught or kept in place
[9] **frostbite:** an injury to the body caused by extreme cold

Think about It Which sentence in Activity 6 has a comma after the adverb clause? Why?

Talk about It Think of two to three more tips to add to each list in Activity 6. Explain them to a classmate.

7 | Identifying Subordinators Underline the subordinator in each adverb clause of reason. Then add a comma where necessary. `6.2 C`

MODERN LIVING

1. <u>Because</u> the cost of living has gone up, many people are working longer hours.
2. More people are working during their vacations now that they have access to the Internet.
3. Since more people are watching TV the programs are getting better.
4. It's easier to do research now because there is so much information on the Internet.
5. Now that people can do research on the Internet they don't go to the library as often.
6. People are driving less now that the price of gasoline has gone up.
7. Because there are so many cars on the road driving has become more dangerous.
8. There is no real need to go shopping in stores as one can buy almost anything online.
9. Since it's easy to travel almost anywhere in the world there are few unspoiled places left.
10. Now that smoking is illegal in many public places more people will probably quit smoking.
11. Since fewer people are smoking deaths from lung cancer should go down.
12. Because people are living longer it's even more important for them to have health insurance.

> **RESEARCH SAYS...**
>
> The subordinator *as* sounds more formal and is used less often to introduce a reason.

Talk about It Does each sentence above describe a positive result or a negative result? Why do you think so? Share ideas with your classmates.

Write about It Rewrite each sentence above using a different main clause.

1. Because the cost of living has gone up, fewer people are traveling overseas.

Write about It Write three of your own opinions about modern living. Use *because, since, as,* or *now that*.

8 | Usage Note: *Since* and *As* Read the note. Then do Activity 9.

Some subordinators have more than one meaning: they can be used to introduce different types of adverb clauses. For example, *as* and *since* can be used to begin a time clause or a reason clause.

ADVERB CLAUSES OF TIME	ADVERB CLAUSES OF REASON
1 I've known him **since I was a child***.	**3** **Since no one is using this room**, I'm going to use it.
2 She called just **as I was leaving**.	**4** **As the president couldn't be here today**, the vice president has come instead.

* When we use *since* in a time clause, the verb must always refer to an earlier time (present perfect, simple past, past perfect, etc.).

9 | Adverb Clause of Time or Reason? Underline the adverb clauses with *as* or *since*. Then identify each adverb clause as a time clause or a reason clause. Check (✓) your answers. `6.2 A–C`

Statements from Professors

	TIME CLAUSE	REASON CLAUSE
1. "If you look at the course syllabus[10], you'll notice that I've marked three items in blue. These are the things I'm going to emphasize <u>as we go through the course</u>."	✓	☐
2. "I'd like to show you some pictures of the poet T. S. Eliot since I'm going to be talking about him in today's lecture."	☐	☐
3. "As I was reading through your papers, I noticed that some of you had trouble understanding a few of the concepts we discussed last week."	☐	☐
4. "There are several things you need to remember as we move forward in our study of basic chemistry. I'm going to post these online for you to refer to."	☐	☐
5. "I'm going to read the poem to you in class since some of you weren't able to get the packet of class materials from the bookstore."	☐	☐
6. "As the semester goes on, I'll go into more detail about different styles of architecture[11]."	☐	☐
7. "There have been several new developments in the field since we last met, and I'll be discussing these over the next few weeks."	☐	☐
8. "I can't tell you exactly when the final exam will be since the department hasn't made the schedule yet. But I'll let you know soon."	☐	☐
9. "Since I published my research paper on animal extinction[12], there's been a lot of interest in the subject."	☐	☐
10. "As none of you will be here next semester, we'll end this course with a review of European economics."	☐	☐

Think about It In which sentences above can you use a different subordinator? Which subordinator would you use?

These are the things I'm going to emphasize while we go through the course.

10 | Exploring Ways to Give Reasons Rewrite sentences 1–8 using an adverb clause of reason. Then complete sentences 9–12 with your own ideas. Pay close attention to the time frame and verb forms you use. `6.2 D`

GOOD EXCUSES/BAD EXCUSES

1. We couldn't understand him because of his strong accent.

   We couldn't understand him because he had a strong accent.

2. My brother's car broke down, so he missed his flight.

3. I couldn't get to class because of the bad weather.

4. I didn't exercise because of the heat.

---

[10]**syllabus:** a list of all the things that you must study in a class
[11]**architecture:** the study of designing and making buildings

[12]**extinction:** the disappearance of a type of plant or animal (it no longer exists)

5. I don't have any money, so I can't go out this weekend.

6. I don't have a computer, so I can't email my family.

7. I couldn't go away for the weekend. I had to work.

8. We don't see her very often because of her job.

9. I couldn't do my homework because of _____

_____.

10. I _____,

so I couldn't do my homework.

11. I couldn't come to class last week. _____

_____

12. I _____,

so I had to stay home.

Talk about It Share some of your ideas from sentences 9–12 in Activity 10 with your classmates. Ask your classmates to say if they are good or bad excuses.

11 | Error Correction Correct any errors in these sentences. (Some sentences may not have any errors.)

1. It's hard to compare schools in the United States and Mexico. Because my country has a different educational system.

2. I did not do very well on the examination because of I did not read the instructions carefully.

3. Since you weren't here yesterday you didn't get the assignment.

4. I couldn't sleep last night because I worry about the test.

5. Now that I have some money I'm going to take a vacation.

6. When I arrived here, I was happy because my sister was here and I hadn't seen her in a long time. At the same time, I was sad because I left my friends behind and I knew I will miss them.

7. I'm proud of myself because now I could communicate with people in English, I have a good job, and I'm going to start college soon.

8. My parents always encouraged me to make my own decisions. This was very important to me. Because made me trust myself.

9. I thought my parents would come here until the day my father call me.

10. After I left my country, I moved to Germany. While I living there, I studied at a university.

11. I want to go back home as long as I can.

12. When I will get older I will look back at this time and laugh.

13. After finished eating, they went to the bride's house.

14. At noon all my friends arrived, as soon as they arrived, they started to decorate my apartment, they finished at 5:00.

15. Because my country, Cambodia, has a very different educational system.

6.3 Adverb Clauses of Contrast

An **adverb clause of contrast** adds unexpected, surprising, or contrasting information to a main clause, as in **1 – 2**.

A

main clause   adverb clause

1 | My grandfather still works | **even though he's in his eighties.** | (= unexpected or surprising information)

adverb clause   main clause

2 | Though cell phones have solved some problems, | they have created many others. | (= contrasting information)

B

SHOWING CONTRAST

3 **Although she's been teaching for ten years,** she still feels nervous at the beginning of the school year.
(= She's been teaching for ten years, but she still feels . . .)

4 **Though she said she wanted to help,** she didn't do anything. (= She said she wanted to help, but she . . .)

5 He wouldn't eat anything **even though he was hungry.**
(= He was hungry but he wouldn't eat anything.)

Adverb clauses of contrast often begin with the subordinator *although*, *though*, or *even though*, as in **3 – 5**. These subordinators usually include a meaning of concession or "but . . ."

Although, *though*, and *even though* are similar in meaning. However:
- *although* is more formal
- *even though* expresses a stronger contrast or emphasis

C

CONTRASTING ASPECTS OF THE SAME THING

6 **While smokeless tobacco may be safer than cigarettes,** it is not safe enough. (= Smokeless tobacco may be safer than cigarettes, but it is not safe enough.)

7 **While a college education is useful,** it doesn't guarantee a job after graduation. (= A college education is useful but it doesn't guarantee a job.)

CONTRASTING TWO DIFFERENT THINGS

8 Hawaii is warm **while Alaska is cold.**

9 My mother was an artist and very high-strung **while my father was quite calm.**

We can also use *while* to introduce an adverb clause of contrast.

- When we use *while* to contrast two aspects of the same thing, it usually includes a meaning of concession or "but . . ." as in **6 – 7**. With this use of *while*, the adverb clause usually comes before the main clause.

- We can also use *while* to make a direct contrast between two different things, as in **8 – 9**. With this use of *while*, the adverb clause usually comes after the main clause.

D

COMPARE: OTHER WAYS TO SHOW CONTRAST

independent clause + *but* + independent clause

10 My grandfather is in his eighties, but he still works. (*but* = conjunction)

11 Cell phones have solved some problems, but they have created many others.

despite + noun phrase

12 Despite **his age**, he has never had a job. (*despite* = preposition)

13 Despite **being hungry**, he wouldn't eat anything.

in spite of + noun phrase

14 In spite of **his age**, he has never worked. (*in spite of* = preposition)

ADVERB CLAUSES   **183**

12 | Noticing Adverb Clauses of Contrast Match the questions with the answers. Then underline each adverb clause of contrast and circle the subordinator. 6.3 A–B

FACTS ABOUT HISTORICAL PEOPLE

Questions

1. What university did George Washington attend? _d_
2. How many children did Washington have? ____
3. Did George Washington wear a wig[13]? ____
4. Is he buried[14] under the U.S. Capitol? ____

George Washington,
first president of the U.S.

1. Did Christopher Columbus discover America? ____
2. Where was Columbus trying to go in 1502? ____
3. Did Columbus sail in very large ships? ____
4. Was Christopher Columbus married? ____

Christopher Columbus,
Italian explorer

1. What did Mozart call himself? ____
2. Was Mozart very rich? ____
3. What sort of music did Mozart compose[15]? ____
4. How old was he when he began to compose? ____

Wolfgang Amadeus Mozart,
Austrian composer

Answers

a. No, he didn't. Even though wigs were fashionable, Washington didn't wear one. Instead, he powdered his hair.

b. None. George Washington had no children of his own although he helped raise two of his wife's children from her first marriage.

c. No, he isn't. Although Congress built a room under the Capitol Building for this purpose, Washington is not buried in it.

d. He did not attend college. Although Washington believed strongly in formal education, the death of his father ended his formal schooling.

a. Yes, he was. Although no one writes about her often, Columbus had a wife named Filipa Perestrelo, a Portuguese lady. Their wedding was on the Portuguese island of Porto Santo in 1479.

b. No, he didn't. Columbus's biggest ship, the *Santa Maria*, sailed across the Atlantic Ocean even though it was only 70 feet long and not designed for exploration.

c. In 1502, Columbus sailed to America for the fourth time and explored Central America though he was still hoping to land in China!

d. Although people have said Columbus discovered America, this isn't in fact true. There were many people living there already, but of course, Columbus didn't know that.

a. Even though it's hard to believe, Mozart was only eight years old when he composed his first symphony.

b. No, he wasn't. Although he was very famous, Mozart was extremely poor when he died in 1791. His grave[16] didn't even have a stone on it.

c. Though Mozart is often remembered for writing cheerful music and funny operas, not all his music was happy. He also wrote serious music and even funeral music.

d. Mozart's official name was Joannes Chrysostomus Wolfgangus Theophilus although he called himself Gottlieb until 1769. Then he began to call himself Amadeo.

[13] **wig:** a covering for your head made of hair that is not your own
[14] **bury:** to put a dead body in the ground

[15] **compose:** to write something, especially music
[16] **grave:** a hole in the ground where a dead person's body is buried

Think about It Look at the sentences with adverb clauses of contrast in Activity 12. What verb forms does the writer use in the main clause and the adverb clause of each?

Talk about It What was the most surprising thing you learned about each person? Tell a partner.

13 | Using Adverb Clauses of Contrast Add unexpected or surprising information to these sentences. (Many different answers are possible.) `6.3 A–B`

1. I got up early this morning even though _____.

2. Although _____,
   I drank several cups of it.

3. Although _____,
   I usually take the bus.

4. Although _____,
   I still got to work on time.

5. I worked all day even though _____.

6. I didn't eat lunch even though _____.

7. Although _____, I stayed up late watching TV.

8. Though it seemed like a bad idea, I _____.

9. I never learned to drive a car even though _____.

10. _____ though I had plenty of time.

> **FYI**
>
> In a sentence with an adverb clause of contrast, we sometimes use the word still in the main clause to add emphasis.
>
> Even though she's 24, she **still** acts like a child.

Talk about It Share one of the sentences you completed above with your classmates. Think of different ways to complete the sentence.

"I got up early this morning even though it was a holiday."

14 | Using *While* in Contrast Clauses Complete these sentences to make a contrast between the adverb clause and the main clause. (Many different answers are possible.) `6.3 C`

Opinions about Television

1. While the number of programs on TV is increasing, _____
   _____.

2. While many parents don't want their children to watch a lot of TV,
   _____.

3. Some of the news programs on TV are OK while others _____
   _____.

4. Some people prefer news programs while others _____.

5. While many people admit that they watch too much TV, _____.

6. While TV is still a popular source of news, _____.

7. While TV _____, it can also be harmful for children.

8. While many TV channels show only sports programs, _____.

Think about It Which of the sentences you completed in Activity 14 use *while* to contrast two aspects of the same thing? Which make a direct contrast between two different things?

Talk about It Read your opinions from Activity 14 to a classmate. Ask your classmate to agree or disagree.

15 | Usage Note: *While* Read the note. Then do Activity 16.

We can use *while* to introduce a contrast clause or a time clause. In a contrast clause, *while* is similar in meaning to *although*. In a time clause, *while* is similar in meaning to *during the time that*.

1 Why are some people afraid of snakes **while others aren't**? (contrast clause)
2 A fire broke out **while people were still in the building**. (time clause)

Sometimes the word *while* could have either meaning.

3 While I do the dishes, he does the laundry. (contrast clause or time clause?)

16 | Understanding Clauses with *While* Underline the adverb clauses in these sentences. Then decide if the subordinator *while* introduces a contrast clause or a time clause. Check (✓) your answers. 6.3 C

	CONTRAST CLAUSE	TIME CLAUSE
1. <u>While this disease can be deadly in humans and animals</u>, it is treatable.	✓	☐
2. While people are being treated for the disease, they need constant care.	☐	☐
3. While animals can get this disease, people cannot.	☐	☐
4. While the river is being cleaned up, swimming will not be allowed.	☐	☐
5. While the river is being cleaned up, the surrounding area is not.	☐	☐
6. While it would be wonderful to clean up the river, it is unlikely to happen.	☐	☐
7. We couldn't see or hear anything while we were swimming across the river.	☐	☐
8. While it can be challenging to swim across the river, it can be done.	☐	☐
9. Several protestors had to be taken from the room while the president was giving her speech.	☐	☐
10. While the president's speech was informative, she didn't address several important issues.	☐	☐
11. While it would be nice to think that we don't need this law, we do.	☐	☐
12. The crime rate went down while the law was in effect.	☐	☐
13. While the law was effective, it was very unpopular.	☐	☐

🔊 17 | Pronunciation Note: Contrasting Information Listen to the note. Then do Activity 18.

In sentences with adverb clauses of contrast, we may sometimes stress the information (or words) that we are contrasting.

1 He went to WORK even though he had been SICK all night.
2 Even though most people here speak SPANISH, I want to practice speaking ENGLISH.
3 While this book was written for CHILDREN, ANYONE can enjoy it.

18 | Noticing Contrasting Words Listen and underline the contrasting words. Then listen again and repeat the sentences. `6.3 A–C`

1. Even though she's <u>older</u>, she's not really any <u>wiser</u>.
2. While it may help to take vitamins, it's not absolutely necessary.
3. Someday I may want to move although I doubt it.
4. Even though I can understand Spanish, I can't speak it.
5. He was kind to me even though I didn't deserve it.
6. I live a quiet life although I'm really a city person.
7. I respect your decision even though I don't like it.
8. Although I disagree with many of the changes, I'm willing to try them out.
9. Even though I dislike politics, I think it's important to vote.
10. While solar panels[17] are a good source of energy, they're very ugly.
11. Although I don't like loud music, I love listening to modern jazz.
12. I rarely get any exercise even though I know I should.

> **RESEARCH SAYS...**
>
> Clauses with *although* and *(even) though* come more often at the beginning of a sentence.
>
> CORPUS

Talk about It Look back at Activities 13 and 14. Practice reading some of your sentences to a partner using stress to show the contrasting information.

19 | Exploring Different Ways to Contrast Ideas Rewrite each sentence using the **bold** subordinator. `6.3 D`

1. Bamboo looks like a tree, but it is actually a grass.

   Despite _____ *looking like a tree, bamboo is actually a grass* _____.

2. Most people think water always boils at 212 degrees Fahrenheit, but this only happens at sea level.

   While _____

   _____.

3. Some bacteria are harmful, but the vast majority of bacteria are harmless.

   Although _____.

4. Some deserts are hot, dry places; others are cold and ice-covered.

   While _____.

5. Despite the earth's being slightly flat at the poles, we say it is round.

   Even though _____.

6. Despite looking like a tree, the banana plant is actually a very large herb.

   Although _____.

7. In spite of the distractions, the researchers were able to focus on their work.

   Even though _____.

8. Despite being extremely small, ants are very strong insects.

   While _____.

Think about It How else could you rewrite each sentence above? Compare ideas with your classmates.

---

[17] **solar panels:** groups of solar cells that collect radiation from the sun, used to produce electricity

20 | Error Correction Correct any errors in these sentences. (Some sentences may not have any errors.)

1. Although she is a good wife, we are a happy family.
2. I don't know much about U.S. history. Although I took several courses.
3. Even they look very different, they have similar personalities.
4. Even though I was a good student, but I couldn't get a scholarship.
5. Although I had heard that word many times, so it sounded strange to me.
6. Although it was an old car, it didn't run very well.
7. He is very generous even though he doesn't have much money he gives everything to his friends.
8. My family lives in a small house near Seattle, Washington. Despite the only three rooms that the house has, we never feel crowded.

6.4 Adverb Clauses of Manner

A

1 She called me last night **as she always does.**

2 I prefer to leave things **as they are.**

3 **As I said at the last meeting,** I expect to finish this task by the end of next month.

MANNER VS. TIME VS. REASON CLAUSES WITH *AS*

4 Please carry the box **as I showed you.** (manner)

5 **As we were driving home,** there was a huge storm. (time)

6 We stopped at a gas station **as we were running out of fuel.** (reason)

An **adverb clause of manner** answers the question *how* or *in what way*. Adverb clauses of manner begin with the subordinator *as*. In these clauses, *as* means "in the same way that," as in **1 – 3**.

WARNING! We can use the subordinator *as* to begin an adverb clause of manner, time, or reason, as in **4 – 6**.

B

USING *AS THOUGH* AND *AS IF*

7 He **looks as though he needs to sit down.**
(Based on looking at him, I think this.)

8 It **doesn't sound as if Jim is going to get the job.**
(Based on the things I've heard, I believe this.)

9 She **feels as though she is being punished.**
(Based on her experience, this is her feeling.)

We can use adverb clauses beginning with *as though* or *as if* after a linking verb like *look*, *sound*, or *feel*, as in **7 – 9**.

We use these adverb clauses to say how we imagine something or how someone seems to be.

GO ONLINE

---

21 | Distinguishing Types of Adverb Clauses Underline the adverb clauses. Then decide how each adverb clause is used. Check (✓) *Manner*, *Reason*, or *Time*. 6.4 A

	MANNER HOW?	REASON WHY?	TIME WHEN?
1. My mother runs her house <u>as you would run a hotel</u>.	✓	☐	☐
2. My sister always gets up just as the coffee is ready.	☐	☐	☐
3. My father has a good pension as he worked many years for the government.	☐	☐	☐
4. He recited the poem perfectly as he always does.	☐	☐	☐
5. She raised herself on her elbows as she stared into the night.	☐	☐	☐
6. As I have said before, I'll be leaving early tonight.	☐	☐	☐
7. She dragged her feet as she made her way out of the house.	☐	☐	☐
8. He is in great demand as he is a good speaker.	☐	☐	☐

	MANNER HOW?	REASON WHY?	TIME WHEN?
9. The event was a failure as only 20 people came.	☐	☐	☐
10. The hotel was not a depressing place as I had imagined it.	☐	☐	☐
11. People stood and applauded as the parade went by.	☐	☐	☐
12. She looked down as her mother kissed her goodbye.	☐	☐	☐
13. As the musicians were late, there was no entertainment for the first hour.	☐	☐	☐
14. He's taking a nap as he always does in the afternoon.	☐	☐	☐
15. That's a picture of me as I used to look.	☐	☐	☐
16. As she opened the door, she heard a sharp crack.	☐	☐	☐

22 | Using Adverb Clauses of Manner Write a sentence about the people in each picture below. Use *as though/as if* and ideas from the box. (More than one answer may be possible.) Then compare with a partner. **6.4 B**

In picture 1, the woman looks as though she is in a hurry.

confused about something	going to have a good time	has a lot to do	really surprised
feel pretty cold	happy to be there	in a hurry	very relaxed

Talk about It Think of another sentence for each picture above using *as though/as if*. Share your ideas with classmates.

6.5 Adverb Clauses of Purpose and Result

<table>
<tr><td>A</td><td>

ADVERB CLAUSES OF PURPOSE

1 Cover it with glass **so that the contents are visible.**

2 It's important to keep the cables vertical **so you know where they are.**

3 We took a map **so we wouldn't get lost.**

</td><td>

An adverb clause of purpose answers the question *for what purpose* or *why.* Purpose clauses often begin with *so that,* as in **1**. The word *that* is often omitted, as in **2 – 3**.

We often use the modals *can, may,* and *will / would* in purpose clauses, as in **3**.

</td></tr>
<tr><td>B</td><td>

ADVERB CLAUSES OF RESULT

4 He talked **so fast** that I couldn't understand him.

5 I met **so many people** that I'll never remember all their names.

6 I ate **so much food** that it made me sick.

7 She is such a **generous person** that she always agrees to everything we ask for.
(NOT: ~~a such generous person~~)

8 The birds flew in such **large numbers** that the sky became dark.

9 That's such **good advice** that I should pay you for it.

10 I'm so **happy** I could cry.

</td><td>

An **adverb clause of result** shows the result of something in the main clause, as in **4 – 10**. The main clause usually includes *so* or *such;* the result clause usually begins with the connecting word *that.* Clauses of result almost always come after the main clause.

There are a number of ways to signal in the main clause that an adverb clause of result follows:

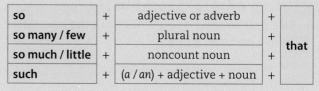

so	+	adjective or adverb	+	
so many / few	+	plural noun	+	**that**
so much / little	+	noncount noun	+	
such	+	(*a / an*) + adjective + noun	+	

The word *that* is often omitted when the meaning of the sentence is clear, as in **10**.

</td></tr>
</table>

23 | Using Adverb Clauses of Purpose Choose an adverb clause from this box to complete each sentence below. `6.5 A`

so that you don't spread germs	so that you don't have health problems later	so that you lose weight
so that you feel less stressed	so you catch any health problems early	so you don't get a sunburn
so you don't get dehydrated	so you don't have too much to do at once	so you don't get cavities
so it doesn't become infected	so you feel rested when you wake up	so you raise your heart rate

Health Advice

1. You should always wash a cut _____ *so it doesn't become infected* _____.

2. It's a good idea to wash your hands frequently _____.

3. Drink plenty of water _____.

4. You should exercise energetically _____.

5. You should cover your skin when you are in direct sunlight _____.

6. Quit smoking _____.

7. Brush your teeth twice a day _____.

8. Get an annual checkup _____.

9. Eat more fruit and vegetables _____.

10. Do small tasks immediately _____.

11. Try yoga or meditation _____.

12. Aim for seven hours of sleep _____.

24 | Understanding Adverb Clauses of Result
Match each main clause with an adverb clause of result. (More than one answer may be possible, but only one is correct.) **6.5 B**

DESCRIPTIONS FROM FICTION

Main clause

1. She was **so beautiful** _d_
2. He was **so funny** ____
3. He'd been **so busy** ____
4. The pain was **so strong** ____
5. He had gained **so much weight** ____
6. She sounded like **such a fascinating person** ____
7. Joe let him go, pushing him back **so hard** ____
8. He looked at me with **such sad eyes** ____

Adverb clause of result

a. **that** no one recognized him.
b. **that** I wanted to cry.
c. **that** I couldn't stop laughing.
d. **that** he couldn't find the words to describe her.
e. **that** he'd completely forgotten to call her.
f. **that** he almost fell.
g. **that** I wanted to meet her.
h. **that** she nearly fainted.

Think about It Write the **bold** words above in this list.

1. *So* + adjective + *that*: _so beautiful that_ _____
2. *So* + adverb + *that*: _____
3. *So much* + noncount noun + *that*: _____
4. *Such* + adjective + plural noun + *that*: _____
5. *Such* + *a/an* + adjective + singular noun + *that*: _____

Think about It Circle the word that best completes each sentence.

1. We **can** / **can't** use *so* before a singular noun.
2. We **can** / **can't** use *such* before an adjective or adverb alone.
3. We **can** / **can't** use *such* before *a/an* + an adjective + a singular noun.

Write about It Think of a different adverb clause of result for each main clause above.

She was so beautiful that people often stared at her.

25 | Using Adverb Clauses of Result
Rewrite these sentences with *so* or *such*. **6.5 B**

1. I'm studying very hard. I'm sure to do well in this course.

   I'm studying so hard that I'm sure to do well in this course.

2. She has a strong accent. I can hardly understand her.
3. I have very little money. I can't afford to buy a car.
4. He was feeling quite ill. He went home.
5. She takes good care of her car. It looks new.
6. He was very grateful. He couldn't stop thanking me.
7. The flowers in the garden were pretty. I wanted to pick them.
8. It happened a long time ago. She can't remember the details.
9. I was late for class. I took a taxi.
10. It was a beautiful day. I didn't want to think about my problems.

Good Design

<u>When digital audio players (DAPs) first appeared in the 1990s</u>, they weren't very popular. In 2000, Apple realized that customers were not interested in DAPs because the players weren't designed well. Apple soon developed a new product: the iPod. It was attractive and had a fast computer connection so that songs could quickly transfer from a computer to the player. Since Apple released the first iPod in 2001, it has released many different versions. Most iPods now have touch screens to play videos. Others are so small that they can fit in your hand. Apple has also developed similar products, such as the iPhone and the iPad. Because of their excellent design, these products are some of the most popular devices for mobile communication and entertainment.

1. How many adverb clauses did you find in the paragraph above?
2. How many of these adverb clauses show the result of something in the main clause?
3. How many of these adverb clauses show the purpose for something?
4. What other expression in the paragraph shows the purpose for something? Circle it.
5. How is the Apple iPod different from earlier digital music players?

6.6 Reduced Adverb Clauses of Time and Contrast

A

COMPARE FULL AND REDUCED ADVERB CLAUSES

same subjects

1a Although **the house** is small, **it** has lots of closets.
1b Although **small,** the house has lots of closets.

different subjects

2 Although **the house** is small, **I** still like it.
(NOT: ~~Although small, I still like it.~~)

We can sometimes shorten an adverb clause of time or contrast when the subject of the adverb clause and the subject of the main clause are the same, as in **1a**. We call this a **reduced adverb clause**, as in **1b**.

When the subjects are different, the adverb clause cannot be reduced, as in **2**.

B

REDUCED ADVERB CLAUSES WITH THE VERB *BE*

3a While I **was** in school, I played a lot of football.
3b While **in school,** I played a lot of football.

4a Although my father **was** bothered by the news, he did his best to ignore it.
4b Although **bothered by the news,** my father did his best to ignore it.

5a When you**'re** looking for a job, you should be sure to keep your resume up to date.
5b When **looking for a job,** you should be sure to keep your resume up to date.

REDUCED ADVERB CLAUSES WITH OTHER VERBS

6a The train stopped several times before it finally **arrived.**
6b The train stopped several times **before finally arriving.**

7a Since David **graduated** from college, he's worked in three different banks.
7b Since **graduating from college,** David has worked in three different banks.

The way we reduce an adverb clause depends on the verb in the clause:

- When the adverb clause has a form of the verb *be* (as a helping verb or a main verb), we drop the subject and the form of the verb *be*, as in **3 – 5**.

- When the adverb clause has a verb other than *be*, we drop the subject and any helping verb, and we use the *-ing* form of the main verb, as in **6 – 7**.

WARNING! When you use a reduced adverb clause, make sure the subject in the main clause is clear, as in **4b** and **7b**.

We use these subordinators in reduced adverb clauses:

after	when	since	although
before	while		though

27 | Analyzing Reduced Clauses of Time and Contrast Underline the subject in each main clause and each adverb clause. Then check (✓) the adverb clauses you can reduce. 6.6 A–B

1. ☑ Although <u>my sister</u> was tired, <u>she</u> refused to stop working.
2. ☐ Lots of people listen to the radio while they are driving.
3. ☐ They left the room before we announced the good news.
4. ☐ Brothers and sisters share a lot of experiences while they are growing up.
5. ☐ I always feel good after I exercise outdoors.
6. ☐ Although this method is complicated, it is highly reliable.
7. ☐ Although the directions were written simply, they were difficult to follow.
8. ☐ After the committee members discussed the issues, they made a final decision.
9. ☐ Although the engine was new, we couldn't get it started.
10. ☐ Although this issue is important, we aren't ready to make a decision.
11. ☐ Though the findings are based on only a few studies, they are very promising.
12. ☐ You should think about your career goals before you apply to a college or university.
13. ☐ Since Joe and I started to eat more healthily, we've both felt fitter[18] and better.
14. ☐ We aren't allowed to use our cell phones while we are at work.
15. ☐ When I think about the future, I see myself changing careers completely.

Write about It Rewrite the sentences you checked above using a reduced adverb clause. Change pronoun subjects to full noun subjects if necessary.

1. Although tired, my sister refused to stop working.

28 | Using Reduced Clauses Underline the subject in each main clause and adverb clause. (If the clause uses an imperative, write *you*.) Where possible, rewrite each sentence using a reduced adverb clause. 6.6 A–B

TRAVEL ADVICE

1. When <u>you</u> travel with children, <u>you</u> should carry plenty of water and snacks.

   When traveling with children, you should carry plenty of water and snacks.

2. When you pack your suitcase, you should roll your clothes instead of folding them.
3. When you carry your own luggage on an airplane, it is less likely to get lost.
4. Although checked luggage rarely gets lost, you should put extra clothes in your carry-on luggage.
5. Make sure your flight is on time before you leave for the airport.
6. When you go through airport security, take your computer out of your carry-on bag.
7. Most passengers have to take off their shoes when they go through airport security.
8. When people are on an airplane for a long time, they should do foot and leg exercises.
9. You have to have a passport when you travel to a foreign country.
10. When you visit a foreign country, follow the customs of that country.
11. Hotel rates are often cheaper when you travel with a large group of people.
12. Take a small dictionary with you when you are traveling to a foreign country.

> **F Y I**
>
> The subject of an imperative statement is always *you*. Notice how we can reduce adverb clauses when the main clause is an imperative.
>
> (**You**) Don't forget to make a hotel reservation before **you** leave home.
>
> Don't forget to make a hotel reservation **before leaving home**.

Write about It Write your own travel advice using reduced clauses.

[18]**fitter:** healthier or stronger

6.7 Conditional Adverb Clauses (Real Conditionals)

A

	condition	result
1	If I'm not too tired,	(then) I usually go out in the evening.

	condition	result
2	If you mix red, green, and blue light,	you get white light.

	result	condition
3	I can come over	if you need some help.

A **conditional adverb clause** shows what must happen first (the condition) so that another thing (the result) can happen, as in **1 – 3**.

A conditional clause:
- usually begins with the subordinator *if*
- can come before or after the main clause

B

PRESENT REAL CONDITIONALS

4 If eggs aren't properly cooked, they can make you sick.

5 If we want to go downtown, we usually take the bus.

6 If you don't know the meaning of a word, look it up in your dictionary.

PAST REAL CONDITIONALS

7 When I was a child, if my father wasn't working, we usually did something outdoors.

8 Our teachers were very strict. If you didn't do all your homework, you failed the course.

We often use conditional adverb clauses to talk about real situations or events. These could be:
- facts or general truths, as in **4**
- events that happen regularly, as in **5**
- commands or advice, as in **6**
- events that happened regularly in the past, as in **7 – 8**

In these clauses, it is possible to use *when* or *whenever* in place of *if*.

GRAMMAR TERM: The present and past real conditionals are sometimes called the **zero conditional**.

C

FUTURE REAL CONDITIONALS

9 If he's had a bad day, he probably **won't come** over.

10 This hypothesis **will need** to be tested to determine if it is accurate.

11 If I can get home early, I **will call** you.

12 We **might cancel** the meeting if they **can't come.**

13 If you need some help tomorrow, **call** me.

14 If I take two classes next summer, I'll graduate early.
(NOT: ~~If I will take two classes next summer, I'll graduate early.~~)

We sometimes use a conditional adverb clause when we make a prediction or talk about future events. In these sentences, we usually use a present verb form in the *if-* clause, as in **9 – 14**.

IF- CLAUSE	RESULT (MAIN) CLAUSE
present verb form *can* + base form *must* + base form	modal + base form imperative

Notice that we use a present form in the *if-* clause even when it has a future time expression, as in **14**.

GRAMMAR TERMS: This use of the future real conditional is sometimes called the **future-possible conditional** or **first conditional**.

29 | Noticing Conditional Clauses Underline the conditional clauses in this article. Then write each conditional and result clause under the correct group in the chart on page 195. **6.7 A**

Five Warning Signs You're Headed Toward Credit Card Debt[19]

1. **You skip[20] one credit card bill to pay another.**
   Skipping payment of one credit card bill to pay another is unwise. <u>If you usually find yourself unable to make your credit card payments</u>, you are already in trouble.

---

[19] **debt:** money you must pay back to someone   [20] **skip:** to not do something that you should do

2. **You charge more than you pay.**
   Imagine trying to fill a hole while someone digs[21] out more dirt than you put in. The hole would never get filled, would it? It's the same with credit card debt. If you're charging more than you're paying, your debt will always continue to increase.

3. **You don't have a plan to pay off your credit card debt.**
   "Failing to plan is planning to fail." If you're not actively working to pay off your credit card bill, you could end up paying for years to come.
4. **You use credit to "afford" expensive items.**
   Credit cards trick us into thinking we can afford to buy more than we really can. You are endangering your future income if you're getting into debt to have a lifestyle you really can't afford.
5. **You have reached the limit on your credit cards.**
   If your credit cards are maxed out, you're not headed for credit card debt; you're already in it. What can you do? Make a decision to pay off your credit card debt and to make wiser choices when you use your credit cards in the future.

Condition	Result
you usually find yourself unable to make your credit card payments	*you are already in trouble*

30 | Using Conditionals to Talk about Real Situations Match each clause on the left with a clause on the right. `6.7 B`

LANGUAGES

1. Any language is in trouble __*d*__
2. If you can speak two languages fluently, ____
3. If my grandparents came to visit, ____
4. It's difficult to travel in a foreign country ____
5. If no one speaks a language anymore, ____
6. You have a better chance of getting a job ____
7. I can understand Chinese ____
8. In the past, children were punished ____
9. In Spanish, if you know how a word is spelled, ____
10. If you travel extensively, ____

a. if you can't speak the language.
b. the language has become extinct.
c. if you know more than one language.
d. if it is spoken by only a few people.
e. if they didn't speak the official language at school.
f. you are bilingual.
g. we spoke with them in Italian.
h. if people speak it slowly.
i. you probably know some basic words in many languages.
j. you almost always know how it is pronounced.

Think about It Which sentences above describe a fact or general truth? An event that happened regularly in the past?

[21] **dig:** to move earth by making a hole in the ground

31 | Using *If-* Clauses in Predictions Complete these predictions with the correct present or future form of the verbs in parentheses. Then check (✓) *Fact* or *Myth*. **6.7 C**

HOW MUCH DO YOU KNOW ABOUT HEALTH?

		FACT	MYTH

1. If you _____*cross*_____ your eyes, they _____*will stay*_____ that way. ☐ ✓
   (cross)   (stay)

2. If both parents _____ poor eyesight, their children will, too. ☐ ☐
   (have)

3. If you _____ a lot of carrots, you _____ good eyesight. ☐ ☐
   (eat)   (have)

4. If both parents _____ blue eyes, they usually _____ ☐ ☐
   (have)   (not have)
   a child with brown eyes.

5. You _____ longer if you _____ frequently. ☐ ☐
   (live)   (exercise)

6. You _____ a cold if you _____ outside in cold weather ☐ ☐
   (catch)   (go)
   with a wet head.

7. You _____ smarter if you _____ a lot of fish. ☐ ☐
   (get)   (eat)

8. You _____ if you _____ swimming after a big meal. ☐ ☐
   (drown²²)   (go)

9. Your heart rate _____ if you _____ smoking. ☐ ☐
   (decrease)   (quit)

10. If you _____ deeply, you _____ calmer. ☐ ☐
    (breathe)   (feel)

Talk about It Discuss your answers above with a partner. Do you know other health myths or facts?

32 | Usage Note: *Unless* Read the note. Then do Activity 33.

> We sometimes use the subordinator **unless** to begin an adverb clause of condition. *Unless* is similar in meaning to *except if*, as in **1a – 3a**. We can sometimes replace *unless* with *if + not* in these sentences, as in **1b – 3b**.
>
> **1a** You shouldn't make personal phone calls from work **unless** it is an emergency.
>   (= You shouldn't make personal phone calls from work except if it is an emergency.)
> **1b** You shouldn't make personal phone calls from work **if** it **isn't** an emergency.
>
> **2a** She isn't happy **unless** she's working.   **3a** I won't go **unless** you go.
> **2b** She isn't happy **if** she **isn't** working.   **3b** I won't go **if** you **don't** go.

33 | *Unless* or *If*? Complete these sentences with *unless* or *if*. **6.7 B–C**

1. Generally I can sleep anytime, anywhere, anyplace, _____*unless*_____ I'm anxious about work.
   (Natalie Imbruglia, singer)

2. _____ you dream it, you can do it. *(Walt Disney, entrepreneur)*

3. Fishing is boring _____ you catch an actual fish, and then (if you do) it is disgusting.
   (Dave Barry, humorist)

4. _____ you can't explain it simply, you don't understand it well enough. *(Albert Einstein, physicist)*

5. You can't push anyone up the ladder _____ he is willing to climb. *(Dale Carnegie, writer)*

6. Mistakes are always forgivable _____ one has the courage to admit them. *(Bruce Lee, martial artist)*

7. _____ you don't practice, you don't deserve to win. *(Andre Agassi, tennis player)*

²² **drown:** to die underwater because you cannot breathe

8. _____ we remember, we cannot understand. *(E. M. Forster, writer)*

9. You may be deceived _____ you trust too much. *(Frank Crane, writer)*

10. Nothing will work _____ you do. *(Maya Angelou, writer)*

Write about It Look at the sentences in Activity 33 that use *unless*. Rewrite them using *if* + *not*.

Generally I can sleep anytime, anywhere, anyplace, if I'm not anxious about work.

6.8 Conditional Adverb Clauses (Unreal Conditionals)

A

1 It's too bad that my brothers are away. **If they were here,** I know they would help me. (They aren't here.)

2 You'd feel better **if you exercised.** (You don't exercise.)

3 I wouldn't have met my wife **if I had moved to London.** (I didn't move to London.)

4 **If you had studied harder,** you would have passed the test. (You didn't study hard enough.)

5 **If there were no air,** sound could not travel.
(There is air.)

We can use some **conditional adverb clauses** to describe unreal, imaginary, unlikely, or impossible situations, as in **1 – 5**. We might use an unreal conditional:

• when we wish the situation were true, as in **1**

• to give advice, as in **2**

• to express cause and effect, as in **3**

• to criticize, as in **4**

• to give surprising information, as in **5**

GRAMMAR TERM: This use of the unreal conditional is sometimes called the **third conditional**.

B

PRESENT UNREAL CONDITIONALS

6 If it **weren't raining, I'd go** for a walk. (= It is raining.)

7 If my sister **were** here now, she **would know** what to do. (= She's not here now.)

8 If I **didn't have to work** today, I **could go** hiking.
(= I do have to work today.)

9 If I **could do** anything I wanted, I'd **move** to Japan.

FUTURE UNREAL CONDITIONALS

10 If I **had** time next month, I'd **go** to Hawaii.
(= I don't have time next month.)

11 If I **had to work** next week, I **wouldn't be able to go** with you. (= I don't have to work next week.)

To show that we are talking about an unreal or imaginary situation, we use special verb forms.

When both the condition and the result refer to a present or future time frame, as in **6 – 11**, we use:

UNREAL CONDITION IN PRESENT OR FUTURE	UNREAL RESULT IN PRESENT OR FUTURE
if + a past verb form	*would* + base form
	could + base form

WARNING! When we use the verb *be* in the *if-* clause, we usually use *were* instead of *was*, as in **6 – 7**.

PAST UNREAL CONDITIONALS

12 If I **hadn't eaten** earlier, I **would have gone** to lunch with you. (= I did eat earlier.)

13 If I **had had** any vacation days last month, I **could have gone** to Hawaii. (= I didn't have any vacation days last month.)

When both the condition and the result refer to past time, as in **12 – 13**, we use:

UNREAL CONDITION IN PAST	UNREAL RESULT IN PAST
if + a past perfect verb	*would have* + past participle
	could have + past participle

C

THE TWO CLAUSES REFER TO DIFFERENT TIME FRAMES

14 If we **had left** earlier, I **would be** home by now.
(unreal past condition + present result)

15 If he **hadn't been helping** me, I **would** still **be living** an hour away from school.
(unreal past condition + present result)

As with other adverb clauses, the time in an *if-* clause may be different from the time in a result clause, as in **14 – 15**.

GO ONLINE

34 | Identifying Uses of Unreal Conditionals Why did each speaker or writer below use an unreal conditional? Read the reasons in the box. Then write *a*, *b*, *c*, *d*, or *e*. (More than one answer may be possible.) `6.8 A`

> a. because the person wishes the situation were true
> b. to give advice
> c. to express cause and effect
> d. to criticize
> e. to give surprising information

1. If I had known you were coming, I would have cooked something special. _c/d_
2. If the ice at both the North and South Poles melted, the seas would rise by over 70 meters. ____
3. It would help if you wrote the instructions down. ____
4. If something happened to her, her parents would be devastated. ____
5. If there were no gravity, things would spin off the earth. ____
6. I'd laugh if I weren't so tired. ____
7. If you hadn't wasted so much time, you'd be finished by now. ____
8. If he had the skills to work, he would be able to find a job. ____
9. If you had listened to me, we wouldn't have gotten lost. ____
10. If she had known the ice was thin, she wouldn't have gone out on the lake. ____
11. If I had told you the truth, you wouldn't have believed me. ____
12. You would have been disappointed if I hadn't come. ____
13. If you got up earlier, you wouldn't be late. ____
14. I would go to the doctor more often if I had health insurance. ____
15. Your essay would be better if it had a more interesting introduction. ____

Think about It In each sentence above, what didn't happen or isn't true?

> *1. I didn't know you were coming.*

35 | Talking about Unreal Situations Match each clause on the left with a clause on the right. (More than one answer is possible.) Then circle the verbs in the main clause and the *if-* clause of each sentence. `6.8 B`

1. If I (won) a lot of money, _e_
2. If I were the leader of my country, ____
3. If everyone could speak the same language, ____
4. If there were fewer people in the world, ____
5. If I could choose my dream job, ____
6. If we were at the beach, ____
7. If you didn't have any water to drink, ____
8. If I had more free time, ____
9. If I could take tomorrow off, ____
10. If I had a good boss, ____

a. I would be the president of a company.
b. you probably wouldn't live for more than a few days.
c. we could go surfing.
d. my job would be great.
e. I (would share) it with my friends.
f. our cities wouldn't be so crowded.
g. we wouldn't need translators anymore.
h. I would learn a new sport.
i. I would change the tax system.
j. I would go for a long hike.

Think about It What verb forms are used in the *if-* clause and main clause of each sentence in Activity 35? What time frame is each sentence in?

Write about It Write new sentences using each *if-* clause in Activity 35. Use your own words to write a different main clause.

36 | Identifying the Time Frame
Underline the verb forms in the *if-* clause and main clause for each sentence. Then decide if each **bold** result clause describes an imaginary result in the *past*, *present*, or *future*. `6.8 B–C`

1. a. If we <u>hadn't learned</u> how to use electricity, **we <u>might still be using</u>** candles at night. ___*present*___

   b. If we hadn't learned how to use electricity, **computers couldn't have been invented.** _____

2. a. If I hadn't lost my job, **I would be able to afford a new car.** _____

   b. If I hadn't lost my job, **I wouldn't be able to travel with my family next week.** _____

3. a. If he hadn't been wearing his seat belt, **he wouldn't have survived the crash.** _____

   b. If he hadn't been wearing his seat belt, **he wouldn't be alive today.** _____

4. a. If she hadn't spent so much money, **she could have afforded a new car.** _____

   b. If she hadn't spent so much money, **she would still have some money in the bank.** _____

5. a. If the earth didn't rotate, **there would always be daylight on one side of it.** _____

   b. If the earth didn't rotate, **there would be very little life.** _____

6. a. If I didn't have to work, **I would have gone shopping this morning.** _____

   b. If I didn't have to work, **I'd feel a lot more relaxed.** _____

7. a. If my brother had become a lawyer, **he'd probably be working at a law firm.** _____

   b. If my brother had become a lawyer, **he wouldn't have been very happy.** _____

8. a. If our city wasn't so expensive, **I'd buy a bigger house next year.** _____

   b. If our city wasn't so expensive, **I would have moved into a bigger apartment.** _____

Write about It Write another main clause for each *if-* clause above. Which time frame did you use in each sentence?

1. *If we hadn't learned how to use electricity, life would be much more difficult.*

37 | Usage Note: Contrasting Real and Unreal Conditionals
Read the note. Then do Activity 38.

> Future real and unreal conditionals may be used in similar contexts. However, with the real conditional, the speaker believes the situation is more likely to happen.
>
> **Future Real:** If I **get** a new car, I**'ll drive** across the country. (= I think there is a good chance that I will get a new car.)
> **Future Unreal:** If I **got** a new car, I**'d drive** across the country. (= I am just imagining what getting a new car is like.)
>
> We sometimes use *would* to describe a regular event in the past. Be careful not to confuse a past real conditional with *would* and a present/future unreal conditional.
>
> **Past Real:** I really liked my fifth-grade teacher. If we all did our homework, he **would give** us a treat.
> (describes something that happened regularly in the past)
> **Present/Future Unreal:** If we all did our homework, our teacher **would give** us a treat. Why don't we do it?
> (describes something that is not true now; the speaker expresses something he or she wishes would happen)

38 | Identifying Real and Unreal Conditionals Does each *if-* clause describe a real condition (something likely) or an unreal condition (something less likely or impossible)? Check (✓) your answers.

6.8 A–C

	REAL	UNREAL
1. She'll be worried if you're late.	✓	☐
2. I'd be happier if I lived near the ocean.	☐	☐
3. If you tell me the truth, I won't get mad.	☐	☐
4. If my brother remembers my birthday, I'll be very surprised.	☐	☐
5. We would finish this work faster if we could talk on the phone.	☐	☐
6. This will taste great if you add a little salt.	☐	☐
7. If you take a vacation, you'll feel a lot better.	☐	☐
8. If you took the train, you'd save some time.	☐	☐
9. I'd love it if you came to dinner.	☐	☐
10. If you book the hotel, I'll pay you back.	☐	☐
11. If he fixes my laptop, I'll be amazed.	☐	☐
12. If I'd gone to the meeting, I'd know the decision.	☐	☐
13. I'd feel better if I were more organized.	☐	☐
14. When I was young and got sick, I would always feel better if my mother brought me a cup of tea.	☐	☐
15. When we were younger, my sister would always help me if she could.	☐	☐
16. My sister doesn't have much money, but I know she would help me if she could.	☐	☐
17. My mom doesn't like to criticize anyone. If I did something wrong, I don't think she would say anything.	☐	☐
18. When I was a child, if I did something wrong, my mom would always say the same thing.	☐	☐
19. If I hadn't eaten so much last night, I'd feel much better than I do now.	☐	☐
20. If I hadn't had bad teeth as a kid, I wouldn't have needed to go to the dentist so often.	☐	☐

Think about It Work with a partner. For 1–12 above, change the real conditions to unreal ones and the unreal conditions to real ones.

1. She would be worried if you were late.

Talk about It Work with a partner. Choose one of the sentences from 13–20 above, and use it to create a short conversation. Present your conversation to the class.

A: Were you close to your sister as kids?
B: Very close. When we were younger, my sister would always help me if she could.

39 | Usage Note: *As If* and *As Though* Read the note. Then do Activity 40.

We can use *as if* and *as though* to compare a real situation (in the present or past) to something unreal or imaginary. These subordinators express a sense of both manner (*how*) and condition. Notice that the main clause may use a present or past verb form. The adverb clause uses a past verb form to show that the situation is distant from reality.

PRESENT REAL SITUATION COMPARED TO SOMETHING UNREAL	PAST REAL SITUATION COMPARED TO SOMETHING UNREAL
1 He feels **as though he were a character in a book.** (He is not a character in a book.)	**3** She acted **as though nothing had happened.** (Something did happen.)
2 She speaks Mandarin **as if she were born in China.** (She wasn't born in China.)	**4** He acted **as if he were the president of the company.** (He was not the president of the company.)

40 | Using *As If* and *As Though* Match each clause on the left with a clause on the right. (More than one answer may be possible.) `6.8 A–C`

1. I asked her to stop, but she went ahead __g__
2. There is a photograph on his desk; it looks ____
3. He looked around and leaned toward me ____
4. She was so thin. She looked ____
5. He was walking ____
6. Her eyes were very wide, and she looked ____
7. He looked very red, ____
8. I remember my graduation day ____
9. This isn't a big problem but she feels ____
10. They spoke in low voices ____
11. He bent down suddenly ____

a. as though he wanted to tell me a secret.
b. as if they were in the library.
c. as though he'd hurt himself.
d. as if he'd been out in the sun for hours.
e. as if it were taken in the 1950s.
f. as though she hadn't eaten for weeks.
g. as though she hadn't heard me.
h. as if it were enormous.
i. as if he were going to pick up something.
j. as if it were yesterday.
k. as though she'd had a terrible scare.

Write about It Think of a different way to complete each sentence above. Then think of a different way to begin each sentence.

1. She kept talking as though she hadn't heard me.

41 | Error Correction Correct any errors in these sentences. (Some sentences may not have any errors.)

1. As if she had all that she needs.
2. If I know more about grammar, I wouldn't make so many mistakes.
3. If this happened in my country, he would have gone to jail.
4. If nobody would tell me to get glasses, I would not be successful in my classes.
5. If you ever go to California, you should go to Los Angeles.
6. You didn't wear a uniform, you can't go to this school.
7. If you want to buy something, you can probably order it on the Internet.
8. I knew I would have a better life if I study hard.
9. It is safer if you would travel with another person.
10. If you don't have self-confidence, you can't lead other people.
11. If my parents was here, I wouldn't have learned the language so quickly.
12. Her business wouldn't have been successful. If I hadn't supported her.

6.9 Using Adverb Clauses in Speaking

A	**1** A: When can I go there by myself?
	   B: **When you're 16.**
	
	2 A: I don't think I got the job.
	   B: **Because they didn't call back?**
	
	3 I have an idea. (*pause*) **If you're interested.**
		In conversation, we sometimes use an **adverb clause** alone (without a main clause), as in **1 – 3**. Sometimes the adverb clause completes another person's idea or question, as in **2**. Sometimes the adverb clause is an afterthought, as in **3**.

B	**4** If that's Elvis, then I'm John Lennon! **5** If you need anything else, just holler. **6** If I've said anything I shouldn't have, I'm truly sorry. **7** If you really want my advice, don't bother with making a reservation. Just go there. **8** If you'll cook dinner, I'll wash the dishes. **9** If you won't open it, I will.	We often use real conditional sentences to: • speak humorously or sarcastically, as in **4** • make an offer, as in **5** • make an apology, as in **6** • give advice, as in **7** • make a deal with someone, as in **8 – 9**. Notice that we use a future form in both the main clause and the *if-* clause for this special situation.
C	**10** If everyone could look this way, please. **11** If I might have your attention . . . **12** If you'll excuse me, . . . **13** I'd like to go to sleep now if that's OK with you. **14** If you don't mind, I'd like to eat soon.	In conversation, we sometimes use conditionals to: • make a polite request, as in **10 – 12**. (Here the *if-* clause is often used without a result clause.) Notice that we sometimes use a future form in the *if-* clause for this special situation. • show formality or request permission, as in **13 – 14** The conditional clause softens the request or statement by offering the listener a choice.

D	**15** A: **What if I** run into any problems?
	     (= What should I do if I run into any problems?)
	   B: Just call me.
	
	16 A: Is fencing dangerous?
	   B: **Not if** you're wearing the right clothes.
	     (= It's not dangerous if you're wearing the right clothes.)
		In conversation, we sometimes ask a question with *what if*, as in **15**. In these questions, the result clause is implied.
		
		We sometimes answer a question with *not if*, as in **16**.

GO ONLINE

42 | Using Real Conditionals in Conversation Choose an adverb clause from the box to complete each conversation. Listen and check your answers. Then practice with a partner. **6.9 A**

1. A: Why do we have to spend so much money?

   B: We can talk about it. (*pause*) _____ *If you want.* _____

   A: I don't think there's anything to talk about. (*pause*)

   _____

2. A: How long have you lived here?

   B: _____

3. A: How are you doing?

   B: _____

   (*pause*) I don't know. Could be better.

4. A: How did you know Amanda was lying?

   B: _____

> Because she wouldn't look at me.
> Because we can't really afford it.
> Because you're crazy?
> If you insist.
> If you think I should.
> If you want.
> If you're interested.
> Since I was 13.
> Since the last time we talked?
> Whenever you're ready.

5. A: Do you think I should drive or take the train?

    B: Take the train. Definitely take the train.

    A: OK. _____

    B: I do. I really do.

6. A: This is a great place for a vacation.

    B: I told you it was.

    A: I know but I was hoping I wouldn't enjoy it. You know why?

    B: _____

7. A: I'm getting bored! When can we go?

    B: _____

8. A: I have something to tell you about James. (*pause*) _____

    B: Of course I am! What is it?

9. A: Can we have pizza for dinner again tonight?

    B: I suppose so. _____

6.9 B

43 | Using Real Conditionals in Conversation Why does each speaker below use a real conditional sentence? Choose *a*, *b*, *c*, *d*, or *e* from the box. Then practice with a partner. **6.9 B**

> a. to speak humorously or sarcastically
> b. to make an offer
> c. to make an apology
> d. to give advice
> e. to make a deal

1. A: I just can't do this math problem.

    B: Come on. If you stick with it, you'll figure it out. _*d*_

2. A: That's not a nice thing to say!

    B: If I offended you, I'm sorry. I didn't mean to. ____

3. A: I'll drive you to Chicago if you pay for the gas. ____

    B: That seems reasonable. You're on!

4. A: If you could just listen for a minute, I'll explain.

    B: Sure. I'm sorry. Go ahead. ____

5. A: Well, goodbye. It was nice working with you.

    B: Yeah. I'm sorry if things didn't work out so well. ____

    A: Me too.

6. A: If you want to chat later, I'll be up till midnight. ____

    B: Thanks a lot. I might do that.

7. A: If you think I'm smart, then you're a genius. ____

    B: Oh, come on. You're a lot smarter than me.

8. A: Look, if you hate this job, you should quit. ____

    B: I guess you're right.

9. A: If that's art, my two-year-old son is Picasso. ____

    B: I know what you mean. It's not very good, is it?

10. A: If I can be honest, I think that tie is terrible. ____

    B: Really? It doesn't go with the shirt?

    A: It doesn't go with anything.

11. A: OK, I'll try a raw oyster if you will. ____

    B: Let's do it!

12. A: If you have any questions, just call me. ____

    B: Great. Thanks so much.

44 | Softening a Request or Statement Listen and write the missing words. Then practice the conversations with a partner. [6.9 C]

1. A: Do you mind _____ *if I turn down the music* _____?

   B: No, please, go ahead.

2. A: Anna seems really distracted and I don't know why.

   B: _____, I can talk to her.

3. A: I'm leaving for the bank.

   B: OK _____?

4. A: I'm going to study here _____.

   B: No, please.

5. A: _____, I have to make a phone call.

   B: Talk to you later, then.

6. A: I don't think I want to work tonight.

   B: Look, _____, that's OK.

7. A: This is delicious.

   B: Thanks. You could have a little more, _____.

8. A: _____, Mr. Jones . . .

   B: Please, Tom, come in, come in.

9. A: Hey! Let's go see a movie.

   B: Hmm. _____, could we get some food instead? I haven't eaten.

10. A: _____, I'd like to talk to you.

    B: Sure. How can I help?

---

45 | Using *What If* and *Not If* Choose a sentence from the box to complete each conversation. Listen and check your answers. Then practice with a partner. [6.9 D]

1. A: Are you going to work at home today?

   B: *Not if I don't have to.* _____

2. A: I don't feel like cooking tonight.

   B: _____

   A: Sounds good to me.

3. A: What happened to your car?

   B: A car ran into it.

   A: Wow! _____

   B: Yeah, I know. It would have been bad.

4. A: Is there any cake left?

   B: Yeah, one piece—but it's mine.

   A: _____

5. A: Stop! There's a car coming!

   B: Yikes! He's going fast.

   A: That's crazy. _____

   B: I would have hit him for sure.

> Not if I don't have to.
> Not if I get there first.
> Not if you stay relaxed.
> Not if you want to get there on time.
> What if I hadn't seen him?
> What if I pick you up at 8?
> What if I refuse?
> What if we go out instead?
> What if you hadn't had your seat belt on?

6. A: Do I have time for a shower before we leave?

   B: _____

7. A: Will you lend me some money?

   B: _____

   A: Then I'll tell Dad about the scratch[23] on the car.

8. A: What's the matter?

   B: I'm just nervous. I'm afraid I'm going to forget everything.

   A: _____

9. A: What time do you want to leave?

   B: _____

   A: Sounds good to me.

Will you lend me some money?

6.10 Using Adverb Clauses in Academic Writing

We often use **adverb clauses** to connect two or more ideas. We can do this in a single sentence or across two or more sentences, as in **1a – 1b**. This makes our writing cohesive; it helps each sentence flow smoothly into the next.

COMPARE

1a	The area of China is only slightly larger than that of the U.S. However, the population of China is more than four times greater.	**1b**	Although the area of China is only slightly larger than that of the U.S., its population is more than four times greater.

A

A **subordinator** shows the relationship between the ideas, as in **2 – 8**.

2 Now I'm not so shy **when** meeting new people. (time)
3 **Because** we live in an increasingly multicultural society, it is important to study other languages. (reason)
4 **Even though** I was 26, I had never been outside of my city. (contrast)
5 The company collects and cleans used clothes **so that** they can be used again. (purpose)
6 Cell phones have become **such** an important part of our lifestyle **that** it would be difficult to live without them. (result)
7 **If** you maintain a healthy lifestyle, then you are less likely to get sick. (condition)
8 Please complete the test exactly **as** I showed you. (manner)

An adverb clause can come at the beginning or end of a sentence. We often choose to put an adverb clause at the beginning of a sentence to set the scene for the following ideas, as in **9 – 11**.

9 **When you sleep**, you dream about 20 percent of the time. For example, if you sleep one night for eight hours, you dream for about 96 minutes of those eight hours.
10 A baby has 270 to 300 bones—more than an adult's 213. **As you grow up**, some of your bones grow together.
11 **When you cut yourself**, you may lose some blood, but the body can replace blood and other cells[24].

B

We may also use an adverb clause at the beginning of a sentence to make a connection back to information in a previous sentence, as in **12 – 14**. The adverb clause acts as a bridge between the previous sentence and the new information in the main clause.

12	I got up quickly and went down to the kitchen.	**As I entered the room,** my uncle jumped up from his chair.
	previous sentence	adverb clause · new information in main clause

13 Ching-He Huang studied economics in college, but her passion was cooking. **After she graduated**, she started a food and drink company.
14 In Turkey, high school students take a national achievement exam in March. **If they pass that exam**, they take another exam in June.

---

[23] **scratch:** a cut or mark from something sharp   [24] **cells:** the smallest parts of any living thing

46 | Identifying the Connection between Ideas Underline the adverb clauses in these sentences and circle the subordinators. Then identify the connection between the adverb clause and the main clause. Write *time*, *reason*, *contrast*, *purpose*, *result*, *condition*, or *manner*. `6.10 A`

HOW TO FALL ASLEEP FAST

time

1. Turn the television off and step away from the computer at least one hour (before) you go to bed because they stimulate[25] your brain rather than relax it.

2. Before you get in bed, lie flat on the floor and stretch[26].

3. Although it's sometimes difficult to find a comfortable position when falling asleep, it's a good idea to lie on your back and relax until you feel comfortable. If that doesn't work, lie on your side.

4. Some people use visualization[27] to relax. You imagine yourself in a beautiful place such as the beach. If you are successful, you feel as if you are really there.

5. Deep breathing can help you sleep better. Slowly breathe in so that your chest fully expands. Hold your breath for three seconds. Then breathe out. Repeat five to ten times. You should feel your body relax as you breathe.

6. You may want to fall asleep so much that you become too tense to let it happen. If this is the case, get out of bed and take a walk. Try stretching again before getting back into bed.

Write about It Write two to three more sentences giving advice on how to fall asleep. Use adverb clauses. Then share your sentences with a partner. Ask your partner to identify the types of adverb clauses you used.

47 | Combining Ideas Combine each pair of ideas into one sentence, and make any other necessary changes to the sentence. (More than one answer may be possible.) `6.10 A`

1. I don't drink coffee in the evening.
   Drinking coffee interferes with my sleep.

   I don't drink coffee in the evening because it interferes with my sleep.
   Because coffee interferes with my sleep, I don't drink it in the evening.

2. Hassan came to the U.S.
   Hassan began studying automotive engineering.

3. People don't have to spend so much time preparing food.
   People are better off now than they used to be.

4. Clara Jbour's parents sent her to the U.S. to attend college.
   Clara Jbour graduated from high school.

5. Parents are not teaching their children correct behavior.
   Parents may need coaching in parenting skills.

6. You maintain a healthy lifestyle.
   You are less likely to get sick.

7. Cody Huelskamp works as a wildlife photographer.
   Cody Huelskamp has traveled to 70 countries.

8. I missed most of the movie.
   I was worrying about my job.

Clara Jbour

Cody Huelskamp

---

[25] **stimulate:** to make something active or more active
[26] **stretch:** to push your arms and legs out as far as you can

[27] **visualization:** having a picture in your mind about someone or something

9. I love sweets.

   I try not to eat candy.

10. Many mothers work outside of the home.

    Fathers must share the responsibilities of running a house.

11. He continued to play football.

    His knee got worse.

12. Roughly 36 percent of New Yorkers were born outside of the U.S.

    It's very common to hear people speaking different languages.

Think about It How many different ways can you combine each pair of ideas in Activity 47? Which one do you think is the most effective?

48 | Using Subordinators Read the science article. Choose the subordinator that best completes each sentence. `6.10 A–B`

Protecting Your Skin

_____ _When_ _____ summer comes, I get sun crazy. I like to eat on the patio and lie on the beach. I walk and
(1. because / when)

bike everywhere. _____ I was younger, I played in the sun without worry. _____
(2. although / when)   (3. now that / when)

I'm 30, I realize how important it is to protect myself. That's _____ the ultraviolet (UV) rays[28]
(4. because / when)

from the sun harm the cells in our skin. You can't see the damage _____ you're young, but its
(5. although / when)

effects often show up much later. _____ crowds of young people go to beaches and tanning
(6. as / when)

salons[29], skin cancer is becoming more common, says Mandeep Kaur. She's a dermatologist, or skin doctor,

at Wake Forest University School of Medicine.

_____ our skin works hard to protect us, few people work to protect it. The sun's UV rays
(7. although / because)

are the biggest threat _____ they damage the cells of your skin. The tricky thing is that this
(8. because / while)

process can take 30 or more years to become evident. "It's surprising how long it takes," says Meenhard

Herlyn, a biologist at the Wistar Institute in Philadelphia. "Even _____ kids have big,
(9. because / if)

blistering[30] sunburns every summer, they're fine _____ they're kids."
(10. although / while)

Think about It Circle the sentences above that begin with an adverb clause. Why do you think the writer put the adverb clause at the beginning of the sentence?

- to set the scene for the following ideas
- to make a connection back to information in a previous sentence

Talk about It What is something new you learned from the article above? Tell a partner.

---

[28] **ultraviolet rays:** light from the sun that cannot be seen
[29] **tanning salons:** places where you can expose your skin to ultraviolet light to darken your skin

[30] **blistering:** having small, painful places on your skin that are full of liquid

49│Using Adverb Clauses Read this story and underline the adverb clauses. Then answer the questions below. 6.10 A–B

THE LEMON STORY

Alberto Alvaro Ríos

When the writer's parents buy a new house, his mother gets to choose the color for each room.

When I was about four, or maybe five, my parents bought a new house in what would later become a small suburb of Nogales, Arizona, on the border of Mexico, some four miles outside town. As we kept driving out to watch the house being built, my mother got to make a number of choices regarding details, among which was the color of various rooms.

My mother, when asked what color she wanted the kitchen, said to the workers, who were all Mexican and who spoke very little English, *limón*. She said it both because she wanted the kitchen to be yellow and because she wanted to start learning Spanish. The workers nodded yes. But when she came back the next day, the kitchen was painted bright green, like a small jungle[31]. Mexican *limónes*, my mother found out, are small and green, that color exactly, no mistake.

So that's the color that wall stayed for the next 14 years, until I left home for college. She said it was a reminder to us all that there was a great deal to learn in the world. You might laugh at first, but after 14 years you start to think about it.

QUESTIONS

1. In which sentences does the writer use an adverb clause to make his writing more cohesive?
2. In which sentences does the adverb clause set the scene for the following ideas?
3. In paragraph 1, in the sentence beginning *As we kept driving*, what does the subordinator *as* mean?
4. In your own words, retell the story to a partner.

50│Making Your Writing Cohesive Combine the two ideas on the right to form the next sentence on the left. Decide if you think the adverb clause or the main clause should come at the beginning to make the sentence cohesive. 6.10 B

1. Americans should be required to learn another language. *Because we live in an increasingly multicultural society, this will benefit them in the future.*
   - this will benefit them in the future
   - because we live in an increasingly multicultural society

2. Many people around the world are learning to speak English as a second language.
   - communication would be even better
   - if more Americans learned to speak foreign languages

3. Yoga improves your flexibility[32]. Also, . . .
   - it is a great way to meet people
   - if you do classes

4. My favorite pastime is rock climbing.
   - I enjoy it
   - because it is something I can do inside or outside

5. In the U.S., children must be vaccinated[33] against certain diseases.
   - they must receive vaccinations
   - before they can start school

6. Competition can be very good for children.
   - it is only a problem
   - when too much emphasis is placed on it

---

[31] **jungle:** a thick forest in a hot part of the world
[32] **flexibility:** the ability to bend easily without breaking

[33] **vaccinate:** to put a substance in a person's blood using a needle, to stop them from getting a disease

7. In many families, both parents have full-time jobs. This can create problems at home.

8. Brothers and sisters spend a lot of time together. They help each other and take care of each other.

9. People like to read essays that are well organized and interesting.

10. Having children is very stressful and time-consuming, but . . .

11. Every home should have a pair of small, foldable scissors.

12. The writer Chinua Achebe was born in Nigeria.

13. Plastic bags in the ocean are dangerous for sea turtles.

14. A report concluded that 100,000 ocean mammals die each year by eating or getting caught in plastic.

15. In the 1970s, there was just one Pinta tortoise in the Galapagos Islands.

16. In the past, people brought goats to the Galapagos to raise for food. Unfortunately, the goats liked to eat the same food that the tortoises ate.

- children have to spend all day at school or daycare
- when neither parent can be at home
- they understand each other very well
- because they share so many experiences while growing up
- readers will be able to follow your ideas easily
- if you organize your essay well
- the job can be easier
- if parents are patient with their children
- they fit easily in a purse or pocket
- because they fold up and are very small
- he chose to write in English
- even though he was African
- because the bags look like jellyfish[34]
- the sea turtles try to eat the bags
- when they get caught in plastic
- they may drown or become exhausted and die of starvation
- because it was the last remaining Pinta tortoise that scientists knew of
- the *Guinness Book of World Records* called it the "rarest living creature"
- the food supply for tortoises disappeared
- as the number of goats on the island increased

51 | Making Your Writing Cohesive Rewrite each paragraph. Connect the ideas in different ways to make the writing cohesive. You will probably want to move ideas around and change words. 6.10 B

A	B
I spend a lot of time on the road. That's why I've seen a lot of stupid behavior. I could list at least 15 driving pet peeves. I'll limit myself to two. One thing really bothers me. It's when people forget to turn off their turn signal. It's very distracting. I hate to drive for miles behind someone with a flashing turn signal. Second, people sometimes flash their headlights. I don't understand why people get so impatient. It's really irritating.	One of my biggest pet peeves is irritating cell phone users. Many people talk very loudly on their phone. You can hear everything they say. This is very annoying. Sometimes you are trying to read and you can't. Sometimes you are trying to talk to someone else and you can't. It also bothers me when people always answer their phone. You can be having a conversation with them, and they stop and answer the phone. This is extremely rude.

Talk about It Compare the paragraphs you rewrote above with your classmates. What are some of the different ways people combined the ideas into a new paragraph?

Write about It Write about one of your pet peeves. Try to use two adverb clauses in your writing.

[34] **jellyfish:** an animal with a soft, pale body that lives in the ocean

A | WRITING Study these pictures from movies. Choose one picture, and write a paragraph to explain what might be happening. Use time clauses, reason clauses, manner clauses, and *if*- clauses.

I chose the third picture. When the main character goes out into the ocean, a big storm begins. If the boy can't reach the shore before night, he'll be in a lot of danger. As soon as he realizes that his life is in danger, he starts to panic.

B | TIC-TAC-TOE Follow these instructions:

1. Work with a partner. Student A is X. Student B is O.
2. Student A: Choose a square and complete the sentence.
3. Students A and B: Check the sentence together. If the sentence has no errors, write an X in the square. If the sentence is not correct, do not write an X in the square.
4. Student B: Take your turn. Choose a square and complete the sentence.
5. Students A and B: Check the sentence together. If the sentence has no errors, write an O in the square. If the sentence is not correct, do not write an O in the square.
6. Continue to take turns. The first person to get three Xs or three Os in a line is the winner.

Before I came to this school, I _____ _____.	If I'm good-looking, _____ _____.	Even though it wasn't a good idea, I _____ _____.
If it's OK with you, _____ _____.	As soon as I get home, _____ _____.	Once you've tried _____, you _____ _____.
My brother is so _____ that he _____ _____.	I won't _____ unless _____.	You look as though _____ _____.

C | PERSONAL REFLECTION Read this advice. Choose one piece of advice that you strongly agree or disagree with. Make notes to support your opinion. Then explain to your classmates why you agree or disagree with the advice. Use adverb clauses in your writing.

1. You should follow your dreams no matter how crazy they seem.
2. It's better to be cautious than to make mistakes.
3. Never have regrets. Leave the past in the past.
4. Live for today!
5. Always look after No. 1: that's you.
6. Don't make promises.

I completely disagree with the first piece of advice. If you have crazy dreams, you're probably not going to achieve them. Although it may seem like a good idea to have dreams, it can be hard to make them come true. Instead, you should set yourself easier goals so that you succeed. Even if you think that's unambitious, it's a good idea to think about it. For example, if you wanted to become a famous detective, you'd still have to learn the job. You can't become famous until you've proved you're good.

D | WEB SEARCH Look online for information about an interesting city to visit. Copy the information and underline the adverb clauses you see. Then write an advertisement to describe the city.

As soon as you get off the plane in Belgium, you'll start feeling hungry! Before you start visiting the main tourist sites, be sure to get a good lunch in the town square. If you like mussels, you're sure to love Brussels!

6.11 Summary of Adverb Clauses

TYPE OF ADVERB CLAUSE	COMMON SUBORDINATORS	EXAMPLES
Time *When?*	*after, as, as soon as, before, by the time, once, since, until, when, whenever, while*	**As soon as** he graduates, he'll get a job. **Whenever** I see her, I feel happy. **Once** you travel the world, you're never the same again.
Reason *Why?*	*as, because, now that, since*	**Since** none of the students were ready, the test was postponed. **Now that** all the results are in, I'll announce the winners.
Contrast	*as though, even though, though, while*	**Even though** it was very cold, we decided to go ahead with the hike. I was determined to become a doctor **although** my parents didn't want me to.
Manner *How?* *In what way?*	*as, like*	Please check your spelling **as directed in the instructions.**
	as if, as though	He looks **as though he has a bad cold.**
Result	*so* + adjective or adverb + *that* *so many/few* + plural noun + *that* *so much/little* + noncount noun + *that* *such* + (*a/an*) + adjective + noun	She was **so beautiful that people stared at her.** There were **so many** people in the audience **that we could hardly see the stage.** It was **such a funny movie that I couldn't stop laughing.**
Purpose *For what purpose?* *Why?*	*so that*	I closed the blinds **so that I wouldn't wake up too early.**
Real Conditional	*if, unless, when, whenever*	**If it rains**, we'll change our plans. Don't go to Arizona **unless you love hot climates.** **Whenever I exercise**, I feel great.
Unreal Conditional	*if*	**If I weren't working next week**, I'd go to the beach.
	as if, as though	She felt **as if she had been running a marathon.**

7 Nouns and Pronouns

It takes a lot of courage
to show your dreams
to someone else.
—ERMA BOMBECK, WRITER
(1927–1996)

Talk about It Do you agree or disagree with the quotation above? Why?

WARM-UP

A | Match the beginnings and endings of the quotations. Then choose one quotation and tell a partner if you agree or disagree with it and why.

Famous Quotations

1. **Everything** has its **beauty**, but ___*f*___

2. **Children** are ____

3. Criticize a **friend** in **private**, but ____

4. **It** is not enough to have a good **mind**; ____

5. An angry **man** opens his **mouth** and ____

6. **One** may smile, and smile, and ____

a. praise **him** in front of **others**. *(Leonardo da Vinci, artist)*

b. the main **thing** is to use **it** well. *(René Descartes, philosopher)*

c. be a **villain**[1]. *(William Shakespeare, writer)*

d. shuts his **eyes**. *(Marcus Cato, statesman)*

e. our most valuable natural **resource**. *(Herbert Hoover, U.S. president)*

f. not **everyone** sees **it**. *(Confucius, philosopher)*

B | The words in blue in the quotations above are nouns. The words in green are pronouns. Based on these examples, what can you say about nouns and pronouns? Check (✓) *True* or *False*.

	TRUE	FALSE
1. Nouns always come before verbs.	☐	☐
2. Plural nouns always end in *-s*.	☐	☐
3. We use a singular verb after the pronouns *everything* and *everyone*.	☐	☐
4. Pronouns sometimes take the place of a noun or noun phrase.	☐	☐
5. We can use pronouns to talk about people or things in general.	☐	☐

C | Look back at the quotation on page 212. Identify any nouns or pronouns.

[1] **villain:** a bad person, usually in a book, play, or movie

7.1 Overview of Nouns

A

We use nouns to identify people, places, things, and ideas. Sometimes a group of words acts like a single noun—we call these **noun phrases**. We use nouns and noun phrases in different ways in a sentence, as in **1 – 2**.

subject			subject		indirect object	direct object
1 Studies	have shown	that	music	gives	people	energy.

subject			object of preposition		object of preposition
2 Both cooperation and competition	are needed	for	success	in	a global economy.

B

COUNT NOUNS

3 Nowadays, **computers** are essential for **students**.
The average **student** will pay $1,200 for **a computer**.

Count nouns have both singular forms and plural forms, as in **3**. We almost always use a determiner (in this case, *the* and *a*) with a singular count noun.

NONCOUNT NOUNS

4 **Love makes** the world go around. (NOT: ~~Love make~~ . . .)

5 You can get **information** about it online.
(NOT: ~~an information~~ OR ~~informations~~)

6 The **news** is so depressing. (NOT: ~~The news are~~ . . .)

Noncount nouns do not have plural forms, so we don't use plural verbs with them, as in **4**. We do not use *a* or *an* with noncount nouns, as in **5**. A few noncount nouns end in -s, as in **6**.

For information on determiners, see Unit 8, page 254. For a list of common noncount nouns, see the Resources, page R-9.

C

COMPARE

7a I want a good **education** for my child.
7b **Education** is a basic human right.

8a Japan and India are **democracies** with close ties.
8b **Democracy** is a form of government.

9a Prices have increased on many **foods**.
9b Some snakes eat twice their weight in **food** a day.

Some nouns have both a count meaning and a noncount meaning.

- We use the count meaning when we think of the noun as a single, separate thing, as in **7a**, **8a**, and **9a**.
- We use the noncount meaning when we think of the noun as a substance, material, or general concept, as in **7b**, **8b**, and **9b**.

D

CORRECT THE COMMON ERRORS (See page R-12.)

10 ✗ She gave me some good advices.

11 ✗ I didn't have time to do my homeworks.

12 ✗ When I have a stress, I can't study hard.

13 ✗ Recycled papers are used to produce newspapers.

 GO ONLINE

1 | Exploring Categories of Nouns Read this text. What do the **bold** nouns identify—people, places, things, or ideas? Write each noun under the correct group in the chart on page 215. **7.1 A**

JOSEPH PRIESTLEY

Many people think you need to focus on one **profession** to be truly successful. They say that if you pursue[2] many different **interests**, you won't accomplish[3] anything worthwhile. A number of famous people have proven that this is not true. **Joseph Priestley** (1733–1804), for example, was able to accomplish an extraordinary **number** of things in many different **fields**. He first studied to become a **minister**, and during his **lifetime**, he wrote many books about **religion** and **politics**. He was also interested in **education**, and he started a special **school** for **children** in **England**. When he couldn't find a good grammar **book** for his **students**, he wrote one.

[2] **pursue:** to try to do something over a period of time   [3] **accomplish:** to succeed in doing something

Priestley never studied **science** in school, but he liked to do **experiments** and eventually wrote a book about **electricity**. When he couldn't find an **artist** to do the **illustrations**, Priestley taught himself to draw and did the illustrations himself. Later in **life** Priestley became interested in the study of different **gases**, and he is credited[4] with the **discovery** of carbon dioxide, carbon monoxide, and **oxygen**. Can you think of another famous person who did so many different kinds of things?

People	Places	Physical things	Abstract nouns
			profession

Think about It Are any of the nouns in the passage in Activity 1 difficult to put into the categories? Which ones? Why is this?

Write about It Think of another person who has done many different things. Write about five things this person has done.

> **FYI**
>
> Abstract nouns describe ideas, not physical things.
>
> cooperation   love
> information   success

2 | Grouping Noncount Nouns Write each noncount noun under the correct group in the chart. 7.1 A–B

art	diabetes	gasoline	loneliness	rice	snow
cancer	equipment	hair	music	salt	surfing
clothing	fire	information	oil	self-confidence	transportation
darkness	furniture	karate	physics	smoke	yoga

NONCOUNT NOUNS			
Sports, physical activities	**Gases, liquids, materials**	**Abstract ideas**	**School subjects**
baseball soccer judo	air metal clay paper	experience safety knowledge truth love *art*	biology mathematics chemistry
Names of categories	**Natural occurrences**	**Things with tiny parts too small to count**	**Illnesses**
food meat fruit	electricity rain heat weather	dirt sugar grass	asthma heart disease malaria

[4] **credit:** to say that something is because of someone

Think about It Think of two more words to add to each category in the chart in Activity 2. Then share ideas with your classmates.

3 | Using Noncount Nouns Complete each question with a noncount noun from the box. (More than one answer may be possible.) `7.1 B`

advice	happiness	homework	music	pollution
anger	history	information	news	truth

1. Where can you get ____information____ about your ancestors[5]?
2. How often do you have trouble controlling your _____?
3. What was the best _____ someone gave you?
4. What was the most interesting thing in the _____ yesterday?
5. Do you think it's possible to find _____?
6. Do you always do your _____?
7. How can we reduce air _____?
8. Did you enjoy studying _____ in school?
9. Do you always tell the _____?
10. Do you listen to _____ every day?

Talk about It Ask a partner the questions above.

A: *Where can you get information about your ancestors?*
B: *On the Internet. It has lots of information about people's ancestors.*

4 | Collocations with Noncount Nouns Choose one collocation from each group below. Write six questions using them. `7.1 B`

Does a dictionary <u>provide information</u> about the pronunciation of a word?

get **information** have **information** provide **information**	follow (someone's) **advice** get (someone's) **advice** take (someone's) **advice**	carry out **research** conduct **research** do **research**
know the **truth** speak the **truth** tell the **truth**	be interested in **politics** discuss **politics** enter **politics** talk **politics**	buy **furniture** have **furniture** move **furniture**

F Y I

Words that are often used together are called collocations. For example, *tell the truth* and *have homework* are collocations with noncount nouns.

Talk about It Ask a partner the questions you wrote above.

A: *Does a dictionary provide information about the pronunciation of a word?*
B: *Yes, it does.*

[5] **ancestors:** the people in your family who lived a long time ago

5 | Distinguishing Count and Noncount Nouns Read this text. Decide if each **bold** noun is a count noun or a noncount noun. Write *C* above the count nouns. Write *N* above the noncount nouns. **7.1 B**

Why Do Doctors Wear White Coats?
by Pat MacEnulty

For about a hundred **years**, white **coats** were the standard **uniform** for most **doctors**. Doctors didn't always wear white coats. Up until the early **part** of the twentieth century, they wore street **clothes**—or even black clothes out of **respect** for the **dead**! They also did not have much **training**, and their **methods** were primitive[6]. In the late 1900s, doctors began to rely on scientific **evidence** when it came to medical **treatment**. **Scientists** wore knee-length white coats while doing **experiments** to protect their **clothing** and **skin** from **chemicals**. Soon doctors started wearing the white lab coats of the scientist to reassure[7] their **patients** that their **care** was based on **science** and not **superstition**[8]. So, wearing white coats became a **tradition** for physicians. That tradition is changing, however, and your doctor may very well wear a business **suit** during your next examination.

Think about It Which nouns above were the most difficult to identify as count or noncount? Why?

6 | Count or Noncount Meaning? Do the **bold** nouns in these sentences have a count meaning or noncount meaning? Check (✓) your answers. **7.1 C**

PAPER	COUNT	NONCOUNT
1. In the past, people recorded important information on **paper**. Today most people use computers.	☐	☑
2. A 2005 planning **paper** considered several alternatives[9].	☐	☐
3. Recycled **paper** is used to produce newspapers.	☐	☐
4. Ross has written several **papers** on climate change.	☐	☐
5. To get a PhD, you have to write a very long **paper**, or dissertation.	☐	☐
6. **Paper** used to be made from pieces of cloth.	☐	☐
7. Recycling one ton of **paper** saves about 17 trees.	☐	☐
8. You can go to the Internet to get suggestions for writing a **paper**.	☐	☐

[6] **primitive:** very simple; not developed
[7] **reassure:** to do something to make someone feel safer
[8] **superstition:** a belief in good luck, bad luck, and other things that cannot be explained
[9] **alternatives:** things we can choose instead of other things

EDUCATION	COUNT	NONCOUNT
9. Many schools work hard to get parents involved with their kids' **educations**.	☐	☐
10. A recent poll[10] reported that 90 percent of Americans believe the government should spend the same or more on **education**.	☐	☐
11. For some careers—law, medicine, engineering—a college **education** is necessary.	☐	☐
12. Many cities have their own laws regulating[11] **education**.	☐	☐
13. In tough economic times, an **education** is more important than ever.	☐	☐

TIME	COUNT	NONCOUNT
14. As **time** went on, more people wanted to join the team.	☐	☐
15. They asked eight people at a **time** to play the game.	☐	☐
16. This website has been visited more than 11,000 **times**.	☐	☐
17. There was a **time** when no one had a television.	☐	☐
18. It is **time** to rethink our priorities[12].	☐	☐

7 | Using Count and Noncount Meanings Use the dictionary definitions to write one sentence using the noncount meaning of each word and one sentence using the count meaning of the words. 7.1 C

beau·ty 🔊 /ˈbyuṭi/ *noun* (*pl.* **beau·ties**) **1** [U] the quality that gives pleasure to the senses; the state of being beautiful: *the beauty of the mountains* ◆ *He wrote music of great beauty.* **2** [C] an especially good example of something: *Look at this tomato – it's a beauty!* **3** [C] (*old-fashioned*) a beautiful woman: *She grew up to be a beauty.*

food 🔊 /fud/ *noun* **1** [U] something that people, animals, or plants take into their bodies in order to keep them alive and healthy: *Plants get food from the soil.* ◆ *a shortage of food* **2** [C, U] a particular type of food that you eat: *baby food* ◆ *Mexican food* ◆ *frozen foods* ◆ *health foods* ⊃ Look at the note at **cooking**. **IDM food for thought** an idea that makes you think seriously and carefully

tel·e·vi·sion 🔊 /ˈtɛləvɪʒn/ (also **TV**) *noun* **1** [C] (also **ˈtelevision set**, ˌ**TˈV set**) a piece of electrical equipment in the shape of a box. It has a glass screen which shows programs with moving pictures and sounds: *to turn the television on/off* **2** [U] the programs that are shown on a television set: *Paul's watching television.* **3** [U] the electrical system and business of sending out programs so that people can watch them on their television sets: *in the days before television* ◆ *cable/satellite television* ◆ *the major TV networks* ◆ *She works in television.* ⊃ Look at **public television**.

STUDY STRATEGY

A good dictionary will identify the count and noncount meanings of a word. Some dictionaries, such as the *Oxford American Dictionary for learners of English*, use the words *countable* (C) and *uncountable* (U) to identify these meanings.

All dictionary entries are from the *Oxford American Dictionary for learners of English* © Oxford University Press 2011.

Talk about It Read some of the sentences you wrote above to your classmates. Have them identify the noun as count or noncount.

Write about It Choose two more nouns from your dictionary with both a count meaning and a noncount meaning. Write sentences using each meaning. Read your sentences to a partner and have your partner identify the noun as count or noncount.

[10]**poll:** a way of discovering opinions by asking a group of people questions

[11]**regulating:** controlling something

[12]**priorities:** things that are more important

8 | Error Correction Correct any errors in these sentences. (Some sentences may not have any errors.)

1. We had a lot of funs on our way to the beach.

   We had a lot of fun on our way to the beach.

2. People should just practice to get experiences speaking English.

3. People see a lot of advertisements when they watch televisions.

4. Being a good parent requires loves and caring. Good parent tell their children every day that they love them.

5. In school, we had a physical education every afternoon for an hour.

6. Radio remains popular because our society is very mobile. People who use the automobile as their main form of transportations usually listen to the radio while they are driving.

7. If you don't have a self-confidence, you might appear nervous at a job interview. Having information about the job and the company can help you feel more confident.

8. Many people believe that the Internet will greatly improve education, but I don't agree. In the past, we had to spend a lot of times searching for informations. Now, a quick Internet search often gets us all the informations we need. This is a good things, but it isn't everything. Once we have informations, we need to analyze it and discuss it.

7.2 Personal Pronouns and Possessive Determiners

A

1 A: Where's **Jeff**?
   B: **He** went out. (he = Jeff)
   A: Did **he** take **the car**?
   B: No, **it's** still in the driveway. (it = the car)

2 A: Did **you** call **Anita**?
   B: Yes, but **she** was busy. **She** asked **me** to call **her** back tonight.

3 If **you** have any problems, give **us** a call. **We'll** be happy to help **you** get started.

We use personal pronouns to refer to people and things quickly and easily, as in **1 – 3**. Often a pronoun refers back to a noun or noun phrase that was mentioned earlier.

Subject pronouns and **object pronouns** are personal pronouns. They have different forms:

SUBJECT PRONOUNS	I	you	he	she	it	we	they
OBJECT PRONOUNS	me	you	him	her	it	us	them

GRAMMAR TERM: An **antecedent** or **referent** is the noun or noun phrase that a pronoun refers back to.

B

4 Jules and Jim want us to have **our meeting** at **their house**, but I think it's too small.

5 This film school is the only one of **its kind**.

The words *our*, *their*, and *its* in **4 – 5** look like pronouns, but they aren't. We use these forms before nouns. They are called **possessive determiners** (or possessive adjectives).

POSSESSIVE DETERMINERS	my	your	his	her	its	our	their

6 A: Does anyone have a phone I can use?
   B: Here. Use **mine**. (= my phone)

7 A: Is this Sue's book?
   B: No, it's **yours**. (= your book)

Possessive pronouns are personal pronouns. We use them in place of a possessive determiner + a noun, as in **6 – 7**.

POSSESSIVE PRONOUNS	mine	yours	his	hers	—	ours	theirs

8 Some **friends of mine** are going to a movie, so I might go, too. (NOT: ~~friends of me~~)

9 I love that **dress of yours**.

We can also show possession with a noun + *of* + a possessive pronoun. This possessive form can be used as either a subject or an object, as in **8 – 9**.

 GO ONLINE

9 | Noticing Personal Pronouns Circle the personal pronouns in these riddles. Then choose an answer for each riddle from the box. `7.2 A`

RIDDLES

1. If (you) have (it), (you) want to share (it), but if (you) share (it), (you) don't have (it).
   What is (it)? _d_

2. The more of them you take, the more you leave behind. What are they? ____

3. It has a face, two arms, and two hands, but it cannot move. It counts to 12, but it cannot speak. It can still tell you something every day. What is it? ____

4. If you take off my skin, I won't cry, but you will. What am I? ____

5. I look at you and you look at me. I raise my right hand and you raise your left. What am I? ____

6. I run, but I have no legs. What am I? ____

> **ANSWERS TO RIDDLES**
> a. An onion.
> b. Water.
> c. A mirror.
> d. A secret.
> e. Footsteps.
> f. A clock.

10 | Distinguishing Subject and Object Pronouns Write the missing pronouns in these conversations. Then practice with a partner. `7.2 A`

1. A: Did you call me?
   B: Yes, I was wondering if you could help Ann and ____me____.

2. A: Do you know who John Bell is?
   B: Sure. I listen to _____ on the radio all the time.

3. A: How is your sister doing?
   B: _____'s OK. We had to take _____ to the hospital, but _____'s OK.

4. A: Are these your keys?
   B: Yes, thanks. Where did _____ find _____?
   A: _____ were on the floor in the library.

5. A: Is something wrong?
   B: I don't know.
   A: Sure _____ do. Now, come on, tell _____.

6. A: How do you folks like our hotel so far?
   B: Oh, _____'s just wonderful. ·

7. A: Are Tom and Lisa coming to the meeting?
   B: Oh, I forgot to tell _____ about _____.
   A: That's OK. _____'re usually too busy to come anyway.

8. A: I'd like to check in, please.
   B: How long are you planning on staying with _____?
   A: Just tonight.

9. A: Can you and John help me tomorrow?
   B: Afraid not. _____ both have to work.
   A: I thought John didn't have a job.
   B: No, _____ just got one. His brother hired _____ to work on his house.

> **RESEARCH SAYS...**
>
> In very formal English, speakers may use the subject form of a pronoun after the verb *be*. However, object forms are more typical.
>
> A: John, is that you?
> B: It is **I**. *(very formal)*
>
> A: John, is that you?
> B: Yes, it's **me**. *(typical)*
>
> CORPUS

◄)) 11 | Pronunciation Note: Reduced Words Listen to the note. Then do Activities 12–13.

When *he, his, him, her,* or *them* comes in the middle of a phrase, we don't usually pronounce the initial sound. For example:

1 did he	*sounds like*	"diddy"	**4** tell her	*sounds like*	"teller"
2 at his house	*sounds like*	"addiz house"	**5** lost her phone	*sounds like*	"loster phone"
3 about him	*sounds like*	"abowdum"	**6** find them	*sounds like*	"findum"

◄)) 12 | Pronouncing Reduced Words Listen and practice saying these questions. `7.2 A–B`

1. Why don't you let her answer?
2. Did you tell her the truth?
3. Has she forgotten her promise?
4. Did her boss call you?
5. Do you know where he is?
6. Why doesn't he leave?
7. Is he absent because he's sick?
8. Where are his parents?
9. Can I have his phone number?
10. Do you know his name?
11. What made him angry?
12. Who's standing behind him?
13. Did you give him the book?
14. Have you seen them?
15. Did you get them a present?
16. Where did she meet them?

Talk about It Circle the reduced words in the questions above.

◄)) 13 | Listening for Reduced Words Listen and complete the answers to these questions. Then practice with a partner. `7.2 B`

1. A: What did you say to Jim?
   B: I ____*told him to*____ come back later.

2. A: Have you seen Paula today?
   B: No, but I _____.

3. A: Do you know Tom and Ron?
   B: I've _____, but
   I don't _____ very well.

4. A: How's your new boss?
   B: Everyone _____.

5. A: Are you in touch with Andrew?
   B: No, but I _____
   brother every day.

6. A: What should I say?
   B: I think you should _____
   the truth.

7. A: Would you mind taking your brothers to the movie?
   B: But I don't want to go _____.

8. A: Can my friend Steve come, too?
   B: _____

9. A: Why isn't Sarah here?
   B: I _____ come,
   _____ are visiting.

10. A: How's your new teacher?
    B: I _____ great.

11. A: Mr. Evans is waiting for you.
    B: How long _____ here?

12. A: Where are Tim and Lisa?
    B: I don't know. Can you _____?

13. A: Why did you _____
    I got a new job?
    B: I didn't know it was a secret.

14. A: What did you think of Lisa?
    B: I don't know. I only spent a few minutes
    _____.

14 | Distinguishing Personal Pronouns and Possessive Determiners Read this text. Choose the correct word from each box to complete it. `7.2 A–B`

CARL SAGAN: 1934–1996
by Ray Jayawardhana

Not so long ago, when I was in college, I wrote a paper on Carl Sagan. I wanted to find out as much as I could about Sagan's research as well as ___*his*___ writings. So I called
1
_____ secretary at Cornell University and asked _____ if she could send
2   3
_____ Sagan's vita. A vita is a brief list of a person's education, jobs, awards, and
4
publications. _____ usually a few pages long. She asked, "Are you sure _____
5   6
want the whole thing?" I didn't really understand what _____ meant, but I said,
7
"Yes." A few days later, _____ got this thick package in the mail. Inside was
8
Sagan's vita. _____ was 233 pages long! That's how many pages it took to list this
9
extraordinary man's achievements[13], scientific papers, and popular articles. Although
Carl Sagan died in 1996, _____ influence is still felt in books, TV series, articles,
10
and even movies based on his ideas.

| 1. him/his |
| 2. her/his |
| 3. him/her |
| 4. I/me |
| 5. it's/its |
| 6. you/your |
| 7. her/she |
| 8. I/me |
| 9. it/its |
| 10. him/his |

15 | Pronunciation Note: Possessive Pronouns Listen to the note. Then do Activity 16.

Sometimes we use possessive pronouns when we are contrasting two things. In these cases, we stress the possessive pronoun. In **1**, the speaker stresses *mine* to say, "They are **my** keys, not **Pam's** keys." In **2**, the speaker is not contrasting two things. Compare:

1 A: Are these Pam's keys?
B: No, they're **MINE**. (They are my keys, not Pam's keys.)

2 A: Whose notebook is this?
B: I think it's yours.

16 | Pronouncing Possessive Pronouns Listen and write the missing pronouns. `7.2 B`

1. A: Is this my book?
   B: No, it's ___*mine*___.

2. A: Whose book is this?
   B: It's _____.

3. A: Is this Stella's computer?
   B: No, she told me it was _____.
   A: Well, it's definitely not _____.

4. A: I forgot to bring my homework.
   B: Yeah, I forgot _____, too.

5. A: Here's Tom's book.
   B: But this isn't _____.
   A: If it's not _____, then whose is it?

6. A: Why is Cathy wearing your coat?
   B: Because she doesn't like _____.

7. A: Do you want to take my car?
   B: No, I can use _____.
   A: But _____ needs gas.

8. A: So when are they getting married?
   B: I don't know. The decision is _____.

[13] **achievements:** things that someone has done after trying hard

Think about It Listen again. Circle the pronouns that are stressed in the conversations in Activity 16. Which possessive pronouns are not stressed? Why? Share ideas with your classmates.

Talk about It Practice the conversations in Activity 16 with a partner.

17 | Using Pronouns and Possessive Determiners Choose the correct words from the box to complete these conversations. Then practice with a partner. **7.2 A–B**

1. A: Where do you want me to park _____my_____ car?
   ₁

   B: Why don't you leave _____ here? I'll put _____ over there.
           ₂   ₃

   A: OK, but what about Jack and Tom? Where are _____ going to park
                                          ₄

   _____?
   ₅

   B: I don't know. We'll figure something out.

1. my/mine
2. it/its
3. my/mine
4. they/their
5. theirs/them

2. A: Does anyone here know Ben Wilson?

   B: Actually, my brother is a good friend of _____.
                                    ₆

   A: Really? How long has he known _____?
                                 ₇

   B: _____ met in college.
     ₈

   A: Does your brother see _____ very often?
                             ₉

   B: No, but _____ children go the same school.
            ₁₀

6. him/his
7. he/him
8. they/their
9. his/him
10. they/their

3. A: How did you get in?

   B: Jason gave me his key.

   A: Why didn't you use _____?
                      ₁₁

   B: Because I left _____ at school.
                ₁₂

11. your/yours
12. me/mine

4. A: What do you think of _____ new house?
                              ₁₃

   B: It's nice but it's not as big as _____.
                             ₁₄

   A: Are you sure? I thought _____ was bigger.
                           ₁₅

13. their/theirs
14. our/ours
15. they/theirs

5. A: I can't believe Martha is quitting _____ job.
                                ₁₆

   B: Well, it's true, and the decision was entirely _____.
                                      ₁₇

   A: Someday she's going to regret _____.
                              ₁₈

16. her/hers
17. her/hers
18. it/its

18 | Error Correction Correct any errors in these sentences. (Some sentences may not have any errors.)

FAMILY AND FRIENDS

1. My friends and me usually get together after class. Sometimes we go out for coffee and sometimes we have lunch together. Whatever we do, we have a good time.

   My friends and I usually get together after class. Sometimes we go out for coffee and sometimes we have lunch together. Whatever we do, we have a good time.

2. My best friend and I are in the same class. I usually sit next to he, and during the break we talk and laugh.

3. Last weekend, my best friend and I spent the day at the beach. My friend, he borrowed a car and we got there early in the morning when it was still cool. By ten o'clock, however, its was very hot. We put up a huge umbrella and sat under it for the next few hours.

4. My parents were strict with my older brother and me. They didn't allow us to travel alone until we were in college. Even then, they worried about us a lot.

5. Last year, my parents moved to my neighborhood. It made me happy to see them almost every day.

6. This girl she said I should apply for a job where she works. I didn't know her very well, but I decided to take hers advice and apply for a job. I talked to the owner of the business and he liked mine a lot, but he didn't offer me a job.

7. Several months ago, my friend and I had a big argument. Of course, she thought it was my fault, and I thought it was her.

8. My sister drives to school every day with a friend of her.

9. My sister and I have always been good friends. I can honestly say I have never gotten angry with she.

7.3 Indefinite Pronouns

A

1 A: Did **anyone** call?
B: Yeah. **Someone** called at nine, but there was no message.

2 A: Why didn't Rachel come?
B: I don't know. **Something** is wrong with her.

3 A: Are you still leaving at five?
B: Yes, but we have plenty of time to go over **everything** before then.

We use an **indefinite pronoun** when we can't or don't want to name a specific person or thing, as in **1** – **3**. Indefinite pronouns do not refer back to a specific noun or noun phrase.

INDEFINITE PRONOUNS			
somebody	anybody	nobody	everybody
someone	anyone	no one	everyone
something	anything	nothing	everything

B

SUBJECT-VERB AGREEMENT

4 Everyone likes it here.

5 Nobody has finished the assignment.

We use a singular verb with an indefinite pronoun, as in **4** – **5**.

DESCRIBING INDEFINITE PRONOUNS

6 Can **somebody tall** help me reach this?

7 There's **something I have to tell you.**

8 I've already contacted **everyone in our class** about the assignment.

9 Is **anyone else** going? (= Is any other person going?)

We sometimes use other words after indefinite pronouns to describe them. For example:

• adjectives or adjective phrases, such as *tall*, as in **6**

• adjective clauses, as in **7**

• prepositional phrases, such as *in our class*, as in **8**

• *else*, as in **9**

C

10 There wasn't **anyone** there to help me.
(NOT: ~~There wasn't somebody there to help me.~~)

11 Hardly anyone knew the answer.

12 There was **no one** there to help me.
(NOT: ~~There wasn't no one . . .~~)

13 There's **nothing** to do.

In statements, indefinite pronouns with *any-* and *no-* can both give a negative meaning, but they are used differently.

• We can use *any-* forms after negative verbs or other negative words (such as *never* and *hardly*), as in **10** – **11**.

• We use *no-* forms after positive verbs, as in **12** – **13**.

WARNING! We don't usually use *some-* forms after negative verbs.

19 | Identifying Indefinite Pronouns Underline the indefinite pronouns in these sentences. Then choose one caption for each cartoon below. `7.3 A`

CARTOON CAPTIONS

1. "You work harder than <u>anyone</u> else."
2. "Everybody feels a little depressed at this time of year."
3. "You think I do nothing all day."
4. "I'll be at lunch. If anyone calls, say I'm at the health club."
5. "Does anyone know what the date is?"
6. "Nothing for me, thanks."
7. "Nobody lives forever."
8. "I'd like my daughter to know something about engines."
9. "I like things nobody else likes."
10. "I think everybody bought everything they needed three or four years ago."

____ a.

____ b.

____ c.

____ d.

20 | Using Indefinite Pronouns Rewrite these sentences. Use an indefinite pronoun in your new sentence. (More than one answer may be possible.) `7.3 A`

1. I prefer to travel with a person I know.

   I prefer to travel with someone I know.

2. Every person should have enough food to eat.
3. No person in my class has a full-time job.
4. There isn't a person in my class who speaks Spanish.
5. If a person wants to be a success, he or she must work hard.
6. Every person needs time to relax and have fun.
7. I couldn't find a person to help me.
8. I need a thing to write with.
9. I can't think of a thing better than being a teacher.
10. A fad is a thing that becomes popular quickly for a short period of time.

21 | Singular or Plural Verb? Complete these questions. Use *is*, *are*, *do*, *does*, *has*, or *have*. `7.3 B`

QUESTIONS ABOUT YOUR CLASS AND CLASSMATES

1. _____*Is*_____ anyone absent today?

2. _____ there enough chairs in the room for everyone?

3. _____ there anything interesting on the walls of our classroom?

4. _____ we have everything we need in our classroom?

5. _____ everyone in our class come from the same country?

6. _____ anybody married?

7. _____ somebody in the class have children?

8. _____ someone wearing a red shirt?

9. _____ anyone traveled to another country this year?

10. _____ anybody in the class been to Japan?

11. _____ we learned everything in this book?

12. _____ someone in your class helped you understand something better?

Talk about It Work in a small group. Answer the questions above. (Say more than just yes or no.)

22 | Describing Indefinite Pronouns Add words to describe each indefinite pronoun in these conversations. (Many different words—such as adjectives, adjective clauses, or prepositional phrases—are possible.) Then practice with a partner. `7.3 B`

1. A: Julia just bought something _*really expensive*_____.

   B: Oh, no! What was it?

   A: A gold bracelet.

2. A: You're in big trouble.

   B: Why? I didn't do anything _____.

   A: Well, then, who broke the car window?

3. A: Was there anything _____ in the newspaper?

   B: Yeah. There's a pretty good article about Greece.

4. A: I have something _____ to tell you.

   B: What is it?

   A: I just lost my job.

5. A: Let's do something _____ today.

   B: Like what?

   A: Like, um, like . . . let's go swimming at the lake.

6. A: Are you going on the school trip?

   B: Is everyone _____ going?

   A: Yes, I think so.

7. A: Have you ever met someone _____?

   B: No, but I once saw the musician Yo-Yo Ma on the street.

8. A: Do you know anything about _____?

   B: (Give your own answer.) _____

23 | Using *Any-* and *No-* Rewrite each sentence using an indefinite pronoun with *any-* or *no-*. `7.3 C`

1. There's nobody here named Chris.

   There isn't anybody here named Chris.

2. I think nobody's home.
3. There wasn't anything good on TV last night.
4. I had nobody to talk to all day.
5. There's nothing better than a glass of cold water.
6. We didn't have anything to do with the accident.
7. They did nothing at all for two days.
8. It doesn't cost anything to look at a beautiful sports car.
9. We've had nobody sign up for the workshop.
10. There isn't anything wrong with your car.
11. It doesn't seem as if anybody was surprised.

> **F Y I**
> A positive statement with *no-* (*body, one, thing*) is stronger than a negative statement with *any-* (*body, one, thing*).
>
> I saw **nothing**. Honest.
>
> I don't think I saw **anything**.

24 | Using *Some-* and *Any-* Complete these statements of advice. Use the appropriate form of *someone/something* or *anyone/anything*. In some cases, either *some-* or *any-* is possible. Then decide if you agree with the advice. Check (✓) your answers. `7.3 C`

PERSONAL ADVICE	AGREE	DISAGREE
1. Don't do _____*anything*_____ active just before you go to bed. You might not be able to sleep.	☐	☐
2. If you have money problems, don't tell _____ in your family.	☐	☐
3. When you get angry about _____, count to ten before speaking.	☐	☐
4. When you don't feel well, it helps to wear _____ comfortable.	☐	☐
5. You shouldn't take _____ that doesn't belong to you.	☐	☐
6. Every day, take a few minutes to notice _____ positive about life around you.	☐	☐
7. Don't go to sleep while you're mad at _____. Resolve[14] your disagreement first.	☐	☐
8. Always try to think of _____ good about each person you work with.	☐	☐
9. Don't buy _____ you can't afford.	☐	☐
10. Do _____ fun or creative with your friends every week.	☐	☐

Talk about It Take turns reading the advice above aloud with a partner. See if your partner agrees or disagrees and why.

A: Don't do anything active just before you go to bed. You might not be able to sleep.
B: I agree with that because . . .

Write about It Write three to five statements of advice using *someone, anyone, anything,* and *something*. Share one with your classmates and see if they agree or disagree.

---

[14]**resolve:** to find a solution to a problem

Think about It If we don't usually use *somebody*, *someone*, or *something* after a negative verb, why is it correct to use *something* in the sentence below?

*When you can't sleep, you should drink **something** warm.*

25 | Review of Indefinite Pronouns Complete these questions with your own ideas. **7.3 A–C**

1. Have you ever done something _scary_____?
2. Do you know anyone _____?
3. Have you met anyone _____ recently?
4. In school, did you learn anything about _____?
5. Have you ever forgotten something _____?
6. Do you know anybody who lives in _____?
7. Do you know anyone who speaks _____?
8. Is there anything you don't like about _____?
9. Do you know anything about _____?
10. Does anyone else in your family _____?
11. Have you ever made someone _____?
12. Did you do anything _____ on your last vacation?

Talk about It Ask a partner your questions above. When your partner answers yes to your question, ask another question to get more information.

A: *Have you ever done something scary?*
B: *Well, one time I took a flying lesson.*
A: *Really? What happened?*

flying lessons

Talk about It Tell your classmates about your partner.

"Sarah has done something scary. Once she took a flying lesson, and she was so afraid that she got sick."

7.4 Noun-Pronoun Agreement

<table>
<tr><td rowspan="4" style="vertical-align: middle;">**A**</td><td>

noun phrase   pronoun

1 When **people here** read the news, **they** were shocked.

2 When **people** heard **the news,** **it** surprised **them.**

3 **Every country** has **its** problems.

4 **(You)** Come closer so I can see that smile of **yours.**

</td><td>

Pronouns and **possessive determiners** often refer back to **nouns** or **noun phrases** mentioned earlier, as in **1 – 4**. A singular form refers back to a singular or noncount noun. A plural form refers back to a plural noun.

Notice that *yours* refers back to the implied subject *you* in imperative sentences, as in **4**.

</td></tr>
<tr><td rowspan="1">

B

5 My **mother** sent me **her** new email address.

6 My **father** asked me to call **him.**

7 It should be against the law for **people** to drive while **they** are talking on **their** phones.

COMPARE SINGULAR AND PLURAL FORMS

8a A **doctor** should be honest with **his** patients.
8b A **doctor** should be honest with **his or her** patients.
8c **Doctors** should be honest with **their** patients.

</td><td>

A feminine form refers back to a female person, as in **5**. A masculine form refers back to a male person, as in **6**.

Since plural forms are neutral (not male or female), they are often the best choice in writing, as in **7**.

If we don't know if a person is male or female, we can:

- use either form, as in **8a**. This is problematic because a doctor can be male or female.
- use both forms, as in **8b**. This is somewhat formal and can become repetitive.
- use plural forms, as in **8c**.

</td></tr>
<tr><td>

C

INFORMAL AGREEMENT

9a We think **everyone** can reach **their** potential.

MORE FORMAL AGREEMENT

9b We think **everyone** can reach **his or her** potential.
9c We think **all people** can reach **their** potential.

</td><td>

In informal contexts, we often use a plural form to refer back to an indefinite pronoun, as in **9a**. We do this even though indefinite pronouns are singular.

In formal contexts, **9b – 9c** are more acceptable.

</td></tr>
<tr></tr>
</table>

GO ONLINE

26 | Referring Back to Nouns Choose the correct words to complete these sentences. Then, where possible, circle the noun or noun phrase the pronoun refers back to. **7.4 A**

LISTENING AND SPEAKING STRATEGIES

1. Listen carefully to (other people) when ____*they*____ speak, and don't interrupt when you are part of
    (you / they)
   the audience.

2. Show other speakers that you respect _____ viewpoints[15] even when you don't agree with them.
    (your / their)

3. Think about the speaker's main idea and try to put _____ in _____ own words.
    (it / them)   (your / their)

4. Remember to turn off your cell phone before the speaker begins. You don't want _____ to ring
    (it / them)
   during the talk.

5. When you are planning a presentation, think about your listeners. What _____ already know
    (does it / do they)
   about your topic?

---

[15] **viewpoints:** different ways of thinking about something

6. Try starting your presentation with a personal story. _____ will get the attention of your audience.
   (it / they)

7. Be sure that you don't talk too fast, or no one will understand _____.
   (them / you)

8. If you use pictures, make sure the people in the back of the room can see _____.
   (it / them)

9. Be willing to answer questions at the end of your presentation. If you don't know an answer, volunteer to find out and share _____ later.
   (it / them)

10. If you are making a series of points, organize _____ from most important to least important.
    (it / them)

11. A good conversation is an exchange of ideas. Everyone needs to be included in _____.
    (it / them)

12. During a class discussion, encourage your classmates to talk by asking _____ questions.
    (him / them)

Write about It Write three more speaking or listening strategies like the ones in Activity 26 and then read them to your classmates.

27 | Identifying Pronoun References Read this article. What does each **bold** pronoun or possessive determiner refer to? Write your answers in the boxes. 7.4 A

Subway Hero

Toronto, Dec. 5—Subway riders aren't usually asked to perform acts of bravery. Yesterday, however, one of **them** became a hero. Anna Fischer, a
1
24-year-old woman, saved the life of a small child. The child was waiting with **his** babysitter at the 9ᵗʰ Street subway station when **he** fell onto the
2   3
tracks. Ms. Fischer jumped onto the tracks and saved the child.

When Ms. Fischer was interviewed about the rescue, she said, "I was standing near the tracks when I saw the little boy playing with a ball. **His**
4
babysitter looked sort of worried, and **she** said to be careful. But the kid
5
threw the ball, which rolled onto the tracks. I saw him run after **it**, and he
6
fell off the platform. The babysitter screamed and called for help. There was no train, but **it** as coming in two minutes, so I jumped onto the tracks and
7
lifted the kid up. Luckily there was enough time to get **him** to safety."
8
One witness[16] summed up[17] the situation. "I never saw anyone move so
9
quickly. **It** was a miracle."
10

1. *subway riders*	
2.	
3.	
4.	
5.	
6.	
7.	
8.	
9.	
10.	

Talk about It Retell the story above from the point of view of the babysitter or the little boy.

"Yesterday something terrible almost happened while I was babysitting.
In the morning, I took the child to the grocery store. . . . "

---

[16] **witness:** a person who sees something happen and can describe it to others

[17] **sum (something) up:** to state the main points in a short, clear way

28 | Using Plural Forms Rewrite these statements. Replace the **bold** words with a plural noun, and make any other necessary changes to make the sentence correct. **7.4 B**

JOB REQUIREMENTS

1. **A good doctor** listens carefully to his or her patients.

    Good doctors listen carefully to their patients.

2. **A carpenter** needs to take good care of his or her tools.
3. **A horse trainer** must be gentle with his or her horses. He or she should never lose his or her temper.
4. **A good parent** encourages his or her children to talk to him or her.
5. **An office manager** needs to be organized so that he or she can make good decisions.
6. **A good employer** can communicate clearly with his or her employees.
7. **A good teacher** is able to change to meet his or her students' needs.
8. **A lawyer** must pass a state exam before he or she can practice law.
9. **A pilot in training** must get 250 flight hours before he or she can fly commercially.
10. **A supervisor** must be well-spoken so he or she can explain clearly what needs to be done.

Think about It In the past, the masculine forms (*he/his/him*) were used to refer to all people. Why are plural forms (*they/their/them*) more common now?

Write about It Complete this question with your own idea: *What makes a good . . . ?* Then write three or more sentences to answer the question.

29 | Using Plural Forms Rewrite this essay to make the language neutral. **7.4 B**

It takes a special kind of person to be an effective leader. ***Effective leaders*** *have a confident attitude.* ***They know*** . . .

An Effective Leader

It takes a special kind of person to be an effective leader. An effective leader has a confident attitude. She knows what her goals are and how she wants to reach them. At the same time, she is flexible. A good leader can make changes to her plan when it is necessary. The people around her can feel sure that she will be a good guide.

An effective leader is a good listener. She pays attention to other people's needs. She lets people know that she is working for everybody's interest, not just her own. Finally, an effective leader knows that she can't do everything alone. She knows how to ask other people for help. She knows how to divide responsibilities among several people. Being a good leader takes a certain kind of talent. Not everyone can do it well.

WARNING!

When we use a plural subject, we sometimes need to decide if we should use a singular or plural object. For example:

Children need their **mothers**.
Children need their **mother**.

Both are correct. We might choose *mothers* because we are describing more than one child. Or we might choose *mother* because a child only has one mother.

30 | Referring Back to Indefinite Pronouns Rewrite the informal language using plural forms. **7.4 C**

COMPLAINTS

1. I hate it when someone uses their cell phone in a restaurant. They should at least get up and leave the table.

    I hate it when people use their cell phones in a restaurant. They should at least get up and leave the table.

2. It bothers me when someone sends text messages while they are talking to me.

3. It drives me crazy when someone chews their food with their mouth open.

4. I don't like it when someone drives their car really close behind me.

5. When I call someone in the evening, I'm always afraid I'll disturb them.

6. It bothers me when someone doesn't do their job.

7. I don't understand why anyone smokes. They should quit.

8. It's irritating[18] when someone is late and they don't even call to tell you.

9. I don't like it when someone disagrees with me and they won't listen to my viewpoint.

10. I don't like it when someone borrows something and they don't return it.

Write about It Complete these statements with your own ideas. Then read your statements to your classmates. Ask them if you used formal or informal language.

It bothers me when someone/people . . .
I don't like it when someone/people . . .
It drives me crazy when someone/people . . .

7.5 It, One, Some, Any, Other, You, and They

<table>
<tr><td rowspan="4">A</td><td>**COMPARE *IT* AND *ONE***

1a I can't eat **this sandwich**. Do you want **it**?
(*It* refers to a specific sandwich.)

1b I'm making **a sandwich**. Do you want **one**, too?
(*One* refers to another sandwich, not a specific sandwich.)</td><td>When we refer back to specific people or things, we usually use a personal pronoun like *it*, as in **1a**.

When we refer back to nonspecific things, we use a pronoun like *one*, as in **1b**.</td></tr>
<tr><td>**2** I need **a tripod**. Does anyone here have **one**?

3 We have a new box of discs but **some** are broken.

4 I offered her some coffee but she didn't want **any**.</td><td>We use *one* to refer back to singular count nouns, as in **2**. *Some* and *any* refer back to both plural nouns and noncount nouns, as in **3 – 4**.</td></tr>
<tr><td>**5** **One person** in my class is from Brazil and **another** is from Turkey.

6 **Some people** can stop smoking on their own while **others** need help.</td><td>We often contrast *one* or *some* member(s) of a group with *another* or *others*, as in **5 – 6**. *Another* refers to a singular noun. *Others* refers to plural nouns.</td></tr>
<tr><td></td><td></td></tr>
<tr><td>B</td><td>**7** "Sometimes **one** pays most for the things **one** gets for nothing." (*Albert Einstein*)

8 The more **you** look at the world, the more **you** see how people value things differently.

9 **They** say that Paris is the most romantic city in the world.</td><td>We sometimes use *one*, *you*, or *they* to make general statements about people (not a specific person), as in **7 – 9**. *One* is more formal than *you* or *they*.

GRAMMAR TERM: Pronouns that refer to any person in general are called **generic pronouns**.</td></tr>
<tr><td>C</td><td>**10** **It** was dangerous to go to some of these places.
(= To go to some of these places was dangerous.)

11 **It's** impossible to do this quickly.
(= To do this quickly is impossible.)</td><td>In sentences with *to-* infinitives, we can use *it* as a placeholder for a subject, as in **10 – 11**. (This is often called an **empty subject**.) This allows us to put new information at the end of a sentence where it is easier to notice.

For information on using *it* with *to-* infinitives, see Unit 11, page 354.</td></tr>
</table>

---

[18]**irritating:** making someone angry

31 | One or It? Complete these conversations with *one* or *it*. Then practice with a partner. `7.5 A`

1. A: Do you need your book back?

   B: No, you can give _____*it*_____ to me later.

2. A: Sorry I broke your glass.

   B: No problem. I can replace _____ tomorrow.

3. A: Is that a new hat?

   B: Yeah, I bought _____ online.

   A: Nice. I like _____.

4. A: Did you buy a new hat?

   B: Yeah, I found _____ online. I'll bring it in tomorrow.

5. A: Can I get you a cup of coffee?

   B: No, thanks. I've already got _____.

6. A: Have you seen any good movies lately?

   B: Yeah, I saw _____ last week. _____ was called *The 39 Steps*.

7. A: Can you do the grocery shopping?

   B: Yeah, but I need a list.

   A: OK, I'll put _____ together for you.

8. A: My allergies are terrible today.

   B: Did you take your allergy pill?

   A: Yeah. I took _____ an hour ago.

---

32 | What Does the Pronoun Refer To? Who or what does each **bold** word refer to? `7.5 A`

1. The researchers found two possible explanations, but there may be **another**.

2. Scientists now report discovering why some people are chocoholics[19] and **others** are not.

3. People express grief[20] in different ways. One person may cry for weeks while **another** may scream and yell.

4. Some people think eating chocolate or oily foods causes acne[21]. **Others** blame dirty skin or nervous tension.

5. Some people can't say no to food if **any** is available.

6. Different sleep problems are treated differently. **Some** can be treated with medications, whereas **others** may be helped with special equipment.

7. Some people quit smoking because a friend quit. If we can get a few people to quit, they might go on to help **others** quit.

8. There are a few things you should know about Dr. Brown. **One** is that she asks a lot of questions. **Another** is that she is going to tell you to get more exercise.

9. Not all marathons[22] are the same. **Some** are run in the heat. On **some** the course is flat, and on **others** it is hilly.

10. Scientists don't agree about climate change. **Some** think the climate is changing a lot, but **others** think it is not.

1. another = *another explanation*
2. others = *other people*
3. another =
4. others =
5. any =
6. some =   others =
7. others =
8. one =   another =
9. some =   some =   others =
10. some =   others =

---

33 | One, Another, Some, and Others Write a short paragraph about each topic. `7.5 A`

1. There are several ways to cook eggs. • fry them in a pan • boil them in water	2. There are many different ways you can get the news. • read it online • watch it on TV	3. Travelers have many options for buying airline tickets. • buy them through a travel agent • buy them online

There are several ways to cook eggs. One is to fry them in a pan. Another is to boil them in water. . . .

---

[19] **chocoholics:** people who like chocolate and eat a lot of it
[20] **grief:** great sadness, especially because someone has died

[21] **acne:** a skin problem that causes red spots
[22] **marathons:** very long races

34 | Making General Statements about People

What do the quotations mean to you? Share ideas with your classmates. Then complete each general statement in a new way and share ideas with a partner. `7.5 B`

QUOTATIONS

1. You can't win unless you know how to lose. *(Kareem Abdul-Jabbar, athlete)*

2. You cannot shake hands with a clenched[23] fist. *(Indira Gandhi, Indian prime minister)*

3. If you can dream it, you can do it. *(Walt Disney, entrepreneur)*

4. The excess[24] of one is the shortage[25] of another. *(Arabian proverb)*

5. All you need in life is ignorance and confidence, and then success is sure. *(Mark Twain, writer)*

6. They say the world has become too complex for simple answers. They are wrong. *(Ronald Reagan, U.S. president)*

GENERAL STATEMENTS

1. You can't _____ unless you know how to _____.

2. You cannot _____ with a _____.

3. If you can _____ it, you can _____ it.

4. The _____ of one is the _____ of another.

5. All you need in life is _____ and _____, and then success is sure.

6. They say _____ has become _____. They are wrong.

35 | Using *It* as a Placeholder

Choose the adjective that best completes each statement. `7.5 C`

STATEMENTS FROM PERSONAL ESSAYS

1. It is ____*important*____ to take care of your body and stay healthy, and there are many different ways you can do this.

2. It's not _____ to stay calm when someone makes you angry.

3. It's not always _____ to do well in school.

4. It isn't _____ to be a good parent.

5. Today it is _____ for mothers as well as fathers to have a career.

6. When you travel to a foreign country, it is _____ to visit someone's home.

7. It is _____ for doctors to listen to their patients.

8. It is _____ to work seven days a week.

9. Because of modern health care, it is not _____ for people to live into their eighties.

10. It's _____ to get some exercise every day.

11. It's _____ to have a good relationship with someone who doesn't tell the truth.

12. With modern technology, it is _____ to keep in touch with friends and relatives.

> 1. important/unusual
> 2. acceptable/easy
> 3. good/possible
> 4. easy/possible
> 5. common/interesting
> 6. essential/fun
> 7. easy/essential
> 8. essential/unhealthy
> 9. acceptable/uncommon
> 10. important/interesting
> 11. difficult/necessary
> 12. easy/unusual

[23]**clenched:** closed tightly
[24]**excess:** more than is necessary or needed
[25]**shortage:** less than is necessary or needed

Talk about It Take turns reading the statements in Activity 35 aloud with a partner. See if your partner agrees or disagrees and why.

Write about It Choose five of the *it* + *be* + adjective examples in Activity 35 and write sentences with your own ideas. Share one with your classmates and see if they agree or disagree.

> *It is important/easy/common to . . .*
> *It is not difficult/easy to . . .*

7.6 Compound Nouns

A

Some nouns in English are made up of two or more words. The words work together as one word or concept and have a unique meaning. We call them **compound nouns**. Many compound nouns are made of:

noun + noun	noun + verb	adjective + noun	-*ing* verb + noun
newspaper	headache	software	swimming pool
spacecraft	role-play	solar system	washing machine
light year	homework	easy chair	walking stick
energy costs	rainfall	highway	running shoes

B

1 **Climate change** is a popular topic these days.

2 **Solar panels** on a house absorb the sun's energy.

3 Using fluorescent **light bulbs** can save money.

4 **Landslides** are becoming more common in the Philippines.

5 In Nepal, the amount of water in the **glacier-lakes** is increasing.

The first word in a compound noun gives information about the second word. It often says "what kind or type."

- In **1**, *climate* identifies the type of change.
- In **2**, *solar* identifies the kind of panel.
- In **3**, *light* identifies the kind of bulb.

Most compound nouns are written as either two separate words, as in **1 – 3**, or a single word, as in **4**. A few compound nouns have a hyphen, as in **5**.

C

6 A **heat wave** is hot weather that lasts for a long time.

7 Hurricanes are **wind storms** that start in the ocean.
(NOT: ~~winds storms~~ or ~~winds storm~~)

8 In western India, **rainfall** has doubled.

9 **Solar power** is becoming a more popular source of energy.

Some compound nouns are count nouns, as in **6 – 7**. For the plural form of these compound nouns, we usually make the last noun plural, as in **7**.

Some compound nouns are noncount nouns, as in **8 – 9**. These compound nouns do not have a plural form.

36 | Pronunciation Note: Compound Nouns Listen to the note. Then do Activities 37–38.

Sometimes it is difficult to tell the difference between a compound noun and an adjective + noun. Most compound nouns have the main stress on the first part of the compound. This is different from the stress on adjective + noun forms, which have more equal stress on both words. Compare:

Compound nouns	Adjective + noun	Compound nouns	Adjective + noun
1 VOICE mail	undelivered mail	4 LIGHT year	next year
2 FINGERnail	bent nail	5 EASY chair	uncomfortable chair
3 NEWSpaper	recycled paper	6 SOLAR system	efficient system

37 | Pronouncing Compound Nouns Listen to these sentences. Are the words compound nouns or adjectives + nouns? Check (✓) your answers. `7.6 A–B`

1. ☐ compound noun   ☐ adjective + noun   6. ☐ compound noun   ☐ adjective + noun
2. ☐ compound noun   ☐ adjective + noun   7. ☐ compound noun   ☐ adjective + noun
3. ☐ compound noun   ☐ adjective + noun   8. ☐ compound noun   ☐ adjective + noun
4. ☐ compound noun   ☐ adjective + noun   9. ☐ compound noun   ☐ adjective + noun
5. ☐ compound noun   ☐ adjective + noun   10. ☐ compound noun   ☐ adjective + noun

Talk about It Listen again and write the words. Practice saying the words with the correct stress.

1. _____   6. _____
2. _____   7. _____
3. _____   8. _____
4. _____   9. _____
5. _____   10. _____

38 | Identifying Compound Nouns Listen and read the articles. Circle the compound nouns. (Listen for the stress of the words to help you identify them.) Then compare ideas with your classmates. `7.6 A–B`

The Huntsman Spider

Imagine driving in your car. Suddenly, a huge spider runs across the (windshield.) If you are in Australia, it is probably a huntsman spider. Although the name is scary, the spider doesn't actually hunt men. In fact, the spiders are very beneficial[26] creatures because they eat insects. They are large (as large as your hand) and hairy, and in Australia you can find them everywhere. They live in woods, in living rooms, and even in bedrooms. They can run really fast and are hard to catch. In Sydney, people often come home from work to find a huntsman spider on their dining table or sitting in their favorite armchair. This often happens after a thunderstorm as the spiders come inside for shelter. Most Australians have learned to live with them. They catch the spiders rather than kill them.

F Y I
We don't usually capitalize the names of animals and plants (*huntsman spider, bighorn sheep*) unless there is a proper noun in the name (*African violet*).

---

[26] **beneficial:** improving a situation; helpful

Water Found on Distant Planet

Water has been discovered on a planet beyond our solar system. A telescope detected water vapor in the atmosphere of a gas giant[27] that is 64 light years away from Earth. Although the planet is too hot to support life, the discovery suggests that water may be commonly found on planets throughout the galaxy[28]. According to Giovanna Tinetti of University College London, who led the research group, the team will be able to use this method in the future to study other planets that are "life-friendly."

39 | Using Compound Nouns Choose a compound noun from the box to complete each sentence below. Where necessary, make the compound noun plural. `7.6 C`

blood type	fingernail	kneecap	muscle power	springtime	thighbone
eyelash	jawbone	lifespan	nerve cell	tennis court	tongue print

THE HUMAN BODY

1. You use about 200 muscles when you take one step. That's a lot of _____*muscle power*_____.
2. Children grow faster in the _____.
3. _____ grow four times faster than toenails.
4. Each hair on your head has a _____ of three to seven years.
5. The surface area of the human lungs[29] is equal to a _____.
6. Your _____ are the bones in your upper legs. They are stronger than concrete[30].
7. In addition to unique fingerprints, humans have unique _____.
8. There are four main _____ in the world. The most common is Type O.
9. There are about 86 billion _____ in the human brain.
10. Your _____ is the hardest bone in your body.
11. When they fall out, _____ take seven to eight weeks to grow back.
12. Babies are born with soft _____. They don't turn into bone until a child is two to five years old.

Think about It Decide if each compound noun above is a count noun or a noncount noun. Write *C* above the count nouns. Write *N* above the noncount nouns.

Think about It What are some other compound nouns that you have noticed? Look back through the unit or another English text you read recently. Make a list of compound nouns.

---

[27] **gas giant:** a large planet made mostly of gases
[28] **galaxy:** a large group of stars and planets in outer space

[29] **lungs:** the two parts inside your body that you use for breathing
[30] **concrete:** a hard, gray material used for building things

7.7 Forming Nouns Using Suffixes

Some verbs and adjectives can be changed into nouns by adding a suffix (a word ending), as in Table **1** and Table **2**. The meaning of some nouns can also be changed by adding a suffix, as in Table **3**. Notice that small spelling changes are often necessary.

A

TABLE 1			
verb	+	suffix =	noun
define describe evaluate explain imagine investigate participate realize		-tion -ation	definition description evaluation explanation imagination investigation participation realization
conclude decide		-sion	conclusion decision
act employ		-or -er	actor employer
accomplish achieve agree fulfill invest		-ment	accomplishment achievement agreement fulfillment investment
arrive deny		-al	arrival denial
assist reside		-ant -ent	assistant resident
assist depend rely		-ance -ence	assistance dependence reliance
discover inquire		-ry	discovery inquiry

TABLE 2			
adjective	+	suffix =	noun
complex possible real similar valid		-ity	complexity possibility reality similarity validity
happy lonely sad		-ness	happiness loneliness sadness
free wise		-dom	freedom wisdom
urgent		-cy	urgency
important silent		-ce	importance silence
just		-ice	justice
brave		-ery	bravery

TABLE 3			
noun	+	suffix =	noun
terror		-ism	terrorism
friend member		-ship	friendship membership
bag mile		-age	baggage mileage
child neighbor		-hood	childhood neighborhood
art		-ist	artist
hand mouth		-ful	handful mouthful

40 | Noticing Spelling Changes Choose five words in the chart above that change their spelling. Write the words in the chart and explain the spelling change. Then compare ideas with your classmates. **7.7 A**

	Word	Word + suffix	Spelling change
1.	*describe*	*description*	*Drop the -e, change -b to -p, and add -tion.*
2.	*happy*	*happiness*	*Change the -y to -i and add -ness.*
3.			
4.			
5.			
6.			
7.			

41 | Identifying Nouns with Suffixes Each of these book titles has a noun with a suffix. Find the noun and underline the suffix. Then say how each noun is formed. Check (✓) your answers. `7.7 A`

WELL-KNOWN BOOKS	VERB + SUFFIX	ADJECTIVE + SUFFIX	NOUN + SUFFIX
1. *A Portrait of the Art<u>ist</u> as a Young Man* by James Joyce	☐	☐	✓
2. *Childhood's End* by Arthur C. Clarke	☐	☐	☐
3. *The Importance of Being Earnest*[31] by Oscar Wilde	☐	☐	☐
4. *Crime and Punishment* by Fyodor Dostoyevsky	☐	☐	☐
5. *Appointment in Samarra* by John O'Hara	☐	☐	☐
6. *The Loneliness of the Long-Distance Runner* by Alan Sillitoe	☐	☐	☐
7. *A Handful of Dust* by Evelyn Waugh	☐	☐	☐
8. *Great Expectations* by Charles Dickens	☐	☐	☐
9. *Teach Us to Outgrow Our Madness* by Kenzaburo Oe	☐	☐	☐
10. *The House of Silence* by Orhan Pamuk	☐	☐	☐

Talk about It Think about the titles of the books above. What do you think each one is about? Use other forms of the nouns in the titles to make a guess.

"Great Expectations might be about someone who expects something great."

42 | Forming Nouns with Suffixes Add the correct suffix to these words to make the noun form. Then use them to complete the quotations below. (You will not use one of the nouns. More than one noun may be possible but only one is correct.) `7.7 A`

1. act _____*action*_____
2. agree _____
3. brave _____
4. free _____
5. friend _____
6. fulfill _____
7. happy _____
8. imagine _____
9. punish _____

FAMOUS QUOTATIONS	AGREE	DISAGREE
a. _____*Actions*_____ speak louder than words. (*American proverb*)	☐	☐
b. Success is getting what you want. _____ is wanting what you get. (*Dale Carnegie, writer*)	☐	☐
c. Let the _____ match the offense[32]. (*Cicero, statesman*)	☐	☐
d. _____ is never given; it is won. (*A. Philip Randolph, activist*)	☐	☐
e. Laughter is not at all a bad beginning for a _____. (*Oscar Wilde, writer*)	☐	☐
f. The goal of life is living in _____ with nature. (*Zeno, philosopher*)	☐	☐
g. A promise is a cloud; _____ is rain. (*Arab proverb*)	☐	☐
h. _____ is more important than knowledge. (*Albert Einstein, physicist*)	☐	☐

Talk about It What do the quotations above mean to you? Check (✓) if you agree or disagree. Then compare with a partner.

[31] **earnest:** serious; also a man's name   [32] **offense:** a crime; breaking the law

43 | Forming Nouns with Suffixes Read each pair of sentences. Complete the second sentence with a noun form of the **bold** word. `7.7 A`

1. I can't **decide**. = I can't make a _____*decision*_____.

2. I am proud of the things I have **achieved**. = I am proud of my _____.

3. My work isn't ready to be **evaluated**. = My work isn't ready for _____.

4. It's important to be **free**. = _____ is important.

5. I don't understand why this news is **urgent**. = I don't understand the _____ of this news.

6. How many **miles** is it to the nearest city? = What is the _____ to the nearest city?

7. I'm not interested in becoming a **member** of this group. = _____ in this group doesn't interest me.

8. I can't **explain** this. = I don't have an _____ for this.

9. Do you need someone to **assist** you? = Do you need an _____?

10. Why is this assignment **important**? = What is the _____ of this assignment?

11. You should be proud of the things you have **accomplished**. = You should be proud of your _____.

12. It's important to **participate** in class discussions. = _____ in class discussions is important.

13. The archeologists **discovered** something important this year. = The archeologists made an important _____ this year.

14. About 4,000 people **reside** in this area. = There are about 4,000 _____ in this area.

15. The two teams **agreed** to postpone the game. = The two teams made an _____ to postpone the game.

Think about It Look back through the unit or another English text you read recently. Find five more words with the suffix -*tion*. Then use each word in a sample sentence.

Words	Sample sentences
1. *education*	*I want to get a good education.*
2. *election*	*I have never voted in an election.*
3.	
4.	
5.	
6.	
7.	

7.8 Using *This* and *That* to Refer Back

A

1 A: Why is Matt **angry all the time**?
B: I don't know. He didn't use to be like **that**.

2 I can't believe **my brother left without me**. How could he do **this** to me?

We frequently use **this** or **that** to "point to" or focus attention on a thing, an action, or an idea mentioned earlier, as in **1 – 2**.

3 There was **a decline in the unemployment rate last week**. **This** suggests that the job market is still in good shape.

4 **Mathematics is typically taught in a traditional way**. Too often, **that** means students learn by memorizing facts.

5 **Sleep is necessary for every animal that has ever been studied**. **This** includes whales, octopuses—even fruit flies.

Sometimes we can use either *this* or *that*. However:

- We often use *this* to refer to things that are "closer" to us in time, in location, or in how we feel about them, as in **3**.
- We often use *that* to refer to things that are "farther away" from us, as in **4**.

This or *that* can sometimes refer back to an entire sentence or paragraph, especially in academic writing, as in **5**.

B

COMPARING CONVERSATION AND WRITING

6 A: I think **our garden got washed out by the rain**.
B: Oh, no, **that's** terrible!

7 In recent years, **banks have begun charging higher interest rates**. **This** suggests that they are becoming more careful about who they are lending money to.

That is more common in conversation, as in **6**, while *this* is more common in academic writing, as in **7**. In academic writing, we often use *this* with these verbs:

explains	indicates	makes	seems
implies	involves	means	shows
includes	is	requires	suggests

C

8 To understand a word, we first have to **retrieve its meaning from memory**. Most of the time, **this** happens quickly, but sometimes **it** doesn't.

9 If you have problems with a product, **try contacting the manufacturer**. **This** will help you get useful information, and **it** may solve your problem.

In academic writing, we can use **this** or **that** to refer back to an idea that we have just mentioned. (This brings attention to the previous idea and indicates that the ideas are closely related.) In later sentences, however, we often use **it** to refer to the idea again (not *this*), as in **8 – 9**.

44 | Identifying Pronoun References What do the pronouns *this* or *that* refer back to in each news report? Circle the correct words. (You may circle a whole sentence.) **7.8 A**

NEWS REPORTS

1. With the new public transportation system, (fewer people are driving their cars to work.) **This** could be good for the environment because cars give off pollution.

2. Many scientists believe that gases in the air are causing the earth to gradually become warmer. **That** is called global warming.

3. Young children learn new words very quickly. Researchers have called **this** the "vocabulary explosion."

4. The Apple computer company has sold over 15 billion digital songs from its iTunes program. **This** has made a lot of money for record companies.

5. In 1997, about 12 million people in the United States worked at home at least one day a month. **That** is very different from today's numbers.

6. Most green buildings[33] have lights that automatically turn off when people leave the room. They are also designed with lots of windows. During the day, **this** allows people to use the sun instead of lamps for light.

7. To cope[34] with stress, many people practice yoga every evening. **This** helps them relax after a long day. It also helps them get a good night's sleep.

[33] **green buildings:** buildings designed with environmentally friendly systems   [34] **cope:** to deal with something difficult

8. People use a lot of unfamiliar words when they talk about the inventor Buckminster Fuller. **This** is because Fuller invented words to describe his ideas and inventions.

9. In the Peruvian Amazon, there is a type of ant that kills all kinds of trees except one. **That**'s the finding of Megan Frederickson, a doctoral student at Stanford University.

10. The most intensive[35] period of language development is during the first three years of a child's life. **This** is the time when the brain is developing.

45 | Listening for *This* and *That* in Conversation Listen and write the missing lines in these conversations. Pay special attention to the choice of *this* or *that*. `7.8 A–B`

WORKPLACE CONVERSATIONS

1. Employee: Sorry I'm late. My car broke down.

   Employer: _Is that so?_____

   Employee: Yeah, um, I had to take the bus.

2. Employee: I need to take a few days off. We've had a death in the family.

   Employer: _____

3. Employee 1: I think we should send everyone an email.

   Employee 2: _____

4. Employee 1: Did you hear the boss is quitting?

   Employee 2: _____

   Employee 1: It's true.

5. Employee: Is there anything else I can do before I leave?

   Employer: _____

6. Employee 1: Guess what? We have to work late again tonight.

   Employee 2: Oh, no. _____

7. Employee: I heard you're leaving the company.

   Employer: _____

8. Official: May I see your documents, please.

   Passenger: _____

   Official: Yes, I'm required to check all identification.

> **F Y I**
> All of the missing lines in Activity 45 are common expressions in conversation.

Think about It The pronoun *that* is more common in conversation. However, in two of the conversations above, the speakers chose to use the pronoun *this*. What reasons can you give to explain this? (There is more than one possible answer.)

Talk about It Work with a partner to write a conversation using one of the expressions above. Then present your conversation to your classmates.

46 | Common Verbs Used with *This* and *That* Choose the best verb to complete the sentences. `7.8 B`

1. Successful supervisors give good feedback[36] to their employees. This

   _____*includes*_____ correcting their work and praising them for a job well done.

   > 1. includes/indicates

2. If I only had a few months to live, I would eat my favorite food as often as

   I could. That _____ I would eat pizza every night for dinner.

   > 2. means/shows

[35] **intensive:** involving a lot of activity in a short time   [36] **feedback:** information on how well or badly you have done something

3. Sunlight mixes with pollution to create ozone. Ozone is helpful because it blocks the sun's harmful rays. But close to Earth, ozone can be harmful to people. That _____ why some people have health problems when the ozone level is high.

3. explains/suggests

4. There are several ways to use the sun's power to make electricity. One is called concentrating solar power. This _____ using mirrors to focus[37] the sun's rays. This provides heat, which helps power generators.

4. explains/involves

5. A team of researchers has found the bones of four different kinds of dinosaurs[38] at the same site in New Mexico. This _____ that many different kinds of dinosaurs existed at the same time.

5. requires/suggests

6. In science fiction movies, the characters always refer to "outer space." This _____, somehow, that there's also an "inner space."

6. includes/implies

7. After a job interview, it's a good idea to send the interviewer a thank-you letter or email. This _____ that you are interested in the job.

7. indicates/requires

8. The college admissions process should help students evaluate their strengths. This _____ careful thought and self-awareness.

8. explains/requires

Think about It What does the word *this* refer to in the sentences in Activity 46? Underline the words. Then compare ideas with your classmates.

47 | Recognizing *This*, *That*, and *It* References Read these paragraphs. What does each **bold** pronoun refer to? Write your answers in the boxes. 7.8 C

1. Recreation involves doing an activity just for the fun of **it**. **That** could be doing something outdoors such as playing a sport. **It** could also be simply spending time with friends and family.

> 1. it = *doing an activity*
> that = *doing an activity for the fun of it*
> it =

2. Managing people is an important part of a supervisor's job. **This** is more than making sure a job gets done. **It** requires supervisors to interact[39] closely with employees.

> 2. this =
> it =

3. Plagiarism is the act of taking someone else's work and pretending **it**'s your own. **This** happens in writing, art, music, and other fields and will usually destroy a person's career.

> 3. it =
> this =

4. Hacking is the process of breaking through computer security for some reason. Some people do **this** for profit[40], some do **it** out of protest, and some do **it** for fun.

> 4. this =
> it =
> it =

5. A good friend is someone I get along with. **This** means we like to spend time together, and we enjoy many of the same activities. **It** also means that we can talk about many different things.

> 5. this =
> it =

---

[37] **focus:** to aim light at a particular point
[38] **dinosaurs:** animals that lived millions of years ago
[39] **interact:** to communicate
[40] **profit:** money made from doing something

6. When you get angry, try breathing deeply and counting to ten. **This** will help you to calm down quickly. **It** will also stop you from saying or doing something you will regret[41] later.

6. **this** =   **it** =

7. In many classrooms, mathematics is taught in a traditional way. Too often, **that** means students learn by memorizing facts. Worse, **it** is often taught as if all the students have exactly the same ability and learning style.

7. **that** =   **it** =

8. My most prized possession is my Greek dictionary. **That** might sound silly but **it** is true. I've had **it** since I was in high school.

8. **that** =   **it** =   **it** =

Think about It In the sentences in Activity 47, *this*, *that*, and *it* often refer back to the same thing or idea. Why do you think the writers used different pronouns?

7.9 Using Nouns and Pronouns in Speaking

A	**1** She's good at making **things** with her hands. **2** There's one **thing** I need to tell you. **3** A: Are you going out tonight? B: No, I have a lot of **stuff** to do at home.	In everyday conversation, we sometimes use the **nouns** *thing* and *stuff* to talk in general about objects, actions, ideas, etc., as in **1 – 3**.
	4 I like rock climbing, skateboarding, **and stuff like that.** (*stuff* = actions like rock climbing and skateboarding) **5** She reads a lot and goes to museums **and things like that.** (*things* = actions like reading and going to museums)	We also use the **nouns** *thing* and *stuff* in expressions like *and things like that* or *and stuff like that*, as in **4 – 5**. We do not usually use these expressions in writing.
B	**6** I need a **thingamajig** for removing staples. **7** A: Do you have one of those **whatchmacallits**? B: You mean a hammer? **8** Don't forget to call **whatshisname** tomorrow.	When we can't think of the exact name for something or someone, we sometimes use nonspecific **nouns** like *thingamajig, whatchmacallit, doohickey,* and *whatsitsname*, as in **6 – 8**. These expressions are very informal.
C	**9** Nice day, **isn't it?** **10** Your brother's silly, **isn't he?** **11** You're tired, **aren't you?**	About 25 percent of the questions we ask are tag questions with **pronouns** at the end, as in **9 – 11**. We often use tag questions with falling intonation to ask for confirmation of the previous statement.
D	COMPARE ACADEMIC AND INFORMAL USES **12a** She goes to the same school as **he does.** **12b** *You may hear:* "She goes to the same school as **him.**" **13a** I can do it better than **she can.** **13b** *You may hear:* "I can do it better than **her.**" **14a** **She** and I are going to a movie. **14b** *You may hear:* "**Her** and I are going to a movie." **15a** Can you send the email to John and **me?** **15b** *You may hear:* "Can you send the email to John and **I?**"	The first sentence in each pair, **12a – 15a**, is considered more appropriate for academic use. However, you may hear some English speakers use **pronouns** in ways that are different from standard usage, as in **12b – 15b**.

[41] **regret:** to feel sorry about something

48 | Interpreting the Meaning of *Things* What does the word *things* refer to in these sentences—physical objects, actions, or ideas? Check (✓) your answers. `7.9 A`

STATEMENTS FROM TEACHERS	OBJECTS	ACTIONS	IDEAS
1. I'm going to pass out a couple of **things** before we get started. The first is a program evaluation.	✓	☐	☐
2. There are seven **things** you can do to get organized.	☐	☐	☐
3. There are three important **things** I'd like to share with you about being a teacher.	☐	☐	☐
4. Of all the **things** I do during the day, the best is interacting with students.	☐	☐	☐
5. I rarely have large blocks of time when I can get **things** done.	☐	☐	☐
6. I try not to take a lot of work home with me on the weekend, but sometimes I have to read students' papers and **things** like that.	☐	☐	☐
7. My subject area is environmental science, which has to do with climate change and **things** like that.	☐	☐	☐
8. There are some **things** you need to bring to every class.	☐	☐	☐
9. That's one of the important **things** to ask when you are interviewing for a job.	☐	☐	☐
10. You need to pay more attention to the details. Here I'm talking just about your writing—commas, periods, spelling, and **things** like that.	☐	☐	☐

Think about It Why do you think we use *things* in the plural form in all of the sentences above? Do an online search for more examples of the words "thing/things" or "things like that." Decide what the words refer to in each case.

49 | Recognizing Vague Words Listen to the conversations and circle the word you hear. `7.9 B`

1. thingamajig	doohickey	whatsitsname
2. waddayacallit	thingy	whatchmacallit
3. whatshisname	whatshername	whatsitsname
4. thingamajig	doohickey	whatsitsname
5. waddayacallit	whatshisname	whatchmacallits
6. whatshisname	whatshername	waddayacallit

50 | Using Pronouns in Tag Questions Complete these tag questions. Listen and check your answers. Then practice with a partner. `7.9 C`

1. A: That was a great meal, wasn't ___*it*___?

   B: Yeah, wonderful.

2. A: Your sister isn't coming, is _____?

   B: No, I don't think so.

3. A: That was really funny, wasn't _____?

   B: Yeah, sure. I guess so.

4. A: Ann's really nice, isn't _____?

   B: Yeah, the best.

5. A: That was your idea, wasn't _____?

   B: I can't remember.

6. A: You were here yesterday, weren't _____?

   B: Yeah, all day.

7. A: John seemed nervous, didn't _____?

   B: Yeah, a little bit.

8. A: Cold today, isn't _____?

   B: Yeah, freezing.

9. A: The test was hard, wasn't _____?

   B: Not really.

10. A: Your parents are coming, aren't _____?

    B: Yes, and my grandparents, too.

11. A: Your brother didn't go, did _____?

    B: No, he stayed at home.

12. A: Time for lunch, isn't _____?

    B: Absolutely.

51 | Choosing Appropriate Pronoun Forms Rewrite the underlined part of each conversation with the more formal pronoun form(s). (You may also need to add a verb.) Then practice with a partner. `7.9 D`

1. A: Why is Sam making dinner?

   B: Because no one else can cook like ~~him~~. *he can* ∧

2. A: Who should I send the package to?

   B: Just send it to <u>Bill and I</u>.

3. A: Are you worried about the deadline?

   B: Well, just between <u>you and I</u>, I think it's a serious problem.

4. A: Who taught you how to paint houses?

   B: My father taught both <u>my brother and I</u> when we were teenagers.

5. A: Are you doing something with Tom tomorrow?

   B: Yeah. <u>Him and I</u> are going to play tennis.

6. A: Are you worried about Tom and Jill?

   B: Not really. A lot of people have less money than <u>them</u>.

7. A: If Irene can go out, why can't I?

   B: Because you're younger than <u>her</u>.

8. A: Anne should go first because she's the tallest.

   B: But I'm as tall as <u>her</u>.

9. A: Have you seen Sarah lately?

   B: Yeah. <u>Her and I</u> had coffee yesterday.

10. A: I need a ride to the meeting.

    B: Do you want to come with <u>Jim and I</u>?

> **F Y I**
>
> When speakers use subject pronouns as objects, it is called hypercorrection. It means the speaker makes a mistake by trying too hard to sound "correct."
>
> This award is a great honor for **Linda and I**. (hypercorrection)
>
> This award is a great honor for **Linda and me**. (standard)

A

REPEATING KEY WORDS

1 On May 25, 1961, President Kennedy **announced** his goal to land an astronaut on the moon. His **announcement** came only a month after the Soviet Union sent the first human into space.

2 On May 25, 1961, President Kennedy **announced** his goal to land an astronaut on the moon. His **declaration** came only a month after the Soviet Union sent the first human into space.

Writers often repeat key words to connect ideas. To give variety, they may use different forms of a key word, such as a **noun** or **noun phrase**, as in **1**.

To avoid repetition, writers may also use words that have similar meanings, as in **2**.

WRITING TERM: Repeating key words is one way we make writing more **cohesive**. In a cohesive paragraph, each sentence connects smoothly to the other sentences before and after it.

B

COMPARE VERB AND NOUN FORMS

3a Many people **were unemployed**, and as a result, crime rates **rose** in most parts of the country.

3b **Unemployment** resulted in **a rise in crime rates** in most parts of the country.

Using a **noun** or **noun phrase** instead of a verb makes it possible to include more information in fewer words, as in **3b**. This is a common characteristic of academic writing.

C

USING PRONOUNS AND POSSESSIVE DETERMINERS

4a Last year, a **scientist** from California fell while hiking. The **scientist** hurt his back so badly that the **scientist** could hardly walk. The **scientist's** relatives told the **scientist** to try acupuncture. (no pronouns)

4b Last year, a scientist from California fell while hiking. **He** hurt his back so badly that **he** could hardly walk. **His** relatives told **him** to try acupuncture.

5 At first, people in Europe and America were skeptical about **acupuncture**. By the 1970s, however, **a few doctors** were beginning to experiment with **it**. **They** found that **this form of treatment** was the only thing that gave **their** patients relief from pain.

In writing, it would be very repetitious to use the same noun or noun phrase many times, as in **4a**. Instead, we often replace a **noun** or **noun phrase** with a **pronoun** or **possessive determiner**, as in **4b**.

Writers often use nouns, nouns phrases, and pronouns in a chain of several references that all refer back to the same thing, as in **5**. This also makes writing cohesive.

In **5**, the pronoun *it* refers back to the word *acupuncture*. The noun phrase *this form of treatment* also refers back to *acupuncture*. The pronoun *they* and the possessive determiner *their* refer back to *a few doctors*.

GO ONLINE

52 | Using Different Forms of the Same Word Complete these sentences with the noun form of the bold word. (Use a dictionary if necessary.) **7.10 A**

MEDICAL SCIENCE

1. Studies show that certain parts of the brain become **active** during sleep. This _____activity_____ could be the brain moving memories from short-term to long-term memory.

2. Tests for cancer can **fail** to find problems. A _____ like this can be disastrous when a patient does not get treated right away.

3. More than 50 percent of patients **feel** rushed[42] when they visit their doctor. This _____ is more common among elderly patients.

4. As early as the 1950s, medical researchers **investigated** the connection between smoking and cancer. The _____ led to the first anti-smoking laws.

5. Medical insurance costs have **increased** dramatically in the last ten years. As a result of this _____, many people cannot afford insurance.

> **STUDY STRATEGY**
>
> You can look in a dictionary to find a different form of a word. Keep a chart like the one in the *Think about It* on page 248 to help build your vocabulary.

[42] **rushed:** made to hurry

6. Over the years, many governments have **invested** heavily in medical research. This _____ has led to several important medical breakthroughs[43].

7. Not all medical _____ are made in a scientist's youth. The scientist Benjamin Duggar **discovered** the use of tetracycline antibiotics when he was 76.

8. In 1777, General George Washington had his entire army **vaccinated**. This action was controversial[44] at the time because few doctors believed in _____.

9. Some doctors are starting to use computers to help **diagnose** Alzheimer's disease. This method of _____ is more accurate and faster than current methods.

10. Many people are **allergic** to peanuts. Some researchers say the number of peanut _____ found in children has increased dramatically in the last ten years.

11. Tension headaches are caused by muscle contractions[45] that cause mild _____. This type of headache may not be extremely **painful**, but it lasts for a long period of time.

12. We cough in order to clear **irritated** airways so we can breathe better. However, too much coughing can cause further _____ to the lungs and throat.

Think about It Look again at sentences 4 and 5 in Activity 52. Can you think of another way to complete each sentence using a word that is similar in meaning to the **bold** word?

Think about It Draw a chart like the one below. Add the different forms of the **bold** words in Activity 52. Then continue to add any new words you see or hear.

Noun	Verb	Adjective	Adverb
activity action	activate act	active	actively

53 | Using Fewer Words Each pair of sentences has been combined into one shorter sentence. Complete the shorter sentence with the noun form of the **bold** word. (You can use your dictionary for help.) `7.10 B`

1. Things become **extinct**. It's a natural process.

   Extinction is a natural process.

2. Many species of fish are **disappearing** from the ocean. This is now accelerating.

   The _____ of many species of fish from the ocean is now accelerating.

3. AZT is a very **effective** treatment for AIDS. This is well known.

   The _____ of the AZT treatment for AIDS is well known.

4. Some companies have **decided** to sell AZT at a discount. This will save many lives.

   The _____ of some companies to sell AZT at a discount will save many lives.

5. Humans **express** many emotions. These emotions may be universal.

   The _____ of many human emotions may be universal.

6. After World War II, the government of the United Kingdom **invested** in a national health-care system. This greatly improved the health of the British nation.

   The government's _____ in a national health-care system greatly improved the health of the British nation.

[43] **breakthroughs:** important discoveries
[44] **controversial:** causing a disagreement or argument
[45] **muscle contractions:** movements of muscles that make them tight

7. Nowadays, doctors **emphasize** the psychological side of human health. This has led to changes in patient care.

The _____ on the psychological side of human health nowadays has led to changes in patient care.

8. Many scientists have **concluded** that climate change is caused by human activity. Some others, however, do not accept this.

The _____ that climate change is caused by human activity is accepted by many—but not all—scientists.

54 | Understanding a Chain of References Read the text. What does each **bold** word refer to? Write your answers in the boxes. (If the word *it* doesn't refer back to something, write "empty *it*.") `7.10 C`

Learning to Ride a Bike
by Pat MacEnulty

I learned how to ride a bike when I was about eight years old. As soon as I could ride that bike, I realized I had the freedom to travel far and wide. Being outside on my bicycle provided me with hours of entertainment. So when I recently learned that my 12-year-old nephew had never learned to ride a bike, I decided to teach **him**.[1]

Our first efforts were disastrous. For one thing, **it** was the middle[2] of June and the temperature was in the 90s. In addition to the problem of heat, the bike **we** were using had defective[46] brakes, and[3] the seat wobbled[47] and was uncomfortable for **him**. To make things[4] even harder, my nephew was afraid. I know he wanted to ride **it**, but[5] he couldn't keep his balance, and the heat was making **him** sick.[6]

I wasn't ready to give up. I couldn't control the temperature, but I could do something about the bike. The next day I took **it** to a shop[7] and had the brakes and the seat repaired. We kept at **it**, and a few[8] days later, **he** finally rode down the street on his own. I don't know[9] if he'll ever enjoy riding a bike the way I do, but at least now he has the chance to find out. And he'll have more confidence, knowing that something may seem hard at first, but once you get the hang of **it**, it[10] can be a lot of fun.

1. him = *my 12-year-old nephew*

2. it =

3. we =

4. him =

5. it =

6. him =

7. it =

8. it =

9. he =

10. it =

[46] **defective:** not working correctly   [47] **wobble:** to move from side to side

55 | Usage Note: Repeating Nouns Read the note. Then do Activity 56.

> In order to be clear, writers sometimes repeat a noun instead of replacing it with a pronoun. In the example below, the writer repeats the noun *Solaire* in the second sentence to be clear.
>
> A building called the Solaire was perhaps the first green building in the U.S. In addition to using solar power for energy, the **Solaire** (NOT: ~~it~~) has lights that automatically turn off when people leave the room. The building also has a lot of windows.
>
> Using pronouns can sometimes create confusion for the reader. For example:
>
> My father fed my baby brother before **he** took a nap. (Who took a nap—the father or the baby brother?)
> She couldn't get the boot off her leg, so she had to cut **it** off. (What did she cut off—the boot or her leg?)

56 | Using Pronouns in Writing Replace some of the nouns and noun phrases in these paragraphs to make the writing less repetitive, but not confusing. (To help you practice, the first three paragraphs have **bold** words that show which to replace.) `7.10 C`

1. My favorite sport is volleyball. I like ~~volleyball~~ *it* because **volleyball** is fast-paced. And I like how I have to stay focused on the game while I am playing **the game**. Volleyball is also a team sport, and I like being part of a team.

2. If I could have a conversation with a famous person, I would talk with Mahatma Gandhi. **Gandhi** has definitely inspired me in my life. I'd like to talk with **Gandhi** about how we can change the world without violence. Gandhi said we should be the change we desire to see. I think this is a wise saying, and I would talk to **Gandhi** about it.

3. My main goal is to become financially secure. For me, financial security means not having to worry about having enough money for next month's bills. **Financial security** means having enough money to save for something you really want. **Financial security** means not worrying that you will lose your apartment if you get injured and can't work.

4. Your skin is the largest organ in your body. Your skin keeps your stomach and other organs from falling out. And your skin keeps germs from coming in. Skin allows you to feel pain, heat, and cold, and through sweat, skin rids your body of extra water and salt. Can you imagine life without your skin?

5. Lance Eton is an assistant professor of marine biology at the University of Manchester. Eton has always been interested in science and how things work. Living by the ocean made Eton curious about sea life, and Eton studied sea life in school.

6. People are finding new ways to make money. People might rent a room in their house or make stuff in their home and try to sell the stuff.

7. Most doctors tell their patients to stop smoking. The doctors explain to their patients that smoking is bad for their health. But some of their patients continue smoking anyway.

8. Antioxidants are chemicals in the body that fight cancer-causing substances called free radicals. Free radicals naturally occur in the body, but if there are too many of these free radicals, the free radicals can damage the body and cause cancer.

Think about It Compare your answers with a partner. Did you replace the same nouns in the sentences above?

57 | Evaluate Read the student essay and answer the questions below. 7.10 A–C

Essay Prompt: The Internet is the best thing that has ever happened to education. Agree or disagree?

1 Many people believe that the Internet will greatly improve education, but are they right? Students like
2 to use the Internet because it gives them instant access to large amounts of information. In the past,
3 students had to spend a lot of time searching through libraries to find things out. Now a quick Internet
4 search often gets them the information they need. This is a good thing, but it is not everything. Education
5 is not only about getting information. It is also about learning to process that knowledge. The Internet
6 cannot help with this. Once students have information, they need to discuss it, analyze it, and decide
7 what to do with it. Working with teachers and classmates to learn to process information is vital. The
8 Internet is a useful tool for education, but it is only one tool.

QUESTIONS

1. What key words does this writer repeat?

   The writer repeats the word "Internet" in line 2, line . . .

2. Does the writer ever use a word with a similar meaning to replace a key word?

3. What do the pronouns in this paragraph refer back to?

4. In a cohesive paragraph, each sentence connects smoothly to the sentence before and after it. Do you think this paragraph is cohesive? Why or why not?

58 | Using Nouns and Pronouns in Writing Write several sentences about each topic. Try to use several of the words in each box. 7.10 A–C

1. Write about a difficult decision you made (or didn't make).

decision	decide
choice	choose

2. Write about one of your accomplishments.

accomplishment	accomplish
achievement	achieve

3. Write about one of your goals.

plan	plan
aim	aim

   Some decisions are easy to make while others are very difficult. For example, it's usually easy to decide what you want to do for fun, but choosing a career can be very difficult. One of my most difficult decisions was choosing where to go to college. . . .

WRAP-UP Demonstrate Your Knowledge

A | REPORT Choose one of these topics. Ask five classmates your question and take notes on their answers. Then prepare a report (oral or written) explaining your findings to the class.

TOPICS

1. What does *bravery* mean to you?
2. What is one *investment* you are making in your life now that will help you in the future? How will it help you?
3. What is one important personal *discovery* or *realization* you have made recently (or an *accomplishment* you have achieved)? Why was it important?
4. What is one *inquiry* or *investigation* that you would like to conduct in the near future? Why?

B | DISCUSSION What are eight important personal qualities for each person in the chart? Work with a small group to list your ideas. Then say which is the most important quality for each person. Why? Report your group's answers to the class.

Parent	Boss/Supervisor	Leader of a country	Friend
dependability *flexibility* *creativity* *patience*			

C | PRESENTATION With your classmates, watch several short "how to" videos on YouTube. Discuss what the presenter did well or poorly in each demonstration. Then individually prepare your own short "how to" demonstration and present it to the class. If possible, videotape your demonstration and post it to a class website.

D | WEB SEARCH Look back at Chart 7.8, Section B, and choose one of the verbs commonly used after the pronoun *this*. Go to the website of any English language newspaper and do a search for "this + [one of the verbs]." For example, if you search for "this involves," you may find it used this way:

*A focus on testing <u>does not prepare students for careers in business</u>. **This involves** learning things such as teamwork, interpersonal skills, and creative problem solving.*

Choose one of the search results and print out the article. In class, read aloud *just* the complete sentence with "this + [verb]." Ask your classmates to guess what "this" refers to. Read aloud the preceding sentence in the article so that your classmates can check their guesses.

E | PERSONAL REFLECTION Think of your ideal world—where everything is just the way you want it to be. What would that world be like? Explain this (orally or in writing) to your class.

In my ideal place, everyone has a job, but work doesn't take more than half of each day to complete. In my ideal place, there is something called a Justice Committee. The job of this committee is to . . .

7.11 Summary of Nouns and Pronouns

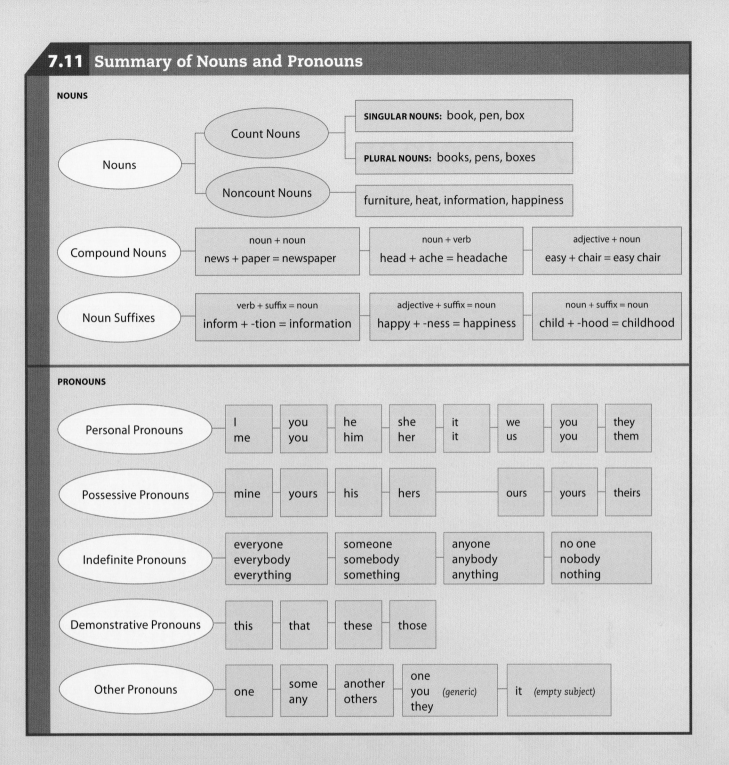

NOUNS

Nouns
- **Count Nouns**
  - **SINGULAR NOUNS:** book, pen, box
  - **PLURAL NOUNS:** books, pens, boxes
- **Noncount Nouns**
  - furniture, heat, information, happiness

Compound Nouns

noun + noun	noun + verb	adjective + noun
news + paper = newspaper	head + ache = headache	easy + chair = easy chair

Noun Suffixes

verb + suffix = noun	adjective + suffix = noun	noun + suffix = noun
inform + -tion = information	happy + -ness = happiness	child + -hood = childhood

PRONOUNS

Personal Pronouns

I me	you you	he him	she her	it it	we us	you you	they them

Possessive Pronouns

mine	yours	his	hers		ours	yours	theirs

Indefinite Pronouns

everyone everybody everything	someone somebody something	anyone anybody anything	no one nobody nothing

Demonstrative Pronouns

this	that	these	those

Other Pronouns

one	some any	another others	one you they *(generic)*	it *(empty subject)*

Determiners

Most people spend
more time and energy
going around a problem
than in trying to solve it.

—HENRY FORD,

INDUSTRIALIST AND INVENTOR

(1863–1947)

Talk about It Do you agree or disagree with the quotation above? Why?

WARM-UP

A | Read these statements and circle your answers. Then compare with a partner.

Geography Quiz

1. There are (**seven** / **five**) oceans on **this** planet.

2. **Most** of **the** world's population lives in **the** (southern / northern) hemisphere.

3. North America and Europe move (about **an inch** / **a few** inches) apart **every** year.

4. About (**10,000** / **1.3 million**) earthquakes occur **each** year around **the** globe.

5. (**Most** / **All**) of **the** world's tallest mountains are in **the** Himalayas.

6. There are (not **many** / **no**) rivers in **the** Bahamas.

7. Canada gets **its** name from **a** Native American word meaning (**the** village / **the** city).

B | The words in blue in the statements above are determiners. Based on these examples, what can you say about determiners? Check (✓) *True* or *False*.

	TRUE	FALSE
1. We can use a noun immediately after a determiner.	☐	☐
2. We can use an adjective immediately after a determiner.	☐	☐
3. We can use a verb immediately after a determiner.	☐	☐
4. A determiner can give information about quantity.	☐	☐
5. A determiner can give information about color or shape.	☐	☐
6. A determiner can give information about possession.	☐	☐

C | Look back at the quotation on page 254. Identify any determiners.

8.1 What Are Determiners?

A

determiner   noun

1 I read | **an** | interesting **article**.
noun phrase

determiner noun

2 I read | **the** | **article** you recommended.

determiner   noun

3 Every place has | **its** | own unique **history**.

determiner noun

4 I need | **a little** | **help**.

determiner   noun

5 I'm nervous and I hate | **this** | **feeling**!

Determiners are words like *a, an, the, two, this, his,* and *a little*. They are one part of a noun phrase, as in **1**.

We use determiners to identify different qualities of a **noun**. These qualities include:

- new information for the listener, as in **1**
- information the listener already knows about, as in **2**
- possession, as in **3**
- quantity or amount, as in **4**
- information we want to "point to" or focus attention on, as in **5**

Charts 8.2–8.8 give more information on the uses of determiners.

B

6 I have **a new computer**. (NOT: ~~I have new computer.~~)

7 She's **my best friend**. (NOT: ~~She's best friend.~~)

8 College **students** need **time** to explore new **ideas**.

A singular count noun always needs a determiner, as in **6 – 7**.

Plural count nouns and noncount nouns can be used without a determiner, as in **8**.

 GO ONLINE

1 | Understanding Determiners Each **bold** determiner describes a noun. Underline the noun. Then answer the questions below. **8.1 A**

PRIZED POSSESSIONS

1. **My** most prized <u>possession</u> is **my** computer. It lets me stay in contact with **my** friends on **several** continents. Computers make **the** world seem like **a** really small place.

2. One of **my** prized possessions is **my** Greek dictionary. It might sound silly, but it's true. With **my** dictionary, I can read some of **the** most beautiful literature in **the** world. It is also special to me because it was **a** gift from **my** teachers. It reminds me of **the** good experiences I had as **a** student in Greece.

3. **My** most prized possession is **my** guitar. **This** guitar is very special to me because it was **my** father's guitar, and he got it from **his** father. **My** wife and I hope to give it to one of **our** children someday.

4. I have **many** prized possessions, but none are valuable. They are just things like old photographs and school papers. I also have **lots of** old letters that **my** grandparents wrote. There are even **a few** letters from **my** great-grandparents.

QUESTIONS

a. Which of the bold determiners above give information about possession? _____

b. Which give information about quantity or amount? _____

c. Which give some other kind of information? _____

Write about It Write a paragraph about one of your prized possessions. Circle the determiners you use and underline the nouns.

> **F Y I**
>
> In a dictionary, quantity words like *a little, many,* and *several* are sometimes identified as adjectives.

2 | Identifying Determiners Underline the determiners in each paragraph. The number in parentheses is the number of determiners in the paragraph. `8.1 A–B`

Heat Waves

1. <u>Several</u> hot days that follow each other are called a heat wave. Experts say heat waves often become dangerous when the nighttime temperature does not drop much from the highest daytime temperature. This constant[1] heat causes great stress on the human body. (6)

2. There are many things people can do to protect themselves from the dangers of extreme[2] heat. Drink lots of cool water. Try to stay out of the sun. Wear light-weight clothes made from natural materials. Make sure the clothing is loose to allow freedom of movement. (5)

3. Heat stress is the most common health problem linked to[3] hot weather. The causes of heat stress include clothing that is too heavy, physical work or exercise, hot weather, and high humidity (the amount of water in the air). (4)

4. Most people suffer muscle pain because of heat stress. The pain is a warning that the body is becoming too hot. Doctors say those individuals suffering from muscle pain could be in danger. They should stop all activity and rest in a cool place. Doctors say not to return to physical activity for a few hours. (8)

Think about It Circle the plural count nouns and the noncount nouns in the sentences above. Which ones are used **without** a determiner? Write them under the correct group in the chart below.

No determiner + plural count noun	No determiner + noncount noun
experts heat waves	stress

Talk about It What do you and your classmates do to stay cool in hot weather? Make a list of ideas. Then identify the determiners in your list.

3 | Using Determiners with Singular Count Nouns Underline the singular count nouns in these quotations. Then add the determiners in parentheses. `8.1 B`

QUOTATIONS

1. You cannot shake hands with _a clenched <u>fist</u>[4]. (a) *Indira Gandhi, stateswoman*

2. If you want to lose friend, lend him money. (a) *Greek proverb*

---

[1] **constant:** staying the same; not changing
[2] **extreme:** the highest or lowest

[3] **linked to:** connected with
[4] **clenched fist:** a hand with the fingers closed tight

3. Laughter is not at all bad beginning for friendship. (a/a)   *Oscar Wilde, author*

4. Hold true friend with both your hands. (a)   *Friedrich Nietzsche, philosopher*

5. I have never been in country where they did not do something better than we do it. (any)

   Maria Mitchell, scientist

6. Even honey tastes bitter to sick man. (a)   *Russian proverb*

7. Music is universal language of mankind. (the)   *Henry W. Longfellow, poet*

8. Giving son a skill⁵ is better than giving him a thousand pieces of gold. (your)   *Chinese proverb*

9. Banks are places where they lend you umbrella in fair weather and ask for it back when it begins

   to rain. (an)   *Robert Frost, poet*

10. I always tried to turn disaster⁶ into opportunity. (every/an)   *John D. Rockefeller, Jr., industrialist*

11. Judge man by his questions rather than his answers. (a)   *Voltaire, writer*

12. Hope is good breakfast, but it is bad supper. (a/a)   *Francis Bacon, philosopher*

Talk about It Choose a quotation from Activity 3. Tell a partner a personal story to show the meaning.

8.2 Articles with Singular Count Nouns

Articles are a kind of determiner. We can use the articles **a / an** or **the** with a singular count noun.

A

A / AN + SINGULAR COUNT NOUNS

1 I have **a very good doctor.**
(= a specific doctor; my doctor)

2 There is **a beautiful lake** near here. You'll love it.
(= a specific lake)

3 This essay needs **an introduction.** (= any introduction)

4 I don't have **a dictionary.** (= any dictionary)

5 My trip to China was **a great experience.**

6 My sister is **a doctor.**

We use **a / an** for many reasons—for example, because:
- we are talking about a specific person or thing, but we think the listener doesn't know which one, as in **1 – 2**
- we are not talking about a specific person or thing, as in **3 – 4**
- we are classifying or describing a type of person or thing, as in **5 – 6**

In **1** and **2**, the speaker is talking about a person or thing for the first time. This is why the noun is unknown to the listener.

GRAMMAR TERM: *A* and *an* are called **indefinite articles**.

B

THE + SINGULAR COUNT NOUNS

7 When I moved to England, I couldn't speak **the language.** (There is only one English language.)

8 Tell me your story from **the beginning.**
(A story has only one beginning.)

9 Jill is **the youngest person in the class.**

10 I was in a meeting for **the whole day.**

11 I want to help **the children in our community.**

12 A simple remedy for **an insect bite** is to place an ice pack on **the bite.** It will relieve both **the itching** and **the swelling.**

We use *the* when we think the listener knows which person or thing we are talking about. We do this when the person or thing:
- is unique (the only one) in the world or in a particular context, as in **7 – 8**
- is identified by other words, like superlatives, unique adjectives, or prepositional phrases, as in **9 – 11**
- was mentioned before or is related to previously mentioned information, as in **12**

GRAMMAR TERM: *The* is called the **definite article**.

⁵ **skill:** the ability to do something well

⁶ **disaster:** something very bad that happens

4 | Using _A_ and _An_ Add the missing article _a_ or _an_ to these questions. `8.2 A`

1. Can you recommend ^a^ good movie?

2. Is there university near your home?

3. Did you get good night's sleep last night?

4. Are you outgoing person?

5. Do you have good sense of humor?

6. How many minutes are in hour?

7. What is major source of air pollution?

8. Is wood synthetic[7] material?

9. What are the qualities of good boss?

10. Can you name famous work of art?

11. Did you ever dream of becoming actor?

12. Have you ever met famous person?

13. Is there difference between American English and British English?

14. Do you know the name of good, inexpensive restaurant around here?

> **F Y I**
>
> Remember: We use _a_ before a word that begins with a consonant sound. We use _an_ before a word that begins with a vowel sound.
>
> **an** essay
> **a** paragraph

Talk about It Ask a partner the questions above.

A: Can you recommend a good movie?
B: Sure. I really liked . . .

5 | Using _A/An_ with Singular Count Nouns Complete the sentences in each group with information about yourself. Then compare ideas with your classmates. `8.2 A`

Group 1

1. I have never seen an _____.

    I have never seen an opera in person.

2. I don't own an _____, but I wish I did.

Group 2

3. I would like to be a _____ someday.

4. My best friend is a _____.

Group 3

5. There is a _____ in my classroom.

6. I bought an _____ last month.

7. When I was a child, my parents gave me an _____.

8. There is a _____ in my city.

---

[7] **synthetic:** not natural; made by a chemical process

Think about It Answer these questions about each group of sentences in Activity 5. Write the group number.

1. In which group is the speaker talking about a specific person or thing? Group # ____

2. In which group is the speaker NOT talking about a specific person or thing? Group # ____

3. In which group is the speaker classifying or describing a person or thing? Group # ____

6 | Exploring Uses of *The* Read the excerpt below. Why did the writer use *the* in the **bold** noun phrases? Choose the correct reason from the box. Write the number of the reason above each *the*. `8.2 B`

REASONS FOR USING *THE*
1. The noun is unique.
2. The noun is identified by a superlative or unique adjective.
3. The noun is identified by a prepositional phrase.
4. The noun is related to previously mentioned information.

The History of Paper-Making

1. **The earliest process for making paper** was invented by Egyptians in **the Nile Valley** almost 5,000 years ago. In those days, strips of a papyrus plant were stuck together to form paper.

2. About 2,000 years ago, **the ancient Chinese** invented our modern paper-making process. In this process, raw materials like straw, wood, or **the bark of trees** are used. **The raw materials** are pounded again and again until they become loose, and then they are soaked in water. After removing **the water**, a flat, thin form remains. When **the form** dries, it becomes a sheet of paper.

3. Europeans started using large machines for making paper near **the end** of **the sixteenth century**. In modern times, paper-making is a very big business. However, it is still possible to make paper by hand using **the same steps** as those used with **the large machines**.

papyrus paper

Think about It Where does the writer use the article *a* in the excerpt above? In each case, why did the writer choose *a* instead of *the*?

Talk about It Describe a process you know about to a partner. Pay special attention to the articles you use.

7 | Using *The* Read this paragraph. Add the missing article *the* where necessary. 8.2 B

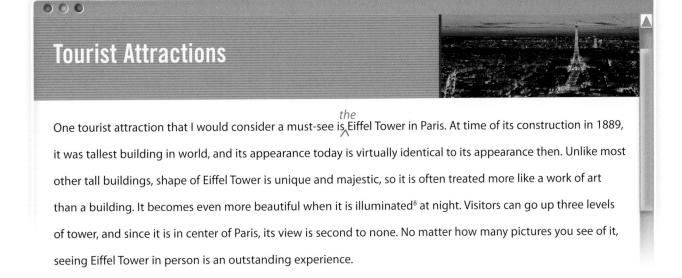

Tourist Attractions

One tourist attraction that I would consider a must-see is ^*the* Eiffel Tower in Paris. At time of its construction in 1889, it was tallest building in world, and its appearance today is virtually identical to its appearance then. Unlike most other tall buildings, shape of Eiffel Tower is unique and majestic, so it is often treated more like a work of art than a building. It becomes even more beautiful when it is illuminated[8] at night. Visitors can go up three levels of tower, and since it is in center of Paris, its view is second to none. No matter how many pictures you see of it, seeing Eiffel Tower in person is an outstanding experience.

Think about It Why did you add *the* in each case above? Look at the reasons in Activity 6. Write the number of the reason next to each *the*.

Write about It Describe a tourist attraction you are familiar with.

Central Park is a popular tourist attraction in New York City. On a sunny day, the park is full of people. . . .

8 | Using *The* for Something Mentioned Before Read the first sentence in these descriptions of dreams. Then make up the next sentence in the description. Use *the* and the **bold** noun. 8.2 B

TALKING ABOUT DREAMS

1. One of the strangest dreams I ever had took place in a **shopping mall**. *It was in the middle of the day, but the shopping mall was empty.*

2. I once dreamed that I was trying to climb to the top of a **mountain**, but I wasn't wearing any shoes. _____

3. I had a dream that I was in a strange **house** with no windows. _____

4. In my dream, I heard a loud knocking **noise**. _____

5. One time I dreamed that I was all alone in an **airplane**. _____

6. Last night I dreamed that I was riding an elephant in a **desert**. _____

7. I once had a dream that I was in a big city standing on the roof of a tall **building**. _____

Write about It Write about a dream that you once had. Pay special attention to the articles you use.

[8]**illuminated:** lighted

9 | Distinguishing *A* and *The* Why did the speaker use *a* or *the* in each sentence below? Choose the correct reason from the box. **8.2 A–B**

REASONS FOR USING A/AN OR THE
The speaker thinks the listener:
1. knows which person or thing he or she is talking about
2. doesn't know which person or thing he or she is talking about

1. a. I'm taking **a** day off next week. __2__

   b. I need to leave early **the** day after tomorrow. ____

2. a. We need **a** new refrigerator. ____

   b. Could you put my lunch in **the** refrigerator? ____

3. a. We went to **the** Museum of Modern Art while we were there. ____

   b. We went to **a** museum while we were there. ____

4. a. I brought **a** computer with me. ____

   b. I brought **the** computer with me. ____

5. a. I'm having **a** small problem with my car. ____

   b. They couldn't fix **the** problem with our TV. ____

Think about It For each sentence above, explain why the speaker thinks the listener knows or doesn't know which person or thing he or she is talking about.

10 | Choosing *A* or *The* Complete this essay with *a* or *the*. **8.2 A–B**

Essay Prompt: If you could have a conversation with a famous person (living or dead), who would you choose? Discuss.

If I could have a conversation with __*a*__ famous person, I would choose to talk with ____ leader of our
    1   2
country. I have many questions to ask him, both about his personal life and about his job.

Being ____ leader of this country must be ____ difficult and stressful job. I would like to ask him how he
      3   4
makes important decisions. Does he take advice from people who work for him? Does he research problems

to make his own decisions? I would also like to know what personal life is like for ____ world leader. Does
                                                                                    5
he have any free time? What does he do to relax? Does he ever just sit back and watch TV or read ____ book
                                                                                                    6
for fun?

I would also choose to talk to ____ leader of our country because I appreciate his doing such ____
                               7   8
difficult job. I would like to thank him for thinking about and trying to improve ____ quality of life for ____
                                                                                  9   10
people of his country.

Think about It In each answer above, why did you choose *the* or *a*? Share ideas with your classmates.

In #1, I chose "a" because the writer is not talking about a specific person.

Write about It Write your own answer to the essay prompt above.

8.3 Articles with Plural Count Nouns and Noncount Nouns

We can use *some*, **no article (Ø)**, or *the* with plural count nouns or noncount nouns.

A

SOME + PLURAL COUNT NOUNS OR NONCOUNT NOUNS

1 I have **some good grammar books** for beginners.
(= specific grammar books; my books)

2 He gave me **some great advice**.
(= specific advice; the advice he gave me)

3 What are **some good grammar books**?
(= any good grammar books)

4 I need **some advice**. (= a little bit of advice)

We use *some* for many reasons—for example:

- because we are talking about specific people or things, but we don't think the listener knows which ones, as in **1 – 2**
- because we are not talking about specific people or things, as in **3 – 4**

Some usually means a small number or amount, as in **4**.

B

Ø + PLURAL COUNT NOUNS OR NONCOUNT NOUNS

5 She prefers to travel with Ø **good friends**.
(= with good friends in general)

6 He has written Ø **novels**, Ø **essays**, and a little poetry.

7 Ø **Travel** is valuable for a number of Ø **reasons**.

We also use **no article (Ø)** when we are not talking about specific people or things. In this case, we are talking about types of people or things in general, as in **5 – 7**.

WARNING! Using no article means you are not using any determiner at all. For example, in **6**, the determiner *a little* is used before *poetry*—not no article.

C

THE + PLURAL COUNT NOUNS OR NONCOUNT NOUNS

8 **The North and South Poles** are warming quickly.

9 She has to get a job because she needs **the money**.
(= the money from the job)

10 We couldn't find an artist to do **the illustrations for our book**. (*for our book* tells us which *illustrations*)

11 In the 1900s, doctors started wearing **the white coats of scientists**. (*of scientists* tells us which *white coats*)

We can use *the* when we think the listener knows which people or things we are talking about, as in **8 – 11**.

Remember: We can use *the* before singular count nouns as well. Chart 8.2B explains many reasons why we choose *the*.

11 | Using *Some* Complete these questions with your own ideas. **8.3 A**

YOUR EXPERIENCES

1. Did you have some _____ for lunch yesterday?

2. Did you drink some _____ this morning?

3. Do you have some _____ with you today?

4. Are there some _____ in your city?

5. Did you have some _____ yesterday?

6. Did you ever find some _____ on the street?

7. Do you need some _____?

> **PRONUNCIATION**
> When *some* is used as an article, it is not stressed, and we pronounce it "sm."

Talk about It Ask a partner your questions above.

A: Did you have some rice for lunch yesterday?
B: Yes. I have rice for lunch every day.

Think about It What other plural count nouns could you use in each question above? What other noncount nouns could you use?

Did you have some sandwiches for lunch yesterday?   *Did you have some soup for lunch yesterday?*

12 | Noticing No Article Underline the **bold** nouns that use no article (Ø). (Remember: Using no article means you are not using any determiner at all. Don't underline nouns that have words like *a, the, some, many,* or *our* before them.) 8.3 B

1. Many **doctors** have noticed an **increase** in <u>eye problems</u> among <u>children</u>.

2. Many **things** can trigger⁹ **allergies**.

3. Throughout **history**, many **items** have been used as **money**, including **shells** and **salt**.

4. Some **experts** say that drinking several **liters** of **water** each **day** will help **adults** lose **weight**.

5. **Carrots** are high in **beta carotene**, which is important for normal **vision**.

6. **Scientists** at Cornell University found that hot **cocoa** may help fight **cancer**.

7. A recent **study** suggests that the **number** of severe **hurricanes** this **year** is normal.

8. In the past few **years**, **hurricanes** have brought **destruction** to the eastern U.S.

9. The sun makes **life** on our **planet** possible by providing great **amounts** of **light** and **heat**.

10. Traditional **sources** of **energy** like **oil** and **gas** may someday run out.

Think about It Is each underlined noun above a plural count noun or a noncount noun? Write *p* (plural count noun) or *n* (noncount noun) above the noun.

13 | Grouping Noun Phrases Read the text. Write each **bold** noun phrase under the correct group in the chart on page 265. 8.3 B–C

The Mystery of Stonehenge

Stonehenge, one of **the world's best-known monuments**, stands in southern England. Stonehenge is made of huge stones set up in four circles. A circular ditch and mound form a border around the site. **Shallow**¹⁰ **dirt holes** also circle **the stones**.

Stonehenge was built over a period of more than 2,000 years. **The earliest construction** probably began about 3100 BCE. The outer ring of **large pillars**, topped with horizontal¹¹ rocks, was built about 2000 BCE. An inner ring of stone pillars also supports **horizontal stones**.

There was no source of **stone** nearby, so **workers**

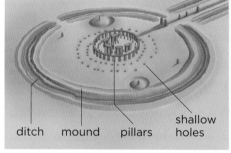

ditch   mound   pillars   shallow holes

Stonehenge

carried it from an area that was about 20 miles (32 kilometers) north. The stones are huge—up to 30 feet (9 meters) long and 50 tons (45 metric tons) in weight. Before putting the stones in place, workers smoothed and shaped them. They cut joints¹² into the stones so that they would fit together perfectly. Then **the builders** probably used levers¹³ and **wooden supports** to lift the stones into position.

About 500 years later, **builders** added **the third and fourth rings** of stones. This time they used bluestone, which an earlier group of **people** had transported 240 miles (386 kilometers) from the Preseli Mountains of Wales.

---

⁹**trigger:** to cause something to start or happen
¹⁰**shallow:** not deep
¹¹**horizontal:** in a side-to-side position (not up and down)

¹²**joints:** places where things are connected
¹³**levers:** strong bars that are used to lift and move things

Most experts agree that Stonehenge was probably used as a place of worship. Some believe that **the series** of holes and stones were used as a calendar. By lining up **particular holes and stones**, people could note **the summer and winter solstices**. They could also keep track of **the months**. Some scientists think that early people used the site to predict **solar and lunar eclipses**.

Ø + plural count noun	Ø + noncount noun	*The* + plural count noun	*The* + noncount noun
		the world's best-known monuments	

Think about It Why did the writer use *the* in each noun phrase in Activity 13? Choose the reason.

1. The noun is unique.	3. It is identified by a prepositional phrase.
2. It is identified by a superlative or unique adjective.	4. It is related to previously mentioned information.

Talk about It Close your book. Share three things you learned about Stonehenge.

14 | Choosing No Article or *The* Underline the plural nouns and noncount nouns in these questions. Then add *the* to the underlined nouns where necessary. `8.3 B–C`

1. What do <u>rings</u> *the* on the Olympic flag represent?
2. Do you have experience with computers?
3. Do you need energy and determination to play football well?
4. How big were first electronic computers?
5. Why do people live longer today?
6. How many sides does a hexagon have?
7. What are most serious problems in the world today?
8. Do you like to talk about movies?
9. Have you ever seen sights of Paris?
10. What are names of your two best friends?
11. Do you know how to make bread?
12. Is the Internet a good place to get information?

Talk about It Ask a partner the questions above.

A: What do the rings on the Olympic flag represent?
B: I'm not sure. Continents?

15 | Choosing *A/An, The,* or No Article Read the text. Add *a, an,* or *the* to the **bold** noun phrases where necessary. 8.3 B–C

Threadless.com

Jake Nickell has always been ^*a* **creative guy**. When he was just 20 years old, he designed **T-shirt** for **online competition**. He won, and **hour** later, he decided to start his own competition. He asked **people** to submit their own T-shirt designs, and he promised to print **best designs** for everyone to wear. That's how his successful company, Threadless.com, began.

Through **company's website**, Jake asks everyone to submit **T-shirt designs**. In **beginning**, he enjoyed looking at **T-shirt designs** for fun, but when more people started to submit **designs**, **website** grew, and Jake's career took off. Today, Threadless.com has 1.7 million users who submit **T-shirt designs**. Jake and his staff print 2,000 T-shirts each year for sale to **general public**. Jake is **example** that you can turn a passion into a career.

Jake Nickell

Think about It Write each **bold** noun phrase above under the correct group in the chart below. Include any articles you added.

Singular count noun	Plural count noun	Noncount noun
a creative guy		

16 | Error Correction Correct any errors in these sentences. (Some sentences may not have any errors.)

1. Weather in my city isn't very nice. Sun rarely comes out.

   The weather in my city isn't very nice. The sun rarely comes out.

2. I don't like vegetables.
3. He is most optimistic person I know.
4. Now I live in Canada, and my friend lives in the my country.
5. People need to spend more time in the nature.
6. Their actions changed the history.
7. He was diagnosed with the cancer.
8. I have a brown eyes and long black hair.
9. At first my sister had a hard time in the U.S. because a culture was very different.
10. My interests are traveling anywhere, listening to music, and playing with computer.

> **RESEARCH SAYS...**
>
> The most common determiners are the articles *a/an, the, some,* and no article (often called *zero article* or Ø).

C CORPUS

266

8.4 Articles in Generic Statements

Generic statements usually give information about an entire group or type of something. The person or thing we are describing in a generic statement usually comes at the beginning of the sentence.

A

SINGULAR COUNT NOUN

1 A laptop computer is a useful tool.
(= any laptop computer)

PLURAL COUNT NOUN

2 Ø Laptop computers are useful. (= all laptop computers)

NONCOUNT NOUN

3 Ø Money is the root of all evil. (= all money)

4 Ø Italian food is delicious. (= all Italian food)

We usually make generic statements with:

A(n)	+ a singular count noun, as in **1**
Ø	+ a plural count noun, as in **2**
Ø	+ a noncount noun, as in **3 – 4**

GRAMMAR TERM: The noun in a generic statement is called a **generic noun**.

B

5 The laptop computer is a useful tool.
(= the type of machine called a laptop computer)

6 The African elephant is an intelligent animal.

7 During the seventeenth century, **the potato** became a major source of food in Europe.

8 A good father spends time with his children.
(NOT: ~~The good father spends~~ . . .)

9 Ø Computers have changed the way we communicate. (NOT: ~~The computers~~ . . .)

10 Ø English parsley has curly leaves.
(NOT: ~~The English parsley~~ . . .)

In some cases, we can also use *the* + a singular noun to make a generic statement. This is more common in academic writing when we are writing about things such as inventions, plants, and animals, as in **5 – 7**.

We don't usually use *the* when we make a generic statement about a person or people, as in **8**.

We don't use *the* with plural nouns or noncount nouns to make generic statements, as in **9 – 10**.

GO ONLINE

17 | Identifying Generic Statements Is each statement about an entire group or type of something (*generic*) or about specific people or things (*not generic*)? Check (✓) your answer. **8.4 A**

	GENERIC	NOT GENERIC
1. A cell phone will not work in all locations.	✓	☐
2. Cell phones are much less expensive today.	☐	☐
3. The cell phone on the desk is mine.	☐	☐
4. Parents are the best advisors.	☐	☐
5. My best friend's parents are getting divorced.	☐	☐
6. A parent has many responsibilities.	☐	☐
7. The parents at our school meeting learned a lot.	☐	☐
8. Young people should have opportunities to travel.	☐	☐
9. The youngest person in my family is six years old.	☐	☐
10. A young person doesn't understand how quickly time goes by.	☐	☐
11. An eagle is a large bird.	☐	☐
12. Eagles can fly 60 miles per hour.	☐	☐
13. The eagle on a U.S. one-dollar bill is a bald eagle.	☐	☐

18 | A/An or No Article? Write *A/An* or Ø at the beginning of these generic statements. If you write Ø, change the first letter of the sentence to a capital letter. Then decide if each statement is a fact or an opinion. Check (✓) your answer. `8.4 A`

		FACT	OPINION
1.	_Ø_ T̶elevision can be educational and entertaining.	☐	✓
2.	___ television set has a tuner, a screen, and speakers.	☐	☐
3.	___ soccer ball weighs between 14 and 16 ounces.	☐	☐
4.	___ people should be more considerate[14] with their cell phone use.	☐	☐
5.	___ women are more patient than men.	☐	☐
6.	___ man has more job opportunities than a woman.	☐	☐
7.	___ male babies are 25 percent more likely to die in infancy than female babies.	☐	☐
8.	___ children have fewer bones than adults.	☐	☐
9.	___ teenagers aren't mature[15] enough to make their own decisions.	☐	☐
10.	___ good advice is priceless.	☐	☐
11.	___ money doesn't grow on trees.	☐	☐
12.	___ apple a day keeps the doctor away.	☐	☐
13.	___ long-distance race of 42 kilometers is called a marathon.	☐	☐
14.	___ baby whales are called calves.	☐	☐
15.	___ stress is a part of many people's lives.	☐	☐
16.	___ effective leader is a good listener.	☐	☐
17.	___ honesty is very important in most situations.	☐	☐
18.	___ sports have become a multibillion-dollar industry.	☐	☐
19.	___ studies show that watching too much TV leads to poor performance in school.	☐	☐

Write about It Each generic statement above introduces a topic. Choose one fact and one opinion above. Write two more sentences about each one.

Television can be educational and entertaining. In fact, the best programs are both. . . .

19 | Exploring Different Ways to Write Generic Statements Rewrite each generic statement in two different ways. `8.4 A–B`

ANIMAL FACTS

1. Toads are poisonous.

   A toad is poisonous. The toad is poisonous.

2. A giraffe's tongue is blue.
3. Mosquitoes have 47 teeth.
4. Emus can't walk backward.
5. A dolphin sleeps with one eye open.
6. A bull is color-blind.
7. Crocodiles can go without food for two years.
8. The female lion does about 90 percent of the hunting.

firebelly toad

---

[14]**considerate:** thoughtful of others   [15]**mature:** fully developed

9. Elephants can smell water that is several miles away.

10. A camel has three eyelids to protect itself from blowing sand.

Write about It What animals do you know about? Write a description of one animal using generic statements like the ones in Activity 19.

20 | Completing Generic Statements Choose a noun phrase from the box to complete each generic statement below. 8.4 A–B

a human brain	hair	infants	the heart
adult lungs	human thigh bones	the average human head	the right side of the brain
an adult skeleton	humans		

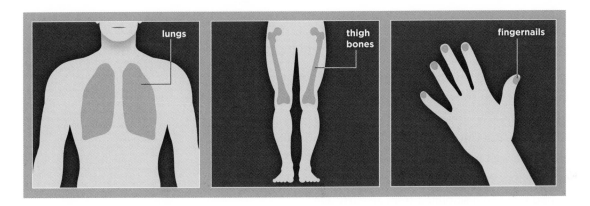

TEN FACTS ABOUT THE HUMAN BODY

1. *An adult skeleton* _____ has 213 bones.

2. _____ beats more than 2.5 billion times in an average lifetime.

3. _____ blink[16] once or twice a minute; adults blink about ten times a minute.

4. _____ has about 100,000 hairs.

5. _____ have a surface area of about 70 square meters.

6. _____ are stronger than concrete[17].

7. _____ is made of the same substance[18] as fingernails.

8. _____ uses 15 to 20 percent of the body's blood.

9. _____ have unique tongue prints and fingerprints.

10. _____ controls the left side of the body.

Think about It Which generic statements above can you rewrite using a different article and form of the noun? (You may need to make other changes as well.) Why is it not possible to rewrite all the statements?

The adult skeleton has 213 bones.   *Adult skeletons have 213 bones.*

---

[16] **blink:** to close and open the eyes quickly

[17] **concrete:** a hard gray material used for building things

[18] **substance:** any solid, liquid, or gas

21 | Writing Generic Statements Add your own ideas to make ten generic statements. [8.4 A–B]

1. A wireless keyboard _____ *is very useful* OR *needs batteries.* _____.

2. A piano _____.

3. A good friend _____.

4. American food _____.

5. Homework _____.

6. New technology _____.

7. A cactus _____.

8. Universities today _____.

9. The giraffe _____.

10. The palm tree _____.

22 | Error Correction Correct any errors in these sentences. (Some sentences may not have any errors.)

1. Fifty years ago, the bathing suits were made of cotton.

2. I think the woman shouldn't work.

3. The parents need to guide their children.

4. Nile crocodile can stay underwater for more than an hour.

5. The airplane was an important invention.

6. The blue whale may be the largest animal that ever lived.

7. The child must be disciplined from an early age.

8. The French food is better than the Italian food.

8.5 Possessives

A

POSSESSIVE DETERMINERS

1 My **uncle** lives near me. **His house** is on the next street.

2 Employers need to respect **their employees.**

3 At the time of **its construction** in 1889, the Eiffel Tower was the tallest building in the world.

We can show possession with a **possessive determiner**, as in **1 – 3.**

POSSESSIVE DETERMINERS						
my	your	his	her	its	our	their

B

POSSESSIVE NOUNS

4 Aging is **one of life's biggest challenges.**

5 The company was pleased with **the plan's success.**

6 My **children's names** are Henry and James.

7 We should respect **other countries' laws.**

8 On **today's date** in 1547, Ivan IV became czar of Russia.

9 You need to be ready to leave at **a moment's notice.**

10 The job requires **two years' experience.**

We can also show possession with a **possessive noun**. Possessive nouns are often related to people, organizations, animals, or countries, as in **4 – 7.** Time expressions are also used as possessives, as in **8 – 10.**

Notice: We can use a possessive noun together with another determiner, as in **5 – 7** and **9 – 10.**

- We add **-'s** after singular nouns, noncount nouns, and irregular plural nouns, as in **4 – 6** and **8 – 9.**
- We add **-'** after plural nouns and other nouns that end in -s, as in **7** and **10.**

C

CORRECT THE COMMON ERRORS (See page R-12.)

11 ✗ What do you think of today young people?

12 ✗ A lot of the cities restaurants have closed.

13 ✗ One researchers' findings were completely different.

14 ✗ Can you give me your the number?

GO ONLINE

23 | Using Possessive Determiners Replace the **bold** words with a possessive determiner. `8.5 A–B`

FAMILY FOCUS

1. My parents enjoy the company of other people. ~~My parents'~~ *Their* favorite thing to do is to have people over for dinner.

2. I have two brothers, and **my brothers'** names are Manuel and José.

3. My first teacher was a young man. **My first teacher's** name was Mr. Cast.

4. My aunt and uncle have three children. **My aunt and uncle's** oldest child is 18.

5. My youngest sister has lots of interests, but **my youngest sister's** favorite thing to do is write plays.

6. My father and I like to prepare meals together. **My father's and my** favorite dish to make is lasagna.

7. My mother and I are very close. I have always depended on **my mother's** helpful advice.

8. My sister and I live in Madrid, but **my sister's and my** parents live in Lebanon.

> **FYI**
>
> Notice how the placement of an adjective changes the meaning of a sentence:
>
> **My first teacher's name** was Mr. Cast. (*first* describes *teacher*)
>
> **My teacher's first name** was Thomas. (*first* describes *name*)

Write about It Rewrite each pair of sentences above to tell about people you know. Use a possessive determiner in your sentences.

1. My friends enjoy music. Their favorite thing to do is to go to concerts.

24 | Using Possessive Nouns Complete each sentence below with the possessive (-'s / -') form of a noun from the box. `8.5 B`

computer	dolphin	everyone	Los Angeles	South Asia	week	world
cow	earth	giraffe	person	sun	women	year

FACT BOOK

1. About 70 percent of the _____*earth's*_____ surface is covered by water.
2. The _____ light and warmth make it possible for life to exist on earth.
3. Mount Everest is located in _____ Himalayan mountain range.
4. Only half of a _____ brain goes to sleep. The other half stays awake to tell the animal to come up for air.
5. Goats' milk has more calcium than _____ milk.
6. _____ hair turns gray as they become older.
7. _____ full name is El Pueblo de Nuestra Señora la Reina de los Ángeles de Porciuncula.
8. In general, _____ hearts beat faster than men's hearts.
9. Twenty-five percent of a _____ bones are in the feet.
10. The _____ libraries now store more than 100 million books.
11. A _____ neck weighs about 600 pounds (272 kilograms).
12. Two scientists shared this _____ Nobel Prize in Physics (2010).
13. You can drive from New York to Los Angeles in about a _____ time.
14. A _____ memory is similar to a human's—it can memorize both short and long things.

We use a group of determiners called **quantifiers** to identify the quantity or amount of something.
We use certain quantifers with certain types of nouns (singular, plural, or noncount).

A

quantifiers	singular count nouns	plural count nouns	noncount nouns
each	student	-	-
every	teacher	-	-
either	day	-	-
neither	answer	-	-
many	-	books	-
several	-	problems	-
both	-	people	-
a few	-	dollars	-
few	-	words	-
fewer	-	days	-
much	-	-	fun

quantifiers	singular count nouns	plural count nouns	noncount nouns
a little	-	-	money
little	-	-	time
less	-	-	food
all	-	teachers	information
a lot/lots of	-	trucks	equipment
plenty of	-	glasses	water
some	-	people	noise
more	-	problems	fun
most	-	days	food
any	key*	pens	paper
no	child	men	rice

*Any + a singular noun usually means "it doesn't matter which." *You can open the lock with **any** key.*

B

USING *OTHER*

1 Thomas has moved on to **other things**.

2 This would be easy for **most other people**.

3 What **other advice** do you have for me?

4 Do you need **any other information**?

5 **The other afternoon class** is also studying grammar.

6 I'll leave **another message** on her desk.

7 What's **another word** for *expensive*?

Other is a determiner that means "a different one / different ones" or "one, two, or several more." We can use *other* alone or after determiners like *most, any, the,* or *an*, as in **1 – 7**. We use *other* before:

• plural nouns, as in **1 – 2**
• noncount nouns, as in **3 – 4**
• singular nouns, as in **5 – 7**

Notice: *An* + *other* is spelled as one word: *another*.

C

QUANTIFIERS AS DETERMINERS AND PRONOUNS

8 I have **many friends** here, but only **a few** in Canada.
(a few = a few friends)

9 I don't need **any help**. I have **plenty**.
(plenty = plenty of help)

10 I have **many friends** in Canada, but **none** here.
(none = no friends)

11 Nancy is a hard worker, but **the others** don't do anything. (the others = the other workers)

We can use a quantifier as a **determiner** or as a **pronoun**, as in **8 – 11**.

WARNING! When we use quantifiers as pronouns, we:

• use *a lot* or *plenty* without *of*, as in **9**
• use *none* instead of *no*, as in **10**

We also use *(the) others* instead of *(the) other* in place of a plural noun, as in **11**.

D

CORRECT THE COMMON ERRORS (See page R-13.)

12 ✗ He has to worry about another things.

13 ✗ You can get many informations on the Internet.

14 ✗ A lot people ride bicycles there.

15 ✗ Few months after I moved home, I quit school.

25 | Noticing Quantifiers Underline the quantifiers and circle the nouns in these sentences. Then decide if you agree with the statement. Check (✓) your answers. **8.6 A**

WHAT'S YOUR OPINION?	AGREE	DISAGREE
1. It takes only <u>a few</u> (days) to learn a new language.	☐	☐
2. Zoos and aquariums are fun for people of all ages.	☐	☐
3. Sleeping five hours a night is plenty of sleep.	☐	☐
4. If you want to be healthy, you should avoid both coffee and tea.	☐	☐
5. There's no good reason to ban cigarettes.	☐	☐
6. You can enjoy the outdoors in any weather.	☐	☐
7. Coffee gives you energy but it only lasts for a few hours.	☐	☐
8. All young people should have the opportunity to travel abroad.	☐	☐
9. Most people like potato chips and French fries, but neither food is good for you.	☐	☐
10. There are many ways to look at any situation.	☐	☐
11. All students should be encouraged to study several languages.	☐	☐
12. Automobiles improve our lives in many ways, but they also cause a lot of problems.	☐	☐
13. A lot of stress is a bad thing, but a little stress can be a good thing.	☐	☐
14. It's impossible to have good relationships with other people when there is no trust.	☐	☐
15. Even if you don't watch much television, you still see many advertisements each day.	☐	☐
16. People should eat a lot of vegetables, just a little meat, and no sweets.	☐	☐

Talk about It Take turns reading the statements above aloud with a partner. See if your partner agrees or disagrees and why.

A: It takes only a few days to learn a new language.
B: I disagree with that. It takes a long time to learn a new language.

Think about It Write each noun phrase above under the correct group in the chart below.

Quantifier + singular count noun	Quantifier + plural count noun	Quantifier + noncount noun
	a few days	

26 | Choosing Quantifiers Complete these opinions with the correct quantifier. `8.6 A`

OPINIONS ABOUT EDUCATION

1. In my opinion, there should be _____*a few*_____ free universities in every country.
   (a little / a few)

2. I think that _____ famous universities don't provide a good education to their students.
   (many / much)

3. In my opinion, a university should encourage students to look at _____ career paths.
   (every / several)

4. _____ people go to a university because they don't know what else to do.
   (a little / many)

5. I think that _____ college student should take physical education classes.
   (all / every)

6. I think that college students need _____ free time to explore new ideas.
   (many / plenty of)

7. Every university student should work for _____ hours a week while in school.
   (a few / a little)

8. I think that _____ students should take a year off before they start college.
   (all / every)

9. In my opinion, students should take only _____ classes outside of their major course
   (a few / a little)
   of study.

10. _____ student should get a free education.
    (all / every)

11. I believe the Internet helps provide _____ opportunities for education.
    (more / most)

12. Students should be able to attend _____ university they choose.
    (all / any)

13. I think that students should spend _____ time taking tests.
    (fewer / less)

Talk about It Which of the opinions above do you agree with? Why?

Write about It Write two more opinions you have about education. Then share your opinions with
your classmates.

27 | Using Quantifiers Make true statements about yourself. Use quantifiers. (Many different answers
are possible.) `8.6 A`

MY LIFE AND TIMES

1. I have _____ things to do tonight.

2. I read _____ good books last year.

3. I get _____ mail every week.

4. _____ people in my family live far away from me.

5. I work _____ hours a week.

6. I'm happy when I have _____ money.

7. I saw _____ good movies last year.

8. There are _____ countries that I want to visit someday.

9. There are _____ interesting things to do in this neighborhood.

10. I had _____ free time yesterday.

11. When I want to have _____ fun, I sometimes _____.

12. When I have _____ free time, I like to _____.

Talk about It Read your statements in Activity 27 to a partner. Answer any questions your partner asks for more information.

A: *I have a lot of things to do tonight.*
B: *Are you planning to go out?*
A: *No, I have to . . .*

28 | Using *Other* Circle the correct form to complete these sentences. **8.6 B**

1. Living in **another** / **the other** country gives you the opportunity to learn many new things.

2. Today, we have greater access to information from around the world than at **any other** / **the other** period in history.

3. Self-discipline is necessary for success, but **other** / **the other** things such as talent, patience, and confidence are important, too.

4. If you want to lose weight, you should avoid eating cakes, cookies, and **other** / **some other** sweet things.

5. In many parts of the U.S., people speak and hear only English. They never hear **another** / **any other** languages spoken, and they don't see any value in learning to speak **another** / **the other** language.

6. My father often told me to treat **the other** / **other** people the way that I wanted to be treated. Now, whenever I have a problem with **another** / **other** person, I think of that advice. I don't try to change **some other** / **the other** person, but I try to understand his or her point of view. This helps me get along with **another** / **most other** people.

7. Television and radio are similar in some ways but very different in **the other** / **some other** ways. For example, fictional shows are popular on television, but you are more likely to hear music and talk shows on the radio. **Most other** / **Another** difference between radio and television is the way people use them. People don't usually do **other** / **the other** things while they are watching television, but they do when they are listening to the radio.

Think about It Look at the noun phrases you completed above. Write each one under the correct group in the chart below.

Quantifier + singular count noun	Quantifier + plural count noun
another country	

29 | Determiner or Pronoun? Decide if each **bold** word is a determiner or a pronoun. Write *D* (determiner) or *P* (pronoun) above each word. **8.6 C**

1. In Europe, **most** people hear languages other than[19] their own. And **many** speak more than one language.

2. The majority of New Yorkers speak English as a first language, and many **more** are fluent in one **other**.

3. Traveling from one country to **another** used to take days or weeks.

4. It's not fair that **some** workers do all the work while **others** are lazy.

5. In **many** offices, **a few** people do all the work while the **others** are wasting time.

6. Lazy people try to get **more** money for doing **less** work than **other** people.

7. **Some** kids like to study, but **most** would rather watch TV.

8. When children play games, they learn to interact with **others**.

9. Parents today have **less** time and energy to give to their children.

10. Ads tell us that **some** products work better than **others**.

11. Fast food is usually high in sodium and fat, and **both** are bad for your health.

12. **Most** bacteria are harmless, and **a few** are even helpful to humans.

Think about It What does each **bold** pronoun above mean?

In #1, many = many people.

Write about It Choose one of the sentences above. What could the writer say next? Write your ideas. (You don't need to use the bold word in your sentence.)

In Europe, most people hear languages other than their own, and many speak more than one language. This is because European countries are very close to each other, so students usually learn foreign languages at an early age.

30 | Using Quantifiers Answer these questions. Try to use quantifiers as determiners and pronouns in your answers. **8.6 C**

TALKING ABOUT GROUPS OF PEOPLE

1. How much homework do the teachers at your school give?

Most teachers give some homework, but some don't give any. Only a few give a lot!

2. How do the students at your school feel about homework?

3. How do people communicate these days (by phone, by text, online, in person, etc.)?

4. What sports do the people in your country like?

5. What color hair do your classmates have?

6. What languages do your classmates speak?

31 | Error Correction Correct any errors in these sentences. (Some sentences may not have any errors.)

1. We knew there were a many opportunities here.

We knew there were many opportunities here.

2. I have other sister who is two years younger than me.

3. You can get information about every famous people on the Internet.

4. I had to speak in front of the others student in my class.

[19] **other than:** different from; besides

5. It's hard to learn another languages like English.

6. I wish I had much money.

7. I don't have a work experience in this field.

8. My sister believes all people is good.

9. Algebra is not an easy subject for almost students.

10. Each seasons have different weather.

11. I think I need to find the another job.

12. At the school where I work, the most children like to play games outdoors.

8.7 Quantifiers with *Of*

A

COMPARE QUANTIFIERS WITH AND WITHOUT *OF*

1a **Many of the international students in my class** speak several languages. (refers to a particular group of international students—the ones in my class)

1b **Many international students** speak several languages. (refers to international students in general)

We can use a **quantifier + *of*** to identify a quantity or amount of something in a particular group, as in **1a**.

When we aren't talking about a particular group, we usually use a **quantifier without *of***, as in **1b**.

2 We met **most of the new people at work**. (NOT: ~~most of new people at work~~)

3 The class misunderstood **some of the homework**.

4 **All of Maria's friends** attend the university.

5 She spends **most of her money** on tuition.

6 I can only answer **a few of these questions**.

We usually use a quantifier + *of* with plural count nouns or noncount nouns. The quantifier + *of* is almost always followed by one of these determiners:

- *the*, as in **2 – 3**
- a possessive (*my, your, Maria's*, etc.), as in **4 – 5**
- *these* or *those*, as in **6**

B

7 Write a topic sentence for **each of the paragraphs**. (NOT: ~~each of the paragraph~~)

8 We can't complete **either of these projects**.

9 My boss rejected **every one of my ideas**. (NOT: ~~every of my ideas~~)

10 Luckily, **none of the students** failed the exam.

We use plural nouns after *each of, every one of, neither of*, and *either of*, as in **7 – 9**, not singular nouns. We can also use a plural noun after *none of*, as in **10**.

WARNING! When we use a quantifier + *of*, we use:
- *every one* instead of *every*, as in **9**
- *none* instead of *no*, as in **10**

11 **Three of my closest friends** live in Italy.

12 Einstein has always been **one of my heroes**.

We can also use *of* after numbers, as in **11 – 12**. We use a plural noun after *one of*, as in **12**.

C

SUBJECT-VERB AGREEMENT

13 Some of the **information** in this article **is** incorrect.

14 Most of the **men** in my office **were** married.

15 **Each of** my brothers **has** three children.

16 **Neither of** my parents **speaks** Chinese.

17 **None of** the rooms **is** available this afternoon.

18 **One of** the students in my class **was** trilingual.

When we use a quantifier + *of* as a subject, the verb usually agrees with the main noun after *of*, as in **13 – 14**.

However, we usually use a singular verb after *each of, every one of, neither of, either of, none of*, and *one of*, as in **15 – 18**. (The verb agrees with the singular quantifier.)

D

19 I don't know all of the members, but I know **most of them**.

20 I'm going to speak to **each of you** separately.

We can also use an object pronoun after a quantifier + *of*, as in **19 – 20**. The pronoun often refers back to a noun or noun phrase that was mentioned earlier.

32 | Quantifiers with and without *Of* Read these paragraphs. Add *of* after the quantifiers where necessary. `8.7 A`

JAMESTOWN, VIRGINIA

The English formed a settlement at Jamestown,

Virginia in 1607. They chose the area because there

were a few ____ rivers nearby, the water was deep,
         1

and the native tribes[20] didn't live there. Unfortunately,

much ____ that land was not good for farming, and many
      2

____ these settlers didn't have the skills to grow crops[21]
3

on such difficult land. When they first arrived, some ____ natives had welcomed the settlers and
                                                          4

had given them food. However, as time passed, the settlers began to demand more ____ the natives'
                                                                                    5

supplies. War broke out between them. Overall, things did not look promising for Jamestown, and a

large number ____ the settlers died during the first four years.
             6

CAVE PAINTINGS

A lot ____ information about our earliest ancestors[22] has been lost.
      7

But there are several ____ caves in France and Spain where visitors
                      8

can still see some ____ the most fascinating paintings in the history
                   9

of art. Thousands of years ago, artists drew murals[23] on the walls

of the caves. Most ____ these paintings show animals in movement,
                   10

and a few ____ the images have a stunning three-dimensional effect.
          11

> **F Y I**
>
> Some quantifiers always use *of*, including *a lot of*, *plenty of*, and *a great deal of*.
>
> **A lot of the questions on the test** confused me.
>
> I have a lot of **questions** about the test.

Think about It Look again at the paragraphs above. Where did you NOT add *of*? Why not?

33 | Noticing Quantifiers + *Of* Choose a noun from the box to complete each sentence. `8.7 A–B`

attention	buildings	diseases	mountains	qualities	things	water
bones	cities	languages	museums	styles	time	ways

1. Many of the _____cities_____ in Japan are large and densely populated. That's because much of the country is mountainous.

2. English, Spanish, Chinese, and Arabic are important languages in the world today. Students should study at least two of these _____.

[20] **native tribes:** groups of people who originally lived in an area
[21] **crops:** plants that are grown by farmers
[22] **ancestors:** people who lived in the past
[23] **murals:** large paintings done directly on the wall

3. One of the world's largest _____ is the Hermitage in Saint Petersburg, Russia. It contains about 3 million works of art.

4. Vaccinations have eliminated[24] many diseases that were once common. Some of these _____ are measles, mumps, and smallpox.

5. Some of the _____ of a good manager are patience, fairness, and a sense of humor.

6. None of the _____ in Honduras is volcanic.

7. The first offices in the area were built about 150 years ago. Many of those _____ are still in use today.

8. When couples have children, their lives change. Suddenly they have to focus most of their _____ on the children.

9. Most of the _____ in the ground comes from precipitation[25].

10. Young children shouldn't spend most of their _____ playing competitive sports.

11. Walking is one of the best _____ to explore a new city.

12. A number of specific things have increased life expectancy. Some of these _____ are vaccinations, workplace safety rules, and a decrease in smoking.

13. Jazz is one of the few uniquely American _____ of music.

14. There is a joint between each of the _____ in the spine that allows them to move.

34 | Choosing Quantifiers Write true statements using quantifiers from the box + *of*. You can use a positive or negative form of the verb. (More than one answer is possible.) 8.7 A-B

a few	a lot	(not) any	(not) either	many	much	several
a little	all	both	every one	most	one	some

TRUE STATEMENTS

1. I live near . . . my relatives.

   I don't live near any of my relatives.

2. I am in touch with . . . my cousins.
3. I can write clearly with . . . my hands.
4. I know . . . my classmates' names.
5. I can see well with . . . my eyes.
6. I am younger than . . . my siblings.
7. I email . . . my parents very often.

8. I have visited . . . the big cities in my native country.
9. I miss . . . my English classes every week.
10. When I go shopping, I usually spend . . . my money.
11. I do . . . my homework in the morning before class.
12. I know the names of . . . the best restaurants in this city.
13. I have seen or read . . . William Shakespeare's plays.
14. My friends and I enjoy . . . the same activities.
15. In the evening, I spend . . . my time working on a computer.

Talk about It Compare your answers above with a partner. How are you the same or different?

A: I don't live near any of my relatives.
B: Neither do I.

---

[24] **eliminate:** to remove or get rid of

[25] **precipitation:** water that falls to the ground as rain, snow, etc.

35 | Using the Correct Verb Complete these sentences with the correct form of the verb in parentheses. 8.7 C

1. Most of the people in my class ____are____ from
(is / are)
   South America.

2. None of the movies that she recommended _____
(was / were)
   interesting to me.

3. All of the bad things that happened on that day

   _____ my fault.
(was / were)

4. Several of the things he said _____ untrue.
(was / were)

5. Many of my friends from high school _____ to visit
(wants / want)
   me here.

6. Some of her advice _____ helpful but not all of it.
(was / were)

7. Most of the movie _____ pretty good, but I didn't like the ending.
(was / were)

8. Every one of my students _____ able to pass the test.
(was / were)

9. One of the students in my class _____ trilingual.
(is / are)

10. Some but not all of my money _____ in the bank.
(is / are)

11. Each of the schools _____ two teams of students to the debate.
(sends / send)

12. All of the information in this article _____ incorrect.
(is / are)

13. Neither of my parents _____ how to speak English.
(knows / know)

14. Most of his books _____ science fiction stories and mysteries.
(is / are)

> **RESEARCH SAYS...**
>
> Traditionally, we use singular verbs after *each of*, *neither of*, and *none of*. Today, many people use a plural verb after these quantifiers.
>
> **None of my brothers** has any children.
> (typical agreement)
>
> **None of my brothers** have any children.
> (less formal agreement)

36 | Using Quantifiers with Pronouns Complete each sentence with *it, them,* or *us*. Where possible, circle the noun or noun phrase that the pronoun refers to. 8.7 D

TRAVEL AND TRANSPORT

1. New York has more than 20 different (subway lines). Some of ____them____ were built more than 100 years ago.

2. Some of New York's subway system runs above ground, but much of _____ operates beneath the city.

3. During the 1930s, bridges were built all over the U.S. Many of _____ are still used today.

4. Canada is building a new bridge to Detroit, Michigan. The Canadian government believes that the bridge is a good investment, so it is willing to pay for almost all of _____.

5. Public transit reduces traffic and pollution for everyone, but few of _____ are willing to stop driving.

6. Because of budget cuts, public transit is being reduced in many communities. Several small towns could lose some or all of _____ within a year.

7. Suburban commuters in Copenhagen have many options for traveling to work. However, most of _____ choose to drive.

8. The majority of people say they enjoy driving to work. However, as gas becomes more expensive, each of _____ will need to explore alternatives[26].

9. Mopeds have become the number-one method of transportation in Vietnam. However, driving one of _____ in city traffic can be difficult.

Think about It In the sentences in Activity 36, which pronouns do NOT refer back to a noun or noun phrase mentioned earlier? What do the pronouns refer to?

37 | Choosing Quantifiers Add the quantifiers to complete the story. `8.7 A–D`

Cat Burglar on the Loose!

A recent newspaper headline read: "Cat Burglar on the Loose[27]!" However, this wasn't _____ those stories about a thief who
(1. another of / one)
climbs up the outsides of buildings. This was about an actual cat.

When Paula Steen discovered that she was missing _____ her necklaces,
(2. one of / some)
she thought she had lost it. However, when _____ her jewelry disappeared, she
(3. both / more of)
started to get worried. One day, she was talking with _____ her neighbors at the door.
(4. one of / some)
_____ them noticed a neighbor's
(5. neither / neither of)
cat, Mimi, sneak into Paula's house. After a few minutes, Mimi returned with _____
(6. some / some of)
earrings sticking out of her mouth.

_____ women were surprised,
(7. both / both of)
but then immediately started laughing. They

went to that neighbor's house and, after a quick search, found Paula's jewelry in Mimi's basket.

_____ it was there—along with
(8. every one of / all of)
_____ neighbors' jewelry. When the
(9. other / one of)
women told their friends, _____ them
(10. no one / none of)
believed the story. But then Mimi did it again—this time she stole _____ towels and
(11. some / some of)
_____ household items!
(12. other / another of)

Think about It Which quantifiers + *of* are followed by pronouns? What do the pronouns refer to?

Write about It Rewrite the story above using different determiners where possible. You can also change other words and phrases.

A recent newspaper headline read: "Cat Burglar on the Loose"! However, this wasn't <u>one of</u> those stories about a thief who climbs up the outsides of buildings. . . .

---

[26] **alternatives:** choices or options

[27] **on the loose:** able to move freely—often used to describe a dangerous person or animal

38 | Error Correction Correct any errors in these sentences. (Some sentences may not have any errors.)

1. Most of time I get up before six.
2. None of my friend think I should go to a school far away.
3. Last year I had to make one of the most important decision in my life.
4. Birthdays are one of a special day for young people.
5. Please give a paper to each one person.
6. For many of my friends, attending college won't be possible.
7. Most of people in Singapore speak English as a first language.
8. Every one of the books that I read were different.
9. One of the purpose of art is to make people think.
10. Some of scientists believe that people are causing global warming.

8.8 Using Determiners in Speaking and Academic Writing

A

SHORT RESPONSES WITH QUANTIFIERS

1 A: Did we get any phone calls?
  B: Yeah, **a lot.**

2 A: Did you talk to your friends today?
  B: **A few of them.**

3 A: Do you have a lot of homework tonight?
  B: No, **not much.** I did **a lot of it** yesterday.

4 A: Were there a lot of people on the bus?
  B: No, **not too many.**

5 A: Do you want more coffee?
  B: **Just a little,** please.

In speaking, we often give a **short response using a quantifier.** This may be:

- a quantifier alone, as in **1**
- a quantifier with *of* + a pronoun, as in **2**
- *not (very) much / many,* as in **3**
- *(not) too much / many,* as in **4**
- *just a few / a little* or *very few / little,* as in **5**

Too usually means "more than you want."

B

INFORMAL MEASURE WORDS IN SPEAKING

6 I'm afraid I can't help you. I have **tons of work** to do!

7 He made a **bunch of promises** last year.

8 Just a **handful of people** came to the lecture.

9 Can I give you a **little bit of advice**?

USING MEASURE WORDS IN ACADEMIC WRITING

10 There are **many advantages** to having a cell phone.
  (NOT: ~~There are a bunch of advantages~~ . . .)

11 The board did not spend a **great deal of time** considering the issues.
  (NOT: ~~The board didn't spend a lot of time~~ . . .)

In everyday conversation, you will sometimes hear informal **measure words** + *of* to describe large amounts, as in **6 – 7**. These include *bunch(es), heap(s), hundreds, loads, mountain(s), pile(s), ton(s),* and more general expressions like *lots of.*

There are also a few informal measure words + *of* that mean a small amount, as in **8 – 9**.

In more formal contexts, such as academic writing, we use more formal **quantifiers**, as in **10**. We also use more formal **measure words** + *of,* such as *a great deal of, a large amount of,* or *a (large) number of,* as in **11**.

C

MAKING GENERAL STATEMENTS IN SPEAKING

12a American classrooms are quite informal. **Everyone** feels free to interrupt and ask questions. This is difficult for **international students.**
  (This is not true for all American classrooms or all international students.)

MAKING GENERAL STATEMENTS IN ACADEMIC WRITING

12b Many American classrooms are quite informal. **Most students** feel free to interrupt and ask questions. This is difficult for **some international students.**

In speaking, we sometimes make general statements that aren't entirely true or accurate, as in **12a**. This is because we usually do not have time to plan what we are going to say in conversation.

In academic writing, we often need to quantify our statements to make them more accurate. We can use **quantifiers** like *some, most,* and *many* to avoid making statements that are too general, as in **12b**.

39 | Using Simple Quantifiers in Conversation Complete each conversation with a short response from the box. (More than one answer may be possible.) Then practice with a partner. `8.8 A`

all of it	a lot	a little	too many of them	too much	just a few
all of them	not a lot	very little	not very many	not much	some

1. A: So, did you get some sleep?

   B: No, _____*not much*_____, unfortunately.

   A: Me neither. I woke up at 6:00 and couldn't get back to sleep.

2. A: Would you like some juice to drink?

   B: Sure, I'll have _____. Thanks!

3. A: Hey, you don't look so good. Are you OK?

   B: I ate _____. I think I need to sit down.

4. A: If gas prices go down, I think we'll save some money on our trip.

   B: I guess, maybe _____.

5. A: I'm excited about the trip. So everyone in our class is coming?

   B: Yeah, _____. It'll be great!

6. A: I'm going to get rid of this coat. Do you want it?

   B: Oh, thanks. It's nice, but I have

   _____.

7. A: How many chairs should I set up?

   B: _____! It's going to be a really big event.

8. A: Everybody's sick these days. Have a lot of your classmates been out lately?

   B: Fortunately, _____.

9. A: Hey, the ice cream is gone! How much did you eat?

   B: _____! Sorry.

10. A: How's your business doing? Have you gotten some new customers?

    B: Well, _____, unfortunately.

11. A: I hear they're starting a new program at your university. Have you heard anything about it?

    B: No, _____, actually.

12. A: Do you speak Japanese?

    B: Yes, but _____. It's a difficult language.

40 | Describing Amounts with Measure Words Listen and write each missing measure word + *of*. `8.8 B`

1. Next week's weather could cause _____*a load of*_____ trouble.

2. I've seen this film _____ times.

3. _____ people came to protest the event.

4. I'm supposed to get _____ money at the end of the month.

5. I don't want to go see the boss. He's just going to give me _____ extra work to do.

6. When I went to the store, there were _____ people already waiting in line.

7. My job started out slow at first, but now I'm getting _____ business.

8. I have _____ unpaid bills. What am I going to do?

9. Everyone appreciates _____ kindness.

> **F Y I**
>
> English speakers may use informal measure words to exaggerate. They may also include the adjective *whole* to emphasize the amount.
>
> He gave me **a whole bunch of roses**!
>
> There are **a whole ton of people** waiting for you!

10. They've made a website that has _____ information on it.

11. The computers at the public library have _____ kid-friendly software.

12. _____ us are going to the movie at 3:00 on Saturday.

13. The writing center is there for students who need _____ help.

14. Last year I got _____ tomatoes from my garden.

15. I have _____ papers to write before the end of the semester.

Talk about It Work with a partner. Choose one of the sentences in Activity 40. Write a conversation with it. Present your conversation to the class.

A: Next week's weather could cause a load of trouble.
B: Really? What's the forecast?
A: We're going to have heavy rain, and it's going to be really windy.

41 | Using Quantifiers in Academic Contexts Circle the quantifier or measure word in each statement below. Then rewrite each statement using a more formal quantifier or measure word from the box. (More than one answer is possible in many cases.) `8.8 B`

few (of)	many (of)	little (of)	a great deal of
a few (of)	a large number of	a little (of)	a large amount of
a number of	most (of)	much (of)	

1. The school will pay for (almost all of) the travel expenses.

   The school will pay for most of the travel expenses.

2. A couple of errors were discovered during review.

3. Despite a new advertising campaign, there was hardly any improvement in sales.

4. A lot of the expert's argument is based on guesswork.

5. Nearly all of the experiments have proven nothing.

6. We can find a bunch of information about the environment online.

7. A bit of knowledge can be more dangerous than no knowledge at all.

8. The exhibition was attended by plenty of people.

9. The situation could easily be resolved[28] with a bit of understanding.

10. There aren't a lot of scientists who now subscribe to that view[29].

11. We made a handful of attempts to contact the head of the company.

12. I have spent a ton of time reading about the problem.

Write about It Rewrite the sentences in Activity 40 using more formal ways of describing amounts. (You may also change some of the other informal words in the sentences.)

Next week's weather could cause a great deal of difficulty.   OR   *Next week's weather could result in many problems.*

---

[28] **resolve:** to settle or solve something   [29] **subscribe to that view:** to have that specific opinion or belief

42 | Recognizing Quantified Statements Circle the quantifiers that are used to make each statement more accurate. 8.8 C

1. (Many) people think a bicycle is a toy for children, not a serious machine for cardiovascular[30] exercise.
2. Most scientists believe our climate is changing because we produce too much CO_2.
3. Researchers believe that violent video games cause behavior problems in some children.
4. Most Americans get the protein in their diet from meat.
5. In a few Western countries, people believe that parents should let teenagers make their own decisions.
6. The negative effects of smoking became clear after the completion of some long-term studies in the 1990s.
7. Many vegetarians say that eating meat is bad for health, wastes resources, and creates pollution.
8. Most of the parents in a recent study believe that homework is helpful, not harmful.
9. Some people believe that actors and professional athletes are paid too much.
10. Most wind energy comes from windmills that are as tall as a 20-story building and have 60-meter-long blades.

Think about it Look at the quantifiers you circled above. Why are they important?

43 | Making Accurate Statements Use a quantifier to make each statement less general. Some sentences need two quantifiers, and you may need to make other changes. (There are several different ways to rewrite each sentence.) 8.8 C

many	a large number of	few	fewer	more	most	some

STATEMENTS ABOUT COLLEGE EDUCATION

1. The benefits of a college education are well known.

   Many benefits of a college education are well known.

2. People from low-income families don't go to college or earn a degree.
3. Children of educated parents begin elementary school with basic knowledge.
4. People with only a high school education need public assistance[31], but college graduates do not.
5. College graduates pay 80 percent more in taxes each year than typical high school graduates.
6. People with advanced degrees[32] have never smoked, have quit, or are trying to quit.
7. People with less education do not exercise, while people with higher education do.
8. College graduates reported that they were very satisfied with their jobs.
9. High school dropouts[33] said their jobs were not satisfying.
10. People with low education levels lose their jobs in difficult economic times.

Write about It What do you think are the benefits of a college education? Write three sentences stating the benefits you believe a college education can give.

---

[30] **cardiovascular:** connected with the heart and lungs
[31] **public assistance:** money that the government gives to people who are poor or disabled
[32] **advanced degrees:** higher levels of education, such as master's degrees and doctoral degrees
[33] **high school dropouts:** people who don't complete high school

WRAP-UP Demonstrate Your Knowledge

A | DISCUSSION Complete these statements about leaders and leadership. Work in a small group to compare your ideas. Then share your ideas with the class.

STATEMENTS ABOUT LEADERS AND LEADERSHIP

1. A good leader has . . .
2. Most leaders have a few . . .
3. The best leaders have a little . . .
4. Some leaders have none of . . .
5. More leaders need some . . .
6. Most good leaders care about their . . .
7. All leaders should want the . . .
8. Every leader should want a . . .

A good leader has the ability to influence other people.

B | PRESENTATION Find some information about a country or a city that you have never visited. Write 6–8 interesting facts about it and then present your findings to a group.

One of the world's largest art museums is in Saint Petersburg.
Many people died there during World War II.

C | PERSONAL NARRATIVE Think of the plot of a movie that you enjoy. Make notes in the chart about the main characters in the story, the places where it occurs, and three or four of the main events.

Characters	Places	Events

Use the notes in your chart to write a one- or two-paragraph version of the story. Underline all of the determiners you used.

The movie "Dirty Pretty Things" is about two immigrants in London. They work together in a hotel and become good friends. The man is a doctor from Africa, but now he is working at the front desk in the hotel. The woman cleans rooms in the hotel. . . .

D | WEB SEARCH Search the Internet for images of bar graphs. (You can just Google "bar graphs" or "bar graphs for college students" and then click Images.) Choose one graph and describe it to your classmates.

This graph shows how many hours a week students study and do homework. According to the graph, most of these students set aside between 5 and 14 hours for homework and studying. However, some set aside 4 hours or less. Only a few study more than 14 hours.

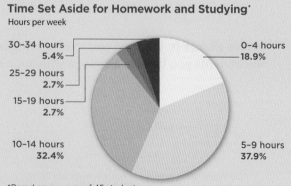

Time Set Aside for Homework and Studying*
Hours per week

30–34 hours 5.4%
25–29 hours 2.7%
15–19 hours 2.7%
10–14 hours 32.4%
0–4 hours 18.9%
5–9 hours 37.9%

*Based on a survey of 45 students

ARTICLES

ARTICLES		NOUNS		
		singular count	plural count	noncount
a / an	+	✓		
some			✓	✓
Ø			✓	✓
the		✓	✓	✓

POSSESSIVES

my	your	his	her	its	our	your	their		singular count	plural count	noncount
								+	✓	✓	✓

POSSESSIVE NOUNS

				singular count	plural count	noncount
singular noun + 's **the plan's** success	irregular plural noun + 's **the children's** tests	noncount noun + 's **life's** challenges	+	✓	✓	✓
name ending in -s + ' **Chris'** success	regular plural noun + ' **the students'** tests	-		✓	✓	✓

QUANTIFIERS

							singular count	plural count	noncount
each	every	either	neither				✓		
many	several	both	a few	few	fewer			✓	
much	a little	little	less			+			✓
all	a lot of	plenty of	some	more	most			✓	✓
any	no						✓	✓	✓

QUANTIFIERS WITH *OF*

							singular count	plural count	noncount
each of	every one of	either of	neither of					✓	
many of	several of	both of	a few of	few of	fewer of			✓	
much of	a little of	little of	less of			+			✓
all (of)	a lot of	plenty of	some of	more of	most of			✓	✓
any of	none of						✓	✓	✓

OTHER

		singular count	plural count	noncount
another		✓		
(Ø / some / most / many / both / etc.) other			✓	
(Ø / some / most / much / little / etc.) other	+			✓
the other		✓	✓	✓

DEMONSTRATIVES

this	that		singular count	plural count	noncount
these	those	+	✓		✓
				✓	

Noun Phrases

The love of family and the admiration of friends is much more important than wealth and privilege.

—CHARLES KURALT,
JOURNALIST
(1934–1997)

Talk about It Do you agree or disagree with the quotation above? Why?

WARM-UP

A | Read the movie titles and check (✓) *I liked it, It was OK, I didn't like it,* or *I haven't seen it.* Then compare lists with a partner.

Ten Famous English Language Films

	I liked it.	It was OK.	I didn't like it.	I haven't seen it.
1. *The Last Emperor*	☐	☐	☐	☐
2. *A Hard Day's Night*	☐	☐	☐	☐
3. *A Streetcar Named Desire*	☐	☐	☐	☐
4. *The Thirty-Nine Steps*	☐	☐	☐	☐
5. *Empire of the Sun*	☐	☐	☐	☐
6. *Million Dollar Baby*	☐	☐	☐	☐
7. *A Beautiful Mind*	☐	☐	☐	☐
8. *The Wizard of Oz*	☐	☐	☐	☐
9. *Rebel Without a Cause*	☐	☐	☐	☐
10. *The Man Who Knew Too Much*	☐	☐	☐	☐

B | Each movie title above is a noun phrase. Based on these examples, what can you say about noun phrases? Check (✓) *True* or *False.*

	TRUE	FALSE
1. A noun phrase has at least one noun or pronoun.	☐	☐
2. Noun phrases sometimes include adjectives.	☐	☐
3. Noun phrases always begin with *a, an,* or *the.*	☐	☐
4. There is always a noun at the end of a noun phrase.	☐	☐

C | Look back at the quotation on page 288. Identify any noun phrases.

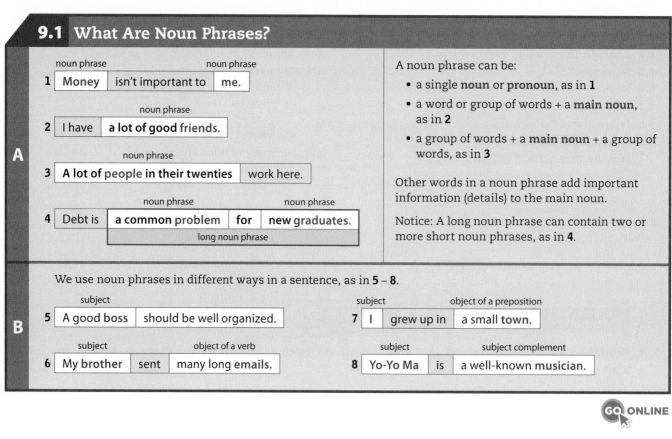

9.1 What Are Noun Phrases?

A

1 | Money | isn't important to | me. |
noun phrase · noun phrase

2 I have | **a lot of good** friends. |
noun phrase

3 | **A lot of** people in their twenties | work here. |
noun phrase

4 Debt is | **a common** problem | for | new graduates. |
noun phrase · noun phrase
long noun phrase

A noun phrase can be:

- a single **noun** or **pronoun**, as in **1**
- a word or group of words + a **main noun**, as in **2**
- a group of words + a **main noun** + a group of words, as in **3**

Other words in a noun phrase add important information (details) to the main noun.

Notice: A long noun phrase can contain two or more short noun phrases, as in **4**.

B

We use noun phrases in different ways in a sentence, as in **5 – 8**.

5 | A good **boss** | should be well organized. |
subject

6 | My **brother** | sent | many long **emails**. |
subject · object of a verb

7 | **I** | grew up in | a small **town**. |
subject · object of a preposition

8 | Yo-Yo Ma | is | a well-known **musician**. |
subject · subject complement

GO ONLINE

1 | Adding Noun Phrases Choose a noun phrase from the box to complete each sentence. Then compare answers with your classmates. **9.1 A**

CAREERS IN MUSIC

1. A lot of people love music, but it's not easy to find
   _____*many full-time jobs*_____ in this field.

2. A professional singer has a glamorous[1] job, but it's not usually
   _____.

3. Many musicians teach in _____.

4. A music teacher at _____ must have
   at least a master's degree in music.

> **NOUN PHRASES**
> many full-time jobs
> public and private schools
> the university level
> well-paid work

CAREERS IN SPORTS

5. _____ are possible in
   professional sports.

6. A sports reporter watches a sports event and gives other people
   _____.

7. There is always _____ for
   photographers and camera operators at sports events.

8. Teaching is _____.

> **NOUN PHRASES**
> a detailed description of it
> a need
> another possible career in sports
> many different careers

[1] **glamorous:** attractive in an exciting way

290

9. Toy companies employ chemists to come up with

_____.

10. Many chemists work in laboratories to improve

_____ like paint or soap.

11. Chemists work in many different fields and have

_____.

12. Some chemists are writers for _____.

> **NOUN PHRASES**
> a wide variety of jobs
> everyday items
> new things to entertain children
> newspapers and magazines

Think about It How many other noun phrases can you find in the sentences in Activity 1? (Remember: A noun phrase can be a single noun or pronoun.)

Talk about It What other careers in music, sports, or chemistry do you know about? Tell a partner.

2 | Identifying Uses of Noun Phrases How is each **bold** noun phrase used in these sentences? Check (✓) your answers. 9.1 B

FAMILY FACTS	SUBJECT	OBJECT OF VERB	OBJECT OF PREPOSITION	SUBJECT COMPLEMENT
1. **Everyone in my family** lives in the same town.	✓	☐	☐	☐
2. I have **many cousins**.	☐	☐	☐	☐
3. My parents met in **high school**.	☐	☐	☐	☐
4. I am **the only person in my family who has lived abroad.**	☐	☐	☐	☐
5. My father works as **an engineer**.	☐	☐	☐	☐
6. My mother is **a doctor**.	☐	☐	☐	☐
7. On **special holidays**, my whole family gets together.	☐	☐	☐	☐
8. I visit **my aunts and uncles** whenever I go home.	☐	☐	☐	☐
9. **My mother-in-law** is one of the nicest people I know.	☐	☐	☐	☐
10. When **my brother and I** were children, we played basketball all the time.	☐	☐	☐	☐
11. Not all sisters and brothers are **good friends**.	☐	☐	☐	☐
12. My parents sent **all of their children** to good universities.	☐	☐	☐	☐

Think about It What other noun phrases can you find in the sentences above? How is each one used in the sentence?

Write about It Write four sentences about your family like the ones above. Find the noun phrases and say how they are used.

9.2 Adding Information to a Main Noun

We can give more information about a main noun by adding words before or after it.

The information **before** a **main noun** usually comes in a particular order, as in **1 – 5**.

NOUN PHRASE

A

		determiner	number	adjective	noun	main noun	
1	This is	a	-	thorough	research	project.	-
2	What are	your	two	favorite	childhood	memories?	-
3	Is there	any	-	new	-	information	on this?
4	Look at	the	first	-	-	chart	on page 30.
5	There are	a few		-	-	problems	that I can't solve.

For more information on determiners and nouns, see Units 7 and 8, pages 212 and 254.

Notice the kind of information that comes **after** a **main noun** in a noun phrase, as in **6 – 9**.

NOUN PHRASE

B

			main noun	appositive	prepositional phrase	adjective clause
6	We just met	our new	boss,	Mr. Wilson.	-	-
7	I answered	all the	questions	-	on the test.	-
8	The U.N. is	an international	organization	-	-	that works for peace.
9	There were	so many	people	-	in my past	who helped me.

C

10 | I didn't know | anyone at the meeting.

11 | We are looking for | those who are responsible.

12 | This essay is clearer than | the one that I wrote.

We can also add more information to certain **pronouns**, such as:

- indefinite pronouns, as in **10**
- *these* or *those*, as in **11**
- *one*, as in **12**

This information usually comes after the pronoun.

GO ONLINE

3 | Understanding Noun Phrase Word Order Put the words for each noun phrase in the correct order to complete the sentences. 9.2 A

1. I have _____*a lot of good friends*_____. (good/a lot of/friends)

2. I wish I had _____. (dollars/million/a few)

3. I can speak _____. (languages/several/foreign)

4. There is _____ near my house. (grocery/a/store/large)

5. I would like to have _____ someday. (job/a/government)

6. In high school, _____ was biology. (subject/my/favorite)

7. I am _____. (movie/a/famous/star)

8. I don't need _____. (any/clothes/new)

9. I would like to live in _____. (modern/building/a/apartment)

10. I do _____ to stay healthy. (different/many/things)

Talk about It Which sentences above are true for you? Tell a partner.

4 | Exploring the Parts of a Noun Phrase Choose a word from the box to complete the **bold** noun phrases in the paragraph below. `9.2 A`

DETERMINERS		ADJECTIVES		NOUNS	
his	the	architectural	geometric	assistant	development
several	their	famous		building	

I. M. Pei

I. M. Pei, one of **the most** _____ (1. adjective) **architects in the world**, was born in China in 1917. Pei came to _____ (2. determiner) **U.S.** to study architecture when he was 17 years old. He worked for _____ (3. determiner) **years** as an _____ (4. noun) **professor** at Harvard University while he was studying for his master's degree in architecture. Then he joined **a New York real estate** _____ (5. noun) **corporation** called Webb & Knapp in 1948. In 1955, Pei started **his own** _____ (6. adjective) **office**. His designs soon became well-known for **their** _____ (7. adjective) **patterns** and _____ (8. determiner) **unique use of glass**. Among **his famous** _____ (9. noun) **designs** are the East Building of the National Gallery of Art in Washington and the New York City Convention Center. _____ (10. determiner) **accomplishments** also include updating the Louvre in Paris with a glass pyramid in one of its courtyards.

5 | Finding the Main Noun Underline the main noun in each noun phrase. `9.2 B`

1. the tallest <u>person</u> in your family
2. your favorite part of the Olympic Games
3. a member of a sports team
4. the second month of the year
5. a city that you would like to visit
6. your favorite subject in high school
7. the best job that you have ever had
8. your favorite thing for breakfast
9. one thing that you really need
10. the last item that you bought

> **F Y I**
>
> When the main noun is a very general word (e.g., *person*, *part*, *member*, or *thing*), we often add other words to make it more specific.
>
> Did you see **the thing**? (too general; not clear)
> Did you see **the beautiful thing on the table**?
> Did you see **the strange thing on TV about wild animals**?

Talk about It Use the noun phrases above to ask a partner questions.

A: Who is the tallest person in your family?
B: My brother is.

6 | Identifying Noun Phrases Underline the long noun phrase in each sentence below. Then choose a noun from the box to complete the sentence. **9.2 A–B**

eyelid	fingernail	head	heel	nose	toes
eyes	foot		heart	knee	thigh	torso

BODY PARTS

1. The part of your leg that you stand on is your _____*foot*_____.
2. The back part of your foot is your _____.
3. The part of your face that you use to smell things is your _____.
4. The body part above your neck is your _____.
5. The five things on your foot are your _____.
6. The piece of skin that covers your eye is your _____.
7. The two things that you see with are your _____.
8. The main part of your body (not your head, arms, and legs) is your _____.
9. The part of your body that pumps your blood around inside is your _____.
10. The part that bends in the middle of your leg is your _____.
11. The body part between your hip and your knee is your _____.
12. The thin, hard part at the end of your finger is your _____.

Think about It Circle the main noun in each underlined noun phrase above.

7 | Adding Information to Pronouns Complete each question below with information from the box. (More than one answer may be possible.) **9.2 C**

in the wild²	at the grocery store	that tasted really good	who can pay for it
in this book	in your family	that you saw last year	who lives in Canada
on TV			who want accurate news

1. Did you buy anything _____*at the grocery store*_____ yesterday?
2. Do you know everything _____?
3. When was the last time you ate something _____?
4. Did you watch anything _____ last night?
5. Do you know anyone _____?
6. Do you like movies? Can you name one _____?
7. What is the best magazine for those _____?
8. Does anyone _____ live in Europe?
9. Do you think everyone should get medical care or just those _____?
10. Many people have seen an elephant in a zoo, but have you ever seen one _____?

Talk about It Ask a partner the questions above.

²**in the wild:** in nature

9.3 Adjectives

A

	determiner	adjective	main noun
1 I need to make	some	important	decisions.

2 The two cars were traveling at **the same speed.**

3 What's **the main idea** of this essay?

4 Tom is **a typical teenager.**

We use **adjectives** to describe or give more information about nouns. In a noun phrase, an adjective usually goes between a determiner and a main noun, as in **1 – 4.**

Most of the time, we use only one or two adjectives before a noun.

B

5 Medicine is an **interesting profession.**
(The profession of medicine interests me.)

6 Bookmarks have a **surprising number** of uses.
(The number of uses for bookmarks surprises me.)

7 Planes have **limited space** for luggage.
(The space for luggage on planes is limited by the airline.)

8 English is a **required course.**
(English is required by the university.)

We can use the -*ing* and -*ed* forms of verbs as adjectives, as in **5 – 8.** Notice the difference in meaning between the -*ing* and -*ed* adjectives.

GRAMMAR TERM: We call the -*ing* form of a verb the **present participle.** The -*ed* form of a verb is the **past participle.**

C

9 Liz is looking for | **a full-time job.**

10 Your essay has | **well-developed ideas.**

11 Joe is | **a hard-working man.**

12 Heart disease is | **an age-related illness.**

13 We had to do | **group-building exercises.**

14 *Toy Story* is | **a full-length animated movie.**

15 The restaurant serves | **delicious slow-cooked meals.**

Multi-word adjectives are formed from more than one word, as in **9 – 15.** Most are spelled with a hyphen. Examples of multi-word adjectives include:

adjective	+	noun	full-time
adverb	+	-*ed* participle	well-developed
adverb	+	-*ing* participle	hard-working
noun	+	-*ed* participle	age-related
noun	+	-*ing* participle	group-building

Notice that we can also use more than one adjective in a noun phrase, as in **14 – 15.**

8 | Using Adjectives Add an adjective from the box to each **bold** noun phrase. (More than one answer may be possible.) **9.3 A**

1. I have *long* **a list of the job qualifications.**

2. **A study in the *Journal of Modern Science*** provides new information on this topic.

3. Volunteering teaches kids **a lesson.**

4. **The sources of energy** today are fossil fuels such as natural gas, oil, and coal.

5. Tai chi is **a type of exercise.**

6. Archeologists discovered **a pyramid** at an ancient burial site near Cairo, Egypt.

7. This course covers **a range of topics.**

8. The sun is **a source of energy.**

9. English is **the language of business.**

10. We now have vaccines to prevent **the spread of some diseases.**

deadly
graceful
international
long
lost
main
recent
renewable
valuable
wide

9 | Noticing -ing and -ed Adjectives Underline the *-ing* and *-ed* adjectives in these questions. `9.3 B`

1. Do all universities have <u>required</u> courses?
2. What are some examples of industrialized nations?
3. Are there many unemployed people in your city?
4. Can you name an outstanding restaurant?
5. Does it bother you to ride in a crowded subway car?
6. What's an interesting topic for a class discussion?
7. Do you like to have unexpected visitors at home?
8. Did you learn some complicated math formulas in school?
9. What was the most exciting period in history?
10. What should two friends do when they have opposing views about something?
11. Why is it important to make an informed decision when you buy something expensive?
12. Why shouldn't you eat spoiled meat?
13. What is the most terrifying experience you've ever had?
14. Do you hope to have a challenging career?

> **RESEARCH SAYS...**
>
> *-ing*/*-ed* adjectives and multi-word adjectives are used most often in academic writing.

Talk about It Ask a partner the questions above.

A: *Do all universities have required courses?*
B: *Many do, but not all.*

10 | Choosing -ing or -ed Adjectives Choose the correct word to complete each sentence. `9.3 B`

1. a. We couldn't believe the _____ news.
      (shocked / shocking)
   b. The whole class fell into _____ silence.
      (shocked / shocking)
2. a. It was a very _____ situation for everyone.
      (confused / confusing)
   b. Irene had a _____ look on her face.
      (confused / confusing)
3. a. Coughing is the body's way of clearing _____ airways to help you breathe.
      (irritated / irritating)
   b. The most _____ habit I have is that I love to talk.
      (irritated / irritating)
4. a. Heat can be one of the _____ annoyances³ of working in Antarctica.
      (surprised / surprising)
   b. I could tell from the _____ look on her face that she wasn't expecting us.
      (surprised / surprising)
5. a. My husband and I have a _____ approach to parenting.
      (relaxed / relaxing)
   b. I just want to have a _____ time on my vacation.
      (relaxed / relaxing)
6. a. Librarians offer useful information to students, teachers, and other _____ individuals.
      (interested / interesting)
   b. This study raises some _____ questions about classroom management.
      (interested / interesting)
7. a. What do you think was the most _____ part of the movie?
      (excited / exciting)
   b. I couldn't see the children but I could hear their _____ voices.
      (excited / exciting)
8. a. He probably would have gotten the job, but he didn't even apply for it. That was a
      _____ opportunity.
      (missed / missing)
   b. I don't understand this report. There's just too much _____ information.
      (missed / missing)

³**annoyances:** things that bother you or make you angry

9. a. Given the _____ expression on her face, I'm guessing she got the job.
   (pleased / pleasing)
   b. They painted the house to give it a more _____ appearance.
   (pleased / pleasing)

Think about It Look at each pair of sentences in Activity 10. How does the meaning of the *-ing* adjective differ from the meaning of the *-ed* adjective?

11 | Learning Multi-Word Adjectives Use the context of each sentence to guess the meaning of the adjective in the **bold** noun phrase. Then write your own sentence using the noun phrase. `9.3 C`

1. **Big-name actors** earn a substantial amount of money.

   big-name = famous   Johnny Depp is a big-name actor.

2. **A front-row seat** at a concert is usually expensive.
3. Some people enjoy driving fast, but for others it is **a hair-raising experience**.
4. There are **few single-story buildings** in any city. The land is too expensive.
5. It is difficult to get from one part of the city to another in **the slow-moving traffic**.
6. There is little information on **the long-term effects** of a new medicine.
7. You will get a good grade for **a carefully planned presentation**.
8. **Newly married couples** have to adjust to a new way of life.
9. Bright red is **an eye-catching color**.
10. The majority of people obey the laws. They are **law-abiding citizens**.
11. It's easy to find things in **a well-organized desk**.
12. The economy is helped by **hard-working families**.
13. It's a pleasure to travel with **well-behaved children**.
14. There are many challenges for the teachers and staff at **a newly opened school**.
15. **Poor-quality products** can be harmful and sometimes dangerous to buyers.
16. *The Help* is **an award-winning novel** written by Kathryn Stockett.

Think about It Write each **bold** adjective above under the correct group in the chart below.

Adjective + noun	Adverb + *-ed* word	Adverb + *-ing* word	Noun + *-ed* word	Noun + *-ing* word
big-name				

12 | Using Multi-Word Adjectives Complete these sets of questions with the multi-word adjectives in the boxes. (More than one adjective may be possible.) `9.3 C`

1. How often do you eat at _____*fast-food*_____ restaurants?
2. Would you rather eat in a restaurant or have a _____ meal?
3. What is one _____ food?

awful-tasting
fast-food
home-cooked

4. Puzzles are one type of _____ game. What are some others?

5. Trivial Pursuit is a _____ game. You need to know a lot of facts. Can you think of any other games like this?

6. What are some common _____ activities?

knowledge-based
mind-stimulating
time-consuming

7. Is there a _____ team for the next World Cup?

8. Why are _____ movies so popular?

9. What is the _____ sport?

action-packed
fastest-growing
highly favored

10. Would you rather have a _____ job or a part-time one?

11. What are the advantages of working in a _____ business?

12. Do _____ people always succeed?

family-owned
full-time
hard-working

13. Should all students go to a _____ university after secondary school?

14. Should education be a _____ experience?

15. Should _____ students study separately from average students?

four-year
high-achieving
lifelong

Talk about It Ask a partner the questions in Activity 12.

A: How often do you eat at fast-food restaurants?
B: A few times a week, maybe.

Write about It Choose three multi-word adjectives from Activity 12 and write new questions. Then ask a partner your questions.

What is your favorite action-packed movie?

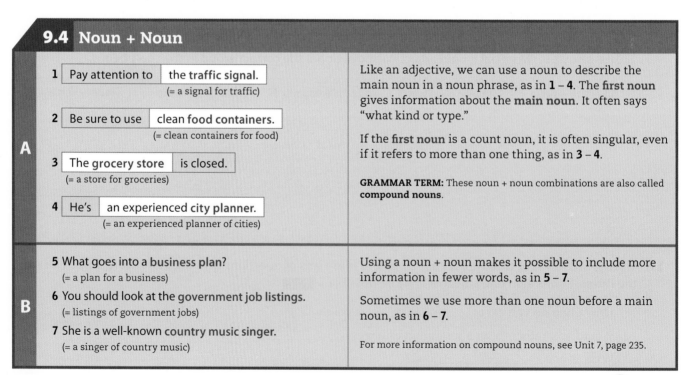

9.4 Noun + Noun

A

1 | Pay attention to | the traffic **signal**.
(= a signal for traffic)

2 | Be sure to use | clean food **containers**.
(= clean containers for food)

3 | The grocery **store** | is closed.
(= a store for groceries)

4 | He's | an experienced city **planner**.
(= an experienced planner of cities)

Like an adjective, we can use a noun to describe the main noun in a noun phrase, as in **1 – 4**. The **first noun** gives information about the **main noun**. It often says "what kind or type."

If the **first noun** is a count noun, it is often singular, even if it refers to more than one thing, as in **3 – 4**.

GRAMMAR TERM: These noun + noun combinations are also called **compound nouns**.

B

5 What goes into a business **plan**?
(= a plan for a business)

6 You should look at the government job **listings**.
(= listings of government jobs)

7 She is a well-known country music **singer**.
(= a singer of country music)

Using a noun + noun makes it possible to include more information in fewer words, as in **5 – 7**.

Sometimes we use more than one noun before a main noun, as in **6 – 7**.

For more information on compound nouns, see Unit 7, page 235.

13 | Noticing Noun + Noun Underline the noun + noun combinations in these sentences. `9.4 A`

The World's Best Airport?

1. <u>Singapore's Changi Airport</u> has won many awards from travel groups.

2. The airport has many comfortable areas for sleeping or watching TV, as well as work desks and free Internet service.

3. If you are tired, you can rent a nap room for a few hours.

4. The airport offers a free bus tour of Singapore.

5. There is a hotel with a rooftop hot tub.

6. There are several movie theaters.

7. The airport has a butterfly garden and an orchid garden.

8. If you spend $10 at one of the many airport stores, you get free admission to the four-story tube slide (an enclosed slide made from a long tube).

9. Terminal 3 is a little city with a pharmacy, grocery store, flower shop, and jewelry stores. It even has an indoor amusement park for kids.

Write about It Write your own sentences using three of the noun + noun combinations you underlined above.

14 | Forming Noun + Noun Combinations How many noun + noun combinations can you make with the words in the box? `9.4 A`

business	city	food	insurance	report
car	community	government	plan	school
center	family	health	police	world

city school   *school community*
business school   *school food*
police school   *school report*

Think about It Choose one of the nouns above. What other nouns do we commonly use with it? Look in the dictionary or online to find other nouns. Then report to the class.

school system   *school bus*   *graduate school*
school year   *school day*   *art school*
schoolteacher   *school library*   *law school*

Write about It Choose five of the noun + noun combinations above and write sentences with your own ideas.

The school year in Japan runs from April to March.

15 | Using Noun + Noun Rewrite the **bold** noun phrases using a noun + noun combination. `9.4 B`

1. Which country has **a good system of health care**?

   Which country has a good health-care system?

2. Is the post office **an agency of the federal government?**
3. What do you think **an expert on sleep** does?
4. How many people in your family are **speakers of a second language**?
5. What does **a manager of a project** do?
6. What can you put on **a bite of an insect** to make it stop itching?
7. What is **the normal temperature of your body**?
8. Do you usually take **a nap in the afternoon**?
9. Do you use **plastic or cloth bags for your groceries**?
10. Have you ever written an essay for **a class in college**?
11. Are you currently **a student at a university**?
12. What are **some common symptoms of a cold**?

Talk about It Ask a partner the questions above.

A: Which country has a good health-care system?
B: I think Canada does.

16 | Identifying the Main Noun When we use several nouns together, it's sometimes difficult to identify the main noun. Can you find the main noun in each **bold** noun phrase? Underline it. `9.4 B`

From the News

1. **A bristlecone pine <u>tree</u> in California** is **the oldest recorded living tree**. It is believed to be more than 4,600 years old.
2. The Large Hadron Collider is **the world's highest-energy particle accelerator**.[4]
3. In 2012, Joe Ayoob broke **the long-distance paper airplane flight record** when he threw a paper airplane 226 feet, 10 inches.
4. Many scientists believe that **an asteroid impact**[5] caused the extinction of the dinosaurs.
5. **The first coast-to-coast airplane flight** in the U.S. took place in 1911 and lasted 49 days.
6. **Fish species loss** is accelerating, and soon we may have no more fish to eat from the oceans.
7. Pollution causes **poor air quality**, and it can be bad for your health.
8. **The orbiting Spitzer Space Telescope** found water vapor in the atmosphere of a distant star.
9. Some scientists think that **music training** may help students with **language problems**.
10. **The fastest-growing plant in the world** is **the giant timber**[6] **bamboo from China**. It reaches **its adult height of up to 18.3 meters** in just two months.
11. **Movie director James Cameron** broke **the world depth record** when he descended nearly 7 miles in the Pacific Ocean.

[4]**particle accelerator:** a device that speeds up small matter; used in scientific experiments

[5]**asteroid impact:** a small planet hitting the earth
[6]**timber:** a tree that is grown to produce wood

9.5 Appositives

A

appositive

1 | Mr. Adrian, **my lawyer,** | can answer this question. |

appositive

2 | Mount Everest, **the world's highest mountain,** | is 60 million years old. |

appositive

3 | There is little water on | **Jupiter, the largest planet in the solar system.** |

We can add information after a main noun with an **appositive**, as in **1 – 3**. An appositive describes or gives another name to a main noun.

GRAMMAR TERM: An **appositive** is usually also a noun phrase. *Apposition* means that two noun phrases are set side by side.

B

4 *Flat Earth*, **a fascinating book,** was published in 2008.
5 Part of this exam **(Section 2)** focuses on vocabulary.
6 Mount Everest—**Mount Chomolungma in Tibetan—** is 8,848 meters high.

We usually use a comma before and after an appositive, as in **4**.

We sometimes use a dash—like this—or parentheses ( ) instead, as in **5 – 6**.

C

COMPARE

7a Mount Everest is the world's highest mountain. Climbing it can be very expensive.
7b Climbing **Mount Everest, the world's highest mountain,** can be very expensive.

Using an appositive is a useful way of combining information from several clauses or sentences into one sentence, as in **7b**. This is a short way to give a lot of information.

17 | Noticing Appositives Underline each appositive in this paragraph. Then circle the noun phrase it renames or describes. **9.5 A**

GUSTAVO DUDAMEL

by Matt Cody

(Gustavo Dudamel), <u>the 31-year-old Venezuelan conductor</u>, is at the center of the classical music world. In 2009, Dudamel became the music director of the Los Angeles Philharmonic, a leading orchestra in the U.S. Yet as famous as Dudamel is for his conducting, he is also much admired for his leadership in music education. He is one of the leaders of El Sistema, Venezuela's widely praised music education program. El Sistema has put musical instruments in the hands of about 250,000 Venezuelan children. Many of them play in the program's top orchestra, the Simón Bolivar Symphony Orchestra. Dudamel, a graduate of El Sistema, is the orchestra's conductor. Whether leading musicians young or old, Gustavo Dudamel is the most charismatic young conductor in the world today.

RESEARCH SAYS...

Appositives are common in news and academic writing. They often describe a proper noun or technical word.

CORPUS

18 | Adding Appositives Choose an appositive from the box to complete each sentence below. `9.5 A–B`

a 147-meter-high tomb	input/output
a 4,000-year-old invention	New York City's largest open space
a favorite destination for skiers	pieces of wood with rounded corners
a language spoken well before 4000 BCE	the frozen continent
a star made of intensely hot gases	the only food that never spoils
a sudden and briefly popular behavior	World Court

DESCRIBING PLACES

1. Central Park, _____*New York City's largest open space*_____, is a model for city parks around the world.

2. The Great Pyramid, _____, was completed in 2600 BCE.

3. The International Court of Justice (_____ _____) is located in the Netherlands.

4. The sun—_____—is the only source of light and the main source of heat in the solar system.

5. Antarctica, _____, surrounds and covers the South Pole.

6. The lower slopes of the Alps—_____ _____—are covered with forests.

Central Park in New York City

DESCRIBING THINGS

7. Honey, _____, was once used as a kind of money.

8. Computers work with a number of different I/O (_____ _____) devices to exchange information.

9. Unlike a fad—_____—trends may become popular slowly and may have long-term effects.

10. Toothpaste, _____, was originally made with vinegar and ground stone.

11. About half of the world's population speaks a language that originally comes from Proto-Indo-European, _____.

12. As far back as 3600 BCE, the Sumerian people used simple wheels (_____).

Honey was once used as a kind of money.

Think about It Which of the appositives above give another name for the noun phrase? Which describe the noun phrase?

In #1, "New York City's largest open space" describes the noun phrase.

19 | Adding Information with Appositives Rewrite each sentence below, adding an appositive from the box. Remember to include commas, dashes, or parentheses. **9.5 A–B**

a city in Bolivia	one of the most beautiful cities in Italy
a city in Brazil	the capital of South Korea
a mausoleum in India	the largest city in California
a popular tourist attraction in Australia	the largest of the seven continents
Bolivia and Colombia	the second largest desert in the world

PLACES AROUND THE WORLD

1. Seoul is located on the Han River. _Seoul, the capital of South Korea, is located on the Han River._

2. Much of the Sahara is uninhabited[7]. _____

3. Asia is home to more than one out of every two people in the world. _____

4. Two countries in South America were named for famous people. _____

5. La Paz is at about the same height as the top of Japan's Mount Fuji. _____

6. Venice is slowly sinking. _____

7. Curitiba has one of the best public bus systems in the world. _____

8. The Taj Mahal is one of the most popular tourist attractions in the world. _____

9. Los Angeles is a major center for shipping, manufacturing, and finance. _____

10. Ayers Rock is located in the center of the country. _____

Write about It Choose a city you know well. Make a list of facts about the city. Then write three sentences to describe the city, using appositives.

Chongqing, my birthplace, is located on the Jialing River.

20 | Combining Information with Appositives Combine each pair of sentences into one sentence, using an appositive. **9.5 C**

DESCRIBING FAMOUS PEOPLE

1. Stephen Hawking is a renowned theoretical physicist. He writes about black holes.

Stephen Hawking, a renowned theoretical physicist, writes about black holes.

2. Fred Leverentz is a 72-year-old mountain climber. He has climbed mountains all over the world.

3. Emily Dickinson is a famous American poet. She published only seven poems during her life.

[7] **uninhabited:** not lived in by people

4. Irène Curie was the second woman in history to win a Nobel Prize in science. She was the daughter of the first woman to win the same prize.

5. The first person to orbit the earth was Yuri Gagarin. He died seven years later in an airplane crash.

6. Aesop was a Greek storyteller in the sixth century BCE. He used animal stories to teach lessons about life.

7. Amelia Earhart was the first woman to cross the Atlantic Ocean in an airplane. She disappeared while trying to fly around the world.

8. Mahatma Gandhi is a symbol of the power of peace. He led the nonviolent movement for independence in India.

9. Alfred Hitchcock is one of the most famous movie directors in history. He made many film classics, including *North by Northwest* and *The Birds*.

10. Agatha Christie was a British crime writer of novels, short stories, and plays. She is the best-selling novelist of all time.

11. The Rolling Stones are the longest-performing rock band of all time. The band first performed in 1962.

12. Lang Lang has been called the superstar Chinese piano player. He loves opera, jazz, and hip-hop.

13. Andrew Johnson was the seventeenth president of the U.S. He was a tailor before he was president.

Write about It Look for information about three famous people and write a sentence about each one. Use an appositive in each sentence. Then read your sentences to the class.

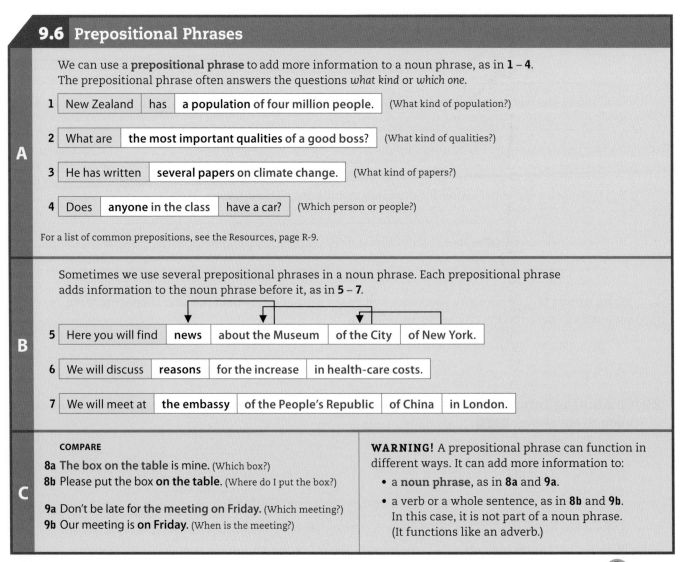

9.6 Prepositional Phrases

A

We can use a **prepositional phrase** to add more information to a noun phrase, as in **1 – 4**. The prepositional phrase often answers the questions *what kind* or *which one*.

| 1 | New Zealand | has | **a population** of four million people. | (What kind of population?) |

| 2 | What are | **the most important qualities** of a good boss? | (What kind of qualities?) |

| 3 | He has written | **several papers** on climate change. | (What kind of papers?) |

| 4 | Does | **anyone** in the class | have a car? | (Which person or people?) |

For a list of common prepositions, see the Resources, page R-9.

B

Sometimes we use several prepositional phrases in a noun phrase. Each prepositional phrase adds information to the noun phrase before it, as in **5 – 7**.

| 5 | Here you will find | **news** | about the Museum | of the City | of New York. |

| 6 | We will discuss | **reasons** | for the increase | in health-care costs. |

| 7 | We will meet at | **the embassy** | of the People's Republic | of China | in London. |

C

COMPARE

8a The box **on the table** is mine. (Which box?)
8b Please put the box **on the table**. (Where do I put the box?)

9a Don't be late for the meeting **on Friday**. (Which meeting?)
9b Our meeting is **on Friday**. (When is the meeting?)

WARNING! A prepositional phrase can function in different ways. It can add more information to:

• a **noun phrase**, as in **8a** and **9a**.

• a verb or a whole sentence, as in **8b** and **9b**. In this case, it is not part of a noun phrase. (It functions like an adverb.)

GO ONLINE

21 | Adding Prepositional Phrases Choose a prepositional phrase from the box to complete each **bold** noun phrase. 9.6 A

1. **The most important qualities** _____*of a good parent*_____ are patience and a sense of humor.

2. Traveling to foreign countries is valuable for **a number** _____.

3. **The primary goal** _____ is to make money.

4. **Some technological advances** _____ had a negative effect on the earth's atmosphere.

of a good parent
of any business
of reasons
of the twentieth century

5. You can easily learn about **life** _____ by looking on the Internet.

6. **The land** _____ **of a city** should be a public park.

7. My teachers have been **important figures** _____.

8. Fathers play **an important role** _____.

in my life
in other countries
in the center
in their children's lives

9. Stress is one of **the worst things** _____.

10. **There are many opportunities** _____ in a big city.

11. There is **very little need** _____ in today's world.

12. There should be **a separate section** _____ **on all public transportation**.

for children
for money
for work and entertainment
for your health

Think about It Circle the main noun in each noun phrase you completed above.

Talk about It Take turns reading the statements above aloud with a partner. See if your partner agrees or disagrees and why.

A: The most important qualities of a good parent are patience and a sense of humor.
B: I disagree. I think it's more important to be a good listener than to have a sense of humor.

22 | Noticing Prepositional Phrases Underline all the prepositional phrases in each **bold** noun phrase. Then say which fact was the most interesting to you. Why? 9.6 B

IN THE NEWS

1. **A team <u>of researchers</u>** recently found **the bones <u>of four different kinds of dinosaurs</u>** at **the same site <u>in New Mexico</u>**.
2. The first time that **sales of computers to homes in the U.S.** were greater than **sales of computers to businesses** was in 1994.
3. As a person ages, **the thickness of each hair on the head** gets smaller.
4. **Many species of fish in the oceans** are now disappearing.
5. A meteorite crashed through **the roof of a house in New Zealand**.
6. **The placement of an ice pack on an insect bite** will relieve the itch.
7. **The caffeine in three cups of coffee or tea** may help to maintain **mental sharpness[8] in older women**.
8. **Researchers at the Erasmus University Medical School in Rotterdam, the Netherlands,** found that boiled coffee significantly increased cholesterol[9].

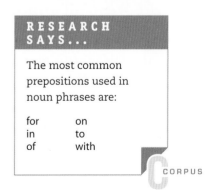

RESEARCH SAYS...

The most common prepositions used in noun phrases are:

for	on
in	to
of	with

CORPUS

[8] **mental sharpness:** the ability to understand something easily   [9] **cholesterol:** a potentially dangerous substance in the blood

9. The most recent survey of time use in the U.S. suggests that women still do most of **the work at home**.

10. **Everything in the factories of the future** will be run by smarter software.

11. **A fifth of respondents to a Chinese local-newspaper survey** said they had over 5,000 *yuan* of digital property[10].

12. One researcher found that **managers with more money invested in their companies** take fewer vacations.

23 | Identifying Prepositional Phrases in Noun Phrases Read this article. If a **bold** prepositional phrase adds more information to a noun, underline the noun it describes. (Only some describe noun phrases. Others function as adverbs.) `9.6 C`

Ocean Storms

Ocean storms form when the <u>temperature</u> **in one area** is different from the temperature **in another nearby area**. Warm air rises and cool air falls, creating a difference **in atmospheric pressure**.

If the pressure changes **in a large area**, winds start to blow **in a huge circle**. High-pressure air is pulled **toward a low pressure center** and thick clouds form. As the storm gains speed and moves **over the ocean**, very heavy rain begins to fall. And storms can get even stronger if they are moving **over warm waters**.

Under certain conditions, an ocean storm can strengthen and become a hurricane. The center **of the storm**, known as the eye, is fairly calm. However, the strongest, fastest winds **of a hurricane** blow **in the area** around the eye known as the eyewall, which can be **about 16 to 80 kilometers wide**.

Wind speeds **in the most severe ocean storms** have reached more than 250 kilometers per hour. Some storms have produced more than 150 centimeters **of rain**. Many ocean storms cause high waves and ocean surges. An ocean surge is a constant movement **of water** that can reach as high as 6 meters or more. This can cause major damage **to shore areas**.

Think about It What kind of information does each **bold** prepositional phrase above give?

"In one area" explains which air temperature.
"In atmospheric pressure" explains what kind of difference.

9.7 Using *Of* to Show Possession

A

1 I don't know **the title** of the book. (NOT: ~~the book's title~~)
2 He walked to **the end** of the hallway. (NOT: ~~the hallway's end~~)
3 Water is needed for **the production** of electricity. (NOT: ~~electricity's production~~)
4 **The success** of the plan depends on cooperation. (= the plan's success)
5 **The appointment** of the new sales manager will be announced soon. (= the new sales manager's appointment)

Sometimes we use a **prepositional phrase with** *of* to show possession. This is common when we:

- talk about a nonliving thing, as in **1 – 2**
- talk about an abstract thing or idea, as in **3 – 4**
- use a possessive phrase that is more than two words long, as in **5**

WARNING! In **1 – 3**, it would usually be incorrect to use a noun phrase + -'s. In **4 – 5**, it is the speaker's choice.

B

CORRECT THE COMMON ERRORS (See page R-13.)

6 X Please don't drink from that water's glass.   7 X The parents of Sylvia are here.

[10]**digital property:** for example, audio and video clips that can be downloaded online

◄)) 24 | Pronunciation Note: *Of* Listen to the note. Then do Activity 25.

> Before vowel sounds, *of* is pronounced /əv/. For example:
>
> **1** the heat **of** August   *sounds like*   "the heatuv August"
>
> Before consonant sounds, *of* is reduced to /ə/. For example:
>
> **2** the problems **of** the world   *sounds like*   "the problemsuh the world"
>
> You don't have to use the reduced form, but you need to understand it in conversation.

◄)) 25 | Pronouncing *Of* Listen and write the missing words in each question. Then listen again and check (✓) the sound you hear. `9.7 A`

	OF /əv/	OF /ə/
1. Do we usually have class in the middle _____*of the day*_____?	☐	☐
2. Are you the owner _____?	☐	☐
3. How many years _____ have you had?	☐	☐
4. Who is the author _____?	☐	☐
5. What day _____ is it?	☐	☐
6. Do you ever watch the end _____ first?	☐	☐
7. Do you know the rules _____?	☐	☐
8. Are you a member _____?	☐	☐
9. Have you ever left before the end _____?	☐	☐
10. Are you worried about the state _____?	☐	☐
11. Are you excited about the future _____?	☐	☐
12. What was the result _____?	☐	☐
13. What's on the cover _____?	☐	☐
14. What's the name _____?	☐	☐
15. Is anyone in your family the parent _____?	☐	☐
16. Do you have a good sense _____?	☐	☐
17. Is there a museum _____ in your city?	☐	☐
18. What is the definition _____?	☐	☐
19. How many hours _____ did you do last week?	☐	☐
20. What is your favorite time _____?	☐	☐

Talk about It Ask a partner the questions above. Pay attention to how you pronounce *of*.

A: Do we usually have class in the middle of the day?
B: Yes. Our class is at 2:00.

RESEARCH SAYS...

Using *of* to show possession is much more common than using a possessive *'s*, especially in academic writing.

C CORPUS

Think about It Answer these questions about each prepositional phrase you wrote in Activity 25.
- Is the noun a nonliving thing?
- Is the noun an abstract thing or idea?
- Is the possessive phrase more than two words long?

1. _In #1, a day is an abstract thing._
2. _____
3. _____
4. _____
5. _____
6. _____
7. _____
8. _____
9. _____
10. _____

11. _____
12. _____
13. _____
14. _____
15. _____
16. _____
17. _____
18. _____
19. _____
20. _____

26 | Using *Of* to Show Possession In this paragraph, the writer has used too many possessive determiners. Use prepositional phrases with *of* to rewrite some of them. (More than one answer is possible). **9.7 A**

Manatees

Manatees are water animals sometimes called sea cows because of their large size and gentle nature. Although they do not have many natural predators, ~~people's actions~~ *the actions of people* have interfered[11] with manatees in recent years. **Humans' interference** with **manatees' habitats** is one of the main problems. For example, **Florida's manatees** no longer migrate south as they once did, but now stay near warm waters created by power plants. Another problem is boats. **A boat's paddles** can cut a manatee, killing it or leaving terrible scars. This may occur partly because of **a boat's sound**. Large boats emit low-frequency sounds that manatees cannot hear. However, manatees will swim away from a boat with a higher frequency, according to **some researchers' findings**. Another major problem for manatees is the red tide. **Toxic[12] algae's growth** causes the red tide, and the toxins damage the **manatee's nervous system**.

Talk about It Compare your answers above with a partner. How are your changes different?

[11] **interfere:** to become involved in the activities of someone or something else in an unwanted or harmful way
[12] **toxic:** poisonous

9.8 Recognizing Adjective Clauses

The main goal of this chart is to help you recognize adjective clauses. Adjective clauses are covered in more detail in Unit 10.

A

Another way to give more information about a main noun is by adding an **adjective clause after** it, as in **1 – 4**.

NOUN PHRASE

		main noun	adjective clause
1	We know	a lot of	**people**	who can speak two languages.
2	He is looking for	an interesting	**job**	that pays a lot of money.
3	I have	a	**boss**	who doesn't like to make decisions.
4	I prefer		**activities**	that I can do outdoors.

GRAMMAR TERM: A **clause** is a group of words with a subject and a verb.

B

5 Do you know **everyone** that works here?

6 I would fire an **employee** who was dishonest.

7 Do you want to see the **coat** I bought?
(= the coat that I bought)

8 Many of the **people** I know are artists.
(= the people who I know)

9 When are the **people** who are doing the work going to be finished?

10 The **class** I need to graduate was canceled.

Adjective clauses often begin with a word like *that* or *who*, as in **5 – 6**. This word refers back to the noun or pronoun before it.

Words like *that* and *who* can be the subject of an adjective clause, as in **5 – 6**. However, when there is another subject, we can usually leave out *that* or *who*, as in **7 – 8**.

Notice that a noun + an adjective clause can come in the middle of a sentence, as in **8 – 10**.

C

COMPARE

11a We bought some milk yesterday. Where is it?
11b Where's the **milk** (that) we bought yesterday?

12a I have a good friend. He helps me all the time.
12b I have a good **friend** who helps me all the time.

13a A tornado has very strong winds. They blow in a circle.
13b A tornado has very strong **winds** that blow in a circle.

An adjective clause lets us combine two ideas into one sentence, as in **11 – 13**.

 GO ONLINE

27 | Noticing Adjective Clauses Underline the adjective clause in each sentence. Name or identify each person, place, or thing described. Then compare ideas with a partner. **9.8 A**

1. Name a type of living thing <u>that you are afraid of</u>. _____

_____

2. Identify the countries that you have visited. _____

_____

3. Identify a food that you can't stand[13]. _____

4. Name a place that you enjoyed visiting. _____

5. Name a person who you admire. _____

> **RESEARCH SAYS...**
>
> Adjective clauses are common in all types of writing. In fiction and news, they often identify or describe a person.

 CORPUS

[13] **can't stand:** dislike a lot

6. Name a person who has helped you in an important way. _____

7. Name a famous scientist who lived in the twentieth century. _____

8. Name a job that requires two or more languages. _____

9. Identify a city that is near some mountains. _____

10. Name a tool that you can use to open a bottle. _____

11. Think of a word that means "very good." _____

12. Name an artist who is alive today. _____

28 | Adding Adjective Clauses Match the first part of each sentence on the left with an adjective clause on the right. 9.8 A

INTERESTING AND UNUSUAL JOBS

1. A wind turbine[14] mechanic repairs the turbines _g_

2. Food stylists arrange the food ____

3. A wildlife rehabilitator[15] helps wild animals ____

4. A sports event coordinator is the person ____

5. A sports psychologist helps athletes ____

6. Salvage divers find things ____

7. Flight attendants assist people ____

8. A dietician helps people ____

9. An archeologist studies the past by studying old buildings ____

10. In a movie, a stunt person does the dangerous things ____

a. who are traveling by plane.

b. that have been lost in deep water.

c. that is used in magazine advertisements.

d. who want to lose weight.

e. that are buried underground.

f. that a famous actor isn't allowed to do.

g. that are on top of the 140-foot towers.

h. who plans special events for a game.

i. who want to improve their performance.

j. that have been injured.

Write about It Choose one of the sentences above. Do an online search for more information about the job. Then write a short paragraph with details about the job.

29 | Using Adjective Clauses Guess the language of origin and meaning of each word on the left. Write sentences using words from each column. Then compare ideas with your classmates. 9.8 B

Tycoon is a Japanese word that means "a successful businessperson."

Word	Language of origin	Meaning
1. tycoon	English	a large group of people who sing together
2. revenue	French	the income of a government or company
3. tornado	Greek	a note that you write to someone at work
4. soprano	Chinese	a thick sauce that is made with tomatoes
5. pajamas	Persian	loose pants and a top that you wear to bed
6. catsup	Italian	a successful businessperson
7. chorus	Japanese	the highest singing voice
8. memo	Spanish	a violent storm with strong winds that blow in a circle

[14] **wind turbine:** an engine that gets its power from the wind
[15] **rehabilitator:** someone who brings something back to a normal or healthy condition

30 | Noticing Adjective Clauses Underline the adjective clauses in these test prompts and circle the noun each clause describes. `9.8 B`

ESSAY TEST PROMPTS

1. Are (children) who play sports less likely to get into trouble than (children) who don't play sports?

STUDY STRATEGY

To identify some adjective clauses, look for a noun + a word like *that* or *who*.

a problem that I had . . .

people who know me . . .

2. What is the most important subject that students should study in high school?

3. Neighbors are the people who live near us. In your opinion, what are the qualities of a good neighbor?

4. Do you agree or disagree with the following statement? People should sometimes do things that they do not enjoy doing.

5. Countries, businesses, and schools are three areas that need good leaders. Choose one of these areas and describe the most important qualities of a leader in that area.

6. What is one skill that every person needs to learn?

7. In your opinion, what is the most important characteristic (for example, honesty, intelligence, a sense of humor) that a person can have? Why?

8. Some people choose friends who are different from themselves. Others choose friends who are similar to themselves. What are the advantages of having friends who are different from you?

9. Do you agree or disagree with the following statement? The decisions that people make quickly are always wrong.

10. Do you agree or disagree with the following statement? People should read only those books that are about real events and real people.

Write about It Choose one of the essay test prompts above and answer it in writing.

31 | Identifying Adjective Clauses The adjective clauses in these sentences don't use *that* or *who*. Underline the adjective clauses and circle the noun each clause describes. `9.8 B`

1. The nicest (thing) I own is a piece of jewelry from my mother.
2. Good writing is the most important skill I have learned.
3. Global warming is the most serious problem we face today.
4. There are many things I like about tennis.
5. The first thing I do in the morning is to drink a cup of coffee.
6. A good friend is someone I trust.
7. The best advice I ever received was from my father.
8. The most important aspect of a job is the money a person earns.
9. There are many different things you can do to stay healthy.
10. The worst thing an employee can do is to steal from the company.

STUDY STRATEGY

To identify some adjective clauses, look for a noun + noun/pronoun + verb.

the nicest **thing I own** . . .

some **people I know** . . .

Write about It Rewrite sentences 1–6 above with your own ideas.

The nicest thing I own is a sweater from my mother.

32 | Combining Sentences Combine each pair of sentences using an adjective clause. `9.8 C`

1. I have many friends. They email me all the time.

   I have many friends who *email me all the time* .

2. There were a lot of people on the street. They were wearing costumes.

   There were a lot of people on the street who _____.

3. I read an interesting article. It explains the benefits of crying.

   I read an interesting article that _____.

4. When I was in Turkey, I met some of my relatives. They still live in my parents' village.

   When I was in Turkey, I met some of my relatives _____.

5. My brother is a doctor. He works with cancer patients.

   My brother is a doctor _____.

6. Many people are concerned about their health. They eat a lot of fruit and vegetables.

   _____

7. I have a good friend. She is always giving me advice.

   _____

8. My brother lives in a building downtown. It was once a factory.

   _____

9. An introduction is part of a book or essay. It comes at the beginning.

   _____

10. Two students went to the hospital. They were injured.

    _____

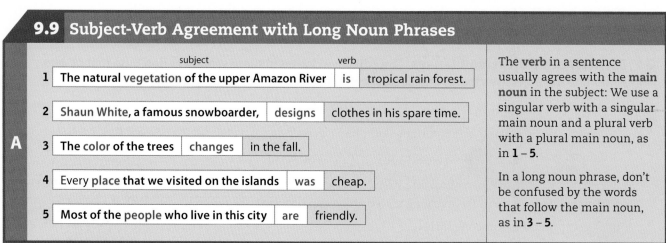

9.9 Subject-Verb Agreement with Long Noun Phrases

A

	subject	verb	
1	The natural **vegetation** of the upper Amazon River	**is**	tropical rain forest.
2	Shaun White, a famous snowboarder,	designs	clothes in his spare time.
3	The color of the trees	changes	in the fall.
4	Every place that we visited on the islands	was	cheap.
5	Most of the people who live in this city	are	friendly.

The **verb** in a sentence usually agrees with the **main noun** in the subject: We use a singular verb with a singular main noun and a plural verb with a plural main noun, as in **1 – 5**.

In a long noun phrase, don't be confused by the words that follow the main noun, as in **3 – 5**.

GO ONLINE

33 | Subject-Verb Agreement Circle the main noun in each **bold** noun phrase. Then write the correct form of the verb in parentheses. `9.9 A`

Facts about Languages and Names

1. **The six official (languages) of the United Nations (U.N.)** _____*are*_____ Arabic, Chinese, English, French, Russian, and Spanish. (is/are)

2. **The most common name in the world** _____ Mohammed. (is/are)

3. In nearly every language, **the word for *mother*** _____ with a /m/ sound. (begins/begin)

4. **The only language that capitalizes the first-person singular (*I*)** _____ English. (is/are)

5. **Seoul, the South Korean capital,** _____ "the capital" in the Korean language. (means/mean)

6. **One of the few people who single-handedly[16] invented an alphabet for a living language**
   _____ Sequoyah, a Cherokee Indian. (was/were)

7. In Chinese, **the characters (or symbols) for *danger* and *opportunity*** _____ the word *crisis*. (forms/form)

8. **Only four common words in the English language** _____ in -*dous: hazardous, horrendous, stupendous,* and *tremendous*. (ends/end)

9. **The only common 15-letter word in the English language that can be spelled without repeating a letter** _____ *uncopyrightable*. (is/are)

10. **Children who study another language** _____ higher on basic skills such as reading and math. (scores/score)

11. **The most widely spoken forms of the Chinese language** _____ Mandarin, Cantonese, Gan, Hakka, Min, Wu, and Xiang. (is/are)

12. **The longest word in the English language with all the letters in alphabetical order** _____ *almost*. (is/are)

13. **A person who speaks several languages** _____ more job opportunities than a person who speaks just one language. (has/have)

14. **The Germanic family of languages** _____ Danish, Dutch, English, German, and Swedish, among others. (includes/include)

15. **Most countries in Europe** _____ a number of regional or minority languages, some of which have become official languages. (has/have)

---

[16] **single-handedly:** done by one person, without help

9.10 Using Noun Phrases in Speaking and Academic Writing

A

STRENGTHENING AND SOFTENING IN SPEAKING

1 That's **a very interesting** question.

2 We had **a really clear** view of the stage from our seats.

3 The president has **some pretty good** ideas.

4 I'm having **such a bad day**. (NOT: ~~a such bad day~~)

5 Kelly doesn't have **a very loud** voice.
(NOT: ~~Kelly doesn't have a pretty loud voice.~~)

STRENGTHENING AND SOFTENING IN ACADEMIC WRITING

6 Japanese is **an extremely difficult** language to learn.

7 When we did the test again, we got **significantly better** results.

8 Based upon our research, we arrived at **quite a different** conclusion. (NOT: ~~a quite different conclusion~~)

We use certain words to strengthen or soften an adjective in a noun phrase.

In speaking, we often use informal words like *very, really, pretty,* and *such,* as in **1 – 5**. Notice:

- We use *such* before *a / an* with singular nouns as in **4**.
- We don't use *pretty* in negative sentences, as in **5**.

In academic writing, we often use more formal words like *very, extremely, significantly,* or *quite,* as in **6 – 8**.

Notice that we use *quite* before *a / an* with singular nouns, as in **8**.

B

COMPARE

9a Gustavo Dudamel is a conductor, and he is 31 years old. He is from Venezuela. He became the music director of the Los Angeles Philharmonic in 2009.

9b **Gustavo Dudamel, the 31-year-old Venezuelan conductor,** became the music director of the Los Angeles Philharmonic in 2009.

Packing a lot of information into longer **noun phrases** is very common in academic writing.

- In **9a**, the writer uses several short sentences to communicate the information. Using many short sentences is common for beginning writers.
- In **9b**, the writer uses longer noun phrases in a single sentence. This allows the writer to communicate a lot of information in fewer words.

C

REFERRING BACK WITH NOUN PHRASES

10 During the 1930s, **roads, bridges, and schools** were built all over the U.S. **Most of these structures** are still in use today.
(structures = roads, bridges, and schools)

11 Today the company made **the announcement that 400 employees would lose their jobs**. **This statement** came during an interview with the company's president.
(statement = announcement)

In writing, we often start a sentence with a **noun phrase** that refers back to an idea in a previous sentence, as in **10 – 11**. Doing this helps connect the ideas from one sentence to the next.

In both **10** and **11**, the writers use *this / that / these / those* to make it clear which ideas they are referring back to. For variety, the writers also use synonyms for words from the previous sentences.

D

INTRODUCING DETAILS AND EXAMPLES

12 The author of the article "The Amazing Effects of Music" explains that **music affects the body in many positive ways**. **One of the obvious effects** is that it can put you in a better mood. **Another benefit** is that it can lower your blood pressure.

In writing, we may introduce details and examples of an earlier idea with words like *one, another,* or *the first,* as in **12**.

 ONLINE

34 | Strengthening/Softening Adjectives in Speaking Choose one strengthening/softening word and one adjective from the box to complete the noun phrase in each conversation below. (More than one answer may be possible.) 9.10 A

STRENGTHENING/ SOFTENING WORDS	ADJECTIVES			
pretty	amazing	careful	hard	smart
really	awful	expensive	important	surprising
such	bad	good	nice	terrible
very	big	great	serious	

1. A: Sarah is graduating next week, but I don't know what to get her.

   B: Hmm. How about a watch?

   A: Oh, yeah. That's a _____ *really nice* _____ idea.

2. A: $120 for a textbook! Can you believe it?

   B: Why do we need _____ a(n) _____ textbook?

   A: I know. It's ridiculous.

3. A: How did you lose your wallet?

   B: I don't know. Sometimes I'm not a _____ person.

4. A: The snow has been falling all morning.

   B: I know—it looks like a _____ storm.

5. A: I think I'm going to quit my job and go back to school.

   B: Really? I don't think that's _____ a(n) _____ decision.

   A: Why not?

6. A: What happened to you? You look exhausted.

   B: I had a _____ day, and I didn't get much sleep last night.

7. A: Where's Carlos today?

   B: Didn't you hear? He was in a _____ bicycle accident.

   A: Oh, no!

8. A: Did you like the pictures I posted online?

   B: Absolutely. You're _____ a(n) _____ photographer!

9. A: What did your father want?

   B: I'm not sure. He said he had a _____ question to ask me.

10. A: My phone keeps turning itself off. Do you think I should get a new one?

    B: That doesn't sound like a _____ problem. Let me see if I can fix it.

Talk about It Work with a partner. Choose two or three of the noun phrases you completed above. Write new conversations with them. Present your conversations (or a conversation) to the class.

A: Why don't we go to the park this weekend?
B: Sure. That's a really nice idea.

Bicycle Transportation Around the World

In some countries today, a (fairly large) percentage of the population uses bicycles for basic transportation. For example, in China, Bangladesh, and some parts of the Netherlands, people use bicycles for more than 40 percent of all trips. Other countries, like the U.S. and Canada, however, have significantly lower bicycle use—an embarrassingly low 1 percent. How do we explain these differences?

bicycling in Amsterdam

In countries like the Netherlands, people think of bicycles as transportation. As a result, their cities have been developed with an extremely large number of bicycle routes. Some streets are marked as "car-free zones," and some traffic lights are timed for bicycles, not cars. These cities are considerably safer places to ride and have very low numbers of bicycle accidents.

In countries like Canada and the U.S., people have quite a different way of thinking about bicycles. People usually ride bicycles for exercise or fun—not transportation. Cities are not designed to accommodate[17] bicyclists. These cities tend to be more spread out, and the long distances between places makes riding a bicycle impractical. Other common problems include a relatively small number of bicycle parking spaces and unfriendly treatment of bicyclists by car drivers.

In some developing countries, there is a completely different type of problem. In India, a bicycle has a substantially greater cost. In fact, a bicycle costs twice as much in India as in other developing countries like China and Brazil. This is unfortunate, since research in Uganda, Tanzania, and Sri Lanka shows that bicycle ownership can lead to a noticeably higher income—as much as 35 percent.

Think about It How are the strengthening/softening words you circled above different from those used most often in conversation?

> **F Y I**
>
> Some adverbs can help writers give their opinion or make a judgment. Compare:
>
> The street had **little traffic.**
>
> The street had **surprisingly little traffic.**
>
> (The writer is surprised by this fact.)

[17] **accommodate:** to provide room for someone or something

36 | Using Longer Noun Phrases Rewrite the information in these sentences using longer noun phrases. (There may be more than one way to rewrite the information.) **9.10 B**

EXERCISE

1. Physical fitness is the result of exercise, proper diet, and nutrition. It can improve mental health and self-esteem[18].

   Physical fitness, the result of exercise, proper diet, and nutrition, can improve mental health and self-esteem.

2. Physical exercise can help with weight loss. It should be frequent and intense.

3. Aerobics is a kind of exercise. It is of relatively low intensity[19]. It increases oxygen available to the body.

4. Bicycling is a kind of low-intensity exercise. It is a fitness activity for the whole body. It is also the second most popular spectator sport in the world.

5. Anaerobic exercise refers to a high-intensity activity. It is of short duration, and it promotes strength and speed.

6. Weight training is popular with professional athletes. It is a kind of strength exercise.

7. Exercise releases endorphins. Endorphins are the body's natural feel-good chemicals. They can even temporarily relieve pain.

8. There is evidence that exercise usually improves sleep. The evidence is convincing[20]—sleep improves for most people.

Think about It What grammar structures did you use in the noun phrases you wrote above?

37 | Language Note: Main Nouns Read the note. Then do Activity 38.

Sometimes it is difficult to find the main noun of a noun phrase, especially when there are many descriptive words before or after the noun. Remember, the information that can come before and after a main noun includes:

determiner(s)	number	adjective	noun	main noun	appositive	prepositional phrase	adjective clause

Today, there are **very few students** who don't have access to a computer.

Universities **in many English-speaking countries** offer students **the possibility** of studying abroad for one or two semesters.

One common pattern in longer noun phrases is a main noun + prepositional phrase + adjective clause.

a list of expressions that I know   **a question** about grammar that she can't answer

---

[18] **self-esteem:** a feeling of respect for yourself
[19] **intensity:** the amount of strength or force something has

[20] **convincing:** causing someone to believe something is true

38 | Identifying the Main Noun Circle the main noun in each **bold** noun phrase. `9.10 B`

1. After we've finished, we'll have a few minutes to relax and take **that much-needed coffee (break.)**
2. *The Thinker*, **one of the most significant works of art in the world**, was created by Auguste Rodin in 1902.
3. **The effects of music on the human body** include **both mental and physical benefits**.
4. The speakers will discuss **reasons for the dramatic increase in health-care costs**.
5. A doctorate is **the highest degree that a student can earn**.
6. **The salaries**[21] **of community college graduates** are higher than **those of people with just a high school education**.
7. **Freshly picked raw green leaves** are **an excellent source of vitamin C**.
8. Traditional African clothing depends on **the natural resources of different areas** and **materials that people can produce cheaply**.
9. After many thousands of years, African people began to make **new kinds of clothes that were lighter and cooler**.
10. India's Internet population was 112 million in 2011, making it **the third largest market in the world after China and the U.S.**

Think about It Did you have trouble finding the main noun in any of the noun phrases? If so, why?

39 | Using Noun Phrases to Connect Ideas Use the **bold** information in the first sentence to complete the noun phrase in the second sentence. Try to use synonyms or add new information to the noun phrase. (There are many different ways to complete each sentence.) `9.10 C-D`

1. There are many **possible ways to solve the problems in our schools.** One _possible solution_ OR _popular idea among teachers_ is to increase funding[22] for education.
2. Some hospitals use music as **a pain management technique**[23] **for their older patients.** This _____ helps calm patients and often results in less pain.
3. **Enrollment at universities has declined a great deal** in the last five years. As a result of this _____, tuition has increased.
4. We really need to **change parts of our voting system in some major ways.** While some of these _____ might be difficult to carry out, they would increase voter turnout.
5. **The government has invested heavily in new energy sources recently.** These _____ have led to several important developments.
6. Many patients **think their doctors don't listen carefully to them.** This _____ is more common among elderly patients.
7. **Speaking and writing differ significantly** in several ways. The most important of these _____ is that speakers usually know who they are talking to, but writers do not.
8. Many scientists believe that gases in the air are causing **earth temperatures to rise.** _____ is called global warming.
9. Young children begin to learn new words very quickly at about **18 to 24 months of age.** Researchers have called _____ the "vocabulary explosion."
10. **Home prices have been increasing rapidly** in some parts of the country. _____ have made it more difficult to get a loan.

---

[21] **salaries:** money that employees are paid each year
[22] **funding:** the money provided for something
[23] **technique:** a way of doing something by using special skill

Think about It Compare ideas with your classmates. How many different ways did you think of to connect the ideas in the sentences in Activity 39? Can you think of any other ways?

40 | Connecting Sentences Write a new sentence to add new information about the previous sentence. Use a noun phrase to help connect the ideas. (There are many possible sentences.) `9.10 C–D`

ADVANTAGES AND DISADVANTAGES OF CELL PHONES

1. There are many advantages to having a cell phone. _One of the most important benefits is that you can call for help in an emergency._

2. If young children are permitted to use cell phones, they need to have some rules. _____

   _____

3. Unfortunately, scientists have also found a number of problems with using cell phones for long periods of time. _____

   _____

   _____

> **FYI**
>
> When we use a noun phrase to refer back to an idea, we can use the noun phrase to add new ideas or opinions.
>
> There are thousands of versions of "Cinderella." **One of the most interesting adaptations of this well-known story** was written by Mary Stewart.

HOME SCHOOLING VS. PUBLIC SCHOOLING

4. Recently, more people have begun to educate their children at home. Home schooling can have both good and bad effects on a child. _____

   _____

5. Attending public schools can provide students with some advantages. _____

   _____

6. However, not all public schools provide good learning environments. _____

   _____

BENEFITS AND DIFFICULTIES OF LIVING IN A FOREIGN COUNTRY

7. There are many benefits to experiencing life in a foreign country when you're young. _____

   _____

8. In their early years, children are influenced by many aspects of the culture around them. _____

   _____

9. At the same time, moving to a new country as a child can also be difficult. _____

   _____

Think about It For each item above, underline the idea introduced in the first sentence. Then circle the noun phrase in the second sentence that helps connect the ideas.

There are <u>many advantages to having a cell phone</u>.

(One of the most important benefits) is that you can call for help in an emergency.

Think about It In addition to connecting ideas, why do writers repeat information from one sentence to the next?

WRAP-UP Demonstrate Your Knowledge

A | REVIEW Choose a restaurant or coffee shop in your area and make a list of noun phrases that describe it. Then experiment with different ways to use the phrases in a short restaurant review. For example:

- a sandwich shop
- tasty food and low prices
- a medium-sized place
- delicious chicken salad sandwich
- homemade vegetable soup
- friendly atmosphere
- high-quality service

Peaches Grill

Peaches Grill is a medium-sized sandwich shop near my apartment. For very little money, you can get a delicious chicken salad sandwich on homemade bread or a large bowl of homemade vegetable soup. The friendly atmosphere at Peaches Grill, the tasty food, the high-quality service, and the low prices will make you want to return many times.

B | VOCABULARY NOTEBOOK Look in an English textbook for examples of noun + noun combinations (compound nouns). Write a list of these in a vocabulary notebook. Write a sentence with each combination.

business trip   *During a recent business trip, my plane was delayed.*

C | PRESENTATION Choose an interesting photograph of people doing a hobby or playing a game or sport. Prepare a description of the people and/or the activity. Then present it to the class. For example:

This is a photograph of some of my friends. When I took this photo, they were playing an Italian game called bocce. In this game, one person throws a small ball toward the end of the playing area. The same person then throws a larger ball toward the small ball. The goal of the game is to get close to the small ball without touching it. The other players then try to throw balls even closer to the small ball. In this photograph, my friend Steven is about to take his turn. None of us could play very well, but we still had fun.

D | WEB SEARCH Do an online search for "World Heritage List," a list of places the U.N. has chosen for special importance. Print a brief description of a place and underline the noun phrases. For example:

Great Barrier Reef

The Great Barrier Reef is a site of remarkable variety and beauty on the northeast coast of Australia. It contains the world's largest collection of coral reefs, with 400 types of coral, 1,500 species of fish, and 4,000 types of mollusk. It also holds great scientific interest as the habitat of species such as the dugong ("sea cow") and the large green turtle, which are threatened with extinction.

Write some of the sentences from the description on the board. Ask your classmates to identify the noun phrases.

9.11 Summary of Noun Phrases

Information before a Main Noun	Main Noun	Information after a Main Noun

DETERMINERS

Articles
(*a, an, the, some, Ø*)

Honesty is	the best **policy**.

A house is not	**a home**.

Possessives
(*my, your, her, etc.*)

You can't have	**your cake**	and eat it.

A fool and	**his money**	are soon parted.

Quantifiers
(*several, a few, many, etc.*)

Many hands	make light work.

Every picture	tells a story.

NUMBERS

Don't put all your eggs in	**one basket**.

Every stick has	**two ends**.

ADJECTIVES

Honesty is	the **best policy**.

Bad news	travels fast.

NOUNS

Don't look	a **gift horse**	in the mouth.

Don't throw the baby out with	the **bath water**.

APPOSITIVES

Proverbs, short popular sayings,
usually state general and practical truths.

PREPOSITIONAL PHRASES

A **thing of beauty**	is a joy forever.

The best **things in life**	are free.

ADJECTIVE CLAUSES

Don't bite	the **hand that feeds you**.

A **man who is his own lawyer**	has a fool for a client.

People who live in glass houses
shouldn't throw stones.

WE COMBINE INFORMATION BEFORE AND AFTER A MAIN NOUN IN MANY WAYS.

	Pictures		tell stories.
A	picture		tells a story.
My	picture		tells a story.
Every	picture	in the world	tells a story.
My family	pictures		tell wonderful stories.
Every motion	picture	that I have ever seen	tells a different story.
My favorite family	pictures		tell wonderful stories.

Adjective Clauses

A person who won't read
has no advantage over
one who can't read.

—UNKNOWN

Talk about It What does the quotation above mean? Do you agree or disagree?

WARM-UP

A | Complete the sentences below with the words in the box. Then check your answers.

| birds | brother | dark | deaf | plant | snakes | toothpaste |

Strange Facts

1. Thomas Edison, **who invented the light bulb**, once said that he was afraid of the _____.

2. The active ingredient in most _____ is sodium fluoride, **which can be lethal[1] if swallowed**.

3. Ireland, New Zealand, Greenland, and Iceland, **which are all islands**, have no native land _____.

4. The man **who invented the phonograph[2]** was almost _____.

5. There are _____ **that can fly over 300 miles a day**.

6. There is a _____ **that was grown in a lab from 2,000-year-old seeds**.

7. Vincent Van Gogh's _____ bought one of the only paintings **Van Gogh sold during his life**.

B | The words in green in each sentence above are adjective clauses. Based on these examples, what can you say about adjective clauses? Check (✓) *True* or *False*.

	TRUE	FALSE
1. Adjective clauses always begin with *who*, *which*, or *that*.	☐	☐
2. Adjective clauses come before the nouns they describe.	☐	☐
3. Adjective clauses can describe both people and things.	☐	☐
4. Adjective clauses are always at the beginning of a sentence.	☐	☐
5. We sometimes use commas before and after an adjective clause.	☐	☐

C | Look back at the quotation on page 322. Identify any adjective clauses.

[1] **lethal:** able to cause a lot of damage or death   [2] **phonograph:** record player

ADJECTIVE CLAUSES   323

10.1 Overview of Adjective Clauses

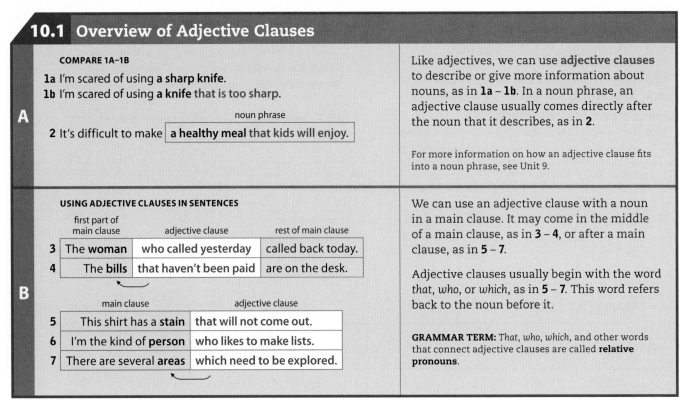

A

COMPARE 1A–1B

1a I'm scared of using **a sharp knife**.
1b I'm scared of using **a knife** that is too sharp.

noun phrase

2 It's difficult to make | **a healthy meal** that kids will enjoy. |

Like adjectives, we can use **adjective clauses** to describe or give more information about nouns, as in **1a – 1b**. In a noun phrase, an adjective clause usually comes directly after the noun that it describes, as in **2**.

For more information on how an adjective clause fits into a noun phrase, see Unit 9.

B

USING ADJECTIVE CLAUSES IN SENTENCES

first part of main clause	adjective clause	rest of main clause
3 The **woman**	who called yesterday	called back today.
4 The **bills**	that haven't been paid	are on the desk.

main clause	adjective clause
5 This shirt has a **stain**	that will not come out.
6 I'm the kind of **person**	who likes to make lists.
7 There are several **areas**	which need to be explored.

We can use an adjective clause with a noun in a main clause. It may come in the middle of a main clause, as in **3 – 4**, or after a main clause, as in **5 – 7**.

Adjective clauses usually begin with the word *that*, *who*, or *which*, as in **5 – 7**. This word refers back to the noun before it.

GRAMMAR TERM: *That, who, which*, and other words that connect adjective clauses are called **relative pronouns**.

1 | Noticing Adjective Clauses in Noun Phrases The **bold** words in this article are adjective clauses. Underline the complete noun phrase that each one is a part of. `10.1 A`

Motion Pictures

It is hard to imagine a time before movies, but before the 1870s, motion pictures did not exist. <u>Early photographers **who first experimented with motion and photography**</u>, such as Eadweard Muybridge, used innovative cameras **that could take as many as 24 pictures per second**. These cameras were the first step toward movies, but there was still no easy way to show these images to an audience. It was two French brothers **who finally accomplished this in 1895**. Auguste and Louis Lumière invented a machine **that they called a Cinématographe**. This was a camera **that could shoot, develop, and project film**. Audiences of all sizes could gather around a screen and watch the brothers' short films, **which showed people sneezing, boarding a train, or leaving work**. Though these movies didn't tell a story, they were the beginning of the biggest art form of our time.

Think about It For each underlined noun phrase in Activity 1, circle the noun that the adjective clause describes. Why is it important for the adjective clause to be close to the noun it describes?

2 | Identifying Adjective Clauses Underline the adjective clauses in these sentences. Circle the main clauses. Then check (✓) *Agree* or *Disagree*. **10.1 B**

Making Generalizations

	AGREE	DISAGREE
1. (People) who have more money (are happier).	☐	☐
2. A student that cheats should be expelled[3] from school.	☐	☐
3. Products that cost more money are usually better.	☐	☐
4. You should never trust a person who has lied to you before.	☐	☐
5. Friends are people who never let you down.	☐	☐
6. Most people want a job which will make them rich and famous.	☐	☐
7. The person that works the hardest has the most success.	☐	☐
8. You should never tell people things that might hurt their feelings.	☐	☐
9. Most people who succeed in life are smart, hard-working, and honest.	☐	☐
10. Any person who commits a crime should be punished.	☐	☐

Think about It Which adjective clauses above come in the middle of the sentence? Which come at the end?

Think about It Write each noun and its adjective clause from the sentences above under the correct group in this chart. Then answer the questions below.

Noun + adjective clause with *who*	Noun + adjective clause with *that*	Noun + adjective clause with *which*
people who have more money		

QUESTIONS

1. Which adjective clauses above describe nouns that are people?
2. Which clauses describe nouns that are things?
3. Which relative pronouns (*who*, *that*, or *which*) do we use to describe nouns that are people or things?

Talk about It Choose four generalizations above. Tell a partner why you agree or disagree with them.

Write about It Rewrite three of the generalizations that you don't agree with to make them true for you. (Don't change the noun phrase with the adjective clause.)

People who have more money are not always happier.

---

[3] **expel:** to force to leave

10.2 Describing People and Things with Adjective Clauses

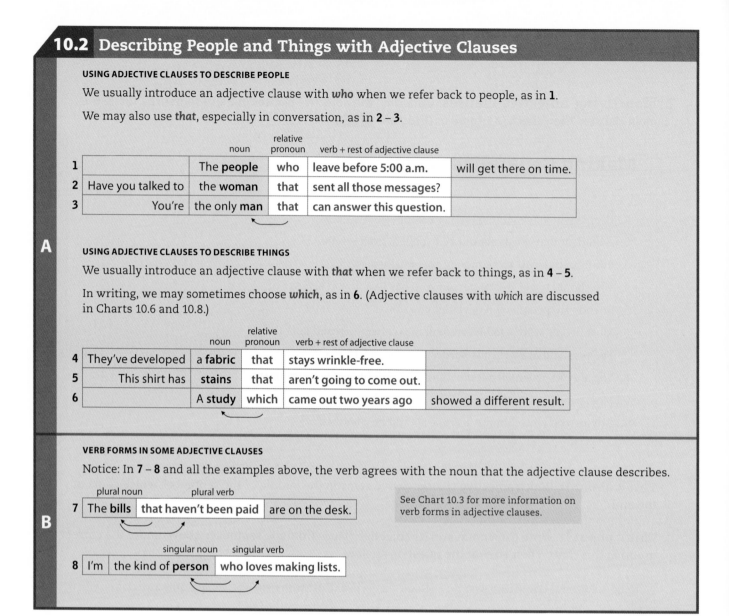

USING ADJECTIVE CLAUSES TO DESCRIBE PEOPLE

We usually introduce an adjective clause with **who** when we refer back to people, as in **1**.

We may also use **that**, especially in conversation, as in **2 – 3**.

	noun	relative pronoun	verb + rest of adjective clause	
1	The **people**	who	leave before 5:00 a.m.	will get there on time.
2 Have you talked to	the **woman**	that	sent all those messages?	
3 You're	the only **man**	that	can answer this question.	

A

USING ADJECTIVE CLAUSES TO DESCRIBE THINGS

We usually introduce an adjective clause with **that** when we refer back to things, as in **4 – 5**.

In writing, we may sometimes choose **which**, as in **6**. (Adjective clauses with *which* are discussed in Charts 10.6 and 10.8.)

	noun	relative pronoun	verb + rest of adjective clause	
4 They've developed	a **fabric**	that	stays wrinkle-free.	
5 This shirt has	**stains**	that	aren't going to come out.	
6	A **study**	which	came out two years ago	showed a different result.

VERB FORMS IN SOME ADJECTIVE CLAUSES

Notice: In **7 – 8** and all the examples above, the verb agrees with the noun that the adjective clause describes.

plural noun   plural verb

7 The **bills** | that haven't been paid | are on the desk.

See Chart 10.3 for more information on verb forms in adjective clauses.

B

singular noun   singular verb

8 I'm | the kind of **person** | who loves making lists.

3 | Noticing Adjective Clauses That Describe People and Things Underline the adjective clauses in these sentences. Circle the noun that each adjective clause describes and the verb in the adjective clause. **10.2 A**

1. The man who repaired my guitar did a great job.
2. What was that dish that tasted like almonds?
3. The customers who came in before 5:00 got a discount.
4. My grandmother had a device that helped her breathe at night.
5. Did you ever talk to that woman who worked in the front office?
6. She never wore clothes that were out of style.
7. They served desserts that were just amazing.
8. They had one son that sang really well and another son that danced really well.
9. The woman who lived in that house was always really friendly.
10. I didn't know the people that lived across the street.

Think about It Which adjective clauses in Activity 3 could use *who* or *that*? Why?

4 | Using *That* or *Who* for People and Things Complete the conversations below with *that* or *who* and the correct form of a verb from the box. Then practice with a partner. `10.2 A-B`

fall	help	meet	own	sit
have	leave	open	pull	start

1. A: David is going to help out today.

   B: Is he the one _____*that helped*_____ last week?

   A: No, that was James.

2. A: How was the restaurant?

   B: It was pretty fancy. There was a guy _____ us at the door and took our coats.

3. A: You remember that woman _____ down the stairs?

   B: Yeah. That was terrible.

   A: Well, I saw her yesterday, and she's doing fine now.

4. A: Where did you buy that T-shirt?

   B: At the new store on Cherry Street. You know, the one _____ last month.

   A: Yeah. I haven't been there yet.

5. A: The woman _____ her glasses here came back.

   B: Oh, I bet she was glad to find them.

6. A: What's the name of that song _____ with a long guitar solo?

   B: Hmm. I know the song, but I don't know what it's called.

7. A: I want to live in a city _____ free Wi-Fi everywhere.

   B: That would be nice.

8. A: Have you seen the student _____ next to the desk?

   B: No. I think she's absent today.

9. A: Do you know the man _____ Java Café?

   B: Yeah. That's my favorite coffee place. His name's John.

10. A: Do you have one of those things _____ staples out?

    B: Yeah, somewhere. Check the desk drawer.

Talk about It Complete these sentences with an adjective clause and your own ideas. Then ask a partner your questions.

1. Have you seen the student . . . ?
2. Do you know the man/woman . . . ?
3. Do you have one of those things . . . ?

5 | Verb Forms in Adjective Clauses Look back at Activity 3 on page 326. Rewrite each sentence using present verb forms. Make sure that the verb in each adjective clause agrees with the noun it describes. `10.2 A-B`

1. *The man who repairs my guitar does a great job.*

6 | Describing People with Adjective Clauses Write ten meaningful sentences using ideas from this chart. Add *who* or *that* and use a form of the verb in parentheses. `10.2 A–B`

PEOPLE PREFERENCES

I'd rather have I'd rather not have	a boss a roommate a teacher co-workers friends neighbors	(be) active. (be) lazy and unreliable. (be) relaxed and friendly. (correct) my work. (explain) everything clearly. (have) a good sense of humor. (let) people leave early. (like) to go out and have fun. (talk) a lot. (treat) people unfairly.

I'd rather not have a boss who treats people unfairly.

Talk about It Read several of the sentences you wrote above to your classmates. Do they agree or disagree?

Write about It Write several more sentences using the words from the first and second columns above. Finish each sentence with your own adjective clause.

7 | Describing Things with Adjective Clauses Write ten meaningful sentences using ideas from this chart. Add *that* and use a form of the verb in parentheses. `10.2 A–B`

THINGS I DO/DON'T LIKE

I don't like I like I'm interested in	books cities movies music neighborhoods new technology	(be) hard to understand. (be) quiet at night. (be) scary or violent. (have) a lot of nightlife. (have) interesting characters. (have) large green areas. (help) me relax. (make) me laugh. (make) my life easier. (teach) me about the world.

I like neighborhoods that are quiet at night.

Talk about It Read several of the sentences you wrote above to your classmates. Do they agree or disagree?

Write about It Write several more sentences using words from the first and second columns above. Finish each sentence with your own adjective clause.

8 | Error Correction Correct any errors in these sentences. (Some sentences may not have any errors.)

1. We read several authors talked about this issue.
2. There were a lot of students missed class yesterday.
3. The employee which works the night shift didn't show up last night.
4. Did you meet the professor who he visited the class last week?
5. I met a really interesting woman that design furniture.
6. There's a photograph shows what he looked like 20 years ago.
7. The toy train was really expensive that looked so realistic.
8. Everybody loves the soccer player who he made the winning goal.
9. Please put this where people who is interested can see it.
10. I have a good friend that go to that school.

10.3 Subjects and Objects in Adjective Clauses

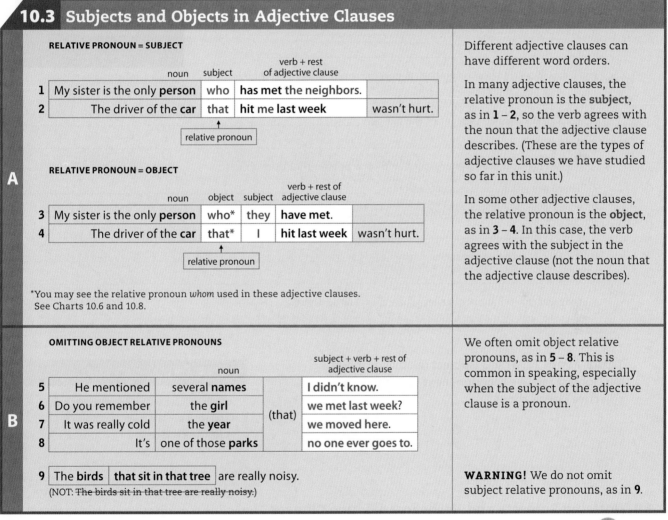

RELATIVE PRONOUN = SUBJECT

	noun	subject	verb + rest of adjective clause	
1	My sister is the only **person**	who	**has met** the neighbors.	
2	The driver of the **car**	that	**hit** me **last week**	wasn't hurt.

↑ relative pronoun

RELATIVE PRONOUN = OBJECT

	noun	object	subject	verb + rest of adjective clause	
3	My sister is the only **person**	who*	they	**have met.**	
4	The driver of the **car**	that*	I	**hit last week**	wasn't hurt.

↑ relative pronoun

*You may see the relative pronoun *whom* used in these adjective clauses. See Charts 10.6 and 10.8.

Different adjective clauses can have different word orders.

In many adjective clauses, the relative pronoun is the **subject**, as in **1 – 2**, so the verb agrees with the noun that the adjective clause describes. (These are the types of adjective clauses we have studied so far in this unit.)

In some other adjective clauses, the relative pronoun is the **object**, as in **3 – 4**. In this case, the verb agrees with the subject in the adjective clause (not the noun that the adjective clause describes).

OMITTING OBJECT RELATIVE PRONOUNS

		noun		subject + verb + rest of adjective clause
5	He mentioned	several **names**		I didn't know.
6	Do you remember	the **girl**	(that)	we met last week?
7	It was really cold	the **year**		we moved here.
8	It's	one of those **parks**		no one ever goes to.

9	The **birds**	**that sit in that tree**	are really noisy.

(NOT: ~~The birds sit in that tree are really noisy.~~)

We often omit object relative pronouns, as in **5 – 8**. This is common in speaking, especially when the subject of the adjective clause is a pronoun.

WARNING! We do not omit subject relative pronouns, as in **9**.

9 | Adding Adjective Clauses Complete each sentence below with an adjective clause from the box.

10.3 A

that doesn't sleep	that is liquid at room temperature	that you can see without a telescope
that enters your bloodstream	that live in most people's eyelashes	that you can stretch out your arms
that had lived for over 400 years	that most people can remember easily	who go into space
that is a thousand years old	that specializes in recognizing faces	

STRANGE FACTS

1. The Andromeda Galaxy is the most distant object
   that you can see without a telescope, 2.4 million light years away.

2. Mercury is the only metal _____
   _____.

3. The longest string of numbers _____
   _____ is seven.

4. Honey doesn't spoil or go bad. A person could safely eat honey
   _____.

Andromeda Galaxy

5. Your brain uses 20 percent of the oxygen _____.

6. A person _____
   experiences problems more quickly than a person that doesn't eat.

7. There are small, microscopic animals _____.

8. There is a part of your brain _____.

9. The width _____ is about the same as your height.

10. In 2007, researchers found a clam _____.

11. People _____
    may get up to 3 percent taller while they are up there.

Think about It Write *S* (subject relative pronoun) or *O* (object relative pronoun) next to each adjective clause above.

10 | Noticing Subjects and Verbs in Adjective Clauses Underline the adjective clauses in these conversations. Circle the subject and verb in each adjective clause. Then practice with a partner. 10.3 A

1. A: Who's Isabel?
   B: She's the girl that (I introduced) you to last week.

2. A: Where's the teacher that we had yesterday?
   B: She's sick. She's supposed to come back
      for the next class.

3. A: There's one thing that I don't understand
      about this movie.
   B: What's that?
   A: Why didn't the hero just call the police
      for help?

4. A: Do you have the money that I left you?

   B: Oh, I do! Sorry I forgot to pay you back.

5. A: Did they change the carpet?

   B: Yeah. The one that used to be here was blue and white.

6. A: This is the best soup that I've ever tasted.

   B: Thanks. It's my mom's recipe.

7. A: I can't stand people who are always late.

   B: I know. It's really annoying.

8. A: What happened to the keys that were on this table?

   B: I don't know. I didn't touch them.

9. A: This guy who I know is starting his own T-shirt business.

   B: Sounds like a hard way to make money.

10. A: What's International Day?

    B: It's a big cultural event that we have here every year. It's fun.

Think about It Write *S* (subject relative pronoun) or *O* (object relative pronoun) next to each adjective clause in Activity 10.

11 | Adding Relative Pronouns Complete these sentences with *who* or *that* if a relative pronoun is necessary. Write an *X* if a relative pronoun can be omitted. `10.3 B`

WHAT DO EMPLOYERS WANT?

1. Nowadays, it's hard to find a job ____*that*____ doesn't require some technical skill.

2. Employers want the people _____ they hire to have good communication skills.

3. Probably the most important personal quality _____ employers look for is honesty.

4. Employers are looking for workers _____ get along well with others.

5. Other skills _____ employers value are leadership, problem solving, and the ability to work independently.

WHAT DO EMPLOYEES WANT?

6. The money _____ an employee earns is important, but it's not the only thing that matters.

7. Most employees want a job _____ gives them responsibility.

8. More and more employees want to work for companies _____ offer flexible hours.

9. Many employees want a boss _____ will give frequent feedback.

10. People like to work for companies _____ allow them to be creative.

Talk about It Tell a partner what you want in an employer. Use adjective clauses.

"I want an employer that listens to my ideas."

12 | Using Adjective Clauses Complete each adjective clause. Use the correct form of the verb in parentheses. Add *who* or *that* if a relative pronoun is needed. **10.3 A–B**

QUESTIONS TO GET TO KNOW SOMEONE BETTER

1. What do you remember about the first time that you _____*came*_____ to this school? (come)

2. What is one thing _____ you really happy? (make)

3. Who is the first person you _____ to every day? (talk)

4. What is one thing _____ you a lot? (annoy)

5. Do you ever buy things you _____? (not need)

6. How often do you have dreams you _____ in the morning? (remember)

7. Who is a famous person you _____ to meet someday? (want)

8. What is the most fun you _____ ever _____? (have)

9. Can you name a movie _____ you? (scare)

10. What is the most beautiful place you _____ ever _____? (see)

Talk about It Ask a partner the questions above.

A: *What do you remember about the first time that you came to this school?*
B: *I remember I couldn't find my classroom.*

Think about It Write *S* (subject relative pronoun) or *O* (object relative pronoun) next to each adjective clause above.

Talk about It Complete these questions with an adjective clause and your own ideas. Then ask a partner your questions.

1. What is one thing . . . ?   2. Who is one person . . . ?   3. What is one book . . . ?

10.4 Adjective Clauses Describing Pronouns

A

	pronoun one(s)	relative pronoun	verb + rest of adjective clause
1	Is Sarah	the **one**	who	lives in Oman?
2	These are	the **ones**	that	don't have a price tag.

	pronoun one(s)	relative pronoun	subject + verb + rest of adjective clause
3	I like	the **one**	that	we usually buy.
4	These are	the **ones**	—	I'm keeping.

We often use **adjective clauses** to describe the pronoun *one* or *ones*. *One* and *ones* can refer to things or people, so the adjective clauses may begin with *who* or *that*, as in **1 – 3**. We may also omit object relative pronouns, as in **4**.

B

5 I can't find **anyone** who understands this.

6 I've already asked **everyone** I know about the assignment.

7 He said **something** that didn't make any sense.

8 Nothing they do is going to make a difference.

We also often use adjective clauses with or without a relative pronoun to describe indefinite pronouns, as in **5 – 8**.

INDEFINITE PRONOUNS FOR PEOPLE

someone	no one	anyone	everyone
somebody	nobody	anybody	everybody

INDEFINITE PRONOUNS FOR THINGS

something	nothing	anything	everything

13 | Noticing Adjective Clauses with Pronouns Underline each adjective clause and circle the pronoun it describes. 10.4 A

WORK DUTIES

1. The receptionist is the (one) who answers the office phone.
2. The desk clerk is the one that talks to clients at the counter.
3. The salespeople are the ones who you ask if you want to place an order.
4. The secretaries are the ones who keep track of all of the orders.
5. The warehouse foreman is the one who creates the schedule for the warehouse workers.
6. The warehouse workers are the ones who put the orders together.
7. The truck drivers are the ones who deliver the product to the stores.
8. The accountant is the one who makes out the paychecks.
9. The boss is the one who signs the paychecks.
10. The office manager is the one that employees talk to about any problems.

Think about It In which sentences above is the relative pronoun *who* or *that* not necessary? Why? Cross those pronouns out.

Talk about It Discuss the responsibilities of people at home, at your job, or in your classroom. Use adjective clauses. Share ideas with your classmates.

"I'm the one who usually takes out the trash."

14 | Adding Adjective Clauses Complete each question below with an adjective clause using information from the box. Add *who* or *that* if a relative pronoun is needed. (More than one answer is possible.) 10.4 B

WHAT DO YOU THINK?

you regret buying	hurt someone's feelings
asked to copy your homework	you miss right now
has a really strange job	always interrupts you
you don't know very well	you will never eat again
most people don't know about you	you would really love to meet

1. How do you help someone _you don't know very well_____?
2. What do you say to someone _____?
3. Have you ever accidentally said something _____?
4. Is there anyone famous _____?
5. Have you ever met anyone _____?
6. Have you ever eaten anything _____?
7. Is there anybody _____?
8. What would you say to somebody _____?
9. Do you have anything _____?
10. Is there something _____?

Write about It Write an answer to each question in Activity 14. Use an adjective clause.

It's not hard to help someone you don't know very well. Just ask the person how you can help.

Talk about It Ask a partner the questions in Activity 14.

10.5 Reduced Adjective Clauses

We can sometimes reduce (or shorten) an **adjective clause** when the relative pronoun is the subject. We call this a **reduced adjective clause**.

A

COMPARE

1a The first **word** that was spoken on the moon was "OK."
1b The first **word** spoken on the moon was "OK."

2a The first **thing** that was mentioned at the meeting was the new tax law.
2b The first **thing** mentioned at the meeting was the new tax law.

3a There are a lot of **movies** that are based on books.
3b There are a lot of **movies** based on books.

We can reduce adjective clauses that have passive verb forms. We omit the relative pronoun and the verb *be*, as in **1 – 3**.

Remember: We form the passive with:

| a form of *be* | + | the past participle of the main verb |

Like a full adjective clause, the reduced adjective clause usually comes directly after the noun it describes.

Some past participles commonly used in reduced adjective clauses include:

based on	given	taken
caused	made	used
concerned with	produced	

B

COMPARE

4a The **boy** who was sitting in front saw everything.
4b The **boy** sitting in front saw everything.

5a I don't know the **woman** who is talking to Maria.
5b I don't know the **woman** talking to Maria.

6a The table was set with large **vases** that contained yellow flowers.
6b The table was set with large **vases** containing yellow flowers.

7a There are a number of **questions** that concern the company's finances.
7b There are a number of **questions** concerning the company's finances.

8 The cake **that they're eating** looks delicious.
(NOT: ~~The cake eating looks delicious.~~)

We can reduce adjective clauses that have present or past progressive verb forms by omitting the relative pronoun and the verb *be*, as in **4 – 5**.

We can reduce adjective clauses that have simple present or past verb forms by:

• omitting the relative pronoun
• replacing the verb with an *-ing* form, as in **6 – 7**

We can use the *-ing* verb form to reduce adjective clauses with many verbs that are not normally continuous. The most common examples are *concerning, containing, having, involving, requiring, resulting in,* and *using*.

WARNING! Because we cannot omit the subject of an adjective clause, we cannot reduce adjective clauses with object relative pronouns, as in **8**.

15 | Noticing Reduced Adjective Clauses with Past Participles Underline the reduced adjective clauses in these news items. Circle the noun that each reduced adjective clause describes. `10.5 A`

In the News

1. (Research) conducted in the Tule Valley of Mexico has identified a new method of filtering water—cilantro! Contaminated[4] water causes a number of problems in the area, but the methods normally used to clean water are too expensive for local residents. So far, tests show that cilantro works well to reduce some of the contamination.

cilantro

2. Most children under age 10 think that the earth is flat. A survey carried out for the U.S. National Science Teachers Association showed that most children are taught that the earth is round at about age 10. Before then, they rely on their own perceptions.

3. The use of a drug known to the ancient Egyptians has been suggested for the treatment of certain cancers. Dr. Richard L. Edelson, in a recent *Scientific American* article, describes how cancerous cells removed from a patient's body are damaged by the drug, known as 8-MOP.

4. Clams collected from rivers can provide information about contamination in the water. A clam eats by pulling in water and absorbing[5] food from it, so any toxins in the water will build up inside the clam's body. By testing clams, biologists have discovered chemicals buried years ago that are now leaking into river water.

clams

5. NASA's *Cassini* spacecraft has discovered a chemical used to make food containers, car bumpers, and other consumer products on Saturn's moon Titan. This chemical is usually put together in long chains to form a plastic called polypropylene. This is the first time the chemical has been discovered on any moon or planet other than Earth.

Think about It Use a full adjective clause to rewrite each sentence above that contains a reduced adjective clause. What verb form do you use in each adjective clause?

Research that was conducted in the Tule Valley of Mexico has identified a new method of filtering water—cilantro! (simple past passive)

16 | Reducing Passive Forms Rewrite each sentence. Use a reduced adjective clause. `10.5 A`

FAMOUS FIRSTS

1. Dr. Antonia Novello was the first woman who was named surgeon general of the United States.

   Dr. Antonia Novello was the first woman named surgeon general of the United States.

2. The first automated banking machines that were connected to computers were made in the 1970s.

---

[4] **contaminated:** dangerous, dirty, or not clean   [5] **absorb:** to take in

3. Golf was one of the first sports that was cut from the modern Olympics.
4. Grover Cleveland was the first president who was married in the White House.
5. The first woman who was pictured on a U.S. stamp was Queen Isabella of Spain.
6. The first U.S. president who was inaugurated[6] in Washington, D.C., was Thomas Jefferson.
7. Herbert Hoover was the first U.S. president who was born west of the Mississippi.
8. The first woman who was awarded a Nobel Prize was Marie Curie.
9. The first living thing that was sent into space was a dog.
10. The first computers that were designed as laptops went on sale in 1982.

17 | Identifying Adjective Clause Forms Underline the adjective clauses in these sentences. Circle the noun each adjective clause describes. Then check (✓) *Reduced* or *Not Reduced*. `10.5 A–B`

Flowers

	REDUCED	NOT REDUCED
1. The markets of the world are full of cut (flowers) grown in Colombia.	✓	☐
2. In 1967, a graduate student named David Cheever wrote a paper suggesting that Bogota, Colombia, would be a good place to grow flowers.	☐	☐
3. Cheever pointed out that the soil[7], water, and weather that Colombia has would be perfect for growing carnations.	☐	☐
4. Nowadays, flowers bought by people all over the world are grown and packaged in Colombia and Ecuador.	☐	☐
5. You may wonder how a delicate flower traveling thousands of miles can stay fresh.	☐	☐
6. Growers quickly discovered that flowers that are kept cold for the entire journey can stay fresh for several days.	☐	☐
7. Flowers going from a field in Colombia to the U.S. spend about 48 hours on the journey.	☐	☐
8. In recent years, Colombian flower growers have had to compete with flower industries expanding in other nations.	☐	☐
9. In addition, growers now have to think about customers who are concerned about the sustainability[8] of the flowers they buy.	☐	☐
10. Particularly in Europe, more customers want to see information describing how the flowers are grown.	☐	☐

Think about It Is it possible to reduce the full (not reduced) adjective clauses above? Why or why not? Write the reduced form if possible.

---

[6] **inaugurate:** to introduce a new official, leader, etc., at a special ceremony
[7] **soil:** earth

[8] **sustainability:** the use of natural products and energy in ways that do not harm the environment

18 | Using Reduced Adjective Clauses Underline the adjective clauses in these sentences. If you can reduce the clause, rewrite the sentences using a reduced adjective clause. `10.5 B`

CHANGING TIMES

1. The number of people <u>who use smartphones</u> has increased dramatically.

    The number of people using smartphones has increased dramatically.

2. There are more laws that require companies to explain their privacy policies.
3. These days there are more students who have trouble paying for college.
4. Nowadays, products that contain dangerous substances must carry warning labels.
5. The cars that we buy these days are safer than cars from ten years ago.
6. In recent years, accidents that involve pedestrians[9] have been on the rise.
7. People who are looking for environmentally friendly products have a lot more choices now.
8. There are more and more jobs that require advanced training.
9. Many surgeries are now performed by doctors that use advanced technology.
10. There are now universities that award degrees to students who take all of their classes online.
11. Most places have laws that concern cell phones and driving.
12. Nowadays, most of the news that people read is online.
13. There are more companies that are offering flexible time schedules and work-at-home options.

Think about It Answer these questions about the sentences above.

1. Which adjective clauses could not be reduced? Why?
2. Which of the reduced adjective clauses do not have a continuous verb in the full adjective clause? Why?

Talk about It Are you unhappy about any of the changes above? Tell your classmates why.

Write about It Complete these sentences with a reduced adjective clause and your own ideas. Share your sentences with a partner.

NOWADAYS

1. There are more laws. . . .
2. There are more companies. . . .
3. There are more people. . . .

19 | Error Correction Correct any errors in these sentences. (Some sentences may not have any errors.)

1. We saw a large seal was lying on the beach.
2. The doctor use methods that based on his experience in combat.
3. We buy a lot of products are made in China.
4. They asked him a lot of questions concern his time overseas.
5. The woman was friendly working at the front desk.
6. I don't want to live in a house that built before 1950.
7. The guy was talking to last night was really smart.
8. We spoke to several people were given promotions.
9. That book is very interesting written by Michael Pollan.
10. People look for a new place to eat dinner should try Millie's Restaurant.

[9]**pedestrians:** people who are walking on or near the street

10.6 Defining and Non-defining Adjective Clauses

A

DEFINING ADJECTIVE CLAUSES

1 The **ideas that the artist gave us** are going to be very useful in the future. (the ideas that the artist gave us = which ideas)

2 A gardener is a person **who takes care of plants**. (a person who takes care of plants = definition of gardener)

So far in this unit, we have studied adjective clauses that we call **defining**, as in **1 – 2**. They help us identify the noun we are describing. Without the adjective clause, the meaning of the sentence would not be complete.

B

NON-DEFINING ADJECTIVE CLAUSES

3 The artist's **ideas, which rely more on imagination than logic**, are going to be useful in the future.

4 Let me introduce you to Tom Jordan, **who is the best gardener I know**.

5 The **principal, whom I had met several times before**, sat across the table from me.

6 My **parents, who came to this country 30 years ago**, had four children. (NOT: ~~My parents, that came to . . .~~)

7 The cup, **which I received from my grandmother as a child**, had a small crack. (NOT: ~~The cup, I received from . . .~~)

Another type of adjective clause gives additional information about the noun we are describing. We call this type of adjective clause **non-defining**. We usually use commas before and after non-defining adjective clauses.

We introduce most non-defining adjective clauses with:

- *which* to refer back to things, as in **3**
- *who* to refer back to people, as in **4**

We can also use the object relative pronoun *whom* (especially in writing) to refer back to people, as in **5**. However, this usually sounds more formal.

WARNING! In non-defining adjective clauses, we do not usually omit relative pronouns or use the relative pronoun *that*, as in **6 – 7**.

 GO ONLINE

20 | Using Defining Adjective Clauses Complete these sentences with defining adjective clauses and your own ideas. (Many different answers are possible.) Share your sentences with a partner. `10.6 A`

DEFINING PEOPLE AND THINGS

1. A friend is someone _who talks to you when you're sad_ .
2. A happy person is a person _____ .
3. Your family are the people _____ .
4. An interesting book is one _____ .
5. A great city is one _____ .
6. The best TV shows are the ones _____ .
7. It's important to have someone _____ .
8. I would like to have a machine _____ .
9. I would like to visit a place _____ .
10. I like music _____ .

Think about It Which of the adjective clauses that you wrote above use subject relative pronouns? Which use object relative pronouns?

Write about It Complete these sentences with defining adjective clauses and your own ideas.

I like . . .
I would like . . .
It's important to . . .
A . . . is someone . . .

338

21 | Noticing Defining and Non-defining Adjective Clauses Underline the adjective clauses and reduced adjective clauses in this story. Label each adjective clause *D* (defining) or *ND* (non-defining).

`10.6 A–B`

Tori Murden McClure

Tori Murden McClure began the adventure of a lifetime when she attempted to be the first woman to row across the Atlantic Ocean. McClure,
ND
<u>who had already skied across Antarctica and climbed mountains</u>, was no stranger to adventure. In June 1998, she departed from the east coast of the U.S. in a 23-foot wooden boat with no motor and no sail. She had many problems, including the loss of her communication equipment, fatigue[10], and loneliness. But the worst thing she encountered[11] in her three months

McClure in her rowboat

at sea was a powerful hurricane that destroyed her boat and almost killed her. She was rescued and taken back home. She felt like a failure.

After her failed attempt to cross the Atlantic in a rowboat, McClure got a job with the famous boxer Muhammad Ali, who encouraged her to try again. Ali told her he didn't get to be "world champ" three times until he'd gotten knocked down twice. So McClure tried again in 1999. She rowed for 81 days and this time she made it across the Atlantic.

McClure, who is now a college president, describes herself as a "seeker of truth" more than an adventurer. She says, "I wanted to row across the ocean because I knew I would learn something that I did not know." She wrote a book that describes her journey called *A Pearl in the Storm: How I Found My Heart in the Middle of the Ocean*. She is an inspiration to many.

22 | Usage Note: Giving Background Information Read the note. Then do Activity 23.

We often use a non-defining adjective clause to provide background information about the subject of a sentence. When we do this, we often must decide what information to emphasize. Compare:

Pelé, who is regarded by many as the world's greatest soccer player, grew up in poverty in Brazil.

Pelé, who grew up in poverty in Brazil, is regarded by many as the world's greatest soccer player.

The first sentence emphasizes that Pele grew up in poverty. The second sentence emphasizes that he is regarded as the world's greatest soccer player.

[10] **fatigue:** great tiredness

[11] **encounter:** to experience something (a danger, difficulty, etc.)

23 | Using Non-defining Adjective Clauses Combine each pair of sentences with a non-defining adjective clause that adds information about the **bold** noun or noun phrase. (More than one answer may be possible.) `10.6 B`

HISTORICAL FACTS

the Great London Fire

Amelia Earhart

1. **The Great Fire of London of 1666** only killed eight people. It destroyed about 13,000 houses.

   The Great Fire of London of 1666, which destroyed about 13,000 houses, only killed eight people.

2. **The Minoan civilization** may have been destroyed by an earthquake. It suddenly disappeared in 1600 BCE.
3. **Amelia Earhart** disappeared in 1937. She was the first female pilot to fly solo across the Atlantic Ocean.
4. Christiaan Barnard performed the first **human heart transplant** in 1967. It was a major medical accomplishment at that time.
5. **The Taj Mahal** is one of the most beautiful buildings in the world. It was completed in 1648.
6. Alexander Fleming discovered **penicillin**. It became the first widely used antibiotic.
7. **Antarctica** was not discovered until the 1800s. It is almost completely covered with ice.
8. **The Polynesian Islands** have been populated for thousands of years. They are spread over 70.1 million miles of ocean.
9. **Oranges** were being grown in China as far back as 2500 BCE. They probably originated in Southeast Asia.
10. **Coffee** was a popular drink in many countries by 1100. It was discovered in Ethiopia.

Think about It Which adjective clauses above describe the subject of the sentence? Which describe an object?

Write about It If possible, write a new version of each sentence you wrote above, exchanging the information in the adjective clause and the main clause. Do you think one version sounds better than the other? Why? Why is there no alternative version for some of the sentences?

   1. The Great Fire of London of 1666, which only killed eight people, destroyed about 13,000 houses.

24 | Using Defining and Non-defining Adjective Clauses Combine these sentences with an adjective clause. Use the information in parentheses to help you decide if the adjective clause should be defining or non-defining. `10.6 A–B`

1. The children stayed out of the water. They couldn't swim. (There were several children at the swimming pool. None of them knew how to swim.)

   The children, who couldn't swim, stayed out of the water.

2. The children stayed out of the water. They couldn't swim. (There were several children at the swimming pool. Some of them didn't know how to swim.)

   The children who couldn't swim stayed out of the water.

3. Mary took a book. It was on the table. (There are a lot of books in the room.)

4. I finally read Coleman's book. It was very interesting. (You know which book I'm talking about.)

5. My sister just learned how to scuba-dive. She has never liked the water. (I have one sister.)

6. Kate's sister lives in Washington. She's getting married. (Kate has three sisters that live in different places.)

7. Sam's plan is to fix up the house. It is in a lovely neighborhood near downtown. (Sam owns one house.)

8. Carlos needs to sell the house. He inherited it from his grandfather. (Carlos owns two houses.)

9. Emma was walking with a friend. I've met her friend several times. (I saw Emma at the park with someone I've met before.)

10. Toshi was playing soccer with his friends. They were much better at the game than he was. (All his friends were much better at the game.)

Think about It What made you decide if each adjective clause in Activity 24 should be defining or non-defining? Compare with a partner and explain your choices.

10.7 Adjective Clauses with *Whose*

A

We sometimes use the relative pronoun **whose** + a **noun** to show possession in an **adjective clause**, as in **1** and **2**. We use *whose* much more often in writing than in speaking.

	whose + noun	verb + rest of adjective clause
1	The teacher filled out a survey for each **child**	whose parents	agreed to participate.

(whose parents = each child's parents)

	whose + noun	verb + rest of adjective clause
2	I have a **friend**	whose father	owns an airplane.

(whose father = my friend's father)

In most adjective clauses with *whose*, *whose* + noun is the subject, but it's possible to use *whose* + noun as an object, as in **3**.

	whose + noun	subject + verb + rest of adjective clause
3	He was talking to a **customer**	whose problem	he couldn't solve.

(whose problem = the customer's problem)

GRAMMAR TERM: Adjective clauses with *whose* are also called **possessive adjective clauses**. *Whose* is the possessive relative pronoun.

B

4 I worked for a **company** whose headquarters were in another state.

5 We should not spend that much money on a **program** whose purpose is not at all clear.

6 My **roommate**, whose family lives in Hong Kong, is coming to my house for the holiday.

Whose usually refers to people, but we also use it to refer to groups, for example, governments, corporations, and organizations, as in **4**.

In writing, *whose* sometimes refers to things, as in **5**.

Adjective clauses with *whose* can also be **non-defining**, as in **6**.

GO ONLINE

25 | Combining Sentences with *Whose* Combine each pair of sentences. Use an adjective clause with *whose*. `10.7 A`

FRIENDS, NEIGHBORS, AND STRANGERS

1. I recently met a woman. Her daughter was a professional violinist.

   I recently met a woman whose daughter was a professional violinist.

2. The professor was talking to a student. I don't know his name.
3. Do you know a woman? Her first name begins with Z.
4. They gave the award to Hassan. His work has been excellent this year.
5. How do I contact someone? I don't know her email.
6. The police were talking to a woman. Her purse was stolen in the park.
7. The police are looking for a man. His car was left by the side of the road.
8. Most people want to have talented co-workers. Their skills are at the same level.
9. The sailor is recovering in the hospital. His boat sank last weekend.
10. I have a great friend. His taste in music is exactly the same as mine.

Talk about It Complete these questions with an adjective clause with *whose* and your own ideas. Then ask a partner your questions.

1. Do you know anyone . . . ?
2. Do you have a friend . . . ?
3. Did you ever talk to someone . . . ?

26 | Noticing *Whose* Underline the adjective clauses in these sentences. Rewrite each adjective clause as a separate sentence using a possessive pronoun. `10.7 A–B`

Space Exploration

1. The early astronauts were test pilots. These were men <u>whose lives were full of excitement and danger</u>.

   Their lives were full of excitement and danger.

2. Today's space programs select astronauts whose skills include working well with others.
3. The International Space Station, whose first component was sent to space in 1988, has been continuously occupied since 2000.
4. Sixteen countries take part in the space station program, whose main goal is scientific experimentation.
5. Several tourists have visited the International Space Station. These private citizens, whose flights cost millions of dollars, have spent as long as two weeks in space.
6. Space station astronauts, whose bones get weak in space without exercise, must work out for at least two hours every day.
7. It's amazing to see astronauts whose spacesuits weigh about 280 pounds floating around in space.
8. NASA has six active missions focused on the planet Mars, whose red color has fascinated humans for hundreds of years.
9. The first "space tourist" was Charles D. Walker, whose private flight on the space shuttle cost $40,000.
10. You would weigh much less on a planet whose gravitational pull is not as strong as the earth's.

International Space Station

Think about It Which adjective clauses in Activity 26 are non-defining?

Think about It Which adjective clauses in Activity 26 refer to people? To things? Which refers to an organization?

10.8 Adjective Clauses with Prepositions

<table>
<tr>
<td rowspan="2">A</td>
<td>

COMMON IN SPEAKING

1 The **woman** (that / who) **David spoke to** said the first month would be free.
(David <u>spoke to</u> the woman.)

2 Someone bought the **house** (that) **I used to live in.**
(I used to <u>live in</u> the house.)

COMMON IN WRITING

3 This was one of the **victims** for whom he sought justice.
(He wanted <u>justice for</u> the victims.)

4 Sarah composed a long **letter**, in which she described everything she had witnessed.
(Sarah described everything she had witnessed **in a long letter**.)

</td>
<td>

If the verb in an **adjective clause** requires a preposition, we can include it in two ways:

- In conversation, we often use the preposition after the verb even though it is not followed by an object, as in **1 – 2**. We usually omit the relative pronoun, but we may also use *who* or *that*.

- Some people consider it unacceptable to use a preposition without an object after a verb. In formal writing, we often begin the adjective clause with the preposition + *which* or *whom*, as in **3 – 4**.

These adjective clauses can also be **non-defining**, as in **4**.

In adjective clauses with prepositions, the relative pronoun is the object of the preposition.

</td>
</tr>
</table>

<table>
<tr>
<td rowspan="2">B</td>
<td>

5 She asked quite a few **questions**, most of which we answered without any problem.
(most of which = most of the questions)

6 The software has been used by hundreds of **people**, all of whom were satisfied.
(all of whom = all of the hundreds of people)

</td>
<td>

We often use quantity words and expressions with *of whom* and *of which* in non-defining adjective clauses, as in **5 – 6**. Some examples include:

five of which / whom
all of which / whom
many of which / whom
most of which / whom
some of which / whom
each of which / whom
none of which / whom

</td>
</tr>
</table>

 GO ONLINE

27 | Noticing Adjective Clauses with Prepositions Underline the adjective clauses in these sentences. Then circle the preposition in each adjective clause. `10.8 A`

MY EXPERIENCES

1. He's the best boss <u>I've ever worked for</u>.

2. She's the person I spoke to the most often when I first moved here.

3. The house that I grew up in was knocked down a few years ago.

4. I went shopping yesterday, but the shoes I was looking for weren't on sale anymore.

5. Having a job that I believed in made me happier.

6. My brother is one of those people you can always rely on.

7. I think I saw a man take something he didn't pay for.

8. Last night I went to the same restaurant that I go to every Wednesday.

9. I would never show up at an event I wasn't invited to.

10. My home is one of the many things I am grateful for.

Write about It Choose five of the underlined adjective clauses in Activity 27 and write your own sentence for each one.

It's the best company I've ever worked for.

Think about It Rewrite five of the sentences in Activity 27 using formal adjective clauses with the preposition + *which* or *whom*.

28 | Using Adjective Clauses with *That* + Preposition Complete these conversations with an adjective clause from the box. Listen and check your answers. Then practice with a partner. [10.8 A]

1. A: Is that the car _____*you came in*_____?

   B: Yeah, it is. It's my brother's.

2. A: We'll be discussing solar energy.

   B: Oh, good. That's something _____.

3. A: Why is James so happy?

   B: He finally got that computer _____.

4. A: What did you get your brother for his birthday?

   B: Oh, no. I knew there was something

   _____.

5. A: What's the name of that song _____?

   B: I'm not sure. It was on the radio.

6. A: You look worried.

   B: Yeah. I just took a test _____.

7. A: Who's that guy _____?

   B: His name is Matt. I don't know why John is so mad at him.

8. A: You seem kind of nervous.

   B: Yeah. A project _____ is being graded today.

9. A: I don't think I did very well on that quiz.

   B: The quiz isn't important. It's next week's test _____!

10. A: Look! There's the hotel _____.

    B: Really? I don't think so.

he's been saving up for
I had forgotten about
I'm interested in
John was shouting at
that I contributed to
that I wasn't prepared for
that we stayed in last time
you came in
you should be worried about
you were listening to yesterday

Think about It Which adjective clauses above don't have a relative pronoun? Which relative pronouns could you use with them?

344

29 | Using Adjective Clauses with Preposition + *Which* or *Whom* Read this TV guide.
Then complete the reviews below with preposition + *which* or *whom* at the beginning of each
adjective clause. **10.8 A**

TV Show Reviews

Deep Waters Based on the best-selling book, but set in modern New York.	*Eat It!* Watch 15 people who will eat anything in order to win big prizes!
Maple Town All of the characters you got attached to last season are back. In this week's episode, Sam is reunited with his brother.	*Dr. Soto* You've been waiting for this show all summer. Tonight, learn who the doctor was speaking to at the end of the last episode.

---

1. You'll find *Deep Waters* very different from the book ____*on which*____ it is based. The hero is much like
   the character in the book, but the setting _____ he works has been changed to modern-day
   New York.

2. *Maple Town* is a heart-warming show with a number of delightful characters _____ you'll get
   very attached by the end of the season. Thursday's episode, _____ Sam is reunited with his
   long-lost brother, is particularly moving.

3. This silly show features a competition _____ contestants win big prizes for cooking and eating
   strange foods. Fortunately, the producers have done a great job choosing people who are fun to watch.
   Last spring they received over a thousand video applications, _____ they chose the funniest
   and most creative. As a result, the show is surprisingly entertaining.

4. Monday night we finally see the return of the show _____ we've been waiting all summer.
   Dr. Soto is back, curing patients and solving mysteries. Last season ended with the doctor's mysterious
   phone call. Monday we learn the identity of the strange woman _____ she was speaking.

30 | Using Quantity Words with *Which* and *Whom* Read about these three tourist destinations.
Then complete the adjective clauses with a quantity word or expression with *of whom* or *of which* from
the box. **10.8 B**

TOURIST DESTINATIONS

Yosemite Valley (U.S.)
about 4 million visitors a year—75% from the U.S.
1,504 campsites—16 for large groups
10 large waterfalls—6 visible from the valley floor

1. Yosemite Valley gets about 4 million visitors a year,
   _____*most of whom*_____ come from the U.S.

2. It has 1,504 campsites, _____ are reserved for large groups.

3. It has 10 large waterfalls, _____ are visible from the valley floor.

a few of which
most of whom
some of which

Teotihuacan (Mexico)

Many pyramids—one is 210 feet tall
Stone temples—painted bright colors
Avenue of the Dead—originally about 3 miles long;
1.4 miles recognizable now
Home to potters, jewelers, and craftsmen

4. In Teotihuacan, you can visit Mayan pyramids, _____
   is 210 feet tall.

5. You can see the ruins of ancient stone temples, _____ were
   originally painted bright colors.

6. Walk along the Avenue of the Dead, about _____ is
   recognizable now.

7. Over 100,000 people lived in the ancient city, _____ were potters,
   jewelers, and craftsmen.

> all of which
> half of which
> one of which
> some of whom

The Terracotta Army (China)

Over 8,000 terracotta soldiers and other figures in large pits—
most still underground
Soldiers are life-sized—most carry real weapons
Different ranks—a few officers, many soldiers
20 soldiers and other artifacts have been shown in other countries
Except for a few important visitors, like Queen Elizabeth,
tourists are not permitted to walk through pits

8. There are three enormous pits containing over 8,000 terracotta
   soldiers and other figures, only _____ have been dug up.

9. The soldiers, _____ carry real weapons, are life-sized.

10. Special viewings of the soldiers have been granted to a few important visitors,
    _____ was Queen Elizabeth.

> a few of which
> most of which
> one of whom

Write about It Write two sentences about places you like to visit. Use adjective clauses with **quantity expressions.**

31 | Error Correction Correct any errors in these sentences. (Some sentences may not have any errors.)

1. The student that I talked on the first day of class was very nice.
2. The study included 45 participants, many of had just graduated from high school.
3. All students need to return the equipment to the department which they borrowed it.
4. He tends to get very angry at people with who he disagrees.
5. We were never given a receipt for the item we paid for it.
6. They watched five movies, most which she had seen before.
7. We still have the pen with which the president signed the document.
8. The room in that the children sleep is down the hall to the left.
9. There were several authorities to whom he had to report the incident to.
10. We have 135 residents here, many of them are over 70 years old.

10.9 Using Adjective Clauses in Speaking

A

1 <u>She said the games are completely sold out</u>, **which is ridiculous.**

2 <u>Amanda says we'll save more money if we buy early</u>, **which is a good point.**

3 <u>He's planning on getting into Harvard</u>, **which is possible, but not likely.**

4 <u>I run 20 miles a week</u>, **which is why I need to wear good shoes.**

5 A: It says that the movie starts at 8.
   B: **Which means it will start at 8:15,** after the previews.

6 A: No one ever goes to that place anymore.
   B: **Which is odd,** when it was so popular a few months ago.

We sometimes use **non-defining adjective clauses with *which*** to make a comment about an entire previous clause or idea, as in **1 – 6**.

In conversation, we usually use these adjective clauses to:

- express an evaluation or a feeling, as in **1 – 2**
- express likelihood, as in **3**
- give a reason, as in **4**
- interpret information, as in **5**

We can attach these clauses to our own sentences, or use them to respond to another speaker, as in **5 – 6**.

32 | Referring to an Earlier Idea Complete these conversations with an adjective clause from the box. Listen and check your answers. Then practice with a partner. **10.9 A**

1. A: Rob just bought a boat, __c__ .

   B: I know! He's always saying he doesn't have any money.

2. A: They said the gift will arrive tomorrow, ____.

   B: But you just ordered it!

3. A: I spent the whole day working in the garden, ____.

   B: Ha! That doesn't sound very relaxing to me.

4. A: Sam's out sick again, ____.

   B: Oh, that's too bad.

5. A: We're supposed to bring the textbook on the first day of class, ____.

   B: Really? Mine came two weeks ago.

6. A: They want us to be there at 5:00, ____.

   B: That's right. You work 'til 4:30, don't you?

7. A: This trip is becoming very expensive, ____.

   B: I know. But we're here, so we may as well make the best of it.

8. A: I got a 91 on the test, ____.

   B: Congratulations!

9. A: Anna is an hour late, ____.

   B: She really needs to get a new one.

10. A: If they beat the Lions next week, ____, they can still make it to the championship.

    B: Well, let's hope for the best!

---

a. which I can't do because mine hasn't arrived yet
b. which is possible, I guess
c. which is pretty surprising
d. which is the best I've done all semester
e. which is too early for me
f. which is why I didn't want to come in the first place
g. which isn't very likely
h. which means that her car probably broke down
i. which means that I have to do all of his work
j. which was really relaxing

Think about It How are the adjective clauses in Activity 32 being used? Write each clause under the correct group in this chart. Then share your answers with a partner. (More than one answer may be possible.)

Evaluation or feeling	Likelihood	Reason	Interpreting information
which is pretty surprising			

Write about It Complete these sentences with your own ideas. Then share your sentences with a partner.

1. _____, which is surprising.
2. _____, which is possible.
3. _____, which I loved.
4. _____, which means _____.
5. _____, which is a bad idea.

33 | Noticing Adjective Clauses as Responses Complete these conversations with an adjective clause from the box. Listen and check your answers. Then practice with a partner. **10.9 A**

1. A: She said she'd be here at 6.

   B: _g_. She's always late.

2. A: I heard they promoted Lonnie to manager.

   B: ____. She's great.

3. A: This coffee is terrible.

   B: ____

4. A: Jake said that he can't help us with the project.

   B: ____

5. A: We have to finish the presentation by Friday.

   B: ____. We need to get to work now.

6. A: Alan never showed up yesterday.

   B: ____. I wonder what's going on.

7. A: Emma left all of her dirty dishes in the sink.

   B: ____. She's kind of a slob[12].

8. A: It says here that he only attended school for two years.

   B: ____. He's so brilliant.

9. A: The new printer broke down already.

   B: ____

> a. Which doesn't give us much time.
> b. Which doesn't sound like him at all.
> c. Which is hard to believe.
> d. Which is the smartest thing they've ever done.
> e. Which is what I told you would happen if you bought the cheap one.
> f. Which is why I always order tea at this place!
> g. Which isn't very likely.
> h. Which probably means that he doesn't want to help.
> i. Which really shouldn't surprise you.

[12] **slob:** a lazy or messy person (used as an insult)

Talk about It Write a new sentence for the first part of each conversation. Read the sentences you wrote to a partner out of order. See if your partner gives the response you expected.

1. A: _____

   B: Which isn't very likely.

2. A: _____

   B: Which is hard to believe.

3. A: _____

   B: Which is the smartest thing you've ever done.

4. A: _____

   B: Which doesn't sound like him/her.

5. A: _____

   B: Which really shouldn't surprise you.

10.10 Using Adjective Clauses in Academic Writing

In academic writing, we often choose a more formal style of adjective clause.

A

LESS COMMON IN WRITING	MORE COMMON IN WRITING
1a It's hard to explain these ideas to **someone** that grew up in a different era.	**1b** It's hard to explain these ideas to **someone** who grew up in a different era.
2a The **experiments** [ ] they did provided some useful information.	**2b** The **experiments** that they did provided some useful information.
3a A **study** that came out several years ago showed a completely different result.	**3b** A **study** which came out several years ago showed a completely different result.
4a This was the first **group** that we had complete data for .	**4b** This was the first **group** for which we had complete data.
5a The **subjects** [ ] we spoke to had already completed the trial.	**5b** The **subjects** to whom we spoke had already completed the trial.
6a They compared newcomers with people who had lived in the country for more than three years.	**6b** They compared newcomers with those who had lived in the country for more than three years.
7a The most successful programs are the ones that offer a variety of ways for people to participate.	**7b** The most successful programs are those which offer a variety of ways for people to participate.
	8 **Systems** [ ] using the new software were found to be much more effective.
	9 **Decisions** [ ] based on these findings will waste time and effort.

IN ACADEMIC WRITING

- In subject adjective clauses, we usually use *who* for people instead of *that*, as in **1a – 1b**.
- We usually use *that* for things, as in **2a – 2b**. We don't usually omit the relative pronoun.
- We sometimes choose *which* for things instead of *that*, as in **3a – 3b**.
- We often use preposition + *whom* or *which*, as in **4a – 4b** and **5a – 5b**.
- Instead of using general nouns like *people* or *thing*, we often use the pronoun *those* + *who* or *which* to refer to a person or noun with a defining adjective clause, as in **6a – 6b** and **7a – 7b**.
- Reduced adjective clauses are very common, as in **8** and **9**.

B

COMPARE	
10a The wheat plant was developed thousands of years ago. It provided communities with a stable food source. It could be grown in large quantities.	In writing, we often use full and reduced adjective clauses to include a lot of information in one sentence. It is not unusual for a sentence to have more than one adjective clause, as in **10b**.
10b The wheat plant, **developed thousands of years ago,** provided communities with a stable food source **which could be grown in large quantities.**	

34 | Identifying Adjective Clauses Underline the full and reduced adjective clauses in each passage. Then answer the questions below. `10.10 A`

Traditional Foods

1. Tlacoyo, a Mexican treat <u>made with corn flour and stuffed with beans, potatoes, or mushrooms</u>, is an ancient food. The first Spaniards who came to Mexico wrote about buying tlacoyos from vendors selling them on the street. But the tlacoyos sold back then were healthier than the ones that are popular now because pre-Hispanic street vendors didn't grill them in oil.

2. Jiaozi is the Chinese name for dumplings, which are eaten throughout the year but are particularly important for holidays in northern China. Dumplings, consisting of dough filled with meat or vegetables, are usually boiled and can be served hot or cold.

3. Baklava is a dessert from the Middle East. It is prepared by spreading out layers of pastry dough separated with melted butter in a large pan and covering them with chopped nuts. After the pastry is baked, a syrup containing honey or rose water is poured over the pastry. At one time, baklava was a food that people ate only on special occasions, but nowadays, it is a popular dessert eaten year-round.

QUESTIONS

1. Which of the adjective clauses above are reduced?
2. Which sentences contain more than one full or reduced adjective clause?
3. Which are subject adjective clauses? Which are object adjective clauses?
4. Which are defining? Which are non-defining?
5. Which adjective clauses can be expressed in a different way (for example, with a different relative pronoun or no relative pronoun)? Does changing the adjective clause make it less or more formal?

35 | Using a More Formal Style Rewrite each sentence that contains an adjective clause in a more formal style. `10.10 A`

CLIMBING MOUNT EVEREST

Edmund Hillary and Tenzing Norgay

1. The first people that tried to climb Mount Everest weren't able to reach the top.

   The first people who tried to climb Mount Everest weren't able to reach the top.

2. There were strong winds that forced the first climbers back down the mountain.

3. Later climbers had oxygen they used to survive in the thin air.

4. In May of 1953, Tom Bourdillon and Charles Evans almost made it to the top. They described the route to the team members that would come after them the next day, Edmund Hillary and Tenzing Norgay.

5. Hillary and Norgay, who the information was very useful for, became the first climbers to reach the top of Everest.
6. Nowadays, reaching the top of Everest is an achievement many mountain climbers aspire to.
7. Falling ice, strong winds, and freezing temperatures are dangers on Mount Everest. But the biggest danger climbers face is the lack of oxygen.
8. Climbers that get injured are in serious trouble because they usually cannot be rescued.
9. There are many climbers that have set records on Everest, including the oldest and the youngest to reach the top (80 years old and 13 years old).
10. The Sherpas that climbers pay to carry their equipment up the mountain have a dangerous job.

36 | Identifying Adjective Clauses   Read these two paragraphs. Underline the full and reduced adjective clauses in the second paragraph.   `10.10 B`

San Francisco

A

San Francisco is a coastal city. It is surrounded by water on three sides. It is famous for its many hills. You can see San Francisco Bay and the Pacific Ocean from the hills. Alcatraz Island sits in the middle of the bay. It used to be a prison, but now it's a popular tourist destination. The famous Golden Gate Bridge spans the bay at its narrowest point. Everyone has seen pictures of the bridge. It is easily recognized by its orange color and elegant structure.

B

San Francisco is a coastal city <u>surrounded by water on three sides</u>. It is famous for its many hills, from which you can see San Francisco Bay and the Pacific Ocean. Alcatraz Island, sitting in the middle of the bay, used to be a prison but is now a popular tourist destination. The famous Golden Gate Bridge spans the bay at its narrowest point. Everyone has seen pictures of the bridge, which is easily recognized by its orange color and elegant structure.

Think about It Why does the second paragraph above sound better than the first?

37 | Connecting Ideas   Rewrite each paragraph. Use full and reduced adjective clauses to connect some of the ideas.   `10.10 B`

CALIFORNIA CITIES

1. Sebastopol is a small town. It is located in Northern California. The town has two main streets. They are lined with small shops. Most of them are small and locally owned. The town is a one-hour drive from San Francisco. It is home to many commuters[13]. They are willing to drive a long distance for the pleasure of living in a small town.

   Sebastopol is a small town located in Northern California. . . .

2. Visalia is a mid-sized town in Central California. It is rarely visited by tourists. It is a few miles off of the main highway. The highway leads to Fresno and the mountains of the Sierra Nevada. Visalia is surrounded by farmland. It is home to many farm laborers. The town is quiet and residential. There is a pleasant downtown. It has a busy farmers' market on the weekends.

Think about It Compare your version of each paragraph above with a partner's. Discuss the differences.

Write about It Write a paragraph about a city you are familiar with. Use three different kinds of adjective clauses.

---

[13] **commuters:** people who travel by bus, train, car, etc., from home to work every day

WRAP-UP Demonstrate Your Knowledge

A | GUESSING GAME Work with a partner to complete each statement with an adjective clause describing something or someone that you are both familiar with. Then meet with another pair and read your sentences. See if they can guess who or what you are describing.

1. This is a famous person who _____.

2. This is a TV show in which _____.

3. This is a date on which _____.

4. This is a place that _____.

5. This is a building that _____.

6. This is a writer who _____.

7. This is an athlete who _____.

8. This is a person to whom _____.

9. This is a person whose _____.

10. This is a food that _____.

B | SURVEY Work in a small group to complete these survey questions with adjective clauses. Use the questions to interview a classmate who is not in your group. Report back on your classmate's answers.

Questions	Answers
1. Tell me about one time _____ _____.	
2. Name one person _____ _____.	
3. What is something _____ _____?	
4. Have you ever done anything _____ _____?	
5. Name one book _____ _____.	
6. What is one place _____ _____?	
7. Name one animal _____ _____.	
8. What is one food _____ _____?	
9. What is one way _____ _____?	
10. What is one reason _____ _____?	

C | WEB SEARCH Do an online search for a famous person that you are interested in. Print a short passage about this person and underline the adjective clauses in it. For example:

Alexander the Great

Alexander founded 20 cities <u>that bore his name</u>, most notably Alexandria in Egypt. Alexander's settlement of Greece resulted in a new Hellenistic civilization, <u>which was still evident in the traditions of the Byzantine Empire in the mid-fifteenth century</u>. Alexander became legendary as a classical hero, and he features prominently in the history and myth of Greek and non-Greek cultures. He became the measure <u>against which military leaders compared themselves</u>, and military academies throughout the world still teach his tactics[14].

10.11 Summary of Adjective Clauses

DEFINING SUBJECT ADJECTIVE CLAUSE

	noun	relative pronoun (subject)	verb + rest of adjective clause	
	The **children**	who	spoke two languages at home	did well on the test.
Do you have	a **knife**	that	has a sharper edge?	
He said	**something**	that	sounded very strange.	
I talked to	a **man**	whose son	had climbed Mount Everest.	

NON-DEFINING SUBJECT ADJECTIVE CLAUSE

	noun	relative pronoun (subject)	
	The **governor,**	who brought up this issue in the first place,	wasn't at the meeting.
They stayed in	**Majorca,**	which is an island off the coast of Spain.	

REDUCED ADJECTIVE CLAUSE

	noun		
	Foods	containing a lot of salt	are not recommended.
We bought	**rice**	grown in Japan.	

DEFINING OBJECT ADJECTIVE CLAUSE

	noun	relative pronoun (subject)	subject + verb + rest of adjective clause	
	The **man**	(that / whom)	we met at the barbecue	was friendly.
Do you have	the **knife**	(that)	I lent you last month?	
I talked to	a **man**	whose son	I had met in China.	
	The **goal**	which	she had worked so hard for	was still out of reach.

		preposition + relative pronoun (object)	subject + verb + rest of adjective clause	
He talked about	the **teacher**	to whom	he was most grateful.	
	The **goal**	for which	she had worked so hard	was still out of reach.

NON-DEFINING OBJECT ADJECTIVE CLAUSE

	noun		
	Tina,	whom we have known all of our lives,	is a unique person.
We went to	**Bolivia,**	which we have never visited before.	

[14]**tactics:** the skillful arrangement and use of military forces in order to win a battle

11 Gerunds and *To-* Infinitives

Learning to write may be part of learning to read. For all I know, writing comes out of a superior devotion[1] to reading.

—EUDORA WELTY, AUTHOR

(1909–2001)

Talk about It Do you agree or disagree with the quotation above? Why?

[1] **devotion:** great love for something

WARM-UP

A | Match the beginnings and endings of the quotations. Then choose one quotation and tell a partner if you agree or disagree with it and why.

Famous Quotations

1. The point of **good writing** is __d__
2. **To teach** is ____
3. The only thing better than **singing** is ____
4. It's better **to be alone** than ____
5. **Reading** is to the mind ____
6. **To sing well** and **to dance well** is ____
7. The essential ingredient in politics is ____

a. in bad company. *(George Washington, U.S. president)*

b. **to learn twice over.** *(Joseph Joubert, writer)*

c. what exercise is to the body. *(Joseph Addison, writer)*

d. **knowing** when **to stop.** *(Lucy Montgomery, writer)*

e. **timing.** *(Pierre Trudeau, Canadian prime minister)*

f. **to be well educated.** *(Plato, philosopher)*

g. **more singing.** *(Ella Fitzgerald, jazz singer)*

B | The green phrases in the quotations above are gerunds. The blue phrases are *to-* infinitives. Based on the examples, are these statements true or false? Check (✓) your answers.

	TRUE	FALSE
1. Gerunds include an *-ing* form of a verb.	☐	☐
2. We always use a gerund before a verb.	☐	☐
3. A *to-* infinitive includes *to* + the base form of a verb.	☐	☐
4. We can use a gerund or a *to-* infinitive as the subject of a sentence.	☐	☐
5. We use both gerunds and *to-* infinitives in different ways in a sentence.	☐	☐

C | Look back at the quotation on page 354. Identify any gerunds or *to-* infinitives.

11.1 Overview of -*ing* Forms

A

	main verb	
1	Within seconds, Ann	**was sleeping**	soundly.

	adjective	
2	They took pictures of the	**sleeping child**.

	noun phrase	
3	I often say that	**sleeping**	is my favorite hobby.

	noun phrase	
4	I love	**taking a nap**	in the afternoon.

We can use the -*ing* form of a verb (e.g., *sleeping*, *taking*) in different ways in a sentence. For example, we can use it as:

- a **main verb**, as in **1**
- an **adjective**, as in **2**
- a kind of **noun phrase**, as in **3 – 4**

Remember: A noun phrase can be a single noun or pronoun or a group of words that includes a main noun.

For a list of spelling rules for the -*ing* form of verbs, see the Resources, page R-4.

B

	gerund as subject	
5	**Studying**	is a full-time job.

	gerund as object	
6	We just started	**studying**.

	gerund with possessive	
7	You're interfering with	**my studying**.

	gerund with prepositional phrase	
8	Are you worried about	**working with him?**

	gerund with object	
9	**Finding a good job**	isn't easy.

	gerund with expression of place	
10	Are you afraid of	**speaking in public?**

	gerund with *not* and expression of time	
11	I suggest	**not quitting before you have another job.**

	passive gerund	
12	She doesn't remember	**being hit by a car.**

When we use the -*ing* form of a verb as a kind of noun phrase, we call it a **gerund**. A gerund lets us talk about an action (a verb) like a thing (a noun phrase). Like a noun phrase, a gerund can appear:

- as the subject of a sentence, as in **5**
- as a kind of object, as in **6**
- with a determiner (such as a possessive), as in **7**
- with a prepositional phrase, as in **8**

Gerunds are also a bit like verb phrases. Like verb phrases, gerunds may include:

- a direct object, as in **9**
- an expression of place or time, as in **10 – 11**
- *not*, as in **11**
- a passive verb form, as in **12**

Charts 11.2–11.4 give more information about the different uses of gerunds.

GO ONLINE

1 | Noticing -*ing* Forms Underline the -*ing* forms of verbs in these sentences. Is the -*ing* form used as a main verb, as an adjective, or in a noun phrase? Check (✓) your answers. **11.1 A**

EXERCISE AND SPORTS	MAIN VERB	ADJECTIVE	NOUN PHRASE
1. <u>Swimming</u> is good exercise.	☐	☐	✓
2. Golf is not an especially exhausting sport.	☐	☐	☐
3. Setting a specific goal can help you stay with an exercise program.	☐	☐	☐
4. Playing on a sports team can build self-esteem[2].	☐	☐	☐
5. You burn about 8.5 calories a minute when you are running.	☐	☐	☐
6. Before they compete, most successful athletes try to avoid any distracting[3] thoughts.	☐	☐	☐

[2] **self-esteem:** a good opinion of yourself

[3] **distracting:** taking your attention away from something

	MAIN VERB	ADJECTIVE	NOUN PHRASE
7. You should stretch[4] frequently to keep your muscles from getting tight.	☐	☐	☐
8. Stretching before you exercise won't necessarily prevent sore muscles.	☐	☐	☐
9. Walking may be the perfect exercise. It's safe and simple and it doesn't require practice.	☐	☐	☐
10. If you dress properly, you can exercise even in the pouring rain.	☐	☐	☐
11. Many children today start specializing in one sport at an early age. This can lead to injuries.	☐	☐	☐
12. Most athletes regularly do exercises for building strength.	☐	☐	☐

Write about It Think of another gerund to use in sentences 1 to 4 in Activity 1.

Playing soccer is good exercise.

2 | Identifying Gerunds Which <u>underlined</u> gerunds are subjects and which are objects of verbs or prepositions? Write *S* over the subjects and *O* over the objects. **11.1 B**

Honesty in Friendships

In most situations, honesty is very important. <u>Having good relationships with people</u> [S] 1 is impossible when there is no trust.

Your friends and colleagues won't trust you if they think you are capable of <u>lying</u>. 2 However, <u>lying in certain situations</u> 3 may actually be good for a friendship. For example, a friend may have cooked a nice dinner for you, but the food doesn't taste very good. In this case, <u>saying the food is delicious</u> 4 causes less harm than <u>telling the truth</u> 5 does. And if you don't like a friend's new haircut, it's better to avoid <u>telling the truth</u>. 6 That would only hurt your friend's feelings.

In my opinion, <u>telling small lies in order to make other people feel good</u> 7 is OK, but <u>the telling of lies for personal gain</u> 8 is never appropriate.

> **F Y I**
>
> A gerund may be only the *-ing* form or a longer phrase including an *-ing* form.
>
> I like **working**.
>
> I don't like **his working late on weekends**.
>
> The entire phrase is a gerund.

Talk about It Do you agree with the writer of the text above? Why or why not? Tell your classmates.

Think about It Find an example of each of these types of gerunds in the text above. Then compare ideas with your classmates.

- one-word gerund
- gerund with an object   *having good relationships with people*
- gerund that begins with a determiner
- gerund with an expression of time or place

[4] **stretch:** to extend the body or parts of the body

11.2 Gerunds as Subjects; *Be* + Gerund

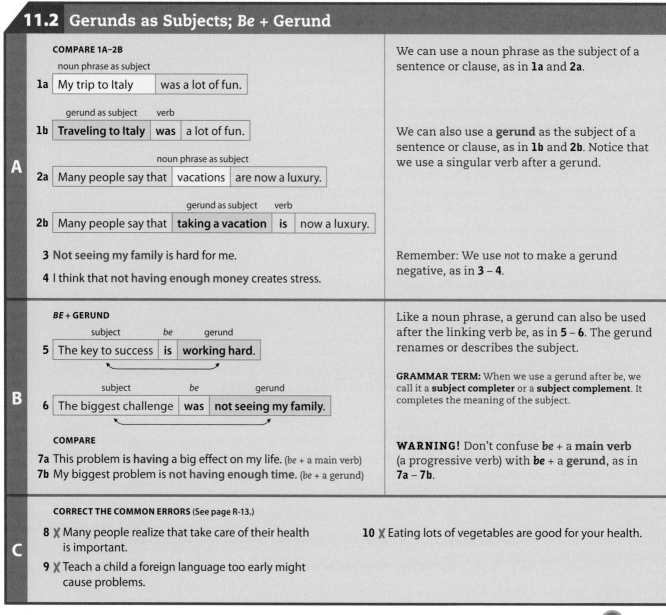

A

COMPARE 1A–2B

noun phrase as subject

1a | My trip to Italy | was a lot of fun.

gerund as subject   verb

1b | **Traveling to Italy** | **was** | a lot of fun.

noun phrase as subject

2a Many people say that | vacations | are now a luxury.

gerund as subject   verb

2b Many people say that | **taking a vacation** | **is** | now a luxury.

3 **Not seeing my family** is hard for me.

4 I think that **not having enough money** creates stress.

We can use a noun phrase as the subject of a sentence or clause, as in **1a** and **2a**.

We can also use a **gerund** as the subject of a sentence or clause, as in **1b** and **2b**. Notice that we use a singular verb after a gerund.

Remember: We use *not* to make a gerund negative, as in **3** – **4**.

B

***BE* + GERUND**

subject   *be*   gerund

5 | The key to success | **is** | **working hard.**

subject   *be*   gerund

6 | The biggest challenge | **was** | **not seeing my family.**

COMPARE

7a This problem **is having** a big effect on my life. (*be* + a main verb)

7b My biggest problem **is not having enough time.** (*be* + a gerund)

Like a noun phrase, a gerund can also be used after the linking verb *be*, as in **5** – **6**. The gerund renames or describes the subject.

GRAMMAR TERM: When we use a gerund after *be*, we call it a **subject completer** or a **subject complement**. It completes the meaning of the subject.

WARNING! Don't confuse *be* + a **main verb** (a progressive verb) with *be* + a **gerund**, as in **7a** – **7b**.

C

CORRECT THE COMMON ERRORS (See page R-13.)

8 ✗ Many people realize that take care of their health is important.

9 ✗ Teach a child a foreign language too early might cause problems.

10 ✗ Eating lots of vegetables are good for your health.

 GO ONLINE

3 | Using Gerunds as Subjects Use ideas from the boxes to complete each opinion with a gerund subject. (More than one answer may be possible.) **11.2 A**

OPINIONS FROM STUDENT ESSAYS

1. _____Voting_____ is an important responsibility of all citizens.

2. _____ is usually one of the most important events in a person's life.

3. _____ is the key to success in life.

4. _____ is bad for your health.

> do something you love
> feel a lot of stress
> get a first job
> vote

5. _____ has several benefits.

6. _____ can make a job better.

7. _____ requires patience and understanding.

8. _____ helps you learn about other cultures.

exercise regularly
have a good boss
live in different countries
raise children

9. _____ is usually unacceptable behavior.

10. _____ is one of the most important jobs a
person has.

11. _____ is a good way to exercise the brain.

12. _____ doesn't have to be boring.

be a parent
cook for yourself
learn a new language
lie

Write about It Think of a different way to begin each sentence in Activity 3. Use a gerund.

Paying taxes is an important responsibility of all citizens.

4 | Using *Not* + Gerund Complete each sentence below with three gerunds from the box. Then add another idea to complete each sentence. 11.2 A

exercising	not eating a lot of sweets	not smoking
going too fast	not listening in class	students' not participating in class
not coming to class on time	not paying attention to the road	talking on the phone while driving

1. a. _Going too fast_____ can cause a car accident.
   b. _____
   c. _____
   d. _____

2. a. _____ drives some teachers crazy.
   b. _____
   c. _____
   d. _____

3. a. _____ can help you stay healthy.
   b. _____
   c. _____
   d. _____

Talk about It Compare your answers above with a partner.

"I think going too fast while driving can cause a car accident."

5 | Be + Gerund or Be + Main Verb? Does each sentence use *be* + a gerund or *be* + a main verb? Circle *be* + a main verb. Underline *be* + a gerund. Then check (✓) your answers. `11.2 B`

	BE + GERUND	BE + MAIN VERB
1. My computer (was working) when I left home.	☐	✓
2. My last job <u>was working with computers</u>.	✓	☐
3. I don't know anyone who is working there.	☐	☐
4. Nothing is working.	☐	☐
5. My favorite way to spend time is working on old cars.	☐	☐
6. My dream is having a car of my own.	☐	☐
7. One common symptom[5] of the flu is having a fever.	☐	☐
8. Seek help if your child is having trouble with homework assignments.	☐	☐
9. The hard drive on my laptop is having problems.	☐	☐
10. The best part of my day is having dinner with my family.	☐	☐
11. My biggest problem is not having a place to study.	☐	☐
12. My problems are getting worse.	☐	☐
13. One of my goals is getting in shape.	☐	☐
14. I think the problem is getting worse.	☐	☐
15. My job is getting harder by the minute.	☐	☐
16. The next step is getting a job.	☐	☐
17. My hope is finding a good place to study.	☐	☐
18. My teacher is finding a good place for me to study.	☐	☐

6 | Using *Be* + Gerund Use gerunds to complete opinions 1 to 5. Then use topics of your choice and gerunds to complete opinions 6 to 10. `11.2 B`

OPINIONS ON MARRIAGE

1. The key to a successful marriage is _communicating with your husband or wife_____.
2. One common cause of arguments is _____.
3. The most difficult thing about marriage is _____.
4. The easiest thing about marriage is _____.
5. The most rewarding thing about marriage is _____.

YOUR OPINIONS

6. The key to _____ is _____.
7. One common cause of _____ is _____.
8. The most difficult thing about _____ is _____.
9. The easiest thing about _____ is _____.
10. The most rewarding thing about _____ is _____.

Talk about It Read your opinions above to a partner. See if your partner agrees or disagrees and why.

---

[5] **symptom:** a sign; something that shows you have an illness

7 | Distinguishing Subjects and Subject Completers Underline the gerunds in this paragraph. Write *S* over the subjects and *SC* over the subject completers. `11.2 A–B`

Irritating[6] Habits Drive Co-Workers Crazy

A third of workers would quit a job because of the irritating behavior of their co-workers, according to a new survey. Examples of annoying behavior

were <u>listening to voicemails on speakerphone</u>, swearing[7] at

SC

computers, and receiving emails from someone who sits nearby. Of the 2,318 people surveyed, 32 percent said that talking loudly was the most annoying behavior. Twenty-two percent said that talking on a speakerphone was the No. 1 pet peeve[8]. Other irritating behaviors were not cleaning up after yourself, bringing strong-smelling food for lunch, and taking things without permission.

> **F Y I**
>
> We sometimes use gerunds in a series. Notice that we use a plural verb when we use more than one gerund as a subject or subject completer.
>
> **Eating well, exercising frequently,** and **getting enough sleep lead to** good health.

Think about It What other *-ing* forms do you see in the text above? Do they function as adjectives or main verbs?

Write about It List the eight irritating behaviors above in order from most irritating (1) to least irritating (8), in your opinion. Then compare ideas with your classmates.

8 | Error Correction Correct any errors in these sentences. (Some sentences may not have any errors.)

1. Came to this country was a dream come true.
2. I don't think that get a lot of money is a good goal.
3. Attending a university help people to get a better job.
4. My father was visiting me when I got sick.
5. The worst thing about it was looked for a place to live.
6. I think that study was an important part of the job.
7. Carrying on a conversation in English is really hard for me.
8. My favorite thing is meet my friends after class.
9. Go to school together is good for girls and boys.

---

[6] **irritating:** annoying
[7] **swearing:** cursing; using bad language

[8] **pet peeve:** something that bothers you

11.3 Gerunds as Objects of Verbs and Prepositions

A

COMPARE 1A–1B

verb	noun phrase as object
1a	I just	**started**	that book.

verb	gerund as object
1b	I just	**started**	reading that book.

2 My boss never **stopped** talking. (Stopped what?)

3 I **miss** seeing my family. (Miss what?)

4 My generation is probably the last one that **remembers not having the Internet in high school.** (Remembers what?)

We can use a noun phrase as the object of a verb, as in **1a**. Like a noun phrase, a **gerund** can also function as the object of certain verbs, as in **1b**.

GRAMMAR TERM: A gerund used as an object of a verb is also called a **verb completer** or a **verb complement**.

The gerund answers the question *what*, as in **2 – 4**. Common one-word verbs followed by gerunds include:

begin	dislike	keep	quit	start
continue	finish	miss	remember	stop

For a list of common verbs followed by gerunds, see the Resources, page R-8.

B

COMPARE 5A–5B

preposition	noun phrase
5a	I left home	**without**	any money.

preposition	gerund
5b	I left home	**without**	eating breakfast.

6 I'm angry with her **for leaving without saying goodbye.**

7 I decided **on not getting a Facebook account.**

8 Videoconferencing is a useful way **of holding a meeting.**

9 The president is responsible **for preparing the budget.**

Like a noun phrase, a gerund can also be used as the object of a preposition, as in **5**.

The gerund answers the question *what*, as in **6 – 9**.

GO ONLINE

---

9 | Using Verbs + Gerunds Complete these sentences with the verbs in parentheses. Use the correct form of the first verb and the *-ing* form of the second verb. **11.3 A**

DEFINITIONS OF PEOPLE

1. An extrovert is someone who _____*enjoys being*_____ around other people. (enjoy/be)

2. An introvert is someone who _____ too much time with other people. (dislike/spend)

3. A couch potato is someone who _____ on the couch all day. (enjoy/sit)

4. A workaholic is someone who can't _____. (stop/work)

5. A homebody is someone who _____ time at home. (prefer/spend)

6. A spendthrift is someone who _____ money. (love/spend)

7. A procrastinator is someone who _____ what he or she needs to do. (postpone/do)

8. A health nut is someone who _____ unhealthy food. (hate/eat)

9. A globetrotter is someone who _____ around the world. (enjoy/travel)

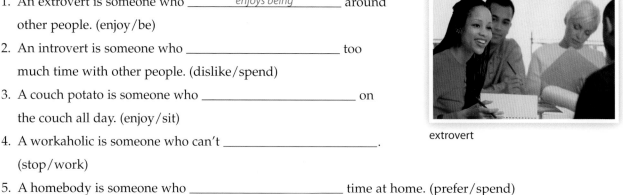

extrovert

10. A control freak is someone who can't _____ in charge. (stand/not be)

11. A slob is someone who doesn't _____ in a messy house. (mind/live)

12. A blabbermouth is someone who can't _____ a secret. (resist/tell)

13. A worrywart is someone who can't _____. (stop/worry)

Write about It Which words in Activity 9 describe you? Why?

I'm an extrovert because I enjoy being around other people. I'm also a worrywart because . . .

10 | Using Verbs + Gerunds Think about your childhood. Use gerunds after the **bold** verbs to write answers to these questions. 11.3 A

TALKING ABOUT YOUR CHILDHOOD

1. What are two things you **enjoyed** doing as a child?

   I enjoyed drawing pictures and eating ice cream.

2. What are two things you **disliked** doing in school?
3. What are two things you **hated** doing as a child?
4. What is something you **regret** doing as a child?
5. What are two things you **regret** not doing when you were younger?
6. What is something you **practiced** doing when you were a child?

Talk about It Ask a partner the questions above. Then tell the class two things about your partner.

"Alberto disliked taking tests in school. He also hated cleaning his room."

11 | Using Prepositions + Gerunds Complete each sentence with the preposition *by, instead of, without,* or *upon.* 11.3 B

Greeting Customs

1. In many countries, people greet each other _____*by*_____ shaking hands.
2. In some cultures, people kiss on the cheeks _____ shaking hands.
3. In some countries, people shake hands _____ taking your hand in both of their hands.
4. Americans sometimes greet people at a distance _____ waving.
5. In some cultures, strangers welcome each other _____ embracing and then rubbing each other's back.
6. It's rude to walk past a friend _____ saying hello.
7. In France, people often kiss each other on both cheeks _____ meeting and leaving.
8. People don't usually leave _____ saying goodbye.

Talk about It What other greeting customs are you familiar with? Tell your classmates.

12 | Usage Note: Common Preposition Combinations Read the note. Then do Activities 13 and 14.

Certain verbs and adjectives are used regularly with specific prepositions. The two words function as a single unit. We can use a gerund after these word combinations.

VERB + PREPOSITION + GERUND

1 I'm **depending on** your helping me with this.
2 I wouldn't **think of** lying.

ADJECTIVE + PREPOSITION + GERUND

3 Are you **worried about** not passing the test?
4 I'm **tired of** doing this.

Nouns such as *possibility*, *chance*, *idea*, and *way* identify a general category of things. After these nouns, we sometimes use *of* + a **gerund** to give more details.

NOUN + *OF* + GERUND

5 We would like to discuss **the possibility of** using a different system.
6 She has **a 50 percent chance of** getting better.

For a list of common verbs + prepositions, adjectives + prepositions, and nouns + *of* that can be followed by gerunds, see the Resources, pages R-7 and R-8.

13 | Using a Verb + Preposition + Gerund Read each direct quote. Then use a gerund with a similar meaning to complete the sentence and explain what happened. (More than one answer may be possible.) `11.3 B`

REPORTING INFORMATION

1. "Sorry I'm late," said David.

   David **apologized for** _being late_.

2. "I'm always afraid I won't get to school on time," said Amanda.

   Amanda **worries about** _____.

3. "I still have Tom's book," said James. "I'm sorry. I forgot."

   James **forgot about** _____.

4. "We're going to New York tomorrow. I can't wait," said Anna.

   Anna **is looking forward to** _____.

5. "I don't want to do anything today. Let's just stay home," said Ava.

   Ava **feels like** _____.

6. "I'm just too hot. I can't study," said Kate.

   Kate **complained about** _____.

7. "I have to go with Nick. I just have to," cried John.

   John **insisted on** _____.

8. "I was supposed to visit my uncle this weekend, but I had to change the date until later," said Matt.

   Matt **put off** _____.

9. "I got the job," said Rob.

   Rob **succeeded in** _____.

10. "I might go home, but I'm not sure," explained Carlos.

    Carlos **is thinking about** _____.

11. "I can't finish the report tonight. It's not worth trying," said Mary.

    Mary **gave up on** _____.

STUDY STRATEGY

Because some verbs + prepositions are always used together, it helps to learn the words together. Keep a list of the verbs with their required prepositions and a sample sentence.

apologize for

He **apologized for** eating all of the ice cream.

12. "I forgot to check my calendar this morning, so I missed a doctor's appointment," said Toshi.

   Toshi **ended up** _____.

13. "I always make the same mistake on tests," said Sam.

   Sam **keeps on** _____.

Write about It Choose five of the **bold** verb + preposition combinations in Activity 13, and write your own sentences. Use a gerund in each sentence. (You can change the form of the bold verb.)

I never feel like getting up in the morning.

14 | Using an Adjective or a Noun + Preposition + Gerund Complete each quotation with an adjective + preposition or a noun + preposition. (More than one answer may be possible, but only one matches the original quotation.) `11.3 B`

ADJECTIVE + PREPOSITION						
afraid of	afraid of	good at	important in	interested in	responsible for	tired of

1. I'm pretty _____*good at*_____ remaining calm. (*Anne Hathaway, actor*)

2. There is nothing more _____ making movies than the screenplay.
   (*Richard Attenborough, actor*)

3. A champion is _____ losing. Everyone else is _____
   winning. (*Billie Jean King, athlete*)

4. The individual person is _____ living his own life and for "finding himself."
   (*Thomas Merton, clergyman*)

5. I'm more _____ enjoying my life and looking after my family than being hugely
   successful. (*James D'Arcy, actor*)

6. I never get _____ hearing compliments. (*John Lithgow, actor*)

NOUN + PREPOSITION			
chance of	idea of	possibility of	way of

7. Science is a _____ thinking much more than it is a body of knowledge.
   (*Carl Sagan, scientist*)

8. Without the faintest _____ finding a job, I decided to devote myself to literature.
   (*José Saramago, writer*)

9. Children born today have a 50–50 _____ living to 100. (*William Greider, writer*)

10. I toyed with[9] the _____ pursuing a career as a lawyer just because I like to
    argue. (*Lexa Doig, actor*)

Write about It Choose two of the adjective + preposition combinations and two of the noun + *of* combinations above, and write your own sentences.

My sister is afraid of flying in airplanes.

---

[9]**toy with:** to think about something, but not seriously

15 | Using Gerunds as Objects Use the *-ing* form of the verbs in the box to complete the article below. (More than one answer may be possible.) Then listen and check your answers. **11.3 A–B**

| attend | become | create | develop | improve | receive | study | work |

JONAS SALK 1914–1995

Jonas Salk is among the most admired medical scientists of the twentieth century. He initially planned on _____becoming_____ a lawyer, but he became
1

interested in _____ biology and chemistry and ended up
2

_____ New York University medical school. There, in 1938, he
3

began _____ with the scientist Thomas Francis, Jr., who was
4

looking for a flu vaccine. Together they developed a flu vaccine for the army to use during World War II.

In 1947, Salk became the head of the Virus Research Lab at the University of Pittsburgh. He felt the flu vaccine could be better, so he concentrated

on _____ it. He also began to study the poliovirus with hopes
5

of _____ a vaccine against polio as well. With help from the
6

research of many other scientists, Salk succeeded in _____ a
7

polio vaccine. In 1952, he vaccinated his first volunteers, including himself, his wife, and their three sons. No one became ill, and in that same year,

thousands of children started _____ the polio vaccine.
8

Talk about It Work with a group of students. Close your books, and list as many facts as you can remember about Jonas Salk. See which group can remember the most information.

16 | Error Correction Correct any errors in these paragraphs.

1. Advertise is everywhere. Wherever we go for news or entertainment, we see advertisements. These ads make us think we need things that we don't really need. I used to pay attention to ads, and sometimes I would even consider to buy the product. Eventually I got tired to see so many ads, and I stopped watch television and listen to the radio. Now I think there should be a law against show ads in public places.

2. Anger is an appropriate response in certain situations. If treated unfairly, for example, is a good reason for feel anger. Examine why you are angry and then take appropriate action is a good way to get a positive result from becoming angry or upset. In fact, suppress anger can be harmful to your health.

3. Do what you love is the key to success. No matter how hard you working, your success depends on do what you love. When you love your job, you are totally committed to do your best. You won't mind work extra hard when something difficult gets in your way.

11.4 Passive Gerunds

A

COMPARE 1A–1B

active form of gerund

1a | I enjoyed | driving around town. |

(= I drove around town and I enjoyed it.)

passive form of gerund

1b | I enjoyed | being driven around town. |

(= I was driven around town and I enjoyed it.)

2 I remember **being bitten by a dog** when I was 6.
(= I was bitten by a dog and I remember it.)

3 I don't like **being told lies**.
(= Sometimes I am told lies and I don't like it.)

4 The meeting kept on **being postponed**.
(= Somebody kept on postponing the meeting.)

Some gerunds can have an active form and a **passive form**, as in **1a – 1b**.

The most common passive form we use is **being** + a **past participle**, as in **1b**. (Remember: The past participle may be an *-ed/-en* form or an irregular form.)

We use a passive form when we want to focus on what happens rather than the person or thing that performs the action, as in **2 – 4**.

For a list of past participles of irregular verbs, see the Resources, page R-3.

B

COMPARE USES OF *BEING*

5a He **isn't being** honest.
5b She **was being** silly.

5c He **is being treated** for an infection.
5d I **wasn't being told** the truth.

5e My brother apologized for **being late**.
5f I remember **being told that story**.

Remember: We can use the word **being** in different ways in a sentence, as in **5a – 5f**. *Being* can be:

• a main verb in a progressive form, as in **5a – 5b**

• a helping verb in a passive form, as in **5c – 5d**

• an active form of a gerund, as in **5e**

• a passive form of a gerund, as in **5f**

 GO ONLINE

---

17 | Using Passive Gerunds
Complete each restatement with a passive gerund form (*being* + past participle) of the **bold** verb. `11.4 A`

1. People are always **telling** me what to do.
   I hate that.
   I hate _____*being told*_____ what to do.

2. I don't like it when people **laugh** at me.
   I don't like _____ at.

3. I love it when people **invite** me to dinner.
   I love _____ to dinner.

4. People sometimes **ignore** me. I don't like that.
   I don't like _____.

5. My sister is always **making** me feel guilty.
   I'm tired of it.
   I'm tired of _____ to feel guilty.

6. I don't like it when people **misunderstand** me.
   I don't like _____.

7. Sometimes people **call** me too early. I don't appreciate that.
   I don't appreciate _____ too early.

8. My brother always **asks** to me to drive when we are going someplace.
   I don't appreciate _____ to drive all the time.

9. When I was a child, people **told** me I was a good athlete. I liked that.
   When I was a child, I liked _____ I was a good athlete.

10. When I was a teenager, my parents wouldn't **allow** me to go out in the evening. I hated that.
    When I was a teenager, I hated not
    _____ to go out in the evening.

Write about It Complete these sentences with passive gerunds and your own ideas.

I like being . . .   *I don't like being . . .*

18 | Passive Gerunds Check (✓) the sentences that have a passive gerund and underline the form. **11.4 B**

1. ☐ a. She is being treated like a child.

   ☑ b. Most people don't like <u>being treated like a child</u>.

2. ☐ a. Stop throwing things at me. I don't like being used as target practice.

   ☐ b. Most people hope that their tax dollars are being used wisely.

3. ☐ a. He's afraid of being hurt again.

   ☐ b. Why did they stop the game? Nobody was being hurt.

4. ☐ a. Am I being punished for something?

   ☐ b. My being punished for this isn't fair.

5. ☐ a. I don't like being called ridiculous.

   ☐ b. She is being ridiculous.

6. ☐ a. I apologized for being mean.

   ☐ b. I don't appreciate being made fun of.

7. ☐ a. Don't worry. The arrangements are being made.

   ☐ b. I'm not happy about being made to do all the work.

8. ☐ a. Their son won't do anything without being told.

   ☐ b. We were just being told the news when he called us.

Think about It How is *being* used in the sentences that you did NOT check above?

- as a main verb in a progressive form
- as a helping verb in a passive form
- as part of an active form of a gerund

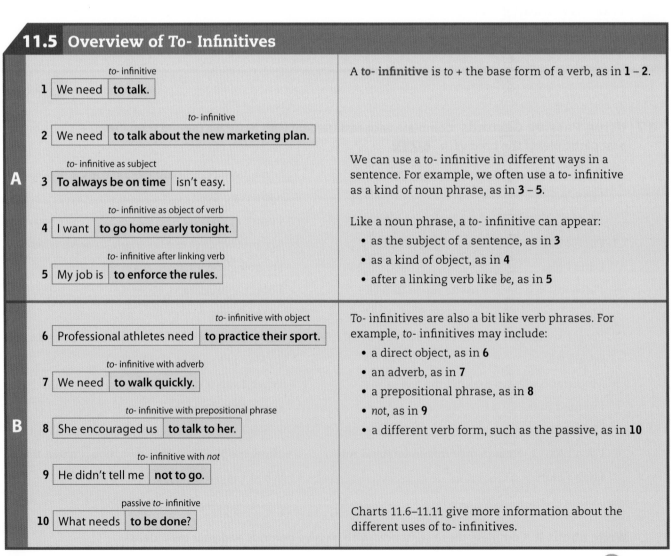

11.5 Overview of *To-* Infinitives

A

to- infinitive
1 | We need | **to talk.**

to- infinitive
2 | We need | **to talk about the new marketing plan.**

to- infinitive as subject
3 | **To always be on time** | isn't easy.

to- infinitive as object of verb
4 | I want | **to go home early tonight.**

to- infinitive after linking verb
5 | My job is | **to enforce the rules.**

A **to- infinitive** is *to* + the base form of a verb, as in **1 – 2**.

We can use a *to-* infinitive in different ways in a sentence. For example, we often use a *to-* infinitive as a kind of noun phrase, as in **3 – 5**.

Like a noun phrase, a *to-* infinitive can appear:
- as the subject of a sentence, as in **3**
- as a kind of object, as in **4**
- after a linking verb like *be*, as in **5**

B

to- infinitive with object
6 | Professional athletes need | **to practice their sport.**

to- infinitive with adverb
7 | We need | **to walk quickly.**

to- infinitive with prepositional phrase
8 | She encouraged us | **to talk to her.**

to- infinitive with *not*
9 | He didn't tell me | **not to go.**

passive *to-* infinitive
10 | What needs | **to be done?**

To- infinitives are also a bit like verb phrases. For example, *to-* infinitives may include:
- a direct object, as in **6**
- an adverb, as in **7**
- a prepositional phrase, as in **8**
- *not*, as in **9**
- a different verb form, such as the passive, as in **10**

Charts 11.6–11.11 give more information about the different uses of to- infinitives.

19 | Noticing *To-* Infinitives Which underlined *to-* infinitives are subjects and which are objects of verbs? Write *S* over the subjects and *O* over the objects. [11.5 A–B]

If You Could Visit Any Country in the World for Two Weeks, Where Would You Want to Go?

1. If I could visit any country in the world,
   I would choose <u>to visit Poland</u>. [*O*] I want
   <u>to visit Poland</u> because my grandparents
   grew up there. I would like <u>to see their</u>
   <u>home and meet my relatives there.</u> I also
   want <u>to learn more about the culture</u>
   <u>and history of Poland.</u>

2. If I could go anywhere in the world for two weeks, I would choose <u>to go</u>
   <u>to Iran.</u> My family is from Iran and I have always wanted <u>to go there.</u>
   <u>To stay in Iran for two weeks</u> would be a dream come true for me.

3. I have always wanted <u>to go to Japan.</u> To me, everything about Japan is
   interesting—the music, the food, the customs. I really want <u>to learn the</u>
   <u>language, too.</u> I would actually prefer <u>not to travel with a friend or family</u>
   <u>member.</u> By traveling alone, I think I would meet people more easily.

Think about It Based on the sentences above, is it more common to use a *to-* infinitive as a subject or object?

Think about It Find all these types of *to-* infinitives in the text above, and write them in this chart. Then compare ideas with your classmates.

To- infinitive with an object	*To-* infinitive with a prepositional phrase	*To-* infinitive with an adverb	*To-* infinitive with *not*
to visit Poland			

Write about It If you could go anywhere in the world for two weeks, where would you choose to go? Why? Write several sentences.

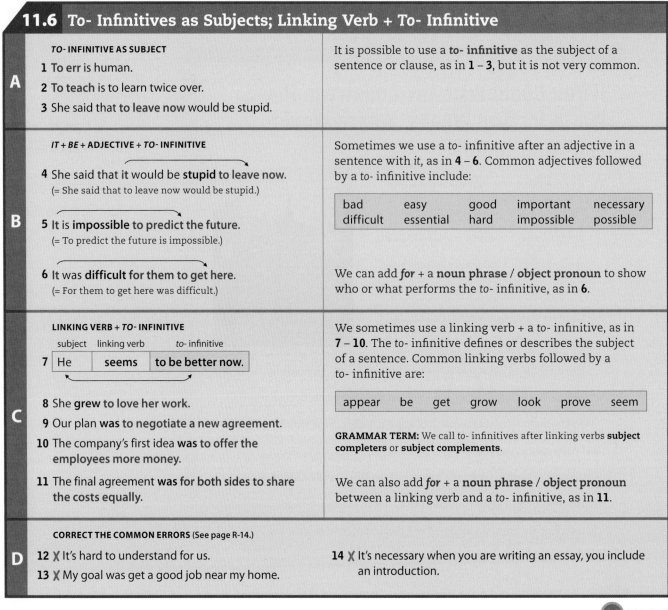

11.6 To- Infinitives as Subjects; Linking Verb + To- Infinitive

A

TO- INFINITIVE AS SUBJECT

1 To err is human.

2 To teach is to learn twice over.

3 She said that **to leave now** would be stupid.

It is possible to use a *to*- infinitive as the subject of a sentence or clause, as in **1 – 3**, but it is not very common.

B

IT + BE + ADJECTIVE + TO- INFINITIVE

4 She said that **it** would be **stupid** **to leave now**.
(= She said that to leave now would be stupid.)

5 **It** is **impossible** **to predict the future**.
(= To predict the future is impossible.)

6 **It** was **difficult** **for them to get here**.
(= For them to get here was difficult.)

Sometimes we use a *to*- infinitive after an adjective in a sentence with *it*, as in **4 – 6**. Common adjectives followed by a *to*- infinitive include:

bad	easy	good	important	necessary
difficult	essential	hard	impossible	possible

We can add *for* + a **noun phrase / object pronoun** to show who or what performs the *to*- infinitive, as in **6**.

C

LINKING VERB + TO- INFINITIVE

subject	linking verb	*to*- infinitive
7 He	seems	to be better now.

8 She **grew to love her work**.

9 Our plan **was to negotiate a new agreement**.

10 The company's first idea **was to offer the employees more money**.

11 The final agreement **was for both sides to share the costs equally**.

We sometimes use a linking verb + a *to*- infinitive, as in **7 – 10**. The *to*- infinitive defines or describes the subject of a sentence. Common linking verbs followed by a *to*- infinitive are:

appear	be	get	grow	look	prove	seem

GRAMMAR TERM: We call *to*- infinitives after linking verbs **subject completers** or **subject complements**.

We can also add *for* + a **noun phrase / object pronoun** between a linking verb and a *to*- infinitive, as in **11**.

D

CORRECT THE COMMON ERRORS (See page R-14.)

12 ✗ It's hard to understand for us.

13 ✗ My goal was get a good job near my home.

14 ✗ It's necessary when you are writing an essay, you include an introduction.

20 | Choosing *To*- Infinitive Subjects Match the sentence beginnings with the sentence endings. (More than one answer may be possible but only one is correct.) Then compare with a partner. `11.6 A`

PROVERBS

1. To be rich ____
2. To deny everything ____
3. To lend [money] ____
4. To talk without thinking ____
5. To be brave from a distance ____
6. To teach ____
7. To travel hopefully ____

a. is to shoot without aiming. *(English proverb)*
b. is to buy a quarrel¹⁰. *(Indian proverb)*
c. isn't everything, but it certainly helps. *(anonymous)*
d. is easy. *(Aesop)*
e. is a better thing than to arrive. *(Robert Louis Stevenson, writer)*
f. is to confess everything. *(Spanish proverb)*
g. is to learn. *(Japanese proverb)*

Write about It Think of a different way to complete each proverb above.

To be rich doesn't mean you are happy.

¹⁰**quarrel:** argument; disagreement

21 | Using *It* + *Be* + Adjective + *To*- Infinitive Choose the best adjective in parentheses to complete each sentence. Then compare with your classmates. `11.6 B`

OPINIONS FROM STUDENT ESSAYS

1. It's _____ to be rich.
   (important / not important)

2. It's _____ to listen to other people.
   (important / not important)

3. It's _____ to know about the past.
   (helpful / unhelpful)

4. When something makes you angry, it's _____ to stay calm.
   (useful / useless)

5. It is _____ to have a brother or sister than to be an only child.
   (better / worse)

6. Today it's _____ for young people to study in other countries.
   (common / uncommon)

7. It used to be _____ to work for the same company your whole life.
   (common / uncommon)

8. Five hundred years ago, it was very _____ to cross the ocean in a boat.
   (dangerous / safe)

9. With a cell phone, it's _____ for me to stay in touch with my friends.
   (easy / difficult)

10. It's _____ to cook something from scratch[11] than heat up a frozen pizza.
    (easier / more difficult)

11. It is _____ to have a good relationship with someone when there is no trust.
    (impossible / possible)

12. It's _____ for high school students to start planning for their future before they graduate.
    (bad / good)

> **FYI**
>
> In these situations, *it* is a placeholder for the subject. This allows us to put new information at the end of a sentence where it is easier to notice.

Write about It Write six opinions using these adjectives and *to*- infinitives. (Many different sentences are possible.) Read your sentences to a partner. See if your partner agrees or disagrees.

I think it's	dangerous difficult good important impossible useful	to be to have to know to make to take to understand to use	_____.

I think it's important to have a job you enjoy.

22 | Noticing Linking Verbs + *To*- Infinitives Circle the linking verbs in these sentences. Underline the *to*- infinitives. `11.6 C`

1. Running my own business (was) difficult at first, but it soon (proved) <u>to be a lot of fun</u>.

2. I didn't make any noise because he seemed to be asleep.

3. I thought she would be nervous but she seemed to be very calm.

4. It's not an idea that proved to be correct.

5. Something appears to be wrong.

6. Over the years, they grew to be close friends.

7. We grew to love our new home.

> **FYI**
>
> Some linking verbs describe or rename the subject: *appear, be, seem*.
>
> Some other linking verbs identify the result of a change: *become, get, grow, prove*.

[11] **from scratch:** making something yourself from the beginning

8. All I need is for you to do the dishes.

9. Their household grew to include four generations.

10. The best advice I ever received was to always tell the truth.

11. My childhood dream was to become a famous photographer.

12. One of my goals is to learn several languages.

Think about It Based on the examples in Activity 22, what other types of words can follow a linking verb?

Write about It Complete these sentences with your own ideas.

When I was a child, my dream was to . . .   One of my goals is to . . .
Over time I grew to . . .   The best advice I ever received was to . . .
All I really need is to . . .   My first year in school proved to . . .

23 | Using Linking Verbs + *To-* Infinitives Complete these restatements. Use *was* + a *to-* infinitive.

`11.6 C`

BUSINESS ISSUES

1. The company hoped to make a profit, but it didn't.

   The company's hope *was to make a profit but it didn't*   .

2. The owner advised the managers to come up with a plan.

   The owner's advice _____ for the managers _____.

3. The managers planned to lay off[12] 20 percent of the employees.

   The managers' plan _____.

4. The employees decided to go on strike[13].

   The employees' decision _____.

5. The owner threatened to close the company.

   The owner's threat _____.

6. The lawyer advised the employees to talk to the owner.

   The lawyer's advice _____ for the employees _____.

7. It was agreed to sit down and discuss the problem.

   The agreement _____.

8. Everyone hoped to come up with a better solution.

   Everyone's hope _____.

Write about It Complete these sentences with information about yourself. Use *to-* infinitives.

My last big decision was . . .   One of my worst decisions was . . .

24 | Error Correction Correct any errors in these sentences. (Some sentences may not have any errors.)

1. Everything I tried seemed making things worse.

2. It is difficult to live on one income for many families. In many households, both the husband and the wife need to work. Under these circumstances, it can be difficult for to take care of the children.

3. My plan for saving money was stop eating out in restaurants.

---

[12] **lay off:** to stop giving work to someone because there is not enough to do

[13] **go on strike:** to stop working because you want something from your employer

4. It is better to have brothers and sisters than be an only child. I say this because I am an only child, and I didn't like not having a sibling.

5. It normal to feel afraid when your life is in danger. If you don't want to get hurt, you should pay attention to your feelings.

6. It is impossible have a good relationship with someone you don't trust. It's necessary in a relationship, you be honest with each other.

11.7 To- Infinitives as Objects

A

1 I **need** to speak to you.
2 They **forgot** to go.
3 Please close the door. We're **trying** to study.

4 Do you **promise** not to tell?
5 We **decided** not to go.

We can use a **to- infinitive** as the object after certain verbs, as in **1 – 3**. Remember: We use *not* to make a to- infinitive negative, as in **4 – 5**.

For a list of common verbs followed by *to-* infinitives, see the Resources, page R-8.

GRAMMAR TERM: An infinitive used as an object of a verb is also called a **verb completer** or a **verb complement**.

B

COMPARE

6a They **expect** to visit. (They are going to visit.)
6b They **expect** us to visit. (We are going to visit.)

7a The story **proved** to be untrue.
7b They **proved** his story to be untrue.

With some verbs, we can (but don't have to) use a **noun phrase / object pronoun** before the to- infinitive, as in **6b** and **7b**. For example:

ask	expect	need	promise	want

8 My parents **encouraged** me to become a doctor.

9 I **warned** my brother not to go in the water.

A few verbs must use a noun phrase or pronoun before the *to-* infinitive, as in **8 – 9**. For example:

advise	help	persuade	teach	urge
encourage	order	remind	tell	warn

10 The school **arranged** for a bus to pick us up.

11 I can't **wait** for the concert to start.

A few verbs can be followed by *for* + a **noun phrase / object pronoun** + to- infinitive, as in **10 – 11**. For example:

arrange	ask	love	pay	wait	wish

C

WH- WORD + TO- INFINITIVE

12 I didn't **know** what to do.
   (= I didn't know the thing that I should do.)
13 He **explained** how to get there.
   (= He explained the way that we could get there.)
14 Do you **know** where to go?
   (= Do you know the place where we should go?)

15 Can you **show** me how to use this?
16 Did she **tell** the driver when to be there?

After certain verbs, we sometimes use a **wh- word** + a **to- infinitive**, as in **12 – 14**. This is a shorter and more informal way to express phrases like *the thing that*, *the way that*, or *the place where*. Common verbs include:

ask	explain	know	remember	wonder
decide	forget	learn	understand	

We can also use a **noun phrase / object pronoun** + a *wh-* word + a *to-*infinitive after certain verbs such as *ask, advise, show, teach,* and *tell,* as in **15 – 16**.

D

CORRECT THE COMMON ERRORS (See page R-14.)

17 ✗ She wants finish her work and watch TV.
18 ✗ He wanted the children worked harder.

19 ✗ I will teach you know how to play the piano.
20 ✗ My parents encouraged me about coming here.

25 | Using Verbs + *To-* Infinitives Complete these conversations with the correct form of a verb from the box. (More than one answer may be possible.) Then practice with a partner. `11.7 A`

1. A: Do you _____ to be home by 9?

   B: Yes, yes. I'll be back by then.

2. A: This is heavy! How did you _____ to get it here by yourself?

   B: I didn't. Hassan helped me.

3. A: Where did you _____ to do that?

   B: What?

   A: Erase everything like that.

   B: Pretty neat, huh? I taught myself.

4. A: Did you _____ to help Sarah?

   B: No, she asked me for help.

5. A: How's David?

   B: He _____ to be better.

| learn |
| manage |
| offer |
| promise |
| seem |

6. A: How long do you _____ to be here?

   B: Oh, until about 3.

7. A: Where's my magazine?

   B: I gave it to Isabel.

   A: To Isabel? Why? She won't _____ to read it.

   B: Probably not. But maybe she'll look at the cartoons.

8. A: I hear Khalid is in trouble at work. What's going on?

   B: Well, now that he's married, he _____ to travel. His boss isn't very happy about it.

9. A: How long have you worked here?

   B: More years than I _____ to remember.

10. A: Ouch! You just stepped on my foot.

    B: Sorry, I didn't _____ to do it.

| bother |
| care |
| mean |
| plan |
| refuse |

26 | Using Verbs + *To-* Infinitives Choose a *to-* infinitive from the box to complete each sentence below. (More than one answer may be possible.) `11.7 A`

to be	to learn	to lose	to read	to stop
to get	to live	to make	to ride	to take

NEW YEAR'S RESOLUTIONS

1. This year I plan _____ organized. I can never find anything and I don't want _____ this way.

2. I haven't been reading enough books, so I decided _____ a book a month. And I really mean _____ my bike more often and _____ about 20 pounds.

3. I've started a new business, so I want my business _____ successful in the new year.

4. This year I want _____ to play my guitar really well. I hope _____ lessons and join a band.

5. This year I intend _____ buying shoes online.

6. I've had a lot of resolutions in the past, and mostly I don't follow through on them. So, this year I've resolved not _____ any resolutions.

Talk about It What plans or resolutions have you made in the past? Tell your classmates.

27 | Using a Verb + Noun Phrase + *To-* Infinitive Read each conversation. Then complete the sentence to explain what happened in each conversation. 11.7 B

1. John: It's late. Don't you think you should go to bed?

   John's son: Yeah, I guess so.

   John **advised** *his son to go to bed* _____.

2. Amanda: I don't want you to leave the house today. Do you hear me?

   Matt: Yeah, Mom. I won't. I promise.

   Matt **promised** _____.

3. Rob: Do you think you can help me tomorrow?

   James: Sure. What do you need me to do?

   Rob: I just need someone to move some furniture.

   Rob **asked** _____.

4. Mika: Don't forget to put some gas in the car.

   Toshi: Right, yeah. Thanks for reminding me.

   Mika **reminded** _____.

5. Sun-Hee: Are you going to drive there?

   Sarah: Yeah, why?

   Sun-Hee: I wouldn't if I were you. The roads are really icy.

   Sun-Hee **warned** _____.

6. Sam: You should go with me. It'll be fun.

   Hassan: Really?

   Sam: Yeah. You'll love it.

   Sam **encouraged** _____.

7. Asad: When do you think you'll get back to school?

   Khalid: By Friday, I'm sure.

   Asad: That's great. I can't wait.

   Asad **can't wait** _____.

8. Isabel: I called Sarah and she's going to meet you for coffee tomorrow.

   Carla: Tomorrow? Where?

   Isabel: At the coffee shop in the hotel. At 9 o'clock.

   Isabel **arranged** _____.

28 | Choosing *Wh-* Words Complete these questions with a *wh-* word (*what, where, who,* or *how*). Then ask a partner the questions. Check (✓) your partner's answers. **11.7 C**

HOW MUCH DO YOU KNOW ABOUT FIRST AID?

	YES	NO
1. Have you ever learned _____*how*_____ to take someone's pulse¹⁴?	☐	☐
2. Do you know _____ to do for a fever?	☐	☐
3. Do you know _____ to do if someone is choking¹⁵?	☐	☐
4. Can you show me _____ to do CPR¹⁶?	☐	☐
5. Do you know _____ to buy a first aid kit?	☐	☐
6. Can you explain _____ to do if someone stops breathing?	☐	☐
7. Do you know _____ to stop a nosebleed?	☐	☐
8. Do you know _____ to buy medicine?	☐	☐
9. Can you teach me _____ to give an injection?	☐	☐
10. Do you know _____ to call if you need emergency help?	☐	☐

Write about It Report your partner's answers to the class. How much do your classmates know about first aid? Write three summary statements.

Very few students know what to do for a fever, but everyone knows how to take someone's pulse.

29 | Using a *Wh-* Word + *To-* Infinitive Rewrite these requests for information. Use a *wh-* word + a *to-* infinitive. **11.7 C**

MAKING REQUESTS

1. How do you turn on the GPS on this phone? Could you show me?

   Could you show me how to turn on the GPS on this phone?

2. Where do I put this? I can't remember.
3. How did you make this? Can you teach me? It's delicious.
4. Where can I buy cheap furniture? Can you tell me?
5. How do I get downtown? Can you show me?
6. How do I fix this? Do you know?
7. How do you do that? Can you explain it to me?
8. How can you save money on airfare? Do you know?

GPS

Talk about It Work with a partner. Choose one of the questions above and use it to create a short conversation. Present your conversation to the class.

30 | Error Correction Correct any errors in these paragraphs.

1. I admire Michelle Kwan, the skater who competed in several Olympic Games but never won a gold medal. While this was a terrible disappointment for her, she continued to work hard. In fact, no getting a gold medal seemed making her even more determined. I think Kwan is a role model for young people because she teaches them know how to keep trying even when things are going badly.

¹⁴**pulse:** the beat of the heart that you feel in your body
¹⁵**choking:** not able to breathe because something is stopping the air

¹⁶**CPR:** a way of trying to save the life of someone whose heart has stopped beating

2. One person who has had an important effect on my life is my boss. She is the person who advised me about improving my English. My job requires me to reading business contracts and studying trade agreements. Many of these contracts and agreements are in English, and I need to understand them perfectly. My boss also encouraged me to studied American culture. She said that cultural differences often caused problems in business and that I needed understanding about these differences.

11.8 Verb + Gerund or *To-* Infinitive

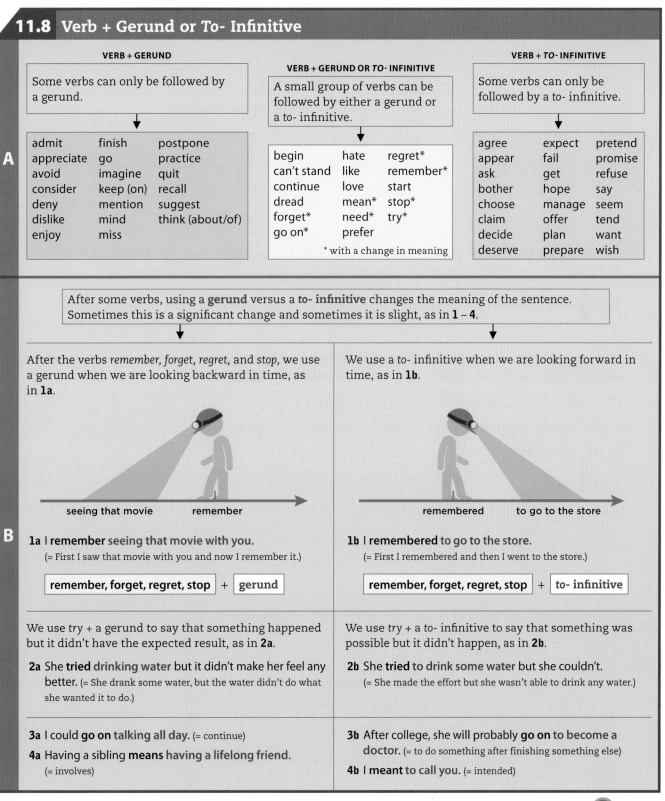

A

VERB + GERUND

Some verbs can only be followed by a gerund.

↓

admit	finish	postpone
appreciate	go	practice
avoid	imagine	quit
consider	keep (on)	recall
deny	mention	suggest
dislike	mind	think (about/of)
enjoy	miss	

VERB + GERUND OR *TO-* INFINITIVE

A small group of verbs can be followed by either a gerund or a *to-* infinitive.

↓

begin	hate	regret*
can't stand	like	remember*
continue	love	start
dread	mean*	stop*
forget*	need*	try*
go on*	prefer	

* with a change in meaning

VERB + *TO-* INFINITIVE

Some verbs can only be followed by a *to-* infinitive.

↓

agree	expect	pretend
appear	fail	promise
ask	get	refuse
bother	hope	say
choose	manage	seem
claim	offer	tend
decide	plan	want
deserve	prepare	wish

B

After some verbs, using a **gerund** versus a **to-** infinitive changes the meaning of the sentence. Sometimes this is a significant change and sometimes it is slight, as in **1 – 4**.

After the verbs *remember, forget, regret,* and *stop,* we use a gerund when we are looking backward in time, as in **1a**.

seeing that movie → remember

1a I **remember** seeing that movie with you.
(= First I saw that movie with you and now I remember it.)

remember, forget, regret, stop	+	gerund

We use *try* + a gerund to say that something happened but it didn't have the expected result, as in **2a**.

2a She **tried** drinking water but it didn't make her feel any better. (= She drank some water, but the water didn't do what she wanted it to do.)

3a I could **go on** talking all day. (= continue)

4a Having a sibling **means** having a lifelong friend.
(= involves)

We use a *to-* infinitive when we are looking forward in time, as in **1b**.

remembered → to go to the store

1b I **remembered** to go to the store.
(= First I remembered and then I went to the store.)

remember, forget, regret, stop	+	to- infinitive

We use *try* + a *to-* infinitive to say that something was possible but it didn't happen, as in **2b**.

2b She **tried** to drink some water but she couldn't.
(= She made the effort but she wasn't able to drink any water.)

3b After college, she will probably **go on** to become a doctor. (= to do something after finishing something else)

4b I **meant** to call you. (= intended)

31 | **Gerund or *To-* Infinitive?** Complete these questions with the correct form of the verb in parentheses. (More than one answer may be possible.) `11.8 A`

> ## Common Job Interview Questions
>
> 1. I saw on your resume that you enjoy _____*playing*_____ chess. How did you get interested in that?
>   (play)
> 2. Why do you want _____ here?
>   (work)
> 3. What kind of people do you like _____ with?
>   (work)
> 4. Were you ever asked _____ a pay cut?
>   (take)
> 5. Where do you hope _____ professionally in five years?
>   (be)
> 6. What made you choose _____ an engineer?
>   (become)
> 7. When you begin _____ with new people, how do you get to understand them?
>   (work)
> 8. Describe a situation where you failed _____ a goal.
>   (reach)

Think about It In which of the questions above could you use either the *-ing* or the *to-* infinitive form of the verb?

Talk about It Choose one of the questions above. Tell your classmates how you would answer it.

32 | **Noticing Differences in Meaning** Complete these conversations with the *-ing* or *to-* infinitive form of the verb in parentheses. Then practice the conversations. `11.8 B`

1. A: Why did you leave the door open this morning?

   B: I left the door open? I don't remember _____*doing*_____ that. (do)

2. A: Where's your computer?

   B: Oh, no. I didn't remember _____ it. (bring)

3. A: Did you pick up some milk on your way home?

   B: Oh, sorry. I forgot _____ at the store. (stop)

4. A: Did you have a good time at the White House?

   B: Absolutely. I'll never forget _____ there. (be)

5. A: Somebody has been smoking in here.

   B: Not me. I stopped _____ a year ago. (smoke)

6. A: Why are you so late?

   B: I stopped _____ to some friends. (talk)

7. A: Why didn't you move the car this morning?

   B: I tried _____ it but it wouldn't start. (move)

8. A: Is David feeling any better?

   B: I don't think so. He tried _____ a vacation but he still doesn't feel very good. (take)

9. A: Are you tired?

   B: Yeah, really tired. I don't think I can go on _____ this much longer. (do)

10. A: What did your sister do after college?

   B: She went on _____ engineering at graduate school. (study)

11. A: Do you enjoy skiing?

   B: Not especially. In my opinion, skiing means _____ cold all day. (be)

12. A: What happened to the window?

   B: I'm sorry. I didn't mean _____ it. (break)

33 | Gerund or *To-* Infinitive? Complete these paragraphs with the correct form of the verbs in parentheses. (More than one answer may be possible.) `11.8 A–B`

How to Prepare for a Vacation

Most people go on vacation because they want ___*to relax*___.

(1. relax)

However, if you are not well prepared, your vacation can turn into a disaster.

First, it is important to bring everything you need with you. Before you

pack, check the weather at your destination so you know what kind of

clothes you will need. Don't forget _____ a bathing suit if you

(2. pack)

are going to the beach. Remember _____ your passport if you

(3. take)

are going to another country.

You also have to think about the things you leave behind. Consider _____ someone

(4. ask)

_____ an eye on your house while you are away. Don't forget _____ a house key and

(5. keep)   (6. leave)

emergency phone numbers for this person. Ask the post office _____ your mail. If you get a daily

(7. hold)

newspaper, ask the newspaper office _____ your subscription while you are away.

(8. stop)

Once you leave, stop _____ about things at home. Relax and enjoy your vacation.

(9. worry)

34 | Understanding Differences in Meaning Complete these quotations with the *-ing* or *to-* infinitive form of the verb in parentheses. `11.8 B`

1. I totally forget about ___*snowboarding*___ in the summertime. (snowboard) —*Shaun White, snowboarder*

2. I forgot _____ hands and _____ friendly. It was an important lesson about
   leadership. (shake/be) —*Lee Iacocca, businessman*

3. Don't call the world dirty because you forgot _____ your glasses. (clean) —*Aaron Hill, poet*

4. Don't forget _____ yourself. (love) —*Soren Kierkegaard, philosopher*

5. I do remember actually _____ chords to Beatles songs. I thought they were great songwriters.
   (learn) —*Mick Taylor, musician*

6. In adversity, remember _____ an even mind. (keep) —*Horace, poet*

7. I don't remember _____ to become a writer. (decide) —*Mark Haddon, writer*

8. I once tried _____ on my toes to see far out in the distance, but I found that I could see much farther by climbing to a high place. (stand up) —*Xun Zi, philosopher*

9. In my early days in Hollywood I tried _____ economical. I designed my own clothes, much to my mother's distress. (be) —*Gene Tierney, actor*

10. I tried _____ classical guitar when I was 16 but it got really hard. I could never play a lead to save my life. (study) —*Kip Winger, musician*

11. I always tried _____ every disaster into an opportunity. (turn) —*John D. Rockefeller, Jr., industrialist*

35 | Gerund or *To-* Infinitive? **Complete these paragraphs with the correct form of the verbs in parentheses. (More than one answer may be possible.)** `11.8 A–B`

Product Review: Allay 7-Cup Rice Cooker

RATINGS
Overall: ★★
Ease of Use: ★
Durability: ★★★
Ease of Cleaning: ★★★

PROS
Not too hard to clean.

CONS
Instructions are wrong and heat timer doesn't always work.

REVIEW

I had problems with this rice cooker from the first time I used it. The instruction booklet says

____to use____ 1 cup of water per 1 cup of rice. When I did this, the rice ended up _____
(1. use)   (2. be)

hard and burned. Next, I tried _____ 1½ cups of water per 1 cup of rice. After cooking the rice
(3. use)

for the correct amount of time, I found that the rice at the top was edible, but the rice at the bottom was

burned. Then I decided _____ 2 cups of water per cup of rice, and that worked just about right.
(4. use)

   A second serious problem with this rice cooker is that the heat timer doesn't always work. The heat

timer has two positions. You press it down when you want _____ the rice and up when you
(5. cook)

just need _____ the rice warm. To cook the rice, you put the water and rice in the cooker and
(6. keep)

press the heat timer down. After about 15 minutes, the heat timer should pop up to the "keep warm"

position. Instead, the rice keeps on _____. This could be dangerous. It also means you can't
(7. cook)

stop _____ the rice.
(8. watch)

Think about It How many other gerunds and *to-* infinitives can you find in the text above?

Write about It Write a product review of something you have used. Pay special attention to the way you use gerunds and infinitives.

11.9 Bare Infinitives as Objects

We use a bare infinitive instead of a *to-* infinitive after certain verbs and other expressions. A bare infinitive looks like the base or simple form of a verb.

A

1 She **made me cry.** (= She caused me to cry.) **2** He **had his brother** do the shopping. (= He caused his brother to do the shopping.) **3** He wouldn't **let anyone come in.** (= He wouldn't allow anyone to come in.)	We use a **noun phrase** + **bare infinitive** after the verbs *make* and *have* when they mean "cause someone to do something," as in **1 – 2**. We also use *let* + a **noun phrase** + **bare infinitive** when *let* means "allow," as in **3**.
4 The IMF **helped (us) stabilize** the world economy. **5** The IMF **helped (us) to stabilize** the world economy.	It is possible to use either a **bare infinitive** or a **to-infinitive** after the verb *help* (+ a **noun phrase**), as in **4 – 5**.

B

COMPARE **6a** I **saw her leave.** (completed) **6b** I **saw her leaving** though the back door. (in progress) **7a** We **heard someone yell.** (completed) **7b** We **heard someone yelling.** (in progress)	We use a **noun phrase** + **bare infinitive** after the verbs *feel, hear, see,* and *watch* when we are describing a completed action, as in **6a** and **7a**. We use a **noun phrase** + **gerund** after these verbs when the action is in progress or unfinished, as in **6b** and **7b**.

36 | *To-* Infinitive or Bare Infinitive? Underline the *to-* infinitives used as objects. Circle the bare infinitives used as objects. `11.9 A`

To Nap or Not to Nap?

Medical researchers say most people need <u>to sleep</u> more. When people don't get enough rest, they often have more health problems and greater difficulty dealing with stress. A recent study suggests that short naps in the middle of the day can help reduce stress and improve general health.

Some companies in Europe and Latin America allow workers to nap in the middle of the day. They have workers go home and rest for a short time. (Some shops even close for a few hours around midday.) Most employers say that the naps make people feel more energetic when they return.

Now some American companies are letting employees nap after lunch, and the results have been positive. When workers stop to rest, it helps them to relax and makes them happier.

> **F Y I**
>
> Don't confuse a *to-*infinitive in a series with a bare infinitive.
>
> I managed **to get up** early and **finish** my work.
> (= I managed to get up early and to finish my work.)

Think about It What verbs are used with the *to-* infinitives and bare infinitives in Activity 36? Write them in this chart.

Verb (+ noun phrase) + *to-* infinitive	Verb (+ noun phrase) + bare infinitive
need to sleep	

Talk about It What do you think about resting/napping at work? Do you think employers should permit this? Explain your opinion to a partner.

37 | Using Bare Infinitives Write ten questions using the information in this chart and your own ideas. `11.9 A`

Do you think	parents teachers children wives husbands employers	should help should let should make	their children their students their parents their husbands their wives their employees	——?

Do you think parents should let their children stay home alone?

Talk about It Ask a partner the questions you wrote above. Answer your partner's questions.

A: Do you think parents should let their children stay home alone?
B: It depends on the age of the child.

38 | Bare Infinitive, *To-* Infinitive, or Gerund? Complete this paragraph with the correct form of the verbs in parentheses. Use bare infinitives, *to-* infinitives, or gerunds. `11.9 A–B`

Online Learning

A few years ago, you couldn't have made me ____*take*____ a

           (1. take)

class online. It seemed to me that the experience of _____

                 (2. sit)

in the same room and _____ a professor face-to-face

       (3. see)

was necessary for _____. After _____

     (4. learn)   (5. take)

an online course, though, I now realize that being able to watch a

lecture whenever I want has helped me _____ better.

               (6. learn)

_____ able to pause and review the lecture over and over

 (7. be)

again lets me really _____ about the information. I'm not worrying the whole time about
                        (8. think)

_____ _____ everything the professor says. And I can still interact with
  (9. try)   (10. write down)

the professor and the other students by _____ small group discussion sessions and by
                                          (11. attend)

_____ the professor. I can definitely see myself _____ more online courses in
  (12. email)   (13. take)

the future.

Write about It What is your opinion of online learning? Write several sentences.

39 | Bare Infinitive or Gerund? Complete these descriptions with the bare infinitive or gerund form of the verbs in parentheses. Then explain your choices. (In some sentences, either form may be possible.) 11.9 B

DESCRIBING SIGHTS AND SOUNDS

1. The last time I was in New York City, I saw a young woman _____*walking*_____ down the street
                                                                  (walk)

   in a wedding dress. It was strange because she was alone.

2. One time my father saw some kids _____ a bag of empty soda cans out of the window of
                                       (throw)

   their car. My father actually picked up the bag, ran after them, and threw the bag back into their car.

3. One time I was on an airplane and we hit some turbulence. The plane started shaking and suddenly we

   all heard a voice _____. It was a very deep laugh, and it sounded as if it was coming from
                        (laugh)

   outside the plane. What was it? Later I found out it was one of those birthday cards with sound. The

   card was in someone's luggage in the overhead compartment, and the turbulence must have set it off.

4. At my college graduation on a hot May day, I felt the sweat _____ down my face and wanted
                                                                  (drip)

   to take off my gown, but I didn't see anyone else _____ that. In that heat, how could my
                                                         (do)

   friend next to me look so cool, even though he was wearing a long-sleeved shirt and dark pants? When

   I asked him, he shrugged and opened his gown. He was wearing only a pair of shorts, two sleeves,

   cut off at the elbows, and two pant legs, cut off at the knees. The sleeves and pant legs were held up

   with rubber bands! With his gown on, you couldn't tell at all!

5. One day I was walking down Lexington Avenue in New York. A handsome man was walking toward

   me. When he got close, he looked up and I saw him _____ at me. That's when I almost did
                                                          (smile)

   a double-take[17]—it was the actor Sean Connery. Imagine, 007 in New York!

Write about It Write your own description like the ones above.

---

[17] **double-take:** a quick or surprised second look

11.10 Other Uses of To- Infinitives

A

LINKING VERB + ADJECTIVE + TO- INFINITIVE

	adjective	to- infinitive
1 She **was**	**happy**	**to help us.**

2 I **was surprised to find** that things weren't so different here.

3 He's **apt to be late.**

We sometimes use a **to- infinitive** after a **linking verb + adjective**, as in **1 – 3**. The to- infinitive gives more information about the adjective.

A few adjectives are almost always followed by a to-infinitive. These include *able, apt, due, inclined, likely, prepared, ready,* and *willing.*

B

NOUN PHRASE + TO- INFINITIVE

	noun phrase	to- infinitive
4 I don't have	**any reason**	**to go there.**

5 Her **ability to manage the office** surprised us.

6 There are **many sights to see** in London.

We can also use a **to- infinitive** after a **noun phrase**, as in **4 – 6**. The to- infinitive gives more information about the noun phrase.

C

EXPRESSING A PURPOSE

7 She exercises **to stay healthy.**

8 He's studying **to become a doctor.**

9 A company needs good management **in order not to fail.**

10 **To be a good manager,** a person must be very organized.

We can also use a to- infinitive to explain *why* or *for what purpose*, as in **7 – 8**. We sometimes include the words *in order* before a to- infinitive (especially before negative infinitives and in more formal writing), as in **9**.

Sometimes we use a purpose infinitive at the beginning of a sentence, as in **10**. This focuses attention on the purpose. We use a comma to separate the purpose infinitive from the main clause of the sentence.

 GO ONLINE

---

40 | Adjectives + *To*- Infinitives Choose the best adjective in parentheses to complete each sentence. `11.10 A`

1. I'm _____sorry_____ to bother you. (happy/sorry)

2. I'd be _____ to help you. (happy/sorry)

3. I'm so _____ to finally have some free time. (excited/sad)

4. I'm _____ to be a citizen of my country. (anxious/proud)

5. The sun is _____ to rise tomorrow morning. (likely/unlikely)

6. I was _____ to get an invitation to the dinner.

    (disappointed/surprised)

7. Teachers are usually _____ to have hard-working students. (pleased/scared)

8. A good manager must be _____ to fire a dishonest employee. (unwilling/willing)

9. On a nice day, I'm _____ to jump on my bicycle and go for a ride. (apt/not likely)

10. I'm _____ to say I can't come to your house for dinner next week. (sorry/happy)

> **FYI**
>
> To- infinitives are especially common after adjectives that describe feelings.

41 | Noun Phrases + *To*- Infinitives Put these words and phrases in the correct order. Include a noun phrase + *to*- infinitive in your sentence. (More than one sentence may be possible.) `11.10 B`

1. don't need/I/to do/anything

   I don't need anything to do.

2. work/have/I/to do
3. San Francisco/to visit/is/a great city
4. an apartment/looking for/to rent/she's
5. anything/didn't give me/he/to say
6. *Mississippi*/a hard word/is/to spell
7. a good way/to meet people/joining a club/is
8. lots of things/I/to keep track of/have
9. to relax/playing a game/a great way/is
10. not everyone/to go/the opportunity/has/to college

42 | Adjectives and Nouns + *To*- Infinitives Match the beginning of each sentence on the left with a *to*- infinitive. (More than one answer may be possible.) Then compare with your classmates. `11.10 A–B`

1. On a rainy day, I'm not likely __e__
2. I'm always ready ____
3. I would never be willing ____
4. Babies are apt ____
5. Newborn babies aren't able ____
6. Teachers are likely ____
7. Many people never have the opportunity ____
8. Exercising is a great way ____

a. to reduce stress.
b. to walk.
c. to steal someone's money.
d. to give homework.
e. to sit outside.
f. to help my friends.
g. to start crying at any time.
h. to travel abroad.

Write about It Write your own ending for the sentences above. Use a *to*- infinitive. Then share your ideas with a classmate.

43 | Using a *To*- Infinitive of Purpose Match the beginning of each instruction on the left with a *to*- infinitive. (More than one answer may be possible.) `11.10 C`

INSTRUCTIONS

1. Put a little water in the pan and cover it __e__
2. Stir the water occasionally ____
3. Store coffee properly ____
4. Clean your coffeemaker frequently ____
5. Allow at least two hours before you exercise ____
6. Stretch after you exercise ____
7. Try drinking hot milk ____
8. Take up a hobby or join a club ____

a. to avoid a bitter taste.
b. to avoid boredom.
c. to digest your food.
d. to ensure a fresh taste.
e. to keep the moisture in.
f. to help you fall asleep.
g. to reduce stiffness and soreness.
h. to separate the pasta.

Write about It Choose three of the sentence beginnings above, and use a *to*- infinitive to write your own ending. Share your ideas with a classmate.

11.11 Progressive, Perfect, and Passive Forms of *To-* Infinitives

A

PROGRESSIVE FORM to *be* + present participle	A **to- infinitive** can also have a progressive, perfect, or passive form, as in **1 – 6**.
1 She seems **to be doing very well.** (= I think that she is doing very well.) **2** **To be living in Italy** is a dream come true. (= The fact that I am living in Italy is a dream come true.)	We use the progressive form of a *to-* infinitive to emphasize that something is in progress at a particular time, as in **1 – 2**.
PERFECT FORM to *have* + past participle	We can use the perfect form of a *to-* infinitive:
3 Jeff looks much better. The treatment seems **to have been effective.** (= I think the treatment has been effective.) **4** They were delighted **to have finally met her.** (= They were delighted because they had finally met her.)	• for something that happened in the past but has a connection to now, as in **3** • to show that one event in the past took place before another, as in **4**
PASSIVE FORM to *be* + past participle	We use the passive form of a *to-* infinitive when the doer of the action is unknown or less important than the action itself, as in **5 – 6**.
5 What needs **to be done?** (= What does somebody need to do?) **6** He didn't want **to be called** *Professor.* (= He didn't want people to call him *Professor.*)	

44 | Noticing Different Forms of *To-* Infinitives   Underline the *to-* infinitives in these conversations. Then practice with a partner. **11.11 A**

1. A: Where's Mary? She should be here by now.
   B: Yeah. She seems <u>to have forgotten about the meeting</u>.

2. A: What's the matter with the refrigerator?
   B: What do you mean?
   A: Well, look at the water. It seems to be leaking.

3. A: Did you tell your sister to do her homework?
   B: I don't think she needs to be told.

4. A: Are you going to help Sam move?
   B: I offered but he doesn't like to be helped.

5. A: Was your new boss at the dinner?
   B: Yes, and I'm so happy to have finally met her.

6. A: Do you have any money on you?
   B: No, I'm still waiting to be paid.

7. A: How's your new job?
   B: I love it. It's so nice to be working for a good company.

8. A: Where's all the food?
   B: Somebody seems to have eaten it all.

9. A: Why is Anne in such a good mood?
   B: I think she's just relieved to have finally finished her project!

10. A: Do you want to be picked up Friday morning? I think I'm going to the same meeting.
    B: Oh, that'd be nice. Then I won't have to drive.

11. A: The snow finally seems to be stopping. Do you want to go out?
    B: Sure.

12. A: So which letters are ready to be mailed?
    B: Well, the ones I put by the front door. The rest can wait.

Think about It Group the infinitives in Activity 44 in this chart.

Progressive form (*to be* + present participle)	Perfect form (*to have* + past participle)
	to have forgotten

Active form (*to* + base form)	Passive form (*to be* + past participle)

Write about It Choose three of the sentences in Activity 44 with a *to-* infinitive. Restate the information in each sentence without using a *to-* infinitive.

1. *I think she has forgotten about the meeting.*

11.12 Using Gerunds and *To-* Infinitives in Speaking

A

USING A *TO-* INFINITIVE BY ITSELF

1 A: Why did you call her?
 B: **To ask if I could stay longer.**

2 A: What's this for?
 B: **To remove staples.**

In conversation, we often answer a question about the purpose of something with a **to- infinitive** by itself, as in **1 – 2**.

B

USING *TO* ALONE

3 A: Can you help me with this?
 B: Sure. I'd be happy **to.** (= I'd be happy to help you.)

4 A: Did you go out last night?
 B: No, we decided not **to.** (= We decided not to go out.)

5 A: Did you send that email?
 B: Oh, sorry. I forgot **to.** (= I forgot to send that email.)

In conversation, we can use **to** alone when answering a *yes/no* question because the meaning is understood from the question itself, as in **3 – 5**.

C

USING A GERUND BY ITSELF

6 A: Why do you keep doing that?
 B: **Doing what?**
 A: **Talking to yourself.**
 B: Sorry. I didn't know I was bothering you.

In conversation, we often use a **gerund** by itself to talk about an action in a short way, as in **6**.

Using a gerund lets us "package" an action as a kind of noun phrase. Then we can use the gerund to talk about the action in different ways.

45 | Answering Questions with a *To-* Infinitive Listen and write the missing *to-* infinitives in these conversations. Then practice with a partner. `11.12 A`

1. A: Why are you calling Matt again?

   B: _To ask_ him a question.

2. A: Why are you going out so early?

   B: _____ some exercise.

3. A: Why did you turn the TV back on?

   B: _____ the weather report.

4. A: Why did you want to see me?

   B: Just _____ .

5. A: Where'd Sam go?

   B: _____ something for dinner.

6. A: What are you going to use all these rocks for?

   B: _____ a wall.

7. A: Do you need some help?

   B: _____ what?

   A: _____ the kitchen.

   B: Sure. I'd love some help.

8. A: Can I use the car today?

   B: What for?

   A: Just _____ to the store.

9. A: What do you need to go to the store for?

   B: _____ some eggs.

10. A: What do you need eggs for?

    B: _____ a cake.

46 | Noticing *To-* Infinitives in Conversation Listen and write the missing responses. Then practice with a partner. `11.12 B`

1. A: Do you want to do something tonight?

   B: _Sure, I'd love to._

2. A: Did you go for a swim?

   B: _____

3. A: Can you help me with this?

   B: _____

4. A: Did you stop at the grocery store?

   B: _____

5. A: Did you play tennis?

   B: _____

6. A: Do you want to join us for lunch?

   B: _____

7. A: We're going for coffee. Want to come?

   B: _____

8. A: Did you get a hold of Anna?

   B: _____

Think about It What words did the speakers leave out in the conversations above? Share ideas with your classmates.

47 | Using Gerunds in Conversation Listen and write the missing gerunds. Then practice with a partner. `11.12 C`

1. A: Would you mind _____helping_____ me with this?

   B: _____ you with what?

   A: _____ this table.

   B: Oh, sure.

2. A: Did you postpone _____ again?

   B: _____ where?

   A: To register the car.

   B: Oh, no. I forgot.

RESEARCH SAYS...

Gerunds are more common in writing than in speaking.

CORPUS

3. A: Don't you love _____ this?

   B: _____ what?

   A: The ice skating.

   B: Oh, is there ice skating on TV?

4. A: I wish you would stop _____ that.

   B: _____ what?

   A: _____ the channel every ten seconds.

5. A: I hate _____ about this.

   B: _____ about what?

   A: The economy. I'm sick of it.

6. A: When are you going to start _____?

   B: _____ what?

   A: You know. The garage.

7. A: I really don't enjoy _____ this.

   B: _____ what? You mean _____ the windows?

   A: Right.

8. A: Did you finish _____ everything?

   B: What do you mean?

   A: You know. _____ the dishes and putting away the food.

   B: Yeah, everything's done.

11.13 Using Gerunds and *To-* Infinitives in Academic Writing

<table>
<tr>
<td rowspan="2">A</td>
<td>**INTRODUCING A TOPIC WITH A GERUND SUBJECT**

1 **Being a responsible member of one's community** is important to the success of representative democracy.

2 **Traveling to foreign countries and experiencing different cultures** is a great opportunity.</td>
<td>In academic writing, we sometimes use a **gerund** to introduce the topic of a paragraph or essay, as in **1 – 2**.</td>
</tr>
</table>

<table>
<tr>
<td rowspan="2">B</td>
<td>**INTRODUCING AN IDEA WITH NOUN + *BE* + *TO-* INFINITIVE**

3 The first rule of letter writing **is** **to make your purpose clear to your audience.**

4 Our primary challenge **is** **to provide good feedback.** A secondary challenge is **to help . . .**</td>
<td>We often use a **noun phrase** + **be** + a **to-** **infinitive** in writing to introduce an important point or idea, as in **3 – 4**. Common nouns used to introduce an important point include:</td>
</tr>
</table>

aim	goal	method	rule	step
challenge	idea	plan	solution	way

<table>
<tr>
<td rowspan="2">C</td>
<td>**GERUNDS AND *TO-* INFINITIVES IN A SERIES**

5 The best things about my trip were **meeting new people, staying on a farm,** and **eating great food.**

6 In conclusion, being a good boss depends on **being organized, giving your employees good feedback,** and **understanding that they are only human.**

7 Someday I hope **to see where my grandparents grew up** and **learn about their culture.**</td>
<td>In writing, we sometimes use a series of gerund phrases or *to-* infinitives in a sentence, as in **5 – 7**.

Remember: When we use a series of *to-* infinitives, it's not always necessary to repeat the word *to*, as in **7**.

Ideas in a series should have the same grammatical form. We call this *parallelism*.</td>
</tr>
</table>

GO ONLINE

48 | Writing Topic Sentences Use a gerund to complete these topic sentences. (Many different answers are possible.) `11.13 A`

TOPIC SENTENCES

1. _Living in many different places_ _____ has had a major impact on my life.

2. _____ has many benefits.

3. _____ is never appropriate.

4. _____ should be one of this country's most important goals.

5. _____ has several disadvantages.

6. _____ is one of the most important duties of a citizen.

7. _____ should be a requirement for every college student.

Write about It Write three more topic sentences beginning with gerunds.

49 | Noticing *To-* Infinitives Underline the *to-* infinitives in these paragraphs. Which of your underlined *to-* infinitives introduce an important point? Underline them twice. `11.13 B`

Writing Work Emails

All work emails need a clear purpose. The first rule of email writing is to make your purpose clear to the reader. What are you telling your manager or coworkers? Write the subject on the subject line. Then tell your reader the point of your message at the beginning of your email. The second rule is to include all the information that your reader needs in as few words as possible. Try to keep a clear focus in your message.

It's also important to keep your words simple and direct. Use short words and sentences and avoid using jargon[18] and slang[19]. When you have finished writing, don't forget to go back and cut any unnecessary words. Editing always improves an email.

> **F Y I**
>
> Writers often use a noun phrase + *be* + a *to-* infinitive to introduce a goal, purpose, plan, or idea.
>
> The first rule of email writing is **to make your purpose clear to your reader**.

50 | Introducing an Important Point Match the beginning of each sentence on the left with a *to-* infinitive. `11.13 B`

1. The first rule of advertising is _h_
2. The first rule of being a good businessperson is ____
3. The first rule of friendship is ____
4. A goal of science is ____
5. The goal of a business is ____
6. One good way to learn a language is ____
7. The first step in any research project is ____
8. The best method for storing tea is ____

a. to surround yourself with good people.
b. to read a lot of books.
c. to make money.
d. to put it in an airtight container.
e. to acquire knowledge of the world.
f. to define the problem.
g. to forgive your friends no matter what they do.
h. to have a good product to advertise.

Talk about It Do you agree or disagree with the sentences above? Tell a partner.

[18]**jargon:** special words used by a particular group of people   [19]**slang:** informal language

51 | Introducing an Important Point Complete these sentences with your own ideas. Use a *to-* infinitive in each sentence. `11.13 B`

1. One way to meet new people is _____.

   Another way is _____.

2. One of my reasons for taking this course is _____.

   Another reason is _____.

3. The first step in buying an airline ticket is _____.

   The next step is _____.

4. One way to discipline a child is _____.

   An alternative way is _____.

5. One challenge for travelers in foreign countries is _____.

   Another challenge is _____.

6. One method for learning new words is _____.

   Another method is _____.

7. One of my goals is _____.

   Another goal is _____.

52 | Writing a Series of Ideas Complete these sentences with your own ideas. Use gerunds or *to-* infinitives. `11.13 C`

THREE IMPORTANT THINGS

1. You can improve your grades by _____,

   _____, and _____.

2. Three of my personal goals are _____,

   _____, and _____.

3. For me, the three worst household chores are _____,

   _____, and _____.

4. For many people, "fun" involves _____,

   _____, and _____.

5. A healthy lifestyle requires _____,

   _____, and _____.

6. The three most difficult things for a parent are _____,

   _____, and _____.

7. Parents can promote good reading habits in their children by _____,

   _____, and _____.

8. Three important human rights are _____,

   _____, and _____.

A | SURVEY Choose one of these statements, and ask ten classmates if they agree or disagree and why. Then report your findings to the class.

- It is important never to contradict your boss at work.
- It is critical for children to have physical education classes in school.
- Adolescents should be allowed to make their own decisions.
- Setting up a bank account for every young child is a good idea.
- It is impossible to have a good life unless you have a certain amount of money.
- You can't learn without making mistakes.

A: Do you agree or disagree with this statement? It is important never to contradict your boss at work.
B: I disagree because nobody is perfect and even your boss can make a mistake. If you think your boss is really saying something wrong, you need to speak up. At the same time, I think you need to be very polite so your boss doesn't get angry.

B | DISCUSSION In a small group, choose one of these scenarios, and give advice and suggestions about what the person should do.

Scenario 1: Carlos was traveling by train on his vacation in a foreign country. Suddenly he realized that his wallet was missing. He checked his pockets and looked all around, but he couldn't find it. Then he noticed that his suitcase was missing, too. Here he was in a foreign country, he didn't speak the local language, and he had no money and none of his belongings. What could he do?

Scenario 2: Irene is taking an important university entrance exam when she notices that several of the students are cheating. She knows that only the top scorers on the exam will get accepted into the university, and she wants to be one of them. What should she do?

Scenario 3: Paul loves his job in the computer industry, but one of his co-workers is driving him crazy. This person spends much of the day on his phone talking to friends and playing games on his computer. As a consequence, Paul ends up doing a lot of his co-worker's work so they can finish their projects on time. What should he do?

"I would advise a person in this situation to . . ."
"I recommend doing . . ."
"I think this person should consider going . . . "
"I would ask, 'Have you ever considered doing . . . ?'"
"I would suggest that he/she not forget to . . ."
"I think it is important for this person to . . ."

C | WEB SEARCH Look online to find a short video that explains the process of doing something (e.g., how to draw a rose, how to tie a necktie, how to make sushi, or how to _____). Without turning on the sound, write your own instructions explaining how to accomplish the process.

In order to ____, you will need to get the following materials/ingredients: ____, ____, ____, etc.
You start by ____.
Next, be sure to ____.
Continue ____ or ____.
Don't forget to check ____.
Finally, remember to ____.

D | WRITING Choose one of your topic sentences from Activity 48 and write a paragraph.

Owning a car has several disadvantages. Perhaps the biggest disadvantage is that having a car is very expensive. When you own a car, it costs money to keep it in good shape. You also need to pay for car insurance and gasoline, and this can get very expensive. Another disadvantage is that you need to have a safe place to park your car at night, and this can be difficult if you live in a big city. While many people think that they can't live without a car, there are actually some good reasons to live without a car. . . .

11.14 Summary of Gerunds and To- Infinitives

Gerund as Subject	• **Reading** is to the mind what exercise is to the body. (Joseph Addison)
Gerund as Subject Completer	• The ony thing better than singing is **more singing**. (Ella Fitzgerald)
Gerund as Object of a Verb	• If we stop **loving animals**, aren't we bound to stop **loving humans** too? (Aleksandr Solzhenitsyn)
Gerund as Object of a Preposition	• Let no one come to you without **leaving better and happier**. (Mother Teresa)
Passive Form of a Gerund	• He who fears **being conquered** is sure of defeat. (Napoleon Bonaparte)

To- Infinitive as Subject (*It + Be* + Adjective + *To*- Infinitive)	• **To teach** is to learn twice over. (Joseph Joubert) • It's better **to be alone** than in bad company. (George Washington)
To- Infinitive as Subject Completer	• The only way to have a friend is **to be one**. (Ralph Waldo Emerson)
To- Infinitive as Object of a Verb	• Everyone wants **to share in a man's success**, but no one wants **to share in his misfortunes**. • Expect the most wonderful things **to happen**, not in the future but right now. (Eileen Caddy)
Wh- Word + To- Infinitive	• Never tell people **how to do things**. Tell them **what to do** and they will surprise you with their ingenuity. (George Patton)
Bare Infinitive	• No one can make you **feel** inferior without your consent. (Eleanor Roosevelt)
Linking Verb + Adjective + To- Infinitive	• Create the kind of self that you will be happy **to live with all your life**. (Golda Meir)
Noun + To- Infinitive	• For every good reason there is to lie, there is a better reason **to tell the truth**. (Bo Bennett)
To- Infinitive of Purpose	• **In order to excel**, you must be completely dedicated to your chosen sport. (Willie Mays)
Progressive Form of a To- Infinitive	• **To be doing good deeds** is man's most glorious task. (Sophocles)
Perfect Form of a To- Infinitive	• In my view you cannot claim **to have seen something** until you have photographed it. (Emile Zola)
Passive Form of a To- Infinitive	• I would like **to be called an inspiration to people**, not a role model— because I make mistakes like everybody else. (Britney Spears)

12 Noun Clauses and Related Forms

What is wrong today
won't be right tomorrow.

—DUTCH PROVERB

Talk about It What does the quotation above mean? Do you agree or disagree?

WARM-UP

A | Read these statements and check (✓) *Agree* or *Disagree*. Then compare your answers with your classmates. What was the most common answer for each question?

Personal Statements

	AGREE	DISAGREE
1. **What I'm doing these days** is interesting.	☐	☐
2. I love **where I live**.	☐	☐
3. I believe **friends are very important to happiness**.	☐	☐
4. I am very concerned about **how other people feel**.	☐	☐
5. I feel strongly **that I can make the world a better place**.	☐	☐
6. I have always thought **that language learning is fun**.	☐	☐
7. I know exactly **what I want to do in the future**.	☐	☐
8. I'm certain **that I'll be successful in life**.	☐	☐
9. I don't know **if I'll live in the same country all my life**.	☐	☐
10. **What people think of me** is very important.	☐	☐

B | The words in green above are noun clauses. Based on these examples, what can you say about noun clauses? Check (✓) *True* or *False*.

	TRUE	FALSE
1. A noun clause always comes at the end of a sentence.	☐	☐
2. Noun clauses usually answer the question *what*.	☐	☐
3. Noun clauses always begin with the word *that*.	☐	☐
4. A noun clause has a subject and a verb.	☐	☐
5. We often use noun clauses in sentences about opinions or feelings.	☐	☐

C | Look back at the quotation on page 394. Identify any noun clauses.

12.1 Overview of Noun Clauses

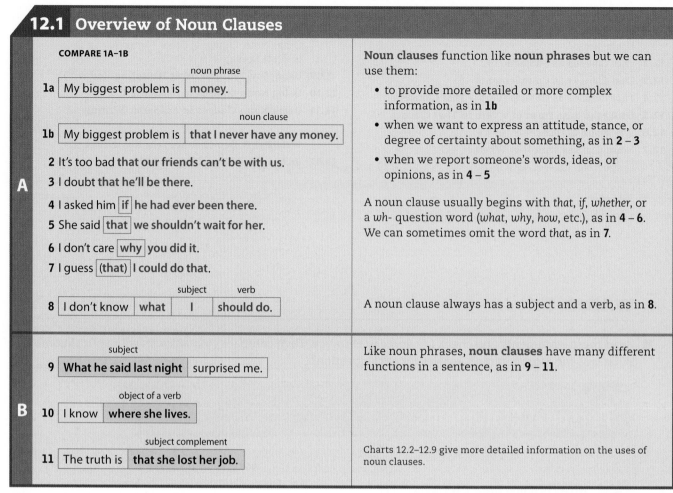

A

COMPARE 1A–1B

noun phrase

1a | My biggest problem is | money. |

noun clause

1b | My biggest problem is | that I never have any money. |

2 It's too bad **that our friends can't be with us.**

3 I doubt **that he'll be there.**

4 I asked him | if | he had ever been there.

5 She said | that | we shouldn't wait for her.

6 I don't care | why | you did it.

7 I guess | (that) | I could do that.

subject   verb

8 | I don't know | what | I | should do. |

Noun clauses function like **noun phrases** but we can use them:

- to provide more detailed or more complex information, as in **1b**
- when we want to express an attitude, stance, or degree of certainty about something, as in **2 – 3**
- when we report someone's words, ideas, or opinions, as in **4 – 5**

A noun clause usually begins with *that*, *if*, *whether*, or a *wh-* question word (*what*, *why*, *how*, etc.), as in **4 – 6**. We can sometimes omit the word *that*, as in **7**.

A noun clause always has a subject and a verb, as in **8**.

B

subject

9 | What he said last night | surprised me. |

object of a verb

10 | I know | where she lives. |

subject complement

11 | The truth is | that she lost her job. |

Like noun phrases, **noun clauses** have many different functions in a sentence, as in **9 – 11**.

Charts 12.2–12.9 give more detailed information on the uses of noun clauses.

GO ONLINE

---

1 | Identifying Subjects and Verbs in Noun Clauses Underline the subject and circle the verb in each **bold** noun clause. What do the quotations mean to you? 12.1 A

QUOTATIONS FROM FAMOUS PEOPLE

1. I'm not interested in **how people move**, but **what moves them**. (*Pina Bausch, dancer and dance teacher*)

2. I don't care **what people say about me**. (*Roger Daltrey, musician*)

3. Keep trying and see **what fate¹ brings**. (*Vietnamese proverb*)

4. Don't ask **whether it is going to be easy**. Ask **whether it is worth it**.
   (*Michael Josephson, law professor and attorney*)

5. Sometimes it is more important to discover **what one cannot do** than **what one can do**.
   (*Lin Yutang, writer and inventor*)

6. Practice **what you preach**. (*Plautus, playwright*)

7. I often think **that the night is more alive and more richly colored than the day**. (*Vincent van Gogh, artist*)

8. My doctor told me **I would never walk again**. My mother told me **I would**. I believed my mother.
   (*Wilma Rudolph, athlete*)

9. It took me a hundred years to figure out **I can't change the world**. I can only change Bessie.
   (*Bessie Delany, civil rights pioneer*)

¹**fate:** things that happen to us

10. I can't understand **why people are frightened of new ideas**. I'm frightened of the old ones. (*John Cage, composer*)

11. I don't know **if a song is going to be a hit or . . . a flop**[2]. I never know. (*T-Pain, musician*)

12. My opinion is **that you never find happiness until you stop looking for it**. (*Zhaungzi, philosopher*)

13. The more I live, the more I think **that humor is the saving sense**[3]. (*Jacob August Riis, journalist*)

14. I worry **that life is getting faster and faster**. (*John Lasseter, movie director*)

Think about It What is the first word of each noun clause in Activity 1?

Think about It Can you find an adverb clause in one of the quotations in Activity 1? Is it inside the noun clause?

Think about It In which of the quotations in Activity 1 does the speaker report someone's words or ideas? In which of the quotations does the speaker express a degree of certainty or an attitude?

2 | Identifying Noun Clauses Underline the noun clauses in these sentences. `12.1 B`

VINCENT VAN GOGH

1. Some experts believe <u>that Van Gogh was the greatest artist of all time</u>.
2. It's hard to believe that Van Gogh was once almost unknown.
3. Most people know that Van Gogh painted *Starry Night*.
4. Many people don't realize that he also painted a large number of pictures of himself.
5. One of Van Gogh's problems was that few people appreciated his art.
6. That he sold very few paintings during his lifetime is surprising.
7. Van Gogh was killed by a gun. Whether or not he killed himself is uncertain.
8. There have been several documentaries focusing on how he died.
9. The truth is that Van Gogh suffered from mental illness all his life.
10. If he shot himself, his illness may explain why he did it.
11. What Van Gogh accomplished in his lifetime is amazing.
12. Today most people agree that he made a huge contribution[4] to the art world.

Think about It How is each noun clause used in the sentences above? Write *S* (subject), *O* (object of a verb), or *SC* (subject complement) above each noun clause.

---

[2] **flop:** something that is not a success
[3] **sense:** the ability to understand or appreciate something

[4] **contribution:** something that a person gives

3 | Usage Note: *That* Read the note. Then do Activity 4.

We use the word *that* in many different ways:

As a demonstrative pronoun	**That**'s my favorite store.
As a demonstrative determiner	I like **that store**.
To introduce an adjective clause	I went to the store **that you like**.
To introduce a noun clause	I forgot **that the store is closed on Mondays**.

4 | Identifying Uses of *That* Find the word *that* in the sentences below. If it's part of a longer phrase or clause, underline the entire phrase or clause. Then identify how it is used. Choose an answer from the box. 12.1 B

USES OF THAT

a. It's a pronoun.
b. It's a determiner.
c. It introduces an adjective clause.
d. It introduces a noun clause.

1. This is <u>the house that Bill Gates lived in</u>. _c_
2. We all know that she's intelligent. ____
3. I like that painting in our classroom. ____
4. She thinks that I'm wrong. ____
5. I decided that I should leave. ____
6. That cannot be true! ____
7. Is this the restaurant that you want to go to? ____
8. Let's rent that new action movie. ____
9. That's not what I said. ____
10. The problem is that I have to work on Saturday. ____
11. He moved! I didn't know that. ____
12. Did you hear that loud noise? ____

12.2 *That* Clauses as Subjects

COMPARE 1A–1B

	that clause as subject	
1a	That he wasn't coming	soon became clear.

	it		*that* clause
1b	It	soon became clear	that he wasn't coming.

It is possible to use a **that clause** as the subject of a sentence, as in **1a**, but it is not very common. Instead, we use *it* as an empty subject and move the *that* clause to the end of the sentence where it is easier to notice, as in **1b**.

A

IT + BE + ADJECTIVE + THAT CLAUSE

2 It is **likely** that a new business will go through a difficult period before it is established.

3 It is **clear** from the statistics that today's families are spending more time at home.

the fact + *that* clause	
4 The fact that she loves to sing	doesn't surprise me.

We can use *it* as an empty subject followed by *be* + adjective + *that* clause, as in **2 – 3**. This is one way we express an attitude or degree of certainty about something, especially in academic and news writing.

We may also use **the fact** + **that clause**, as in **4**. This sounds better than starting a sentence with a *that* clause alone.

398

5 | Noticing *That* Clauses Read these personal opinions about travel. Which sentences contain *that* clauses? Underline them. (Not all the sentences have a *that* clause.) `12.2 A`

Travel

1. It's obvious <u>that you learn a lot when you travel</u>.
2. It surprises me that people travel to other countries. I like staying at home.
3. Traveling allows you to understand the similarities and differences between different people and places.
4. The fact that travel can be expensive doesn't bother me. I love it!
5. I enjoy traveling because it gives me the chance to see beautiful new places.
6. The fact that you can meet new people and experience different cultures is the best thing about visiting a new country.
7. It's very clear that travel can change your view of the world.
8. I think it's possible that traveling makes you more confident in life.
9. I love to simply get on a plane, train, or bus and go somewhere new!
10. For me, it's disappointing that I can't travel all the time.

Think about It Which *that* clauses above are in sentences beginning with *it*? Which are in sentences beginning with *the fact*?

Think about It None of the sentences above begins with a *that* clause. Why do you think this is?

Talk about It Which of the opinions above do you agree with? Why? Share ideas with your classmates.

6 | Giving Opinions with *That* Clauses Use the word(s) in parentheses to write a new sentence with *it* and a *that* clause. `12.2 A`

VISITING PARIS

1. Paris is popular. (obvious)

   It's obvious that Paris is popular.

2. There are long lines for the Eiffel Tower. (annoying)

   _____

3. The food is generally very good. (not surprising)

   _____

4. Paris is called "the City of Light." (appropriate⁵)

   _____

5. They light up the Eiffel Tower at night. (wonderful)

   _____

6. The shopping in Paris is the best in the world. (possible)

   _____

⁵ **appropriate:** right or correct for the situation

7. Many people visit the Louvre Museum just to see the *Mona Lisa*. (too bad)

_____

_____

8. You can go on a boat ride on the Seine River and canals. (great)

_____

_____

9. So many famous people are buried[6] in the Père-LaChaise cemetery[7]. (interesting)

_____

_____

10. The Sorbonne is one of Europe's oldest universities. (well known)

_____

_____

Think about It How is the meaning of each sentence you wrote in Activity 6 different from the meaning of the original one?

7 | Using *That* Clauses Complete these sentences. Use *that* clauses and your own ideas. `12.2 A`

GIVING PERSONAL OPINIONS

1. It's surprising _____ .

   It's surprising that some people don't like to study grammar.

2. The fact _____ worries me.

3. It annoys me _____ .

4. The fact _____ doesn't surprise me.

5. It's strange _____ .

6. It bothers me _____ .

7. The fact _____ makes me happy.

8. It's too bad _____ .

9. It's obvious _____ .

10. The fact _____ pleases me.

Talk about It Take turns reading the sentences you wrote above to a partner. See if your partner agrees or disagrees and why.

Talk about It Talk with a partner. What things are possible, likely, or certain to happen to you next week? Finish these sentences with a *that* clause and your own ideas.

1. It's possible . . .

   A: *It's possible that I won't be in class next week.*
   B: *Why not?*
   A: *I need to go visit my parents.*

2. It's likely . . .

3. It's certain . . .

---

[6] **bury:** to put a dead body in the ground   [7] **cemetery:** a place where people are buried

12.3 *That* Clauses as Complements

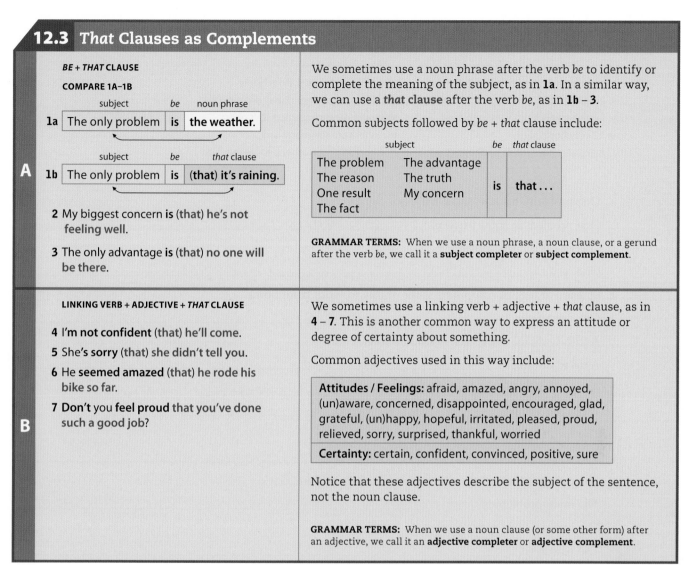

A

BE + *THAT* CLAUSE

COMPARE 1A–1B

	subject	*be*	noun phrase
1a	The only problem	**is**	**the weather.**

	subject	*be*	*that* clause
1b	The only problem	**is**	**(that) it's raining.**

2 My biggest concern **is** (that) he's not feeling well.

3 The only advantage **is** (that) no one will be there.

We sometimes use a noun phrase after the verb *be* to identify or complete the meaning of the subject, as in **1a**. In a similar way, we can use a ***that* clause** after the verb *be*, as in **1b – 3**.

Common subjects followed by *be* + *that* clause include:

subject		*be*	*that* clause
The problem	The advantage		
The reason	The truth	**is**	**that . . .**
One result	My concern		
The fact			

GRAMMAR TERMS: When we use a noun phrase, a noun clause, or a gerund after the verb *be*, we call it a **subject completer** or **subject complement**.

B

LINKING VERB + ADJECTIVE + *THAT* CLAUSE

4 **I'm not confident** (that) he'll come.

5 **She's sorry** (that) she didn't tell you.

6 **He seemed amazed** (that) he rode his bike so far.

7 **Don't** you **feel proud** that you've done such a good job?

We sometimes use a linking verb + adjective + *that* clause, as in **4 – 7**. This is another common way to express an attitude or degree of certainty about something.

Common adjectives used in this way include:

Attitudes / Feelings: afraid, amazed, angry, annoyed, (un)aware, concerned, disappointed, encouraged, glad, grateful, (un)happy, hopeful, irritated, pleased, proud, relieved, sorry, surprised, thankful, worried

Certainty: certain, confident, convinced, positive, sure

Notice that these adjectives describe the subject of the sentence, not the noun clause.

GRAMMAR TERMS: When we use a noun clause (or some other form) after an adjective, we call it an **adjective completer** or **adjective complement**.

GO ONLINE

8 | Identifying *That* Clauses as Subject Complements Read this text. Which of the **bold** *that* clauses are subject complements? Write *SC* over them. Compare your answers with a partner. **12.3 A**

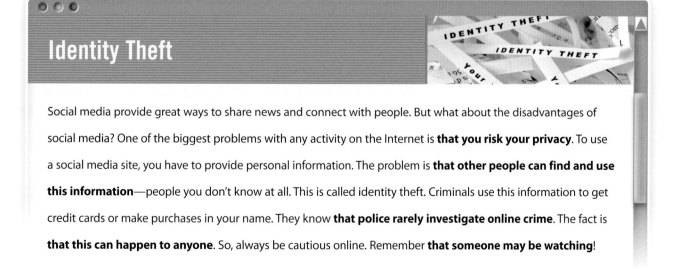

Identity Theft

Social media provide great ways to share news and connect with people. But what about the disadvantages of social media? One of the biggest problems with any activity on the Internet is **that you risk your privacy**. To use a social media site, you have to provide personal information. The problem is **that other people can find and use this information**—people you don't know at all. This is called identity theft. Criminals use this information to get credit cards or make purchases in your name. They know **that police rarely investigate online crime**. The fact is **that this can happen to anyone**. So, always be cautious online. Remember **that someone may be watching**!

Think about It What subject does each *that* clause identify or complete? Underline it.

9 | Using *That* Clauses as Subject Complements Read the first sentence in each pair below. Then complete the new sentence using a *that* clause from the box with a similar meaning. 12.3 A

that countries all over the world owe money	that people can work from home
that employees are unhappy	that people have no money and no jobs
that farmers cannot grow enough food	that public transportation isn't good
that it's very hot and dry	that there are too many cars
that managers have made poor decisions	that you don't see other people regularly

1. a. One problem in some areas is the hot climate.

   One problem in some areas is ___*that it's very hot and dry*___.

   b. One result is crop failure.

   One result is _____.

2. a. One advantage of computers is the ability to work from home.

   One advantage is _____.

   b. A disadvantage is the lack of human interaction.

   A disadvantage is _____.

3. a. A big concern is worldwide debt.

   A big concern is _____.

   b. The result is poverty and unemployment.

   The result is _____.

4. a. The main problem at the office is staff dissatisfaction.

   The main problem is _____.

   b. The reason is bad management.

   The reason is _____.

5. a. The biggest problem in the city is the amount of traffic.

   The biggest problem is _____.

   b. One cause is the lack of public transportation.

   One cause is _____.

Think about It Work with a partner. Read the original sentences and the new sentences above aloud. Which sentences sound more academic or formal? Why?

10 | Using *That* Clauses after Adjectives Read these sentences and circle the correct adjective. Then combine the pairs of sentences using a *that* clause. (More than one answer may be possible.) 12.3 B

SENTENCES ABOUT PROFESSIONALS

1. Their presentation was inaccurate. The sales team was (happy / (worried)).

   The sales team was worried that their presentation was inaccurate.

2. The number of hurricanes is increasing. Climate scientists are (concerned / glad).

   _____

3. The archaeologists were able to excavate the site. They were (frustrated / grateful). _____

_____

4. They would get an interview with the celebrity. The journalists were (sure / sorry). _____

_____

5. She would win the election. The candidate was (confident / annoyed).

_____

6. During the investigation, the detective would solve the case. He was (irritated / convinced).

_____

7. Scientists will find a cure for the disease. They are (certain / sorry).

_____

8. Three students failed the exam. The professor is (disappointed / proud).

_____

9. The patient needs surgery. The doctors are (annoyed / positive).

_____

10. The rescue workers arrived in time to help. They were (sorry / relieved).

_____

11. Her paintings are selling so well. The artist is (angry / amazed).

_____

12. He needed to decrease the workers' wages. The manager was (sorry / encouraged).

_____

11 | Writing *That* Clauses Think about your life and your future. Write sentences that are true for you using the adjectives in parentheses. `12.3 B`

MY LIFE AND FUTURE

1. (positive) _____

   I'm positive that I'll continue to study English.

2. (glad) _____

3. (confident) _____

4. (sorry) _____

5. (concerned) _____

6. (grateful) _____

7. (amazed) _____

8. (encouraged) _____

9. (sure) _____

10. (happy) _____

Talk about It Take turns reading the sentences you wrote above to a partner. See if your partner feels the same way.

12.4 That Clauses as Objects (Verb + That Clause)

A

VERB + *THAT* CLAUSE

verb	*that* clause
1 I can see	(that) we're going to be late.

2 I **couldn't believe** (that) I said it.

3 I **guess** (that) no one is at home.

4 I **told** her (that) I had to work late.

We often use a ***that* clause** as the object of a verb, as in **1 – 3**. In these sentences, the verb in the main clause often expresses thoughts, beliefs, attitudes, or feelings about the information in the *that* clause. Some common verbs we use in this way are:

believe	find	imagine	suppose
feel	guess	know	think

We also use *that* clauses to report what someone said, wrote, or asked, as in **4**. For more information on this use of *that* clauses, see Chart 12.8.

GRAMMAR TERMS: *That* clauses used as the object of a verb are called **verb complements** or **verb completers**.

B

***THAT* CLAUSES IN SPEAKING AND WRITING**

5 A: Somebody needs to clean this room.
　 B: I **guess** I could do it.

6 A: Hi, Jim. Come on in.
　 B: I **hope** I'm not bothering you.

7 A: You can't go in there.
　 B: I **know** I can't. (= I know that I can't go in there.)

8 Scientists **believe** that the animal is extinct.

9 He **explained** that the answers were not in the book.

10 She **argued** that she couldn't afford to pay the fine.

In speaking, we often omit the word *that* at the beginning of a noun clause, as in **5 – 6**.

Sometimes in a short answer, we do not include the full form of the verb in a *that* clause, as in **7**.

In writing, we often use the word *that* because it can make the writing easier to understand, as in **8**.

WARNING! In both conversation and writing, it is usually necessary to include *that* after the verbs *answer*, *argue*, *explain*, *reply*, and *understand*, as in **9 – 10**.

 ONLINE

---

12 | Using *That* Clauses as Objects Rewrite each sentence below using a *that* clause and the appropriate positive or negative form of a verb from the box. Try to use a different verb in each sentence. (Many different answers are possible.) **12.4 A**

assume	feel	imagine	see	think
believe	guess	know	suppose	understand

ENDANGERED BIRDS

1. There are many types of endangered birds.

   I know that there are many types of endangered birds.

2. Many different species of penguins are endangered.

3. Human activity is a threat to birds.

4. One of the biggest threats to birds is agriculture[8].

5. The changing climate is another reason birds are in danger.

6. Some types of birds probably can't be saved.

7. They should be protected.

8. Some governments are protecting areas for birds to live in.

[8] **agriculture:** the farming industry

404

9. Some charities[9] give money to protect birds.

10. People should take an interest in wildlife.

Think about It How is the meaning of each sentence you wrote in Activity 12 different from the meaning of the original one?

Talk about It Look online to find more information about endangered birds, and share three facts with your classmates.

"I learned that there are over 190 kinds of birds in immediate danger."

13 | Reporting Your Thoughts and Beliefs Write ten sentences with a *that* clause using the information in this chart and your own ideas. (More than one answer may be possible.) **12.4 A**

TALKING ABOUT SPACE

I assume	I can't travel into space.
I believe/don't believe	I'll go to the moon.
I doubt	people will take vacations in space someday.
I guess	scientists are searching for signs of life on Mars.
I hope	space exploration is extremely expensive.
I know	space exploration is important.
I regret	space is endless.
I suppose	space travel is becoming cheaper.
I think/don't think	the moon goes around the earth.
I understand	we will discover life on other planets.

I know that the moon goes around the earth.

Talk about It Compare the sentences you wrote above with a partner. Which statements do you agree or disagree on? Why?

14 | Using *That* Clauses as Objects Think of someone you know well. What do you know about him or her? Rewrite each sentence, adding more detailed information with a *that* clause. (You can give specific information or a more general answer.) **12.4 A**

DESCRIBING SOMEONE I KNOW WELL

1. I know his/her occupation.

   I know that he's an accountant. OR
   I know that he works in an office downtown.

2. I know his/her favorite pastime.

3. I know the kind of food he/she likes.

4. I know his/her address.

5. I know his/her family members.

6. I know his/her hopes for the future.

7. I know some abilities he/she has.

8. I know the kind of movies he/she likes.

9. I know the country he/she was born in.

10. I know the things he/she is afraid of.

[9]**charities:** organizations that help those in need

Talk about It Choose a person that everyone in your class knows. Share what you know, think, or believe about this person.

I know that Mahatma Gandhi was from India and that he . . .

15 | Using *That* Clauses in Conversation Listen and complete the response in these conversations. Then practice with a partner. `12.4 B`

1. A: You can leave now.

   B: I know _____ .
      I just need to finish one thing.

2. A: It's late. We should go.

   B: I suppose _____ .

3. A: Is this too expensive?

   B: I think _____ .

4. A: Shall I call Nick?

   B: No, I think _____ .

5. A: It's already noon. Where's the train?

   B: I hope _____ .

6. A: Is there a bank near here?

   B: I believe _____ .

7. A: Where's Amy?

   B: I suppose _____ .

8. A: I love my job.

   B: I imagine _____ .

9. A: I'm hungry!

   B: I guess _____ .

10. A: Joe's getting married.

    B: I know _____ .
       I heard.

Think about It Which responses above use short answers in the noun clause?

Think about It Can you add *that* to the noun clauses in the responses above? How do the sentences sound different? Does the meaning of the statements change?

16 | Omitting *That* in Conversation Listen to these conversations. Cross out *that* if you don't hear it. Listen again and check your answers. Then practice with a partner. `12.4 B`

1. A: What did Professor Cook just say?

   B: He explained that we need to summarize the text.

2. A: You don't look good. Are you tired?

   B: Yes, I suppose that I am.

3. A: Why are you keeping that old watch?

   B: I guess that I just like it.

4. A: Mary seems really mad at you.

   B: I know. I understand that she's upset, but I was trying to help.

5. A: This coffee tastes awful!

   B: I guess that it's gotten cold.

6. A: Is there a pool at the hotel?

   B: I really hope that there is.

7. A: What did the driver say?

   B: He argued that it wasn't his fault. It was an accident.

8. A: Did you hear Joey's news?

   B: Yes, I heard that he'd been promoted.

9. A: What did you do when she asked you to help her?

   B: I just replied that I was too busy.

10. A: I think that we should call the police.

    B: Hmm. I guess so.

Think about It In which conversations above does the speaker have to use the word *that* at the beginning of a noun clause? Why? Discuss with your classmates.

12.5 Using the Base Form of a Verb in *That* Clauses

A

VERB + *THAT* CLAUSE WITH BASE FORM VERB **1** She **demanded** that her employees be on time for work. **2** I **insist** that he see a doctor. (NOT: I insist that he ~~sees~~ a doctor.) **3** We **recommend** that you not go out after dark.	After verbs that express urgency or a requirement, we usually use the base form of the verb in a *that* clause, even with third-person singular verbs, as in **1 – 2**. We form the negative with *not* + the base form of the verb, as in **3**. Common verbs we use this way include *advise, ask, demand, insist, propose, recommend, request,* and *suggest*.
IT + *BE* + ADJECTIVE + *THAT* CLAUSE WITH BASE FORM VERB **4** It is **essential** that she start the work this week. **5** It is **important** that my brother not hear about this from you.	Sometimes we also need to use the base form of a verb in a *that* clause after *it* + *be* + adjective to express urgency or requirement, as in **4 – 5**. Common adjectives we use this way include *critical, crucial, essential, imperative, important,* and *vital*. **GRAMMAR TERM:** When we use the base form of the verb with verbs and adjectives of requirement or importance, we call it a **subjunctive** form of the verb.

GO ONLINE

17 | Using the Base Form Verb in a *That* Clause Read the first sentence. Then complete the second sentence with a positive or negative base form verb. `12.5 A`

1. Don't be late for the lecture! I recommend that you ____*be*____ on time for the lecture.

2. He absolutely has to go to a doctor. It is critical that he _____ to a doctor.

3. Pay your rent! I insist that you _____ your rent.

4. It's a good idea to keep notes. She suggests that we _____ notes.

5. I must see your passports. He demands that he _____ our passports.

6. Get to the exam room on time. It's important that we _____ to the exam room on time.

7. Why doesn't she go back home early? He proposes that she _____ back home early.

8. Please don't make too much noise. She asks that we _____ too much noise.

9. If I were you, I'd leave right now. She advises that he _____ immediately.

10. Everyone has to be careful on board the ship. It's essential that everyone _____ careful on board the ship.

11. Please be quiet in the theater. She asks that we _____ quiet in the theater.

12. Please don't park there. He requests that we _____ there.

Think about It In what situations or places do people give orders or make strong recommendations like the ones above? Share ideas with your classmates.

18 | Using *That* + the Base Form of the Verb Imagine that you're advising some friends who are preparing for job interviews. Complete these sentences with your own ideas to help them succeed at the interviews. `12.5 A`

TEN TIPS FOR SUCCEEDING AT A JOB INTERVIEW

1. I always recommend that everyone _____.

2. It's essential that women _____.

3. I would advise that men _____.

4. I feel it's critical that you (not) _____.

5. It's always very important that we _____.

6. It's vital that an interviewee (not) _____.

7. Many people insist that you _____.

8. I suggest that you (not) _____.

9. Most employers ask that a job candidate _____.

10. Finally, it is important that every interviewee _____.

Talk about It Compare your ideas in Activity 18 with your classmates. Make a list of ideas on the board and decide on the best advice.

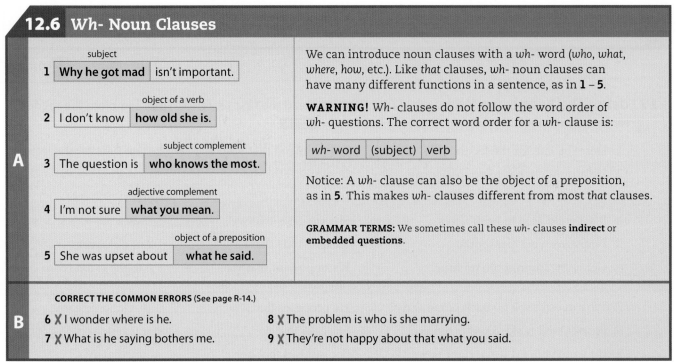

12.6 *Wh-* Noun Clauses

A

subject
1 | **Why he got mad** | isn't important. |

object of a verb
2 | I don't know | **how old she is.** |

subject complement
3 | The question is | **who knows the most.** |

adjective complement
4 | I'm not sure | **what you mean.** |

object of a preposition
5 | She was upset about | **what he said.** |

We can introduce noun clauses with a *wh-* word (*who, what, where, how,* etc.). Like *that* clauses, *wh-* noun clauses can have many different functions in a sentence, as in **1 – 5**.

WARNING! *Wh-* clauses do not follow the word order of *wh-* questions. The correct word order for a *wh-* clause is:

| *wh-* word | (subject) | verb |

Notice: A *wh-* clause can also be the object of a preposition, as in **5**. This makes *wh-* clauses different from most *that* clauses.

GRAMMAR TERMS: We sometimes call these *wh-* clauses **indirect** or **embedded questions**.

B

CORRECT THE COMMON ERRORS (See page R-14.)

6 ✗ I wonder where is he.

7 ✗ What is he saying bothers me.

8 ✗ The problem is who is she marrying.

9 ✗ They're not happy about that what you said.

19 | Identifying *Wh-* Noun Clauses Read this text and underline the *wh-* noun clauses. `12.6 A`

Beauty

A new documentary[10] on TV this spring examines <u>what happens when we see something, or someone, beautiful</u>. It's a program about things that have symmetry, that is, things that are mirror images of one another. The documentary focuses on how symmetry affects us. What's interesting about this is that every human being reacts to symmetry. As far as humans are concerned, symmetry is almost equivalent to[11] beauty. And there's no doubt at all that

mirror image

---

[10] **documentary:** a program or movie that gives facts or information about a topic

[11] **equivalent to:** the same as

symmetry is important. Think about it: almost everything around us is symmetrical. What you're sitting on is symmetrical. Butterflies have symmetry—each half of a butterfly is identical. A glass or a plate has symmetry. In fact, it's pretty hard to think of anything that isn't symmetrical in some way.

The most interesting question is why we find symmetry attractive. It seems that symmetry appeals to us because we like things that match. We are naturally attracted to people whose faces are symmetrical. Take a look at your friends! Essentially, the presenter suggests that we can't help falling in love with symmetry.

Think about It How is each *wh-* clause used in Activity 19? Write *S* (subject), *O* (object of a verb), *OP* (object of a preposition), *SC* (subject complement), or *AC* (adjective complement) above each clause.

20 | Using *Wh-* Clauses Match each **bold** noun phrase with a *wh-* clause that is similar in meaning. `12.6 A`

1. I know **her age**. __*d*__
2. I know **his favorite food**. ____
3. I can't repeat **her words**. ____
4. I don't know **the school he attends**. ____
5. I don't understand **this word**. ____
6. I love **your clothes**! ____
7. I don't know **the problem**. ____
8. I remember **your address**. ____
9. I don't understand **her behavior**. ____
10. I know **the subject of the presentation**. ____
11. I don't know **him**. ____
12. I don't understand **your actions**. ____

a. what the word *fortunate* means
b. where he goes to school
c. what you're wearing
d. how old she is
e. why she acts that way
f. what he likes most
g. where you live
h. what's wrong
i. what it's about
j. why you're doing that
k. who he is
l. what she said

Write about It Work with a partner. Can you think of another *wh-* clause with a similar meaning for each sentence above? Write your ideas and then compare with your classmates.

1. I don't know what her age is.

21 | Word Order in *Wh-* Clauses Read the question on the left. Then complete the question on the right with a *wh-* clause. (Make sure to use the correct verb form.) `12.6 A`

1. How did you get to school today?   Can you tell me __*how you got to school today*__?
2. When is the last day of class?   Do you remember _____?
3. What time is it?   Can you tell me _____?
4. When do we have our next holiday break? Do you know _____?
5. Why did you move to this city?   Can you explain _____?
6. How old are your parents?   Do you know _____?
7. When were your grandparents born?   Can you tell me _____?
8. Where did your grandparents grow up?   Do you remember _____?

9. Why do you study English? Can you explain _____?

10. What did we learn in class today? Do you understand _____?

Talk about It Work with a partner. Take turns asking and answering the questions you wrote in Activity 21. Which of you knows the most answers?

A: Can you tell me how you got to school today?
B: Sure. I usually walk, but today I got a ride.

Write about It Write five new questions like the ones in Activity 21 about these topics. Then ask different classmates each question.

1. (favorite music) Can you tell me _what your favorite music is_____?

2. (spare time) Can you tell me _____?

3. (favorite food) Can you tell me _____?

4. (address) Can you tell me _____?

5. (your best friend) Can you tell me _____?

22 | *Wh-* Clauses with Prepositions Work with a partner. Read each pair of sentences. Then write a new sentence with a similar meaning. Use the *wh-* word and the preposition in parentheses. `12.6 A`

1. I saw something. I can't talk about it.

    (about what) _I can't talk about what I saw._____

2. My friends were upset. You said something.

    (about what) _____

3. He knows nothing. I told him something.

    (except what) _____

4. I'm confused. My father went somewhere.

    (about where) _____

5. She is laughing. No one is interested.

    (in why) _____

6. You seem nervous. He might say something.

    (about what) _____

7. I was fascinated. He was saying something.

    (by what) _____

8. The readers were happy. The story ended.

    (with how) _____

9. There was a lot of discussion. Some people should attend the meeting; others shouldn't.

    (about why) _____

    _____

10. We're thrilled. You've done something.

    (with what) _____

Write about It Choose three verbs + prepositions or adjectives + prepositions above and write sentences that are true for you. Use *wh-* clauses.

I like to talk about what's happening in the news with my friends.

23 | Error Correction Correct any errors in these sentences. (Some sentences may not have any errors.)

1. I have often wondered where do birds go at night.
2. What I think isn't important. You should ask a zoologist.
3. I like what are we listening to. Is it jazz?
4. Please tell me where is the station.
5. What's important is the scene of the crime.
6. What did you tell me isn't correct. It's not the right answer.
7. No, I have no idea where does she live.
8. Tell me about what you liked doing when you were a child.
9. I'm annoyed about that what he did.
10. I don't understand what is the problem.

12.7 Noun Clauses with *If* or *Whether*

A

object of a verb
1 We don't know **if she's right or wrong.**
(= Maybe she's right; maybe she's wrong.)

adjective complement
2 I'm not sure **whether I can join you tonight or not.**
(= Maybe I can join you tonight; maybe I can't.)

subject
3 **Whether or not he will come** isn't certain.
(NOT COMMON: If he will come isn't certain.)

subject complement
4 The question is **whether I should stay or go.**
(NOT COMMON: The question is if I should stay or go.)

object of a preposition
5 We talked about **whether animals can truly communicate or not.**
(NOT COMMON: We talked about if animals can truly communicate or not.)

We use noun clauses with *if* or *whether* to show a choice between two options, as in **1 – 2**. The second option is often negative or contrasting.

Clauses with *whether* can have many different functions in a sentence, as in **1 – 5**.

If- clauses are not used in as many different places as other kinds of noun clauses. We often use them as objects of verbs or adjective complements, as in **1 – 2**. However, they are not common in other places in a sentence, as in **3 – 5**.

B

6 I can't decide **if / whether I should move.**
(= Maybe I should; maybe I shouldn't.)

7 Your doctor can tell you **whether or not you should take your medication.**
(NOT: Your doctor can tell you if ~~or not~~ you should take your medication.)

Sometimes only one option is mentioned in an *if / whether* clause, as in **6**. In these sentences, the second option (*or not*) is implied.

Note that *or not* can directly follow *whether*, but not *if*, as in **7**.

---

24 | Recognizing the Functions of *If/Whether* Clauses Read each sentence. Underline the *if/whether* clause. Say how it is used in the sentence. Check (✓) the correct answer. Then compare with a partner. `12.7 A`

WORLD ISSUES

	Object of a verb	Adjective complement	Subject	Subject complement	Object of a preposition
1. Everyone is talking about <u>whether or not the economy will improve soon.</u>					✓
2. No one is sure if scientists will ever cure cancer.					
3. Everyone wonders if we'll ever have world peace.					

	Object of a verb	Adjective complement	Subject	Subject complement	Object of a preposition
4. Whether or not global warming will ever slow down is a big question.					
5. One question is whether or not we can save our forests.					
6. I don't know if it's a good idea for people to get married when they are young.					
7. Leaders need to make a decision about whether or not they will cooperate[12].					
8. Does anyone know if there's life on other planets?					
9. It's not clear whether or not technology has improved our lives.					

Talk about It Take turns reading the sentences in Activity 24 aloud with a partner. Find out what your partner thinks about each issue.

> A: *Everyone is talking about whether or not the economy will improve soon.*
> B: *I think it will. A lot more people are getting new jobs.*

Talk about It Choose one of the issues in Activity 24 and discuss it with your classmates. What do you think?

25 | Usage Note: Clauses with *If* Read the note. Then do Activity 26.

We can use *if* to begin a noun clause or an adverb clause of condition, but the meaning is very different. Notice that an adverb clause can come before or after the main clause. A noun clause cannot be reversed with the main clause.

IF IN NOUN CLAUSES	*IF* IN ADVERB CLAUSES OF CONDITION
object of verb **1** I **don't know** if she needs help (or not).	adverb clause **3** If you need me, I **can help** you.
adjective complement **2** I'm not **certain** if I should leave yet.	adverb clause **4** I'll **call** you if I'm going to be late.

26 | Distinguishing Noun Clauses and Adverb Clauses Is the *if*- clause in each sentence a noun clause or an adverb clause of condition? Check (✓) your answers. **12.7 A**

TALKING ABOUT ACADEMIC PROBLEMS AND DOUBTS

	NOUN CLAUSE	ADVERB CLAUSE
1. My teacher would be able to help me if she were here.	☐	✓
2. You may feel discouraged if you get a poor grade.	☐	☐
3. Sometimes I'm not sure if I've understood the lectures.	☐	☐

[12] **cooperate:** to work together

	NOUN CLAUSE	ADVERB CLAUSE
4. I don't know if I want to drop this class or not.	☐	☐
5. You won't do well if you wait until the last minute to do the assignment.	☐	☐
6. I'm not certain if I can finish this essay in time.	☐	☐
7. You won't understand everything if you don't do the reading before class.	☐	☐
8. I can't decide if I want to transfer to a different school.	☐	☐
9. I wonder if the academic advisor can help me.	☐	☐
10. You can consider repeating a course if you finish it with a low grade.	☐	☐
11. Ask your classmates for help if you need more ideas.	☐	☐
12. I can't tell if I'm doing well or not.	☐	☐

Write about It Write two more sentences about your academic problems or doubts. Use an adverb clause with *if* in one and a noun clause with *if* in the other.

Think about It Two of the *if-* clauses in Activity 26 are adjective complements. (They come after adjectives.) Which ones are they? Work with a partner to find these two clauses.

27 | Using *or Not* Read each sentence and insert *or not* if possible. (You may be able to put *or not* in more than one place.) [12.7 B]

1. I'm not sure if I'll go to Tibet or Switzerland.
2. My professor and I talked about whether Latin and Greek were important.
3. The question is whether we should move or stay where we are.
4. I just can't decide if I should call the company and complain.
5. A doctor can tell you whether you have a real problem.
6. Whether you join us or stay at home is really your decision.
7. Well, I have no idea whether you need to be worried!
8. I just don't know if I was awake at the time.
9. I wonder if it's a good idea to take so many risks.
10. The real question here is whether to sell the house.

RESEARCH SAYS...

Noun clauses with *if* are much more common than those with *whether*. *Whether* is more common in writing than in speaking.

CORPUS

28 | Using Noun Clauses with *If* and *Whether* Use the phrases in parentheses to complete each sentence with an *if/whether* clause. (More than one answer is possible.) Are you wondering about these things? Check (✓) *Yes* or *No*. [12.7 A–B]

DO YOU WONDER ABOUT ANY OF THESE THINGS?	YES	NO
1. (go to class tomorrow)	☐	☐
I don't know *if I'm going to class tomorrow*_____.		
2. (rain tonight)	☐	☐
I'm not sure _____.		
3. (take English next semester)	☐	☐
I can't decide _____.		

4. (our class/finish on time) ☐ ☐

   I don't know _____.

5. (buy a new computer this year) ☐ ☐

   I'm not sure _____.

6. (the next assignment/be difficult) ☐ ☐

   I don't know _____.

7. (information on the Internet/be always true) ☐ ☐

   I'm not sure _____.

8. (eat in or eat out tonight) ☐ ☐

   I can't decide _____.

9. (ask friends over this weekend) ☐ ☐

   I'm not certain _____.

10. (my favorite TV show/be on tonight) ☐ ☐

   I don't know _____.

Write about It Write three sentences about things you are wondering about. Use *if/whether* clauses. Then read your sentences to a partner. Find out if your sentences are true for your partner as well.

"I don't know if I'll travel much next year. How about you?"

29 | Noun Clause Review Read this text. Underline the noun clauses. Then answer the questions on page 415. Look back at Charts 12.1–12.7 if necessary.

THE ANCIENT ART OF FENG SHUI

Have you ever wondered if you can make your life better? Maybe in the past you've taken up a new sport, started eating more healthily, or changed your lifestyle in some way. But have you considered changing the place you live in? The art of feng shui is well known nowadays because people have been practicing it for years. Whether or not it works is uncertain, but many people arrange their bedrooms, offices, and apartments according to the principles[13] of feng shui. They firmly believe that a few simple actions will have a positive influence on their lives. In 2005, Disneyland Hong Kong even moved its main entrance after talking to a feng shui expert!

But what exactly is feng shui? Feng shui originally came from China. In English, these two words mean "wind and water." It's a belief that we can balance human life with our environment. The main concept behind feng shui is something called *chi*—the Chinese word for energy flow[14]. And the question is whether or not we can encourage this force to move in more positive ways around the spaces we live in. At its simplest, feng shui is the examination[15] of how the placement of objects around you can affect the movement of energy.

Feng shui specialists say that the way you design the space you live in can benefit your life. For example, make sure that your home is tidy and that you have good-quality light and air. It's not certain if you'll see immediate results, of course, but learning a little about this ancient art may make life more pleasant.

---

[13]**principles:** rules
[14]**flow:** slow, steady movement

[15]**examination:** the act of looking at something carefully

1. What is the function of each noun clause? Write *S* (subject), *O* (object of a verb), *OP* (object of a preposition), *SC* (subject complement), or *AC* (adjective complement) next to each clause.

2. Would you arrange your home according to feng shui principles? Why or why not?

12.8 Noun Clauses in Indirect Speech

We often want to report what someone else has said. We can do this by repeating the person's exact words, as in **1a – 2a**. We call this **direct speech**. We can also report someone's words using a *that clause*, as in **1b – 2b**. We call this **indirect speech** (or **reported speech**).

DIRECT SPEECH	INDIRECT SPEECH (MAIN CLAUSE + NOUN CLAUSE)
1a "I'm leaving in a few minutes," she said.	**1b She said** (that) she was leaving in a few minutes.
2a He said, "I don't know."	**2b He said** (that) he didn't know.

When we change direct speech to indirect speech, we often use a past verb form in the main clause, as in **3b – 11b**. Usually, we also "move" the verb form in the noun clause back further into the past. We call this "backshifting."

A

DIRECT SPEECH	CHANGES TO THE VERB IN THE NOUN CLAUSE	INDIRECT SPEECH
3a "I'm tired."	simple present → simple past	**3b He said** he **was** tired.
4a "It **isn't working**."	present continuous → past continuous	**4b She said** it **wasn't working**.
5a "He **hasn't left** yet."	present perfect → past perfect	**5b She said** he **hadn't left** yet.
6a "I **didn't see** them."	simple past → past perfect	**6b He said** he **hadn't seen** them.
7a "We **weren't living** there then."	past continuous → past perfect continuous	**7b She said** they **hadn't been living** there then.
8a "I'll be there." **9a** "I **can't go**." **10a** "He **may not call**." **11a** "He **must quit**."	will → would can → could may → might must → had to	**8b He said** he **would be** there. **9b He said** he **couldn't go**. **10b She said** he **might not call**. **11b She said** he **had to quit**.

B

CHOOSING NOT TO BACKSHIFT

12 A: What time is the movie?
B: **Joe said** that it starts at 7:15.

13 A: Where's Ann?
B: She just called. **She said** she is still at work.

Sometimes we decide not to backshift the verb in the noun clause. We may do this because:

- the state or event is still true, as in **12**
- we are reporting something that someone just said, as in **13**

USING PRESENT REPORTING VERBS

14 He says the school is on Highland Road.

15 John says he doesn't care if we help him or not.

16 They say the building is on fire and everyone's being evacuated.

We can also use a present verb in the main clause. We do this:

- when the information in the noun clause is still true or relevant, as in **14 – 15**
- to make our reporting more vivid, as in **16**

Notice: When we use a present verb form in the main clause, we don't backshift the verb in the noun clause.

C

REPORTED *YES/NO* QUESTIONS

17 She asked if she was late.

18 They asked whether or not we could join them for dinner tonight.

REPORTED *WH-* QUESTIONS

19 They asked when we were coming.

20 He asked why I wasn't interested in reading his book.

We often use *asked* to report questions, as in **17 – 20**. When we report questions with *asked*, we use *if / whether* and *wh-* clauses.

TYPE OF QUESTION	BEGIN NOUN CLAUSE WITH:
YES/NO	*if / whether* (or not)
WH-	*wh-* word (*who, when, why, where . . .*)

GO ONLINE

30 | Using Indirect Speech Rewrite these sentences using indirect speech. Remember to change the verb form used in the original sentence. (More than one answer may be possible.) `12.8 A`

U.S. POLITICS AND PRESIDENTS

1. "The next election will take place in four years."

    She said _(that) the next election would take place in four years_.

2. "The candidates in the election have been chosen."

    He said _____.

3. "George W. Bush has a collection of signed baseballs."

    She said _____.

4. "Thomas Jefferson spoke six different languages."

    He said _____.

5. "The next election will be exciting."

    She said _____.

Theodore Roosevelt

6. "Theodore Roosevelt was the first president to travel outside the United States."

    He said _____.

7. "Theodore Roosevelt was the first president to be known by his initials: T. R."

    She said _____.

8. "Lyndon B. Johnson was an auto mechanic and teacher."

    He said _____.

9. "The capital of Liberia is named after James Monroe."

    She said _____.

10. "Herbert Hoover's son had two pet alligators!"

    He said _____.

31 | Using Indirect Speech Report what these people said. (More than one answer may be possible.) `12.8 A`

QUOTATIONS FROM FAMOUS PEOPLE

1. Hope is a good breakfast [but] a bad supper. (*Francis Bacon, philosopher*)

    He said _(that) hope was a good breakfast but a bad supper_.

2. All children have creative power. (*Brenda Ueland, journalist*)

    She said _____.

3. A quick temper[16] will make a fool[17] of you soon enough. (*Bruce Lee, martial artist*)

    He said _____.

4. It's better to be alone than in bad company. (*George Washington, U.S. president*)

    He said _____.

5. Money is only useful when you get rid of it. (*Evelyn Waugh, writer*)

    He said _____.

6. The only thing better than singing is more singing. (*Ella Fitzgerald, jazz singer*)

    She said _____.

---

[16]**temper:** the act of becoming angry   [17]**fool:** a person who is silly or does something silly

7. It's going to be a season with lots of accidents. (*Ayrton Senna, race car driver*)

   He said _____.

8. We don't know a millionth of one percent about anything. (*Thomas A. Edison, inventor*)

   He said _____.

9. You can only lead . . . from behind. (*Nelson Mandela, president of South Africa*)

   He said _____.

10. You cannot find peace by avoiding life. (*Virginia Woolf, author*)

    She said _____.

11. A man may be a fool and not know it. (*H. L. Mencken, journalist*)

    He said _____.

12. Everybody is talking . . . about the economy. (*Joschka Fischer, politician*)

    He said _____.

32 | Usage Note: Changing Other Forms in Indirect Speech Read the note. Then do Activity 33.

When we use indirect speech, we may need to change certain pronouns and possessive forms in the noun clause. We may also change time and place expressions, but this depends on when and where we report the statement.

DIRECT SPEECH	INDIRECT SPEECH
1a He said, "**You** shouldn't go."	**1b** He said **I** shouldn't go.
2b She said, "**I**'ll be leaving **tomorrow**."	**2b** She said **she** would be leaving **the next day** / **today**.
3c He said, "**My** brother doesn't want to be **here**."	**3b** He said **his** brother didn't want to be **there** / **here**.

Sometimes we omit time words if they aren't necessary or to make the sentence more concise (shorter, simpler).

DIRECT SPEECH	INDIRECT SPEECH
4a Bob said, "**We** just saw him **yesterday**."	**4b** Bob said **they**'d just seen him.
5a Sarah said, "**I really** need to talk to you **later**."	**5b** Sarah said **she** wanted to talk to me.

33 | Using Indirect Speech Rewrite each example of direct speech as indirect speech. Make changes to verb forms, pronouns, and time and place expressions. (More than one answer may be possible.) `12.8 A`

DIRECT SPEECH	INDIRECT SPEECH
1. She said, "I really don't want to go today."	*She said she didn't want to go.*
2. He said, "I saw my brother yesterday."	_____
3. He said, "I'm going on vacation next week."	_____
4. She said, "I left my book here."	_____
5. He said, "We're going to the library today."	_____
6. She said, "We must sell the house."	_____
7. He said, "We enjoyed the match yesterday."	_____
8. She said, "Max is working here with me."	_____
9. He said, "I'm very happy in London."	_____
10. He said, "I'll meet you here at two tomorrow."	_____
11. She said, "I'll call you. I promise."	_____
12. She said, "You can help me with my assignment."	_____

DIRECT SPEECH	INDIRECT SPEECH
13. He said, "I've been working."	_____
14. She said, "We're having a meeting."	_____
15. She said, "She's not here."	_____

Talk about It Work with a partner. Choose three of the sentences you wrote in Activity 33 and use them to create short conversations. Present one of your conversations to the class.

A: Why didn't Sarah come to dinner last night?
B: She said she didn't want to go. I'm not sure why.
A: Well, we missed her!

Write about It Look online to find quotations from people who are interesting to you. Write down what the people said using reported speech. Share some of your sentences with your classmates and explain what they mean.

34 | Reporting Information about Your Classmates Work in groups of three. Ask each other questions and share information using topics from this box. Then write sentences to report what your partners said. `12.8 A`

> **TOPICS**
> a fact about your family
> a plan for this week or this year
> something special that you can do
>
> something you are thinking about doing
> something you are worried about
> something you did last week

A: Hassan, what are your plans this week?
B: I think I'm going to buy a new laptop. Mine's too slow. How about you?
A: Uh, nothing special, I guess.

Hassan said he was going to buy a new laptop.

35 | Reporting Facts Rewrite each example of direct speech with indirect speech. Only make changes to verb forms, pronouns, and time and place expressions if necessary. `12.8 B`

INTERESTING FACTS YOU MAY NOT KNOW

1. Professor: "The total number of people who have ever lived is about 108 billion."

   The professor said *that the total number of people who have ever lived is about 108 billion*_____.

2. Report: "Three percent of the world's energy comes from wind power."

   The report says _____.

3. Artist: "Mickey Mouse's ears are perfect circles."

   The artist told us _____.

4. Coach: "Basketball has been part of the Summer Olympics since 1936."

   Our coach said _____.

5. Tour guide: "Kangaroos can't walk backward."

   The tour guide said _____.

6. Dictionary: "The word *orchestra* means 'dancing place' in Greek."

   The dictionary says _____.

7. Farmer: "The average chicken lays 250–270 eggs a year."

   The farmer told us _____.

8. Professor: "Shakespeare never used the word *October* in his plays."

   Our professor said _____.

Think about It Look back at the sentences you completed in Activity 35. Was it necessary to change the verbs in the noun clauses you wrote? Why or why not?

Talk about It What other interesting facts do you know? Share ideas with a partner. Then report one of your partner's facts to the class.

36 | Reporting Questions Write questions about activities. Use your own ideas. `12.8 B–C`

Activity Survey

1. What _____ *are you doing* _____ tomorrow?
2. What _____ yesterday?
3. Have you ever _____?
4. Are you going to _____ next week?
5. Did you _____ last week?
6. Where does _____?
7. Where is _____?
8. How often _____?
9. Are you _____?
10. Where do you _____?
11. Were you _____?
12. Does _____?

Talk about It Ask and answer the questions above with a partner.

A: What are you doing tomorrow?
B: Well, I have class and then I have to work.

Talk about It Join another pair. Report your questions and answers to another pair of students.

"I asked Sarah what she was doing tomorrow. She said she has class and then she has to work."

12.9 Using *Say*, *Tell*, and Other Reporting Verbs

In reported speech, two of the most common reporting verbs are **say** and **tell**. They are similar in meaning, but we use them in different ways. Compare:

A

USING *SAY*

1	I said (that) I'd meet my roommate at seven.
2	I said (that) I was sorry. (NOT: ~~I said Mary I was sorry.~~)
3	Someone said he wasn't coming. (NOT: ~~Someone said me . . .~~)

• We don't usually include an indirect object with *say*, as in **1 – 3**.

USING *TELL*

4	I told **my roommate** (that) I'd meet her at seven.
5	I told **Mary** (that) I was sorry.
6	Someone told **me** (that) Joey wasn't coming. (NOT: ~~Someone told that Joey wasn't coming.~~)

• With *tell*, we usually include an indirect object (the hearer), as in **4 – 6**.

B

7 In a 2012 study, Smith **argued** that long-term treatment was ineffective.

8 He's always **complaining** that it's too hot.

9 My friend **pointed out** that I had forgotten to turn on the electricity.

We can also use **other reporting verbs**, as in **7 – 9**. These verbs can add important information about our attitude or feelings.

admit	claim	hint	recall	respond
agree	complain	joke	repeat	shout
announce	confess	point out	reply	state
answer	demand	propose	report	whisper
argue	explain			

10 The officials **wondered** if they'd made a mistake.

11 They **wanted to know** what happened.

We may also use **wonder** or **want to know** to report a question, as in **10 – 11**.

GO ONLINE

37 | Using *Say* and *Tell* Complete these sentences with a correct form of *tell* or *say*. `12.9 A`

1. Why didn't you ____tell____ me that you couldn't go?

2. I never _____ that you couldn't go.

3. She didn't _____ me we had to leave.

4. How do you feel now that they _____ you that you've won the prize?

5. He _____ that our presentation will be a great success.

6. _____ anyone _____ the students how to find the lecture hall?

7. She _____ it was going to rain tomorrow.

8. I wish you had _____ me you were coming!

9. The doctor _____ I'm very healthy.

10. Why didn't he _____ me that I should book the flight?

> **F Y I**
>
> Notice: When you use the reporting verb *tell* and omit the word *that* in the noun clause, you may use two pronouns in a row.
>
> I **told her I couldn't meet her**.
>
> She didn't **tell me you couldn't come**.

Talk about It Work with a partner. Choose three of the sentences you completed above and use them to create short conversations. Present one of your conversations to the class.

A: Are you ready to go?
B: Go where?
A: The movie. I asked you last night.
B: Oh, I can't. I've got homework.
A: Well, why didn't you tell me that you couldn't go?

38 | Using *Tell* Report what the first person said to the second one. Use *tell*. `12.9 A`

MAKING STATEMENTS

1. Jim to Tom: "I don't believe you."

   Jim told Tom that he didn't believe him.

2. Maria to Susan: "My book won a prize."

   _____

3. Ann to June: "It's raining."

   _____

4. Martin to Nick: "I'm selling my apartment."

   _____

5. Louise to Bill: "The meeting is tomorrow."

   _____

6. Andrew to James: "I quit my job last month."

   _____

7. Sally to Jo: "My daughter is studying music."

   _____

8. David to Stephen: "I've already been to Rome."

   _____

9. James to Nicky: "It's too late to leave."

   _____

10. Sam to Ben: "I did the research."

    _____

> **F Y I**
>
> We can use *to* + an indirect object after *say*; however, this is less common.
>
> Jim **said to Tom** that he didn't believe him.

39 | Using Different Reporting Verbs Use the correct form of the verb in parentheses that best completes each sentence. (More than one answer may be possible.) `12.9 B`

1. My brother finally _____ that he took my phone. (admit/demand)

2. The customer _____ that the computer is too expensive. (want to know/complain)

3. I _____ if the meeting has started because I can't find my colleagues. (wonder/recall)

4. The terrified child _____ that he was in danger. (announce/shout)

5. Several journalists _____ that the situation was calm. (report/propose)

6. At today's conference, the president _____ that the economy is improving. (complain/announce)

7. In the meeting this morning, a co-worker _____ that I was right. (agree/wonder)

8. My old friend _____ whether we met in 2007 or 2008. (want to know/recall)

9. The team leader _____ that we try a different plan. (propose/respond)

10. Two people _____ that they had seen the suspect. (demand/report)

11. The little girl _____ that she'd seen a dinosaur. (claim/confess)

12. We both _____ whether there is a better solution to the problem. (whisper/wonder)

Think about It Which of the sentences above are reported questions? How do you know? Compare your answers with a partner.

12.10 Using Noun Clauses in Speaking

A

main clause	noun clause
I think	it's delicious.
I guess	she left early.
I don't think	I'll get there in time.
I don't know	if he's right.
I don't care	if you stay there.
I wonder	if anyone will come.

1

Speakers often want to express an opinion or lack of certainty about something. One way they do this is with a main clause containing a mental verb (such as **think**, **know**, **guess**, etc.) + **noun clause**, as in **1**.

COMPARE

2a You should call him.
2b **I think** you should call him.

3a You should go to the lecture.
3b **I guess** you really should go to the lecture.

Speakers often use *I think* / *I guess* + noun clause to soften a suggestion, as in **2b** and **3b**.

They can also add other "softening" words, such as *maybe*, *perhaps*, *probably*, and *really*, as in **3b**.

B

4 A: So you're leaving early tomorrow?
　　B: No, that's not **what I said.**

5 A: I hear you're going to LA to see the Rose Bowl.
　　B: Yes, but that's not **why we're going.**

We sometimes want to contradict someone (say the opposite). To do this, we often use a demonstrative pronoun (usually *that*) + *be* + *not* + *wh-* clause, as in **4** – **5**.

C

Sometimes we want to put extra focus on one part of a sentence. We can use a special type of *wh-* clause to do this, as in **6b**. The *wh-* clause signals that important information is coming next, as in **6** – **10**. This use of *wh-* clauses is common in academic lectures.

COMPARE

6a I'd like to welcome you to this course, Introduction to Anthropology. My name is Dr. Hale and I'm the professor. This is going to be a general introduction to the study of anthropology.
6b I'd like to welcome you to this course, Introduction to Anthropology. My name is Dr. Hale and I'm the professor. **What this course is going to be is** a general introduction to the study of anthropology.

These *wh-* clauses usually have this form: *wh-* clause + *be* + one of the following: noun, gerund, *to-* infinitive, or noun clause, as in **7** – **10**.

noun
7 What I love the most **is** chocolate.

to- infinitive
9 What I want **is** to understand the problem better.

gerund
8 What I love **is** spending time with my family.

noun clause
10 What this means **is** that you need to take good notes.

GRAMMAR TERM: These *wh-* clauses are called **wh- clefts**.

40 | Expressing an Opinion or Uncertainty Write eight meaningful sentences using these main clauses and noun clauses. (Different sentences are possible.) **12.10 A**

	anyone called me.
I don't care	I'll work tonight.
I don't know	if he's home.
I don't think	if it'll rain.
I guess	it's fun to travel.
I think	it's wrong.
I wonder	whether I like this dish.
	you're right.

I think you're right.

Talk about It Work with a partner. Choose three of the sentences you wrote in Activity 40 and use them to create short conversations. Present one of your conversations to the class.

41 | Using Noun Clauses in Speaking
Soften each of these suggestions. Use noun clauses and words like *maybe*, *probably*, or *really*. (Different answers are possible.) `12.10 A`

1. You should see a doctor!

   I think you should probably see a doctor.

2. You ought to study.

3. What you must do is apologize.

4. It's time you went home.

5. The question is whether you want to switch colleges.

6. You should leave as soon as possible. It's late.

7. You need to decide whether to go or not.

8. The problem is that you're making too much noise.

Talk about It Work with a partner. Take turns talking about a problem. Use noun clauses to soften the advice.

A: *I'm falling behind with my assignments.*
B: *I guess maybe you should study more.*

42 | Contradicting Someone
Complete each conversation below. Use *that* + *be* + *not* + a *wh-* clause and the correct form of a verb from the box. Then practice with a partner. `12.10 B`

attach	be	do	leave	move	say	speak	use

1. A: So you said you're buying an apartment?

   B: No, _____ *that's not what I said* _____. I said I was moving to a new apartment! I can't afford to buy one!

2. A: Pam tells me you're moving to Paris! You have family there, don't you?

   B: Yes, but _____. I'm moving because I got a great new job.

3. A: Hey, look, here's your computer. Right here on the table.

   B: Oh. That's weird. _____. I thought I put it over there.

4. A: Thanks for your email. I love the picture of your dog. It's so funny!

   B: What dog? I sent you a document. Let me see that. _____! How did that get there?

5. A: The pasta you made was delicious. You used olive oil in the sauce, didn't you?

   B: Nope. _____. It has cream in it.

6. A: I saw you in the supermarket this morning.

   B: That's impossible. _____. I was at work.

7. A: So this morning I called your company and spoke to your manager.

   B: _____. You spoke to my assistant!

8. A: OK, I've figured it out. To turn the phone's volume down, you press this button.

   B: No, _____. You just press and hold this button for two seconds.

43 | Using *Wh-* Clefts Rewrite the professor's statements. Use a *wh-* cleft to replace the **bold** words. `12.10 C`

The First Day of Class

1. **This class is going to be** a thorough examination of all aspects of sociology.

   What this class is going to be is a thorough examination of all aspects of sociology.

2. First of all, I want you to think about what you already know about sociology. **And I want** your ideas as well as mine for each class discussion.

3. My goal is to provide a framework for you. **I want to explain to you** exactly what the study of sociology is.

4. You'll need to do some research during the semester. **And this means** you'll need to spend time online and in the library.

5. I'm here to help you, of course. **And I suggest** a weekly appointment with me in my office to discuss the topics we cover.

6. It will help you to work with your classmates. So, **I also recommend** that you form study groups and meet regularly in the library.

44 | Focusing on Information Rewrite each sentence using a *wh-* cleft to put extra focus on important information. (More than one answer may be possible.) `12.10 C`

FACTS ABOUT THE FAMOUS

1. **John Travolta likes** flying airplanes **the most**.

   What John Travolta likes the most is flying airplanes.

2. **Barack Obama wanted** cooperation between political parties.

   What Barack Obama

3. His unique style **made Michael Jackson famous**.

   What made

4. **Mahatma Gandhi wanted** independence for India.

   What

5. Surprisingly, **Albert Einstein loved** music **more than anything else**.

6. **Nelson Mandela worked for** peace in his country.

7. **Julius Caesar didn't want anyone to know** that he was bald.

8. Dr. Seuss's ability to write a book with just 50 words **was amazing**.

Talk about It Choose three of the people from the sentences above. Look online to find more information about them. Look for sentences that use noun clauses and share some examples with your classmates.

12.11 Using Noun Clauses in Academic Writing

A

1 Researchers **have found** that people with musical training have an easier time learning Chinese.

2 Prior research **has shown** that people quite naturally begin to feel sleepy in the early afternoon.

3 Hale **notes** that people may think they are avoiding problems by staying in touch.

4 One survey **showed** that Canadians enjoyed, on average, 5.5 hours of leisure time daily.

Academic writers often need to report other people's ideas or research findings. To do this, they can use a reporting verb followed by a **noun clause**, as in **1 – 4**. Common reporting verbs in academic writing include:

argue	explain	report	state
claim	find	say	suggest
conclude	note	show	think
demonstrate	propose		

Writers often use present verb forms when they report on the research of others, as in **1 – 3**. They may do this to:

- emphasize that the research is still true or relevant
- show that they agree with the research

Notice that, in writing, we don't usually omit the word *that* at the beginning of a noun clause.

B

5 There are many qualities that a boss must have in order to be a good supervisor. I **think** (that) it is most important for a boss to be sensible, approachable, and fair.

6 **It is true** that some adults will be unemployed.

7 **It is clear** that different people have different priorities.

In academic writing, writers often want to sound objective. However, sometimes they need to express an opinion or attitude about a topic or idea. They often use a main clause with the verb *think* or *believe* + noun clause, as in **5**. They also use *it* + *be* + adjective + *that* clause, as in **6 – 7**.

For more information on *it* + *be* + adjective + *that* clause, see Chart 12.2.

45 | Identifying Reported Ideas in Academic Writing Underline the noun clauses in this article. Then answer the questions on page 426. **12.11 A**

Spending Time in Nature Makes People Feel More Alive

Staring out the window at the trees and plants outside isn't necessarily a sign that you are daydreaming. You might actually be recharging your batteries[18]. Recent studies published in the *Journal of Environmental Psychology* and reprinted on the website *Science Daily* (www.sciencedaily.com) demonstrate that being around nature can give you more energy and make you feel more alive. A lot of people think that they can wake themselves up with a cup of coffee or an energy drink, but Richard Ryan, author and professor of psychology at the University of Rochester, says that connecting with nature works better.

A number of studies have shown that hiking or walking in the woods gives people energy, but scientists weren't sure if the physical activity or simply being around other people during these activities explained the increase in energy. The new studies went further. The researchers tested college students in natural settings and inside buildings. They found that spending time in nature or even imagining a natural environment increased

[18] **recharge your batteries (idiom):** to get back your strength and energy

the students' vitality[19]. Physical activity was not the key factor. They had more energy simply because of the presence of nature.

The good news is that just 20 minutes a day in nature is enough to create the beneficial effects of greater energy. According to Ryan, "Nature is something within which we flourish[20], so having it be more a part of our lives is critical[21], especially when we live and work in built environments[22]." We all know that we feel tired when we're indoors all day. Now we know how we can make things better.

QUESTIONS

1. Which noun clauses are used to report other people's research or ideas?
2. What reporting verbs are used with these noun clauses? Circle them.

Write about It Complete the short summary, begun for you below, of the article in Activity 45. Use some of the reporting verbs from this box and sentences with noun clauses.

argue	conclude	explain	note	report	show	suggest
claim	demonstrate	find	propose	say	state	think

The article "Spending Time in Nature Makes People Feel More Alive" from <u>Science Daily</u> *states that nature can help people have more energy. The author argues that . . .*

46 | Expressing Opinions Write your own thoughts about the qualities that are needed for each occupation. Then discuss your opinions with a partner. ▨ 12.11 B

PROFESSIONAL REQUIREMENTS

1. actor

    I think *that an actor needs to have an excellent memory*   .

2. doctor

    It's clear _____.

3. teacher

    It's important _____.

4. architect

    I believe _____.

5. writer

    I think _____.

6. attorney

    It's important _____.

7. psychiatrist

    I think _____.

8. business executive

    I believe _____.

---

[19] **vitality:** great energy
[20] **flourish:** to do very well

[21] **critical:** very important
[22] **built environments:** buildings and other structures

Talk about It If you could have any occupation you wanted, what would it be? What are the qualities that are needed for this occupation? Discuss as a class.

A: If I could, I would be a doctor. I think it's important that a doctor be a good listener.
B: Yes, I agree with you. But it's also clear that doctors need good training.

WRAP-UP Demonstrate Your Knowledge

A | WRITING Study these pictures from movies. Choose one picture, and write a paragraph to explain what you think is obvious, probable, or possible about the situation in the picture. Talk about what is happening, might have happened, or will happen. Use noun clauses.

Example (picture 1)
I'm not sure <u>who they are</u>. It's possible <u>that they're a husband and wife and they're on vacation</u>. . . .

B | DISCUSSION Choose one of these statements or think of your own. Make some notes to support your opinion about the statement. Then explain to your classmates why you agree or disagree with the statement.

STATEMENTS

1. If you choose a job you love, you will never have to work a day in your life.
2. One loyal friend is worth 10,000 relatives.
3. Time is money.
4. Anyone who keeps learning stays young.
5. Everything has beauty, but not everyone sees it.
6. There is only one happiness in life: to love and be loved.

I don't completely agree with the first statement. I love the job I have, but I didn't really choose it. What makes it fun is the energy I put into it. I don't know whether I'll do the same kind of work all my life, but for now, it's fine. What people don't realize is that you can make your work satisfying if you try hard enough. The problem is that people often don't see that.

C | TIC-TAC-TOE Follow these instructions.

1. Work with a partner. Student A is X. Student B is O.

2. Student A: Choose a square. On another piece of paper, complete the sentence with a noun clause.

3. Students A and B: Check the sentence together. If the sentence has no errors, write an *X* in the square. If the sentence is not correct, do not write an *X* in the square.

4. Student B: Take your turn. Choose a square and complete the sentence.

5. Students A and B: Check the sentence together. If the sentence has no errors, write an *O* in the square. If the sentence is not correct, do not write an *O* in the square.

6. Continue to take turns. The first person to get three *X*s or three *O*s in a line is the winner.

I feel strongly that . . .	I know I'll . . .	She said . . .
I'm not sure whether . . .	I'm upset about the fact . . .	The problem . . .
I insist that . . .	He told me . . .	Let's talk about . . .

D | RESEARCH Look at several news websites or newspapers. Find examples of the different types of noun clauses from this unit and share them with your classmates.

"I was reading a health and fitness website and this is what I found. It's an example of a <u>wh</u>- noun clause as object. 'People should buy just what they need, serve smaller portions, and understand the difference.'"

"I found this on the BBC News website: 'Martha Lane Fox, co-founder of the travel website Lastminute.com, told the BBC she was confident Twitter could make money.'"

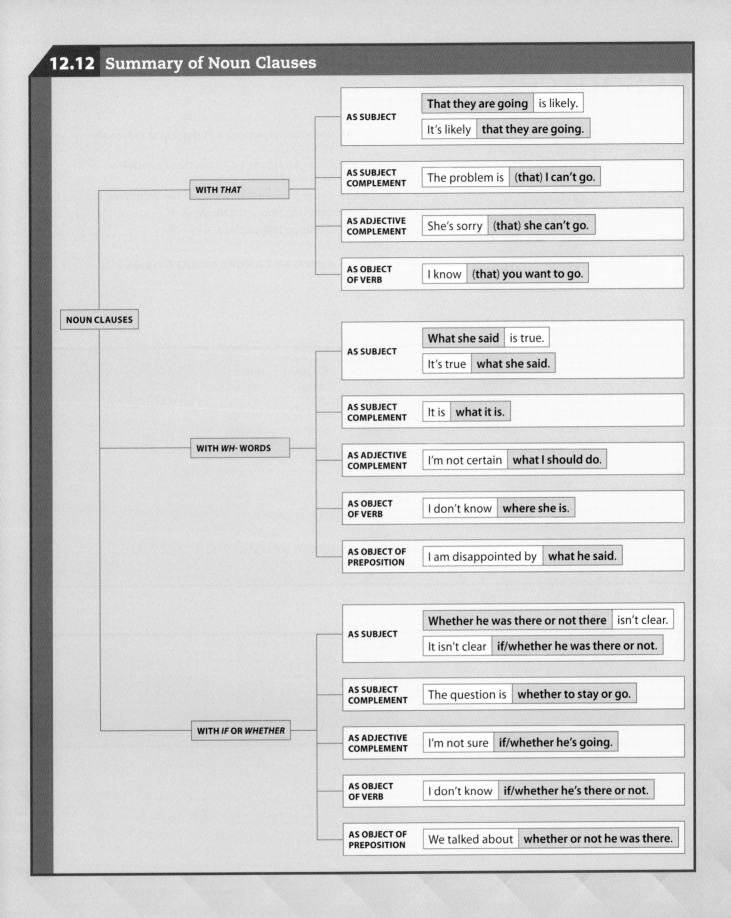

Resources

I. Non-Action Verbs

agree	consist of	fear	include	mind	recognize	think
appear	contain	feel	involve	need	remember	understand
appreciate	cost	fit	know	owe	see	want
be	dislike	hate	like	own	seem	weigh
believe	doubt	have	look	possess	smell	wish
belong	envy	hear	love	prefer	suppose	
conclude	equal	imagine	mean	realize	taste	

Remember:

- A non-action verb describes a state (an unchanging condition).
- Non-action verbs are also called **stative verbs**.
- Some verbs have more than one meaning. They can function as a non-action verb in one context and an action verb in another.

II. Linking Verbs

appear	become	get*	look	seem	sound	turn*
be	feel	grow*	remain	smell	taste	

* with a meaning of *become*

Remember: A linking verb can have an adjective as a complement.

III. Irregular Verbs

BASE FORM	SIMPLE PAST	PAST PARTICIPLE
arise	arose	arisen
beat	beat	beaten
become	became	become
begin	began	begun
bend	bent	bent
bet	bet	bet
bite	bit	bitten
bleed	bled	bled
break	broke	broken
bring	brought	brought
build	built	built
burn	burned	burned
buy	bought	bought
catch	caught	caught
choose	chose	chosen
come	came	come
cost	cost	cost
cut	cut	cut
deal	dealt	dealt
dig	dug	dug
draw	drew	drawn
dream	dreamed	dreamed
drink	drank	drunk
drive	drove	driven
eat	ate	eaten
fall	fell	fallen
feed	fed	fed
feel	felt	felt
fight	fought	fought
find	found	found
fly	flew	flown
forbid	forbade	forbidden
forget	forgot	forgotten
forgive	forgave	forgiven
freeze	froze	frozen
get	got	gotten
give	gave	given
go	went	gone
grow	grew	grown
hear	heard	heard
hide	hid	hidden
hit	hit	hit
hold	held	held
hurt	hurt	hurt
keep	kept	kept
know	knew	known
lay	laid	laid
lead	led	led
leave	left	left
lend	lent	lent
let	let	let
light	lit/lighted	lit/lighted
lose	lost	lost
make	made	made
mean	meant	meant
meet	met	met

BASE FORM	SIMPLE PAST	PAST PARTICIPLE
pay	paid	paid
put	put	put
quit	quit	quit
read	read	read
ride	rode	ridden
ring	rang	rung
rise	rose	risen
run	ran	run
say	said	said
see	saw	seen
seek	sought	sought
sell	sold	sold
send	sent	sent
set	set	set
sew	sewed	sewn
shake	shook	shaken
shoot	shot	shot
show	showed	shown
shrink	shrank	shrunk
shut	shut	shut
sing	sang	sung
sink	sank	sunk
sit	sat	sat
sleep	slept	slept
slide	slid	slid
speak	spoke	spoken
speed	sped	sped
spend	spent	spent
spill	spilt/spilled	spilt/spilled
spin	spun	spun
spread	spread	spread
spring	sprang	sprung
stand	stood	stood
steal	stole	stolen
sting	stung	stung
stink	stank	stunk
strike	struck	struck
strive	strove	striven
swear	swore	sworn
sweep	swept	swept
swim	swam	swum
swing	swung	swung
take	took	taken
teach	taught	taught
tear	tore	torn
tell	told	told
think	thought	thought
throw	threw	thrown
understand	understood	understood
wake	woke	woken
wear	wore	worn
weep	wept	wept
win	won	won
wind	wound	wound
write	wrote	written

IV. Spelling Rules for the -s/-es Form of Verbs

To form the third-person singular (*he/she/it*) for the simple present:

1 Add -*es* to verbs that end in -*sh*, -*ch*, -*ss*, -*s*, -*x*, or -*z*.

| finish | finishes | touch | touches | pass | passes | relax | relaxes |

2 For verbs ending in a consonant + -*y*, change the -*y* to -*i* and add -*es*.

| study | studies | worry | worries | deny | denies | fly | flies |

3 Three verbs have a special spelling:

| go | goes | do | does | have | has |

4 For all other verbs, add -*s*.

| like | likes | buy | buys | see | sees | speak | speaks |

V. Spelling Rules for the -*ing* Form of Verbs

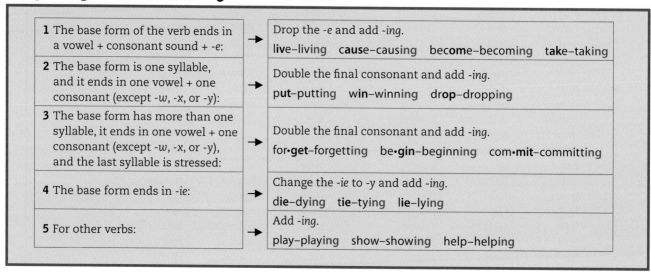

1 The base form of the verb ends in a vowel + consonant sound + -*e*: ➡	Drop the -*e* and add -*ing*. live–living **cause**–causing become–becoming take–taking
2 The base form is one syllable, and it ends in one vowel + one consonant (except -*w*, -*x*, or -*y*): ➡	Double the final consonant and add -*ing*. put–putting win–winning drop–dropping
3 The base form has more than one syllable, it ends in one vowel + one consonant (except -*w*, -*x*, or -*y*), and the last syllable is stressed: ➡	Double the final consonant and add -*ing*. for·**get**–forgetting be·**gin**–beginning com·**mit**–committing
4 The base form ends in -*ie*: ➡	Change the -*ie* to -*y* and add -*ing*. die–dying tie–tying lie–lying
5 For other verbs: ➡	Add -*ing*. play–playing show–showing help–helping

VI. Spelling Rules for the *-ed* Form of Verbs

SPELLING RULES	base form	simple past
When the base form of a regular verb ends in *-e*, **add -d.**	close refuse	closed refused
When the base form ends in a consonant + **-y, change the -y to -i and add -ed.**	study worry identify	studied worried identified
When the base form has one syllable and ends in a **c**onsonant + **v**owel + **c**onsonant (CVC), **double the final consonant and add -ed.** (Warning! Do not double a final *w, x,* or *y: play / played, wax / waxed, row / rowed*).	plan jog drop	planned jogged dropped
When the base form of a two-syllable verb ends in a **c**onsonant + **v**owel + **c**onsonant (CVC) and the last syllable is stressed, **double the final consonant and add -ed.**	re•**fer** re•**gret**	referred regretted
For all other regular verbs, **add -ed.**	open destroy	opened destroyed

VII. Common Transitive Verbs

VERB + DIRECT OBJECT

Examples: *develop a theory; include your name and address; consider several possibilities*

allow	complete	enjoy	introduce	meet*	refuse	take
ask*	consider	expect	invent	move*	remember*	teach
attempt	create	feel*	involve	need	save	tell
begin*	cut*	find	keep*	pass*	say	think*
believe*	describe	follow*	know*	pay*	see*	throw
bring	design	forgive	leave*	produce	send	use
build	destroy	hear*	lend	provide	serve	visit*
buy	develop*	help*	like	put	show	want
call*	discover	hold*	lose*	raise	speak*	wash*
carry	divide*	identify	love	read*	start*	watch*
cause	do	include	make	receive	study*	win*
close*	end*	intend	mean	recognize	surround	write*

* verbs that we can also use intransitively (without a direct object)

Remember: Transitive verbs need an object (a noun phrase or pronoun) to complete their meaning.

VERB + INDIRECT OBJECT + DIRECT OBJECT

Examples: *ask your professor a question; show her the answer*

ask	forgive	lend*	pay	save	teach*
bring	give*	make	promise*	send*	tell*
buy	hand*	offer*	read*	serve*	throw*
find	leave*	owe*	refuse	show*	wish*

* The indirect object can come before or after the direct object.

VIII. Common Intransitive Verbs

Examples: *The movie begins at 8. She doesn't hear very well.*

agree	come	follow*	leave*	rain	sneeze	wait
appear	cough	freeze*	lie	read*	snow	walk*
arrive	cut*	go	live	remember*	speak*	wash*
begin*	decrease*	happen	look	ring*	stare	watch*
belong	die	hear*	lose*	rise	start*	win*
bleed	disappear	help*	matter	see*	stop*	work
break*	dream*	hide*	meet*	shake*	study*	write*
burn*	drown	hurt*	move*	sit	swim	
call*	end*	increase*	occur	sleep	think*	
close*	fall	laugh	pass*	smile	visit*	

* verbs that we can also use transitively (with a direct object)

Remember: Intransitive verbs make sense without an object.

IX. Common Verbs Followed by Gerunds

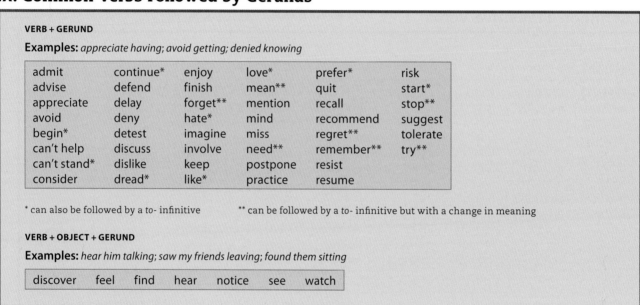

VERB + GERUND

Examples: *appreciate having; avoid getting; denied knowing*

admit	continue*	enjoy	love*	prefer*	risk
advise	defend	finish	mean**	quit	start*
appreciate	delay	forget**	mention	recall	stop**
avoid	deny	hate*	mind	recommend	suggest
begin*	detest	imagine	miss	regret**	tolerate
can't help	discuss	involve	need**	remember**	try**
can't stand*	dislike	keep	postpone	resist	
consider	dread*	like*	practice	resume	

* can also be followed by a *to-* infinitive   ** can be followed by a *to-* infinitive but with a change in meaning

VERB + OBJECT + GERUND

Examples: *hear him talking; saw my friends leaving; found them sitting*

discover	feel	find	hear	notice	see	watch

X. Common Verbs + Prepositions Followed by Gerunds

Examples: *argue about going; apologize for being; cope with losing; dream of becoming*

VERB + *ABOUT*	VERB + *AT*	VERB + *FOR*	VERB + *IN*	VERB + *INTO*
argue about care about complain about forget about talk about think about worry about	aim at work at	apologize for blame for care for forgive for thank for use for	believe in result in specialize in succeed in	look into

VERB + *LIKE*	VERB + *OF*	VERB + *ON*	VERB + *TO*	VERB + *WITH*
feel like	accuse of approve of dream of hear of think of	concentrate on depend on go on insist on keep on plan on work on	admit to confess to object to	cope with deal with

XI. Common Adjectives + Prepositions Followed by Gerunds

Examples: *afraid of being; bad at making; excited about going*

ADJECTIVE + *OF* + GERUND	ADJECTIVE + *AT* + GERUND	ADJECTIVE + *ABOUT* + GERUND
afraid of aware of capable of fond of incapable of proud of tired of	bad at better at effective at good at great at successful at upset at	bad about concerned about enthusiastic about excited about happy about nervous about serious about sorry about worried about

ADJECTIVE + *FROM* + GERUND	ADJECTIVE + *IN* + GERUND	ADJECTIVE + *FOR* + GERUND
different from evident from exempt from free from obvious from safe from tired from	crucial in effective in important in interested in involved in useful in	available for crucial for famous for important for necessary for responsible for sorry for suitable for useful for

XII. Common Nouns + *Of* That Can Be Followed by Gerunds

Examples: *chance of getting; possibility of using*

advantage of*	effect of*	idea of*	point of	prospect of	task of*
chance of*	experience of*	importance of	possibility of*	purpose of*	thought of
charge of	form of*	intention of	practice of*	result of*	way of*
cost of*	habit of	means of*	problem of*	risk of*	
danger of	hope of	method of*	process of*	system of*	

* common in academic writing

XIII. Common Verbs Followed by *To-* Infinitives

VERB + *TO-* INFINITIVE

Examples: *agree to go; asked to leave; decide to stay*

afford	can't stand*	desire	hope	plan	remember**	threaten
agree	claim	dread*	intend	prefer*	request	try**
aim	consent	fall	learn	prepare	say	volunteer
appear	continue*	forbid	like*	pretend	seek	vow
ask	dare	forget**	love*	proceed	seem	wait
attempt	decide	get	manage	promise	start*	want
beg	decline	hate*	mean**	prove	stop**	wish
begin*	demand	help	need**	refuse	struggle	
bother	deserve	hesitate	offer	regret**	tend	

* can also be followed by a gerund   ** can be followed by a gerund but with a change in meaning

VERB + OBJECT + *TO-* INFINITIVE

Examples: *advised me to go; reminded me to call; helped them to move*

advise**	beg*	encourage**	hate*	know**	permit**	teach**
allow**	believe**	expect*	help*	like*	persuade**	tell**
appoint**	challenge**	forbid**	imagine**	love*	prefer*	urge**
assume**	choose*	force**	instruct**	need*	promise*	want*
ask*	consider**	get*	judge**	order**	remind**	warn**

* object is optional   ** object is required

XIV. Common Noncount Nouns

advice	cooperation	food*	glass*	news	rain	traffic
air	courage	fruit*	heat	noise*	research	transportation
baggage	creativity	fun	jewelry	organization*	respect	truth*
beauty	economics	furniture	knowledge	oxygen	rice	violence
behavior*	education*	gasoline	literature	paint*	safety	water
blood	electricity	grammar	luck	participation	salt	weather
bread	entertainment	hair*	luggage	patience	sand	work*
cash	equipment	happiness	mathematics	peace	smoke	
chemistry	evidence	health	medicine*	physics	snow	
clothing	excitement	help	milk	pollution	soap	
coffee*	experience*	homework	money	privacy	spaghetti	
confidence	flour	information	music	progress	sugar	

* often has a count meaning or a noncount meaning

XV. Common Prepositions

ONE-WORD PREPOSITIONS

about	at	beyond	in	on	than	unlike
above	before	by	including	onto	through	until
across	behind	despite	inside	opposite	throughout	up
after	below	down	into	outside	to	upon
against	beneath	during	like	over	toward	with
among	beside	except	near	past	towards	within
around	besides	for	of	per	under	without
as	between	from	off	since	underneath	

GROUPS OF WORDS THAT FUNCTION LIKE ONE-WORD PREPOSITIONS

according to	because of	in exchange for	instead of	owing to
ahead of	but for	in front of	near to	prior to
apart from	by means of	in place of	on account of	rather than
as for	due to	in spite of	on top of	such as
as of	except for	in terms of	out of	thanks to
as well as	in addition to	inside of	outside of	up to
away from				

COMMON ERRORS CORRECTIONS

1.2 The Simple Present (page 6)

CORRECTION	EXPLANATION
13 ✗ Everyone **have** the duty to vote. ✓ Everyone **has** the duty to vote.	We use a singular verb (**has**) with an indefinite pronoun.
14 ✗ My brother always **get** what he wants. ✓ My brother always **gets** what he wants.	<table><tr><td>I / you / we / they</td><td>get . . .</td></tr><tr><td>he / she / it</td><td>gets . . .</td></tr></table>
15 ✗ I very proud to be a part of this group. ✓ I **am** very proud to be a part of this group.	Every sentence needs a verb. We can use the verb *be* before an adjective (**am proud**).
16 ✗ People in a big city **has** more trouble sleeping at night. ✓ People in a big city **have** more trouble sleeping at night.	The noun subject of this sentence is **people** (not *city*). *People* is a plural noun so we use a plural verb (*have*).

C

1.5 The Simple Past (page 16)

CORRECTION	EXPLANATION
12 ✗ Later I **remember** that I was not well prepared to take the test. ✓ Later I **remembered** that I was not well prepared to take the test.	Pay attention to all of the verb forms in a sentence. It's important to use similar verb forms when they refer to the same time frame.
13 ✗ We **didn't** want to leave home because we **want** to take care of our grandparents. ✓ We didn't want to leave home because we **wanted** to take care of our grandparents. ✓ We **don't** want to leave home because we want to take care of our grandparents.	remembered–was didn't want–wanted don't want–want looked–wore–didn't feel got–sat–thought
14 ✗ Although she looked nice when she **wear** that suit, she didn't feel comfortable in it. ✓ Although she looked nice when she **wore** that suit, she didn't feel comfortable in it.	
15 ✗ When I got there, I sat and **think** for a while. ✓ When I got there, I sat and **thought** for a while.	

C

2.2 The Simple Past vs. the Present Perfect (page 45)

	CORRECTION	EXPLANATION
C	**10** ✗ I have seen many things when I was a child. ✓ I saw many things when I was a child.	The time expression *when I was a child* indicates a finished time period. We use the simple past (not the present perfect) with these time expressions.
	11 ✗ I have been here since three weeks. ✓ I have been here for three weeks.	<table><tr><td>since</td><td>+</td><td>a specific time (*January 2014*)</td></tr><tr><td>for</td><td>+</td><td>an amount of time (*for three weeks / for a year*)</td></tr></table>
	12 ✗ I lived in Toronto for three years. I really love it here. ✓ I have lived in Toronto for three years. I really love it here.	We usually use the present perfect (not the simple past) when we are talking about something that started in the past and is connected to *now*.
	13 ✗ He is the most optimistic person I ever know. ✓ He is the most optimistic person I have ever known.	We usually use the present perfect with the time expression *ever*. We form the present perfect with *have / has* + the past participle of the main verb (**known**).

4.3 Transitive and Intransitive Verbs (page 117)

	CORRECTION	EXPLANATION
D	**13** ✗ They thought she was died. ✓ They thought she was dead. ✓ They thought she had died.	The verbs *die* and *happen* are intransitive. Intransitive verbs don't have a passive form.
	14 ✗ These things were happened on Friday evening. ✓ These things happened on Friday evening.	
	15 ✗ The paintings appeared several people. ✓ The paintings showed several people. ✓ Several people appeared in the paintings.	*Appear* is an intransitive verb. We don't use an object (*several people*) with an intransitive verb.
	16 ✗ Three people injured in the accident. ✓ Three people were injured in the accident.	When the subject (*three people*) is the **receiver** of the action, we use a passive verb (*were injured*).

7.1 Overview of Nouns (page 214)

D

CORRECTION	EXPLANATION
10 ✗ She gave me some good advices. ✓ She gave me some good **advice**. **11** ✗ I didn't have time to do my homeworks. ✓ I didn't have time to do my **homework**. **12** ✗ When I have a stress, I can't study hard. ✓ When I **have stress**, I can't study hard. ✓ When I **am under a lot of stress**, I can't study hard. ✓ When I **feel stressed**, I can't study hard. ✓ When I **am stressed**, I can't study hard.	The words *advice*, *homework*, and *stress* are noncount nouns. Noncount nouns do not have plural forms and we don't use them with *a* or *an*. Notice that in 12, we can also use a linking verb + the adjective *stressed*.
13 ✗ Recycled papers are used to produce newspapers. ✓ Recycled **paper is** used to produce newspapers.	The word *paper* has a noncount meaning and a count meaning. In this sentence, *paper* refers to a kind of material and has a noncount meaning.

8.5 Possessives (page 270)

C

CORRECTION	EXPLANATION
11 ✗ What do you think of today young people? ✓ What do you think of **today's** young people? ✓ What do you think of young people **today**? **12** ✗ A lot of the cities restaurants have closed. ✓ A lot of the **city's** restaurants have closed.	We can use certain time expressions and nouns as possessives before a main noun (*today's young people*, *the city's restaurants*). *today's young people = the young people of today* *the city's restaurants = the restaurants of the city* Notice that we can also use a time expression as an adverbial after the noun (*young people today*).
13 ✗ One researchers' findings were completely different. ✓ One **researcher's** findings were completely different.	We add 's after a singular noun to show possession (*one researcher's findings*). We add ' after a plural noun (*two researchers' findings*).
14 ✗ Can you give me your the number? ✓ Can you give me your number?	We don't use an article (*the*, *a*, etc.) together with a possessive determiner (*my*, *your*, etc.).

8.6 Quantifiers (page 272)

CORRECTION	EXPLANATION
12 ✗ He has to worry about **another things**. ✓ He has to worry about **other things**. ✓ He has to worry about **another thing**.	We use: | another | + | singular noun | | other | + | plural count noun / noncount noun |
13 ✗ You can get **many informations** on the Internet. ✓ You can get **much information** on the Internet.	*information* = a noncount noun. We use: | much | + | noncount noun | | many | + | plural count noun |
14 ✗ **A lot** people ride bicycles there. ✓ **A lot of** people ride bicycles there.	We use: | a lot **of** | + | plural count noun / noncount noun |
15 ✗ **Few** months after I moved home, I quit school. ✓ **A few** months after I moved home, I quit school.	We use: | **a** few | + | plural count noun | We can also use (*very*) + *few* + a plural noun, but the meaning is different. *a few months* = a small number of months *very few months* = almost no months

D

9.7 Using *Of* to Show Possession (page 306)

CORRECTION	EXPLANATION
6 ✗ Please don't drink from that **water's glass**. ✓ Please don't drink from that **glass of water**.	For nonliving and abstract things, we don't usually use 's to show possession. We use a prepositional phrase with *of* instead.
7 ✗ **The parents of Sylvia** are here. ✓ **Sylvia's parents** are here.	For living things, we don't usually use a prepositional phrase with *of* to show possession. We use 's instead.

B

11.2 Gerunds as Subjects; *Be* + Gerund (page 358)

CORRECTION	EXPLANATION
8 ✗ Many people realize that **take** care of their health is important. ✓ Many people realize that **taking** care of their health is important.	We can use a gerund (**taking**, **teaching**) as the subject of a sentence or clause. We can't use the base form of a verb (*take*, *teach*) in this way.
9 ✗ **Teach** a child a foreign language too early might cause problems. ✓ **Teaching** a child a foreign language too early might cause problems.	
10 ✗ Eating lots of vegetables **are** good for your health. ✓ Eating lots of vegetables **is** good for your health.	In this sentence, the subject is *eating* (not *vegetables*). We use a singular verb (**is**) with a gerund subject.

C

11.6 To- Infinitives as Subjects; Linking Verb + To- Infinitive (page 370)

D

CORRECTION	EXPLANATION

12 ✗ It's hard to understand for us.
  ✓ It's hard **for us to understand**.
	The correct order is:
	
	  adjective + *for* + object pronoun + to- infinitive

13 ✗ My goal was get a good job near my home. ✓ My goal was **to get** a good job near my home.	We can use a *to-* infinitive (*to get*) after a linking verb, not the base form of a verb (*get*).

14 ✗ It's necessary when you are writing an essay, you include an introduction.
  ✓ It's necessary **to include an introduction** when you are writing an essay.
	We use:
	
	  It + *be* + adjective + to- infinitive

11.7 To- Infinitives as Objects (page 373)

D

CORRECTION	EXPLANATION

17 ✗ She wants finish her work and watch TV.
  ✓ She wants **to finish** her work and watch TV.
 	
18 ✗ He wanted the children worked harder.
  ✓ He wanted the children **to work** harder.
	We can use a *to-* infinitive (not a base form or simple past form) as the object of the verb *want*.

19 ✗ I will teach you know how to play the piano.
  ✓ I will teach you how to play the piano.
	We use:
	
	  teach + object pronoun + *wh-* word + to- infinitive

20 ✗ My parents encouraged me about coming here. ✓ My parents encouraged me **to come** here.	We can use a *to-* infinitive (not a preposition + gerund) as the object of the verb *encourage*.

12.6 Wh- Noun Clauses (page 408)

B

CORRECTION	EXPLANATION

6 ✗ I wonder where is he.
  ✓ I wonder where **he is**.
 	
7 ✗ What is he saying bothers me.
  ✓ What **he is saying** bothers me.
 	
8 ✗ The problem is who is she marrying.
  ✓ The problem is who **she is marrying**.
	The correct word order for a *wh-* noun clause is:
	
	  wh- word | subject | verb

9 ✗ They're not happy about that what you said. ✓ They're not happy about what you said.	We can use a *wh-* clause as the object of a preposition (not a *that* clause).

Index

Class Audio Track List

GO ONLINE For these audio tracks and the audio scripts, go to the Online Practice.

Unit	Activity	Track File Name
Unit 1	Activity 33, p. 27	ELM3_U01_Track01_Activity33.mp3
	Activity 34, p. 28	ELM3_U01_Track02_Activity34.mp3
	Chart 1.9, p. 30	ELM3_U01_Track03_Chart1.9.mp3
	Activity 38, p.31	ELM3_U01_Track04_Activity38.mp3
Unit 2	Activity 6, p. 46	ELM3_U02_Track01_Activity06.mp3
	Activity 7, p. 46	ELM3_U02_Track02_Activity07.mp3
	Chart 2.6, p. 62	ELM3_U02_Track03_Chart2.6.mp3
	Activity 27, p. 63	ELM3_U02_Track04_Activity27.mp3
	Activity 28, p. 63	ELM3_U02_Track05_Activity28.mp3
Unit 3	Activity 33, p. 89	ELM3_U03_Track01_Activity33.mp3
	Activity 34, p. 89	ELM3_U03_Track02_Activity34.mp3
	Chart 3.11, p. 100	ELM3_U03_Track03_Chart3.11.mp3
Unit 4	Activity 6, p. 113	ELM3_U04_Track01_Activity06.mp3
	Activity 7, p. 113	ELM3_U04_Track02_Activity07.mp3
	Activity 25, p. 128	ELM3_U04_Track03_Activity25.mp3
	Chart 4.7, p. 130	ELM3_U04_Track04_Chart4.7.mp3
	Activity 27, p. 130	ELM3_U04_Track05_Activity27.mp3
Unit 6	Activity 17, p. 186	ELM3_U06_Track01_Activity17.mp3
	Activity 18, p. 187	ELM3_U06_Track02_Activity18.mp3
	Chart 6.9, p. 202	ELM3_U06_Track03_Chart6.9.mp3
	Activity 42, p. 202	ELM3_U06_Track04_Activity42.mp3
	Activity 44, p. 204	ELM3_U06_Track05_Activity44.mp3
	Activity 45, p. 204	ELM3_U06_Track06_Activity45.mp3
Unit 7	Activity 11, p. 221	ELM3_U07_Track01_Activity11.mp3
	Activity 12, p. 221	ELM3_U07_Track02_Activity12.mp3
	Activity 13, p. 221	ELM3_U07_Track03_Activity13.mp3
	Activity 15, p. 222	ELM3_U07_Track04_Activity15.mp3
	Activity 16, p. 222	ELM3_U07_Track05_Activity16.mp3
	Activity 36, p. 235	ELM3_U07_Track06_Activity36.mp3
	Activity 37, p. 236	ELM3_U07_Track07_Activity37.mp3
	Activity 38, p. 236	ELM3_U07_Track08_Activity38.mp3
	Activity 45, p. 242	ELM3_U07_Track09_Activity45.mp3
	Chart 7.9, p. 244	ELM3_U07_Track10_Chart7.9.mp3
	Activity 49, p. 245	ELM3_U07_Track11_Activity49.mp3
	Activity 50, p. 246	ELM3_U07_Track12_Activity50.mp3
Unit 8	Activity 40, p. 283	ELM3_U08_Track01_Activity40.mp3
Unit 9	Activity 24, p. 307	ELM3_U09_Track01_Activity24.mp3
	Activity 25, p. 307	ELM3_U09_Track02_Activity25.mp3
Unit 10	Activity 28, p. 344	ELM3_U10_Track01_Activity28.mp3
	Chart 10.9, p. 347	ELM3_U10_Track02_ Chart10.9.mp3
	Activity 32, p. 347	ELM3_U10_Track03_Activity32.mp3
	Activity 33, p. 348	ELM3_U10_Track04_Activity33.mp3
Unit 11	Activity 15, p. 366	ELM3_U11_Track01_Activity15.mp3
	Chart 11.12, p. 387	ELM3_U11_Track02_Chart11.12.mp3
	Activity 45, p. 388	ELM3_U11_Track03_Activity45.mp3
	Activity 46, p. 388	ELM3_U11_Track04_Activity46.mp3
	Activity 47, p. 388	ELM3_U11_Track05_Activity47.mp3
Unit 12	Activity 15, p. 406	ELM3_U12_Track01_Activity15.mp3
	Activity 16, p. 406	ELM3_U12_Track02_Activity16.mp3
	Chart 12.10, p. 422	ELM3_U12_Track03_Chart12.10.mp3

OXFORD
UNIVERSITY PRESS

198 Madison Avenue
New York, NY 10016 USA

Great Clarendon Street, Oxford, OX2 6DP, United Kingdom

Oxford University Press is a department of the University of Oxford.
It furthers the University's objective of excellence in research, scholarship,
and education by publishing worldwide. Oxford is a registered trade
mark of Oxford University Press in the UK and in certain other countries.

© Oxford University Press 2014

The moral rights of the author have been asserted.

First published in 2014

2018 2017 2016 2015 2014

10 9 8 7 6 5 4 3 2 1

Director, ELT New York: Laura Pearson
Head of Adult, ELT New York: Stephanie Karras
Publisher: Sharon Sargent
Senior Development Editor: Andrew Gitzy
Senior Development Editor: Rebecca Mostov
Development Editor: Eric Zuarino
Executive Art and Design Manager: Maj-Britt Hagsted
Content Production Manager: Julie Armstrong
Image Manager: Trisha Masterson
Image Editor: Liaht Pashayan
Production Artists: Elissa Santos, Julie Sussman-Perez
Production Coordinator: Brad Tucker

ISBN: 978 0 19 402826 4 Student Book 3 with Online Practice Pack
ISBN: 978 0 19 402845 5 Student Book 3 as pack component
ISBN: 978 0 19 402879 0 Online Practice website

Printed in China

This book is printed on paper from certified and well-managed sources.

ACKNOWLEDGEMENTS

*Although every effort has been made to trace and contact copyright holders before publication,
this has not been possible in some cases. We apologize for any apparent infringement of
copyright and if notified, the publisher will be pleased to rectify any errors or omissions at the
earliest opportunity.*

*The authors and publisher are grateful to those who have given permission to reproduce the
following extracts and adaptations of copyright material:* p. 17 from "Leonardo da Vinci" in
The World and Its People, Western Hemisphere, Europe, and Russia, Student Edition. Copyright
© 2005. Reprinted by permission of The McGraw-Hill Companies, Inc.; p. 20 "What
Were You Doing When ...?" by Thomas Thurman, www.marnanel.org/. Reprinted by
permission of Thomas Thurman; p. 25 from "FAQ: All About Coal - A Necessary Evil"
by Michael Kanellos, December 3, 2007, http://news.cnet.com. Used with permission
of CBS Interactive, News.com. Copyright © 2013. All rights reserved; p.33 from
the abstract of "Real Men Don't Need Work Life Balance," by Tanvi Gautam,
Forbeswoman, May 23, 2012, www.apaexcellence.org. Used with permission
from the American Psychological Association; p. 67 from "Humans Have Been
Making Art for a Lot Longer Than We Thought" by Sophie Bushwick, June 21, 2012,
http://blogs.discovermagazine.com. Reprinted by permission of Sophie Bushwick;
p. 67 from "Scientists able to study atmosphere of planet outside our solar system
using infra-red" by Eddie Wrenn, Daily Mail (UK), June 27, 2012, retrieved from
http://www.dailymail.co.uk. Reprinted by permission of the Daily Mail; p. 134 from
"Lord Marmaduke Hussey; led BBC, Times Newspapers" by Mark Herlihy and Chris
Peterson, Bloomberg News, December 28, 2006. Used with permission of Bloomberg
L.P. Copyright © 2013. All rights reserved; p. 152 "just" reproduced by permission of
Oxford University Press from *Oxford American English Dictionary for Learners of English*
© Oxford University Press 2011; p. 164 from *Literacy for Life: Education for All Global
Monitoring Report 2006*, http://www.unesco.org. © UNESCO 2005. Used by permission
of UNESCO; p. 207 from "Sun Screen" by Emily Sohn, *Science News for Kids*, June 26,
2006, http://www.sciencenewsforkids.org. Reprinted with Permission of Science
News for Students; p. 208 from "The Lemon Story" by Alberto Álvaro Ríos as appeared
in *Wachale!: Poetry and Prose on Growing Up Latino in America*, edited by Ilan Stavans.
Reprinted by permission of the author; p. 218 "beauty," "food," and "television"
reproduced by permission of Oxford University Press from *Oxford American English
Dictionary for Learners of English* © Oxford University Press 2011; p. 222 "Carl Sagan:
1934-1996." Reprinted by permission of Carus Publishing Company, 30 Grove Street,

Suite C, Peterborough, NH 03458 from MUSE magazine, December 1997, Vol. 1, No. 6,
text © 1997 by Carus Publishing Company. All rights reserved. www.cricketmag.com;
p. 264 from "Stonehenge" in *The World and Its People, Western Hemisphere, Europe, and
Russia, Student Edition.* Copyright © 2005. Reprinted by permission of The McGraw-Hill
Companies, Inc.; p. 320 "Great Barrier Reef" (brief description), http://whc.unesco.
org/en/list/154, © UNESCO 1992-2013. Used by permission of UNESCO; p. 353 from
"Alexander the Great," http://en.wikipedia.org/wiki/Alexander_the_great. Permission
granted under Creative Commons Attribution-ShareAlike 3.0 Unported (cc by-sa 3.0),
http://creativecommons.org/licenses/by-sa/3.0/.

Illustrations by: 5W Infographics: p. 39, 60, 91, 264, 269, 286, 377. John Kaufmann:
p. 141. Jerome Mireault: p. 32. Tablet Infographics: p. 19, 237. Joe Taylor: p. 104.

We would also like to thank the following for permission to reproduce the following photographs:
Cover: blinkblink/shutterstock; back cover: lvcandy/Getty Images; global: Rodin
Anton/shutterstock; p. 2 Alistair Berg/Getty Images; p. 17 AP Photo/Idaho Press-
Tribune, Charlie Litchfield, DeAgostini/Getty Images; p. 21 Steve Smith/SuperStock,
LOOK Die Bildagentur der Fotografen GmbH/Alamy, Mario Tama/Getty Images, Yellow
Dog Productions/Getty Images, Barry Lewis/In Pictures/Corbis, Tetra Images/Getty
Images, Oote Boe 3/Alamy, Rubberball/Mike Kemp/Getty Images; p. 25 Dmitriy Sechin/
istockphoto; p. 38 KidStock/Blend Images/Corbis; p. 43 Caro/Alamy; p. 44 Jacques
Alexandre/age fotostock; p. 48 Studio Ghibli/The Kobal Collection; p. 49 Beowulf
Sheehan/Writer Pictures; p. 50 Jupiterimages/Getty Images; p. 52 imagebroker/
Alamy; p. 55 Yasuyoshi Chiba/AFP/Getty Images; p. 57 GAB Archive/Redferns/Getty
Images; p. 61 2xSamara.com/shutterstock; p. 70 Yannick Tylle/Corbis; p. 72 Jorge
Salcedo/shutterstock; p. 75 Huntstock/Getty Images; p. 78 Pawel Libera/Loop Images/
SuperStock; p. 79 robynmac/istockphoto; p. 85 Rubberball/Mike Kemp/Getty Images;
p. 87 Creative Travel Projects/shutterstock; p. 88 jackscoldsweat/istockphoto;
p. 93 Troy House/Corbis; p. 94 Maksud/shutterstock; p. 98 F1 ONLINE/SuperStock,
stockstudioX/Getty Images; p. 99 Eric Audras/Onoky/Corbis; p. 101 OJO_Images/
istockphoto, Monalyn Gracia/Corbis, keith morris/Alamy, John Fedele/Blend Images/
Corbis; p. 102 Johner Images/Alamy; p. 106 andresrimaging/istockphoto; p. 107
ClassicStock/Alamy, Library of Congress - digital ve/Science Faction/Corbis, akg-
images/Newscom, Bettmann/Corbis, Hulton-Deutsch Collection/Corbis, AP Photo/
Wally Fong; p. 108 Stocksnapper/shutterstock; p. 110 All Canada Photos/Alamy; p. 111
Glow Images, Inc./Getty Images, James Steidl/shutterstock; p. 112 Dudarev Mikhail/
shutterstock, majeczka/shutterstock; p. 118 HANDOUT/KRT/Newscom, Peggy Peattie/
San Diego Union-Tribune/ZUMA Press, copyright San Diego Union-Tribune Publishing
Co./Alamy; p. 119 Corbis, Ralph Gatti/AFP/Getty Images; p. 127 Lebrecht Music &
Arts/Corbis; p. 136 Courtesy of Barb Schwarz at www.Stagedhomes.com; p. 138
Marnie Burkhart/Masterfile; p. 140 OUP/Photodisc; p. 144 Doug Lemke/shutterstock;
p. 146 Scanpix Creative/Masterfile; p. 147 Nagel Photography/shutterstock; p. 148
Cultura RM/Alamy; p.149,150 OUP/Photodisc; p. 154 Brian Snyder/Reuters/Corbis,
Rungroj Yongrit/epa/Corbis; p. 157 Erickson Photography/istockphoto; p. 158
Feng Yu/shutterstock; p. 159 OUP/Photodisc, Eric Audras/PhotoAlto/Corbis; p. 162
Wilfred Y. Wong/Getty Images; p. 167 OUP/Frank Krahmer, prudkov/shutterstock,
VeronikaMaskova/shutterstock; p. 168 ONOKY - Fabrice LEROUGE/Getty Images;
p. 169 OUP/Image Source; p. 172 Raimund Linke/Getty Images; p. 175 ITAR-TASS
Photo Agency/Alamy; p. 179 Dave & Les Jacobs/Getty Images, Giorgio Fochesato/Getty
Images; p. 181 Sean De Burca/Corbis; p. 184 Corbis, PoodlesRock/PoodlesRock/Corbis,
Ken Welsh/Design Pics/Corbis; p. 185 monkeybusinessimages/istockphoto; p. 187
BIHAIB/istockphoto; p. 189 Barry Rosenthal/Getty Images, OJO Images/Getty Images,
Radius Images/Alamy, Southern Stock/Blend Images/Corbis, Asia Images/Getty Images,
Glovatskiy/shutterstock, Vadim Ratnikov/shutterstock, Graham Oliver/Juice Images/
Corbis; p. 192 Ocean/Corbis, D. Hurst/Alamy; p. 195 Brigitte MERLE/Getty Images;
p. 205 JGI/Jamie Grill/Blend Images/Corbis; p. 206 Hero Images/Corbis, Ocean/Corbis;
p. 210 Universal/The Kobal Collection/Jasin Boland, Universal/DNA/Working Title/The
Kobal Collection/Peter Mountain, FOX 2000 Pictures/Dune Entertainment/Ingenious
Media/Haishang Films/The Kobal Collection; p. 212 Taxi/Court Mast/Getty Images;
p. 214 Bettmann/Corbis; p. 217 Stuart Jenner/istockphoto; p. 222 Tony Korody/Sygma/
Corbis; p. 225 Edward Koren/The New Yorker Collection/www.cartoonbank.com, Leo
Cullum/The New Yorker Collection/www.cartoonbank.com, Mike Twohy/The New
Yorker Collection/www.cartoonbank.com, Jack Ziegler/The New Yorker Collection/
www.cartoonbank.com; p. 228 Robert Fried/Alamy; p. 236 Gerry Pearce/Alamy; p. 237
NASA/JPL-Caltech/Harvard-Smithsonian CfA; p. 245 Hill Street Studios/Getty Images;
p. 249 OUP/Mike Stone; p. 254 nobleIMAGES/Alamy; p. 257 Stanley Brown/Getty
Images; p. 260 Jtafalla/istockphoto; p. 261 Sylvain Sonnet/Corbis; p. 266 WWD/Condé
Nast/Corbis; p. 268 Michelle D. Milliman/shutterstock; p. 278 North Wind Picture
Archives/Alamy; p. 281 a witch/Getty Images; p. 288 Ariel Skelley/Blend Images/Corbis;
p. 293 Arcaid Images/Alamy; p. 299 ecostecera2/Alamy; p. 301 Sigi Tischler/epa/Corbis;
p. 302 Songquan Deng/shutterstock, Africa Studio/shutterstock; p. 306 Seth Resnick/
Getty Images; p. 308 Visuals Unlimited/Masterfile; p. 316 Atlantide Phototravel/Corbis;
p. 320 Jupiterimages/Getty Images, Handout/Reuters/Corbis; p. 322 Mijang Ka/Getty
Images; p. 324 Eadweard Muybridge/Time Life Pictures/Getty Images; p. 326 Jose
Jacome/epa/Corbis; p. 330 Novastock/Getty Images; p. 331 Odua Images/shutterstock,
Creativa/shutterstock; p. 333 Hero Images/Corbis; p. 335 Scisetti Alfio/shutterstock,
Dani Vincek/shutterstock; p. 336 Inomoto/shutterstock; p. 339 AP Photo/Patti
Longmire; p. 340 GL Archive/Alamy, Time Life Pictures/Getty Images; p. 345 Stocktrek
Images/Getty Images; p. 345 Roy Bartels/shutterstock; p. 346 Ritterbach/age fotostock,
alantobey/istockphoto; p. 350 lrafael/shutterstock, Chikei Yung/Getty Images, Africa
Studio/shutterstock, Hulton-Deutsch Collection/Corbis; p. 353 Hoberman Collection/
Corbis; p. 354 Rick Friedman/Corbis; p. 359 OUP/Chris Ryan; p. 361 ColorBlind
Images/Corbis; p. 362 Ariel Skelley/Corbis; p. 363 Sergio Pitamitz/Masterfile; p. 364
Jade/Blend Images/Corbis; p. 366 Karen Kasmauski/Science Faction/Corbis; p. 369
UpperCut Images/Masterfile; p. 371 Hero Images/Corbis; p. 376 Oleksiy Maksymenko
Photography/Alamy; p. 379 Africa Studio/shutterstock; p. 380 photosync/shutterstock;
p. 381 Djomas/shutterstock; p. 382 Roy Morsch/age fotostock/SuperStock; p. 386
StockLite/shutterstock; p. 394 LluÁs Real/Getty Images; p. 397 Corbis; p. 399 David
Nunuk/Getty Images, Luciano Mortula/Shutterstock.com; p. 401 Petegar/istockphoto;
p. 403 Keren Su/Corbis; p. 404 Don Kates/Alamy; p. 405 Kritchanut/shutterstock; p. 408
Robert Trevis-Smith/Getty Images; p. 414 Andreas von Einsiedel/Corbis; p. 416 Corbis;
p. 421 4x6/Getty Images; p. 424 Radius Images/Corbis; p. 427 Weinstein Company/
courtesy Everett Collection, Daniel Smith/Warner Bros./courtesy Everett Collection,
Warner Bros/The Kobal Collection.

ELEMENTS *of* SUCCESS
Online Practice

How to Register for Elements of Success Online Practice

Follow these steps to register for *Elements of Success Online Practice*:

1. Go to www.elementsofsuccessonline.com and click  **Register**

2. Read and agree to the terms of use. **I Agree.**

3. Enter the Access Code that came with your Student Book. Your code is written on the inside back cover of your book.

   ☐ ☐ ☐ ☐ **Enter**

4. Enter your personal information (first and last name, email address, and password).

5. Click the Student Book that you are using for your class.

It is very important to select your book.
You are using Elements of Success 3.
Please click the **BLUE** Elements of Success 3 cover.

   If you don't know which book to select, **STOP**. Continue when you know your book.

6. Enter your class ID to join your class, and click NEXT. Your class ID is on the line below, or your teacher will give it to you on a different piece of paper.

   _____ **Next**

   You don't need a class ID code. If you do not have a class ID code, click Skip. To enter this code later, choose Join a Class from your Home page.

7. Once you're done, click Enter Online Practice to begin using *Elements of Success Online Practice*.

   Enter Online Practice

Next time you want to use *Elements of Success Online Practice*, just go to www.elementsofsuccessonline.com and log in with your email address and password.